T0180083

ion about this series at http://www.springer.com/series/7899

More informa

Imran Sarwar Bajwa · Tatjana Sibalija ·
Dayang Norhayati Abang Jawawi (Eds.)

Intelligent Technologies and Applications

Second International Conference, INTAP 2019
Bahawalpur, Pakistan, November 6–8, 2019
Revised Selected Papers

 Springer

Editors
Imran Sarwar Bajwa ⓘ
Islamia University of Bahawalpur
Baghdad, Pakistan

Tatjana Sibalija ⓘ
Metropolitan University
Belgrade, Serbia

Dayang Norhayati Abang Jawawi ⓘ
University of Technology Malaysia
Johor Bahru, Malaysia

ISSN 1865-0929   ISSN 1865-0937 (electronic)
Communications in Computer and Information Science
ISBN 978-981-15-5231-1   ISBN 978-981-15-5232-8 (eBook)
https://doi.org/10.1007/978-981-15-5232-8

This Springer imprint is published by the registered company Springer Nature Singapore Pte Ltd.
The registered company address is: 152 Beach Road, #21-01/04 Gateway East, Singapore 189721, Singapore

Preface

The present book includes accepted papers of the Second International Conference on International Conference on Intelligent Technologies and Applications (INTAP 2019), held in Bahawalpur, Pakistan, during November 6–8, 2019, organized by the Artificial Intelligence Research Group in collaboration with the Sir Sadiq Association of Computing and hosted by the Islamia University of Bahawalpur. The conference was sponsored by Higher Education Commission, Pakistan.

The conference was organized into 13 simultaneous tracks: Internet of Things [8], Intelligent Applications [9], Decision Support Systems [7], Social Media Analytics [6], Machine Learning [8], Natural Language Processing [7], Image Processing and Analysis [9], Intelligent Environments [6], and Cloud and Data Systems [7].

INTAP 2019 received 226 submissions from 23 countries and districts across all continents. After a blind review process, only 60 were accepted as full papers and only 7 were selected as short papers based on the classifications provided by the Program Committee, resulting in an acceptance rate of 29%. The selected papers come from researchers based in several countries including Canada, Australia, New Zealand, France, China, Turkey, Malaysia, Serbia, and the UK. The highly diversified audience gave us the opportunity to achieve a good level of understanding of the mutual needs, requirements, and technical means available in this field of research.

The selected papers reflect state-of-the-art research work in the different domains and applications of artificial intelligence and highlight the benefits of intelligent and smart systems in various fields of life. These high-quality standards will be maintained and reinforced at INTAP 2020, to be held at the Norwegian University of Science and Technology (NTNU), Norway, and in future editions of this conference.

Furthermore, INTAP 2019 include six plenary keynote lectures given by Sule Yayilgan (NTNU, Norway), Giuseppe Boccignoe (University of Milan, Italy), Filippo Sanfilippo (University of Agder, Norway), Saad Naeem Zafar (Riphah International, Pakistan), Khurram Shahzad (Punjab University, Pakistan), and Muhammad Ali Shahid (COMSATS University, Pakistan). We would like to express our appreciation to all those mentioned above and in particular to those who took the time to contribute with a paper to this book.

On behalf of the INTAP 2019 Organizing Committee, we would like to thank all participants. First of all, the authors, whose quality work is the essence of the conference, and the members of the Program Committee, who helped us with their eminent expertise in reviewing and selecting quality papers for this book. As we know that organizing an international conference requires the effort of many individuals. We wish to thank also all the members of our Organizing Committee, whose work and commitment were invaluable.

The proceedings editors wish to thank the dedicated Scientific Committee members and all the other reviewers for their contributions. We also thank Springer for their trust and for publishing the proceedings of INTAP 2019.

November 2019

Imran Sarwar Bajwa
Tatjana Sibalija
Dayang Norhayati Abang Jawawi

Organization

General Co-chairs

Imran Sarwar Bajwa	The Islamia University of Bahawalpur, Pakistan
Mark G. Lee	University of Birmingham, UK
Anna Helena Reali Costa	University of São Paulo, Brazil

Program Co-chairs

Fairouz Kamareddine	Heriot-Watt University, UK
Imran Ghani	Indiana University of Pennsylvania, USA
Jamal Bentahar	Concordia University, Canada
Dayang Norhayati A. Jawawi	Universiti Teknologi Malaysia, Malaysia

Organizing Committee

Amir Hussain	University of Stirling, UK
Irfan Hyder	Institute of Business Management, Pakistan
Omair Shafiq	Carleton University, Canada
M. Abbas Choudhary	Dadabhoy Institute of Higher Education, Pakistan
Noreen Jamil	Unitec Institute of Technology, New Zealand
Ghulam Alli Mallah	SALU, Pakistan
Riaz ul Amin	BUITEMS University, Pakistan
Aman Ullah Yasin	CASE, Pakistan
Imran Memon	Zhejiang University, China
Rafaqut Hussain Kazmi	The Islamia University of Bahawalpur, Pakistan

Program Committee

Adel Al-Jumaily	University of Technology Sydney, Australia
Adina Florea	Politehnica University of Bucharest, Romania
Adriano V. Werhli	Universidade Federal do Rio Grande, Brazil
Agostino Poggim	Università degli Studi di Parma, Italy
Ales Zamuda	University of Maribor, Slovenia
Alexander Gelbukh	National Polytechnic Institute, Mexico
Amin Beheshti	Macquarie University, Australia
Anand Nayyar	Duy Tan University, Vietnam
António Luís Lopes	Instituto Universitário De Lisboa, Portugal
Anna Helena Reali Costa	University of São Paulo, Brazil
Alvaro Rubio-Largo	Universidade NOVA de Lisboa, Portugal
Asif Baba, Tuskegee	The University of Alabama, USA

Invited Speakers

Sule Yayiligan	Norwegian University of Science and Technology, Norway
Giuseppe Boccignone	University of Milan, Italy
Filippo Sanfilippo	University of Agder, Norway
Saad Naeem Zafar	Riphah International University, Pakistan
Khurram Shahzad	PUCIT, Punjab University, Pakistan
M. Ali Shahid	COMSATS University, Pakistan

Contents

Internet of Things

Social Media Analytics

Machine Learning

Natural Language Processing

Image Processing and Analysis

Intelligent Environments

Cloud and Data Systems

Internet of Things

Design of Wearable Prototype Smart Wristband for Remote Health Monitoring Using Internet of Things

Ayesha Masood$^{(\boxtimes)}$, Khan Bahadar Khan, Talha Younas,
and Ali Raza Khalid

Department of Telecommunication Engineering, Faculty of Engineering,
The Islamia University of Bahawalpur, Bahawalpur, Pakistan
ayeshamasood73@gmail.com

Abstract. Remote health monitoring for patients is increasing with the advancements of various types of health related mobile applications. The vital signs such as pulse rate, blood pressure and temperature are the basic parameters, used for monitoring a patient's health. The designed healthcare kit consists of different sensors that are used for sensing and monitoring a patient's health. The data from healthcare kit is transmitted via the internet to save in a cloud-based server, which helps to monitor the consistent health situation of a candidate. The sensing information will be collected constantly over specified intervals of time and will be used to aware the patient about any concealed problem to endure possible diagnosis. The higher and lower range of temperature, blood pressure and heartbeat can be defined by the doctor according to the patient's health. Afterward, the system starts monitoring the patient and sends alert to the concerned doctor as soon as the sensing parameters cross the defined limits. The recorded values are transmitted via internet to the cloud server and a notification in the form of a tweet is also displayed on the doctor's twitter account and as well as the patient's account.

Keywords: IoT · Healthcare kit · Biomedical · Patient's monitoring system · Pulse rate · Temperature

1 Introduction

In the modern era of communication and technology, the electronic devices such as smart phones and tablets become the essential tool of a daily life. These devices are used for both physical and wireless communications [1]. The modern peers of connecting world are IoTs. The IoT is the extension of internet connectivity into physical devices and everyday objects. It is so beneficial that it can connect anything from anywhere at any time. A thing in the IoTs can be a person with a heart rate observer implant, a farm animal with a biochip transponder, a vehicle that has built-in sensors to notify the driver when tire pressure is low or any other natural or man-made object that can be assigned an IP address and is able to transfer information over a network.

Now-a-days, every individual become so much busy in his life that it is difficult to remember to take care of their health. By observing all these circumstances, technological

© Springer Nature Singapore Pte Ltd. 2020
I. S. Bajwa et al. (Eds.): INTAP 2019, CCIS 1198, pp. 3–13, 2020.
https://doi.org/10.1007/978-981-15-5232-8_1

developments get utilized for the benefits to the individuals. At first stage of advancement, lots of smart medical sensors are introduced that observes the activities of patients and forecasts the disorder, such as, pulse sensor can detect the abnormal pulses or it provide an ease to detect the risk of heart attack. However, a normal heart rate depends on the individual, age, gender, diet, heart conditions. For younger and older, a normal resting heart rate is virtually 90 beats per minute. Most commonly, maximum heart rate is calculated by subtracting your age from 220 [2].

The IoT technology is amplified with sensors and specialists approximate that the IoT will comprise of almost 50 billion objects by 2020 [3]. Usually, IoT is anticipated to deliver cutting-edge connectivity of the devices, systems and services that goes beyond machine-to-machine communications and shelters a variety of protocols, domains and applications.

As the number of ageing individuals and long-lasting disease patients propagate swiftly, problems of old-fashioned healthcare facility are progressively more noticeable. The most important one is that healthcare facilities are only accessible in hospitals, so it is difficult for senior or disabled individuals to achieve such facilities under disaster situations [4]. The increasing number of heart attacks is a core enduring disorder in mature adults, accounting for about 260,000 deaths a year [5]. The healthcare system is developed and estimated by using one of the technologies of Identification by Radio Frequencies (RFID). Many survey papers describe the function of a radio frequency technology in utilizing for building a smart hospital [6]. Our designed healthcare kit offerings a real time wearable band for monitoring, envisioning and examining biological signals [7]. A set of non-invasive physical sensors are wirelessly connected to an operator device, which stores, transmits and analyses the physiological data and then it is presented in a suitable way to the medical experts. The proposed remote healthcare kit is based on IoT for monitoring and scanning patient's vital signs.

2   Proposed Method

The designed system is very useful for saving the patient's life at an emergency time. Figure 1 demonstrates the architecture of the designed system.

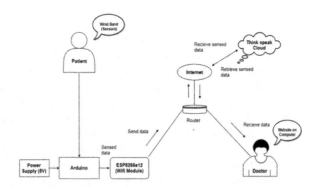

Fig. 1. Architecture of the designed system

The function of the system is classified into two stages: Sensing Phase and Interaction Phase. In Fig. 1, smart wrist band measures the body vital signs (blood pressure, temperature and pulse rate) and transmit the scanned data via internet to the ThinkSpeak platform [8] using the built-in Wi-Fi module.

2.1 Sensing Phase

The pulse rate, blood pressure and temperature sensor modules are used in the designed prototype system. This healthcare kit utilized the Electrically Erasable Programmable Read-Only Memory (EEPROM) chip to store vital signs values. The data can be retrieved by the bus serial clock and serial data lines. The data is collected or extracted in the form of blood pressure and heartbeats from the EEPROM of the wristband to the Arduino UNO board data pins. Figure 2 and Fig. 3 shows the connections the hardware components.

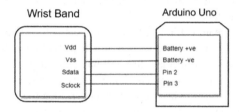

Fig. 2. Connections between Arduino board and wrist band.

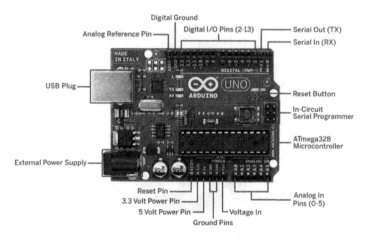

Fig. 3. Arduino board.

After setting the connection between Arduino board and wrist band, the board starts receiving the sensor data in the form of hexadecimal. Which is converted into machine language (binary form), then converted these values into decimal form for displaying on a serial monitor and for understanding of the concerned patient and doctor

Temperature Sensor: It DS18B20 temperature sensor builds relationship between the environmental temperature and the human-body temperature, which is found by suitable difference between environmental temperature and body-temperature [9]. That's why we used DS18B20 for measuring body temperature is a digital sensor which can measure body temperature as well as environmental temperature.

Sphygmomanometer: We used a simple wrist band for a patient's healthcare and implement an IoT technology for remote monitoring of the candidate. If the heartbeat and blood pressure of the patient is in critical condition then the band notifies to the doctor via the internet. It is an extremely straightforward gadget including a cuff, vacuum apparatus, air discharge valves and pressure sensor. A cuff is included around the wrist is overstated to around 200 mmHg or 26 kPa pressure [10]. At this weight the band is adequately constrictive to square blood course to the arm. A weight sensor measures the outright weight in the band, this sensor properly delicate to get the trademark throbs of the heart.

At 200 kPa blood stream is hindered, no heart beat will be detected [5]. The cuff is gradually contracting. At the systolic weight, the heart will have the capacity to defeat the cuff pressure. The microcontroller chip will have the capacity to distinguish a little beating variety in the cuff pressure. The band keeps on lessening pressure until the point that a point is meeting where no heartbeat is identified. This is the diastolic pressure. A controller chip deals with these measurements and displays the results. Figure 4 shows a smart band used in the proposed design.

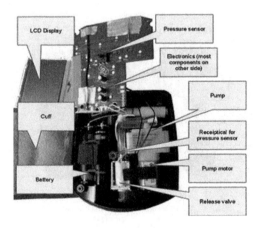

Fig. 4. Smart band [10].

2.2   Interaction Phase

After the sensors results obtained on serial monitor, the next step is the interaction between Wi-Fi module and the cloud server via the internet. There are two access methods: one is local area network and other is wide area network, we worked on both, but our goal is to access body parameters globally. So, the ESP8266 Wi-Fi module is used for wireless communication which transfers the data on server which can be shown on the specified web account using a web browser.

ThingSpeak platform is an open source which can store and recover information from this web by means of Internet or Intranet [11]. At first, a patient record is required to scanned and transmitted on Thinkspeak platform. Then login ID and password is required by the concerned doctor to login to the server for examining these vital signs. Figure 5 demonstrates the flowchart of the proposed framework.

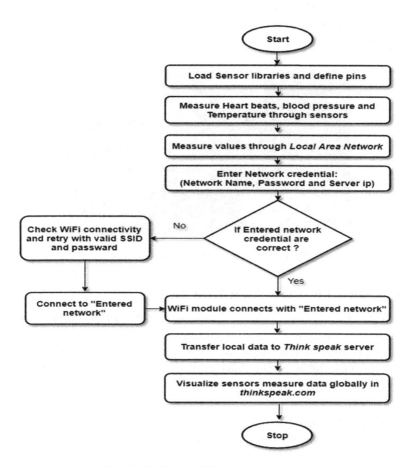

Fig. 5. Flowchart of the proposed system.

3   Results and Analysis

The outcomes validate that the proposed system works in an efficient manner without any delay or loss of information. The sensors acquire the correct readings and send the information to the Arduino memory board which are transmitted to the ThinkSpeak platform via the built-in Wi-Fi module [11]. The ThinkSpeak platform stores the information of every individual in their specified web account. The designed system measures the blood pressure and heart beat which are displayed on the LCD as well as sent to the ThinkSpeak server through a Wi-Fi module just by pushing the start button of the wrist band. Although, we have not compared our results with the existing literature as we have different hardware and different scenarios for result computation. Figure 6 shows the complete hardware which makes the simple band into smart band.

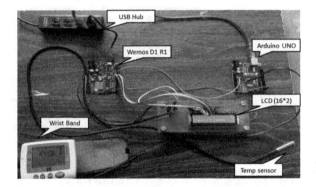

Fig. 6. Hardware component connectivity.

3.1   Experimental Results of Smart Wrist Band

In this article, the different conditions have been considered for monitoring the vital signs which are human pulse rate, blood pressure and temperature. The y-axis of all the obtained graphs represents the amplitude of the signal given by the sensors and x-axis represents the time duration. The different results are obtained on the basis of the following conditions:

- Age based analysis
- Gender based analysis
- Activity (Eating/without eating) based analysis

Age Based Analysis of the Heartbeat and Blood Pressure. The most extreme heart rate diminishes as you get more matured because of the organic impacts of maturing. Your most extreme heart rate can be assessed by subtracting your age from 220 [12].

Figure 7 shows the different heart beats according to the age differences. Figure 7 shows the human heart beats of different ages with respect to time. The heartbeats of 7 to 15 years old candidate are observed up-to 90 bpm by using the designed smart wrist band. Similarly, the average adult heart rate is 72 bpm and 65 bpm for the peoples of the age 40 to 60 years is observed using the designed system. These results are obtained through ThinkSpeak platform.

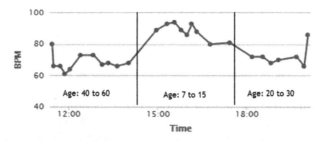

Fig. 7. Human heart rate reading of different ages.

Similarly, blood pressure is measured of different peoples having different ages. Figure 8, shows the human blood pressure of different ages with respect to time. The leftmost section of the graph represents the blood pressure of an elder peoples, afterward a young child blood pressure, which is lower as compared to aged people and right most results shows an adult blood pressure which is normal. The different colors of the graphs show having the normal and abnormal blood pressure.

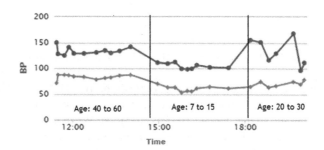

Fig. 8. Human blood pressure reading of different ages.

Gender Based Analysis of the Heart Beat and Blood Pressure. Ladies have higher heart rates than men as shown in Fig. 9. The distinction is that ladies are by and large smaller than men and require a quicker heart beat to encourage digestion. A significant part of the size distinction amongst people is because of ladies having a less aggregate bulk or muscle weight. Since muscle is in charge of a significant part of the body's digestion.

In this chart, the left five peaks demonstrate the heart rate of the ladies and right five peaks demonstrates the man's heart rate. These outcomes demonstrate the heart rate of male and female of the same age. Figure 9 demonstrates the outcomes as per the above characterized hypothesis.

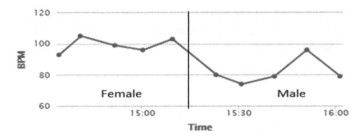

Fig. 9. Human heart rate reading of different gender.

Men are for the most part at more serious danger for heart and renal ailment than ladies having same age. Current investigations utilizing the procedure of 24 h wandering circulatory strain checking have demonstrated that pulse is higher in men than in ladies at comparable ages [13].

Figure 10, demonstrates a similar hypothesis which are examined above left half of diagram demonstrates the female circulatory strain which are marginally lower than the man which are on the right side of the chart.

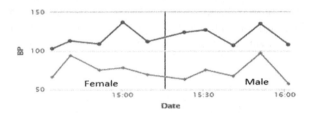

Fig. 10. Human blood pressure reading of different gender.

Activity (Eating vs. Non-eating) Based Analysis of the Heart Beat and Blood Pressure. After eating any food, heart rate increases to help with digestion. More blood is directed to the stomach area to process the food. When large quantities of food are consumed, heart rate may be increased for a longer period of time compared to after eating a small meal or snack.

In Fig. 11, left side shows the heart rate before meals which are much lower than the right side of the graph which indicate the heart beats after a meal.

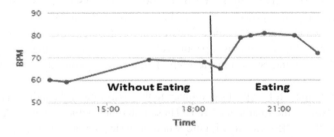

Fig. 11. Human heart rate reading with and without any activity.

A blood pressure slightly higher after a meal due to increase in heart rate, which is shown in Fig. 11. The heart pumps blood faster, right side of the Fig. 12 shows the results after eating a meal and left side of the graph shows without taking a meal.

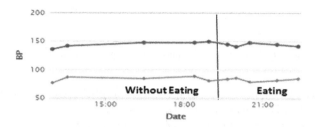

Fig. 12. Human blood pressure reading with and without any activity.

3.2 Experimental Results of the Temperature Sensor

The digital temperature sensor DS18b20 produces an output, digital signal. Micro-controllers receive digital signals as their input directly. Thus, no requirement to convert the analog output signal to digital before serving to a microcontroller's input. Due to this reason, we use a DS18b20.

Age Based Analysis of the Temperature Results. An elderly people usually have a low temperature, as compare to the young peoples. Figure 13 shows that temperature is decreasing, when age of peoples increasing. Therefore, graph proves the inverse relation of temperature of the human body and age of the peoples.

Gender Based Analysis of the Temperature Results. The gender does not effect on human body temperature. The temperature of the human body depends upon physical body part working properly or not, so, body temperature depends upon the body parts functionality either based on male or female. Left side of the graph of Fig. 14, shows the female body temperature with respect to time and the right side shows the male body temperature with respect to time.

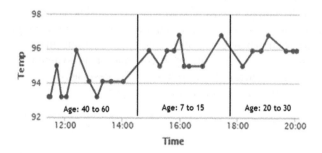

Fig. 13. Human body temperature reading for different ages.

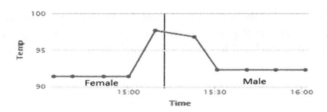

Fig. 14. Human body temperature reading of different gender

Activity Based Analysis of the Temperature Results. Activity (eating) caused a slight increment in body temperature, as your metabolic rate increments, keeping in mind the end goal to permit the assimilation of sustenance.

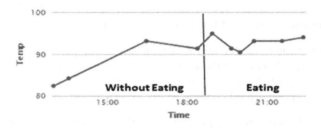

Fig. 15. Human body temperature assessment w.r.t activity (eating).

Your temperature may increment by upwards of 2 °F as the synthetic responses of the stomach related process happen inside in your body. Figure 15 shows the temperature of the human body without taking a meal or eating a meal. If neglected temperature sensor noise almost increment of 2 °F.

4   Conclusions

This proposed system is designed to monitor the patient's health, remotely. One of the main motives of the proposed system is to create a real time communication between doctor and patient in an easier way and require less power consumption. The model actualized is a constant patient screening system, which permits medical consultants to observe their patients on a remote site, to detect their crucial symptoms and to provide them some assistance for medical aid medicines. The designed system is very efficient, accurate, smart, less power consumption and low cost.

References

1. Hossain, M.S., Muhammad, G.: Cloud-assisted Industrial Internet of Things (IIoT)–enabled framework for health monitoring. Comput. Netw. **4**(101), 192–202 (2016)
2. American College of Sports Medicine: ACSM's Health-Related Physical Fitness Assessment Manual. Lippincott Williams & Wilkins, Philadelphia (2013)
3. Malhara, S., Vittal, V.: Mechanical state estimation of overhead transmission lines using tilt sensors. IEEE Trans. Power Syst. **25**(3), 1282–1290 (2010)
4. Li, C., Hu, X., Zhang, L.: The IoT-based heart disease monitoring system for pervasive healthcare service. Procedia Comput. Sci. **1**(112), 2328–2334 (2017)
5. Yadav, Y., Gowda, M.S.: Heart rate monitoring and heart attack detection using wearable device. Int. J. Tech. Res. Appl. **4**(3), 48–50 (2016)
6. Atzori, L., Iera, A., Morabito, G.: The internet of things: a survey. Comput. Netw. **54**(15), 2787–2805 (2010)
7. Lakein, A., Leake, P.: How to Get Control of Your Time and Your Life. New American Library, New York (1973)
8. Gowrishankar, S., Prachita, M.Y., Prakash, A.: IoT based heart attack detection, heart rate and temperature monitor. Int. J. Comput. Appl. **170**(5), 26–30 (2017)
9. Xiahou, K.S., Zeng, X.J., Hu, L.K., Li, G.P., Ye, R.H.: Design of human-body temperature monitoring system based on MLX90614 and ZigBee. Autom. Instrum. **11**, 23–26 (2011)
10. JoeDesbonnet's (2011). http://jdesbonnet.blogspot.com/search/label/Blood%20pressure%20monitor
11. De Nardis, L., Caso, G., Benedetto, M.G.D.: ThingsLocate: a ThingSpeak-based indoor positioning platform for academic research on location-aware internet of things. Technologies **7**(3), 50 (2019)
12. Reimers, A., Knapp, G., Reimers, C.D.: Effects of exercise on the resting heart rate: a systematic review and meta-analysis of interventional studies. J. Clin. Med. **7**(12), 503 (2018)
13. Mendelsohn, M.E., Karas, R.H.: Molecular and cellular basis of cardiovascular gender differences. Science **308**(5728), 1583–1587 (2005)

FireNot - An IoT Based Fire Alerting System: Design and Implementation

Bahman A. Sassani[1(✉)], Noreen Jamil[2], M. G. Abbas Malik[3],
and S. S. Tirumala[1]

[1] Unitec Institute of Technology, Auckland, New Zealand
bsarrafpour@unitec.ac.nz
[2] Fast University, Islamabad, Pakistan
[3] Universal College of Learning, Palmerston North, New Zealand

Abstract. Internet of Things (IoT) based systems have revolutionised the way real world systems are inter-connected through internet. At present the application of IoT based systems is extend to real time detection and warning system. However, cost has been a major factor for development and implementation of IoT systems. Considering the cost, ease of implementation, this paper proposes a low cost yet efficient IoT system called FireNot for warning and alerting fire incidents. FireNot is a cloud-based system that uses sensors (hardware) to detect fire and alert the user through internet and is maintained and monitored using a simple Android app. The FireNot system uses Raspberry Pi programmed through Python language and utilises Google API for location detection. This paper practically demonstrates the FireNot system through extensive testing on various operations and the FireNot system is proven to be efficient.

Keywords: Fire alert system · IoT alter systems · FireNot

1 Introduction

Internet of Things (IoT) initially appeared as an automation of processes, but smart IoT allows to achieve the paradigm of reaching the result, where the goal is a paramount and not methods for achieving it. IoT is a continues support for a man by the things which surround him. IoT is a clarity of processes and focus on result. IoT is not to tell how to do, but what should be in the outcome. Basically, things are agents for performing processes. Life cycle of things are quite simple. First, they collect the information from the real world, then they process it or in the other words, they plan some actions. The actions will be executed by commands.

Agent of a man communicates with agents of things, giving them commands and exchanging information. This relationship between man and surrounding things can provide comfort in living, prevention of disasters and saving lives.

The safety of any person is the most important part of living. Unfortunately, accidents and misfortune can happen even inside of any house. One of the threats is an open fire, which can take place due to uncontrolled cooking, unfinished smoking or

© Springer Nature Singapore Pte Ltd. 2020
I. S. Bajwa et al. (Eds.): INTAP 2019, CCIS 1198, pp. 14–21, 2020.
https://doi.org/10.1007/978-981-15-5232-8_2

simply due to electrical failure. There can be different reasons, but the outcome is always dangerous. Despite domestic fire alarms availability and installation inside premises, there are number of cases, when fire alarm does not function as supposed to or simply when nobody is around, when fire alarm goes off. IoT based Fire Alerting System "FireNot" is designed to give a second cross check in alerting people of possible fire on the premises. When the system senses smoke or fire, it alerts the user through their mobile phone, giving them notification of possible fire on the location. From here, the user can take any additional steps and action to check the premises, ask somebody else to check, if the user is away from the premises, or even call the fire brigade. The system is designed to use modern day technologies of Internet of Things, such as Raspberry Pi minicomputer, compatible smoke sensitive sensors, all of which communicates to an Android mobile application via Google Cloud. There is no man-to-man or man-to-machine interaction involved, therefore, it provides efficient inexpensive solution for a cross check in case of fire. The Fig. 1 below shows the system architecture.

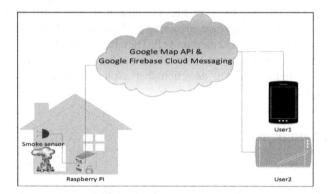

Fig. 1. System architecture

The other aspect, which is added to a business value of the system, is affordability in terms of cost of hardware. The Internet of Things technologies, available today, gives flexibility in terms of functionality, supported pool of open source knowledge, scalability, robustness and continues development. There is a definite demand for this type of solution for every household or business premise. Target audience include basically every layer of society. The development is decided to use Agile Software Delivery methodology due to most suitable project methodology available for software delivery. Its flexibility, clarity and absence of work overload provides great opportunity for successful delivery of the project within the timeframe. The main goal of the project is to provide the efficiently working system, which will be detecting any fire/smoking activity taking place on the premises, and alerting the user, who is located distantly, or in case of failure of fire alarms. The methodology for the development is Agile and Lean Software Delivery with several iterations, each of which has its own backlog of tasks and user stories.

2   Related Work

The rapid advances in IoT development have made possible to employ technology in new fields, such as smart cities [1]. The researchers have also explored the use of wireless sensor technologies and IoT for fire alerts. For example, Saeed et al. [7] propose an IoT-based home fire prevention system which has several sensors. The authors run several simulation experiments and conclude that the system can detect early fire and keeps the energy consumption of the sensors at an acceptable level. In [3], the researchers also build smart home hardware for fire alarm and suppression which is part of an IoT architecture that use cloud services to monitor and control room temperature. The paper aims to implement an IoT scenario based on the use of the MQTT protocol in the AWS platform. In another work, Vijayalakshmi S.R. and Muruganand S. [8] design a low-cost fire detection node and build an experimental WSN to compare two fire exposure algorithms. Maguluri, L. P. and others [4] also propose a fire detection solution based on IoT. They build a smoke alerting device and test it in a smart emergency response network for fire hazards. Our work will be part of those emerging solutions for fire detection that exploits the IoT features to create smarter buildings.

3   System Components

3.1   Raspberry Pi 3

The Raspberry Pi is one of the most popular applications which is used as a small computer in IoT industry. We used Raspberry Pi Model 3B over the 2nd Generation board since it is suitable for increasing CPU speed, power supply efficiency and built-in Wi-Fi chip [6]. The study of comparing the Raspberry Pi's performance and capabilities to the Arduino Uno, BeagleBone and Phidgets boards said that the Pi has limitations such as no Analog to Digital Converter (ADC) or real-time clock (RTC) and the number of digital I/O ports available is limited [5]. Even though most of IoT users suggest Arduino Uno for connecting Smoke sensor like MQ2 because of ADC, this limitation could not be the problem and Raspberry Pi's strengths are much over the other boards since Pi can easily connect to the Internet and support processing power available. Moreover, some users who are using Raspberry Pi and MQ2 sensor for detecting smoke explained that it is fine if we can receive the digital data when the sensor detects smoke (Fig. 2).

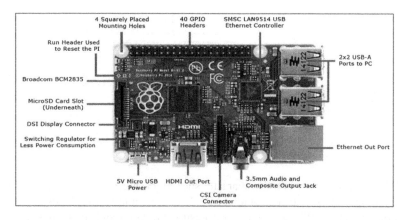

Fig. 2. Raspberry Pi 3

3.2 Smoke Sensor (MQ2)

There are many sensors for detecting smoke and other gases. We chose MQ2 which can detect smoke, LPG, CO, H2, CH4, alcohol and Propane because of detecting smoke. The sensor operation mainly depends on heater coil, the sensor heater uses 5 V Dc supply otherwise PWM pulses from 2 V to 5 V amplitudes. Important thing is No H pins (heater) directly connected to Raspberry Pi because of receiving the output voltage. The sensor gets warm by using this heater and this time taken for warm is called as "burn-in time" it may take up to 3 min for MQ sensors (Fig. 3).

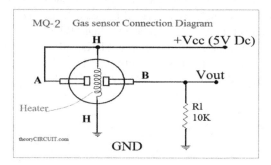

Fig. 3. Gas sensor connection diagram

The sensor which has the own board on the bottom has four pins to connect Raspberry Pi. These are power, ground, analogue output and digital output (Fig. 4).

Fig. 4. Smoke sensor MQ2

MQ2 sensor has the sensitivity characteristics for each gas for detecting. According to these data curves, Resistance value of MQ-2 is different to various kinds and various concentration gases. LPG gas is the most sensitive to detect and smoke is likely to be normal sensitive, and propane gas is the least sensitive. Therefore, it is good to detect smoke in a closed place such as closing home or office when the fire happens.

3.3   Google Firebase Cloud Messaging (FCM)

To send the notification to the mobile device, Google Firebase Cloud Messaging [2], hereafter FCM, is used for our system. FCM is a cross-platform solution for messages and notifications for Android, iOS and web applications which currently can be used at no cost. First of all, user account was registered on Google webpage in order to use Google Firebase Console. And then, our project can be added on Firebase, and can modify the setting of the project for utilising Firebase features. This key is necessary and used for sending notification to mobile devices. Also, users can download the JSON file which should be used for Android mobile application on this webpage.

The Firebase Realtime Database is a cloud-hosted database. Data is stored as JSON and synchronised in realtime to every connected client. When you build cross-platform apps with our iOS, Android, and JavaScript SDKs, all of your clients share one Realtime Database instance and automatically receive updates with the newest data. First, we made an android mobile application by using Android Studio, and the mobile

Fig. 5. Android mobile application page

3.4 Google Map API

Fig. 6. Google map API

devices were registered on Firebase Realtime Database by using the application and have got the tokens for each device from Firebase. After that, all the registered data can be shown on Firebase Realtime Database page. Among the data, the tokens are very important because they should be used when the project system would send notification (Figs. 5 and 6).

3.4   Google Map API

For displaying the location which fire happen, we used Google Maps Android API which can show the map based on Google Maps data to our application. The API automatically handles access to Google Maps servers, data downloading, map display and response to map gestures. Also, developers can use API calls to add markers, polygons, and overlays to a basic map, and to change the user's view of a particular map area. These objects provide additional information for map locations, and allow user interaction with the map. Because our project was already registered Firebase console account, we can get google map API key by just linking our project on the Google Cloud Platform webpage (Fig. 7).

Fig. 7. Google Cloud Platform webpage

This webpage shows the services which Google company supports. And we selected Google Maps Android API on Dashboard category after choosing API and services category in order that the service is available (Fig. 8).

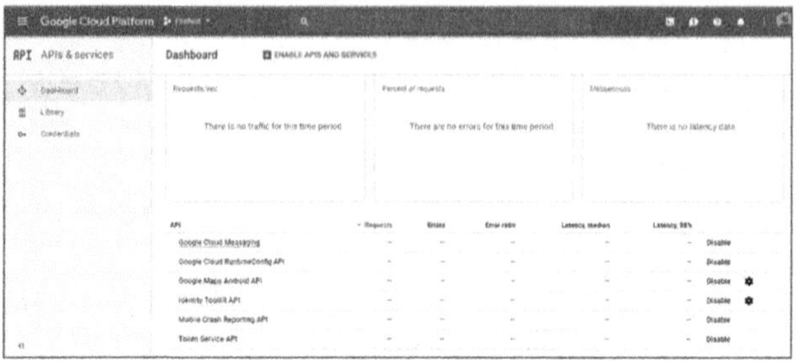

Fig. 8. Google Cloud Platform

And then, go to Credentials category, Android key is available for our application (Fig. 9).

Fig. 9. Google Cloud Platform

4 Conclusion

This paper presents a low cost IoT based fire alerting system called FireNot. The system provides a real time monitoring of the fire incidents and provides an alert to the user through computer and mobile interfaces. FireNot uses Raspberry Pi with the interfaced programmed using Python which provides low cost yet efficient system interns of both hardware and software.

The key contribution of this paper is boosting the IoT research and encouraging the possibility of building IoT systems that are portable, low cost and can be built using open source hardware and software. The ability of proposed FireNot is demonstrated through extensive testing and application. The integration of physical and software systems is been thoroughly tested.

The future implementations are concentrating and looking at developing an interface that could provide customisable interfaces and can report the incident to concern people (may be fire station/emergency or others) to provide an immediate action. The development of an API to provide access to external software and hardware systems is also another direction of research. Further, implementation of multiple locations and multiple systems to provide an overall a cloud-based fire alert service through government or private organisations may also be considered.

References

1. Arasteh, H., et al.: IoT-based smart cities: a survey. In: 2016 IEEE 16th International Conference on Environment and Electrical Engineering (EEEIC), pp. 1–6. IEEE (2016)
2. Firebase: Firebase cloud messaging, October 2019. https://firebase.google.com/
3. Kang, D.H., et al.: Room temperature control and fire alarm/suppression IoT service using MQTT on AWS. In: 2017 International Conference on Platform Technology and Service (PlatCon), pp. 1–5. IEEE (2017)
4. Maguluri, L.P., Srinivasarao, T., Syamala, M., Ragupathy, R., Nalini, N.: Efficientsmart emergency response system for fire hazards using IoT. Int. J. Adv. Comput. Sci. Appl. (IJACSA) 9(1), 314–320 (2018)
5. Maksimović, M., Vujović, V., Davidović, N., Milošević, V., Perišić, B.: Raspberrypi as internet of things hardware: performances and constraints. Des. Issues 3(8) (2014)
6. Raspberrypi.org: Raspberry pi 3 model b, October 2019. https://www.raspberrypi.org/products/raspberry-pi-3-model-b/
7. Saeed, F., Paul, A., Rehman, A., Hong, W., Seo, H.: IoT-based intelligent modeling of smart home environment for fire prevention and safety. J. Sens. Actuator Netw. 7(1), 11 (2018)
8. Vijayalakshmi, S., Muruganand, S.: Real time monitoring of wireless fire detection node. Procedia Technol. 24, 1113–1119 (2016)

Smart Intelligent System for Mobile Travelers Based on Fuzzy Logic in IoT Communication Technology

Imran Memon[1,2]([✉]), Hadiqua Fazal[1], Riaz Ahmed Shaikh[2],
Ghulam Ali Mallah[2], Rafaqat Hussain Arain[2],
and Ghulam Muhammad[1]

[1] Department of Computer Science, Bahria University, Karachi Campus,
Karachi, Sindh, Pakistan
imranmemon.bukc@bahria.edu.pk
[2] Department of Computer Science, Shah Abdul Latif University,
Khairpur, Sindh, Pakistan

Abstract. An internet of thing (IoT) is vulnerable to many identity-based attacks. However, due to the substantial increase in the density of users and nodes mobile travelers are more vulnerable to such attacks in IoT Communication Technology. In this paper, we have tried to explore the potential weaknesses related to security for mobile traveler's Smart Intelligent System environment in nodes mainly for handover conditions. We propose a novel scheme to protect against spoofing that utilizes probability distributions of Received Power based on the regions for mobile (moving) user. We further investigate the impact on secrecy rate of the targeted user in the absence and presence of an eavesdropper. Also, we evaluated our methods through simulation results for sensitive regions information based on fuzzy logic.

Keywords: Fuzzy logic · Smart · Intelligent system · IoT · Communication

1 Introduction

Promising advancement in an integrated circuit (IC), sensing technologies, internet of thing (IoT) and intra- wireless body sensor networks (WBSNs) has enabled a comfortable, affordable and reliable communication/health monitoring [1, 2]. Strategically placed nodes can monitor different vital information such as ECG signals, blood pressure, body temperature, glucose level, EEG, etc [3, 4]. Using hierarchical communication architecture, these nodes forward their sensing information to medical experts without disturbing routine activities of the human. Three-tier communication architecture is required to send the sensing information from nodes to medical experts. IoT is the first tier; a star topology network which is managed and regulated through implant and wearable bio-sensors. These nodes are capable of sensing vital Information, processing and forwarding them to a central controller called mobile network code (MNC). Normally a PDA or a smartphone is used as MNC [5–7]. In the second tier, IoT communication establishes a link between the primary network and beyond-IoT

© Springer Nature Singapore Pte Ltd. 2020
I. S. Bajwa et al. (Eds.): INTAP 2019, CCIS 1198, pp. 22–31, 2020.
https://doi.org/10.1007/978-981-15-5232-8_3

[8]. Data is collected by different MNCs and forwarded to one or more access points called sinks. These are equipped with large storage capacity, high processing speed and excessive energy source as compared to sensors [1, 6, 9, 10].

Mobile ad hoc networks are an infrastructure-free network with mobile nodes. The density of nodes in these networks is comparatively low as compared to sensor networks. The relationship among nodes is temporary often suffering from disconnections [1]. Mobility and reduced node density results in an absence of end to end route between the source and the destination. Due to the delayed delivery of packets mobile ad-hoc networks are also called delay tolerant networks. As discussed earlier, Delay Tolerant Networks (DTNs) are wireless networks [11] comprising of mobile nodes that prepare the possibility of data exchanges in solitude environments. Due to the movement of nodes, the topology of the network is constantly changing and the graph of the network is not wholly connected [2]. In these networks the nodes use saving, carrying, and sending policies to route packets to other stations [2]. Each node makes decision along with neighbors to send the packets between source and destination [1]. In DTN [19] the negotiations between nodes happen abruptly. Mobile Social Networks (MSNs) support a certain pattern for node negotiations. These networks are mainly implemented inhumane populations and the nodes possess some social characteristics [12, 13]. In these independent groups we required an edge survivable network to connect each other. IoT applications are mainly designed having centralized, decentralized and distributed architecture [14]. However, this may not fulfill above issues effectively therefore a hybrid architecture with novel topologies is used. Packet transmission within network is mainly operated in two modes i-e ad-hoc and infrastructure. In ad-hoc mode, there is no need of a central coordinator whereas in infrastructure mode coordinator centralized approach for transmission is used [7]. In many engineering applications, topologies are of prime importance. The basics of these topologies are derived from graph theory, a branch of mathematics, consisting of many specialized graphs e.g. complete graph, mesh, fully connected graphs etc [15].

The main objective of this research are as under

1. To propose mechanism which protects against the interference.
2. To propose MTFLA algorithm that will ensure detection and protection mechanism.

The paper further discusses related work concerning different topologies such as theoretical model, scalability model, survivability models present in IoT communication technologies in Sect. 2. Followed up by developed analytic model for probability distributions for different patterns, which is described in proposed method Sect. 3. Experimental and Evaluations and Conclusion are placed in Sect. 4 and 5 respectively.

2 Related Work

Many data routing algorithms have been proposed since last decade by considering major aspects, such as efficient energy utilization, quick and reliable delivery of sensing data, efficient bandwidth utilization etc. Authors in [17], discussed the packet size optimization for IoT to increase the energy efficiency. Packet size optimization has been discussed for implant as well as wearable bio-sensor nodes through different error control codes. They illustrated that energy efficiency increases with the increase in packet size till optimal packet length. However, the energy efficiency has been found to decrease with further increase in packet size after optimal length.

In [18], authors proposed a cost-effective and an energy-efficient design for IoT by introducing relay nodes. An Energy-aware IoT design model is used for finding an optimum number of relay nodes and their deployed position. Utilizing the integer linear programming model, the proposed scheme minimizes the energy consumption of biosensor nodes as well as that of network and also reduces their installation cost. The authors in [19], exhibited that the placement of MNCs has significantly influenced the energy efficiency and to work a lifetime of IoT. Through proper metric selection, authors have proposed three different routing schemes for the placement of MNC. They showed that the network life time could increase up to 47% through effective placement of MNC. Authors proposed, RE-ATTEMPT [14], an energy efficient routing protocol for IoT. Bio-sensors nodes are placed according to their energy levels. The high energy bio-sensor nodes are deployed near the MNC while MNC is located on center of the human body. Emergency data is directly transmitted (single-hop) to MNC while routine data is delivered through multi-hop communication.

In [20], authors proposed routing scheme iMSIMPLE for IoT. The proposed routing scheme achieved high throughput, energy efficiency and supported body posture movement. Multi-hop communication is utilized to enhance the energy efficiency. Sensing data from bio-sensor nodes is forwarded to MNC through the intermediate node (forwarder node). The selection of forwarder nodes is based on the cost-function. A cooperative data routing mechanism Co- LAEEBA has been proposed which has minimal path loss for the IoT [16]. Multi-hop and single-hop routing schemes are utilized on the basis of data priority. The proposed routing algorithm introduced a cost function to select the most feasible route from bio sensor nodes to MNC. The proposed mechanism maximizes the network stability, network lifetime and throughput at the cost of increased delay. Authors in [21] proposed a relay based reliable cooperative communication scheme for IoT. With different relay nodes, an analytical model for energy efficiency (EE) and packet error rate (PER) has been evaluated. A routing algorithm, enhance incremental cooperative critical data transmission in emergencies for static IoT (EInCo-CESat) has been proposed for IoT. The proposed algorithm achieved better network stability, less packet error rate (PER) and high throughput at the cost of high energy consumption [22].

3 Proposed Method

3.1 Sequence Estimation of Mobile Users

In an uplink transmission system, a sub-frame holds two training sequence, the 3rd and the 10th training sequence, used for frequency offset estimation. The signal received by k subcarrier of mth training sequence of ith sub-frame is shown as formula (1).

$$\Gamma_i^{(u)} = \sum_i R_i^{(u)*}(3, k) R_i^{(u)}(10, k) \tag{1}$$

The frequency offset estimation calculated by the formula [6] is shown in formula (2).

$$(u)_i = \arg\{\Gamma_i^{(u)}\}/14\pi \tag{2}$$

The estimating range of discussed before is only ±0.07, which is a very small scale. While the algorithm described in the literature [6] can only improve the accuracy of frequency offset estimation. The frequency deviation considered in the high-speed situation is roughly 0.107, which means that these methods discussed before cannot reach the estimation range condition. Improved estimating method of frequency deviation is employed to enhance the estimation range, which is shown as formulas (3) and (4).

$$f_i^{\wedge} = \arg\max\{M_{i,M}(\lambda)(f)\} \tag{3}$$

$$M_{i,m}(\lambda)(f) = \frac{\sum_{k=0}^{N_u-1}\left|R_{i,m}^S(\lambda)(k)\right|^2 s_{i,m}(\lambda, k)\big|^2}{\sqrt{\sum_{k=0}^{N_u-1}\left|S_{i,m}^{(\lambda)}(k, f)\right|^4}} \tag{4}$$

Thought the algorithm that performs maximum likelihood calculation on a single training sequence, discussed in the literature [23] might obtain batter estimating performance and the range are larger in the high-speed motion scenario, its estimating accuracy is low. Meanwhile, this literature also draws on the idea of joint estimation to improve the estimating accuracy, which imposes the training sequence calculation on training sequence on the one path and impose phase differ compute on two training sequence on the other path, and then carry correlation calculation on the two path. That is the idea of a united algorithm. According to the literature [24], the normalized frequency offset estimate is calculated out via frequency offset estimating, which is shown as formula (5) and (6).

$$\varepsilon_i^{(u)} = \varepsilon_i^{\wedge(u)} + 15v_i^{2\wedge(u)} \tag{5}$$

Where $\varepsilon_i^{(u)}$ is calculated out by phase, differ compute of two training sequence.

$$v_i^{\wedge(u)} = \arg\min\left(\varepsilon_i^{\wedge(u)} + \frac{2v_i^{(u)}}{15}\right)\varepsilon_i^{\approx(u)^2} \tag{6}$$

Where $\varepsilon_i^{(u)}$ is the estimation of the frequency offset obtained by the maximum likelihood calculation of single training sequence symbol and $v \in Z$, where Z is the set of all integers, the range of the Maximum likelihood estimation algorithm [25] of the method discussed in the literature is $-0.5 \leq \varepsilon_i^{(u)} \leq 0.5$, and the range of phase difference is $-0.07 \leq \varepsilon_i^{(u)} \leq 0.07$. Though the frequency deviation estimation range of this method is relatively large and the estimating accuracy is high, its high computational complexity is not easily employed in an actual communication system. Table 1 depicts fuzzy rules in the algorithm

Table 1. Fuzzy rules in algorithm

Number of neighbors	Distance to BSn	Remaining energy	Protection
Low	Low	Low	Medium
Low	Medium	Low	Medium
Low	High	Low	Very low
Low	Low	Medium	Medium
Low	Medium	Medium	Low
Low	High	Medium	Very low
Low	Low	High	Medium
Low	Medium	High	High
Low	High	High	High
Medium	Low	Low	High
Medium	Medium	Low	Medium
Medium	High	Low	Very low
Medium	Low	Medium	High
Medium	Medium	Medium	Medium
Medium	High	Medium	Low
Medium	Low	High	High
Medium	Medium	High	Medium
Medium	High	High	Low
High	Low	Low	Medium
High	Medium	Low	High
High	High	Low	Low
High	Low	Medium	Very high
High	Medium	Medium	High
High	High	Medium	Medium
High	Low	High	Low
High	Medium	High	Low
High	High	High	Very low

3.2   Time Estimation of Mobile User

Employing the method of cyclic prefix for frequency estimation, in time-division mode of LTE uplink multi-user transmission system, must obtain all users' cyclic prefix and the corresponding data of its other part. Obtaining a cyclic prefix is a method of extracting and reconstructing. And then, dispose the cyclic prefix received by receiving terminal through formula (7) to obtain phase shift owing to frequency deviation.

$$\Gamma_I^{(u)} = \sum_{m=0}^{M-1} \sum_{n=0}^{N_{cp}-1} r_i\left(nT_s + T_0(m)\right)s_i^{(u)}(m,n) \tag{7}$$

Therefore, the final frequency deviation estimate is shown as formula (8).

$$\varepsilon_i^{\wedge(u)} = \left(\frac{<\Gamma_i^{(u)}}{2\pi} + v_{cp}\right) \times 1500 \tag{8}$$

Where v_{cp} is an integer. According to the formula (8), frequency offset range of cyclic prefix auxiliary is $-0.5 \le \varepsilon_i^{(u)} \le 0.5$, which reach the requirement of large frequency deviation estimating range in high-speed.

Railway situation. However, if there are huge delays in the channel or another influence factor, the cyclic prefix may be somewhat mixed, which reduce the accuracy of the frequency offset estimation. Therefore, there is a new frequency offset estimating algorithm described in the literature [7], which reducing the impact of multipath in a Rayleigh channel situation. So, L defined as phase estimating length is shown in formula (9).

$$L(b) = (1 - b/p)N_{cp}, b = [1, p-1] \tag{9}$$

Where p is phase estimating coefficient whose value is 16 when cyclic prefix is relatively longer, or value is 8 when cyclic prefix is comparatively shorter. And the range of frequency offset estimate is $[-L, -1]$. Choose L(b) and L (b + 1) to estimate frequency deviation starting from b. Then describe the two estimate computed as eb and eb + 1, where eb is estimating frequency deviation according to L(b) which is defined as a cyclic prefix, which is shown in formula (10).

$$E(b) = \varepsilon^{\wedge} - \varepsilon_{b+1}^{\wedge \frac{2}{\varepsilon_b^{\wedge 2}}} \tag{10}$$

Plug eb and eb + 1 into formula (10), and if $E(b) \le e - 4$, it is considered as meeting the laboratory criteria in the phase estimating length. And then value L as L(i), let e = eb. Otherwise b will auto-increase 1, which may calculate repeatedly. e − 4 is the coefficient, which may modify owe to the change of actual situation. Table 2 depicts fuzzy Rules in MTFLA Algorithm.

Evidently, the method described in the literature [26] solves other path's interference to some extent. As a result, the outcome is relatively precise. At the same time, it holds a lower realizing complexity. However, the method can only apply to a single user system. In the TDD mode of LTE uplink multi-user system, if based on cyclic prefix auxiliary algorithm to estimate, reconstructing the cyclic prefix for each user, is needed which may greatly increase the complexity.

Table 2. Fuzzy rules in MTFLA algorithm

Distance to BS	Meet a number of mobiles	Protection
Low	Low	Very low
Low	Medium	Low
Low	High	Medium
Medium	Low	Low
Medium	Medium	Medium
Medium	High	Medium
High	Low	Medium
High	Medium	High
High	High	Very high

4   Experimental and Evaluations

4.1   Simulation Parameters

In this section, we give a detailed description of the simulation parameters and path losses information due to the deployment reason. Our proposed method to provide protect the user information while moving through sensitive regions and communication achieve the accuracy with reducing the range as shown in Table 1 and 2. Table 3 shows the simulation parameters below.

Table 3. Simulation parameters

Parameter	Value
Total bandwidth	6 MHz
Location of the base station	(100, 100)
Number of nodes	100
Data packet size	6000 bits
Eelec	50 nJ/bit
εmp	0.0013 pJ/bit/m^4
εfs	10 pJ/bit/m^2
Initial energy	1 J

4.2   Result and Discussion

In this section, we verify our proposed method, and has also analyzed several sensitive regions. We divided our evaluation in the three subpart based on regions of mobile users. The probability of coverage mobile user during moving on the smart environment, we observed that region 1 has low protection because less mobile meet inside the region and medium protection in the 2nd region meet the number of mobile users. Finally, number of users communicate each other get high protection during the various moving regions shown in Fig. 1. In Fig. 2, a high distance very user and less distance

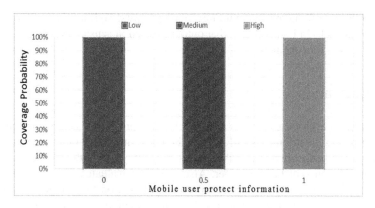

Fig. 1. Regions attacks performance

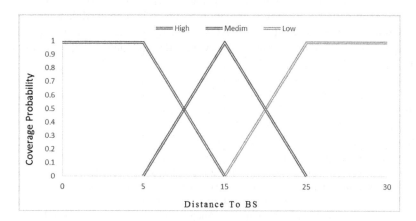

Fig. 2. Distance to BS mobile user protection

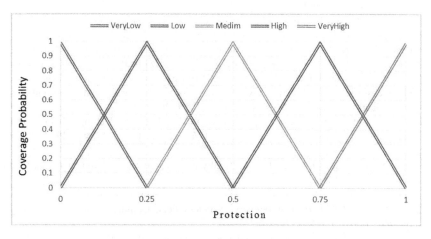

Fig. 3. Output protection information sensitive regions

number of the user to increases communication range and high-level protection against the spoofing attack. In Fig. 3 shows that output protection sensitive region information the fuzzy laws of our method.

5 Conclusion

In this paper, we propose a novel scheme for the protection against spoofing that utilizes probability distributions of Received Power signal based on the regions for the mobile user. We further investigate the impact on secrecy rate of the targeted user in the absence and presence of Eavesdropper. Also, we have evaluated our methods through simulation results for sensitive regions information based on fuzzy logic. On the basis of results, we have suggested mobile travelers' fuzzy logic Algorithm (MTFLA) for the protection of high sensitive regions, i.e. where the probability of attack will be highest. Also, comparisons among various security algorithms are made for energy consumption of different patterns. From the simulation results, it is concluded that our proposed algorithm for protection (MTFLA) proved to be energy efficient (secure harvesting) as it has reduced energy requirement for encrypting the data and resulting in low computational time.

References

1. Verma, P., Sood, S.: Fog assisted-IoT enabled patient health monitoring in smart homes. IEEE Internet Things J. **5**, 1789–1796 (2018)
2. Phoemphon, S., So-In, C., Niyato, D.(Tao): A hybrid model using fuzzy logic and an extreme learning machine with vector particle swarm optimization for wireless sensor network localization. Appl. Soft Comput. **65**, 101–120 (2018)
3. Mshali, H., Lemlouma, T., Magoni, D.: Adaptive monitoring system for e-health smart homes. Pervasive Mob. Comput. **43**, 1–19 (2018)
4. Sendra, S., Parra, L., Lloret, J., Tomás, J.: Smart system for children's chronic illness monitoring. Inf. Fusion **40**, 76–86 (2018)
5. Lochert, C., Mauve, M., Füßler, H., Hartenstein, H.: Geographic routing in city scenarios. ACM SIGMOBILE Mob. Comput. Commun. Rev. **9**(1), 69–72 (2005)
6. Hussain, F., Baek, W.-S., Sthapit, P., Pandey, D., Pyun, J.-Y.: Coordinator assisted passive discovery for mobile end devices in IEEE 802.15.4 (2013). ISBN 978-1-4673-3131-9
7. Zen, K., Habibi, D., Rassau, A., Ahmad, I.: Performance evaluation of IEEE 802.15.4 for mobile sensor networks. In: 2008 5th IFIP International Conference on Wireless and Optical Communications Networks (WOCN 2008), pp. 1–5 (2008)
8. Gubbi, J., Buyya, R., Marusic, S., Palaniswami, M.: Internet of Things (IoT): a vision, architectural elements, and future directions. Fut. Gener. Comput. Syst. **29**, 1645–1660 (2012)
9. Walia, N., Kalra, P., Mehrotra, D.: An IOT by information retrieval approach: smart lights controlled using WiFi (2016)
10. Akhtar, R., Leng, S., Memon, I., Ali, M., Zhang, L.: Architecture of hybrid mobile social networks for efficient content delivery. Wireless Pers. Commun. **80**(1), 85–96 (2014). https://doi.org/10.1007/s11277-014-1996-4
11. Dvir, A., Vasilakos, A.: Backpressure-based routing protocol for DTNs, vol. 40 (2010)

12. Abdo, A.M.A., et al.: MU-MIMO downlink capacity analysis and optimum code weight vector design for 5G big data massive antenna millimeter wave communication. Wirel. Commun. Mob. Comput. **2018**, 1–12 (2018). https://www.hindawi.com/journals/wcmc/2018/7138232/

13. Memon, I., Chen, L., Ali, Q., Memon, H., Chen, G.: Pseudonym changing strategy with multiple mix zones for trajectory privacy protection in road networks. Int. J. Commun. Syst. **31**, e3437 (2017)

14. Mihovska, A., Sarkar, M.: Smart connectivity for Internet of Things (IoT) applications. In: Yager, R.R., Pascual Espada, J. (eds.) New Advances in the Internet of Things. SCI, vol. 715, pp. 105–118. Springer, Cham (2018). https://doi.org/10.1007/978-3-319-58190-3_7. ISBN 978-3-319-58189-7

15. Zhang, D., Zhu, Y., Zhao, C., Dai, W.: A new constructing approach for a weighted topology of wireless sensor networks based on local-world theory for the Internet of Things (IOT). Comput. Math. Appl. **64**, 1044–1055 (2012)

16. Iffert, M., Kuenkel, M., Skyllas-Kazacos, M., Welch, B.: Reduction of HF emissions from the TRIMET aluminum smelter (optimizing dry scrubber operations and its impact on process operations). In: Bearne, G., Dupuis, M., Tarcy, G. (eds.) Essential Readings in Light Metals, pp. 968–974. Springer, Cham (2016). https://doi.org/10.1007/978-3-319-48156-2_143. ISBN 978-3-319-48155-5

17. Srinivas, A., Kalyan Kumar, A., Tulasi, B.: Introduction to TRIMET along with its properties and scope, vol. 1705 (2016)

18. Han, C., Jornet, J., Fadel, E., Akyildiz, I.: A cross-layer communication module for the Internet of Things. Comput. Netw. **57**, 622–633 (2013)

19. Arain, Q.A., et al.: Privacy preserving dynamic pseudonym-based multiple mix-zones authentication protocol over road networks. Wireless Pers. Commun. **95**(2), 505–521 (2016). https://doi.org/10.1007/s11277-016-3906-4

20. Uckelmann, D., Harrison, M., Michahelles, F.: An architectural approach towards the future Internet of Things. In: Uckelmann, D., Harrison, M., Michahelles, F. (eds.) Architecting the Internet of Things, pp. 1–24. Springer, Heidelberg (2011). https://doi.org/10.1007/978-3-642-19157-2_1

21. Rohokale, V., Prasad, N., Rangistty, N.D.: A cooperative Internet of Things (IoT) for rural healthcare monitoring and control (2011)

22. Liu, X., et al.: Distributed cooperative communication nodes control and optimization reliability for resource-constrained WSNs. Neurocomputing **270**, 122–136 (2017)

23. Lee, S., Lim, J., Park, J., Kim, K.: Next place prediction based on spatiotemporal pattern mining of mobile device logs. Sensors **16**, 145 (2016)

24. Lmai, S., Bourre, A., Laot, C., Houcke, S.: An efficient blind estimation of carrier frequency offset in OFDM systems. IEEE Trans. Veh. Technol. **6363**, 1945–1950 (2014)

25. Menze, M., Geiger, A.: Object scene flow for autonomous vehicles (2015)

26. Herrera, L.E., Calliari, F., Villafani Caballero, D.R., Amaral, G., Urban, P., von der Weid, J. P.: Transmitter-embedded AMCC, LTE-A and OTDR signal for direct modulation analog radio over fiber systems (2018)

Perception of Wearable Intelligent Devices: A Case of Fitbit-Alta-HR

Khurram Shahzad[1]([✉]), Muhammad Kamran Malik[1], and Khawar Mehmood[2]

[1] Punjab University College of Information Technology,
University of the Punjab, The Mall, Lahore 54000, Pakistan
{khurram,kamran.malik}@pucit.edu.pk
[2] School of Engineering and Information Technology (SEIT),
University of New South Wales, Canberra, ACT 2600, Australia
k.mehmood@unsw.edu.au

Abstract. Several wearable devices are available in the market they are becoming increasingly popular. These devices have been used for scheduling, time management, energy prediction, as well as for health management. Our thorough analysis of the literature has revealed that the majority of the studies focus on investigating the usefulness, accuracy, or adoption of the devices. However, no study has been conducted to evaluate the perception of these wearable devices among its users. To that end, in this study, we have used the end-user feedback in natural language to evaluate the perception of Fitbit-Alta-HR, which is an award-winning and widely used wearable device. The study reveals that majority of the users talk positively about the device. Furthermore, we have performed experiments using three supervised learning techniques to evaluate their effectiveness for classification. The studies show that state-of-the-art Artificial Neural Networks is the most effective technique, and unigram is the most suitable feature.

Keywords: Wearable devices · Intelligent devices · Sentiment analysis · Machine learning

1 Introduction

We are surrounded by numerous sensors, such as temperature, vision, motion, and medical sensors, that can capture various types of data associated with personals, environment, and their associated objects [1]. Furthermore, several portable products, including wearable devices, has also become available that can track human activities [2]. The examples of modern wearable devices are Pebble smartwatch, Google Glass, and Adidas MiCoach Fit Smart. A key feature of these devices is that they are adequately intelligent to reliably and accurately track human activities [3,4,7]. The data generated by these devices have been used for various purposes, such as food management, activity scheduling, time management, energy prediction, and diet management.

© Springer Nature Singapore Pte Ltd. 2020
I. S. Bajwa et al. (Eds.): INTAP 2019, CCIS 1198, pp. 32–42, 2020.
https://doi.org/10.1007/978-981-15-5232-8_4

A recent report by International Data Corporation (IDC) has highlighted that during the last quarter of 2018 alone, the global market of wearable devices grew 31.4% with a sale of over 172 million wearables shipped [12]. The report further highlighted that `Fitbit Inc.`, was third in terms of the number of shipments, and it was only behind `Apple Inc.` and `Xiaomi Inc.` In this study, we have considered Fitbit-Alta-HR as a representative wearable device due to two reasons: a) it has won the biggest award at the Wearable Tech Awards ceremony for the year 2017 [13], making it the most noticeable device, and b) it is pronounced as the most common activity tracking wearable device in the consumer market [2], making it a widely used device. Furthermore, a leading business data platform `www.statista.com`, has shown that the number of Fitbit devices being sold are continuously increasing [14] making it a market-oriented device.

We have conducted a thorough literature survey of the studies that involved activity monitoring devices, including Fitbit devices, to reveal that a large majority of the studies, such as [2,4,7,15], have focused on investigating the accuracy or reliability of the products in controlled settings [1,16]. However, to the best of our knowledge, no study has been conducted to evaluate the perception of these wearable devices among its users. To that end, in this study, we have used a Natural Language Processing (NLP) based approach to evaluate the perception of a representative wearable device, Fitbit-Alta-HR. In particular, we have crawled the customer feedback publicly available at `Amazon.com` and evaluated the perception of the device.

The rest of the paper is organized as follows. Section 2 presents an overview of the related work. Section 3 provides an overview of the approach that we have used for the evaluation of the perception. Section 4 presents the details of the experiments used for the effectiveness of the proposed approach. The results are discussed in Sect. 5, and finally the paper concludes in Sect. 6.

2   Related Work

We conducted a comprehensive search of the studies related to wearable devices in general, as well as the studies that focus on Fitbit, which is the representative wearable device used in this study. In particular, we used several relevant keywords to search for literature, which includes wearable device, perception, activity tracking, health monitoring, customer feedback, customer reviews, accuracy of a wearable device, and intelligent wearable devices, to search for literature. These key words were used for searching through several widely established digital libraries and search engines, including ACM DL, Springerlink, Sciencedirect, google scholar and PubMed. Our search and screening procedure revealed that there are two major areas of systems science research for wearable devices, a) effectiveness of wearable devices, b) adoption of wearable devices. A brief overview of these areas is as follows:

Effectiveness of Wearable Devices. A large majority of the studies focus on evaluating the accuracy or reliability of wearable devices for patients with different diseases. For instance, a recent study [7], has evaluated the accuracy of

Apple Watch, Fitbit Charge HR, Samsung Gear S, and Mio Alpha, to measure heart rate. Similarly, other studies have also been conducted to evaluate the effectiveness of measuring heart rate [8]. Another study [22], has evaluated and compared the accuracy of two wearable devices, Fitbit Charge HR, and Garmin vivosmart, to track the activities among patients with Parkinson's disease. Furthermore, an evaluation of the effectiveness of these devices has been conducted in various other healthcare settings, such as Aerobic exercises [9], monitoring ICU patients [10], and high-risk surgical patients [11].

More specifically, several studies have been conducted on Fitbit, which is one of the most widely used activity monitoring devices in the market [2]. For instance, an investigation has highlighted that Fitbit reasonably meets the validity and reliability standards and therefore it can be objectively used by primary care physicians to monitor patients' physical activity [2]. Furthermore, similar to other devices, studies have been conducted using Fitbit in different settings, such as during treadmill walking [4], depressed alcohol dependent women [5], physical activities of women [15], and in post-cardiac surgery population [6].

Adoption of Wearable Devices. Several studies have examined the phenomena of the adoption of wearable devices. For instance, a recent study has explored the contributing and inhibiting factors that influence the adoption of wearable devices using Google Glass and Sony Smart watch 3, as representative devices [17]. Some studies, such as [18,23], have investigated the adaption of wearable devices, including Fitbit, from end user perspective. However, these studies have the following limitations: a) they either focus on evaluating the users' acceptance on conceptual level, rather than their perception on the actual usage of the devices [20], or b) they empirically evaluate the tendency of users to recommend the technology to other users [19], or acceptability of these technologies [21], rather than relying on the actual comments of users that are available in natural language text. Therefore, any these quantitative evaluations cannot be used to develop insights about the perception of these devices.

To that end, in this study, we pioneer the use of end-user feedback, publicly available as natural language text, to evaluate their perception of a wearable device. Furthermore, we develop insights about the perception a wearable device.

3   Conceptual Overview

In this section, we have presented an overview of our approach that we have used to evaluate the perception of wearable intelligent device. In particular, we have used a NLP-based approach to evaluate the perception of Fitbit-Alta-HR, which is a wearable and an intelligent device. In contrast to the traditional approaches that rely on the very quantitative customer reviews, represented on a scale of 1-5, our approach takes into consideration the customer feedback given in the natural language. A key benefit of using natural language feedback is that it offers abundant opportunities to synthesize the feedback to identify the strengths and weaknesses of the key features of devices, hence, providing reliable and elaborated insights about the perception of the devices.

An overview of our approach is presented in Fig. 1. As depicted in the figure, we have employed a three-step approach to evaluate the perception of Fitbit-Alta-HR, which are: scrap the web and extract user comments, classify the scrapped feedback, and evaluation the perception of the device. In the following three sub-sections, we present the details of each step of our approach.

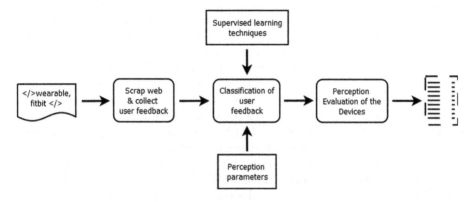

Fig. 1. A conceptual overview.

3.1 Step 1: Extract Customer Feedback

As a first step of our approach, we scrapped the customer feedback about Fitbit-Alta-HR, that is publicly available at www.amazon.com. The key reasons for choosing the amazon portal is that it is widely acknowledged as the most valuable global retailer [25], and it is the most valuable public company in the US, which is the largest market of such device [24]. Furthermore, recent data show that half of the web shoppers go to Amazon to search products, and 50% of consumers planned to do all their holidays shopping on Amazon [26]. Hence, offering a representative of the very large customer base of the Fitbit users. As there are several variants of Fitbit each having different features, therefore, it is highly likely that the customer feedback, as well as the perception of each variant, is different. Hence, combining the customer feedback of different variants may generate misleading perception. To that end, we have parsed all the publicly available comments[1] of a specific variant, Fitbit-Alta-HR, from $March$ 1, 2017 to May 30, 2019.

We scrapped Amazon web pages to extract the real-world and publicly available customer feedback. For the scrapping, we implemented a web crawler in Python that scraped the web and stored it in a text file. It was observed that the scrapped file contained several junk snippets, such as html tags, and non-English content. Given the observation, we implemented a script to omit such snippets, hence, leaving the customer comments written in English language. Accordingly, we collected a total of 4,379 comments that are used in this study for the perception evaluation.

---

[1] http://tiny.cc/blvo8y.

3.2 Step 2: Feedback Classification

A pre-requisite to generate a perception of the device using customer feedback in natural language is to classify the feedback into three categories positive, negative, and neutral. However, the manual processing and classification of our scrapped 4,379 comments is a time-consuming task. Furthermore, as the number of comments continue to increase, which are likely alter the perception of the device, therefore, it is equally important to take into consideration the newly added comments. To that end, in this study, we have employed an automatic approach to classify the comments. In particular, we have used Artificial Neural Network (ANN), which is a state-of-the-art supervised learning technique, to classify the comments. The choice of the technique stems from the experimental comparison of the three supervised learning techniques, Logistic Regression, Naive Bayes, and ANN, that we have performed. The details of these experiments and their results are presented in Sect. 4. The supervised learning techniques require numerical values as features for learning and prediction, whereas, the customer feedback is composed of natural language text. Therefore, we have used unigram features to convert the natural language text into numerical values. Similar to the choice of supervised learning technique, the choice of features stems from the experimental comparison of three features, unigram, bigram, and combination of both. The details of these experiments, as well as their results, are also presented in Sect. 4.

For the classification, the feedback was given as input to the implementation of machine learning techniques available in Scikit-learn. In order to train the model, we performed data prepossessing to convert the text data into numeric format. In the first step, we learnt the vocabulary of the training set, where vocabulary is the unique set of tokens in the training set. In this kind of representation, the word is neither bound to follow any grammatical rule for its appearance nor its position matters in the text. Based on the learnt vocabulary, we built the document-term matrix, where, rows of the documents term matrix are the reviews and its columns are the features. Its values are the numeric counts of the features. The output of this step was a set of 4,379 comments that were classified into positive, negative, and neutral.

3.3 Step 3: Perception Evaluation

In the third step, we have synthesized the comments to develop a perception of the Fitbit-Alta-HR. Our synthesis revealed that the comments can be grouped into two broad but slightly overlapping categories: (a) feature-specific comments, and (b) generic comments. The feedback comments that express feelings about a single or a set of features of the device are considered as feature-specific comments. Whereas, the comments that express a feeling about the device in general, without pointing out to some specific features, are considered as generic comments. For instance, consider a comment 'The doctor and the machine told the same heart-rate, and the battery life is great'. It can be observed that the user has expressed his satisfaction about two features of the device, battery life and the accuracy of measuring the heart rate. In contrast to that the comment 'I love it, highly recommended' expresses a positive feeling about the device, without specifying any specific features of the device.

Table 1. Examples of comments.

Examples of generic comments		
Topic	Sentiment	Comment
Working	Negative	I have owned that mysteriously stopped working around a year after purchase (I had the Charge previously that literally started falling apart after a year)
		The device basically stops giving any HR reading as soon as you start lifting
Ease of use	Positive	She said it is very easy to understand
		It was really easy to set up and it's easy to operate both the device and app
Recommendation	Positive	I love it and highly recommend it to everyone!
		Highly recommend for anyone that works at a desk and doesn't realize how scarily close to a rock they are becoming
Examples of feature specific comments		
Feature	Sentiment	Comment
Battery life	Positive	I would give this 5 stars, my only reason I'm holding off is because I want to see how long the battery lasts on a full charge
		Battery life is great - I get about a week out of it
	Negative	Sensor failed so I cannot turn off the heart-rate monitor, which glows a brilliant green both on and off the wrist, causing the battery to run down to zero in less than an hour
		I gather it just sits there flashing until you fish it out again, which doesn't help battery life. I guess the alternative is slapping some duct tape over it, but you know...
Heart rate	Positive	I checked the Fitbit heart rate against my polar heart monitor every 5 min during a 45 min kickboxing workout. It was EXACTLY in tune with the polar heart rate monitor, always right on or within 5 BPM
		The watch like clasp is great, the clasp on old fitbits were awful, they did a wonderful update with these ones. The continuous heart rate tracker is exactly what I was hoping it would be
	Negative	This Fitbit doesn't record accurate heart data, especially when working out

In addition to the broad categories, we further synthesized the comments by employing a bottom-up approach to further identify the feedback comments, to develop a perception of the device. Accordingly, we identified three key topics of discussion about generic comments, and two key features that are widely discussed by users. The topics are: working of the device, ease of use, and recommendation, whereas, the two key widely discussed features are, battery life and heart-rate. For an illustration, Table 1 shows example comments, their sentiment, as well as the feature or topic discussed in the comment.

Our synthesis of the feature-specific comments revealed that over 800 reviews discussed the use of the device about measuring the heart-rate, especially during work-out. A majority of these users expressed that the device was up to their expectations. Similarly, at least 450 comments discussed battery-life of the device, and a large majority of them talks positively about the battery life. Our synthesis of the generic comments revealed that over 300 reviews expressed that setting-up and use of the device was a pleasure, whereas, over 200 recommended the use of the device. Also, over 200 reported some issues with the working of the device. Based on the discussion, we conclude that the perception of Fitbit-Alta-HR is positive among its users.

4   Evaluation

As discussed in the second step of our approach, we used ANN to classify comments using unigram features, where the choice of the technique and features stem from the experimental comparison of three supervised learning techniques and three features. In particular, we performed experiments using Logistic Regression, Naive Bayes, and Artificial Neural Network, using unigram, bigram, and a combination of both, as features. In this section, we introduce the dataset, the evaluation measures used in this study, and the experimental setup, followed by an analysis of the results in the subsequent section.

4.1   Dataset

To evaluate the effectiveness of the supervised learning techniques, as well as the most suitable features, we scrapped the web to extract the customer reviews available at the Amazon online retail store. For that, we wrote a Python script that scraped the web and stored it in a text file. Subsequently, we identified the junk snippets, such as html tags, as well as non-English content, included in the scrapped content. Notably, we only extracted the real-world and publicly available in natural language. Accordingly, we extracted a total of $4,379$ comments, that were posted from March 1, 2017 to May 30, 2019. Subsequently, we manually classified the comments into three types, positive, negative, and neutral, so that the comments can be used for training and testing of the three supervised learning techniques.

4.2   Evaluation Measures

For the evaluation of the effectiveness of the measures, we have adopted three measures that are widely used in the information retrieval and natural language processing domain. That is, Precision, Recall, and F1 score. For a formal specification of the evaluation measures, let C be the complete set of comments, whereas, C_p^m, C_n^m, and C_u^m, be the set of positive, negative, and neutral comments, respectively. Furthermore, consider C_p^t, C_n^t, and C_u^t be the set of comments that are classified as positive, negative, and neutral comments, respectively, by a technique t. The evaluation measures can be defined as follows:

In the context of comments classification, Precision is the fraction of comments that are correctly classified by a technique, whereas, recall is the fraction of comments that should have been correctly classified by a technique. Formally, the two measures are defined in Eq. 1 and Eq. 2.

$$P = \frac{|(C_p^t \cup C_n^t \cup C_u^t) \cap (C_p^m \cup C_n^m \cup C_u^m)|}{|(C_p^t \cup C_n^t \cup C_u^t)|} \tag{1}$$

RIn the context of comments classification, Recall is the ratio between a) true positives in terms of classification, and b) the sum of true positive an false negative comments in terms of classification. Formally, it is defined in Eq. 2.

$$R = \frac{|(C_p^t \cup C_n^t \cup C_u^t) \cap (C_p^m \cup C_n^m \cup C_u^m)|}{|(C_p^m \cup C_n^m \cup C_u^m)|} \tag{2}$$

Finally, the F1 score is the harmonic mean of Precision and Recall, which is formally defined in Eq. 3.

$$F1 = 2 \times \frac{P \times R}{P + R} \tag{3}$$

4.3   Experimentation

We have performed experiments using the corpus of comments whose details are presented in Sect. 4.1. For the experiments, we used a training and testing ratio of $80 : 20$, that is, 80% of the comments for training and the remaining 20% for testing. Furthermore, we repeated the experiments ten times to neutralize any bias in the selecting of training or test data. That is, we repeated the same process ten-time from the complete corpus to neutralize any bias that may have been induced. The results presented in this paper are an average of the ten iterations that we have performed.

The experiments were performed using three features, unigram, bigram, and a combination of the unigram and bigram. In particular, to compute the value of each N-gram feature, we used Feature Presence (FP), Count of Feature Frequency (CFF) and Term Frequency-Inverse Document Frequency (TFIDF). More specifically, we first learnt the vocabulary set and formed a term-document matrix, where each column of the matrix represents a member from vocabulary set, whereas each row represents a comment. The values of each matrix represent FB, CFF, or TFIDF. The generated matrices have been used as features for learning and prediction.

For the classification, we fed the feedback directly to the implementation of machine learning techniques available in Scikit-learn. To train the models we performed data prepossessing to convert the text data into numeric format. In the first step, we learnt the vocabulary of the training set. Vocabulary is the unique set of tokens in training set. In this kind of representation, the word is neither bound to follow any grammatical rule for its appearance nor its position matters in the text. Based on the learnt vocabulary, we built the document-term matrix. Rows of the documents term matrix are the reviews and its columns are the features. Its values are the numeric counts of the features.

5   Results

A summary results of the experiments are shown in Table 2. As discussed above, each result presented in the table is an average of the ten iterations that we have performed. Following are the key observations from the experiments.

Most Effective Technique: It can be observed from the table that the F1 scores achieved by ANN are comparable with or higher than the F1 scores achieved by NB and LR. Furthermore, the Precision and Recall scores achieved by ANN are comparable or higher than that of NB and LR. The observation is valid for all type of features, unigram, bigram, and a combination of both. These results indicate that ANN is the most effective technique for classification of customer feedback.

Table 2. Results of the experiments.

Feature	Measure	LR	NB	ANN
Unigram	Precision	0.87	0.87	0.87
	Recall	0.88	0.87	0.88
	F1 score	0.66	0.58	0.66
Bigram	Precision	0.68	0.58	0.68
	Recall	0.61	0.57	0.62
	F1 score	0.57	0.54	0.58
Unigram + Bigram	Precision	0.63	0.56	0.63
	Recall	0.59	0.55	0.59
	F1 score	0.61	0.55	0.62

Most Effective Features: It can also be observed from the table that use of unigram features in all the supervised learning techniques achieved the highest Precision, Recall, and F1 score, whereas, the use of bigram feature achieved the lowest Precision, Recall, and F1 score. This indicates that unigram is the most effective feature for the classification and bigram is the least suitable feature for the classification. A key reason stems from the fact that the vocabulary, as well as the formulation of each customer, is different from each other, therefore there is scarcity of a pair of consecutive words that should be used for correctly classifying comments.

6   Conclusion

We have conducted a comprehensive survey of literature on wearable devices to reveal that most of the work has been done to evaluate the effectiveness of the devices in different settings. However, no study has been conducted to evaluate the perception of these wearable devices. To fill this gap, in this study, we have evaluated the effectiveness of a state-of-the-art (award-winning) and widely used wearable device, Fitbit-Alta-HR. In particular, we have scrapped the web to extract the customer feedback publicly available at a widely used online retailer, Amazon. Subsequently, we have data cleansing to extract the feedback available in natural language text. Following that, we employed Artificial Neural Networks (ANN) and unigram features to classify the comments into three types, positive, negative, and neutral, and used the classified comments to develop a perception of the device. Notable, the choice of ANN is based on an experimental comparison of ANN with Logistic Regression and Naive Bayes. Similarly, the choice of unigram also stems from its comparison with bigram and unigram + bigram features. In the future, we plan to classify further comments based on various features of the product.

References

1. Espinilla, M., Madina, J., Garcia-Fernandez, A., Campana, S., Londono, J.: Fuzzy intelligent system for patients with preeclampsia in wearable devices. Mob. Inf. Syt. **2017**(1), 1–10 (2017)
2. Diaz, K., et al.: Fitbit: an accurate and reliable device for wireless physical activity tracking. Int. J. Cardiol. **185**(15), 138–140 (2015)
3. Singh, A.K., Rehab, M.C., Farmer, C., Berg, M.L.E., Killington, M., Barr, C.J.: Accuracy of the FitBit at walking speeds and cadences relevant to clinical rehabilitation populations. Disabil. Health J. **9**(2), 320–323 (2016)
4. Takacs, J., Pollack, C.L., Guenteher, J.R., Bahar, M., Napier, C., Hunt, M.A.: Validation of the Fitbit One activity monitor device during treadmill walking. J. Sci. Med. Sport **17**(5), 496–500 (2014)
5. Abrantes, A.M., Blevins, C.E., Battle, C.L., Read, J.P.: Developing a Fitbit-supported lifestyle physical activity intervention for depressed alcohol dependent women. J. Subst. Abuse Treat. **80**(1), 88–97 (2017)
6. Daligadu, J., et al.: Validation of the Fitbit Flex in an acute post-cardiac surgery patient population. Physiother. Can. **70**(4), 314–320 (2018)
7. Wallen, M.P., Gomersall, S.R., Keating, S.E., Wisloff, U., Coombes, J.S.: Accuracy of heart rate watches: Implications for weight management. PlosOne **11**(5), 1–11 (2016)
8. Wang, R., Blackburn, G., Desai, M.: Accuracy of wrist-word heart rate monitors. JAMA Cardiol. **2**(1), 104–106 (2017)
9. Gillinov, S., et al.: Variable accurcy of wearable heart rate monotirng during aerobic exercise. Med. Sci. Sports Exerc. **49**(8), 1697–1703 (2017)
10. Kroll, R.R., et al.: Use of wearable devices for post-discharge monitoring of ICU patients: a feasibility study. J. Intensive Care **5**(64), 1–8 (2017)

11. Bretelerm, M.J.M., et al.: Reliability of wireless monitoring using a wearable patch sensor in high-risk surgical patients at a step-down unit in the Netherlands: a clinical validation study. BPM Open **8**(2), 1–9 (2018)

12. IDC   Report.   https://www.idc.com/getdoc.jsp?containerId=prUS44901819. Accessed 23 June 2019

13. Wearable Tech Award. https://www.wareable.com/fitbit/wareable-tech-awards-2017-fitbit-alta-hr-wins-wearable-of-the-year-5335. Accessed 23 June 2019

14. Sales   Report.   https://www.statista.com/statistics/472591/fitbit-devices-sold/. Accessed 23 June 2019

15. Cadmus-Bertram, L., Marcus, B.H., Patterson, R.E., Parker, B.A., Morey, B.L.: Randomized trial of a Fit-bit based physical activity intervention for women. Am. J. Prev. Med. **49**(3), 414–418 (2015)

16. Evenson, K.R., Goto, M.M.: Systematic review of the validity and reliability of consumer-wearable activity trackers. Int. J. Behav. Nutr. Phys. Act. **12**(159), 1–22 (2015)

17. Adapa, A., Nah, F.F., Hall, R.H., Siau, K., Smith, S.N.: Factors influencing the adoption of smart wearable devices. Int. J. Hum. Comput. Interact. **34**(5), 399–409 (2018)

18. Pal, D., Funilkul, S., Charoenkitkarn, N., Kanthamanon, P.: Internet-of-Things an smart homes for elderly healthcare: an end user perspective. IEEE Access **6**(1), 10483–10496 (2018)

19. Talukder, M.S., Chiong, R., Bao, Y., Malik, B.H.: Acceptance and use predictors of fitness wearable technology and intention to recommend: an empirical study. Industr. Manage. Data Syst. **119**(1), 170–188 (2018)

20. Kim, K.J., Shin, H.: An acceptance model for smart watches: Implications for the adoption of future wearable technology. Internet Res. **25**(4), 527–541 (2015)

21. Chuah, S.H., Rauschnabel, P.A., Krey, N., Nguyen, B., Ramayah, T., Lade, S.: Wearable technologies: the role of usefulness and visibility in smartwatch adoption. Comput. Hum. Behav. **65**(1), 276–284 (2016)

22. Lamont, R.M., Daniel, H.L., Payne, C.L., Brauer, S.G.: Accuracy of wearable physical activity trackers in people with Parkinson's disease. Gait Posture **63**(1), 104–108 (2018)

23. Jarrahi, M.H.: Digital and physical materiality of information technologies: the case of Fitbit activity tracking devices. In: 48th Hawaii International Conference on System Sciences, USA, pp. 1–2. IEEE (2015)

24. Top   Brands.   https://www.marketingcharts.com/brand-related/top-brands-108621. Accessed 23 June 2019

25. Amazon, Most Valuable Company. http://fortune.com/2019/01/07/amazon-most-valuable-public-company/. Accessed 23 June 2019

26. Amazon Statistics. https://muchneeded.com/amazon-statistics/. Accessed 23 June 2019

Automatic Sun Tracking Smart Wheel Chair with Real Time Navigation

Muhammad Rizwan Masood[1(✉)], Ali Sufyan[1], Usama Khalid[1(✉)],
Muhammad Makki Khan[1(✉)], and Sundus Amin[2(✉)]

[1] Department of Telecommunication Engineering, UCET,
The Islamia University of Bahawalpur, Bahawalpur, Pakistan
rizwanmughal91@gmail.com, ali_sufyan@ymail.com,
usama.khalid6033@gmail.com, makkikhan530@gmail.com
[2] Department of Computer Science, Comsats University, Vehari, Pakistan
sundasramey@ciitvehari.edu.pk

Abstract. Aging is a natural procedure prompt changes in quality and amount of muscles in skeletal, due to which muscle shortcoming and disability in moving of maturing populace. Crumbling pain in the arms and legs in the main cause of movement and the basic cause of disability in the spinal cord, cauda equina, or fringe neuropathy. As a result of seriousness and merits, electric wheelchairs are progressively requested in the recent era. Our proposed work is a smart electric wheelchair control by both joystick and a dependent user recognition voice system. To facilitate the patients in the outdoor environment an automatic sun-tracking solar plate is provided to charge the battery itself and automatically tracks sun position to provide not only power backup but also shadow to walk in sunlight. The navigation device is installed for providing real-time navigation which helps the user to select the shortest and easiest route. The proposed system is cost-effective of existing available in the market and also energy efficient.

Keywords: Joystick · Voice system · Sun tracking · Navigation · Smart · Cost effective · Energy efficient

1 Introduction

Every single individual in this world has a desire to carry on an ordinary human life however street mishaps, disorders and permanent injury make their desires into disability. Also, the mature populace of Pakistan above the '80s suffers from crumbling pain in legs and toes. Due to this issue, they face severe problems in mobility and have a dependence on others. Statistics show approximately 2% of Pakistan's total population suffer from disabilities. Statistics are given in Table 1. As a result of serious effects and percentage of disability, electrically mechanized wheelchairs are requested. We are proposing a framework that facilitates the patients to move independently without any human assistance.

© Springer Nature Singapore Pte Ltd. 2020
I. S. Bajwa et al. (Eds.): INTAP 2019, CCIS 1198, pp. 43–52, 2020.
https://doi.org/10.1007/978-981-15-5232-8_5

Table 1. Pakistan Bureau of Statistics Disability result 2017 [1]

Administrative unit	Total disable population	Crippled %	Mentally retarded %	Multiple disabilities %	Others %
Pakistan	3,286,630	18.93	7.60	8.23	43.37
Rural	2,173,999	20.52	7.32	8.23	42.55
Urban	1,112,631	15.81	8.15	8.22	44.97
Islamabad	8,434	29.79	8.05	4.55	23.73
Rural	3,996	29.65	8.63	4.02	29.73
Urban	4,438	30.10	7.53	5.05	18.32
Punjab	1,826,623	20.83	7.87	8.07	39.84
Rural	1,338,410	20.84	7.63	8.18	40.32
Urban	488,213	20.79	8.51	7.77	38.52
Sindh	929,400	10.56	7.45	8.92	53.29
Rural	385,984	11.25	6.81	9.06	55.28
Urban	543,416	10.07	7.91	8.82	51.86
Khyber Pakhtunkhwa	375,752	31.73	7.43	8.11	31.90
Rural	327,638	32.25	7.26	8.22	31.48
Urban	48,114	28.21	8.63	7.31	34.75
Balochistan	146,421	14.81	5.61	6.35	54.96
Rural	117,971	14.31	5.53	6.24	57.36
Urban	28,450	16.86	5.97	6.83	45.02

This project is made up of a voice recognition module which enables the patient to move freely in any direction just by providing defined voice commands. Speech recognition is a key revolution which can provide a human association with machines for regulating a wheelchair. Sometimes the user has some throat problem or he has some issue with his neck and not able to speak that's why a joystick is provided which can move wheelchair freely in all directions automatically without any hard effort.

Nowadays energy crises are the main issue in Pakistan. To overcome this issue, the proposed project provides a facility to the user in the harsh environment through automatic sun-tracking solar plates that are used to charge the battery in outdoors. Solar plates not only deliver current but also provide shadow to walk in sunlight.

Sometimes the user has to move to unknown places, too overwhelmed this problem this project is accessible with GPS bases real-time navigation aid to ease the patient to move unknown places using an android device. It is cost-effective, easy to use and has simple mobility. The proposed project is 56% cost-efficient as compared to available in markets (Table 2).

Table 2. Cost comparison

Source	Cost range
[11]	US $ 800–1870/piece
[12]	US $ 800–1870/piece
[13]	US $ 900–2400/piece
[14]	US $ 700–1500/piece
Proposed project	US $ 450/piece

2 Literature Review

The objective of this project is to train the available mechanizes wheelchair control framework with a voice recognition command at low-price and with the approachable procedure. For this purpose, the Bluetooth module SR-04 module is connected via Arduino for controlling a wheelchair [2].

To oblige the number of inhabitants in people who discover it troublesome or difficult to work to a power wheelchair, a rare-experts have used advances originally produced for moveable robots to develop smart wheelchairs [3–5]. A smart wheelchair ordinarily comprises of a normal Control Wheelchair base that consist of a PC and an accumulation of sensors have been included, or a versatile robot base attach with a seat has been joined [6]. Pineau et al. 2011 contend that the progress to wheelchairs that collaborate with the client is at any rate as significant as that from physically to controlled wheelchairs, perhaps considerably progressively significant since this would mark a paradigmatic as opposed to only a mechanical shift [7].

The voice-controlled wheelchair is manufactured to overthrown the issues confronted by disabling users and facilitate them to move the wheelchair. The wheelchair engaged by providing voice recognition commands through defined information. The Arduino will operate the wheelchair as the user provide input commands [3].

The point of the design is to build up a smart program that is effectively versatile to an electric wheelchair and to assist numerous persons with physical disabilities and seniors who experience issues moving their joysticks. This control operation depends on an artificial intelligence technique [8].

Solar power is a clean, effectively open and plentifully, accessible elective energy source in the environment. For power generation, solar energy is a beneficial source provided by nature at free of cost. Applications that utilize fixed solar panels for generations of electricity will provide their maximum output only for noon from 12 noon to 2 PM which results in a deficiency of energy produced by them. For this purpose, to improve the efficiency and utilization of solar energy, the mounting of solar tracking plates on the device would be a solar tracking system that follows sunlight's maximum intensity. To get extreme utilization of energy, photovoltaic panels would be paced in perpendicular manners. The system utilized in this work incorporates the execution of Arduino based commands to track solar light. Light Dependent Resistors (LDRs) are utilized to detect the power of daylight and consequently the solar panels are adjusted in fashion is to track maximum sunlight and hence produce much energy accordingly. The instrument utilizes a servo motor to control the mobility of the sunlight based solar panels. The microcontroller is utilized to control the servo motor dependent on the instructions received from light-dependent resistors [9].

Photovoltaic solar tracking plates have a great and biggest application due to its ease of working and implementation in housing and many robots. In this proposed venture, another model of photovoltaic solar plates-based trackers interfaced with Arduino was created. Feedback control framework that permits two axes based solar tracking in which linear actuator and stepper motor are utilizes photodiodes placed on the electronic circuit [10].

The proposed system is an automatic sun tracking smart wheelchair with Real-time navigation for the physically crippled and disabled person. This system is designed to operate the wheelchair based on voice recognition module (command from user is sent to Arduino UNO where it is detected and then desired output of command is generated), joystick control (command being generated from joystick is taken to controller where related output of command is generated through motor driver), solar tracking (LDR is connected to Arduino) tend to move in a direction where intensity of light is maximum and real-time navigation helps the user to navigate towards the shortest route in order to save energy and prevent user from tiredness. Solar plates not only charge the battery but also provide shadow to a user in harsh environments. The proposed work has a vast diversity that multiple devices interface with this project.

3   Proposed System Architecture

The main tool that is used in the proposed project is a microcontroller named Arduino UNO. Arduino UNO is open-source. It has a USB interface and consists of 14 Input/output pins from which 6 can be consumed as PWM output pins. For the operating purpose, it requires 5 V. Input/output pins having 20 mA direct current. It has a clock speed of MHz and 32 KB flash memory from which 0.5 KB utilized by a bootloader. Arduino UNO holding 25 mg weight (Fig. 1).

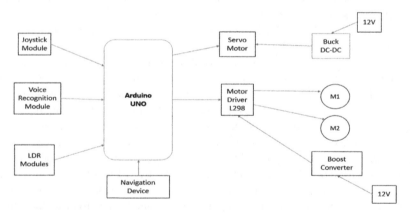

Fig. 1. Block diagram

In the proposed project Arduino is the main component that is used as a controller. The Voice recognition module is linked with analog pins of the Arduino to transfer voice command to the controller. Voice signals are in analog foam so it utilized by analog pins. Joystick module is linked with analog pins for transferring command in the form of voltages. Voltages by joystick are in the foams of continues waves. So, the joystick module is connected to analog pins of Arduino UNO. Similarly, the LDR module's output is in the form of a continuous-wave of voltages. Due to this fact the LDR modules linked with Arduino through analog pins. The navigation device needs power for battery charging. For this purpose, a navigation device is fixed to the Arduino UNO.

Arduino UNO gets commands from the voice recognition module and the joystick module. After processing Arduino UNO generate instructions to the motor driver for operating motors according to the user command. After processing on the commands by LDR modules the Arduino UNO generate instructions to servo motors for moving on the desired angle where sun light's density is high (Fig. 2).

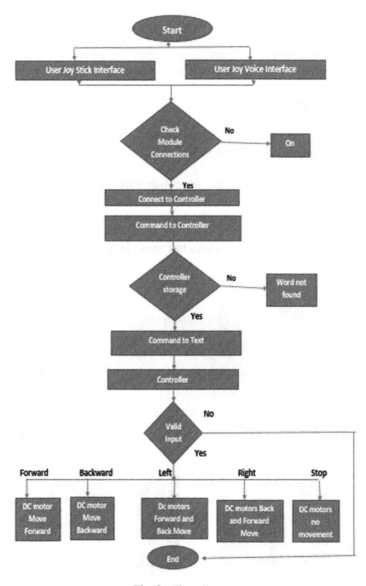

Fig. 2. Flow diagram

In the initial stage, the command generates through a voice recognition module or a joystick module. After that check the connections. If no connections exist with the controller, then create a connection and transfer command to it. The controller checks the command even if it is a valid or invalid command. The valid command transfer into text and marked as valid input. After this process, the output is generated in the foam of motors moving.

4 Results and Discussion

This project consists of sun-tracking with the help of LDR for charging purposes, voice control by using the different commands given to voice reorganization module, joystick control for easy mobility, navigation device to choose the best route for the destination.

4.1 Joystick Results

1. Initially, the wheelchair is in rest as shown in Fig. 3.
2. By moving the joystick Up the wheelchair move in the forward direction as shown in Fig. 4.
3. By moving the joystick Down the wheelchair move in a backward direction as shown in Fig. 5.
4. By moving the joystick Right, the wheelchair move in the right direction as shown in Fig. 6.
5. By moving the joystick Left the wheelchair move in the left direction as shown in Fig. 7.

Fig. 3. Rest position   **Fig. 4.** Forward movement   **Fig. 5.** Backward movement

Fig. 6. Right movement   **Fig. 7.** Left movement

4.2 Voice Recognition Result

1. By using the word 'F' the wheelchair start movement in the forward direction as shown in Fig. 8.
2. By using the word 'Z' the wheelchair start movement in a backward direction as shown in Fig. 9.
3. By using the word 'L' the wheelchair start movement in the left direction as shown in Fig. 10.
4. By using the word 'R' the wheelchair start movement in the right direction as shown in Fig. 11.
5. The word 'O' is used to stop the movement as shown in Fig. 12.

Fig. 8. Forward movement   **Fig. 9.** Backward movement   **Fig. 10.** Left movement

Fig. 11. Right movement   **Fig. 12.** Stop movement

4.3 Sun Tracking Result

1. By emitting light on LDR1, the plate moved in EAST, shown in Fig. 13.
2. By emitting light on LDR2 the plate moved in NOON, shown n Fig. 14.
3. By emitting light on LDR3, the plate moved in WEST, shown in Fig. 15.

Fig. 13. Plate at EAST   **Fig. 14.** Plate at noon   **Fig. 15.** Plate at noon

4.4 Navigation Device Result

1. For testing the system, we select the destination from Engineering old building to Main Canteen of Bagdad campus (Fig. 16).

Fig. 16. Best route result

5 Conclusion and Future Work

The fundamental constituents of our project are Arduino UNO, Voice recognition module V3.1, motor driver L298n and motors. This project exertion aspires to help those people who are relying on a wheelchair for their mobility and portability. This model will be so cost-effective and penny-wise that even common people may have access to it.

We are materializing this automatic wheelchair which acquires numerous advantages and among them, the main gratification is that its ease of being operated and it doesn't need any external help as it is self-directing. It is being executed in two different modules i.e. joystick module and voice recognition module.

This wheelchair has been designed for physically disabled people who cannot walk. They can easily handle it with their hands by using the Joystick and for those people who can't move their hands as well as legs, the voice recognition control wheelchair can overcome this shortcoming. This model can be made remarkably effective and profitable on the occasion of demanding environmental conditions.

In this project, real-time navigation factor has been used to make it more useful. If we tend to move to a new area without knowing about this area, time navigation can be used to reach our destination. This project is comparatively penny-wise than those projects that have been implemented for the same purpose. This project can also be counted as a luminous drive for the advancement of physically crippled and disabled people's lifestyles. This product can be commercialized in Pakistan and patients may get benefit from it and we have commenced our efforts to commercialize it.

Disorder or catastrophe that harms the neural system may cause individuals to lose their capacity to move their voluntary muscle. Sometimes it leads to paralysis which may cause an individual's failure to move their locomotory organs, for say, arms, and legs. In the future, our aim to develop an addition in this system is to provide another controlling feature that is an eye monitoring system. We are proposing a way to control an electric wheelchair is to use the head as a joystick instead of a traditional joystick. Another future aspect is a system named Hand Gesture Controlling wheelchair that is classified into a gesture unit and wheelchair unit and this wheelchair would be controlled with simple hand gestures. A remarkable amendment regarding the future is Human Following Wheelchair. The primary goal of this work is to design and fabricate a model that not only tracks the target but also moves towards it while doing the tracking. A very useful need to be done is to provide obstacle detection and then avoiding that obstacle. The proposed work has a vast diversity that multiple devices interface with this project. Another way to control a smart wheelchair is through mobile by interfacing it with Bluetooth module. The android base application will be used as a commanding source. Android knowledge behaves as a new approach to human communication with machines.

References

1. Pakistan Bureau of Statistics report on disability. http://www.pbs.gov.pk/content/disabled-population-nature-disability
2. Lodhi, D.K., et al.: Smart electronic wheelchair using Arduino and bluetooth module. IJCSMC **5**(5), 433–438 (2016)
3. Kokila, P., Sharmila, R., Sheril, P., Karthik Raj, G.R., Ramkumar, M.: Audio controlled wheelchair using Arduino. Int. J. Intellect. Adv. Res. Eng. Comput. **06**(01), 300–306 (2018)
4. Sinyukov, D., Desmond, R., Dickerman, M., Fleming, J., Schaufeld, J., Padir, T.: Multimodal control framework for a semi-autonomous wheelchair using modular sensor designs. Intell. Serv. Robot. **7**(3), 145–155 (2014). https://doi.org/10.1007/s11370-014-0149-7
5. Rathore, D.K., Srivastava, P., Pandey, S., Jaiswal, S.: A novel multipurpose smart wheelchair. In: IEEE Students' Conference on Electrical, Electronics and Computer Science, Bhopal, pp. 1–4, March 2014
6. Yayan, U., Akar, B., Inan, F., Yazici, A.: Development of indoor navigation software for intelligent wheelchair. In: Proceedings of the IEEE International Symposium on Innovations in Intelligent Systems and Applications, Alberobello, pp. 325–329, June 2014
7. Leishman, F., Monfort, V., Horn, O., Bourhis, G.: Driving assistance by deictic control for a smart wheelchair: the assessment issue. IEEE Trans. Hum.-Mach. Syst. **44**(1), 66–77 (2014)
8. Rabhi, Y., Mrabet, M., Fnaiech, F.: Development of a new intelligent joystick for people with reduced mobility. Hindawi Appl. Bionics Biomech. **2018**, 14 (2018) (Article ID 2063628)

9. Aigboviosa, A.P., Anthony, A., Claudius, A., Uzairue, S., Timilehin, S., Imafidon, V.: Arduino based solar tracking system for energy improvement of PV solar panel. In: Proceedings of the International Conference on Industrial Engineering and Operations Management, Washington DC, USA, 27–29 September 2018

10. Morón, C., Ferrández, D., Saiz, P., Vega, G., Díaz, J.P.: New prototype of photovoltaic solar tracker based on Arduino, 30 August 2017

11. Made in China.com. https://www.made-in-china.com/productdirectory.do?word=smart+wheelchair&subaction

12. Ali express.com. https://www.aliexpress.com/premium/smartwheelchair.html?SearchText=smart+wheelchair

13. ebay.com. https://www.ebay.com/sch/i.html?_from=R40&_trksid=m570.l1313&_nkw=smart+wheelchair

14. daraz.com. https://www.daraz.pk/catalog/smartwheelchair.html

A Blockchain-Based Framework for Information Security in Intelligent Transportation Systems

Wajid Rafique[1,2], Maqbool Khan[1,2], Xuan Zhao[1,2], Nadeem Sarwar[3], and Wanchun Dou[1,2(✉)]

[1] State Key Laboratory for Novel Software Technology, Nanjing University, Nanjing, People's Republic of China
rafiqwajid@smail.nju.edu.cn, douwc@nju.edu.cn
[2] The Department of Computer Science and Technology, Nanjing University, Nanjing, People's Republic of China
[3] Department of Computer Science, Bahria University Lahore, Lahore, Pakistan

Abstract. Efficient utilization of the IoT generated data helps in the decision-making process as well as the realization of the concept of smart cities into a reality. The smart cities utilize Intelligent Transportation System (ITS) to facilitate smart vehicles to operate independently without much human intervention. The ITS system utilizes the data produced by the smart infrastructure to intelligently operate the smart vehicles and make highly precise decisions in the whole smart city ecosystem. Although ITS has been in its evolutionary phase, this is the right time to realize the vulnerabilities present in the ITS infrastructure that can be exploited by the adversaries to render devastating attacks. The ITS network involves highly sophisticated infrastructure where any anomaly provokes threat to human lives. The ITS data can be manipulated by the adversaries for attacks such as password theft, information spoofing, data manipulation, information loss, eavesdropping, and key fob attacks.

Blockchain provides a distributed and tamper-resistant technology by utilizing a privacy-preserving ledger to secure data in an efficient manner. The Blockchain technology eliminates the adversarial impact of the attackers by leveraging the computational capabilities of the trusted nodes in the network. In this research, we provide a secure framework for effective implementation of ITS using Blockchain technology in the centralized management of software defined networking. This framework utilizes edge computing where Blockchain provides security services. This framework is secure, provides interoperability, less information leakage, and seamless integration between versatile smart vehicles and service infrastructure.

Keywords: IoT · SDN · Network security · Blockchain · Privacy · Access control · Information security

© Springer Nature Singapore Pte Ltd. 2020
I. S. Bajwa et al. (Eds.): INTAP 2019, CCIS 1198, pp. 53–66, 2020.
https://doi.org/10.1007/978-981-15-5232-8_6

1   Introduction

The rapid development in the sensor technologies has provided the capabilities to capture real-world data from the physical infrastructure. Internet of Things proved to be one of the promising technology which has brought immense attention of researchers from academia and industry during the past few years [11]. IoT interlinks the physical world with the internet using the prevalent networking infrastructure to enables the concept of ubiquitousness into reality. Figure 1 illustrates the evolution of computing technology from centralized computing in the 1970s to ubiquitous computing recently. IoT facilitates human lives by incorporating sensing capabilities in the physical infrastructure including healthcare, transportation, and industry which enable sophisticated measurements and smart decision making. According to [3], approximately 50 billion devices will be connected to the internet till 2020 generating a cumulative growth of 31% from that of 2016. This rapid increase in the IoT devices results in a huge amount of data generation and transfer. As the IoT devices lack in the computation resources, including memory, storage, and battery, the IoT Big data is handled by the cloud infrastructure to facilitate the decision making [16]. This data generation and transfer to the cloud provoke countless vulnerabilities of privacy and security. The resource limitation in IoT aggravate multiple other attack vectors where resource limitation in IoT becomes a serious threat to the internet infrastructure.

Software-Defined Networking (SDN) offers centralized decision making by separating the infrastructure plane from the control plane [13]. SDN has proved to be a feasible choice in managing heterogeneous IoT infrastructure [19]. The SDN concept is based on the programmability of the networks where the increasing network size can be flexibly managed. The centralized control in SDN lower downs the complexity of the heterogeneous IoT traffic administration. SDN has the capability to manage the complete life-cycle of IoT including service discovery, commissioning, user handover, service migration, and performance optimization. SDN utilizes edge cloudlets to offload the tasks from the resource-limited IoT devices to enable the execution of compute-intensive tasks [5].

From the past few years, the attack vectors employing IoT devices to attack vital infrastructure has been increased extensively [9,12]. The workflow in IoT systems is usually based on the data mobility among different hosts which raises data leakage and information theft-related issues. IoT generated data is highly critical and contains private information which must be protected from leakage and unauthorized access. As IoT devices contain limited resources, complex security algorithms are difficult to implement on such an infrastructure. In this regard, it is necessary to secure such devices using network-based security solutions. Moreover, the distributed nature of the IoT devices makes it challenging for the implementation of centralized security solutions. In this situation, Blockchain provides a distributed privacy preservation strategy to cope with the demands of privacy.

Blockchain is a distributed data storage strategy where every user in the network stores some parts of the Blockchain [4]. It eliminates the adversarial impact

Fig. 1. The evolution of technology from the start of computing era.

of the attackers by leveraging the computational capabilities of the trusted nodes in the network [14]. It operates in a ledger-oriented fashion where each network transaction is verified and documented. The blocks in the Blockchain are linked using the cryptography where non-trusted entities have no access to the blocks. Every member in the Blockchain is responsible for adding the data in the overall Blockchain. The data is updated by adding a new block on top of the previous blocks where the whole chain is updated accordingly. This sequential data-keeping provokes a chaining mechanism which is secure and easy to detect malicious activity on the data. If an adversary tries to manipulate the data, the whole sequence chain analyzes its own block of data and identify the location where it has been changed. Figure 2 illustrates the possibilities of attacks on the Intelligent Transportation System (ITS) networks. The adversary is shown attacking the Vehicle to Vehicle (V2V) and Vehicle to Infrastructure (V2I) communication. ITS utilizes the centralized management of SDN and edge computing to offload the compute-intensive tasks to the cloud [1]. The data manipulation on multiple platforms poses greater security issues including information loss, topology poisoning, password theft, Man-in-the-Middle (MiTM) attacks, eavesdropping, credentials reuse, data manipulation, relay attacks, key fob attacks, and information spoofing [17]. To cater to this problem we propose a Blockchain-based solution for data security for ITS networks which utilize centralized network management using SDN and offloading capabilities using the edge technology. We present the contributions of this paper in the following.

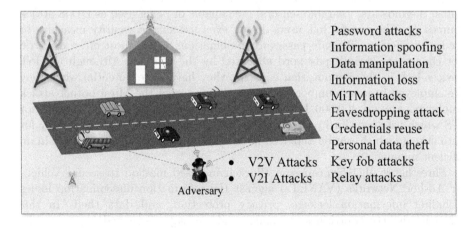

Fig. 2. The attack model on the ITS infrastructure.

- The problem of IoT data security is extensively discussed where the data transfer among different applications provokes security vulnerabilities in ITS.
- A framework for security in ITS networks is proposed which utilizes centralized network management using SDN, computation offloading capabilities using edge computing, and security using Blockchain technology.
- The architecture is extensively discussed where the workflow and the message exchange on different platforms are elaborated in detail.
- The feasibility of implementation of the proposed framework is discussed where the initial results demonstrate the effectiveness of the framework.

This research paper is organized as follows. Section 2 illustrates the related work in the field of IoT security, Blockchain, and limitations of the prevailing research in securing the ITS infrastructure against information spoofing attacks. Section 3 discusses the Blockchain-based ITS security framework including system model, its components, and their configuration. Moreover, we discuss the detailed workflows and the working principle on how different components work together to accomplish the security of heterogeneous ITS networks. Similarly, Sect. 4 provides a discussion on the potential utilization of the proposed framework in the ITS infrastructure. Finally, Sect. 5 provides the conclusion and suggests some future research directions.

2 Related Work

ITS employ a huge number of heterogeneous and resource-limited IoT devices which helps in collecting real-world data using the sensor and actuator technologies [2]. The resource limitation in IoT is exploited by the adversaries to launch a variety of cyberattacks [18],[6]. IoT-based Distributed Denial of Service Attacks (DDoS) and link flooding attacks have been increasingly observed during the past few years due to the lack of hardening of IoT devices [10]. Due to the sensing and data transfer capabilities in IoT, even low-end IoT objects (like light bulbs, thermostats, wearable sensors) are capable of being used as DDoS attack sources [8]. The general IoT users do not even use simple security measures to secure the devices like safe password combinations where most often users do not change the default password allocated by the vendors. Although the IoT devices lack in the computation capacity, they have huge potential when they are employed in large numbers as the world witnessed the Mirai botnet attack employing around 400,000 IoT devices [6]. Blockchain is a novel solution for ITS which uses the third party to store data. It uses distributed technology for data storage which can be deployed in the ITS to secure the data privacy in an efficient manner [9].

Shrestha et al. [15] propose a Blockchain-based method to secure Vehicular Ad-hoc Networks (VANETs) against the information dissemination issues including information leakage, privacy protection, and data theft. In this solution, the trustworthiness of nodes and messages is stored in the public Blockchains. They used public Blockchains in a specific locality (e.g. country) to store and manage the message and node trustworthiness. Similarly, authors in [19] propose an SDN-based 5G-VANET as a security framework using Blockchains. Centralized authentication and distributed trust management are employed to devise a road condition monitoring system. A secure service is provided by sharing the video along with the road condition tagged with the road information to share with other vehicles to avoid inaccurate information. However, the problem with these solutions is that they only consider a part of the problem of V2V or V2I security, however, we propose a comprehensive solution which utilizes Blockchain to secure the data involved in the whole ITS ecosystem including V2V and V2I.

Besides the above-mentioned literature in securing ITS using the Blockchain technology, there is still a lack of research available that considers the whole ITS ecosystem to secure the transactions. The ITS infrastructure includes smart vehicles, smart hospitals, fire stations, weather forecasting systems, smart road signals, smart refueling stations, and many other smart capabilities which need to be considered for security. The data generated from one device to the other traverses diverse platforms which create high-security risks. The current literature also suffers from the scope problem which only considers one part of the problem of securing either the V2V communication, V2I, or securing the payment transactions and there is a lack of literature available which considers the whole ITS ecosystem for security. Therefore, keeping in view the above discussion, there is still a need to improve the ITS paradigm using the Blockchain-based decentralized storage mechanism by utilizing the SDN and edge cloud capabilities. We comprehensively propose an efficient framework to cater to the privacy problems in the ITS using SDNs edge and Blockchain technology.

3   System Model

The proposed system is devised to fulfill the demands of the ITS where heterogeneous systems interact to transfer the data which pose security challenges on the privacy of data, information loss, eavesdropping, and credentials reuse. The ITS involves centralized network management using SDN and traffic offloading using cloud computing. The system model also incorporates the Bloom filtering strategy to analyze the presence of spoofed packets generated by the adversarial vehicles. Bloom filter is a probabilistic data structure which is used to identify the membership of an item in a list. The traditional item search methods like linear search or hash tables are not efficient whereas Bloom filter provides a robust data structure for item search in a list. Bloom filtering comprises up of hash functions and a list of items to search from. The hash function generates the locations in the list where the items are stored and analyzed for the presence or otherwise of an item. The collisions may occur when generating a hash for items, as for some items the hash function produces the same value which impacts the accuracy of the results. This is the reason why this data structure is called as probabilistic. Moreover, we employ the phenomena of learning the parameters of the malicious flows. When the Blockchain identifies the malicious flows, it records them in the database where first the traffic flows are compared with the database information, if the record is found in the malicious database, the flow is instantly dropped which provides an added advantage of instant transaction security.

Figure 3 illustrates the architecture of the SDN-based Blockchain framework to secure the IoT infrastructure. The framework is comprised up of three planes including application, control, and infrastructure plans. The figure illustrates that the Blockchain mechanism has been implemented at the edge cloudlets where the resources in the cloudlets are allocated to the IoT devices using the secure Blockchain technique.

3.1   Intelligent Transportation System

The proposed framework for ITS incorporates the centralized management of SDN, computation offloading using the edge cloudlets, and the secure transaction management using the Blockchain technology. The vehicles generate the transportation data that is maintained using the edge cloudlets stored using the Blockchain technology which offers a secure platform for computation offloading.

In our proposed framework, we employ private Blockchain where the mining task is performed by the resource-efficient edge servers as compared to resource-limited IoT devices. We employ this process as it is less resource-intensive as compared to the public Blockchains. This gives edge servers the control over creating and appending the block to the Blockchains to efficiently store the offloaded data from the ITS. In these circumstances, the ITS infrastructure including smart vehicles and service infrastructure acts as the clients which can only request the transaction services. The ITS uses centralized network management using SDN.

SDN provides flexible network management by employing q centralized control strategy over the network. It enables network programmability by flexibly installing flow rules for customized traffic forwarding. Network devices and hardware act merely as forwarding stations where the brain is the controller which efficiently install forwarding flow rules on the corresponding hardware. SDN employs proactive and reactive flow rule installation mechanism where the proactive methodology is used to install flow rules on the SDN switches prior to the arrival of packets. Whereas in the reactive flow rule installation, the flows are installed as soon as the packets arrive at the switch. In most of the conditions, hybrid flow rule installation strategy is used where some flow rules are proactively installed whereas other rules are installed as soon as packets arrive at the switches. The security framework comprises of the following components.

Application Plane. The application plane of our framework contains the programmable platform that facilitates the custom security application development, Blockchain configuration, edge cloudlet service orchestration, and IoT management. This plane provides accessibility to the application developers to implement customized Blockchain hashes, configuration, and implementation of the algorithms. This plane acts as a service orchestration platform where the vehicles and infrastructure search for the service provisioning and orchestration.

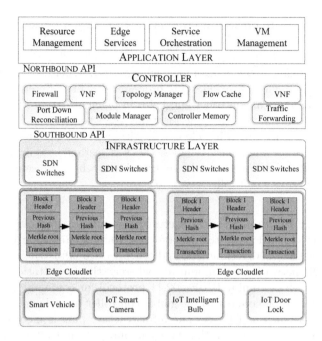

Fig. 3. The basic system architecture.

It provides a platform for the programmability of the ITS where custom applications can be developed for traffic forwarding and processing including security, mobility, routing, virtualization, and topology. The requirements of the vehicles and service infrastructure are ascertained and transmitted to the controller which allocates the required resources to the infrastructure plane. The controller then manages the flow rules and the traffic forwarding requirements of the ITS at the infrastructure plane.

Control Plane. The controller is the brain of our secure ITS framework where all the network intelligence resides. The network policies are implemented at this plane where a global database is maintained to enforce node placement and data flow routes selection in the ITS network. The controller implements virtual instances of the controller using hypervisor in order to serve a maximum number of requests without compromising Quality of Service (QoS). Multiple physical controllers are used in order to avoid a single point of failure. The control plane in our system installs the forwarding rules on the data plane devices which uses southbound RESTful API to communicate with the data plane infrastructure. It acts as an intelligent platform which has a global view of the network and knows where to divert the traffic to orchestrate seamless services. All the decisions to control the network and the policies of the network on how to access the appropriate cloudlets and the Blockchain-based security is implemented at this plane. It monitors the status of the forwarding devices at the data plane where the smart vehicles need to orchestrate the services to make a decision in a spontaneous manner. Our system employs multiple controllers which interact together to provide a centralized view of the network. The network operating system is employed to implement the control logic which uses a hypervisor to perform the network slicing for virtualization. This process helps in the creation of virtual instances of the physical controller and helps in placing Virtual Machines (VM) at the remote controllers. Different locations tend to be at different proximity of the edge service providing cloudlets. Although this architecture provides localized services for the smart vehicles, the VM instances equip the localized controller to fulfill the requests of the smart vehicles where the central controller handles all the remote controller instances.

Infrastructure Plane. The infrastructure plane comprises up of physical hardware including OpenFlow switches, gateways, routers, Roadside Units (RSU), base station, vehicles, edge cloudlets, and other service infrastructure. The vehicles use a P2P network to communicate whereas the base stations, controller nodes, and the RSUs employ IEEE 802.11 protocol for communication. All the RSUs and other nodes connect to the global controller using long-range communication protocol such as LTE-A. The infrastructure plan is incorporated with the edge cloudlets which offer the data computation and offloading capabilities to the resource-limited IoT infrastructure including smart vehicles, service infrastructure, and online transactions. This architecture enhances the overall security and provides seamless integration in the heterogeneous ITS infrastructure. It ensures secure P2P communication among smart vehicles in an intelligent environment. The infrastructure plane in our system consists of two layers where the first layer contains the SDN switches which forwards the network traffic as advised by the SDN controller. Secondly, the cloud services layer offers offloading services to cloud devices to perform compute-intensive tasks.

Blockchain on Edge Cloudlets. The Blockchain in this framework is considered as the distributed database which maintains a growing list of blocks that are connected together and maintain a consistent ledger which is not dependent on centralized storage. A public key is contained in the edge cloudlets to maintain the security of the ITS-generated data. Each cloudlet block is identified by the public key. In the ITS the transactions are identified by the public keys and are broadcast throughout the network where the edge cloudlets verify the transaction using the public key and comparing it with the signature of the transaction generator. The smart vehicles request resources from the edge cloudlets where they need secure transactions. The decentralized Blockchains employ the edge cloudlets where every cloudlet works as a block in the Blockchain-based on the trust mechanism. In such a scenario the trusted nodes act as the data trustee in order to keep the data save which will block the malicious traffic from the adversarial smart vehicles.

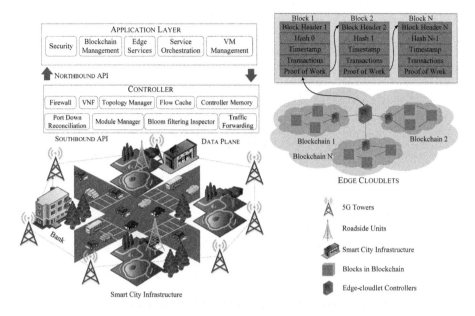

Fig. 4. A detailed system configuration.

3.2 Working Principle to Secure ITS Using Blockchains

A detailed system configuration of the proposed framework is illustrated in Fig. 4. The figure demonstrates a secure ITS framework where smart vehicles request V2V and V2I services from the smart city infrastructure. The edge cloudlets provide the offloading capabilities where the data is continuously being transferred to the cloud. Local controllers manage the respective cloudlets. The blockchain is implemented on every cloudlet controlled by the localized controller. This framework helps in the seamless and secure service orchestration and provisioning in the ITS network.

In the proposed framework, the Blockchain is integrated with the edge cloudlets and the internal coin system of the Blockchain which links the smart vehicles in the ITS to the resources in the edge cloudlets. The mining work is performed at the edge cloudlets as compared to the IoT devices as the edge cloudlets own higher amount of resources as compared to the resource-limited IoT devices. The Blockchain owns an internal security mechanism which is utilized by IoT infrastructure to secure the ITS. The security is performed on the basis of a device's past behavior, consumption of a huge amount of resources, continuous request of the resources, or causing DoS. If any of the devices is happened to be involved in any of the above-mentioned suspicious use-cases, it is categorized as malicious. After the identification of a malicious IoT device, it is added to the blacklists. All the activities are stored on the Blockchain which ensures durable security of the ITS system. Edge cloudlets employ VMs to fulfill the service requests from the IoT devices.

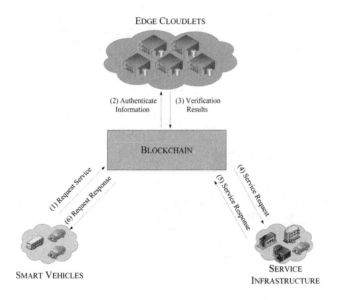

Fig. 5. Request and response of the Blockchain-based ITS.

The idea of using the Bloom filter to analyze the occurrence of a malicious item in the IoT-Fog networks was presented by Li et al. [7]. We extend this idea in our research by using Bloom filters as the first line of defense for the security of the ITS networks. The Bloom filter is employed to check whether a flow is malicious or not. In this technique, the controller in the SDN IoT edge Blockchain framework monitors the Bloom filters in the data plane switches. The switch flows in one path, inserts the packets in the Bloom filters where the inspection engine in the controller analyzes the packets in the Bloom filters. If these packets have not been changed then there is no attack, however, if the packets are changed then it is clearly because of information spoofing from the adversaries. Figure 5 illustrates the request and response propagation mechanism in the proposed framework. An interesting aspect to illustrate here is that we include a smart vehicle in the service infrastructure as the request and response in V2V must also be provided in a secure fashion. The smart vehicles request a resource from the service infrastructure where the request is first delivered to the Blockchain which authenticates the data integrity in the edge cloudlets using the public key mechanism. Once the data authentication is performed the verification results are delivered back to the Blockchain which forwards the results to the corresponding infrastructure or vehicle. The response is also generated in the same manner where the response goes to the Blockchain first and then it is delivered to the requesting station.

Subsequent to discussing all the components of the secure ITS, we demonstrate the working principle of the proposed solution. The ITS is managed and extended form SDN where we employ Blockchain-based edge cloudlets layer. The smart vehicles request services from the edge cloud to offload the tasks where the services are provided by the controller in an intelligent way by considering the overall perspective of the network. The security is maintained by the Blockchain services, Bloom filtering, and incorporating blacklists. The Blockchain technology is implemented at the edge cloudlet layers of the improved SDN architecture. In this scenario, every transaction is recorded using Blockchain technology using key and signature functions. Hence, all the information contained in the Blockchain is secure from the information spoofing and data theft attacks by deploying the Blockchain security measures.

The traffic flow is initiated from the smart vehicles which arrive at the SDN switches which looks for the flow rules in the local Ternary Content Addressable Memory (TCAM), if the rule in not present in the TCAM memory, the packet is sent to the controller for flow rule installation. The controller sends back the packet to the switch containing the flow rule on how to handle the packet. Subsequently, the flow is passed to the Bloom filter which inspects the incoming packet to analyze whether it is an attack packet or not. Subsequent to Bloom filtering operation the Blockchain is initiated and the nodes are also initialized. Subsequently, the Blockchain clients start to perform operation on the edge cloudlets. The incoming packet is inspected whether it is malicious, based on the previous blocklists. If it is malicious, then it is instantly dropped. Alternatively, its behavior is analyzed, if it is found to be normal then the request is fulfilled, otherwise the packet information is recorded in the block list and the flow is dropped. This process is performed for all the incoming packets to secure the ITS infrastructure.

4   Discussion

In this research, we have proposed a framework for securing ITS networks using Blockchain technology. This framework utilizes the capabilities of centralized control from SDN, offloading technology from the edge computing, information sensing by the IoT, and security using the Blockchain and Bloom-filtering to efficiently orchestrate the services for the ITS network. The vehicles in the ITS generate critical information which needs to be processed efficiently in order to orchestrate the services from the smart infrastructure. The ITS data consists of transactions among the vehicles and the refueling stations, V2V synchronization information, boundary sensors, control towers, and service infrastructure communication. This information is critical and any discrepancy in the communication provoke human lives in danger. Moreover, any malicious adversary may get hold of the critical information for data spoofing, data manipulation, data theft, and relay attacks generation. Moreover, the IoT devices are limited in the computation power including the energy, processing, storage, and memory hence the security solutions are challenging to implement on this infrastructure. Therefore, currently, network-based security solutions are widely being adopted to secure the IoT infrastructure. In this research, we employ Bloom filtering and Blockchain technology to secure the ITS infrastructure from the data manipulation attacks. The Bloom filter provides the initial defense against the attacks whereas the Blockchain technology works on the edge cloudlets to store the information in a distributed fashion under the management of a centralized control using SDN. The machine learning technology is also employed to learn the features of the traffic and the remedial measures are taken to mitigate the adversarial flows at first. The blocklists are managed for the adversaries which try to impact the infrastructure continuously, hence, a rapid blocking of these flows increases the efficiency of the security process.

In this research, we provide an extensive framework by comparing the capabilities of different architecture to mitigate the data related attacks in the ITS. This framework can be implemented effectively over the simulated network. We employ the floodlight controller and mininet to simulate the SDN paradigm where 5G simulation is used for the edge cloudlet implementation. Moreover, Ethereum blockchain network is utilized for the implementation of Blockchain. We are performing the experiments to evaluate the effectiveness of the proposed framework where the initial results illustrate the effectiveness of the solution.

5   Conclusion and Future Research Direction

IoT has revolutionized the physical world infrastructure where millions of sensors are collecting real-time information about the physical environments. This data is utilized for smart decision making and realization of the smart city concept where everything is connected with the internet to facilitate decision making without much human intervention. Intelligent Transportation System (ITS) portrays a novel paradigm where the vehicles are becoming smart equipped with the sensors and actuators which efficiently control the vehicles and embeds the service infrastructure from the smart city needed by the smart vehicles. The smart vehicles are capable of reserving a place for a wide range of tasks including refueling, parking, repair, and emergency services moreover, they are connected with the payment infrastructure to pay for the utilized services. However, this infrastructure is vulnerable to data spoofing attacks, information loss, relay, MiTM, key fob, and password attacks.

In the ITS, the information transferred among different physical systems including online transactions, banking detail, and driver information is vital, and any threat can invoke the whole infrastructure in a vulnerable position. The adversaries exploit this vulnerability to spoof information and other data related attacks. To cater to this problem, we devised a framework which uses SDN and secures Blockchain paradigm to secure ITS infrastructure. The Blockchain is utilized to secure the offloaded transactions where the data is stored in terms of blocks, the public key, and signature mechanism to ensure that the transactions are not malicious and direct the benign transactions towards the relevant service infrastructure.

This research provides a framework to secure the ITS infrastructure which effectively utilizes the Blockchain and virtualization using SDN to secure the ITS. We are further performing the experiments to evaluate the proposed framework. The framework will be implemented using the simulation testbed, the initial results illustrate that the framework ensures ITS security and provides a robust solution for the future ITS networks.

References

1. Abbas, M.T., Muhammad, A., Song, W.C.: SD-IoV: SDN enabled routing for internet of vehicles in road-aware approach. J. Ambient Intell. Hum. Comput. **11**, 1265–1280 (2019)
2. Din, S., Paul, A., Rehman, A.: 5G-enabled hierarchical architecture for software-defined intelligent transportation system. Comput. Netw. **150**, 81–89 (2019)
3. Evans, D.: The Internet of Things: how the next evolution of the internet is changing everything, white paper (2017). www.cisco.com/c/dam/en_us/about/ac79/docs/innov/IoT_IBSG_0411FINAL.pdf
4. Hebert, C., Cerbo, F.D.: Secure blockchain in the enterprise: a methodology. Pervasive Mob. Comput. **59**, 101038 (2019)
5. Jindal, A., Aujla, G.S., Kumar, N.: Survivor: a blockchain based edge-as-a-service framework for secure energy trading in sdn-enabled vehicle-to-grid environment. Comput. Netw. **153**, 36–48 (2019)
6. Kolias, C., Kambourakis, G., Stavrou, A., Voas, J.M.: Ddos in the IoT: mirai and other botnets. Computer **50**, 80–84 (2017)
7. Li, C., Qin, Z., Novak, E., Li, Q.: Securing sdn infrastructure of IoT-fog networks from mitm attacks. IEEE Internet of Things J. **4**(5), 1156–1164 (2017)
8. Miloslavskaya, N., Tolstoy, A.: Internet of things: information security challenges and solutions. Cluster Comput. **22**(1), 103–119 (2019)
9. Moin, S., Karim, A., Safdar, Z., Safdar, K., Ahmed, E., Imran, M.: Securing iots in distributed blockchain: analysis, requirements and open issues. Fut. Gener. Comput. Syst. **100**, 325–343 (2019)
10. Rafique, W., He, X., Liu, Z., Sun, Y., Dou, W.: CFADefense: a security solution to detect and mitigate crossfire attacks in software-defined IoT-edge infrastructure. In: Proc. 21st IEEE International Conference on High Performance Computing and Communications (HPCC), pp. 1–10 (2019, to be held in Zhangjiajie, China)
11. Rafique, W., Khan, M., Dou, W.: Maintainable software solution development using collaboration between architecture and requirements in heterogeneous IoT paradigm (Short Paper). In: Wang, X., Gao, H., Iqbal, M., Min, G. (eds.) CollaborateCom 2019. LNICST, vol. 292, pp. 489–508. Springer, Cham (2019). https://doi.org/10.1007/978-3-030-30146-0_34
12. Rafique, W., Khan, M., Sarwar, N., Dou, W.: A security framework to protect edge supported software defined Internet of Things infrastructure. In: Wang, X., Gao, H., Iqbal, M., Min, G. (eds.) CollaborateCom 2019. LNICST, vol. 292, pp. 71–88. Springer, Cham (2019). https://doi.org/10.1007/978-3-030-30146-0_6
13. Rasool, R.U., Ashraf, U., Ahmed, K., Wang, H., Rafique, W., Anwar, Z.: Cyberpulse: a machine learning based link flooding attack mitigation system for software defined networks. IEEE Access **7**, 34885–34899 (2019)
14. Ryu, J.H., Sharma, P.K., Jo, J.H., Park, J.H.: A blockchain-based decentralized efficient investigation framework for IoT digital forensics. J. Supercomput. (2019). In press
15. Shrestha, R., Bajracharya, R., Shrestha, A.P., Nam, S.Y.: A new-type of blockchain for secure message exchange in Vanet. Digital Communications and Networks (2019), In press

16. Sollins, K.R.: IoT big data security and privacy versus innovation. IEEE Internet of Things J. **6**(2), 1628–1635 (2019)
17. Sun, Y., et al.: Attacks and countermeasures in the internet of vehicles. Ann. Telecommun. 283–295 (2016). https://doi.org/10.1007/s12243-016-0551-6
18. Vlajic, N., Zhou, D.: IoT as a land of opportunity for Ddos hackers. Computer **51**(7), 26–34 (2018)
19. Xie, L., Ding, Y., Yang, H., Wang, X.: Blockchain-based secure and trustworthy internet of things in SDN-enabled 5g-Vanets. IEEE Access **7**, 56656–56666 (2019)

Home Automation Security System Based on Face Detection and Recognition Using IoT

Sana Ghafoor$^{(\boxtimes)}$, Khan Bahadar Khan,
Muhammad Rizwan Tahir$^{(\boxtimes)}$, and Maryoum Mustafa$^{(\boxtimes)}$

Department of Telecommunication Engineering, Faculty of Engineering,
The Islamia University of Bahawalpur, Bahawalpur, Pakistan
sanaghafoor935@gmail.com, Kb.khattak@gmail.com,
Rizwantahir085@gmail.com, maryoummustafa968@gmail.com

Abstract. In the modern world security is one of the major issues. As technology is getting advanced many security issues are arising. The existed developed security methods have some flaws and they can be hacked. The proposed system for resolving the security issue is based on face detection and recognition using Internet of Things (IoT). The face of a person is captured by the camera and compared with the acquired database. The authorized user can also utilize mobile application to give access to the premises to any unregistered person. In the case of unauthorized/unknown access, the face image of the person will be captured and notified to the concerned authorities through an email. An Alarm will be generated in the case of unauthorized access. The proposed system produced accurate results in both cases: authorized and unauthorized access. The introduced system provides a low-cost solution for monitoring and controlling the houses, different organizations like banks, universities, etc.

Keywords: Biometrics · Face detection and recognition · Digital image processing · Raspberry pi · IoT

1 Introduction

Face recognition is important not only because it allows us to use our face as a key but also because systems like face identification can read our expressions in real time. As IoT grows, different devices are being developed and face recognition is emerging rapidly. Now-a-days, security is the major issue for every person. People get harassed in their house and old security methods have failed to provide a high level of security. Different electronic devices, such as mobile phones, laptop and ATM, used some type of biometric authentication or passcode but these can be easily accessed by thieves by any means which is not safe.

According to United Nations Office on drugs and crime statistics [1], 5723500 theft cases were reported in the year 2015 in United States of America. However, in Pakistan 38902 cases were reported. The Statistics are given in the Table 1.

© Springer Nature Singapore Pte Ltd. 2020
I. S. Bajwa et al. (Eds.): INTAP 2019, CCIS 1198, pp. 67–78, 2020.
https://doi.org/10.1007/978-981-15-5232-8_7

Table 1. United Nations statistics on drugs and crime

Theft case reports at national level								
	2012		2013		2014		2015	
Pakistan	Count	Rate	Count	Rate	Count	Rate	Count	Rate
	49,148	27.62	45,494	25.04	42,747	23.04	38,902	20.54
United States of America	6,168,874	1968.78	6,019,500	1907.70	5,809,100	1828.38	5,723,500	1788.99
Robbery case reports at national level								
	2014		2015		2016		2017	
	Count	Rate	Count	Rate	Count	Rate	Count	Rate
Pakistan	18,107	0.18	15,164	0.15	13,088	0.13	12,458	0.12
United States of America	322,900	3.23	328,100	3.28	332,800	3.33	319,400	3.19

So, to solve these cases face recognition will help as face is unique identity of every person. Facial recognition combined with IoT will be much more secure than any other biometric systems.

The term "Internet of Things" consists of two sections i.e. first section is "Internet" and the second section is "Things". IoT is referring to the idea of things, especially everyday objects, that are readable, recognizable, capable of being addressed through different sensors and can be controlled via the internet [2]. IoT has totally transformed the technology, as it has capability of connecting multiple devices together on one platform which can be accessed and modified according to our needs.

The proposed home automation security system, utilized face detection and recognition features. The prototype system consists of a raspberry Pi module with attached camera, programmable stepper motor, relay circuit and an internet link. At first, we will install Linux based operating system in raspberry pi and stepper motor will be mounted on the door so that it can be automatically unlocked. The captured face by camera is compared with the database and if the person is recognized the door will be unlocked otherwise the system will send an email to the concerned person. The unregistered person access can be granted by using the mobile application by the owner. Similarly, if light is too low then door can be unlocked by using application via the internet.

2 Literature Review

The authors [3, 14], have proposed the face detection framework using Principal Component Analysis (PCA). The system is fast and efficient, but algorithm was run on MATLAB which uses very high memory and processing power. So, it is costly and also having low processing speed. We use Linus Base Operating System that is more efficient. Senthilkumar et al. [4], implemented the embedded images taking system via raspberry-pi. In this work, they took the picture and contrasted it with database, but have the problem of inefficiency the low light state. We Compared the Particular picture with 500 Database and results are 95% accurate. Sowmiya et al. [5], proposed the system of based on IoT. In this framework, they used PIR (passive infrared) sensor and camera. PIR sensor was exploited for identifying individual and camera utilized for capturing the video of the individual who comes at the entrance. But their proposed model did not give the ability of sending messages to the concerned persons. We will develop a system that will not only send message via Email but also send message on Number. Karri and Daniel [6, 7] proposed SMS based system using GSM, which send notifications via SMS to the house owner replacing conventional SMS. Jayashri and Arvind effectively implemented finger authentication for unlocking of doors. This system prevents unauthorized person and this can be monitored. This system includes extra protection features like leakage of smoke and gas detection. Fingerprint scanning may be costly and costly to some extend. Some experts think it's not a wise decision to rely only on fingerprint seniors because it's easy to replicate them, this can be overcome by addition of PIN password, voice detection or any other technique.

Dwiet et al. [8], have proposed the system of face recognition which used MyRIO 1900 controller. The controller has the program for detection of face. Personal computer is used to display the output and LabVIEW is used for programming. But the problem is that the MyRIO module is very costly. We used Raspberry Pi which is very cheap nd easy to use. Kodali et al. [9], have proposed a system of home security by using TI-CC3200 Launchpad board which uses Wi-Fi and internet to control and manage home appliances. But the limitation is that TI-CC3200 Launchpad board has limited memory, processing power and features than that of raspberry-pi. The earlier face recognition systems used nose, mouths and eyes for identification. These systems used classifier based on use of faces and datasets. These methods were not producing good results due to its low quality and low amount of information [10]. Ramanan et al. [11], proposed a system based on Algorithm of support vector machine (SVM). The algorithm for face scanning and detection upon functioning of static face image or color image. For color image, the colors of image increase in size of data available while mapping on pixels which efficiently reduce processing speed.

Dalal et al. [9], developed a system that was based on linear discrimination analysis (LDA). LDA is used to form an idea of an amount of significance of facial attributes. The datasets divided into different classes each of them has images of the same person, but in different ways, like different frontal faces and facial expressions. It assumed all images have one facial region that is of equal size. But this technique was the old one and makes the processing too slow. The earliest face recognition systems used nose, mouths and eyes for identification. These systems used classifier based on use of faces and data sets. This method was not producing good results due to its low quality and low amount of information. Moghaddam and Poggio [12] addressed the high dimensionality problem by using PCA to linearly take out significant modes of the face. They proposed statistical density model that was based on Eigen faces. But this system did not model for non-face patterns. Kartik et al. [13], developed two systems, One based on GSM and other on camera for scanning or detection. Which is controlled by PC with the help of Internet. It gives sound alarm when the intruder comes in front of the house. Second system based on GSM sends an SMS to the owner, but using this system the owner can monitor only, but can't control his door when he is away from his house. We intend to design an automated door lock system based upon IoT that uses face recognition for its operation. The use of IoT in our home automation system is in line with advancements in modern security technologies which shall dominate all aspects of postmodern life. The microcontroller is used for a robust design that will introduce simplicity and flexibility in the system.

3 Proposed System Architecture

The proposed system for real-time face detection and face recognition is shown in Fig. 1. It can be categorized into five sections: Face Detection, Creation of a dataset of the individuals, Training the classifier, Recognition of the face in the stored dataset and the IoT. The complete working flow of the proposed system is shown in Fig. 2.

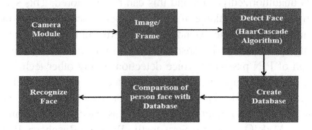

Fig. 1. Block diagram of the proposed system (Color figure online)

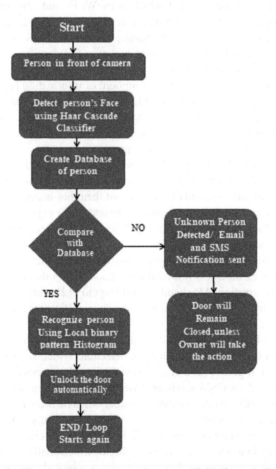

Fig. 2. Flowchart for the proposed system. (Color figure online)

3.1   Face Detection

In this section, we will first test the camera. A person comes in front of the camera. The camera will capture the particular person's frontal face. Then the person's face is detected by using the algorithm. The algorithm we use is Haar Cascade [15, 16]. This classifier is used to detect the objects for which it has been trained before. It is an effective object detection method. A cascade is instructed from a group of positive and negative images. It is needed to take out the features from it. This algorithm covers four stages: Haar feature, creation of integral images, adaboost training and Cascading classifier. First step is to gather Haar feature. Haar features include edge feature, line feature and rectangle feature. It examines adjoin rectangular fields, ranges at special placing in discovering window, sums pixel intensity in each division and calculate the difference. Integral images are the sum of all pixel values present before the current pixel at any location. Adaboost selects the best features among 160000 features and trains them. It provides a huge number of potential features. Cascade classifier is collection of stages in which each stage groups of weak learners. Weak learners are the decision stumps. Each stage is trained by boosting technique which trains highly accurate classifier by taking a weighted average of decision. During the detection distinct period, a window will go in a specific direction over input image and Haar features are calculated. The threshold separates non objects from the objects. To achieve detection's accuracy, we have set number of stages, feature types and other function parameters. The features extracted for face detection are: Gray scale, scale factor, neighborhood connectivity, and size of image, eyes detection and face detection. Gray image is obtained by conversion of the RGB image to Gray image. This scale factor specifies the smoothness and identifies how much image's size lessen at every image scale. The neighborhood connectivity identifies how many neighbors should be shown in the particular person's image. In our project, the neighbor is zero. The size of the image is identified. It defines the size of the rectangle around the picture. The dimension of the rectangle is 640*480. The eyes detection feature is added for more accuracy in the proposed system. Then, the frontal face of the particular person is detected with dimensions. The image is shown is a rectangle which is of 640 * 480's dimension. The images are marked as a blue rectangle.

3.2   Creation of Datasets of the Individuals

In this section, we will create database of each person, each person's id and number of images in grayscale that is used for face detection. The images of the particular person are gathered to create a dataset and store the images in XML file. We have used 1000 samples for each person's id using 1000 samples gives more accuracy about the person's image.

Training Datasets: The generated dataset of the authorized persons is stored in YML file. The Local Binary Pattern Histogram (LBPH) technique is used for training purpose of the images.

The LBPH is used to label the pixels of the images.

The LBPH package provides the following metrics to compare the histograms:

Chi-Square: This equation is used to describe the expression of the person. In our project, it is used to judge the person of the particular person whose database is saved in the XML File.

$$D = \sum_{i=1}^{n} \left(\frac{h_i st_1 i - h_i st^2 i}{h_i st^1 i} \right)^2 \tag{1}$$

D = chi square obtained
$\sum$ = the sum of
hist1 = observed score
hist2 = expected score.

Euclidean Distance: This equation is used to measure the distance between two straight lines. It is used to measure the Dimension of the picture that have stored in dataset.

$$D = \sqrt{\sum_{i=1}^{n} (hist1i - hist2i)^2} \tag{2}$$

Where:
D = chi square obtained
$\sum$ = the sum of
(hist1, hist2) are two vectors.

Normalized Euclidean Distance: The Euclidean distance between points hist1 and hist2 is the length of the line segment connecting them (hist1, hist2). The position of a point in a Euclidean n-space is a Euclidean vector. This formula scaled the length of the image and make a square box around the picture.

$$D = \sqrt{\sum_{i=1}^{n} \left(\frac{hist1i - hist2i}{n} \right)^2} \tag{3}$$

Absolute Value: When the picture is captured through camera it is then trained a number of positive and negative images through the Haar Cascade Classifier. It is used to convert the gray scale images into the colored images.

$$D = \sum_{i=1}^{n} |hist1i - hist2i| \tag{4}$$

3.3 Recognition of Face Through Stored Database

If the particular person's database is created before. Then the recognizer predicts the person's face and it also shows the confidence about the images in terms of percentage.

In our system, the accuracy s about 85–90% of images. If an unknown person comes in front of the camera then it will predict as unknown person.

3.4   IoT Platform

For IoT, we have used Ubidots platform [17]. To make our homes more secure and smart, we have used IoT. When an unauthorized person tried to enter into the home. The picture of unauthorized person will be sent to the owner via email. If owner is far away from his house, he can control and monitor his home's door via internet. If the owner wants to give permission to unauthorized person to enter into the home. He can simply give access and door will be opened.

4   Results and Discussion

The real-time testing of the proposed system is performed using a prototype hardware which consists of webcam for acquisition of an image, servo motor for door locking/unlocking, raspberry-pi 3B+ microcontroller board for controlling functionality. It is a Linux based operating system. We can also use windows and other operating systems but Linux is open source and easily available. The step-wise visual illustration of the proposed method is shown in Fig. 3. The raspberry-pi microcontroller board is shown in Fig. 4. The IoT involvement is for remote monitoring and controlling the premises access.

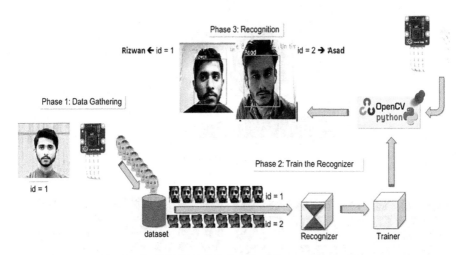

Fig. 3. Steps of proposed face detection and recognition

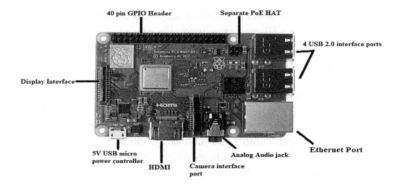

Fig. 4. Raspberry pi

Figure 5, shows the detection of face when a person comes in the front of camera. Figure 6, shows the dataset created. Figure 7, shows the detection and identification of a person through the proposed system. Figure 8, shows the denied access of the unregistered/unauthorized person. Figure 9, shows the image notification via email, in the case of illegal access. Figures 10, 11 and 12, shows the IoT platform used in this project to control and monitoring of home. Figure 13 shows that the owner will receive the SMS also in his mobile phone. User can open and close the door through the internet or via its mobile application remotely.

Fig. 5. Face detection

Fig. 6. Facial datasets

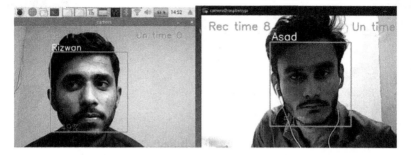

Fig. 7. Face recognition

Fig. 8. Unknown person

Fig. 9. Email notification received

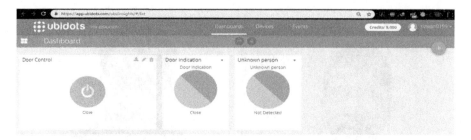

Fig. 10. IOT platform

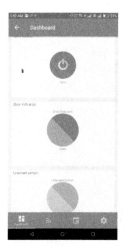 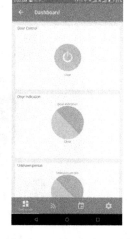

Fig. 11. Door opened using mobile app   **Fig. 12.** Door closed via mobile app

Fig. 13. SMS notification to user

5 Conclusion and Future Work

The proposed automated security scheme is low-cost and low power. The utilization of IoT in the proposed system makes it efficient and enabled for real-time applications. The accuracy is about 95% in our proposed system. System is based on WAN that the owner can monitor and control his house by sitting from far away his house. The utilizing of IoT in this system, provides remotely control and monitoring. The arrangement can be altered easily without interrupting the supplementary elements in the scheme. This system can be used in both online and offline modes.

In future, the IoT based security system can be deployed in the banking system, retailers, private companies and in debit cards in order to avoid frauds. Further, this system can be integrated and synchronized with the local police station's database, for detection and monitoring of the peoples having a criminal record.

References

1. United Nations Office on Drugs and Crime (2017). https://dataunodc.un.org/crime/
2. Patel, K.K., Patel, S.M.: Internet of Things-IOT: definition, characteristics, architecture, enabling technologies, application & future challenges. Int. J. Eng. Sci. Comput. **6**(5), 1–2 (2016)
3. Chin, H.: Face recognition based automated student attendance system. Diss. UTAR (2018)
4. Senthilkumar, G., Gopalakrishnan, K., Kumar, V.S.: Embedded image capturing system using raspberry pi system. Int. J. Emerg. Trends Technol. Comput. Sci. **3**(2), 213–215 (2014)
5. Sowmiya, U., Mansoor, J.S.: Raspberry pi based home door security through 3G dongle. Int. J. Eng. Res. Gener. Sci. **3**, 138–144 (2015)
6. Karri, V., Lim, J.D.: Method and device to communicate via SMS after a security intrusion. In: 1st International Conference on Sensing Technology, vol. 1, pp. 664–668 (2005)
7. Bangali, J., Shaligram, A.: Design and implementation of security systems for smart home based on GSM technology. Int. J. Smart Home **7**(6), 201–208 (2013)
8. Wati, D.A., Abadianto, D.: Design of face detection and recognition system for smart home security application. In: 2017 2nd International conferences on Information Technology, Information Systems and Electrical Engineering (ICITISEE), pp. 342–347. IEEE (2017)
9. Dalal, N., Triggs, B.: Histograms of oriented gradients for human detection. In: International Conference on Computer Vision & Pattern Recognition (CVPR 2005), pp. 886–893. IEEE Computer Society (2005)
10. Kodali, R.K., Jain, V., Bose, S., Boppana, L.: IoT based smart security and home automation system. In: 2016 International Conference on Computing, Communication and Automation (ICCCA), pp. 1286–1289. IEEE (2016)
11. Ramanan, D., Zhu, X.: Face detection, pose estimation, and landmark localization in the wild. In: Proceedings of the 2012 IEEE Conference on Computer Vision and Pattern Recognition (CVPR), pp. 2879–2886 (2012)
12. Moghaddam, B., Pentland, A.P.: Face recognition using view-based and modular eigenspaces. In: Automatic Systems for the Identification and Inspection of Humans, vol. 2277, pp. 12–22 (1994)
13. Kartik, J.S., Kumar, K.R., Srimadhavan, V.S.: Security system with face recognition, SMS alert and embedded network video monitoring terminal. Int. J. Secur. Priv. Trust Manag. (IJSPTM) **2**, 15–17 (2013)
14. Lwin, H.H., Khaing, A.S., Tun, H.M.: Automatic door access system using face recognition. Int. J. Sci. Technol. Res. **4**(6), 210–221 (2016)
15. WILL BERGER (2018). http://www.willberger.org/cascade-haar-explained/
16. Open Source Computer Vision. https://docs.opencv.org/3.2.0/d7/d8b/tutorial_py_face_detection.html
17. Ubidots (2019). http://www.ubidots.com/education/

Smart Reader for Visually Impaired People Based on Optical Character Recognition

Muhammad Farid Zamir[1(✉)], Khan Bahadar Khan[1],
Shafquat Ahmmad Khan[1], and Eid Rehman[2]

[1] Department of Telecommunication Engineering, UCET, The Islamia
University of Bahawalpur, Bahawalpur 63100, Pakistan
mfzamir67@gmail.com, ahmadatlive@gmail.com
[2] Department of Computer Science, International Islamic University Islamabad,
Islamabad, Pakistan
eidrehmanktk@gmail.com

Abstract. There are millions of visually impaired people in the world. According to the World Health Organization (WHO) data on visual impairment, 1.3 billion people are living with some kind of visual impairment while 36 million people are completely visually impaired. Reading is one of the major necessities of visually impaired people. Numerous researchers have worked on developing a mechanism that allows blind people to detect obstacles, to read the labels or specific currencies and to read the written, typed or printed text. We proposed a system which facilitates the visually impaired people by converting the text into voice signal based on raspberry pi. Optical Character Recognition (OCR) scheme is employed for the detection of printed text using a camera. Typed, handwritten characters or text are converted into machine-encoded text. The proposed method is developed on the raspberry pi in which OCR is employed for an image to audio converter which is the output of the system. It is a smart real-time device based on OCR.

Keywords: Optical character recognition · Raspberry pi · Tesseract · Open source · Espeak · Python programming · Real-time · Voice output · Voice signal

1 Introduction

World Health Organization revealed some horrific statistical figures in their report which was titled WHO data on visual impairment 2010 [1]. It can be seen in Table 1 below which describes the blindness and its classification, masses who are suffering from respect to their ages. It can be seen from the table that almost 285 million people are visually impaired. The terrific stats define blindness as a massive and growing health problem in World. Reading is one of the major necessities of blind people.

The earliest method used by blind people to read was the braille system of dots which requires its complete learning and understanding. In the 21st Century of Science & technological revolution, a person has to learn the old fashioned system of braille for just to read. The conversion of text into braille alphabets is itself a very time-consuming task.

© Springer Nature Singapore Pte Ltd. 2020
I. S. Bajwa et al. (Eds.): INTAP 2019, CCIS 1198, pp. 79–89, 2020.
https://doi.org/10.1007/978-981-15-5232-8_8

Table 1. UN WHO data on visual impairment 2010 [1]

Ages	Population in millions	Blind (millions)	Low vision (millions)	Visually impaired (millions)
Till 14 years	1,848.50	1,421	17.518	18.939
Between 15 & 49	3548.2	5,754	74.463	80.248
Older than 50	1,340.80	32.16	154.043	186.203
Overall	6,737.50	39.365 (0.58)	246.024 (3.65)	285.389 (4.24)

For reading books and documents, they are required to be converted into a system of dots which is a major demerit of this system. Figure 1 shows the conversion of basic alphabets into braille language.

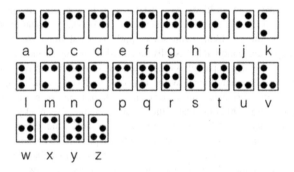

Fig. 1. Braille system of basic character mapping

In this era of technological development, many efforts have been made to assist blind people in reading. Many prototypes were proposed and many devices were made for the purpose. But none of the devices has been completely successful in fulfilling this necessity of less privileged people of our society. Some of those advancements lack versatility, some were not the real-time applications, and some of them had limitations around the text while some had the issues of high processing time. The clarity in the voice and extraction of complete and desired text has been a problem faced by many researchers in the past.

The basic concept behind our research is to propose a system that will assist millions of visually impaired masses as mentioned at the stats in Table 1, in reading the typed, handwritten & printed text without using the old fashioned tough & difficult system of braille mapping. As discussed in the last paragraph, that number of advancements has been made for the same purpose but none of them was completely able to overcome the technical challenges and hurdles. So we aim to overcome all those challenges and propose a versatile and complete system.

So we in this research paper proposed a system that develops a device that will provide reading assistance to blind people in real-time by converting the printed or typed text into voice. Raspberry Pi is the brain of this device that is connected with a camera that will capture the image containing text. OCR is used for the detection of text and computer programming for the conversion into voice signals. Python programming along with the Tesseract library and Espeak open source software is used for processing image capturing & detection, conversion into digital signals, and conversion into voice form.

2   Literature Review

Several systems and methodologies are proposed in the literature, which employs the use of raspberry pi, microcontrollers & sensors using different software tools which includes Python, MATLAB, etc. for making the assistive tool for reading for the visually impaired people. In literature, many systems employ the concept of OCR for image capturing and text to speech synthesis for its conversion in voice signals.

Goel et al. [2] proposed in their paper to develop the system assistive reading system for visually impaired people by implementing OCR through the tesseract library and OpenCV for the detection of text. For conversion into the voice signals, they proposed a text to speech module in their research paper. Mandar et al. [3] proposed a system in their research article which uses two modules that are image processing and voice processing module. He has also employed tesseract in the image processing module and text to the speech synthesizer. The major limitation of this proposed methodology was it recognizes only a font size of 18. Subbiah et al. [4], in his research paper, proposed a system for making a reader for blind people using Raspberry Pi. The researcher proposed their methodology by using the AdaBoost algorithm for the conversion of text to audio. One of the major disadvantages of the Adaboost algorithm is its sensitivity towards noise and outliers which can affect the detection and its conversion into noise. Velmurugan [5], proposed a system to design a reader for visually impaired people by using the OCR and text to speech engine. The author tested the system of image processing and conversion on the software of MATLAB, the major limitation of using MATLAB as software in making the device is the processing time which is comparatively quite slow in recursive systems. Bhargava et al. [6] proposed in their paper, a scheme to design a system that will help blind people by reading the text. The author proposed the scheme using raspberry pi and employed OCR and TTS. Image Magik Open source software was employed for display of edited images. One of the drawbacks in this scheme as it doesn't provide precision and clarity of output voice signal. Shahi et al. [7] proposed in their paper, a mechanism for blind people to identify labels and product packages using raspberry pi and implemented the OCR only for the identification of Labels containing text. The scheme has some major limitations as it wasn't tested for normal printed typed or handwritten text.

Ezhilarasi et al. [8] proposed a mechanism in their research paper for the identification of currency, and text using the SURF and MNS algorithm which is a method based on the comparison. The captured image was to be compared with the already feed image. It was made for the identification of currency notes and color identification. Abinaya et al. [9] proposed in their research work, an assistive device for blind people using the Raspberry Pi and OCR was implemented. The major demerit of this proposed mechanism is the use of MATLAB for the processing image and implementation of

OCR. The processing time in MATLAB is comparatively high which makes it unsuitable for a recursive device in real-time. Pooja et al. [10] proposed the design of a virtual eye for blind people using microcontrollers, ultra-sonic sensors, and raspberry pi. It was designed for object detection. It was a feedback system. As text reading was not involved, and use of sensors, microcontrollers don't make it cost-effective. Saurabh et al. [11] proposed in their paper a mechanism that will convert the normal typed or printed text into braille language. Raspberry Pi & microcontrollers are employed with the implementation of OCR. The major demerit was that the proposed scheme provides the conversion of text into braille language which is not a feasible solution towards the problem of reading for blind people. It is an extremely difficult task to convert the massive text in form of books and documents to braille language. The design is not cost-effective however the same scheme can be employed for getting the voice output.

3 Proposed Method

The proposed Raspberry Pi based smart reader works on the principal framework, which is Raspberry Pi. It is a single board minicomputer that is used in the proposed project for the extraction of text from the captured image and its conversion into audio which is the output of this project (Fig. 2).

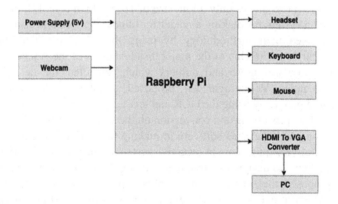

Fig. 2. Block diagram of the proposed model which demonstrates the hard-work implementation.

As shown in the block diagram, the Power supply of 5 V is supplied to Raspberry Pi, through the switched-mode power supply (SMPS). The Conversion of 230 V supply to 5 V takes place through SMPS. The Web Camera is connected to one of four USB Ports of Raspberry Pi. The Operating System of Raspberry Pi is RASPBION, which facilitates the process of conversions. The audio jack of the Pi is used for taking the voice output. An audio amplifier amplifies the converted speech. The Ethernet port of the Raspberry Pi used for the internet connection. The typed or the printed text which is to be read is stationed on the base wall, the camera which is placed in front of the base wall is focused to capture the image. The installed software of OCR processes the captured image and conversion of the captured image is done by using the software.

The Text-to-speech (TTS) engine facilitates the process of converting text into vocalization. Connected speakers are sued to fetch the final output which is processed by the audio amplifier. For the sake of ease & comfort, headphones may be used in place of speakers.

3.1   Architecture of the Proposed Model

The architecture of the proposed model is primarily described in two main phases

1. Image Acquisition and its conversion into text
2. Text-to- Speech Conversion

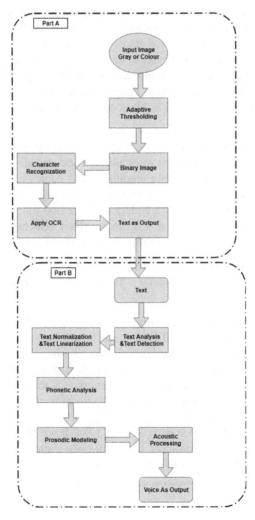

Fig. 3. The architecture of the proposed model which explains the process from text to audible Output.

The image acquisition & its conversion into text and text-to-speech conversion are processed in the steps which are described in the following Sect. 3.2.

3.2 Flow of Process

Image Capturing: As shown in Fig. 3 Part A, The primordial step of the proposed model is the capturing of the image which is of the typed or printed text paper/page. The page is placed in front of the stationed camera. The focus of the camera is set properly for getting a good quality of the image of the text. The high-resolution camera will give a high quality of the image which will help have a fast and clear recognition of text.

Image Processing: It can be seen in Fig. 3 after the image is captured, the goal is to extract the letters of the text and convert them into digital form and then speak them respectively. Image processing is a framework that is applied to the image to collect the information from it. The image is fed into the system, it will be converted into a greyscale image. The converted greyscale image will be in the form of pixels and specified within a range. The letters find out by using this range. The white and black contents of the greyscale indicate that white content will be usually the spacing's between the word or it can be called as blank space, while the words are identified by the black contents.

Optical Character Recognition: Optical character recognition which is commonly referred to as OCR is a mechanism for recognition of text that allows the conversion of handwritten, typed, or printed text into modifiable soft copies or text files. The OCR plays the primary role of extracting the text from the images and transforming them into modifiable text format. OCR is a widely used method for getting the printed or typed text into a digitized format so that it can be edited, searched and used for many purposes like machine learning, text-to-speech or cognitive computing, etc.

Image to Text Conversion: As it is described in the architecture of the proposed model Sect. 3.1, the captured input image is processed by the Tesseract OCR engine to process the image to text conversion.

Tesseract OCR Engine & Its Working: From Fig. 3 part A, the working flow of image to text conversion through Tesseract OCR can be seen, the input image is processed through the adaptive thresholding through the programming, the output image after adaptive filtering is binary image, which is then processed towards character recognition and OCR is applied, which then give us the desired output of modifiable text file. The file extension of the output file given by the tesseract is shown as a .txt file. It provides results in 100% accuracy (Fig. 4).

Tesseract OCR was developed from 1985 to 1984. It was developed on HP-UX at HP, to run at the scanner of a desktop. It was an open-source in 2005. It is an OCR Engine, available for Windows, LINUX, and MAC OS.

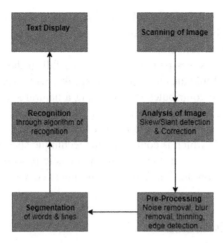

Fig. 4. Block diagram of the optical character recognition process and its stepwise detail

It is a command based tool in which an image containing the text in which an image containing text is fed into the engine as input.

The two arguments of the tesseract commands are

1. The first argument is the filename of the image which contains the text.
2. The other argument is the text file where the extracted text is stored.

Text-to-Speech: The second major step described in proposed model Sect. 3.1, is the conversion of the text into the speech. Text-to-Speech synthesizer which is commonly referred to as TTS is a system that is capable of reciting the text automatically. It is a computer-based system which read the text irrespective of whether the text was scanned input extracted through Optical character recognition OCR, or fed by the computer input stream (Fig. 5).

Fig. 5. Process of Text-to-Speech

TTS Architecture: The TTS architecture is explained in the above block diagram of the architecture of the proposed model Fig. 3 part B, which describes the process in the following way. When the input image contacting text or the text file is fed into the system, it passes through different phases before coming out as voice output.

- In the text analysis phase, the text is arranged into a manageable list of words.
- Text normalization is a conversion of the input text in a pronounceable format. Identification of any pauses or any punctuation mark is the key aim of this process.

- The transformation of the orthographical symbols into phonological ones by taking the phonetic alphabets into account, the process is commonly referred to as grapheme-to-phoneme conversion.
- The amalgamation of stress pattern, the rise, and fall in the speech and rhythm is known as prosody. While the emotion of the speaker while speaking is explained by modeling. This phase contributes to generating a natural synthesized speech.
- Acoustic processing refers to the process in which the type of speech synthesis is decided. The synthesis may be pre-recorded human voice or intelligible speech. Articulatory synthesis which is computational technique speech based on models of the human vocal tract falls in the domain of acoustic processing.
- After all processing through these phases, the intended voice output is taken out.

4   Results and Discussion

Raspberry Pi Model 3B with camera module V2-8 megapixel and speaker/handsets are the prime hardware used for the implementation of the proposed methodology. The software implementation is a major part of the proposed research paper. The following software is used with the operating system of RASPBIAN. Python 2.7.13 is used with a library of Tesseract OCR 4.0.0 and Espeak 1.48.15 was used as a TTS synthesizer and the compiler for the whole process is Thonny 3.1.2. The major advantage of the implementation of the following software is versatility, speed, precision, and efficiency.

The proposed project has been designed to provide the reading assistance to blind people in real-time with swift and precise processing of an image, and its conversion into voice form with clarity. From Figs. 6, 7, 8 and 9 shows the implementation of the proposed methodology on the hardware and results which are obtained. In Fig. 6 it is shown that the proposed methodology is implemented on the hardware, and a raspberry pi camera module captured the image which contains text.

Fig. 6. The Text used for testing on hardware.

In Fig. 7 the captured image is shown after getting fetched into the system, the quality of the image containing text can be seen.

Fig. 7. The captured image by the Raspberry Pi Model 3B with camera module

After getting the captured image containing text fetched in the system, the extraction of text through OCR and its conversion through tesseract is done which can be seen in Fig. 8.

Fig. 8. Conversion of the captured image to a text file by using Tesseract OCR.

We have implemented the proposed model and evaluated its versatility and success towards its objective by comparing it with past and relevant methodologies. The applied method is a very cost-effective economical as the methods applied in the past had many unusual components for getting the same output.

In Fig. 9 it is shown about the conversion of a modifiable text file is converted into voice signal through the python algorithm, which is the output of the system.

Fig. 9. Python algorithm used for conversion of the text file to audio file for blind peoples.

The method is implemented and results are obtained with the least hardware used. The precision and accuracy of the method can be seen in results. The processing time is compared with other methods, and through this approach, we got the best results. The processing time was tested with multiple styles of fonts & with many font sizes. Several samples are applied to verify the results. The output voice clarity was one of the main challenges in previous methodologies. The text-to-speech approach applied in our paper is most efficient as its speed can be varied with own desire and it provides multiple voice format.

5   Conclusion and Future Work

The proposed method was applied to the hardware and it was tested with different samples repeatedly. Our research methodology has successfully done the process of an image containing text and its transformation into audible speech. The experimental results are evident of this conclusion that the proposed method gives exceptional results in the processing of the image, extraction of text and conversion into speech. The experimental results have shown that the extraction of text and its conversion into audible speech is 100%. In the proposed method, speed of voice output can be altered as per one's comfortability and the proposed method gives several audio voices which resolves the issue of voice clarity. The proposed method is feasible and versatile as it had addressed some major limitations & issues, within a very economical cost. It will be proved as a major advancement towards serving the visually impaired people.

As we are living in an era of technological development, so the room for improvement is always there. We have the plan to implement our proposed method for the text of Urdu which will serve millions of people of Subcontinent. Moreover, more enhancements can be achieved by implementing it with high-resolution focused cameras which will then improve the extraction of text and more efficient text to speech engines can be developed for swift conversion into the text.

References

1. https://www.who.int/blindness/GLOBALDATAFINALforweb.pdf?ua=1
2. Goel, A., Sehrawat, A., Patil, A., Chougule, P., Khatavkar, S.: Raspberry Pi Based Reader for Blind People (2018)
3. Jadhav, M.S., et al.: Raspberry pi based reader for blind. Int. J. Innov. Emerg. Res. Eng. **5**(1), 1639–1642 (2018)
4. Subbiah, A.: Camera based label reader for blind people. Int. J. Chem. Sci. **14**(S3), 840–844 (2016). ISSN 0972-768X
5. Velmurugan, D., et al.: A Smart reader for visually impaired people using Raspberry pi. IJESC. https://doi.org/10.4010/2016.699. ISSN 2321 3361 © 2016
6. Bhargava, A., Nath, K.V.: Reading assistant for the visually impaired. **5**(2) (2015)
7. Shah1, P.H., et al.: A portable prototype label reading system for blind. **4**(9) (2015)
8. Ezhilarasi, C., et al.: A raspberry pi based assistive aid for visually impaired users. **3**(2) (2017)
9. Abinaya, R.I., et al.: Compact camera based assistive text product label reading and image identification for hand-held objects for visually challenged people. **3**(1), 87–92 (2015)
10. Sharma1, P., et al.: Design of microcontroller based virtual eye for the blind. **3**(8) (2014)
11. Bisht, S., et al.: Refreshable Braille Display using Raspberry Pi and Arduino, vol. 6, no. 3, June 2016. Accepted 01 June 2016, Available online 06 June 2016

Intelligent Applications

A Survey on Context-Aware Computing Frameworks for Resource-Bounded Devices

Younas Khan[1]([⊠]), Sajjad Ahmad Bhatti[1], and Sohail Khattak[2]

[1] Islamia College University, Peshawar, Pakistan
younaskhattak@gmail.com, Sajjadbhatti25000@gmail.com
[2] Government College Peshawar, Peshawar, Pakistan
sohailkhattak19@gmail.com

Abstract. Internet of Things (IoT) provides ubiquitous computing at any place, at any time and in any data format to any user across a network. Context-awareness is a phenomenon where an entity can portray its behavior in a particular time based on facts, rules, and axioms to form a system that is formally called context-aware computing framework. Several frameworks exist for context-awareness either ported from other platforms to android or explicitly build for android platform. Resource-bounded devices like tablet, smart TV, the smartphone and the wireless sensors nodes have several constraints like memory, power, and time that must be considered while designing a framework for resource-bounded devices. This paper surveys various resource-bounded context-aware computing frameworks that are either ported from desktop to android platform or explicitly build for android platform. The key challenges associated with these frameworks and portability issues from desktop to Android platform have also been discussed in detail.

Keywords: Internet of things · Context-Awareness · Resource-Bounded devices · Smartphones · Android SDK · Ubiquitous computing

1 Introduction

The term context-awareness was employed in ubiquitous computing as an emerging feature at the start of 1990 [1] and was first used in 1994 [2]. A substantial evolution can be observed from ubiquitous computing to the Internet of Things (IoT) that have made available the computation at any place, at any time and in any data format to any user across a network [3, 4]. The smartphones equipped with various sensors such as the accelerometer, camera, heartbeat, Global Positioning System (GPS) and touchscreen have been progressively taking over the desktop systems and are becoming the most attractive and feasible platform for ubiquitous computing among others [4–7]. These sensors produce enough data about the user's movement, location, time, surrounding, and act accordingly. For the purpose, not only an appropriate communication way out would enhance the user's interaction with the application and among the devices [8] but an application framework will also be required to collect the environmental data from the sensors and react accordingly without any intervention from the user [9]. From the scholarly perspective [10, 11], the context is about the facts

© Springer Nature Singapore Pte Ltd. 2020
I. S. Bajwa et al. (Eds.): INTAP 2019, CCIS 1198, pp. 93–105, 2020.
https://doi.org/10.1007/978-981-15-5232-8_9

(certainties), rules (guidelines), and axioms (sayings) that can be utilized to portray the condition of an entity at a particular time. This contextual information may contain different parameters such as time, location, activity, identity, and others as shown in Fig. 1, e.g. an identity, location and the current activity of a person at a particular time.

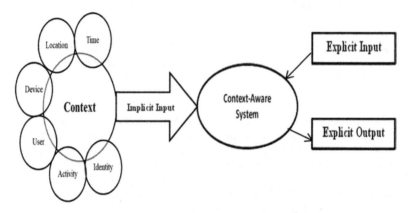

Fig. 1. An illustration of context-aware system.

Context-awareness provides an uncommon sort of formal logic frameworks wherein established artificial intelligence speculations and procedures (algorithms) are used to atomize the process of inferring the new knowledge and reasoning on data representing the user state. Context-aware computing system consists of human agents and various intermingling devices hence form a multi-agent system. The non-human agents are intelligent programs that depict intelligent behavior based on rule-based reasoning skills. Both the rule-based and ontology-based reasoning have been used to develop context-aware systems [12, 13]. As compared to the desktop environment, the smartphones are equipped with less number of resources and are not feasible to use those conventional rule-based engines due to the heterogeneous framework and hardware outlines. Some conventional rule-based engines were also tried to implement in the smartphone environment but found unsatisfactory. Their transfer from desktop to the smartphone environment was only found partially successful [14, 15]. A decentralized computing framework with an appropriate communication model and a declarative rule-based programming language is necessary for the efficient utilization of the smartphone platform for the provision of resource-bounded context-aware information within the environment [16, 17]. Pure smartphone-related context-aware computing frameworks provide ease of development to develop various context-aware applications such as pulse monitoring, traffic control\management, and office security.

The rest of the paper has been arranged as; the Section-II is narrating different aspects of context-aware systems and also highlighting the limitations and challenges regarding these systems. Section-III is discussing the portability issues of desktop-oriented frameworks to Android while Section-IV is elaborating different context-aware frameworks for resource-bounded devices. The Section-V is putting a light on those frameworks which are either ported to or specially designed for the Android platform while the Section-VI is presenting the findings and conclusion.

2 Context-Aware Computing System

Context-aware computing evolved with the development of mobile phones at the start of the 1990s. A company named Olivetti Labs assigned active badges to the staff to locate them in the office at any time [18]. Context-aware frameworks support four main points such as acquisition, representation, dissemination, and reaction to accomplish a context-aware task [19, 20]. Several advanced systems have also been introduced since decades that provide basic functionalities because of two reasons [21]; i) their sensing and reasoning mechanisms are complex to acquire dynamic contextual information over time, and ii) they function on small resource-bounded devices

2.1 Context-Awareness

Various definitions of context have been presented in the literature. Dey and his companions have highlighted the weak points of these definitions in detail [20]. They have claimed that these definitions do not facilitate to identify new contexts. As per Dey [22]: "Context is any information that can be used to characterize the situation of an entity. An entity is a person, place, or object that is considered relevant to the interaction between a user and an application, including the user and applications themselves". Similarly, the term context-awareness is defined as "A system is context-aware if it uses context to provide relevant information and/or services to the user, where relevancy depends on the user's task" [22]. In this survey paper, we will consider these definitions of the terms.

2.2 Raw Facts Vs Contextual Information

There is a difference between raw facts and contextual information [23]. We take a Global Positioning System (GPS) example to understand this concept. GPS sensors generate and disseminate big data. Often, all the generated data is of no use; however, when some data is processed to provide information like the geographical location, then, this kind of information will be named as contextual information.

2.3 Implicit Vs Explicit Context Models

There are two ways outs (implicit and explicit context models) used to develop context-aware applications as shown in Fig. 2 [24]. Implicit context models provide inherent libraries, toolkits, and frameworks to the applications to perform acquisition, pre-processing, storing, and reasoning jobs to build applications quickly, while the explicit context model provides a middleware (also call context management layer) to perform all functions outside from applications [24].

2.4   Limitations and Challenges

Context-aware computing confronts with several limitations for smartphones. Sensors integrated context-aware system gathers the data from the real world and tries to infer implicit context (high-level context) from the explicit context (low-level context) to make the best and the relevant action upon the environment [19, 25]. There are few restrictions need to address when designing and developing context-aware computing systems. These are space, time and communication [26–28]. Smartphones have limited memory to store contextual information. That is why these devices are not allowed to store all contexts acquired by themselves or from other devices. Smartphones have less computational power, unlike desktop computers. The process to infer high-level contexts from the low- level contexts is a time-consuming task [25], but the issues arise here that these time-consuming tasks need to repeat again and again more or less with every context-aware application. So many android context-aware application developers use less mobile features and sensors to speed up the computational process due to this time constraint problem [29]. Context-aware mobile devices intercommunicate through messages in a very dynamic environment by using different wireless communication technologies such as Wifi, Bluetooth, and others [30]. As we know that mobile devices move with the user from one location to another, so communication may be discontinued or interrupted by device and connection failure due to no coverage in the area. The device failure can also be examined due to the reduction of battery power level. In order to avoid the problem, the mobile devices may be switched off or the sensors may be deactivated in the most passive scenarios [31]. It is, therefore, can be concluded that due to these limitations some applications may not be able to execute on smartphones to deliver the expected output.

3   Portability Issues from Desktop to Android Platform

There are various platforms available for resource-bounded devices, especially for mobile devices. Some of them are Android, IOS, Windows Mobile, BlackBerry, and Symbian. Among these, one platform may be chosen to implement any resource-bounded framework in its pure form. Various resource-bounded frameworks have been implemented in Java (an open-source programming language) such as JADE [32], JARE, JESS [33], JASON [34], Cartago [35], are dedicated to being used in the Android environment either in form of add-ons or as an ad-hoc frameworks [36, 37]. These platforms cannot be used directly on smart devices because the Oracle Java has some compatibility issues when porting to smart platforms such as Android or IOS. These smart devices have their own development tools, e.g., in Android, Google's Android Software Development Kit (SDK) and the Android Studio are used to develop pure android based applications. Though the basic syntax for Oracle Java and Android Java Programming is the same, the difference lies at their low-level machine code generations. Oracle-Java uses Java Virtual Machine (JVM) in desktop systems while the resource-bounded devices such as smart TV's, tablets and smartphones uses Dalvik Virtual Machine (DVM) to translate program code into the machine-executable format [38]. The Oracle Java though optimized to be used with Android devices but still do not support all Java Classes that is why Google Android SDK facilitates to program any application for the Android Framework.

4 Context-Aware Resource-Bounded Frameworks

In recent years researchers have shown a keen interest in investigating and proposing different approaches for context modeling considering particular architectures based on some reasoning methods to develop context-aware systems [13, 17, 26]. The development of these systems has also elevated the importance of application use in different smart devices. Table 1 is depicting different ontology-based context-aware frameworks for resource-bounded devices discussed in this section with programming tools, constraints considered and the challenges.

Table 1. Different ontology-based context-aware frameworks for resource-bounded devices

S. #	Framework	Programming tool	Constraint(s)	Challenges
1	GCOM	OWL	Power	Space and time
2	OPEN	Java 2	time, power, space	Resource sharing framework has limitation in a distributed environment
3	Modelling & Verifying Resource-Bounded CA Agents	OWL 2 RL & SWL	time, power	Memory requirement
5	L_{DROCS}	-do-	time, power, space	Properties not automated
4	L_{OCRS}	OWL 2 RL	time, power, space	Inconsistency occurs in agent memory
6	Maude LTL model	OWL 2	time, memory, communication	The heterogeneous multi-context system is not specified

4.1 Gcom

A prototype of ontology-based generic context management (GCOM) is proposed in [39]. This prototype (model) provides a structure for context, rules, and rules semantic. GCOM model is dynamic and can be reused in different domains where resource limitation is an issue. This model also supports interoperability, an abstraction for programming, and efficient reasoning while utilizing low power. GCOM has three components; i) context semantic (ontology), ii) context instance data, and iii) context-related rules. The context semantics represents the characteristics of an entity and its relationship within a domain while context-related rules are used to govern the context-aware data. GCOM framework considers user-defined as well as the ontology-based rules to perform modeling of the context. These rules may be entered either through the user interface or can be implicitly learned by the system itself. The author has not identified the space and time limitations for this model, that is why, the rules which are not frequent, occupy more memory space.

4.2   Open

In [13], OPEN, an ontology-based programming framework, is proposed for rapid prototyping of application development, sharing and for personalization of applications. The author's goal of developing this framework is to support a wide variety of user's categories. It has four main components; i) the context-provider that separates context sensing from context manipulation, while, ii) the context-manager provides a middle layer to separate context processing from its usage, iii) the programming toolkit consists of context-aware programming languages, while, iv) the resource sharing server share and reuse resources and support different users with different technical skills (high level, middle level or low-level) by providing three different programming modes; the mode used for the creation of new context-aware applications called the incremental mode, while, the composition mode is as like incremental mode, however, in this mode, the developers can also reuse and modify already created rules, and, the parameterization mode is used to customize already developed rules. Though this framework provides different modes and options to users with diverse technical skills but this framework's resource sharing server has some limitations when implemented in a distributed environment.

4.3   Modeling and Verifying Resource-Bounded Context-Aware Agents

Authors of [26] provide an ontological rule-based theoretical approach to model resource-bounded multi-agent context-aware systems using OWL 2 RL and SWRL rules oriented languages. The OWL 2 RL and Semantic Web Rule Language (SWRL) are rules oriented languages used to define the static and dynamic contexts of the system respectively. Both the formal representation and verification of resource bound multi-agent context-aware systems have considered in this framework. Context ontologies are translated into Horn clause rules and these rules used to build rule-based agents. This framework provides a problem-solving technique for rule-based agents communicating in a context-aware system. This framework is time-bound and emphasis on the number of messages traded to infer an objective (communication bound), however, lacks memory requirement that is necessary for reasoning.

4.4 L_{ocrs}

A logical framework called L_{OCRS} has designed in [27] as a formal logical model for representing and verifying the resource-bounded multi-agent context-aware systems using OWL 2 RL web ontology rule-based language. Context ontologies have translated into Horn clause rules, and these rules are used to build rule-based agents. In this framework, the authors have considered the bound on time, communication and memory. A monotonic reasoning technique is used to develop rule-based agents. In monotonic reasoning, the beliefs of an agent cannot be looked over (revised) based on some conflicting evidence. The Authors of [16] reveal that to some extent inconsistencies may happen in an agent's memory that is why an agent might show an untrustworthy response in certain situations.

4.5 L_{drocs}

Another logical framework L_{DROCS} for the resource-bounded multi-agent-based context-aware system has been proposed in [28] to handle the inconsistency problem in L_{OCRS} framework [27]. L_{DROCS} framework uses non-monotonic reasoning to design rule-based agents. This framework makes bounds on time, space and resources allocated for communications. The OWL 2 RL and Semantic Web Rule Language (SWRL) are rules oriented languages and are used to define the static and dynamic contexts of the system respectively. L_{DROCS} framework uses defeasible reasoning [40] technique to reason with incomplete and inconsistent facts to resolve the conflicting evidence based on rules priorities. This framework is implemented in [41] for smartphones using the Google Android SDK.

4.6 The Maude LTL Model

This paper [42] is a compliment for a previous work already done in [28], focuses upon automated analysis and verification. The Maude LTL model [43] has been used to determine and verify the context properties of resource-bounded multi-agent context-aware system. For the purpose, a case study consisting of three different scenarios have been considered and evaluated by analyzing and verifying non-conflicting contextual information using Maude LTL model based on message passing techniques among the multi-agents.

5 Context-Aware Rule-Based Frameworks for Mobile Devices

Only a few resource-bounded frameworks have been designed for context-aware systems since decades [16]. Literature reveals [17, 44] that there does not exist even a single comprehensive design and the developmental environment with integrated modules for methodology, communication protocols, languages, inference engines, and others for designing and developing comprehensive context-aware applications for resource-bounded mobile devices. Some open-source frameworks such as JADE [32], JASON [34] and Cartago [35] were dedicated to being used in the Android environment either in the form of add-ons or as ad-hoc frameworks [36, 37]. Table 2 is depicting different rule-based context-aware frameworks\models for mobile devices discussed in this section with their design, programming tools, working environment, constraints considered and the challenges.

Table 2. Analysis of rule-based context-aware frameworks for mobile devices

S. #	Framework	Design	Programming tool	Constraint (s)	Environment	Challenges (separated by ',')
1	JADE	ported as add-on to android	Java	time, space, power	client/server	Ambient Intelligence, Communication
2	JASON	-do-	agent oriented programming	-do-	-do-	Lack of agent Conjunctive goals, Parallel goals not available
3	Cartago	-do-	Java, agent-oriented programming	-do-	-do-	Artifacts types not mentioned, Lack of methodologies for testing and validating artifact-based environment, Lack of cognitive selection of artifact
4	ContextDroid	android-based	general purpose language	time, battery	-do-	Memory constraint is not considered
5	Knowledge-based agents in android	-do-	JESS	time, space, power	-do-	Not purely distributed
6	Decentralized context-aware model	-do-	google android SDK	space, power	distributed, open-peer	Time constraint is not considered
7	Rule-Engine	-do-	-do-	time, space, power	-do-	Working memory length not specified, Rule reversal is not possible

5.1   JADE in Android

The authors of [36] have proposed to import the JADE framework to Android by implementing its add-on to develop an interoperable multi-agent system based on peer to peer communication model. This add-on exploits the features of both the JADE and the Android platform and provides an application interface that allows working as a local agent, triggers actions, and discover Androids as well as other mobile objects (located remotely) to perform probable complex dialogues/communication among them. This JADE add-on uses ontological based reasoning to process all the messages and background activities. This problem in this framework is that this JADE add-on works in a client-server environment where the JADE framework works as a server and its add-on works as a client in the Android devices.

5.2 Contextdroid

ContextDroid [45] is an expression-based, centralized and a generic context-aware framework designed for the developers to develop multiple context-aware applications that run on Android mobiles. This framework provides efficient utilization of smartphone resources especially the time and the battery. This framework considers past history and also assigns termination time to different context readings to provide more accurate context figures. Requirements such as usable, efficient, extensible and portable were considered to design to reduce the development time for developers.

5.3 Knowledge-Based Agents in Android

A framework has been proposed in [14] to provide Computer Aided Knowledge Engineering environment to allow programmers to program agents based on the knowledge artifacts [46]. This technique has been used to generate executable rule-based agents written in Java Expert System Shell (JESS) which consequently minimizes the knowledge engineering efforts. This framework works in a client-server environment, where the knowledge-based agent acts as a server while the reactive agent (simple agent) acts as a client. The former performs two functions; i) the creation of rule-based agents as per user's indications and ii) the execution of rule-based agents based on the client's given data, while the latter is used to send and receive data to and from the knowledge-based agent.

5.4 Decentralized Context-Aware Computing Model

An actual android based logical model is proposed in [16], based upon the work done in [28] that used defeasible reasoning [40, 47] technique to reason with incomplete and inconsistent facts to resolve the conflicting evidence based on rules priorities. This framework is being developed in a Google's Android SDK with support of decentralized computing and with an appropriate communication (Open Peer) model using rule-based programming language for android platforms. By using this framework, the smart device shares only the facts using message passing. Numerous agents are considered in this framework where each agent works as a module and react as per the current contexts. Each agent has the capability to generate high-level contexts based on low-level contexts. The rules are distributed in a customized mode, and no change occurs in the rules when they are in execution. The proposed framework is a theoretical model and covers some issues of resource-bounded devices.

5.5 Rule Engine

An efficient rule-based distributed reasoning logical framework\model has proposed especially for Android devices (also works on any resource-bound device) in [17, 47] and is implemented using Android Studio. This framework incorporates a Rule Engine with a broad range of user preferences to minimize the mass of rules while inferring personalized contexts. This minimization of rules helps the Rule Engine to optimize the execution speed of the inference engine that ultimately results in less execution time and execution cost. This Rule Engine lacks working memory length and rule reversal.

6 Findings and Conclusion

Context-awareness can be a multi-agent system which can provide a logical framework for artificial intelligence to infer new knowledge representing user state. Most of the frameworks developed for resource bounded devices are theoretical and are centralized based (works in a client server scenario). Decentralized context-aware computing in addition with some declarative languages is in dire need for operating and designing context-aware systems for mobile devices. Frameworks that have designed for the desktop platform and later on ported to the android (either in the form of add-ons or as ad-hoc frameworks) have some portability issues in the android environment which consequently, lacks the provision of full functionality. Ontology-based reasoning would be feasible for mobile devices as smartphones have limitations in memory. On the other hand, rule-based reasoning generally requires more space (feasible for desktop applications). As discussed in this paper, there are two types of Context models i.e. implicit and explicit context models. Implicit context models are associated with inherited libraries, toolkits, and frameworks, while explicit context model uses middleware to develop context-aware systems for resource-bounded devices. Explicit context model should be lightweight that occupy less space in the mobile devices. Smartphones have several limitations like space, time, and communication. Due to these limitations, some context-aware application might not be able to execute on smartphones to deliver the expected output. Therefore, it is suggested that the mobile devices may be switched off, or the sensors may be deactivated in the most passive scenarios. To develop android-based context-aware frameworks, Google's Android Software Kit (SDK) is the best option, natively designed to develop android based applications for smartphones.

This survey provides a detailed study of already available context-aware frameworks for resource-bounded devices. The context-aware systems\frameworks use some logic or guideline to compel an entity to act according to a specific condition. Different context-aware frameworks\models designed for the resource-bounded device including the mobile devices have been elaborated and discussed along with their designs, programming tools, working environments, constraints considered and the challenges. In this survey paper, we have provided a background for a new researcher to consider constraints such as time, space, communication and power while designing such a system for resource-bounded devices especially for Android or other mobile devices. In the future, we would like to address the challenges associated with Rule Engine as shown in Table 2. The working memory length of the Rule Engine has not been specified in the algorithm which directly affecting the memory constraint in resource-bounded devices. Moreover, if a rule is added in the Rule Engine, then there is no way out provided in the Rule Engine to reverse it.

References

1. Weiser, M.: The computer for the 21st century. Sci. Am. **265**(3), 94–105 (1991)
2. Schilit, B.N., Theimer, M.M.: Disseminating active map information to mobile hosts. IEEE Netw. **8**(5), 22–32 (1994)
3. Andrade, R.M.C., Carvalho, R.M., de Araújo, I.L., Oliveira, K.M., Maia, M.E.F.: What changes from ubiquitous computing to Internet of Things in interaction evaluation? In: Streitz, N., Markopoulos, P. (eds.) DAPI 2017. LNCS, vol. 10291, pp. 3–21. Springer, Cham (2017). https://doi.org/10.1007/978-3-319-58697-7_1
4. Gochhayat, S.P., et al.: LISA: lightweight context-aware IoT service architecture. J. Clean. Prod. **212**, 1345–1356 (2019)
5. Karlson, A.K., et al.: Mobile taskflow in context: a screenshot study of smartphone usage. In: Proceedings of the SIGCHI Conference on Human Factors in Computing Systems, ACM (2010)
6. Want, R.: When cell phones become computers. IEEE Pervasive Comput. **8**(2), 2–5 (2009)
7. Nalepa, G.J., Kutt, K., Bobek, S.: Mobile platform for affective context-aware systems. Future Gener. Comput. Syst. **92**, 490–503 (2019)
8. Raento, M., et al.: ContextPhone: a prototyping platform for context-aware mobile applications. IEEE Pervasive Comput. **2**, 51–59 (2005)
9. Deshmukh, S., Shah, R.: Computation offloading frameworks in mobile cloud computing: a survey. In: 2016 IEEE International Conference on Current Trends in Advanced Computing (ICCTAC), IEEE (2016)
10. Mehra, P.: Context-aware computing: beyond search and location-based services. IEEE Internet Comput. **16**(2), 12–16 (2012)
11. Kim, J.-D., Son, J., Baik, D.-K.: CA5W1HOnto: ontological context-aware model based on 5W1H. Int. J. Distrib. Sens. Netw. **8**(3), 247346 (2012)
12. Esposito, A., et al.: A framework for context-aware home-health monitoring. Int. J. Auton. Adap. Commun. Syst. **3**(1), 75–91 (2010)
13. Guo, B., Zhang, D., Imai, M.: Toward a cooperative programming framework for context-aware applications. Pers. Ubiquit. Comput. **15**(3), 221–233 (2011)
14. Sartori, F., Manenti, L., Grazioli, L.: A Conceptual and Computational Model for Knowledge-based Agents in ANDROID, pp. 41–46 (2013)
15. Ughetti, M., Trucco, T., Gotta, D.: Development of agent-based, peer-to-peer mobile applications on ANDROID with JADE. In: Second International Conference on Mobile Ubiquitous Computing, Systems, Services and Technologies IEEE, Editor, pp. 287–294. IEEE (2008)
16. Uddin, I., Ul Haque, H.M., Rakib, A., Segi Rahmat, M.R.: Resource-bounded context-aware applications: a survey and early experiment. In: Vinh, P.C., Barolli, L. (eds.) ICTCC 2016. LNICST, vol. 168, pp. 153–164. Springer, Cham (2016). https://doi.org/10.1007/978-3-319-46909-6_15
17. Uddin, I.: A Rule-Based Framework for Developing Context-Aware Systems for Smart Spaces, University of Nottingham (2019)
18. Sehic, S., et al.: Entity-adaptation: a programming model for development of context-aware applications. In: Proceedings of the 29th Annual ACM Symposium on Applied Computing, Gyeongju, p. 436–443. ACM (2014)
19. Perera, C., et al.: Context aware computing for the Internet of Things: a survey. IEEE Commun. Surv. Tutorials **16**(1), 414–454 (2014)

20. Dey, A.K., Abowd, G.D., Salber, D.: A conceptual framework and a toolkit for supporting the rapid prototyping of context-aware applications. Hum. Comput. Interact. **16**(2–4), 97–166 (2001)

21. Bardram, J.E., et al.: A context-aware patient safety system for the operating room. In: Proceedings of the 10th International Conference on Ubiquitous Computing, Seoul, pp. 272–281. ACM (2008)

22. Abowd, G.D., Dey, A.K., Brown, P.J., Davies, N., Smith, M., Steggles, P.: Towards a better understanding of context and context-awareness. In: Gellersen, H.-W. (ed.) HUC 1999. LNCS, vol. 1707, pp. 304–307. Springer, Heidelberg (1999). https://doi.org/10.1007/3-540-48157-5_29

23. Sanchez, L., et al.: A generic context management framework for personal networking environments. In: 2006 Third Annual International Conference on Mobile and Ubiquitous Systems: Networking & Services (2006)

24. Hu, P., Indulska, J., Robinson, R.: An autonomic context management system for pervasive computing. In: 2008 Sixth Annual IEEE International Conference on Pervasive Computing and Communications (PerCom), IEEE (2008)

25. Elazhary, H.: A cloud-based framework for context-aware intelligent mobile user interfaces in healthcare applications. J. Med. Imag. Health Inform. **5**(8), 1680–1687 (2015)

26. Rakib, A., Faruqui, R.U.: A formal approach to modelling and verifying resource-bounded context-aware agents. In: Vinh, P.C., Hung, N.M., Tung, N.T., Suzuki, J. (eds.) ICCASA 2012. LNICST, vol. 109, pp. 86–96. Springer, Heidelberg (2013). https://doi.org/10.1007/978-3-642-36642-0_9

27. Rakib, A., Ul Haque, H.M., Faruqui, R.U.: A temporal description logic for resource-bounded rule-based context-aware agents. In: Vinh, P.C., Alagar, V., Vassev, E., Khare, A. (eds.) ICCASA 2013. LNICST, vol. 128, pp. 3–14. Springer, Cham (2014). https://doi.org/10.1007/978-3-319-05939-6_1

28. Rakib, A., Haque, H.M.Ul: A logic for context-aware non-monotonic reasoning agents. In: Gelbukh, A., Espinoza, F.C., Galicia-Haro, S.N. (eds.) MICAI 2014. LNCS (LNAI), vol. 8856, pp. 453–471. Springer, Cham (2014). https://doi.org/10.1007/978-3-319-13647-9_41

29. Alnanih, R., Ormandjieva, O., Radhakrishnan, T.: Context-based and rule-based adaptation of mobile user interfaces in mHealth. Procedia Comput. Sci. **21**, 390–397 (2013)

30. Hofer, T., et al.: Context-awareness on mobile devices - the hydrogen approach. In: Proceedings of the 36th Annual Hawaii International Conference on System Sciences (HICSS 2003) - Track 9, vol. 9, p. 292.1. IEEE Computer Society (2003)

31. Toutain, F., et al.: Interpersonal context-aware communication services. IEEE Commun. Mag. **49**(1), 68–74 (2011)

32. Bellifemine, F., Poggi, A., Rimassa, G.: JADE–A FIPA-compliant agent framework. In: Proceedings of PAAM, London (1999)

33. Petcu, D., Petcu, M.: Distributed jess on a condor pool. In: Proceedings of the 9th WSEAS International Conference on Computers, World Scientific and Engineering Academy and Society (WSEAS) (2005)

34. Bordini, R.H., Hübner, J.F., Wooldridge, M.: Programming Multi-Agent Systems in Agentspeak Using Jason, vol. 8. Wiley, Hoboken (2007)

35. Ricci, A., Piunti, M., Viroli, M., Omicini, A.: Environment programming in CArtAgO. In: El Fallah Seghrouchni, A., Dix, J., Dastani, M., Bordini, R.H. (eds.) Multi-Agent Programming, pp. 259–288. Springer, Boston, MA (2009). https://doi.org/10.1007/978-0-387-89299-3_8

36. Ughetti, M., Trucco, T., Gotta, D.: Development of agent-based, peer-to-peer mobile applications on ANDROID with JADE. In: 2008 The Second International Conference on Mobile Ubiquitous Computing, Systems, Services and Technologies, IEEE (2008)

37. Santi, A., Guidi, M., Ricci, A.: JaCa-android: an agent-based platform for building smart mobile applications. In: Dastani, M., El Fallah Seghrouchni, A., Hübner, J., Leite, J. (eds.) LADS 2010. LNCS (LNAI), vol. 6822, pp. 95–114. Springer, Heidelberg (2011). https://doi.org/10.1007/978-3-642-22723-3_6
38. Jackson, W.: Android apps for absolute beginners: covering Android 7, Apress (2017)
39. Ejigu, D., Scuturici, M., Brunie, L.: An ontology-based approach to context modeling and reasoning in pervasive computing. In: Fifth Annual IEEE International Conference on Pervasive Computing and Communications Workshops (PerComW 2007) (2007)
40. Antoniou, G., et al.: Representation results for defeasible logic. ACM Trans. Comput. Logic 2(2), 255–287 (2001)
41. Uddin, I., Rakib, A., Haque, H.M.U.: A framework for implementing formally verified resource-bounded smart space systems. Mob. Netw. Appl. 22(2), 289–304 (2017)
42. Rakib, A., Haque, H.M.U.: Modeling and verifying context-aware non-monotonic reasoning agents. In: 2015 ACM/IEEE International Conference on Formal Methods and Models for Codesign (MEMOCODE) (2015)
43. Eker, S., Meseguer, J., Sridharanarayanan, A.: The maude LTL model checker and its implementation. In: Ball, T., Rajamani, S.K. (eds.) SPIN 2003. LNCS, vol. 2648, pp. 230–234. Springer, Heidelberg (2003). https://doi.org/10.1007/3-540-44829-2_16
44. Nalepa, G.J., Bobek, S.: Rule-based solution for context-aware reasoning on mobile devices. Comput. Sci. Inf. Syst. 11(1), 171–193 (2014)
45. Van Wissen, B., et al.: ContextDroid: an expression-based context framework for Android. In: Proceedings of PhoneSense (2010)
46. Bandini, S., Sartori, F.: From handicraft prototypes to limited serial productions: exploiting knowledge artifacts to support the industrial design of high quality products. AI EDAM 24 (1), 17–34 (2010)
47. Hecham, A., Croitoru, M., Bisquert, P.: Argumentation-based defeasible reasoning for existential rules. In: AAMAS: Autonomous Agents and MultiAgent Systems (2017)
48. Rakib, A., Uddin, I.: An efficient rule-based distributed reasoning framework for resource-bounded systems. Mob. Netw. Appl. 24(1), 82–99 (2019)

A Real-Time Driver Drowsiness Detection and Warning System Based on an Eye Blinking Rate

Mubeen Arif$^{(\boxtimes)}$, Khan Bahadar Khan, Khizar Fiaz, and Ayesha Niaz

Department of Telecommunication Engineering, Faculty of Engineering,
the Islamia University of Bahawalpur, Bahawalpur, Pakistan
mubeenarif2014@gmail.com

Abstract. Every year many people lose their lives due to fatal road accidents around the world and drowsy driving is one of the primary causes of road accidents and deaths. The other causes of traffic accidents are due to human errors and/or due to mechanical failures. Driver fatigue is one of the leading causes of Road Traffic Accidents (RTA) in Pakistan. Numerous systems are invented that minimize the impact of these accidents. The research in this area began sixty years ago, to determine the drowsiness of driver using computer assisted techniques. In this paper, we have purposed a method that will detect the drowsiness of driver by its eye behavior, such as, eye blink rate and patterns. This paper presents a system for detecting driver drowsiness, based on analysis of the eyes. The system has the ability to adapt to any person, works in real driving conditions, under varying lighting and generating drowsiness index at every moment, which measures the wakefulness of the driver. In several experiments, the proposed system has shown excellent results regarding the objectives and the problems have been successfully overcome.

Keywords: Driver drowsiness system · Eye blinking rate · Haar-Cascade classifier

1 Introduction

The traffic accident is a problem that troubles the world population. According to the World Health Organization (WHO), cardiac morbidity (deaths due to traffic accidents) will be the second leading cause of death in the world by 2020 (World Health Organization, 2012) [1]. According to a recent research the incident rate for a motor vehicle crash changed in to marginally higher for urban drivers in comparison with rural drivers (urban: IR = 4.2/10,000 riding days; Rural: IR = three.7/10,000 driving days [2]. According to the report of American National Highway Traffic Safety (NHTSA), the most common factor that is responsible in a every vehicle run-off-road crashes is the driver performance related factors [3]. Traffic accidents are one of the most serious threats to the health and life of people around the world. The problem is motivated by the fact that those injured in accidents are usually young and healthy (before the accident) people. According to the available statistics, nearly 1.3 million peoples die on the road accidents and 20 to 50 million people suffer non-fatal injuries [4]. The NFTSA

© Springer Nature Singapore Pte Ltd. 2020
I. S. Bajwa et al. (Eds.): INTAP 2019, CCIS 1198, pp. 106–117, 2020.
https://doi.org/10.1007/978-981-15-5232-8_10

statistics shows that there are 72000 crashes, 44000 injuries and 800 deaths in 2013 due to drowsy driving [5]. According to the WHO [6], about 1.25 million people die as a result of road accidents every year in the world and up to 50 million suffers from non-fatal injuries.

Driver drowsiness is also one of the major causes of road accidents in Pakistan. According to National Highway and Motorway Police (NHMP), from 2003 to 2012 the number of road accidents on the motorways was 1750 out of which 497 were fatigue related. From the year 2003 to 2011 the number of accidents on national highway were 5080 out of which 483 were fatigue related. The average percentage of fatigue related accidents on Pakistani roads are 38% [7]. Drowsiness causes a decrease in recognition and control of the vehicle and at the same time, increasing the probability of suffering an accident or a jolt on the road. Many drivers behind the wheel of a vehicle find themselves in a state of fatigue and at the same time are not even aware that they are in such a state. Driver drowsiness depends on many factors such as quality of the last sleep, the biological time (time of day) and the rise within the period of the driving task [8], so a person will feel drowsy if these factors are not full filled.

Driving in a state of weakened attention is hazardous. It is quite similar to driving in a drunk condition, as evidenced by an analysis of the number of deaths and injuries sustained while driving. In order to increase the level of safety on the roads by global manufacturers of cars and trucks are developed and built into cars modern driver assistance systems (CCAS). These systems are designed to prevent drivers from a road traffic accident (MTA) or mitigate its consequences [9].

Since the 1950s, control techniques have been developed to minimize the impact of accidents or prevent them. The active systems and passive systems are developed to monitor the driver. The passive systems are those that are present in a car, but their effect is only seen at the moment in which the accident occurs. These systems minimize the impact on the people involved in the accident, this is the case of the Air bags. The active security systems are mostly electronic or electromechanical. These systems involve the study of the behavior of the driver, the vehicle or machinery and its mode of operation or behavior on the road. As these systems are continuously monitoring behavior, so accidents can be avoided. Among the most prominent active systems is the drowsiness state monitoring system. There are several methods proposed to detect the drowsiness of the driver and some of them are described with their limitations.

2 Literature Review

Traffic accidents have become a great pain for many families, in traffic accidents, people carry lifelong disabilities, deaths leave nothing to compensate for people. When the driver is fatigued, they are detected in various physiological symptoms. For example, fatigue produces changes in brain waves, eye activity varies, facial expressions change, head movements decrease, the cardiac pulse decelerates, pressure is exerted on the brain, pressure on steering wheel decreases, etc.

The methods to detect the drowsiness of the driver have been classified into three main categories as shown in Fig. 1. (1) analysis based on driving patterns, (2) analysis based on physical changes of the eyes and facial expressions using image processing and (3) analysis based on the change of physiological measurements [10].

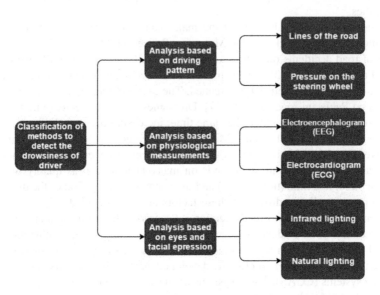

Fig. 1. Classification of methods to detect drowsiness

The approaches to detect the drowsiness of the driver are further classified into invasive and non-invasive methods as shown in Fig. 2. Those methods that somehow affect the comfort of the driver are called Invasive methods. Non-Invasive methods are those methods that do not interfere with the way of driving while minimizing inconvenience. The above defined categories can be further classified as intrusive and non-intrusive methods.

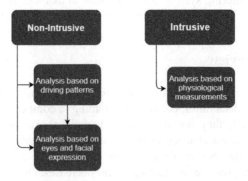

Fig. 2. Classification of the Invasive and non-invasive approach

The following subsections briefly summarize the methods used to detect the drowsiness and describe their limitations.

Analysis Based on the Driving Patterns: These methods detect the condition of the driver through the constant analysis of certain metrics, such as the position of the car, movements of the steering wheel, pressure of the accelerator or the brake, the change of gears (among others) and if it is true, the threshold is exceeded, the driver is likely to be drowsy or distracted.

This method is non-intrusive, since it does not affect the driver. Driving patterns must be generated from measurable parameters and on characteristics of both the driver and/or the vehicle with its surroundings. For example, the pressure of the hands that the driver exerts on the steering wheel is a driving pattern. This method is not easy to model and in many cases, it may be necessary to design a different model according to the characteristics of the vehicle and/or the driver [5]. A driver may change the lane due to some reasons other than the drowsiness, but the system will generate an alarm indicating that the driver is drowsy. So these systems much rely on the characteristics of the external environment and perform well in particular environment only.

Analysis Based on the Change of Physiological Measures: The second group is based on the analysis of physiological variables used for the detection of drowsiness. These are very robust methods because they allow the detection of drowsiness in its initial phases with a low rate of false positives. In this group, the methods for detecting drowsiness are based on Electroencephalogram (EEG), Electromyogram (EMG), Electrocardiogram (ECG), Electrooculogram (EOG).

Among all these methods, the most common method for the detection of drowsiness is the EEG, where different frequency bands are analyzed [11]. The methods focused on measuring physiological changes such as the variability of the heart rate, the EMG and the EEG of the driver are considered as a means to detect human cognitive states [5].

The advantages that present are the precision in the diagnosis of the state. While one of the biggest drawbacks is the use of sensors connected to the driver's body. For example, for the EEG several electrodes are connected to the head during the driving and thus be able to record the brain waves.

Methods Based on the Analysis of Eyes and Facial Expressions: According to the results of several researchers, the monitoring systems based on the analysis of the images of the eyes and facial expressions are difficult to implement due to several complicated factors to control in a vehicle. But despite this, it is considered the most appropriate methodology to deal with the problem of driver drowsiness analysis [12].

Based on the previous premises, the objective of this paper is to propose, construct and validate an architecture based on the analysis of visual characteristics through the use of artificial vision and self-learning techniques. The methods that base their analysis on physical changes of the eyes and face are highly reliable and have the advantage of not being invasive [13], that is, they do not generate discomfort or discomfort in the driver.

3 Proposed Method

The following constraints are considered for designing system of detection and warning of the driver sleepiness. The designed system constraints are 1) a non-invasive system 2) camera acquired image to be processed 3) a real-time environment validation. The simplified general flow diagram of the proposed system is shown in Fig. 3. Firstly, the image containing the driver's face from the driving simulation medium is obtained by means of a camera. Then, the face of the driver is detected. The evaluation of eye images obtained in this region is performed in two stages. The images obtained in the first stage are recorded. The recorded eye images are classified by labeling the eyes in the image according to their open or closed condition. After the classification process, the data files were created by subtracting the attributes of these images. These data files are used to test the proposed method. Eye images obtained in the second stage are not recorded. The live camera image is classified with the previously created learning model and is used to determine the driver's sleepiness according to the open or closed eye results.

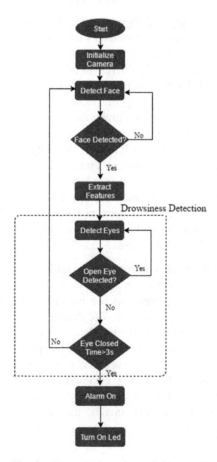

Fig. 3. General Flow chart of the system

3.1   Image Acquisition

The cameras used in this study is positioned in front of the driver to detect the driver face area and its surroundings. By means of the camera operating in the visible area at sufficient light intensity the image is obtained. These images will be obtained with the help of real-time video images of the person's eyes when they are open and closed and standard cleaning and filtering operations have been applied.

Converting Image to Grey Scale. The first step after capturing the image in real time is to convert (RGB image) it into grey scale image. The treatment of images is very important for the detection of facial features, eyes, lips etc. OpenCV libraries allow you to make changes to RGB to Scale of Grays as shown in Fig. 4.

Fig. 4. RGB to Gray scale

3.2   Detection of Face

After Acquisition of the image from the camera and converting it to grey scale, the very first step is to detect the face from the image. For the face detection we have use viola jones algorithm [14].

Viola Jones Algorithm. The algorithm of Viola-Jones is a method of object detection that stands out for its low computational cost, which facilitates its use in systems that require real-time processing. The algorithm is based on a series of weak classifiers called Haar-like features, which can be calculated from a general image efficiently.

The nodes are sorted from less to more complex, that is, initially fewer features are used than at the end. For each node, a negative result at any stage ends the computation, and the algorithm declares that there is no face in that location. We can see this operation in the Fig. 5.

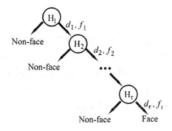

Fig. 5. Cascading stages of Viola jones face detection

The face detection system with cascade classifier using a Haar-like feature that can work in real time consists of three stages. The first performs a transformation of the original image in another so-called integral image, the second stage extracts characteristics using Haar filters, and the latter uses an AdaBoost classifier for the construction of cascaded cascade structure.

Integral Image. The integral image is used for the effective calculation of the quadrilateral properties of the input data in the cascade classifier method. This image allows to quickly extract characteristics at different scales, it does not work directly with the values of the pixels, it works with accumulative image of the value of its original pixels. An integral image can be defined according to Eq. (1).

$$ii(x,y) = \sum x' \leq x, y' \leq y^{\wedge}(i(x',y'))\tag{1}$$

Where ii (x, y) is the point of the integral image in the coordinates (x, y) and i (x ', y') is the point of the original image in the same coordinates. Figure (6a) shows an original image, while Fig. (6b) illustrates the corresponding integral image. The integral image can be calculated from the original image by performing the operations described in the equations:

$$s(x,y) = s(x,y - 1) + i(x,y)\tag{2}$$

$$ii(x,y) = ii(x - 1,y) + s(x,y)\tag{3}$$

Where s (x, y) is the sum of an entire row considering that s (x, −1) = 0, and ii (−1, y) = 0. With the integral image you can obtain the sum of all the points located in a rectangle, using only the four values shown in Fig. (6c).

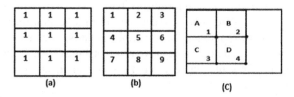

(a)   (b)   (c)

Fig. 6. (a) Original image, (b) Integral image, (c) Integral image calculation, Calculation of the sum in an integral image [14].

Feature Extraction Using Haar-Cascade. Classification features are geometric shapes used to detect areas of an image that may contain parts of a face. These can be simple structures composed of two, three or four gray and white rectangles called Haar filters, as shown in Fig. 7. [15]. The features can have 6, 8 or 9 significant points, corresponding to the corners of each rectangle.

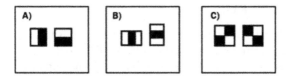

Fig. 7. Haar Filters A) Characteristics of two B) Characteristics of three C) Characteristics of Four

These structures are usually associated with the eyes, nose, forehead, hair, etc. Figure 8 illustrates the correspondence of two possible classification features with parts of a face.

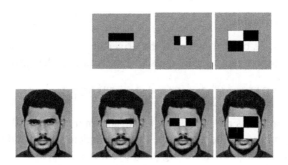

Fig. 8. Haar filters and its correspondence on the face

To evaluate each feature, the sum of the points of the white and gray regions and the subtraction between those sums are required, this is done efficiently by having an integral image.

Classifier. The third characteristic of the Viola-Jones algorithm is the use of a cascade combination of groups of increasingly complex classifiers (with a greater number of traits). In our project we have used AdaBoost classifier for the face detection.

AdaBoost is a contraction of Adaptive Boosting, the algorithm seeks to create a strong classifier whose base is the linear combination of weak learner classifiers.

The first stages of the cascade have a smaller number of classifiers, these allow faster windows to be discarded without faces, concentrating the computational effort in the following stages that have a greater possibility of containing a face Fig. 9 [16] illustrates a distribution of cascade classifiers of multiple stages.

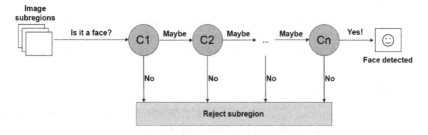

Fig. 9. Illustration of a cascade of classifiers

3.3   Detection of the EYE

Once the face is detected from an image the very next step is to detect the eyes from it. We have used deep learning open source software Dlib tool.

This method is based on the shape of the eyes, this measurement can be performed using OpenCV functions using the Hough circles function. What this function does basically is to find in the image forms that resemble circles.

Once the front face of the driver is detected by the Haar classifier, a rectangle object belonging to the Dlib class is created with the coordinates obtained in the detection. Given this bounding box of the face, we can obtain 68 highlights used to locate the eyes, eyebrows, nose, mouth and jaw [17].

3.4   Detecting Drowsiness

To determine the state of drowsiness of the driver in this system, the calculation of a metric called eye aspect ratio (EAR) is used. EAR can be calculated as follows:

$$EAR = (\|p2 - p6\| + \|p3 - p5\|)/(2\|p1 - p4\|) \tag{4}$$

Where the coordinates p1, p2, p3, p4, p5 are shown in the Fig. 10. In the lower left corner as shown in Fig. 12, there is an eye that is completely open and the facial points of the eye traced. Then, in the lower right, an eye that is closed. The lower part traces the aspect ratio of the eye over time.

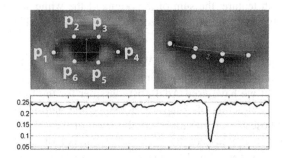

Fig. 10. Open and closed eyes with landmarks pi automatically detected by [18]. The eye aspect ratio EAR in Eq. (4) plotted for several frames of a video sequence. A single blink is present.

By performing different test, we have adjusted a threshold value of 0.25 EAR, so a scale greater than or equal to 0.25 EAR shows a state of no drowsiness, while a scale lower than 0.25 EAR and for a time of three seconds will indicate a drowsiness state.

3.5   Alarm Activation

Drowsiness alarm is formed by a tone and a voice. When drowsiness is detected, a tone followed by a voice code announcing "Drowsiness alert" is executed. The Python library called "Pygame" was used to play the audio files, which can be played by a simple command by loading the audio file in "wav" format.

4   Results

In this study, a real-time driving safety system is implemented with the Raspberry Pi 3 development card using the open source Computer Vision (OpenCV) library including image processing algorithms. Python software was chosen as a programming language due to its great flexibility. Raspberry Pi, which is frequently used in real-time image processing applications with camera-compatible hardware, has a 1.2 GHz 64-bit Quad-core ARMv8 central processing unit. The block diagram of the image processing based embedded system is given in Fig. 11. The Raspberry Pi 3 Model B development board is powered by a 12 V DC battery through the 5 V regulator circuit. With the A4 TECH 1080P FULL HD webcam, the image processing software running in the development card is applied to the fluid image taken and the eye opening and closure of the driver are detected.

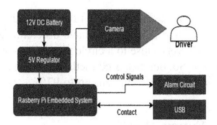

Fig. 11. Block Diagram of hardware system

4.1   Tests of the Driver Fatigue Detection Hardware

At different hours and in different day-weather conditions, it was decided that light intensity was the most affected by the system. Although the angle of the camera and the physical condition of the driver are effective on the system, it is obvious that the most important factor is the light intensity. As a result of the tests, even if the light intensity is low, the system yielded successful results as shown in Fig. 12.

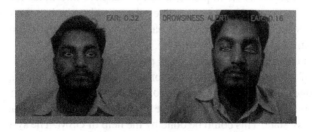

Fig. 12. Implementing the system in real time environment on person 1

As it can be seen that as the EAR falls below the threshold value the drowsiness is detected and an alarms is generated to awake the driver. These results are quite appropriate and can detect the drowsiness of the driver.

We have compared our method with another method in which the Haar-Cascade classifier is used. The color of the eyes is different in each person, but all of them have a common characteristic that is the white color of the eyeball. As for color, an open eye contains a higher density of white pixels than a closed eye as shown in Fig. 13. Therefore, it is possible to set a threshold value of white pixels.

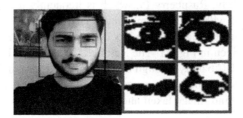

Fig. 13. Haar Cascade algorithm for eyes detection

The main problem with this method was due to obtaining the threshold value of the grayscale image. As for the shape, people can have different sizes of eyes, but all of them have an elliptical shape very close to a circle, depending on each person the eyes will be more or less circular. So, our proposed method is reliable as the threshold value can be fixed. The purposed system is efficient up to 97%.

5   Conclusion and Future Work

In this study, real-time hardware device has been developed to determine driver's fatigue status and to warn the driver in case of danger situation to ensure driving safety. The results obtained in the detection of blinking to determine drowsiness are positive, since few errors have been obtained, which, in most cases, occurred due to the influence of illumination. The use of Dlib tool in conjunction with Haar waterfalls has served to build an efficient method to detect the state of drowsiness and distraction of the driver. Detecting if an eye is open or closed in situations of variable illumination was a difficult task.

A noteworthy aspect is the implementation of adaptive thresholds for the estimation of the flicker parameters, that is, the values that decide whether the eye is open or closed. To evaluate the flicker detector, each frame processed by the software was analyzed, resulting in an efficiency of 97%.

The system cannot work properly if the person has worn dark color lenses so there is still a need of improvements. The vibrations that occur in a vehicle slightly affect the capture of images, but not the processing of these. Moreover, there should be a procedure that should inform the traffic police by an email or text message, if driver is driving in drowsy state. This could be done by the help of GSM. The system can't work if the driver has worn googles the system need advancement in this respect.

It can be affirmed that the method implemented in this project has allowed to fulfill the main objectives, leaving open many options of improvement and extension of functionalities that invite and motivate to continue working on its improvement.

References

1. Sharma, B.R.: Road traffic injuries: a major global public health crisis. Public Health **122** (12), 1399–1406 (2008)
2. Stevenson, M.R., Palamara, P.: Behavioural factors as predictors of motor vehicle crashes: differentials between young urban and rural drivers. Aust. N. Z. J. Public Health **25**(3), 245–249 (2001)
3. Liu, C., Subramanian, R.: Factors Related to Fatal Single-Vehicle Run-Off-Road Crashes, U. S. Department of Transportation, American National Highway Traffic Safety Administration, DOT HS 811 232, Washington, D.C., November (2009)
4. Sahayadhas, A., Sundaraj, K., Murugappan, M.: Detecting driver drowsiness based on sensors: a review. Sensors **12**(12), 16937–16953 (2012)
5. Wang, J.-Q., et al.: Longitudinal collision mitigation via coordinated braking of multiple vehicles using model predictive control. Integr. Comput. Aided Eng. **22**(2), 171–185 (2015)
6. World Health Organization: Global status report on road safety 2015. World Health Organization (2015)
7. Azam, K., et al.: Comparison of fatigue related road traffic crashes on the national highways and motorways in Pakistan. J. Eng. Appl. Sci. **33**, 2 (2014)
8. Salih, J.H.K., Kulkarni, L.: Fatigue detection system for the drivers using video analysis of facial expressions. In: 2017 International Conference on Computing, Communication, Control and Automation (ICCUBEA), IEEE (2017)
9. Liang, Y., Reyes, M.L., Lee, J.D.: Real-time detection of driver cognitive distraction using support vector machines. IEEE Trans. Intell. Transp. Syst. **8**(2), 340–350 (2007)
10. Galarza, E.E., Egas, F.D., Silva, F.M., Velasco, P.M., Galarza, E.D.: Real time driver drowsiness detection based on driver's face image behavior using a system of human computer interaction implemented in a smartphone. In: Rocha, Á., Guarda, T. (eds.) ICITS 2018. AISC, vol. 721, pp. 563–572. Springer, Cham (2018). https://doi.org/10.1007/978-3-319-73450-7_53
11. Eskandarian, A., Ali, M.: Evaluation of a smart algorithm for commercial vehicle driver drowsiness detection. In: 2007 IEEE Intelligent Vehicles Symposium, IEEE (2007)
12. Prajapati, N.G., et al.: Driver drowsiness detection with audio-visual warning. Int. J. **3**, 294–300 (2016)
13. Sharma, N., Banga, V.K.: Drowsiness warning system using artificial intelligence. World Acad. Sci. Eng. Technol. **4**(7), 1771–1773 (2010)
14. Viola, P., Jones, M.J.: Robust real-time face detection. Int. J. Comput. Vis. **57**(2), 137–154 (2004)
15. Viola, P., Michael, J.: Rapid object detection using a boosted cascade of simple features. CVPR **1**(1), 511–518 (2001)
16. https://realpython.com/traditional-face-detection-python/
17. Baltrušaitis, T., Peter, R., Louis-Philippe, M.: Openface: an open source facial behavior analysis toolkit. In: 2016 IEEE Winter Conference on Applications of Computer Vision (WACV), IEEE (2016)
18. Soukupova, T., Jan, C.: Eye Blink Detection Using Facial Landmarks. 21st Computer Vision Winter Workshop, Rimske Toplice, Slovenia (2016)

Optimization of Bug Reporting System (BRS): Artificial Intelligence Based Method to Handle Duplicate Bug Report

Afshan Saad[1(✉)], Muhammad Saad[2], Shah Muhammad Emaduddin[1], and Rafi Ullah[1]

[1] PAF-Karachi Institute of Economics and Technology, Karachi, Pakistan
Afshan@pafkiet.edu.pk
[2] 10Pearls Limited, Karachi, Pakistan

Abstract. Bug tracking and reporting are some of the most critical activities/steps in software engineering and implementation which has a direct impact on the quality of tested software and productivity of resources allocated to that software. Bug Reporting System (BRS) plays an important role in tracking all essential bug reports during software development life cycle (SDLC). Duplicate Bug Reports (DBR) have an adverse effect on the software quality assurance process as it enhances the processing time of bug triager whose job is to keep track of all bug reports and also on application developers, to whom bug tickets are assigned by the triager. Duplicate bug reports if remain unidentified may result in enhancing bug handling time (rework) and decreasing overall team performance. However identification of duplicate bug report remains as a critical task as it is a tough job to manually identify all second images of earlier reported bug. In this paper we have proposed an enhancement in existing BRS which uses artificial intelligence based intelligent techniques to detect the existence of a duplicate bug. Every new bug reported to the system will be marked with an identification tag. A bug containing duplicate tag will be phased out from the bug repository which will not only reduce the additional effort on bug triage but also improve the system's performance.

Keywords: Bug tracking optimization · Triager · Software quality assurance

1 Introduction

Bug Reporting System (BRS) is intended to facilitate software Quality-Assurance (QA) engineers and developers to monitor reported bugs in their work for the sake of enhancing system's quality [1]. Bugs are common software issues are found in the greater part of the software system and software products. Reporting a bug procedure [2] is an approach to get feedback from clients, customers and end users. To help tracking bugs in software and develop more quality and reliable software systems, Bug Reporting (BR) tools have been introduced by different people and organization as a part of process (like Mantis, Bugzilla, Jira etc.). The users of system software report bugs that exist already in bug reporting system. These reported bugs often called "duplicates" [3]. Removal of these reports may decrease the efforts of software

© Springer Nature Singapore Pte Ltd. 2020
I. S. Bajwa et al. (Eds.): INTAP 2019, CCIS 1198, pp. 118–128, 2020.
https://doi.org/10.1007/978-981-15-5232-8_11

developers in fixing related defects helps by identifying duplicated bug reports. However, identifying duplicate bug reports manually is quite challenging because there are a huge quantity of Bug Reports (BRs) mainly dependent on software size and scope. Typically, Bugs Reporting Tools (BRT), contains reported bugs is examined by a Triager (triager has the knowledge and information of projects and products) for carrying out tasks such as: check the quality to make sure if the reports contain all the required and useful information, duplicate identification, assigning it to the suitable programmer for editing and correcting some project-specific properties and metadata connected with the reports (such as severity and priority level, assigned to developer, current status and estimated time to closure). Without checking and finding bug reports duplication, the Triagers assign duplicated reports to various software programmers. Once bug is resolved, pointing out the duplicates as a separate bug is a time wastage. DBR are usually processed manually by the Triage. Filtering to find duplicates in a large and complex projects demands the extensive number of Triagers (an informative and knowledgeable person) knowledge, manual work, and information of the developing system. Solutions to automate above mentioned the process of identifying the duplicates can speed-up process/procedure of defect management, increased the productivity of the Triager and result in reduced system maintenance cost.

Rest of the paper is distributed as follow, Sect. 2 is the study of available tools and techniques observed in literature review, Sect. 3 is all about of overview of bug reporting tools most frequently used by industry in software development life cycle, Sect. 4 is the detail discussion of proposed methodology, Sect. 5 is about the applications, problems and their solution and Sect. 6 is about future work and concluding the topic.

2 Literature Review

Authors of [7] propose a framework we propose a feeling based programmed way to deal with anticipate the need for a report. At first, they exploit regular dialect preparing methods to pre-process bug reports. Secondly they distinguish feeling words that are related to the depiction of the bug reports and appoint it a feeling of esteem. Finally, for bug report, they make a component vector and anticipate its need using machine-learning (ML) techniques that are prepared with history/past information gathered from the different sources such as Internet. Eclipse IDE was used by authors to assess proposed approach and consequences of the cross venture assessment which results in enhancing the F1 score by over 6%.

Authors in [8] proposed a screen stream-based model of the framework. With extra metadata, the model serves as a computerized route process for an analyzer. Contrasted and exploratory test is physically performed in two contextual investigations, the proposed structure enables the analyzers to investigate a more noteworthy degree of the tried framework and empowers more prominent identification of the imperfections introduced in the framework.

The web bug is a sites blunder or a questioned document that is set on the site page or in the email so to screen the conduct of the framework client or to bring the private data of the client. There as of now exist different bug recognition instruments with a specific end goal to enhance site security. These instruments have diverse capacities as per the different parameters of sites. However, they are not that productive for giving the outcome and security to a site. Alongside that much time and endeavors get contributed and no certification of exact comes about. As there are a great many diverse sites with different Web administrations having their distinctive renditions running on the sites they can be called as one of the segments of the sites alongside spaces, subdomain, IP, ports, and so on. This apparatus will facilitate the activity of bug analysts [9].

Authors in [10] Suggested an approach based on machine learning for identifying duplicate bug reports. For individual order of bug reports, set of bug reports recognized by connection esteem that relates to particular highlights. A design is created in the shade of author classification and connection esteem to distinguish any sorting of bug reports as non-duplicate or duplicate reports. This prototype is paired to illustrate a particular bug and an expected bug report as duplicate or non-duplicate bug reports.

In paper [11], the authors proposed a semi administered contents order approach for bug triage. Technique aimed to keep a strategic difference from the insufficiency of marked bugs' reports in pre-existing managed procedures. That novel technique consolidates the credulous Naïve-Bayes Machine learning model and desire boost to explore both marked and unlabeled BRs. Mentioned approach prepares a model (ML classifier) with a small amount of named reports. Discussed approach, named unlabeled reports iteratively and trained another classifier with marks of all the BR. DBR portrays issues report in a bug file. For some of the open-source/free available solutions expands, the amount of duplicate bugs addresses an enormous level of the document, so customized distinctive verification of duplicate reports is needed.

Authors of [12] have demonstrate a methodology which facilitate duplicate bug report recognizing evidence more effectively. The mentioned methodology uses Natural Language Processing technique named n-gram for duplicate bug report revelation. Whenever a BR is submitted to the vault, a man, called a triage, looks it is copy of current bug report. In the event that it is, the triage marks it as "duplicate".

In paper [13], authors demonstrate another technique that further consolidates execution data. In their approach, when another bug report arrives, its trademark tongue data and execution data are separated and those of the current bug reports. By that point, few available bug reports are endorsed to the triage as closest matched bug reports to the new found bug report. At long last, triage looks proposed bug reports to pick if the new bug copies a current bug. The utilization of open bug following vaults like Bugzilla is basic in numerous product applications. They permit designers, analyzers, and clients the capacity to report issues related to the framework and track determination status. Research in copy report location has fundamentally centered on token/word recurrence based comparability measures paying less respect to specific situation or detailing dialect's structure. In this way, in substantial storehouses, reports portraying diverse issues might be set apart as copies due to the incessant utilization of normal words. In this paper, authors introduce Factor LCS, an approach which uses basic arrangement coordinating for copy report location [14].

Bug following frameworks is imperative apparatuses that guide the support exercises of programming designers. The utility of these frameworks is hampered by an exorbitant number of copy bug reports– in a few undertakings upwards of a fourth of all reports are copies. Designers should physically distinguish copy bug reports, yet this recognizable proof process is tedious and worsens the officially staggering expense of programming upkeep. Authors proposed a framework that naturally orders copy bug reports as they land to spare designer time. This framework utilizes surface highlights, printed semantics, and chart grouping to anticipate copy status. Utilizing Mozilla Venture's dataset containing 29,000 bug reports and perform tests that incorporate a reenactment of a constant bug revealing condition [15].

In an overview we found that most engineers have encountered copied bug reports, be that as it may, few thought about them as a significant issue. This repudiates well-known knowledge considering bug copies as significant issue for open source ventures. Designers additionally called attention to that the extra data gave by copies makes a difference to determine bugs faster. In this paper, we in this manner propose to combine bug copies, as opposed to treating them independently. We evaluate the measure of data that is included for designers and demonstrate that programmed triaging can be made strides also. Furthermore, we talk about the distinctive reasons why clients submit copy bug reports in any case [16].

Deformity reports are created from different testing and advancement exercises in programming building. At times two reports are presented that portray the same issue, prompting copy reports. These reports are for the most part written in organized normal dialect, and in that capacity, it is difficult to think about two reports for likeness with formal strategies. Recognizing copies as an end goal, authors in this paper examines utilizing Natural Language Processing methods to help the distinguishing proof. A model apparatus is created at Sony Ericson Mobile Communications and assessed for a situation consider breaking down deformity reports. The assessment demonstrates, around 66% of the copies could be discovered utilizing NLP procedures. Distinctive variations of procedures give just minor outcome contrasts, demonstrating a hearty innovation. Client testing demonstrates that the general state of mind towards the strategy is sure and that it has a development potential [17].

Bug revealing and settling the announced bugs plays a vital part in the advancement and support of programming frameworks. The product designers and end users/clients can work together in this procedure for enhancing the dependability of programming frameworks. Different clients, reports imperfections they have faced in the product while using and how these bugs affect their product usage. Be that as it may, the same deformity might be accounted for autonomously by a few clients prompting countless bug's reports. Various available strategies for recognizing copy reports, however best outcomes till now record for just 24% of real copies. Authors proposed another strategy in light of grouping to recognize a bigger extent of copy reports while classifying bogus positives of miss identified non-copies (novelty) low. That approach is tentatively assessed on extensive example of bug reports from three open area informational collections. The outcomes demonstrate that this approach accomplishes better execution as far as a consonant measure that joins genuine positive and genuine negative rates when analyzed to the current strategies [18].

It is found that most engineers have encountered copied bug reports, be that as it may, few thought about them as a significant issue. This repudiates well-known knowledge considering bug copies as significant issue for open-source/free available ventures. Also, designers additionally called attention to that the extra data gave by copies makes a difference to determine bugs faster. In paper [19], the authors propose to combine bug copies, as opposed to treating them independently. They evaluate the measure of data that is included for designers and demonstrate that programmed triaging can be made strides also.

Bugs are overpowering in programming languages frameworks. To push ahead the dependability of programming languages frameworks plans once in a while permit end users to give the commitment to bugs that they have experienced. Clients send bug report in some specific format such as Bugzilla. This procedure is that as it may is ungainly and scattered, which proposes that different clients could submit bug reports pronouncing a practically identical issue. These are recommended as copy bug reports. Proximity of different copy of bug reports may results various futile manual endeavors as reliably a triage needs to be physically mark reports as copies. Beginning late, there exists different assemblies that take a gander at copy bug report issue which essentially answers the running with the demand: given another bug report, recover k other basically indistinguishable bug reports. All considered things still demands substantive manual exertion which could or might be diminished. Jalbert at el. are the first to show the quick distinctive verification of copy bug reports; it responds to demand: given another bug report, total in the event that it's copy of bug or obviously not. Broaden Jalbert et al. tried to enhance the exactness of mechanized copy bugs perceiving confirmation. Authors examine various streets regarding bug reports from Mozilla bug following framework [20].

3 An Overview of Bug Reporting Tools

3.1 Mantis

An open-source freely available bug following framework frequently used is Mantis Bug Tracker. Most widely recognized utilization of MantisBT is, tracking programming surrenders. Notwithstanding, MantisBT is frequently arranged by clients to fill in as a more conventional issue following framework and undertaking administration tool. The logo and name of Mantis alludes to the Mantidae group of bugs, known for following of bugs and benefiting from different creepy crawlies, casually alluded to as "bugs". Venture's name is regularly abridged to either MantisBT or just Mantis [4].

3.2 Bugzilla

Bugzilla is a vigorous, featureful and develop deformity following framework, or bug-following framework. Imperfection following frameworks enables groups of engineers to monitor extraordinary bugs, issues, issues, improvement and other change asks for in their items successfully. Straightforward imperfection following capacities is frequently incorporated with coordinated source code administration situations, for example, GitHub or other electronic or privately introduced reciprocals. We discover associations swinging to Bugzilla when they exceed the capacities of those frameworks - for instance, since they need work process administration, or bug deceivability control (security), or custom fields [5] (Fig. 1).

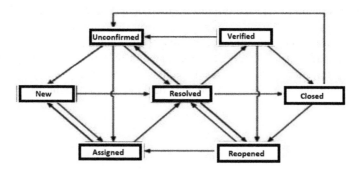

Fig. 1. The bug status transition graph [21]

3.3 JIRA

JIRA is a popular project of Atlassian - and bug tracking tool which is frequently used by the technical support staff to get work done efficiently and faster. It is available on a monthly subscription as SAAS (software-as-service) or it might be deployed over servers. It provides end to end solution from issue appearance to issue resolution. To plan projects and to guide project processes, an iterative approach called agile project management is used [6].

3.4 Duplicate Bug Reports-DBR

Bug Report comprises of a few fields normally it incorporates synopsis, depiction, classification, venture name, need, seriousness, connections et cetera. Each field conveys distinctive sort of data. E.g. rundown is a sort of short portrayal of the bug while depiction is the point by point framework of what is, where it comes from, how it happened, sometimes it has a solution how it will be fixed. Following are the critical issues in case of duplicate bug report. Triager needs to detect which new bug reports are duplicates of last reported reports. In large projects where there are large amount of reports to search through, detecting duplicate bugs can be a daunting task.

- If Triager did not find the duplicate bug and the duplicate bug assigned to developer then the developer spend time on that to fix the bug which is already reported earlier.
- fixing duplicate bugs again and again is a waste of time and effort for both developers and organization.

3.5 Bug Tracking Systems

A BRS is a system/process that monitors reported bugs in projects or products. Many available open-source bug reporting systems allow end-user to enter bug reports directly in the system. Rest of the systems are used by an organization internally as part of their process performing software implementation. A major part of a bug reporting tool is a database which monitor information about known bugs. Information may include the time of a bug was reported in tool and updated, its severity and priority, the program behavior, information and details on how to reproduce that bug; as well as to identify the bug reporter (person) and any developer who might be working on resolving it (Fig. 2).

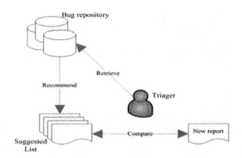

Fig. 2. Duplicate Bug Reporting System

3.6 Bug Reporting Process

At whatever point an issue is found amid programming improvement, testing or activity, it must be distinguished to the person who is in charge of conspicuous of the fundamental abuse and its revision. To assist this, Bug Reporting Systems or "bug following" frameworks are utilized. With this instrument, the analyzer, or whoever finds an issue, can present a Defect Report, generic process describing "how defect report works"

- A bug is found in any project and a bug report is setted in BRS or bug reporting system.
- Report is analyzed and identified by Triage to isolate the main reason of a bug.
- Bug report by reporter is then assigned to a programmer for resolving.
- The programmer reproduces the bug and fix it.
- Fixed bug is tested by the programmer or by a tester after the bug closed.

4 Proposed Methodology

Novel approach has been proposed in this paper to improve DBR detection's accuracy in SDLC. It can improve similarity identification between old bug reports which is in the database and the new submitted reports.

4.1 Generate Tags for New Report

The process starts by generating tags for every new report using the words used in that report. The pseudo code for generating tags for report is as follows:

Algorithm 1: Generating Tags

1. Initialize an empty tagsArray
2. Initialize fieldsArrayIndex to Zero
3. Do While fieldsArrayIndex < size of feildsAr
   a. Convert fieldsArray[fieldsArrayIndex] to an array as wordsArray
   b. Initialize wordsArrayIndex to zero
4. Do while wordsArrayIndex is less than size of wordsArray
   a. Initialize tagsArrayIndex to zero
   b. Initialize Found to False
5. Do while tagsArrayIndex < size of tagsArray
   a. If tagsArray [tagsArrayIndex] = = wordsArray [wordsArrayIndex]
      i. Set found to True
      ii. Break the Do While loop
6. If Found is False
   a. Push wordsArray [wordsArrayIndex] at the end of tagsArray
7. wordsArrayIndex = wordsArrayIndex + 1
8. fieldsArrayIndex = fieldsArrayIndex + 1

4.2 Comparing Tags

Once the tags will be generated new reports, a comparison will be done on these tags with the tags of the reports that are already stored in the database. The pseudo code for comparing tags is as follows:

Algorithm 2: Comparing Tags

1. Initialize tagsArrayIndex to zero
2. Do while tagsArrayIndex < size of tagsArray
   a. SQLQUERY   +   =   "'reports'.'tags'   LIKE   %"
      +tagsArray[tagsArrayIndex]+"%"
   b. tagsArrayIndex = tagsArrayIndex + 1
   c. If tagsArrayIndex < size of tagsArray
      i. SQLQuery += "OR".

4.3 Sorting Fetched Reports

Once all the similar Reports are collected, they will be sorted to find numbers of similar tags. For this number of similar tags will be counted using the following pseudo code:

Algorithm 3: Finding Similar Tags

---

1.   Initialize similarReportsArrayIndex to zero
2.   Do while similarReposrtArrayIndex is less than size of similarReports
   - a.   Add a new element in similarReports
   - b.   [similarReportsArrayIndex] with the key of tagsCount
   - c.   Initialize similarReports [similarReportsArrayIndex] [tagsCount] to zero
   - d.   Initialize tagsArrayIndex to zero
3.   Do while tagsArrayIndex is less than size of tagsArray
   - a.   If similarReports
     - i.   [similarReportsArrayIndex] [tags] contains tagsArray[tagsArrayIndex]
     - ii.   similarReports[similarReportsArrayIndex][tagsCount] = similarReports[similarReportsArrayIndex][tagsCount]
   - b.   tagsArrayIndex = tagsArrayIndex + 1
4.   similarReportsArrayIndex = similarReportsArrayIndex + 1
5.   fieldsArrayIndex = fieldsArrayIndex + 1

---

5   Problems and Solutions

5.1   How Duplicate Bug Report Can Be Detected in Our System?

We have used artificial intelligence algorithm in which we compare the old and new bug reports. Generating tags for every new report using the words used in that report and save them in our database and compare similar reports. Hence each word of each report should have a unique tag.

5.2   What Are the Required Fields for Detection Duplicate Bugs?

We compare fields such as summary, descriptions, category, steps to reproduce, tags, OS and OS versions.

5.3   How Old Bug and New Bug Will Be Linked?

We found the somewhat similar reports which have not exactly the same information. These types of reports I have to merge or link together because different users enter different information in a different way, but the reason behind is the same, telling the same issue in different styles.

5.4 Why Are We not Discarding Old Bug Report?

When the Triager finds the exactly same bug reports then these bug reports should be merged or linked instead of discarding the old bug. This will capture the maximum information in on place. Merging the duplicate bug reports will help the developers to resolve bugs. Discarding the old bug would result in loss of information such as who fix this issue earlier, comments on this issue, how it issue was fixed.

6 Conclusion and Future Work

In open source development, bug report has an important role. Currently manual processes are there to detect duplicate bugs. This paper presents an intelligent approach that save Triager and developer time by automatically categorizing duplicate bug reports. Unlike other approaches, the proposed system is capable to reduce efforts and cost required for development by filtering out maximum number of duplicate reports. Improving bug duplication performance organization can save wastage of cost and efforts on bug triage and finding bug's duplicate. Further work includes two more features in which old bug report in the repository is linked or merged with the new bug report reported by users. This feature facilitates developers to find all relevant information together. If the Triager think that all the information is not provided in old bug report then the Triager can link or merge the report. Hence all the information gathered in one place. Another feature is changing the status of old bug report if the new one has exactly the same information. When the issue is resolved, the users get notified. If the new reported bug has not the same or some information then the Triager will continue the process, set the priority of bug and assign the bug to developers to fix the issue.

References

1. Fischer, M., Pinzger, M., Gall, H.: Analyzing and relating bug report data for feature tracking. In: WCRE, vol. 3 (2003)
2. Dal Sasso, T., Mocci, A., Lanza, M.: What makes a satisficing bug report? In: 2016 IEEE International Conference on Software Quality, Reliability and Security (QRS). IEEE (2016)
3. Aggarwal, K., et al.: Detecting duplicate bug reports with software engineering domain knowledge. J. Softw. Evol. Process 29(3), e1821 (2017)
4. https://en.wikipedia.org/wiki/Mantis_Bug_Tracker
5. https://www.bugzilla.org/about/
6. https://www.quora.com/What-is-JIRA-What-is-it-used-for
7. Umer, Q., Hui, L., Yasir, S.: Emotion based automated priority prediction for bug reports. IEEE Access 6, 35743–35752 (2018)
8. Bures, M., Frajtak, K., Ahmed, B.S.: Tapir: automation support of exploratory testing using model reconstruction of the system under test. IEEE Trans. Reliab. 67, 557–580 (2018)
9. Kadam, S., Shinde, S., Patekar, N., Rain, S.: Bug detection tool for websites. Int. J. Eng. Sci. 16440 (2018)
10. Bagal, P.V., et al.: Duplicate bug report detection using machine learning algorithms and automated feedback incorporation. U.S. Patent Application 14/992,831, filed 13 July 2017

11. Xuan, J., Jiang, H., Ren, Z., Yan, J., Luo, Z.: Automatic bug triage using semi-supervised text classification. arXiv preprint arXiv:1704.04769 (2017)
12. Minh, P.N.: An approach to detecting duplicate bug reports using n-gram features and cluster chrinkage technique. Int. J. Sci. Res. Publ. (IJSRP) **4**(5), 89–100 (2014)
13. Wang, X., Zhang, L., Xie, T., Anvik, J., Sun, J.: An approach to detecting duplicate bug reports using natural language and execution information. In: Proceedings of the 30th International Conference on Software Engineering, pp. 461–470. ACM (2008)
14. Banerjee, S., Cukic, B., Adjeroh, D.: Automated duplicate bug report classification using subsequence matching. In: 2012 IEEE 14th International Symposium on High-Assurance Systems Engineering, pp. 74–81. IEEE (2012)
15. Jalbert, N., Weimer, W.: Automated duplicate detection for bug tracking systems. In: IEEE International Conference on Dependable Systems and Networks with FTCS and DCC 2008, DSN 2008, pp. 52–61. IEEE (2008)
16. Sureka, A., Jalote, P.: Detecting duplicate bug report using character n-gram-based features. In: 2010 17th Asia Pacific Software Engineering Conference (APSEC), pp. 366–374. IEEE (2010)
17. Runeson, P., Alexandersson, M., Nyholm, O.: Detection of duplicate defect reports using natural language processing. In: Proceedings of the 29th International Conference on Software Engineering, pp. 499–510. IEEE Computer Society (2007)
18. Gopalan, R.P., Krishna, A.: Duplicate bug report detection using clustering. In: 2014 23rd Australian Software Engineering Conference (ASWEC), pp. 104–109. IEEE (2014)
19. Bettenburg, N., Premraj, R., Zimmermann, T., Kim, S.: Duplicate bug reports considered harmful... really? In: IEEE International Conference on Software Maintenance 2008, ICSM 2008, pp. 337–345. IEEE (2008)
20. Tian, Y., Sun, C., Lo, D.: Improved duplicate bug report identification. In: 2012 16th European Conference on Software Maintenance and Reengineering (CSMR), pp. 385–390. IEEE (2012)
21. D'Ambros, M., Lanza, M., Pinzger, M.: "A bug's life" visualizing a bug database. In: 4th IEEE International Workshop on Visualizing Software for Understanding and Analysis 2007, VISSOFT 2007, pp. 113–120. IEEE (2007)

A Review of Star Schema
and Snowflakes Schema

M. Zafar Iqbal[1], Ghulam Mustafa[1], Nadeem Sarwar[1]([⊠]),
Syed Hamza Wajid[1], Junaid Nasir[1], and Shaista Siddque[2]

[1] Department of Computer Science,
Bahria University Lahore Campus, Lahore, Pakistan
zafarkarmani6@gmail.com, gmustafa.bulc@bahria.edu.pk,
Nadeem_srwr@yahoo.com, hamzawajid3301@gmail.com,
Junaid.jans@gmail.com
[2] Lahore College for Women, Lahore, Pakistan
shaistasiddique21@gail.com

Abstract. In the new age, digital data is the most important source of acquiring knowledge. For this purpose, collect data from various sources like websites, blogs, webpages, and most important databases. Database and relational databases both provide help to decision making in the future work. Nowadays these approaches become time and resource consuming there for new concept use name data warehouse. Which can analyze many databases at a time on a common plate from with very efficient way. In this paper, we will discuss the database and migration from the database to the data warehouse. Data Warehouse (DW) is the special type of a database that stores a large amount of data. DW schemas organize data in two ways in which star schema and snowflakes schema. Fact and dimension tables organize in them. Distinguished by normalization of tables. Nature of data leads the designer to follow the DW schemas on the base of data, time and resources factor. Both design-modeling techniques compare with the experiment on the same data and results of applying the same query on them. After the performance evaluation, using bitmap indexing to improve the schemas performance. We also present the design modeling techniques with respect to data mining and improve query optimization technique to save time and resource in the analysis of data.

Keywords: Data Warehouse · Data mart · Star schema · Snowflakes · Relational database management system RDBMS

1 Introduction

Data Warehouse is one of the emerging and mainly focused technology and nowadays being used almost in every enterprise to increase business performance. DW is a system that fetches data from different sources within an organization, to deduce some reports or analytical information and predict some patterns for further research. To organize data in DW, different schemas can be handy like star schema (SS) and snowflake (SF) schema. Both of the schemas use around the globe in the process [1] of Excerpt, Convert and Load (ETL). ETL is mainly a three-step process in the making of

© Springer Nature Singapore Pte Ltd. 2020
I. S. Bajwa et al. (Eds.): INTAP 2019, CCIS 1198, pp. 129–140, 2020.
https://doi.org/10.1007/978-981-15-5232-8_12

a data warehouse. There are many things which are to be compared between to both of these, star and snowflake schema before there usage. However, their roots are same or they originate from the same base but they have many differences when it comes to their usage, performance, storage limitations, etc. Both these schemas use fact table as the main table which is linked with the dimensions or the dimension tables, that make the arrangement of tables to be called as data marts and data warehouses, on which queries are applied and these schemas then further are also responsible for query performance which can grow really complex [2]. The importance of both these schemas must be review to make sure the performance of DW and to ensure productive and effective results for the enterprise's growth. As there is also not much work available on the specific domain of these schemas importance and considering its use nowadays that is growing exponentially, so this will definitely be a contribution to the knowledge. We had a database to store data files and use this according to our need. However, the access of data from the database has some limitations that restrict the user to access the open way. We use some programming techniques to access this data according to our requirement. In the new age after the Relational model's data can be used for a lot of ways to get the results [3]. For this purpose, we use data warehouses. DWs use to manage big data for our business purposes.

1.1   Database and Relational Database

Collection of data that holds the tables called database [4] database play a vital role in the world to store data with efficient way but in the simple database have some discrepancies that cannot meet in the new age needs therefor introduce RDBMS. In this way data store more efficient way and can access more easy ways. When we use the large database, we want to real-time analysis for this purpose speed, and resources consumption go very high therefor to hold these aspects we use DWs [5].

In Fig. 1 represent the process of transforming the data from a database towards the knowledge discovery process. For this purpose first, collect data from the OLAP system then refine it for the specific purpose and put in the DW. This data cleansing and remove the ambiguity for fit in the DW select the specific data and design data marts of them. Different data marts design for different purpose of analysis for example sales analysis products impact and price effect on the business area. For all analysis design individual data marts [6].

1.2   Data Warehouse

In the database, data store simultaneously time by time and become big to bigger. For the sake of analysis and management, become difficult to handle this data to overcome this problem we felt the need for data warehouses and DataMart. A data warehouse is the collection of many databases that are combined for the analysis purpose via quantitatively or qualitatively. This enables us to get the required test data for further process [3]. DWs like a database that uses the information for reports in a different way to establish new information from previous. DWs is not a full database also can be the specific relevant data that is beneficial for our industry or company [7]. DWs holds the raw data that will not be part of our research.

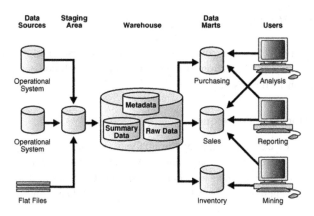

Fig. 1. Data transform to data marts via DWs [2]

1.3 Data Marts

In Data warehouse whole databases, data stored that is memory consuming. We create DWs to combine data from many sources that need to store memory in terabytes. In "Corporate America" data Marts use in the implementation of DWs [8]. Therefore a more abstract form of DWs, we use Data Marts. DMts contain the specific domain data that captured for analysis on a specific topic [9]. For example, we create a DWs that contain the data of laboratory in which store previous 20 years data but we extract only 5 years data for a specific disease prediction or growth rate of disease in last 5 years [5].

1.4 Data Mining

Data mining is the next step of DMts in which we make patterns from data use organized data to analyze using various methods. It is a computational process in which use organized data to get future predictions and some exploring knowledge with a different way. It basically provides a certain kind of intelligence for the company. Set of queries are run the result of which is further considered to obtain help for the decision making [10].

2 Problem Statement

A data warehouse can be managed in many ways but two commonly used types are star schema (SS) and snowflakes schema (SF). The questions are that how can distinguish which schema is best in which DW because in the industry time and resources have much value in the eye of financers. For this purpose, we analyze these schemas with structured efficiency. First, we describe the working of a star schema in which also include an example that helps us for results after this describe SF schema. Comparison of these schemas helps us to lead the best approach for future work.

3   Literature Review

In current literature, we analyze some DW techniques that use to knowledge discovery from selected databases. Collection of data mine in these techniques and fetch out the useful information as the result.

3.1   Design Modeling Techniques

For the selection of exact schema for the analysis, various modeling techniques are used on both the relational database and DWs. The creator ought to have a clear comprehension of the relevance and inability of the techniques. Two main models follow to design schema also in relational database and DWs are Data Model and Process Model [11].

Process Model: Process model when dealing with data warehouse, it cannot be suitable because of the reason that it deals with requirement assumptions which obviously is not suitable for the DW. As it treats more requirement assumptions so it is better to be used for some operational environment and because of this the other model which is data model comes in. Following are the domains where process models are applicable [12–14].

1. Functional breakdown.
2. Environment-level diagram.
3. Data flow diagram.
4. Operational chart.
5. State-run diagram.
6. Hipo chart.
7. Pseudocode [1].

Data Model: Now modeling of data is the one considered compared to the process model for the data warehouse. It basically carries two main techniques which are Entity relational and dimension modeling.

Dimensional Modeling: Dimension modeling focus on the behavior of fact table in any schema because in the fact table whole PKs lies as the foreign key that shows exactly one record for specifying index this behavior also called the star schema. In the expression of element relationship compelled adaptation are utilized for creating dimensional DW. In star schema accentuation is on one table (Fact table) with the basic principle depicting the association, not at all like conventional schema no specific table has a complete thought.

3.2   Evaluation of Schemas

As per after some time the manner in which things being done changes, the thought behind data model structure of related application may encounter intense change. Measurement changes, instant changes, actuality changes, level changes, property changes, limitation changes and quality changes are conceivable emerging changes in the outline plan particularly for DW. The outline advancement challenges are ever-lasting and relevant to each database for all intents and purposes conceivable [15]. Data warehouse center is created iteratively with the goal that key choice, later on, could be conceivable.

3.3   Star Schema

In the ETL process that is follow to design a DW, dimension modeling is used that is done on different models, one of which is star schema. As the name suggests "star", its shape is actually like SS consists of dimensions, which are in dimension tables and a central fact table that carries facts [16, 17]. Fact table carries in it the PKs that lies in dimension tables add with the name of foreign keys, which is the means of connectivity between dimension and fact table. Dimension tables have qualitative data and as dis-cussed above with the FK fact table contains measures that can be summed to analyze or to carry some process [1].

Properties of a Star Schema: Following are a few properties of star schema.

a. Dimensions tables pass the PK add with the name of the FK in fact or base table.
b. Firstly, it contains tables that distinguished with, mainly fact table and dimension tables.
c. Star schema usually not in normalized form except the fact table in the schema.
d. Whenever tables are not normalized it obviously due to redundancy memory will need more, more space will be required.
e. Star schema use all dimensions table's PKs, therefore, fact table look less complex instead of snowflakes.
f. DE normalized means lesser tables and lesser tables mean less complex queries. Queries that are used in star schema to access data are "star join queries".

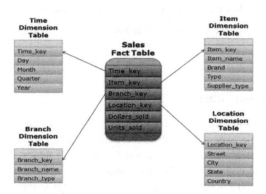

Fig. 2. Star schema represent in pictorial [18].

To explain the results for the query performance of star schema, considering the following Example (Fig. 2).

Table 1. Required specifications for the experiment [19].

Physical memory	Storage disk	Operation system	RDBMS
8 GB	1 TB	Win 2008 server	MS SQL SERVER 2008 R2

Environment under which tests were performed, we required 8 GB RAM and 1 TB hard disk for storage and use Operating system Windows 2008 Server or 2012, SQL server 2008. These hardware specifications are not hardcode for these schemas these are only for the purpose of the experiment.

Table 2. Star schema query [1].

```
SELECT     d1.att2,     d3.att2,     d1.att1,
SUM(f.measure1)

from  Fact1  f  inner  join  dim1  d1  on
d1.dimkey1 = f.dimkey1

GROUP BY d1.att1
```

Star schema used in the example has one fact (main) table and three dimensions (connecting) tables. In Table 2 query used for the SS.

Things which we are going to judge through this query used will be the time taken for execution and memory used by it in the query d1 dimension Table 1 and column att1 and att2 with dimension Table 3 were exist att2 values and accrue these entire columns and sum their values. Results will be obtained just by applying the query to the designed schema. The results obtained are:

Table 3. Star schema query performance [1].

Query	Memory occupied by process	Real time query execution in seconds	DW size
Star join	72%	21 s	0.78 GB

Compensations of Star Schema

a. In a SS, not all tables are normalized but only till first normal form.
b. In Star schema, the execution time of the query is fast when we use large data.
c. Because a star schema database has a small number of tables and clear join paths, Small single-table queries, usually of dimension tables, are almost instantaneous.
d. SS design is easy to follow and especially, with respect to the joined query, which tends with only through the fact table. These joints help to boost the performance of schema.

Only simple queries use because all tables less complex therefore time to run and output result show less time.

3.4   Snowflakes Schema

Like SS, the name of snowflake schema also comes through its resemblance with a snowflake. Like star schema, it is also used in the ETL process and at the same level. There is a choice between using either of them. Unlike star schema, snowflake schema consists of three types of tables, which are, fact table, dimension tables, and sub-dimension tables. Working of the fact table is the same as it carries Foreign keys as of dimension tables as FK and contains its own other values. The fact or base table connected with dimension tables and dimension tables more time connect to normalize dimension tables through keys. Due to sub-dimensions or the splitting of dimensions into the sub-dimensions concept of hierarchy is introduced in snowflake schema [19].

Snowflake apply on a simple database environment also works with different outsider devices and administrations, for example, Informatics, Looker or Tableau notwithstanding, it likewise furnishes the likelihood to collaborate with the framework utilizing only an internet browser [20] (Fig. 3).

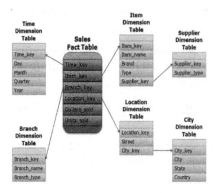

Fig. 3.   Snowflakes schema [21].

Properties of Snowflake Schema

a. It contains three types of tables, fact table, dimension tables, and sub-dimension tables.
b. Sub dimension tables constructed by splitting or normalizing dimension tables, so it can be call snowflake schema is in normalized form.
c. As this schema is, normalize so data is not redundant, repetitions are not present and values are atomic.
d. As the redundancy removed from the tables so lesser memory will be required, means a decrease in storage space required.
e. SF structure more complex because many tables arranged when we normalize database till 3rd normal forms.
f. One problem is there which can be considered, due to increase in a number of tables, querying the data from these tables will be a tough job because linking tables from the sub-dimension of one table to sub-dimension of another table can be complex [22].

Advantages of Snowflakes: Abig online industry uses snowflakes schema due to some important benefits.

Relational: This schema support all transactions of major plate forms like SQL, ANSI, and ACIDS. The big benefit is that u can migrate from one to another platform without a big change.

Semi-structured: The query performance increase with the built-in functions that help for navigating, destruction and organize semi-structure data that use in nested form. Also with the help of JSON and Avro. Fewer operations perform due to the auto discovery of schema and storage operations less perform with respect to efficiency and save the efforts.

Elastic: Usually called the portable schema because of scale and resource independent schema. Port to another schema without damaging the availability and queries concurrent.

Highly Available: Snowflakes schema take less time to recover and rare chances to failure there for tolerance node and cluster less effect the performance. Without down can change the hardware.

Durable: Snowflake can be called durable due to some properties of cross-region backup. Another backup performed this schema with the help of cloning undrop.in this way any damage cannot highly affect the schema.

Cost-Efficient: Snowflake highly cost-efficient because fewer resources required and compressed data stored.

Secure: Whole data that store in the schema is end to end encrypted include all traffic over the network and temp files. Additionally, access control also help the user to protect the data.

Performance: Discussing about star schema and snowflake schema, with bigger fact tables which means containing greater amount of data or the FK in fact tables can reduce the performance of star schema or can be said the lesser the FK in fact table and more the partitioned is the table the faster and more efficient it will work [19]. When using star and snowflake schema in a similar environment it is obvious (considering the example from):

a. It is evident that when dimension tables are bigger it is good to use snowflake schema because it is in normalized form the dimension tables are partition and hence it reduces the size leading to less memory consumption.
b. Query processing time increases when using star schema with large data.

Table 4. Required specifications for the experiment [1].

Physical memory	Storage disk	Operation system	RDBMS
8 Gb	1 TB	Win 2008 server	MS SQL SERVER 2008 R2

The example of SS taken consists of one fact (Main) table with three dimensions (connecting) tables and further having two sub-dimensions. The query used to test the performance of snowflake schema is the following (Tables 4 and 5):

Table 5. Snowflakes schema query [1].

```
SELECT                    fact2.fact2_att1,
fact2.fact2_att2,fact2.fact2_att3,
d11.d11_att1,             fact2.fact2_att3,
fact2.fact2.att3

FROM  d11 LEFT JOIN  d1

ON  d11.d11_att1 = d1.d11_att1  LEFT JOIN
fact2 ON d1.d11_att1 = fact2.fact2_att1

GROUP BY fact2.fact2_att1;
```

Same parameters will be checked for snowflake schema as they were checked for star schema and the results obtained are also from directly querying through schema no optimizations were done, following are the results.

Table 6. Snowflakes schema performance [1].

Query	Memory occupied by process	Real time query execution in seconds	DW size
Snowflake join	49%	17 s	0.61 GB

For obvious reasons, the size of the data warehouse will a bit smaller due to the fact that snowflake schema is in the normalized form so no redundancy is present. The memory occupied by the query is 49%.

3.5   Star vs Snowflakes Schema

The example above for both of the schemas mention or clear the results according to various aspects. These results were accruing from performing an experiment on large data set and it can be said that these figures are accurately applicable dealing with large data sets. Below under the headings, the results compared to clear the reasons for the difference in results obtains.

Query Complexity: It is evident that star and snowflake schema both perform differently due to their nature or properties. When it comes to query complexity, always snowflake schema is more complex for querying. Star schema has lesser number of tables because it is not in normalized form, which makes it easier to gather data from different tables, and in a snowflake, schema tables are normalized resulting in a greater number of tables and making it very much complex to query data. Complex joins are sometimes very difficult to handle and execute because a number of tables sometimes is far greater.

Execution Time: There is also a difference between their execution time. Star schema carries in it also the redundant data so traversing through that causes a bit time delay too, table size is also bigger because tables not split so traversal through the bigger table is a bit expensive. On the other hand snowflake schema is normalized tables are split carrying mostly relative data and no redundancy is there thus making the queries execute faster. Like according to the above example star schema takes 21 s whereas snowflake schema takes 17 s for execution. Therefore, for large data sets, star schema always takes more execution time than snowflake schema.

Effect on the Size of Data Warehouse: Normalization is again a key role in discussing the size of data warehouse size. Star being the one having DE normalized dimensions will always occupy larger space because it will have a lot of redundant data hence requiring for space and memory and snowflake schema being completely normalized will require less space and memory than star schema. As mentioned in the table snowflake used 0.61 GB and star schema used 0.78 GB.

Results: When we apply star schema, execute the query and get results we noted that the results of snowflakes have some difference from star schema. The query applies in Table 6 and Table 3. They show clearly the query execution time and resource consuming for the same data set.

Query Optimization: Star schema's performance figures gathered from the above-carried example are not much prompting to use them in the construction of our data warehouse. The performance of star schema can be improved by adding bitmap indexing. Performance of snowflake can also be enhanced but comparing both snowflakes already have good figures, but the example can be carried for both the schemas [17].

4 Conclusion

In dimension modeling, both star and snowflake schema are major roots that can be considered for the construction of a data warehouse. Everything that we have discussed in detail through the examples it is clear that both of the schemas have their own significant importance. At the time there are two categories like in simple execution snowflake schema is always going to have an upper hand due to the factors discussed above, but if some of the optimizations are, apply to star schema it can also consider efficient, like using or adding bitmap indexes to it. The question above cannot really be considered important because all of the use of snowflake and star schema lies in the fact that you need or your requirements. Because the examples that are discussed above are discussed over some concrete results which specify that whether you consider or give more importance to the size of a data warehouse or you want the maintain the other factors more efficient that is up to you. So in the start snowflake was looking a bit more to consider but it's not true even star schema can be made better with applying optimization techniques.

5 Future Work

In future, some other effective ways can be considered to make these schemas more optimized to be used hence giving a completely new dimension to the data warehouse field, which can be more beneficial for the companies to perform business intelligence.

References

1. Sidi, E., El, M., Amin, E.: Star schema advantages on data warehouse: using bitmap index and partitioned fact tables. Int. J. Comput. Appl. **134**(13), 11–13 (2016)
2. Jan, B., Alharbi, M., Mujeeb-ur-rehman, Khan, F.A., Imran, M., Ahmad, A.: Efficient data access and performance improvement model for virtual data warehouse. Sustain. Cities Soc. **35**, 232–240 (2017)
3. Yusuf, A.: A design comparison: data warehouse schema versus conventional relational database schema. In: CEUR Workshop Proceedings (2016)
4. North, M., Thomas, L., Richardson, R., Akpess, P.: Data warehousing: a practical managerial approach. Comput. Sci. Inf. Technol. **5**, 18–26 (2017)
5. Angelini, M., Catarci, T., Mecella, M., Santucci, G.: The visual side of the data. In: Flesca, S., Greco, S., Masciari, E., Saccà, D. (eds.) A Comprehensive Guide Through the Italian Database Research Over the Last 25 Years. SBD, vol. 31, pp. 3–25. Springer, Cham (2018). https://doi.org/10.1007/978-3-319-61893-7_1
6. Flesca, S., Greco, S., Masciari, E., Saccà, D. (eds.): A Comprehensive Guide Through the Italian Database Research Over the Last 25 Years. SBD, vol. 31. Springer, Cham (2018). https://doi.org/10.1007/978-3-319-61893-7
7. Abdalaziz Ahmedl, R., Mohamed Ahmed, T.: Generating data warehouse schema. Int. J. Found. Comput. Sci. Technol. **4**(1), 1–16 (2014)
8. Sandhu, M.K., Kaur, A., Kaur, R.: Data warehouse schemas. Int. J. Innov. Res. Adv. Eng. (IJIRAE) **2**, 47–51 (2015)
9. Cherniack, M., Lawande, S., Tran, N.: Optimizing snowflake schema queries (2014)
10. Priyadharsini, C., Thanamani, D.A.S.: An overview of knowledge discovery database and data mining techniques. Int. J. Innov. Res. Comput. Commun. Eng. **2**(1), 1571–1578 (2014)
11. Ristoski, P., Paulheim, H.: Feature selection in hierarchical feature spaces. In: Džeroski, S., Panov, P., Kocev, D., Todorovski, L. (eds.) DS 2014. LNCS (LNAI), vol. 8777, pp. 288–300. Springer, Cham (2014). https://doi.org/10.1007/978-3-319-11812-3_25
12. Maimon, O., Rokach, L.: Introduction to Knowledge Discovery and Data Mining, pp. 1–15 (2016)
13. Pavya, K., Srinivasan, D.B.: Feature selection techniques in data mining: a study. Int. J. Sci. Dev. Res. **2**(6), 594–598 (2017)
14. Maimon, O., Rokach, L.: Data Mining and Knowledge Discovery Handbook, pp. 1–15. Springer, Boston (2005). https://doi.org/10.1007/b107408
15. Golfarelli, M., Rizzi, S.: From star schemas to big data: 20+ years of data warehouse research. In: Flesca, S., Greco, S., Masciari, E., Saccà, D. (eds.) A Comprehensive Guide Through the Italian Database Research Over the Last 25 Years. SBD, vol. 31, pp. 93–107. Springer, Cham (2018). https://doi.org/10.1007/978-3-319-61893-7_6
16. Bhide, M.A., Mittapalli, S.K., Padmanabhan, S.: Star and snowflake schemas in extract, transform, load processes (2016)
17. Sidi, E., El, M., Amin, E.: The impact of partitioned fact tables and bitmap index on data warehouse performance. Int. J. Comput. Appl. **135**, 39–41 (2016)

18. Difference Between Star and Snowflake Schema. https://techdifferences.com/difference-between-star-and-snowflake-schema.html
19. Benjelloun, M., El, M., Amin, E.: Impact of using snowflake schema and bitmap index on data warehouse querying. Int. J. Comput. Appl. **180**(15), 33–35 (2018)
20. Dageville, B., et al.: The snowflake elastic data warehouse. In: SIGMOD/PODS 2016, San Francisco, CA, USA, 26 June–01 July 2016 (2016)
21. Difference between snowflakes schema and star schema (2016). https://techdifferences.com/difference-between-star-and-snowflake-schema.html#
22. Cheng, X., Schneider, P.: Star and snowflake join query performance (2017)

A Region-Based and a Unified Team's Strength in the Game of Cricket Using Principal Component Analysis (PCA)

Akbar Hussain and Yan Qiang$^{(\boxtimes)}$

College of Information and Computer, Taiyuan University of Technology,
Taiyuan 030024, Shanxi, China
akbar_hussain555@yahoo.com, qiangyan@tyut.edu.cn

Abstract. In sports, one of the primary measures for assessing the performance of a team is their team's strength. The "team's strength" is the combination of various factors of a team such as batting, bowling and fielding strengths. In cricket, it is significant to measure the strengths of the teams across the region/venue because every region has different playing condition which affects their performance. The selectors should be aware of their team's strength against the opposite team from the visiting region so that the team's management, the coach and the captain select a strong combination from his team. A lot of research has done for player's performance measurement, team's selection, team's ranking, etc. but there is no research done in finding the strength of a team across the region. In this paper, we computed the Region-based Team's Strength (RTS) and a Unified Team's Strength (UTS) based on several parameters of a team using Principal Component Analysis (PCA). In addition, we also used the Weighted Average System (WAS) to compute the region-based team's strength. The intuition is to distinguish a stronger and a weaker team across the region. The results show that the proposed method provides quite promising insights into a region-based and a unified team's strength in cricket sports.

Keywords: Batting · Bowling and fielding strength · Principal Component Analysis · Region strength · Weighted Average System

1 Introduction

Cricket is a bat and ball game played between two teams having 11 players each side. For each phase of play, or an innings, a batting side tries to score as many runs as possible after striking the cricket ball thrown at the wicket with the bat, while a bowling/fielding side tries to prevent and dismiss each player. The batting side gives a target score in the first innings. In the second innings, the first inning's batting side starts bowling and the first inning's bowling side starts batting and they are going towards the target. They will either complete the target in the specific overs or they will lose the match[1].

---

[1] http://www.espncricinfo.com/ci/content/story/239757.html.

© Springer Nature Singapore Pte Ltd. 2020
I. S. Bajwa et al. (Eds.): INTAP 2019, CCIS 1198, pp. 141–161, 2020.
https://doi.org/10.1007/978-981-15-5232-8_13

There are three formats in international cricket; Twenty20, One Day International (ODI) and Test cricket format. T-20 cricket is the latest and fastest international cricket format, in which each team has permitted to play 20 over maximum. ODI cricket is a 50-50 over match, it can be played during the day or day-night and it is faster than test cricket. Test cricket matches can last up to five continues days with each day split into three sessions interrupted by lunch and tea breaks[2]. An 'over' is defined as a set of 6 consecutive balls bowled by a bowler.

In cricket, one of the primary measures for assessing the performance of a team is their teams' strength. The "teams' strength" is the foundation of several parameters of a team such as batting, bowling and fielding strengths. Consistent performance of the players in batting, bowling and fielding department will automatically improve their team's strength. The teams with higher strength are usually considered higher in rank. Ahmed et al. proposed the modified NSGA-II procedure was able to find a set of high-performing teams demonstrating a trade-off between their overall batting and bowling strength. They explained that in cricket team formation, batting and bowling strengths of a team are the two significant factors that affect its performance [2].

In cricket, the region/venue is significant to measure players' and teams' performance because every region has different playing conditions that affect their performance. There are five a region in the world in which cricket is played internationally. These regions are Asia, Africa, the Americas, Europe, and Oceania Region[3]. Region-based ranking classifies the team's strengths and weaknesses across the region/venue which entirely ignored by the ICC.

In this paper, we have considered region-based teams' batting, bowling and fielding strengths of Twenty20, One-day international and Test cricket format to compute the strength of each team across the region using Principal Component Analysis (PCA). We merged the region-based teams' bating, bowling and fielding strengths and then computed the aggregated strengths of all the regions called a Unified Region-based Team Strength (URTS) using several features. Besides, we also computed the region-based team's strength using Weighted Average System (WAS). The intuition is to distinguish a stronger and a weaker team. The results show that the proposed method provides quite promising insights into a region-based and a unified team's strength in cricket sports.

2 Literature Review

Research has identified a limited material set of references regarding region-based and a unified team's strength; however, a comprehensive review revealed the following. The author developed two comprehensive measures, called a combined bowling rate and a dynamic bowling rate to measure the current bowling performance of the bowlers in ODI and test cricket respectively [11, 12]. Irvine and Kennedy identified some key performance indicators that clearly affect the outcome of the T20 cricket match. It was concluded that the number of dot balls, the number of wickets taken and the run rate

---

[2] https://www.icc-cricket.com/about/cricket/game-formats/the-three-formats.

[3] https://www.icc-cricket.com/about/members.

factor completely change the result of a T20 match [8]. Sharma introduced an advanced statistical technique of factor analysis to analyze the performance of the player's capabilities in T20 Cricket [18]. Prakash et al. proposed a new machine learning-based approach named Deep Performance Index (DPI), used to create a new index that reflects the player's performance required for the T20 cricket [15]. Haseeb et al. applied machine learning techniques in cricket sports to predict the rising stars (i.e. batsmen & bowlers) for the future [1]. Authors compared a range of cross-sectional models to study the factors determining the performance of cricketers in different forms of the game including IPL [13]. Lakkaraju and Sethi defined a Saber-metrics style principle to analyze the batting performance in cricket sports [10]. Shah Parag has defined a new measure for the players facing the quality opposition [16]. The author modeled the players' batting and bowling datasets and features to predict an accurate run scored and wickets were taken using classification algorithms [20].

There are many articles found in sports' ranking & prediction but no article found in the region-based team's strength. The author has used Principal Component Analysis (PCA) in cricket sports to reduce high dimensional match datasets into the lower-dimensional dataset in order to improve the predictive performance and to detect frequently occurring play patterns [19]. Manage, Ananda B.W. Scariano, Stephen M. applied the PCA technique for ranking those players who have played Indian Premier League 2012 [14]. Federolf et al. proposed the application of PCA to quantify different techniques in cricket sports [5]. Parag Shah and M.N Patel proposed PCA to rank captains in cricket sports. They ranked captains based on several parameters using PCA. In addition, they also included a weighted average to rank captains based on z-score of performance of a team, individual performance of captain as batsman and bowler [17]. Hussain at el in [6, 7] investigated the team's strength but they ignored some important features for the team's batting, bowling, and fielding parameters.

The purpose of the article is to determine the batting, bowling and fielding strengths of the teams and then finding out the aggregated strengths for all crickets format across the region because every region has different playing condition which affects their performance. Consequently, the teams' management, the coaches and the captains select a strong combination from his team against the opposite team from the visiting region.

This research is perhaps the first generalized approach to apply PCA in the Region-based team's strength in the game of cricket sports and contributes substantially to the application of sophisticated methods in cricketing literature. Daud at el. carried out a similar study by using a region-based player's link fusion algorithm but their work was limited to region-wise players ranking using ODI cricket matches [4]. We used a statistical technique to build a model that can be used to compute the performance of any teams across the region/venue.

3   Materials and Method

3.1   Region-Based Team's Strength

In cricket, the team's strength is the foundation of batting, bowling and fielding strengths. The players showing consistent performance in each department of batting, bowling and fielding will improve their team strength. Deeper analysis and statistics are required to find out the batting, bowling and fielding strength of a team across the region.

In the proposed method we created three datasets from the online website[4] using scraping tools (i.e. parsehub and import.in) then created different features for each of the datasets of batting, bowling and fielding respectively. We applied Principal Component Analysis (PCA), a machine-learning algorithm to reduce the dimensions of the features and find out the strengths and weaknesses of each parameter across the region. In conclusion, we merged the strengths of all the regions and find out the aggregated score of each team we call a Unified Team's Strengths. The parameters are ascertained as follows (Fig. 1).

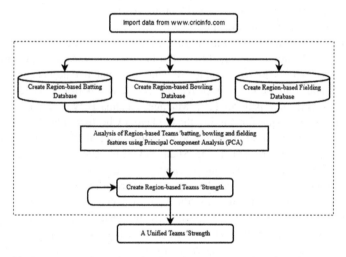

Fig. 1. Graphical representation of region-based team strength using Principal Component Analysis (PCA)

Region-Based Team's Batting Features

Batsmen always perform against the opponent team's bowling and fielding strengths. The following are the most important features for a team that is highly affected by their batting strength. The mathematical notions of each feature are presented as follows.

i. *Region-based Teams Average Runs Scored (RTAR)*

RTAR is defined as the total number of runs scored by team t in region r divided by the number of innings played. Mathematically $\sum_{t,r=1}^{n} RTAR$ can be defined as:

$$\sum_{t,r=1}^{n} RTAR = \frac{Region - basedtotalrunsscored}{Region - basedcompledtedinnings} \tag{1}$$

---

[4] https://www.espncricinfo.com.

ii. *Region-based Teams Strike Rate (RTSR)*

RTSR of a team t in region r is defined as the total number of runs scored per k balls, where k is taken to be 100.

$$\sum\nolimits_{t,r=1}^{n} RTSR = \frac{Region - basedtotalrunsscored}{Region - basedtotalnumberofballsfaced} * 100 \qquad (2)$$

iii. *Region-based Batsmen Average Runs Scored (RBAR)*

RBAR of a team t in region r is defined as the total number of runs scored divided by total number of wicket lost.

$$\sum\nolimits_{t,r=1}^{n} RBAR = \frac{Region - basedtotalrunsscored}{Region - basedtotalwicketlost} \qquad (3)$$

iv. *Region-based Batsmen Economy Rate (RBER)*

RBER of a team t in region r is defined as the total number of runs per k balls, where k is usually taken to be 6.

$$\sum\nolimits_{t,r=1}^{n} RBER = \frac{Region - basedtotalrunsscored}{Region - basedtotalnumberofballsfaced} * 6 \qquad (4)$$

v. *Region-based Boundaries Scored Per Innings (RTBPI)*

Region-based Boundaries Scored per Innings (RTBPI) of a team t in region r is defined as:

$$\sum\nolimits_{t,r=1}^{n} RTBPI = \frac{Region - basedtotalboundaries(4s + 6s)scored}{Region - basedtotalnumberofinningsplayed} \qquad (5)$$

vi. *Region-based Batting Milestone Reaching Ability (RBMRA)*

RBMRA of a team t in region r is defined as the total number of (100s and 50s) scored by the batsmen per inning.

$$\sum\nolimits_{t,r=1}^{n} RBMRA = \frac{Region - based(100s + 50s)scored}{Region - basedinningsplayed} \qquad (6)$$

The collection of the above features can be used to study the region-based team's batting strength through PCA. Some of the features have a strong correlation with each other. Making it difficult to construct an overall batting strength, this is our goal.

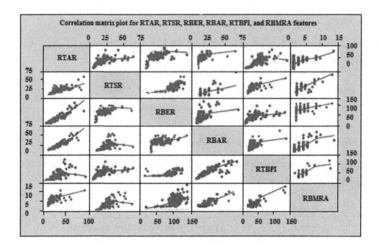

Fig. 2. Correlation between region-based teams batting features

Figure 2 shows a matrix plot between region-based batting features where we can see some significant correlations between the variables. The higher the values of the features indicate a better team's batting strength and each feature measures a different quality of a batsman. But, the primary concern is their joint contribution to batting strength in a multivariate sense. Constructing an overall measure of batting strength by collapsing these correlated variables is a key goal.

Region-Based Teams' Bowling Features

Bowlers always perform against the opponent team's batting line-up. The total number of wickets taken, balls bowled, extra runs, average runs, strike rate and economy rate conceded by a bowler against the opponent team will affect the team's bowling strength. Some of the features are very important for a team which is highly affected by their bowling strength. The mathematical notions of each feature are presented as follows.

i. *Region-based Teams' Extra Runs Conceded Per Innings (RTERCPI)*

RTERCPI of a team t in region r is defined as the total number of extra runs conceded divided by the innings played.

$$\sum_{t,r=1}^{n} RTERCPI = \frac{Region - basedtotalextrarunsconceded}{Region - basedtotalinningsplayed} \quad (7)$$

ii. *Region-based Team's Average Runs Conceded (RTARC)*

RTARC of a team t in region r is defined as the total number of runs conceded divided by total innings played.

$$\sum_{t,r=1}^{n} RTARC = \frac{Region - basedtotalrunsconceded}{Region - basedinningsplayed} \quad (8)$$

iii. *Region-based Team's bowling Average Conceded (RbARC)*

RbARC of a team t in region r is defined as the total number of runs conceded divided by total wickets taken.

$$\sum_{t,r=1}^{n} RbARC = \frac{Region - basedtotalrunsconceded}{Region - basedtotalwicketstaken} \quad (9)$$

iv. *Region-based Team's bowling Economy Rate Conceded (RTbERC)*

RTbERC of a team t in region r is defined as the total number of runs per k balls conceded where k is taken to be 6.

$$\sum_{t,r=1}^{n} RTbERC = \frac{Region - basedtotalrunsconceded}{Region - basedballsbowled} * 6 \quad (10)$$

v. *Region-based Team's bowling Strike Rate Conceded (RbTSRC)*

RbTSRC of a team t in region r is defined as the total number of balls bowled per wicket taken.

$$\sum_{t,r=1}^{n} RbTSRC = \frac{Region - basedtotalballsbowled}{Region - basedtotalwicketstaken} \quad (11)$$

vi. *Region-based bowlers Milestone Reaching Ability (RbMRA)*

RbMRA of a team t in region r is defined as the total number of (4s and 5s) wickets taken by the bowlers per inning.

$$\sum_{t,r=1}^{n} RbMRA = \frac{Region - based(4s + 5s)wicketstaken}{Region - basedinningsplayed} \quad (12)$$

Similarly, for the region-based team's bowling strength we also used the collection of the six features to study the region-based team's bowling strength via Principal Components Analysis (PCA).

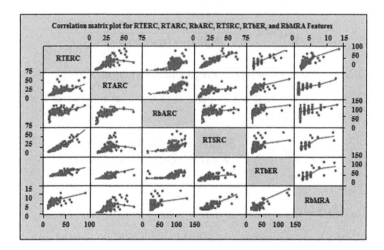

Fig. 3. Correlation between region-based team's bowling features

Figure 3 shows a matrix plot between bowling features where we can see some significant correlations between the features. The higher the values of the variables indicate better bowling strength of a team and each feature measures a different quality of a bowler. But, the primary concern is their joint contribution to bowling strength in a multivariate sense. Constructing an overall measure of bowling strength by collapsing these correlated variables is a key goal of the article.

Region-Based Team's Fielding Features
In the game of cricket, the fielding strength is a significant measure for team strength. In fielding, saving more runs increased the winning probability. The number of Region-based Fielders Catches (RFC), Region-based Wicket-Keeper Catches (RWKC), Region-based Run-out (RRO) and Region-based Wicket-Keeper Stumps (RWKS) are the most important parameters to measure the teams' fielding strengths and weaknesses. The collection of these features study the region-based team's fielding strength via PCA. All of the features are highly correlated with each other.

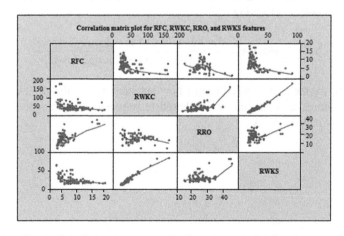

Fig. 4. Correlation between region-based team's fielding features

Figure 4 shows a matrix plot between the region-based team's fielding strength. There is a strong correlation between these features. The higher the values between the features show better fielding strength of a team and each feature measures a different quality of a fielding strength. Constructing an overall measure of fielding strength by collapsing these correlated variables is a key goal of the article.

3.2   Principal Component Analysis (PCA) and a Region-Based Team's Strength

Principal Component Analysis (PCA) is a nonparametric variable reduction technique well-suited for correlated data that can be effectively used in the proposed method. The objective of PCA is to collapse a set of correlated variables into fewer uncorrelated variables as linear combinations of the original variables [9]. PCA is a multivariate method utilized when data on a number of useful variables has been gathered, and it is plausible that there is some redundancy in those variables. Here, redundancy is taken to mean that our region-based teams batting, bowling and fielding features are correlated with one another because, in some unknown sense, they might be measuring similar team-performance attributes. PCA aims to reduce the observed variables down to a smaller number of principal components, which account for most of the variation occurring in the originally observed variables.

If the first few PC capture a large percentage of the total variance, then it is plausible that these new variables can be used in place of the original variables without much loss of information. Customarily, features measured on different scales should first be standardized [4]. If standardization is not performed, the resulting PCs will be dominated by the features with maximum variance, which does not meet the goal of an overall performance measure.

Region-Based Team's Batting Strength Using PCA

For region-based team's batting strength the analysis includes RTAR, RTSR, RBER, RBAR, RTBPI and RBMRA variables for the team who have played at least eight international matches across the region. Values for each of these features were collected together in the form of (RTAR, RTSR, RBER, RBAR, RTBPI, RBMRA)^t for each team's batting strength. These we call the region-based team's batting-features. Once data have been obtained, the (n x n) sample correlation matrix associated with the sample batting vectors may be examined for the correlation structure inherent in these features. They must be standardized before PCA analysis. However, the process of finding the Principal Components (PCs) by using the standardized variables is equivalent to finding PCs by using the correlation matrix instead of the covariance matrix.

Table 1. Correlation matrix of the team's batting strength

	RTAR	RTSR	RBAR	RBER	RTBPI	RBMRA
RTAR	1	0.96	0.95	0.96	0.70	0.96
RTSR	0.96	1	0.94	1	0.69	0.94
RBAR	0.95	0.94	1	0.94	0.58	0.96
RBER	0.96	1	0.94	1	0.69	0.94
RTBPI	0.70	0.69	0.58	0.69	1	0.70
RBMRA	0.96	0.94	0.96	0.94	0.70	1

Table 1 shows the correlation matrix of the team's batting strength for all teams played at least eight matches. Table 2 gives the ordered eigenvalues &percentage of total variability attributed to batting strength, while Table 3 shows the eigenvector coefficients for the team's batting strength for all six principal components. The eigenvalue-eigenvector pair for the first principal component (PC1) is highlighted in Table 3 for the team's batting strength.

Table 2. Eigenvalues & corresponding percentages of the total variability of team's batting strength

Eigenvalues for the teams' batting strength	9.70	5.34	5.13	4.98	3.74	2.51
Total variability	30.89%	17%	16%	15.85%	11.91%	7.99%

Table 3. Component score coefficient matrix for the team's bating strength

Eigenvalues	9.70	5.34	5.13	4.98	3.74	2.51
Variables	PC1	PC2	PC3	PC4	PC5	PC6
RTAR	0.42	0.09	−0.11	−0.89	−0.02	0.01
RTSR	0.43	0.10	0.53	0.14	0.08	−0.70
RBAR	0.41	0.33	−0.36	0.31	0.10	−0.35
RBER	0.43	0.11	0.53	0.15	0.08	0.71
RBPI	0.32	−0.92	−0.08	0.08	−1.17	−0.02
RBMAR	0.42	0.09	−0.54	0.24	0.68	0.03

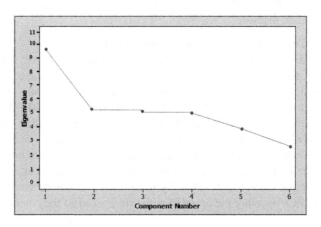

Fig. 5. Screen plot for the teams' batting strength

All the features in Table 2 are standardized. The first entry in Table 3 shows that 31% of the total variability should be explained by the PC1. If the ordered eigenvalues are plotted sequentially then the resulting plot is called a screen plot, which is used to ascertain the appropriate number of PCs to retain a particular application. Figure 5 shows the screen plot for the team's batting strength.

Region-Based Team's Bowling Strength Using PCA

For region-based team's bowling strength the analysis includes RTERC, RbARC, RTbERC and RbMRA variables for a team that has played at least eight matches across the region. Values for each of these features were collected together in the form of (RTERC, RTARC, RbARC, RTSRC, RTbER, RbMRA)^t for each team's bowling strength. These we call the region-based team's bowling-vectors. They must be standardized before PCA analysis.

Table 4. Correlation matrix of the teams' bowling strength

	RTERC	RTARC	RbARC	RTbERC	RbSRC	RbMRA
RTERC	1	−0.18	0.11	−0.28	0.22	−0.15
RTARC	−0.17	1	0.22	0.69	0.05	0.14
RbARC	0.11	0.22	1	0.77	0.98	−0.81
RTbERC	−0.27	0.69	0.77	1	0.62	−0.47
RbSRC	0.22	0.05	0.98	0.62	1	−0.84
RbMRA	−0.15	0.14	−0.81	−0.47	−0.84	1

Table 4 shows the sample correlation matrix of teams' bowling strength. Table 5 gives the ordered eigenvalues & percentage of total variability attributed to bowling strength, while Table 6 shows the eigenvector coefficients for the team's bowling strength for all six principal components (PC1–PC6). The eigenvalue-eigenvector pair for the first principal component is highlighted in Table 6 for the teams' bowling strength.

Table 5. Eigenvalues & corresponding percentages of the total variability of teams bowling strength

Eigenvalues for the teams' bowling strength	3.34	1.63	0.83	0.16	0.038	−0.0039
Total Variability	55.72%	27.19%	13.84%	2.67%	0.63%	−0.065%

Table 6. Component score coefficient matrix for teams' bowling strength

Eigenvalues	3.34	1.63	0.83	0.16	0.038	−0.0039
Variables	PC1	PC2	PC3	PC4	PC5	PC6
RERC	0.04	−0.51	0.82	−0.08	−0.23	−0.04
RTARC	0.17	0.64	0.51	−0.25	0.45	0.10
RbARC	0.54	−0.06	−0.01	0.35	0.02	0.76
RbERC	0.45	0.43	0.03	−0.02	−0.74	−0.35
RbSRC	0.52	−0.21	−0.02	0.44	0.37	−0.54
RbMR	−0.56	0.30	0.25	0.78	−0.13	−0.02

All the features in Table 5 are standardized. The first entry in Table 6 shows that almost 56% of the total variability should be explained by the PC1, while Fig. 6 shows the screen plot for the team's bowling strength.

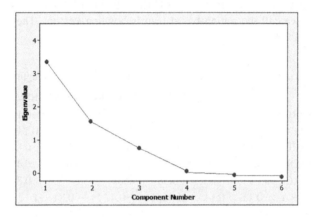

Fig. 6. Screen plot for the team's bowling strength

Region-Based Team's Fielding Strengths Using PCA

Similarly, for the region-based teams' fielding strength the analysis includes the number of region-based fielders catches (RFC), wicket-keeper catches (RWKC), Region-based Run-out (RRO) and Region-based Wicket-Keeper Stumps (RWKS) features. Values for each of these features were collected together into a $(4 \times 1)^t$ column vector of the form (RFC, RWKC, RRO, RWKS)^t for each team's fielding strength. These we call the region-based team's fielding-vectors. All the features must be standardized before PCA analysis. However, the process of finding the principal components (PCs) by using the standardized variables is equivalent to finding PCs by using the correlation matrix instead of the covariance matrix.

Table 7. Correlation matrix of the teams' fielding strength

	RFC	RWKC	RRO	RWKS
RFC	1	0.96	0.97	0.98
RWKC	0.96	1	0.94	0.94
RRO	0.97	0.94	1	0.97
RWKS	0.98	0.94	0.97	1

Table 7 shows the sample correlation matrix of the teams' fielding strength. Table 8 gives the ordered eigenvalues and percentage of total variability attributed to fielding strength, while Table 9 shows the eigenvector coefficients for the team's fielding strength for all four principal components (PC1–PC4). The eigenvalue-eigenvector pair for the PC1 is highlighted in Table 9 for the team's fielding strength.

Table 8. Eigenvalues & corresponding percentages of the total variability of teams' fielding strength

Eigenvalues for teams fielding	3.88	0.075	0.034	0.011
Total variability	97.12%	1.75%	0.85%	0.28%

Table 9. Component score coefficient matrix for the teams' fielding strength

Eigenvalues	3.88	0.075	0.034	0.011
Variables	PC1	PC2	PC3	PC4
RFC	0.50	0.81	0.28	0.07
RWC	0.49	−0.21	−0.09	−0.84
RRO	0.49	−0.08	−0.77	0.39
RWS	0.50	−0.54	0.57	0.37

All the features in Table 8 are standardized. The first entry in Table 9 shows that 97% of the total variability should be explained by the PC1. If the ordered eigenvalues are plotted sequentially then the resulting plot is called a screen plot, which is used to ascertain the appropriate number of PCs to retain a particular application. Figure 7 shows the screen plot for the team's fielding strength.

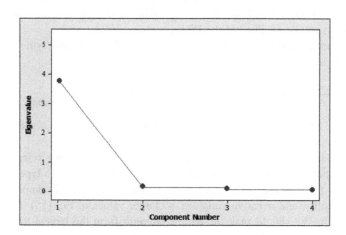

Fig. 7. Screen plot for the teams' fielding strength

Consequently, aggregating the region-based team's batting, bowling and fielding variables for the First Principal Component (PC1)for Region-based twenty20 cricket, the teams' strength is calculated as;

$$\sum_{t,r=i}^{n} \mathbf{RT}_{\text{Strength}} = RTAR * 0.42 + RTSR * 0.43 + RBAR * 0.41$$
$$+ RBER * 0.43 + RBPI * 0.32 + RBMAR * 0.42 + RERC * 0.04$$
$$+ RTARC * 0.17 + RbARC * 0.54 + RbERC * 0.45 + RbSRC * 0.52$$
$$- RbMR * 0.56 + RFC * 0.50 + RWC * 0.49 + RRO * 0.49 + RWS * 0.50$$

$$(13)$$

We refer to the PC1 as the general region-based teams' strength for twenty20 cricket, which is a type of weighted average of all features used. The coefficients of the PC1 are the mixture of positive and negative variables, so larger values of Eq. (13) indicate a better team's strength. This justifies that we should rank the team's strength from the largest to the smallest values of the PC1.

Similarly, the first principal component (PC1) for region-based team's strength for One-day cricket teams is;

$$\sum_{t,r=i}^{n} \mathbf{RT}_{\text{Strength}} = RTAR * 0.23 + RTSR * 0.26 + RBAR * 0.12 + RBER * 0.51$$
$$+ RBPI * 0.48 + RBMAR * 0.11 + RERC * 0.04 + RTARC * 0.19$$
$$+ RbARC * 0.23 + RbERC * 0.55 - RbSRC * 0.52$$
$$- RbMR * 0.56 + RFC * 0.40 + RWC * 0.49 + RRO * 0.21 + RWS * 0.19$$

$$(14)$$

We refer to the first principal component as the general region-based strength for One-day cricket teams, which is a type of weighted average of all features used. The coefficients of the PC1 are the mixture of positive and negative variables, so larger values of Eq. (14) indicate a better team's strength. We should rank the team's strength from largest to smallest values of the PC1.

Finally, the first principal component for Region-based Teams' strength for Test cricket teams is;

$$\sum_{t,r=i}^{n} \mathbf{RT}_{\text{Strength}} = RTAR * 0.11 + RTSR * 0.13 + RBAR * 0.20$$
$$+ RBER * 0.43 + RBPI * 0.61 + RBMAR * 0.33 + RERC * 0.44 - RTARC * 0.19$$
$$+ RbARC * 0.22 + RbERC * 0.52 - RbSRC * 0.33$$
$$+ RbMR * 0.56 + RFC * 0.31 + RWC * 0.42 + RRO * 0.12 + RWS * 0.11 \quad (15)$$

Similarly, for region-based and unified test cricket teams we refer to the first principal component as the general region-based strength, which is a type of weighted average of all features used. The coefficients of the first principal component are the mixture of positive and negative variables, so larger values of Eq. (15) indicate better teams' strength. We should rank the team's strength from the largest to the smallest values of the PC1.

3.3 Region-Based Team's Batting, Bowling and Fielding Strengths Using Weighted Average System (WAS)

In the weighted average system (WAS), we used six features to each team's batting and bowling strengths and four features to the team's fielding strength. In this method, we have assigned 33.33% weightage to each team's batting, bowling and fielding strengths. Whereas the value of $\alpha + \beta + \gamma = 1$

$$RT_{WeightedAverageSystem}{}_{t}^{r} = \frac{\left(RT_{Batting\_Strength}{}_{t}^{r} * \alpha\right) + \left(RT_{Batting\_Strength}{}_{t}^{r} * \beta\right) + \left(RT_{Batting\_Strength}{}_{t}^{r} * \gamma\right)}{100}$$

$$(16)$$

For region-based team's batting strength, we have assigned 10% weightage to each RTAR, RTSR, RBAR and RTBPI features while 30% to each RBER and RBMRA features, Whereas the value of $\alpha + \beta + \gamma + \delta + \lambda + \varepsilon = 1$

$$RT_{Batting\_Strength}{}_{t}^{r} = \sum_{t,r=i}^{n} \frac{(RTAR * \alpha) + (RTSR * \beta) + (RBAR * \gamma) + (RTBPI * \delta) + (RBER * \lambda) + (RBMRA * \varepsilon)}{100} \quad (17)$$

Similarly, for the region-based team's bowling strength, we have assigned 10% to RTERC, *RTARC*, RbARC and *RbSRC* features while 30% to each RTbERC and RbMRA features. The aggregated value of the region-based team's strength is inverted because conceding a lower number of average runs, economy rate, and strike rate, etc. for a bowler means better performance.

$$RT_{Bowling\_Strength}{}_{t}^{r} = \sum_{t,r=i}^{n} \frac{(RTERC * \alpha) + (RTARC * \beta) + (RbARC * \gamma) + (RbSRC * \delta) + (RTbERC * \lambda) + (RbMRA * \varepsilon)}{100}$$

$$(18)$$

Finally, for region-based team's fielding strength, we have assigned 25% to each RFC, RWKC, RRO and RWKS features.

$$RT_{Fielding\_Strength}{}_{t}^{r} = \sum_{t,r=i}^{n} \frac{(RFC * \alpha) + (RWKC * \beta) + (RRO * \gamma) + (RWKS * \delta)}{100}$$

$$(19)$$

3.4   A Unified Team's Strength

A Unified team's strength $\left(\bigcup_{r=1}^{n} Teams\_Strength\right)$ of team t can be computed as follows:

$$\bigcup_{r=1}^{n} Teams\_Strength = \frac{\sum_{t,r=1}^{n} UTS}{n} \quad (20)$$

Where, "$\sum_{t,r=1}^{n} UTS$" is the unified team's strength of team t in region r and n is the total number of regions.

4 Results and Discussion

This section explains the detailed dataset and performance evaluation. It also provides comparisons of the region-based team's strength, a unified team's strength and a weighted average system (WAS) of the team's strength.

4.1 Datasets and Performance Evaluation

The dataset is taken from the ESPNcricinfo[5] website using scrapping tools (parsehub and import.in) from all T-20, ODI and test cricket matches played so far. We considered only those teams which have played at least eight International matches across the region.

The proposed method determined the strengths and weaknesses for each team across the region. If a team visits to play a match against the opponent team having regional team strength, the team's management, the coach and the captain should be aware of their teams' strength against the opposite team from the visiting region so that they can select a strong combination from his team. There is no statistical test to say which team has better strength however, we used nonparametric correlations (Spearman rho) to assess the validity and reliability of the proposed methods as shown in Table 10, Table 11, and, Table 12 respectively for T20, ODI and Test cricket teams which had a strong correlation with our proposed methods. We combined the region-based team strengths of all the regions of RTS and WAS methods respectively and computed the Unified Team Strength (UTS) and the Unified Weighted Average System (UWAS) for T20, ODI, and Test cricket respectively as shown in Table 13, Table 14,

Table 10. Correlation of the ICC Twenty20[a] current ranking with the UTS & UWAS and UTS with the UWAS team's strength using Spearman's rho

Teams	ICC Rank	UTS	UWAS	Correlation between ICC and UTS	Correlation between ICC and UWAS	Correlation between UTS and UWAS
Pakistan	1	1	1	0.813828	0.697102	0.933257
England	2	7	8			
South Africa	3	2	3			
India	4	3	4			
Australia	5	4	5			
New Zealand	6	6	6			
Afghanistan	7	7	7			
Sri Lanka	8	5	2			
West Indies	9	8	9			
Bangladesh	10	9	10			
Zimbabwe	14	10	11			

[a]http://www.espncricinfo.com/rankings/content/page/211271.html

---

[5] www.espncricinfo.com.

Table 11. Correlation of the ICC ODI current ranking[a] with the UTS & UWAS and UTS with the UWAS team's strength using Spearman's rho

Teams	ICC Rank	UTS	UWAS	Correlation between ICC and UTS	Correlation between ICC and UWAS	Correlation between UTS and UWAS
England	1	3	7	0.825175	0.405594	0.804196
India	2	4	4			
New Zealand	3	5	9			
Australia	4	1	1			
South Africa	5	2	2			
Pakistan	6	6	5			
Bangladesh	7	10	11			
Sri Lanka	8	9	8			
West Indies	9	8	6			
Afghanistan	10	7	3			
Ireland	11	11	10			
Zimbabwe	12	12	12			

[a]http://www.espncricinfo.com/rankings/content/page/211271.html

Table 12. Correlation of the ICC Test current ranking[a] with the UTS & UWAS and UTS with the UWAS team's strength using Spearman's rho

Teams	ICC Rank	UTS	UWAS	Correlation between ICC and UTS	Correlation between ICC and UWAS	Correlation between UTS and UWAS
India	1	4	6	0.584127	0.435232	0.963636
New Zealand	2	8	8			
South Africa	3	2	2			
England	4	3	3			
Australia	5	1	1			
Sri Lanka	6	7	7			
Pakistan	7	5	4			
West Indies	8	6	5			
Bangladesh	9	9	9			
Zimbabwe	11	10	10			

[a]http://www.espncricinfo.com/rankings/content/page/211271.html

and Table 15. The results and discussions prove that our proposed methods are highly correlated and very useful in terms of computing the strengths and weaknesses of cricket teams across the region. The ICC only presents a general ranking based on the most recent performance of the teams. However, a T20, ODI and Test rating systems from the ICC is used as a baseline for comparing our region-based and unified team's strength.

In Table 13, we compare the Region-based Unified Team Strength (UTS) and the Unified Weighted Average System (UWAS) methods of Twenty20 international cricket teams. Pakistan, South Africa, and India are the top-3 teams in the UTS method, while in the UWAS method Pakistan, Sri Lanka, and South Africa are the top-3 teams.

Table 13. A Region-based, a Unified and a Weighted Team Strength for T20 crickets teams

Teams	Asia	Africa	America	Europe	Oceania	UTS	UWAS
PAK	286	273	256	249	281	269	0.7811
IND	312	265	224	221	286	262	0.5827
SRI	217	232	259	251	301	252	0.7141
BAN	186	221	222	219	NA	212	0.2285
AUS	243	241	265	214	327	258	0.5266
ENG	273	219	239	235	275	248	0.3810
NZ	252	243	234	213	313	251	0.4047
SA	293	249	238	247	292	264	0.6230
WI	231	225	235	234	265	238	0.3125
ZIM	193	186	209	256	NA	211	0.1300
AFG	317	NA	201	197	NA	238	0.3957

Table 14 shows the comparison of the RTS, UTS and a UWAS method of ODI cricket teams. Australian cricket team has excellent team strength in batting and bowling, while English and South African teams are better in bowling and fielding but a little poor in batting. Therefore, they are 2nd and 3rd in UTS. In the UWAS method Australia, South Africa, and Afghanistan cricket teams are first, 2nd and 3rd respectively. Afghanistan cricket team is a new team and has not played in most of the regions but recently, it has shown excellent team's strength because of better batting and bowling strength in the Asian region.

Table 14. A Region-based, a Unified and a Weighted Team Strength for ODI crickets teams

Teams	Asia	Africa	America	Europe	Oceania	UTS	UWAS
PAK	123	111	114	81	93	104	0.3263
IND	126	116	108	93	95	108	0.3342
SRI	116	91	116	77	78	96	0.2879
BAN	111	77	106	71	66	86	0.1525
AUS	125	119	119	112	113	118	0.5503
ENG	120	109	103	117	99	110	0.3165
NZ	110	106	99	109	107	106	0.2757
SA	119	123	117	89	109	111	0.5319
WI	115	87	111	94	105	102	0.3260
ZIM	109	81	85	66	71	82	0.0986
AFG	115	101	NA	94	NA	103	0.4027
IRE	113	89	87	84	NA	93	0.1954

Table 15 shows the comparison of the RTS, UTS and a UWAS method of test cricket teams. Australian cricket team has excellent team strength in batting, bowling, and fielding, while South Africa and English cricket teams are better in bowling and fielding but a little poor in batting. Therefore they are 2nd and 3rd in UTS and UWAS.

Table 15. A Region-based, a Unified and a Weighted Team Strength for Test crickets teams

Teams	Asia	Africa	America	Europe	Oceania	UTS	UWAS
PAK	156	140	137	133	123	137	0.2364
IND	154	139	136	141	121	138	0.1794
SRI	152	143	132	132	113	134	0.1652
BAN	131	116	108	108	108	114	0.0338
AUS	143	151	146	146	143	146	0.4599
ENG	141	146	135	149	136	141	0.3219
NZ	135	144	133	111	138	132	0.1381
SA	149	149	147	137	139	144	0.3969
WI	140	131	143	143	126	136	0.2156
ZIM	121	125	101	101	NA	112	0.0212

5   Conclusions

Measuring the team's strength in cricket sports is an exciting task. To sum up our work, we studied the strengths and weaknesses of Twenty20, One Day and Test cricket teams across the region. We investigated the region-based team's batting, bowling and fielding strengths across the regions by scrutinizing some new features. We proposed two methods the Region-based Team's Strength (RTS) and a Unified Team's Strength (UTS) based on several parameters of a team using PCA. Besides, we also used the Weighted Average System (WAS) to compute the region-based & a unified team's strength. This paper is the first attempt to create a region-based strength for cricket teams globally. Similar studies can also be utilized to find the region-based team's strength in other sports as well.

Acknowledgement. This work was supported by the National Natural Science Foundation of China (61872261).

Disclosure Statement. The authors have not been reported any potential conflict of interest.

References

1. Ahmad, H., Daud, A., Wang, L., Hong, H., Dawood, H., Yang, Y.: Prediction of rising stars in the game of cricket. IEEE Access **5**, 4104–4124 (2017). https://doi.org/10.1109/ACCESS. 2017.2682162

2. Ahmed, F., Jindal, A., Deb, K.: Cricket team selection using evolutionary multi-objective optimization. In: Panigrahi, B.K., Suganthan, P.N., Das, S., Satapathy, S.C. (eds.) SEMCCO 2011. LNCS, vol. 7077, pp. 71–78. Springer, Heidelberg (2011). https://doi.org/10.1007/978-3-642-27242-4_9

3. Daud, A., Hussain, A., Abbasi, R.A., Aljohani, N.R., Amjad, T., Dawood, H.: Region-wise ranking of sports players based on link fusion. In: Companion of the Web Conference (2018). https://doi.org/10.1145/3184558.3186335

4. Desarbo, W.S., Hausman, R.E., Kukitz, J.M.: Restricted principal components analysis for marketing research. J. Model. Manag. 2(3), 305–328 (2007). https://doi.org/10.1108/17465660710834471

5. Federolf, P., Reid, R., Gilgien, M., Haugen, P., Smith, G.: The application of principal component analysis to quantify technique in sports. Scand. J. Med. Sci. Sports 24(3), 9 (2014). https://doi.org/10.1111/j.1600-0838.2012.01455.x

6. Hussain, A., Qiang, Y., Bilal, A.Q.M., Wu, K., Zhao, Z., Ahmed, B.: Region-wise ranking for one-day international (ODI) cricket teams. Int. J. Adv. Comput. Scie. Appl. (IJACSA) 10(10), 39–46 (2019). https://doi.org/10.14569/IJACSA.2019.0101007

7. Hussain, A., Qiang, Y., Bilal, A.Q.M., Ullah, U., Ullah, N.: Region-based teams ranking in the game of cricket using PageRank algorithm. Int. J. Comput. Appl. 177(16), 10–15 (2019). https://doi.org/10.5120/ijca2019919458

8. Irvine, S., Kennedy, R.: Analysis of performance indicators that most significantly affect International Twenty20 cricket. Int. J. Perform. Anal. Sports 17(3), 350–359 (2017). https://doi.org/10.1080/24748668.2017.1343989

9. Johnson, R.A., Wichern, D.W.: Applied Multivariate Statistical Analysis, 6th edn. Prentice Hall, Upper Saddle River (2007)

10. Lakkaraju, P., Sethi, S.: Correlating the analysis of opinionated texts using SAS® text analytics with application of sabermetrics to cricket statistics. In: Proceedings of SAS Global Forum 2012, 136-2012, pp. 1–10 (2012)

11. Lemmer, H.: The combined bowling rate as a measure of bowling performance in cricket. S. Afr. J. Res. Sport Phys. Educ. Recreat. 24(2), 37–44 (2002). https://doi.org/10.4314/sajrs.v24i2.25839

12. Lemmer, H.: A method for the comparison of the bowling performances of bowlers in a match or series of matches. S. Afr. J. Res. Sport Phys. Educ. Recreat. 27(1), 91–103 (2005). https://doi.org/10.4314/sajrs.v27i1.25909

13. Lenten, L.J.A., Geerling, W., Kónya, L.: A hedonic model of player wage determination from the indian premier league auction: further evidence. Sport Manag. Rev. 15(1), 60–71 (2012). https://doi.org/10.1016/j.smr.2011.01.002

14. Manage Ananda, B.W., Scariano, S.M.: An introductory application of principal components to cricket data. J. Stat. Educ. 21(3), 1–22 (2013). https://doi.org/10.1080/10691898.2013.11889689

15. Prakash, C.D., Patvardhan, C., Singh, S.: A new machine learning based deep performance index for ranking IPL t20 cricketers. Int. J. Comput. Appl. 137(10), 42–49 (2016)

16. Parag, S.: New performance measure in cricket. IOSR J. Sports Phys. Educ. 4(3), 28–30 (2017). https://doi.org/10.9790/6737-04032830

17. Shah, P., Patel, M.N.: Ranking the cricket captains using principal component analysis. Int. J. Physiol. Nutr. Phys. Educ. 3(2), 477–483 (2018). https://doi.org/10.13140/RG.2.2.33455.38564

18. Sharma, S.K.: A factor analysis approach in performance analysis of t-20 cricket. Math. Sci. Res. J. 6(1), 69–76 (2013)

19. Umamaheswari, P., Rajaram, M.: Principal component analysis-based frequent pattern evaluation on the object-relational data model of a cricket match database. Int. J. Data Anal. Tech. Strateg. **1**(4), 364–384 (2009). https://doi.org/10.1504/IJDATS.2009.027514
20. Passi, K., Pandey, N.: Increased prediction accuracy in the game of cricket using machine learning. Int. J. Data Min. Knowl. Manag. Process (IJDKP) **8**(2) (2018). https://doi.org/10.5121/ijdkp.2018.8203

A Unit Softmax with Laplacian Smoothing Stochastic Gradient Descent for Deep Convolutional Neural Networks

Jamshaid Ul Rahman[1], Akhtar Ali[2(✉)], Masood Ur Rehman[1], and Rafaqat Kazmi[3]

[1] School of Mathematical Sciences, University of Science and Technology of China, Hefei 230026, Anhui, People's Republic of China
{jamshaid,masood}@mail.ustc.edu.cn
[2] Department of Mathematics, Government College University Faisalabad, Faisalabad, Pakistan
utm.akhtar@gmail.com
[3] Department of Computer Science, The Islamia University Bahawalpur, Bahawalpur, Pakistan
rafaqutkazmi@gmail.com

Abstract. Several techniques were designed during last few years to improve the performance of deep architecture by means of appropriate loss functions or activation functions. Arguably, softmax is the traditionally convenient to train Deep Convolutional Neural Networks (DCNNs) for classification task. However, the modern deep learning architectures have exposed its limitation towards feature discriminability. In this paper, we offered a supervision signal for discriminative image features through a modification in softmax to boost up the power of loss function. Amending the original softmax loss and motivated by the A-softmax loss for face recognition, we fixed the angular margin to introduce a unit margin softmax loss. The improved alternative form of softmax is trainable, easy to optimize and stable for usage along with Stochastic Gradient Descent (SGD) and Laplacian Smoothing Stochastic Gradient Descent (LS-SGD) and applicable to classify the digits in image. Experimental results demonstrate a state-of-the-art performance on famous database of handwritten digits the Modified National Institute of Standards and Technology (MNIST) database.

Keywords: Angular softmax · Deep Convolutional Neural Networks · Laplacian Smoothing Stochastic Gradient Descent · Softmax loss · Stochastic Gradient Descent

1 Introduction

In the present era of Artificial Intelligent (AI), Deep Convolutional Neural Networks (DCNNs) have remarkable improvement in the state-of-the-art

© Springer Nature Singapore Pte Ltd. 2020
I. S. Bajwa et al. (Eds.): INTAP 2019, CCIS 1198, pp. 162–174, 2020.
https://doi.org/10.1007/978-981-15-5232-8_14

performance in numerous computer vision tasks including object recognition, face recognition, speech recognition and hand-written digit recognition (see all Agarwal et al. (2018), Voulodimos et al. (2018), Zhang et al. (2018), LeCun et al. (2015), Schmidhuber (2015), Bhatia (2014), Ba et al. (2014), Liu et al. (2017) and Ren et al. (2015)). Modern digital world is full of shapes, design and patterns, moreover these patterns can be physically viewed, recognized or derived via mathematical modeling and simulate by theoretical and computational algorithms Ren et al. (2015), Suleman et al. (2019), Ul Rahman et al. (2009) and Zhang et al. (2018). Pattern recognition is beneficial to avoid poor classification of data by recognizing the exact assembly of data in dataset. Identifying a pattern is the computational process to get the particular match and predictabilities of data. Even though the digits identification and recognition has been a research topic for many years, modern researchers still have a keen interest to improve the accuracy and performance of machine. Recognition system is being conventionally associated to the field of AI in which computational mathematics plays a major role in the development and enhancement of methods and algorithms Ul Rahman et al. (2009) and Zhang et al. (2018). An appropriate, ideal and better recognition approach would contemplate classification matters as well as representation and demonstration. Day by day AI applications facing challenges owing to large amount of complex data structures, on the other hand neural network refining deeper architecture and new nonlinear activation functions.

DCNNs architecture is renowned for the extraction of complex features and the important problem in the neural network architectures is to explore appropriate loss functions. A loss function is incredibly simple method of evaluating how the algorithm models the dataset. Most deep learning processes use some sort of loss function in the process of optimization, or to search the appropriate weights for given data. A number of techniques has been proposed by modifying the loss function to improve the performance of DCNNs Liu et al. (2017), Ranjan et al. (2017), Liu et al. (2004), Ashiquzzaman and Tushar (2017), Sun et al. (2014) and Schroff et al. (2015), where the Euclidean loss and softmax loss gain a significant importance in development of deep feature learning and tendency towards learning with robust features is to emphasize DCNNs with extra discriminative information. Few techniques based on combined Euclidean losses and softmax loss has been used to construct a dual supervision that are not sound motivated, as the features learned by softmax loss have inherent angular distribution and softmax loss is also incompatible with Euclidean margin loss.

On this concern, researchers propose alternative methods to combine angular margin by presenting different margin parameters to restrict the boundary closer to the weight vector of each class. To make it optimizable in DCNN, authors introduced a monotonically decreasing angle function by adjusting monotonic element Liu et al. (2017). In recognition task initiate with the dataset into training stage, that containing random projection and extraction of the features with different architectures and loss functions used to extract discriminative deep feature, the Fig. 1 represents a simple structure for performance evaluation of loss function.

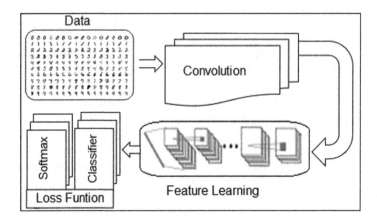

Fig. 1. Structure of Deep convolutional neural networks (DCNNs) for performance evaluation supervised by the modified softmax loss used for Handwritten Digit Dataset MNIST

A theoretically attractive angular margin used in A-Softmax Liu et al. (2017) have amazing performance on face recognition and is introduced to push the classification boundary closer to weight of each class to encourage the discriminability of features. That famous contribution offer a new direction for the researchers to focus on different margin to restrict the boundary closer to the weight vector of each class. Several techniques with motivated concepts and structure are presented during the last two years by introducing multiplicative angular margin, additive angular margin and additive cosine margin Liu et al. (2016), Wang et al. (2018) and Deng et al. (2018).

For optimization task to train the network with loss function, typically used Stochastic Gradient Descent (SGD) Bottou (2010) a gradient based optimization processes circumvent spurious local minima, but it slows down the convergence of regular gradient descent Schmidhuber (2015) and Osher et al. (2018).

Numerous stimulating variance reduction techniques Defazio et al. (2014) and Johnson and Zhang (2013) have been proposed for strongly convex functions to recover the linear convergence rate, but not appropriate to train DCNNs. Laplacian Smoothing Stochastic Gradient Descent (LS-SGD) Osher et al. (2018) is beneficial to reduce noise in SGD and appropriate to use for training of deep neural network. The optimization difficulty of A Softmax, that incorporate the angular-margin in a multiplicative manner, could be handle by adjusting the loss function parameters and by using alternative forms of Stochastic Gradient Descent.

To improve the discrimination power of softmax loss function, we propose a special case of multiplicative angular margin entitled a unit softmax by fixing the margin to integer value ($m = 1$) with a additive parameter ($\epsilon = 0.25$) Ul Rahman et al. (2019) and setting the convolutional layers to train the model on MNIST dataset. We build a deep model on MNIST dataset using the proposed approach, during training phase, A unit softmax monitors the ConvNet to learn deep features and in the testing phase, the digit features are extracted from the ConvNet to perform characters recognition. Moreover, we experiments the modified softmax loss with the SGD and LS-SGD, both optimizer achieved state-of-the-art performance with consistent improvements.

2   Preliminaries

Modern research in deep learning approaches on loss function and optimization strategy Voulodimos et al. (2018), Zhang et al. (2018), LeCun et al. (2015), Bhatia (2014), Ba et al. (2014), Liu et al. (2017), Ranjan et al. (2017) and Osher et al. (2018) play a most important role in deep recognition system. Naturally, softmax loss is considered good to optimize inter-class difference and effective to stabilize un-normalized vector to a probability distribution, that's why classification loss functions for DCNNs are habitually constructed by softmax loss. Mostly, loss function is modified using the original softmax loss Zhang et al. (2018), Liu et al. (2017), Ranjan et al. (2017), Sun et al. (2014), Schroff et al. (2015) and Liu et al. (2016) and the optimizer is adjusted on the base of gradient based optimization techniques Osher et al. (2018), Ruder (2016) and Zhang et al. (2015). If x_i and y_i be the input feature and its labels respectively then the simple form of original softmax loss L_S for N number of training samples is given as

$$L_S = \frac{1}{N}\Sigma_i(-log\frac{e^{f_{y_i}}}{\Sigma_j e^{f_j}})$$ (1)

The notation f_j is the jth element corresponding to the class vector f. In last year, the softmax loss attained good results on its modified form, the angular-margin and cosine-margin loss Liu et al. (2017), Deng et al. (2018) and Wang et al. (2018) has been designed to learned features theoretically separable with angular distance. That work on sofmax loss with adjustment on angular discriminative strategy is considered beneficial for classification task to improve the performance of DCNNs for recognition system and has been discussed in next subsection.

2.1   Angular Margin Softmax

To increase the learn capability of DCNNs through the angular margin approaches for softmax loss, A-Softmax Liu et al. (2017) achieved remarkable progress and has strong geometric explanation towards the discriminative angular distance metric and can be taken as compiler for discriminative feature on a hypersphere manifold that essentially matches the prior that images lie on a manifold. A hypersphere embedding method A-Softmax $(L_{\psi_1(\theta_{y_i})})$ used to learn discriminative image features with angular margin, that is given as

$$L_{\psi_1(\theta_{y_i})} = -\frac{1}{N}\Sigma_i \log \frac{e^{||x_i||\psi_1(\theta_{y_i})}}{e^{||x_i||\psi_1(\theta_{y_i})} + \Sigma_j e^{||x_i||cos\theta}}$$ (2)

where θ is the angle between x_i and W_i, and $\psi_1(\theta_{y_i}) = (-1)^k cos(m\theta) - 2k$ is a monotonically decreasing angle function fixed by $k = \frac{m\theta}{\pi}$.

2.2   Stochastic Gradient Descent

In the era of deep learning, the speed of processors is slower as compared to the data sizes. Stochastic gradient descent optimization strategy is a workhorse for solving a large scale learning of linear classifiers under convex loss functions Bottou (2010) and Bottou et al. (2018). SGD performs a parameter update for each training sample x_i with label y_i and allowed the processors to access shared memory, where every iteration estimates the gradient by randomly picked sample. If L_{obj} represent a differentiable objective function on the stochastic process $\{f_t; t = 1, 2...\}$ with the γ as an adequately chosen gain, the simple form of SGD is given as

$$f_{t+1} = f_t - \gamma_t \nabla_f [L_{obj}(x_i, f_t)] \tag{3}$$

There is no doubt, it beneficial for gradient-based optimization procedures circumvent spurious local minima but it decelerates the convergence of conventional gradient descent. LS-SGD Osher et al. (2018) proposed for progressive learning and to reduce noise in SGD, that is introduced in the next section.

2.3   Laplacian Smoothing Gradient Descent

In the optimization techniques, the Stochastic gradient descent (SGD) have signification performance for handling large scale recognition task in deep learning problems. It gives rise to a family of algorithms that make the training of DNNs practical, which is believed to somehow implicitly smooth the loss function of the DNNs. To find the better minima, the Laplacian Smoothing Gradient Descent Osher et al. (2018) proposed on the basis of theoretical explanation of Hamilton-Jacobi partial differential equations Laval and Leclercq (2013) and Evans (2010) via pre-multiply the gradient by the inverse of the tri-diagonal circular convolution matrix and is applicable to reduces the optimality gap in SGD. The resulting surrogate tends to reduce noise in SGD and improve the training process of DNNs. It is ideally proved and demonstrated that the performance of Deep Relaxation Chaudhari et al. (2018) is better but computationally expensive as the Laplacian smoothing implicit gradient descent requires inner iterations. LS-SGD Osher et al. (2018) used explicit to relax the implicit strategy to perform layer-wise gradient smoothing that assistances to sidestep sharp minima to reach the global minima.

$$f_{t+1} = f_t - \gamma_t A_\sigma^{-1} \nabla_f [L_{obj}(f_t)] \tag{4}$$

3   Proposed Approach

For deep understanding of loss function in DCNNs, researchers presented Cosine Margin based loss functions to make learned features potentially separable with a larger cosine distance, that enables convolutional neural networks to learn angularly discriminative features. The normalization of image features and weights makes the predictions only be subject to the angle between the feature and the weight. A-Softmax loss function observed as imposing discriminative constraints on hypersphere manifold that basically matches the prior that digits lie on the manifold. The model of A Unit Softmax loss is based on the additive and multiplicative angular margin Liu et al. (2017), where the non-monotonicity of the cosine function has been adjusted through fitting a piece-wise element. We modify the original softmax loss with the angular margin m, that can be represent by $L_{S_{m\theta}}$ and modeled as

$$L_{S_{m\theta}} = -\frac{1}{N}\Sigma_i \log \frac{e^{||W||\ ||x_i||cos(m\theta)+b}}{e^{||W||\ ||x_i||cos(m\theta)+b} + \Sigma_j e^{||W||\ ||x_i||cos\theta_j}} \tag{5}$$

For learning task, a monotonically decreasing function $\psi_\epsilon(\theta) = [(-1)^{\lfloor k\rfloor}cos(\theta) - 2k] - \epsilon$ defined to remove nonmonotonicity of cosine by fixing the bias $b = 0$ and normalize the weight to 1, where $\theta \in [\frac{k\pi}{m}, \frac{\pi(k+1)}{m}]$ and ϵ is the additive margin. The values of the ϵ variate from 0 to 0.49 Ul Rahman et al. (2019), and the behavior of the monotonic element is observed decreasing. The Fig. 2 represents the monotonically decreasing phenomena of $\psi_\epsilon(\theta)$.

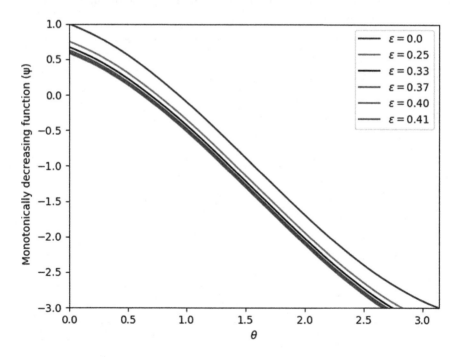

Fig. 2. Monotonically decreasing element $\psi_\epsilon(\theta)$ with the different values of ϵ.

It is clear that the modification based on normalization of features and weights makes the predictions only be subject to the angle between the feature vector and the weight. The modified angular margin based softmax is given as

$$L_{\psi_\epsilon(\theta,m)} = -\frac{1}{N}\Sigma_i \log \frac{e^{||x_i||\psi_\epsilon(\theta)}}{e^{||x_i||\psi_\epsilon(\theta)} + \Sigma_j e^{||x_i||\cos\theta_j}} \tag{6}$$

Final form of a unit softmax is defined by setting angular margin $m = 1$ and fixing the value of additive margin $\epsilon = 0.25$ to generate modified monotonically decreasing parameter $\psi_{\epsilon=0.25} = [(-1)^{\lfloor k\rfloor}\cos(\theta_{min}) - 2k] - 0.25$, where $\theta_{min} \in [k\pi, (k+1)\pi]$. Upgrade the Eq. (6) by adjusting the proposed parameters, a unit softmax is given as

$$L_{\psi_\epsilon(\theta_{min},1)} = -\frac{1}{N}\Sigma_i \log \frac{e^{||x_i||\psi_\epsilon(\theta_{min})}}{e^{||x_i||\psi_\epsilon(\theta_{min})} + \Sigma_j e^{||x_i||\cos\theta_j}} \tag{7}$$

There is just a minor slipping in the angular margin case towards the modified form with ϵ, that can be observed in Fig. 3, the angle is taken at $x - axis$ in radian form and represented in decimal form for better understanding. After the inner product of weight and feature vectors in angular margin approach, a better action is essential that is computationally expensive. The proposed a unit softmax approach is theoretically slight similar to the original sofmax loss

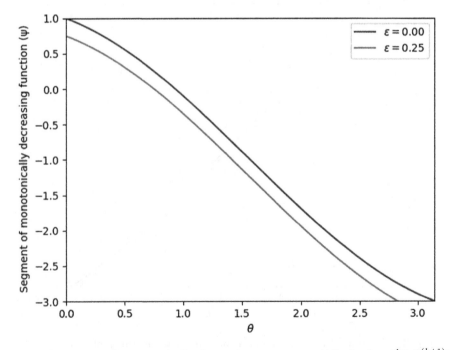

Fig. 3. A segment of monotonically decreasing parameter $\psi(\theta)$, for $\theta \in [\frac{k\pi}{m}, \frac{\pi(k+1)}{m}]$ with angular margin (m) and additive margin $\epsilon = 0.00$ and $\epsilon = 0.25$.

and computationally it is more appealing and bifacial because of its combined effect of additive and angular margin and it is proficient to adjust with both optimization techniques SGD and LS-SGD. The adjustment of a unit softmax is simple to take gradient during the forward and backward propagation and is trivial to optimize the modified softmax loss using SGD and LS-SGD.

3.1 Experiments

For evaluation of a unit softmax, we use a vision application for classification task to recognize hand-written digits (from 0 to 9) using famous benchmark MNIST LeCun et al. (1998), containing 60,000 training images and 10,000 test images and is well-known for pattern recognition and learning approaches. Few samples from the dataset MNIST are shown in Fig. 4 with different patterns.

a   b   c

Fig. 4. Samples of handwritten digits from (training and testing patterns) the MNIST Dataset.

We adjust the network architecture by setting the convolutional units containing multiple convolution layers consist of a set of filters with output channels on the input by adjusting stable and learnable size of kernel (followed by the structure of A-Softmax Liu et al. (2017)), the detailed structure is exposed in the Table 1.

For experiment of a unit softmax with both SGD and LS-SGD optimization strategy, we begin with a learning rate of 0.1 and divide it by 10 at 10k and 12k iterations to generate 50 epochs and other default parameters are set for PyTorch implementation on GPU. Begin with the dataset into training stage that containing random projection and extraction of the features. In this phase to visualize all digits clearly, each letter in dataset is attentive to displayed in haphazard style and then respective characters are extracted individually to examine its assembly and forward to the learning process for training. This process is iterated until all the objects in the dataset get trained completely.

3.2 Results and Discussions

The following Fig. 5 represents the training on the Dataset MNIST using SGD and LS-SGD, accuracy (is taken on vertical axis) corresponding to 50 epochs (on

Table 1. Convolutional layers structure for neural network. The notation Conv1.x, Conv2.x and Conv3.x represents the convolutional units containing multiple convolution layers and FC1 is the fully connected layer.

Layer	CNN structure
Conv 1.x	$\begin{bmatrix} 3 \times 3, & 64 \end{bmatrix} \times 1$
Conv 2.x	$\begin{bmatrix} 3 \times 3, & 64 \end{bmatrix} \times 3$
Conv 3.x	$\begin{bmatrix} 3 \times 3, & 64 \end{bmatrix} \times 3$
Conv 4.x	$\begin{bmatrix} 3 \times 3, & 64 \end{bmatrix} \times 3$
$FC1$	256

horizontal axis) and the Fig. 6 represents the loss (on vertical axis) corresponding to 50 epoch (horizontal axis).

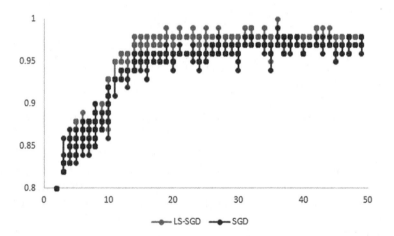

Fig. 5. Training using SGD and LS-SGD. Accuracy (%) is taken on vertical axis corresponding to 50 epochs on horizontal axis.

Its observed from the Fig. 5, that a unit softmax is efficiently work with both the optimization schemes and the performance of LS-SGD to train data is significantly improved after the epoch 10 and smoothly exhibits the better heightening as compared to SGD. The Fig. 6 exposed that, a unit softmax along with LS-SGD attain the notable results on the loss during the training instead of SGD. The minimum loss through SGD is 0.434 and as a result of LS-SGD is 0.384.

From the Table 2, it can be observed that the loss of a unit softmax is 0.384 with LS-SGD and 0.434 with SGD, its notable that the results of a unit softmax with both optimization techniques achieves the state-of-the-art performance

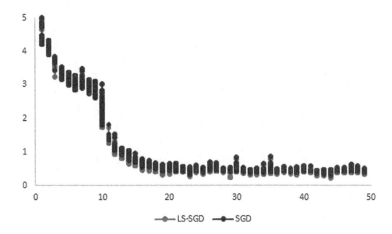

Fig. 6. Loss using SGD and LS-SGD. Loss is taken on vertical axis corresponding to 50 epochs on horizontal axis.

Table 2. Comparison of the both SGD and LS-SGD on a unit softmax loss with the other state-of-the-art loss functions on MNIST dataset.

Method	Error rate
DropConnect Wan et al. (2013)	0.57
CNN Jarrett et al. (2009)	0.53
FitNet Romero et al. (2014)	0.51
Softmax Liu et al. (2016)	0.40
L-Softmax Liu et al. (2016) at m = 2	0.32
L-Softmax Liu et al. (2016) at m = 3	0.31
L-Softmax Liu et al. (2016) at m = 4	0.31
Maxout Goodfellow et al. (2013)	0.45
GenPool Lee et al. (2016)	0.31
A Unit Softmax with SGD (m = 1, $\epsilon = 0.25$)	0.434
A Unit Softmax with LS-SGD (m = 1, $\epsilon = 0.25$)	0.384

compared to the other deep CNN architectures. L-Softmax with the large margin (m = 2, m = 3, m = 4), archived better then our a unit softmax but the our alternative form of softmax (m = 1) is easily trainable with both SGD and LS-SGD and stable. For evaluation, we simply construct the final ensemble classifier and use it with the discriminative feature to predict labels. To generate some clusters, the handwritten digits with similar structure and vector-value are assembled together under a single label and every digit feature is analyzed to find the pattern by proposed algorithm. On both SGD and LS-SGD schemes, the testing accuracy corresponding to 16 randomly selected models (RM 01, RM 02, RM 03, .. RM 16) is shown in Fig. 7. Testing accuracy is taken on vertical axis

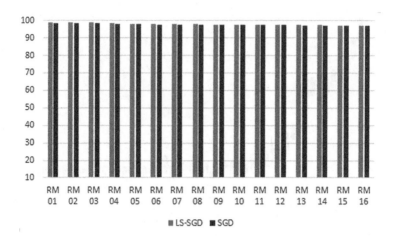

Fig. 7. Testing accuracy on randomly selected models RM 01, RM 02, RM 3, . . RM 16.

and randomly selected models (RM 01, RM 02, RM 03, . . RM 16) on horizontal axis.

The training and testing accuracy represents the proficiency of a unit softmax loss to improve the power of DCNNs along with the both optimization techniques SGD and LS-SGD. However, the results on training and testing demonstrate the advantage of the smoothed gradient as compared to stochastic gradient, but there is a minor difference in results of the modified softmax with SGD and LS-SGD, both optimization schemes are adjustable and stable for a unit softmax loss and helps to find better minima.

4   Conclusion

Motivated by the A- Softmax and the optimization strategy of LS-SGD, we proposed a unit softmax for Deep Convolutional Neural Networks, that expresses a flexible learning job with adjustable additive margin and is flexible to amend with SGD and LS-SGD. The experimental results on MNIST dataset demonstrated the advantages of our a unit softmax loss consistently outperforms the state-of-the-art. We believe that our strategy towards DCNN will be helpful for other deep learning tasks like object detection, recognition and tracking.

Acknowledgements. J.U. Rahman[1], supported by CAS-TWAS President's Fellowship at University of Science and Technology of China, No. 96, JinZhai Road Baohe District, Hefei, Anhui, 230026, P.R.China. We would also like to thanks Mr. Muhammad Ajmal from University of science and technology of China (USTC) for his valuable comments and suggestions.

References

Agarwal, S., Terrail, J.O.D., Jurie, F.: Recent advances in object detection in the age of deep convolutional neural networks. arXiv preprint arXiv:1809.03193 (2018)

Ashiquzzaman, A., Tushar, A.K.: Handwritten Arabic numeral recognition using deep learning neural networks. In: 2017 IEEE International Conference on Imaging, Vision & Pattern Recognition (icIVPR), pp. 1–4. IEEE (2017)

Ba, J., Mnih, V., Kavukcuoglu, K.: Multiple object recognition with visual attention. arXiv preprint arXiv:1412.7755 (2014)

Bhatia, E.N.: Optical character recognition techniques: a review. Int. J. Adv. Res. Comput. Sci. Softw. Eng. **4**(5) (2014)

Bottou, L.: Large-scale machine learning with stochastic gradient descent. In: Lechevallier, Y., Saporta, G. (eds.) Proceedings of COMPSTAT'2010, pp. 177–186. Springer, Heidelberg (2010). https://doi.org/10.1007/978-3-7908-2604-3_16

Bottou, L., Curtis, F.E., Nocedal, J.: Optimization methods for large-scale machine learning. SIAM Rev. **60**(2), 223–311 (2018)

Chaudhari, P., Oberman, A., Osher, S., Soatto, S., Carlier, G.: Deep relaxation: partial differential equations for optimizing deep neural networks. Res. Math. Sci. **5**(3), 1–30 (2018). https://doi.org/10.1007/s40687-018-0148-y

Defazio, A., Bach, F., Lacoste-Julien, S.: SAGA: a fast incremental gradient method with support for non-strongly convex composite objectives. In: Advances in Neural Information Processing Systems, pp. 1646–1654 (2014)

Deng, J., Guo, J., Xue, N., Zafeiriou, S.: ArcFace: additive angular margin loss for deep face recognition. arXiv preprint arXiv:1801.07698 (2018)

Evans, L.C.: Partial Differential Equations. Graduate Studies in Mathematics, vol. 19, 2nd edn. American Mathematical Society, Providence (2010)

Goodfellow, I.J., Warde-Farley, D., Mirza, M., Courville, A., Bengio, Y.: Maxout networks. arXiv preprint arXiv:1302.4389 (2013)

Jarrett, K., Kavukcuoglu, K., LeCun, Y., et al.: What is the best multi-stage architecture for object recognition? In: 2009 IEEE 12th International Conference on Computer Vision, pp. 2146–2153. IEEE (2009)

Johnson, R., Zhang, T.: Accelerating stochastic gradient descent using predictive variance reduction. In: Advances in Neural Information Processing Systems, pp. 315–323 (2013)

Laval, J.A., Leclercq, L.: The Hamilton-Jacobi partial differential equation and the three representations of traffic flow. Transp. Res. Part B Methodol. **52**, 17–30 (2013)

LeCun, Y., Bengio, Y., Hinton, G.: Deep learning. Nature **521**(7553), 436 (2015)

LeCun, Y., Cortes, C., Burges, C.J.: The MNIST database of handwritten digits, 1998, vol. 10, p. 34 (1998). http://yann.lecun.com/exdb/mnist

Lee, C.Y., Gallagher, P.W., Tu, Z.: Generalizing pooling functions in convolutional neural networks: mixed, gated, and tree. In: Artificial Intelligence and Statistics, pp. 464–472 (2016)

Liu, C.L., Sako, H., Fujisawa, H.: Discriminative learning quadratic discriminant function for handwriting recognition. IEEE Trans. Neural Netw. **15**(2), 430–444 (2004)

Liu, W., Wen, Y., Yu, Z., Li, M., Raj, B., Song, L.: SphereFace: deep hypersphere embedding for face recognition. In: Proceedings of the IEEE Conference on Computer Vision and Pattern Recognition, pp. 212–220 (2017)

Liu, W., Wen, Y., Yu, Z., Yang, M.: Large-margin softmax loss for convolutional neural networks. In: ICML, vol. 2. p. 7 (2016)

Osher, S., Wang, B., Yin, P., Luo, X., Pham, M., Lin, A.: Laplacian smoothing gradient descent. arXiv preprint arXiv:1806.06317 (2018)

Ranjan, R., Castillo, C.D., Chellappa, R.: L2-constrained softmax loss for discriminative face verification. arXiv preprint arXiv:1703.09507 (2017)

Ren, S., He, K., Girshick, R., Sun, J.: Faster R-CNN: towards real-time object detection with region proposal networks. In: Advances in Neural Information Processing Systems, pp. 91–99 (2015)

Romero, A., Ballas, N., Kahou, S.E., Chassang, A., Gatta, C., Bengio, Y.: FitNets: hints for thin deep nets. arXiv preprint arXiv:1412.6550 (2014)

Ruder, S.: An overview of gradient descent optimization algorithms. arXiv preprint arXiv:1609.04747 (2016)

Schmidhuber, J.: Deep learning in neural networks: an overview. Neural Netw. **61**, 85–117 (2015)

Schroff, F., Kalenichenko, D., Philbin, J.: FaceNet: a unified embedding for face recognition and clustering. In: Proceedings of the IEEE Conference on Computer Vision and Pattern Recognition, pp. 815–823 (2015)

Suleman, M., Lu, D., Yue, C., Ul Rahman, J., Anjum, N.: He-Laplace method for general nonlinear periodic solitary solution of vibration equations. J. Low Freq. Noise Vib. Act. Control. **38**, 1297–1304 (2019). https://doi.org/10.1177/1461348418816266

Sun, Y., Chen, Y., Wang, X., Tang, X.: Deep learning face representation by joint identification-verification. In: Advances in Neural Information Processing Systems, pp. 1988–1996 (2014)

Ul Rahman, J., Chen, Q., Yang, Z.: Additive parameter for deep face recognition. Commun. Math. Stat., 1–15 (2019)

Ul Rahman, J., Suleman, M., Lu, D., He, J.H., Ramzan, M.: He-Elzaki method for spatial diffusion of biological population. Fractals (2009)

Voulodimos, A., Doulamis, N., Doulamis, A., Protopapadakis, E.: Deep learning for computer vision: a brief review. Comput. Intell. Neurosci. (2018)

Wan, L., Zeiler, M., Zhang, S., Le Cun, Y., Fergus, R.: Regularization of neural networks using dropconnect. In: International Conference on Machine Learning, pp. 1058–1066 (2013)

Wang, H., et al.: CosFace: large margin cosine loss for deep face recognition. In: Proceedings of the IEEE Conference on Computer Vision and Pattern Recognition, pp. 5265–5274 (2018)

Zhang, Q., Yang, L.T., Chen, Z., Li, P.: A survey on deep learning for big data. Inf. Fusion **42**, 146–157 (2018)

Zhang, S., Choromanska, A.E., LeCun, Y.: Deep learning with elastic averaging SGD. In: Advances in Neural Information Processing Systems, pp. 685–693 (2015)

Scientific Map Creator: A Tool to Analyze the Author's Affiliation and Citations by Producing Mind Maps

Sahar Maqsood ul Hassan[✉], Khizra Tariq, and Tooba Dar

Department of Software Engineering, University of Sialkot, Sialkot, Pakistan
sahar.maqsood@uogsialkot.edu.pk, khizra009@gmail.com,
tubadar2016@gmail.com, taroobdar@gmail.com

Abstract. Citations have been considered a parameter to gauge the importance of research paper in the scientific society. Scientific societies consider citations to evaluate the authors to rank them for deserving positions such as assigning those researchers PHD supervisions, presenting them award, hiring them as a reviewer or editor in the Journal. With the help of "Scientific Map Creator", we can provide web-based concept mapping application with a Database. Our main research focus is to extract the information from the bulk of data. The data that has been stored in several online databases for research papers such as JUCS, IEEE Explore and Scopus is intended to be managed and extracting influential author and present that meta data in the form of mind maps with the help of "Scientific Map Creator".

Keywords: Mind maps · Citation networks · Visualization · Brainstorming

1 Introduction

Since 90s, with the gigantic growth of literature, reading and understanding of complete research paper is considered to be heart taking activity. As researchers have to critically read the paper to grab its concept. There are normally two type of papers; Journal and Conferences. As compared to conference papers, Journal papers take more time to understand its core semantics because their numbers of pages are large as well as writing is technical. In order to understand the techniques and terminologies in the paper, critical reading is required. In the era of computing and IT, every developer and researchers is coming forth with modern ways to technologies to deal with science. In computer sciences and other disciplines of studies, researchers are busy in producing the plethora of scientific literature in which numerous unique techniques have been proposed. With the help of those techniques, researchers are dealing with data statistically i-e Correlation Analysis, ANOVA, and Regression and so on. Other than researchers, developers are developing tools to reduce the scientific paper reading time in term of digging useful information. In this way, association between researcher and developer has been mapped to produce the present state of the art work in the research. For this reason, we have designed a tool named as "Scientific Map Creator" which is

© Springer Nature Singapore Pte Ltd. 2020
I. S. Bajwa et al. (Eds.): INTAP 2019, CCIS 1198, pp. 175–180, 2020.
https://doi.org/10.1007/978-981-15-5232-8_15

dedicated to generate mind maps of keywords, co-author network and author's affiliation. Below sections have been designed to provide clear picture of our proposed approach.

1.1 Mindmapping

Mind mapping is a way to portray ideas and concepts graphically. It is a tool that helps structuring information, helping you in generating new ideas, also have better understanding and judgment. Henceforth, mind-maps are useful for;

- Communication within our trans-disciplinary team.
- Brainstorming,
- Interviews
- For sharing ideas and documents.
- Representing combined stakeholder knowledge in an easily accessible format.
- For organizing and planning literature reviews. Focus groups with a diverse range of stakeholders.

1.2 Types of Mind Mapping

- Concept mapping
- Argument mapping
- Conceptual mapping
- Web mapping
- Thinking mapping
- Band mapping

"Scientific Map Creator" is a web-based concept mapping application integrated with Database in which data is stored from heterogeneous sources, i-e; IEEE Explore, JUCS, and CiteSeer. With the help of this tool, researchers, students or either faculty can portray the trending topics, influential authors and active research institutions and departments globally. Also, Maps are noticed to be very effective in bringing structured learning in academic community and enabling students to scaffold their learning.

2 Summarized Literature Review

Our proposed mind map generator is automated tool which collectively gathers the data against the user query and present the information in the form of hierarchical graphs. The graphs are composed of nodes with interactive colors, sizes and edges connected to it which convey its own meaning. On contrary, the "Mind Meister" a web tool, proposed by MeisterLabs GmbH, launched in 2007 to produce mind map against central ideas of the users. The narrated tool is not dedicated to produce the mind map of researchers from the scientific society but for business analysis and decision making. The application of proposed tool is directly implementable in terms of identifying the influential authors and ranks them to assign one of the above discussed positions. Hence the accuracy of the tool will be analyzed against the dataset in which the affiliations and list of co-authors against every author has been stored manually. The proposed mind map is expandable in terms of keywords, sections and subsections.

2.1 Mind Maps

Mind map is a way to portray ideas and concepts graphically. It is a tool that helps structuring information, helping you to generate new ideas, also have better understanding and judgment. It was developed by Tony Buzan in 1970 who introduced this concept in his book "use your head" and developed a system. He did to give up insisting on using the traditional methods for creative minds, but he focus to reflect the brain functioning the human. These maps allow us to reach the in creditable potential of our brain easily. "Buzan's mind maps make you smarter". (Buzan 2000) (Table 1).

Table 1. Comparison between mapping methods

Map methods	Limitations	Benefits
Concept map	• Not easy to apply by novices; requires extensive training (M 2005) • Concept maps tend tobe idiosyncratic (M 2005) • The overall pattern does not necessarily assist memorability (Eppler 2016)	• Rapid information provision (E P. 1997) • Systematic, proven approach to provide overview (E P. 1997) • Emphasizes relationships and connections among concepts (M 2005)
Mind map	• Represents mostly hierarchic relationships (T. 1995) • Can be inconsistent (Eppler 2016) • Can become overly complex (loss of big picture) (Eppler 2016)	• Easy to learn and Apply (T. 1995) • Provides a concise hierarchic Overview (T. 1995) • Easy to extend and add further content (T. 1995)
Conceptual map	• Can be difficult to understand without knowledge of category meanings (Eppler 2016) • Does not provide mnemonic help (Eppler 2016) • Does not foster creativity or self-expression (Eppler 2016)	• Provides a concise overview (E T. 1990) • Structures a topic into systematic • building blocks (Eppler 2016) • Can be applied to a variety of situations in the same • Manner (Eppler 2016)
Visual metaphor	• Cannot easily be extended or modified (Eppler 2016) • May be misunderstood, may trigger wrong associations (Eppler 2016) • Can be manipulative or misunderstood (Blackwell AF 1999)	• Activates prior knowledge • About metaphor domain (Lakoff G 1980) • Draws attention and inspires curiosity. (Eppler 2016) • Facilitates understanding by triggering functional associations (Lakoff 1980)
Augment mapping	• May have over other forms of mapping tools is that it focuses on a certain sub-class of relationships • Puts limitations around the items being mapped. (Davies 2011)	• Argument mapping does not capture looser, more tangential relationships, e.g., cause and effect. (Davies 2011)

3 Importance of Citation Analysis

The analysis of scholarly communication through citation patterns has been extensively used to detect scientific collaboration, assess the impact of research outputs, and observe knowledge shared across domains. Papers and their citations have been used to form networks (e.g., co-author networks, author co-citation networks, affiliation network and keywords based network) where nodes represent papers, authors, or journals, and edges indicate the number of times each paper has been cited, co-authored, or co-cited. The simple citation count remains one of the most central problems for researchers in ranking domain. Citations are considered to be the limited source of information, as citations neither determine the indication explicitly nor the semantics of a reference (Ding 2013).

4 Research Problems

- Crawling huge amount of data, storing in database and transforming into useful information requires complex automated training.
- Different mechanisms and tools have been proposed by researchers to present information such as concept map, conceptual map and mind map.

5 Research Methodology

Our main research focus is to extract the information from the bulk of data. The data that has been stored in different online databases for research papers such as JUCS, IEEE Explore, and CiteSeer is intended to be managed using Mind maps. To narrow down the research idea, we have selected the data from IEEE explore and in the proposed framework, we have built the offline database in which we have stored data along with the authors affiliations and their co-authors.

The architecture diagram of proposed system has been shown in Fig. 1.

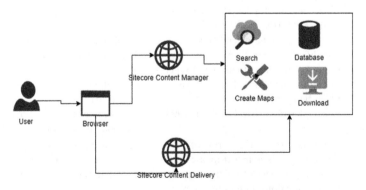

Fig. 1. Architecture design

According to Fig. 1, the user (researcher) will enter the query (input) and the system will process the query according to available database to return results against query. On finding results, based on the produced mind maps, user will interpret those results accordingly.

6   Implementation of Proposed Tool

Table 2 shows us the comparison between Mind Meister and Scientific Map Creator and also tells us about their distinct features.

Table 2. Comparison of Mind Meister and Scientific Map Creator

Mind Meister	Scientific Map Creator
Mind Meister is an online mind mapping tool that gives graphical representation of information	Scientific Map Creator is a web-based Mind mapping tool that gives graphical representation of data from papers
It allows you to choose between classic mind map layout and org chart mode	It allows a user to generate a mind maps by choosing from different Research papers
User can Draw mind maps systematically	User can generate 3 types of mind maps: Affiliation, Keyword, Co-Author
The mind maps created are based on common ideas	The mind maps are created based on Research ideas
Supports: Windows, linux	Supports: Windows
It costs you in order to get good features e.g. Pro 8.9 $ and Business 12.49 $	Free

Figure 2 shows us the difference between two applications graphically. There's an obvious difference of map creation and features. Mind Meister deals with the creation of maps only however, Scientific Map Creator deals with the generation of mind maps from research papers as mentioned in the Table 2 (Comparison of Mind Meister and Scientific Map Creator).

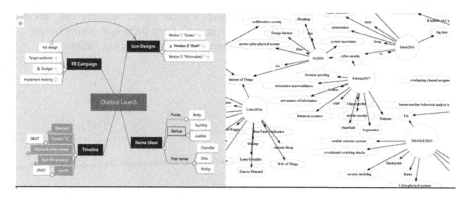

Fig. 2. Mind Meister vs. Scientific Map Creator

7 Conclusion

Mind maps are valuable when our main focus is on time saving in search of colossal or extensive amount of data. In order to introduce smart way of utilizing technology, we have developed the tool "Scientific Map Creator". With the help of this tool, extraction of meta-data, analyzing influential authors and targeting research oriented institutions expected to become easier for the researchers. Our entire focus circulates around building mind maps and our web based application is designed to facilitate researchers to produce related information graphically. In such related information, researcher will be able to analyze co-author's information, author's affiliation and keywords meta-data. This useful information will be presented in the form of mind maps that will provide easiest way to extract and use the information.

At current stage of research, our dataset contains around 500 papers from heterogeneous sources. In future, we are intended gather large amount of papers to sharpen the efficiency of our tool with automated crawler.

References

Meier, P.S.: Mind-mapping: a tool for eliciting and representing knowledge held by diverse informants. Soc. Res. Update **52** (2007). http://sru.soc.surrey.ac.uk/SRU52.pdf

Beel, J.: Retrieving data from mind maps to enhance search applications. Bull. IEEE Tech. Committee Digit. Libr. **6**(2), 1–10 (2010)

Weideman, M.: Concept Mapping – a proposed theoretical model for implementation as a knowledge repository, 10 June 2003

Beel, J., Langer, S.: An exploratory analysis of mind maps. In: Proceedings of the 11th ACM Symposium on Document Engineering, DocEng 2011, Mountain View, California, USA, pp. 81–84. ACM (2011). www.docear.org

Zenios, M., Holmes, B.: Knowledge creation in networked learning: combined tools and affordances. CSALT/Educational Research, Lancaster University

Miertschin, S.L.: Mind maps as active learning tools. JCSC **21**, 4 (2006)

Wheeldon, J.: Framing experience: concept maps, mind maps and data collection in qualitative research. Internship Instructor George Mason University

Faubert, J.: Adjunct Professor Simon Fraser University (2009). Wheeldon. http://creative commons.org/licenses/by/2.0

Beel, J.: Evaluating the CC-IDF citation-weighting scheme: how effectively can 'Inverse Document Frequency' (IDF) be applied to references, Corinna Breitinger, Stefan Langer

von Guericke, O.: University Magdeburg, Department of Computer Science, Germany

Prediction and Analysis of Sun Shower Using Machine Learning

Nadeem Sarwar[1]([envelope]), Junaid Nasir[1], Syed Zeeshan Hussain Shah[4],
Alishba Ahsan[1], Sameer Malik[2], Sarousha Nasir[1], M. Zafar Iqbal[1],
and Asma Irshad[3]

[1] Department of Computer Science,
Bahria University, Lahore Campus, Lahore, Pakistan
Nadeem_srwr@yahoo.com, junaid.jans@gmail.com,
alishbaahsan127@gmail.com, sapisces97@gmail.com,
zafarkarmani6@gmail.com
[2] Department of Computer Science, University of Sialkot, Sialkot, Pakistan
Sameer.malik@uskt.edu.pk
[3] Department of Life Science, University of Management & Technology,
Lahore, Pakistan
asmairshad76@yahoo.com
[4] Department of Software Engineering, University of Sialkot, Sialkot, Pakistan
zgellani@gmail.com

Abstract. Climate is the absolute most occasions that influence the human life
in each measurement, running from nourishment to fly while then again it is the
most tragic wonders. In this manner, expectation of climate wonders is of significant enthusiasm for human culture to keep away from or limit the devastation
of climate risks. Climate forecast is unpredictable because of clamor and missing
qualities dataset. Various endeavors were made to make climate forecast as
precise as would be prudent, yet at the same time the complexities of commotion
are influencing exactness. In this paper, the five-year rainfall record of weather is
used for predicting the rainfall by calculating the performance and accuracy
through 10 cross-fold validation technique. Its initial step is gathering, isolating,
sorting, and detachment of datasets dependent on future vectors. Arrangement
strategy has numerous calculations, some of them are Support Vector Machine
(SVM), Naïve Bayes, Random Forest, and Decision Tree. Prior to the execution
of each strategy, the model is made and afterward preparing of dataset has been
made on that model. Learning the calculation created model must be fit for both
the information dataset and estimate the records of class name. Various classifiers, for example, Linear SVM, Ensemble, Decision tree has been utilized and
their precision and time broke down on the dataset. At last, all the calculation
and results have been determined and analyzed in the terms of accuracy and
execution time.

Keywords: Classification · Naïve Bayes · Decision tree · SVM · Confusion
matrix

© Springer Nature Singapore Pte Ltd. 2020
I. S. Bajwa et al. (Eds.): INTAP 2019, CCIS 1198, pp. 181–186, 2020.
https://doi.org/10.1007/978-981-15-5232-8_16

1 Introduction

During the process of inferring knowledge from datasets we use data mining techniques [1]. It has three fundamental methods known as Classification, Clustering and Association Rule mining. Grouping of datasets is one of the most confused undertakings in pre-time. Arrangement of information is finished by three stages which are preparing set, deflect mine class traits and objective. Taken information is constantly circulated into 2 sections preparing set and testing information and for right expectation 10 cross overlay system is utilized generally [2–4]. Rainfall prediction is used for forecasting of weather. The state of atmosphere for a particular location is predicted by machine learning algorithms. It is one of the most scientific and challenging problems from the last century, which is due to two main factors one is human activities and second is opportunism created by various technological advances.

Information mining (some of the time called information or information revelation) is the movement of dissecting information from exceptional points of view and truncation into helpful information data that can be utilized to expand the income, diminish cost and both. Information mining programming is individual and has number of coherent instruments for breaking down the information. It permits the clients to break down information from different measurements or points and survey the affiliations perceived. Actually, the information mining is the procedure of choice relationships or examples between fields in gigantic social databases. It is the electronic utilization of specific systems/calculations in trains to perceive specific model from the immense informational collections.

The examination work is created by means of learning origination by utilizing PC part of territory information mining called as machine learning.

Climate anticipating thought about two techniques,

(a) The experimental methodology
(b) The dynamical methodology.

The experimental methodology is the principal approach and it depends on frequency of analogs and is again and again alluded by meteorologists as simple gauging. It is a lot valuable methodology for anticipating neighborhood scale atmosphere conditions whenever recorded information's are plenteous.

The other hand on dynamical methodology depends on conditions and forward recreations of the impression and is over and over alluded to as PC demonstrating. It is as it were helpful for demonstrating huge scope climate conditions wonder and may not predicts impermanent climate capably. The larger part meteorological procedures often show fleeting and spatial variability. To experience of issues of nonlinearity of physical procedures, inconsistent spatial and fleeting reach and uncertainty in limitation gauges

In this paper, classification techniques are applying on weather dataset to analyses and prediction of weather, there will be rain tomorrow or not. We will measure their accuracy rate along with execution time [5–8]. The dataset is taken from Kaggle Repository (https://www.kaggle.com/datasets), that is a public dataset repository.

2   Review of Literature/Algorithm Study

The utilization of examples in prescient models is a subject that has been internal a great deal of mindfulness lately. Example mining can help to acquire models for arranged areas, for example, charts and groupings, and has been anticipated as a way to discover increasingly great and progressively interpretable models. Even with the tremendous measure of productions focused on this territory, it considers then again that a synopsis of what has been fulfilled right now not there. This work presents our perspective on this creating region. The fundamental convictions of example mining that are critical when digging designs for models and make accessible an outline of example based arrangement techniques. In inventory these techniques other than the ensuing extents: (1) regardless of whether they post-process a pre-figured situate of examples or iteratively execute design mining calculations; (2) whether they settle on designs model autonomously or whether the example choice is guided by a model. Audit the outcomes that have been gotten for every last one of these strategies [9].

Meteorologists advancement and break down atmosphere estimates utilizing mind flight in order to watch the practices of and relationship with atmosphere highlights. Right now led with meteorologists in result convey jobs, we perceived and endeavored to manage two noteworthy successive difficulties in climate nebulous vision: the work of clashing and over and again ineffective visual encoding rehearses cross ways a huge scope of perceptions and an absence of hold up for straight envisioning how differing climate depiction describe over an assortment of potential estimate results. Right now, a grouping of the effort and information associated with meteorological estimating, we expect a lot of acquainted default programming decisions that join existing meteorological shows with effective representation arrangement, and we make longer a lot of systems as an essential advance toward sincerely envisioning the correspondences of various highlights over a gathering figure. We speak the consolidation of these foundation enthused about an intentional model apparatus, and just as impersonate on the various reasonable difficulties that happen when working with climate information [10, 11].

Combination of two or more than two classifiers is known as ensemble classifier. The ensemble learning has an increasing interest in the computational educations society by generating better quality results as compared to the single hypothesis model [12–14]. Incremental learning algorithm has an ability to learn from the new incoming instances even after the classifier is already generated. It learns the novel information and preserves formally acquire knowledge without accessing the formally seen data so far [15, 16]. One of the biggest benefits of incremental model is it is space and time-efficient. But, while training it requires the small stable time per sample, there should be only one sample at the time in memory, it builds the model by scanning the database and preserve previously obtained data. The advantage of using incremental ensemble is that it uses more than one classifier and multiple hypotheses which will be combined by using voting rule [17].

3 Methodology

For the prediction and analysis of weather forecasting, we perform the steps mentioned in the Fig. 1.

Data Collection, Data preprocessing, Dimensional Reduction, Suitable clustering Algorithm, Verification of data and Forecasting are major components of our methodology.

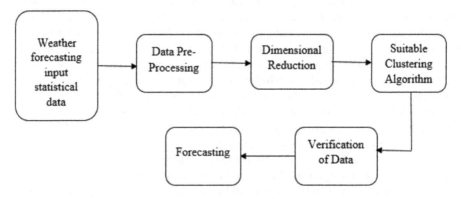

Fig. 1. General forecasting block diagram

The weather Australia datasets are going to be classified. Dataset name, number of instances, attributes and classes are given as follows (Table 1):

Table 1. Dataset used for classification

Dataset	No. of attributes	No. of instances	Response
Aus – Weather	24	142193	Rainfall

4 Results on Applied Algorithms

The selected 22 features show the accuracy 100% in fine tree, medium tree, and coarse tree. In logistic regression 71.9% accuracy is achieved in linear support with 10 features, vector machine 71.4% is achieved using 10 features and quadratic support vector machine 69.1% results are achieved using 10 features.

Using cubic SVM 67.4%, fine Gaussian SVM 71.4% results are achieved. In medium Gaussian support vector machine and coarse Gaussian support vector machine is also shown 71.4% results with 10 features. Using ensemble (boosted trees) and ensemble (bagged trees) shows the 69.3% accuracy with 10 features shown in Fig. 2 (Table 2).

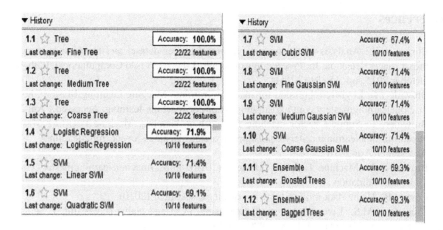

Fig. 2. Algorithm results

Table 2. Best results given by algorithms on datasets

Dataset	Best algorithm	Accuracy	Prediction speed	Training time	True positive rate for class 1 & class 2	False negative rate for class 1 & class 2	Positive prediction value for class 1 & class 2	False discovery rate for class 1 & class 2
Weather Aus	Decision tree algorithm	78.7%	~490000 obs/sec	10.267 s	100%, 100%	0%, 0%	100%, 100%	0%, 0%

The above table shows the dataset name as "Weather Aus" take 10.267 s take training time with 490000 obs/sec prediction speed. Decision tree algorithm shows 78.7% accuracy.

5   Conclusions

In this paper, we analyzed the performance of 12 classifiers, all of them are described above. Performance factors such as classification accuracy, recall, precision, f-measure, speed and execution time are compared. From the experimental results, it is found that the different algorithms are best for different types of datasets. For our dataset tree algorithm proved best and gave 78.7% accuracy because our dataset was consists of 24 attributes and around 1.5 lac instances. Tree algorithm makes rules and performs well on wide and large datasets. In future, we use this algorithm for the prediction and analysis of lungs diseases, kidney dieses and for the critical kidney dieses based creatinine range.

References

1. Borges, L.R.: Analysis of the wiscons in breast cancer dataset and machine learning for breast cancer detection. In: Proceedings of XI Workshop de Visão Computational, 05th–07th October 2015, pp. 15–19 (2015)
2. Brownlee, J.: Logistic regression for machine learning. Machine Learning Mastery. https://machinelearningmastery.com/logistic-regression-for-machine-learning. Accessed 1 Apr 2016
3. Brownlee, J.: Support vector machine for machine learning. Machine Learning Mastery. https://machinelearningmastery.com/support-vector-machines-for-machine-learning/. Accessed 1 Apr 2016
4. Brownlee, J.: Machine Learning Mastery (2018). https://machinelearningmastery.com/k-fold-cross-validation
5. Cortez, P.: Using data mining for wine quality assessment (2010)
6. Vijayarani, M.S.: Liver disease prediction using SVM and Naive Bayes. Int. J. Sci. Eng. Technol. Res. (IJSETR) 4(4), 816-820 (2015)
7. Olaniyi, E.O.A.: Liver disease diagnosis based on neural networks. In: Advances in Computational Intelligence, pp. 48–53 (2015)
8. Woods, W.P.K.: Combination of multiple classifiers using local accuracy estimates. IEEE Trans. Pattern Anal. Mach. Intell. 19(4), 405–410 (1997)
9. Zhou, C., Cule, B., Goethals, B.: Pattern based sequence classification. IEEE Trans. Knowl. Data Eng. 28(5), 1285–1298 (2016)
10. Quinan, P.S., Meyer, M.: Visually comparing weather features in forecasts. IEEE Trans. Vis. Comput. Graph. 22(1), 389–398 (2016)
11. Sheena Angra, S.A.: Machine learning and it's applications: a review. In: 2017 International Conference on Big data and Computational Intelligence, pp. 57–60 (2017)
12. Ahmed, F., et al.: Wireless mesh network IEEE 802.11 s. Int. J. Comput. Sci. Inf. Secur. 14(12), 803–809 (2016)
13. Aslam, N., Sarwar, N., Batool, A.: Designing a model for improving CPU scheduling by using machine learning. Int. J. Comput. Sci. Inf. Secur. 14(10), 201 (2016)
14. Bilal, M., Sarwar, N., Saeed, M.S.: A hybrid test case model for medium scale web based applications. In: 2016 Sixth International Conference on Innovative Computing Technology (INTECH), pp. 632–637 (2016)
15. Bajwa, I.S., Sarwar, N.: Automated generation of express-g models using NLP. Sindh Univ. Res. J. -SURJ (Sci. Ser.) 48(1), 5–12 (2016
16. Cheema, S.M., Sarwar, N., Yousaf, F.: Contrastive analysis of bubble & merge sort proposing hybrid approach. In: 2016 Sixth International Conference on Innovative Computing Technology (INTECH), pp. 371–375 (2016)
17. Sarwar, N., Latif, M.S., Aslam, N., Batool, A.: Automated object role model generation. Int. J. Comput. Sci. Inf. Secur. 14(9), 301–308 (2016)

Electroencephalography Based Machine Learning Framework for Anxiety Classification

Aamir Arsalan[1]([⊠]), Muhammad Majid[1]([⊠]), and Syed Muhammad Anwar[2]

[1] Department of Computer Engineering,
University of Engineering and Technology Taxila, Taxila, Pakistan
{aamir.arsalan,m.majid}@uettaxila.edu.pk
[2] Center for Research in Computer Vision (CRCV), University of Central Florida,
Orlando, FL 32816, USA
s.anwar@knights.ucf.edu

Abstract. Anxiety is a psycho-physiological phenomenon related to the mental health of a person. Persistence of anxiety for an extended period of time can manifest into anxiety disorder, which is a root cause of multiple mental health issues. Therefore, accurately detecting anxiety is vital using methods that are automated, efficient and independent of user bias. To this end, we present an experimental study for the classification of human anxiety using electroencephalography (EEG) signals acquired from a commercially available four channel headset. EEG data of 28 participants are acquired for a duration of three minutes. Five different feature groups in time domain are extracted from the acquired EEG signals. Wrapper method of feature selection is applied, which selects features from two feature groups among the five feature groups initially extracted. Classification is performed using logistic regression (LR), random forest (RF), and multilayer perceptron (MLP) classifiers. We have achieved a classification accuracy of 78.5% to classify human anxiety by using the RF classifier. Our proposed scheme outperforms when compared with existing methods of anxiety/stress classification.

Keywords: Anxiety · Electroencephalography · Feature extraction · Feature selection · Classification

1 Introduction

All individuals are prone to face situations causing stress or anxiety in daily life activities. This affects the quality of life of a person which is related to the level of stress or anxiety being faced. Stress and anxiety are considered to be the same in general perception, despite the fact that there is a difference between these two states. In particular, anxiety and stress have different origin, but have physical and mental indications which are mostly similar (such as headaches, uneasiness, tension, high blood pressure and sleeplessness) [2,13]. It is important to understand the difference between the two states so that an appropriate action

© Springer Nature Singapore Pte Ltd. 2020
I. S. Bajwa et al. (Eds.): INTAP 2019, CCIS 1198, pp. 187–197, 2020.
https://doi.org/10.1007/978-981-15-5232-8_17

can be taken for prevention and cure. Stress is generally provoked as a result of an external stimulus (e.g., deadline of a project, a quarrel with a friend or a financial crisis) and it diminishes away once the stressful situation goes away. Stress is categorized into two categories i.e., instantaneous (acute stress) and chronic (long-term stress) [14].

Anxiety is an individual reaction to stress and its origin lies within the internal emotional state of a human being and the response to unknown potential threats that could occur in future (e.g., before appearing for an exam or before taking some important decisions). Unlike stress, anxiety persists even after the cause of its origin goes away. A prolonged persistence of anxiety can transform into anxiety disorder, which can cause serious damage to a person's mental and physical health. According to a report of American Psychological Association (APA), various forms of anxiety disorders are the most commonly faced mental issue in the United State population. These include social anxiety, phobias, post-traumatic stress disorder (PTSD), and obsessive-compulsive disorder. Anxiety is categorized into two types: i) state anxiety and ii) trait anxiety. State anxiety corresponds to a frightening arousal in the current situation. A situation might seem frightful to some individuals, whereas for someone else the same situation may be an exciting. Trait anxiety of a person is the inherent response of an individual to a threatening situation and it is consistent throughout a person's life [20]. People who have a higher trait anxiety level tends to have more frequent episodes of state anxiety and are highly exposed of being targeted by anxiety disorders [17].

The level of anxiety can be quantified using both subjective and objective measures. Subjective measures include an interview with a psychologist and filling of standard questionnaires developed by researchers and psychologists (Beck anxiety inventory (BAI) [9], state trait anxiety inventory (STAI) [9], and hospital anxiety and depression scale-anxiety (HADS-A) [9]). These measures could be unreliable in multiple cases such as when a subject is illiterate, or the questions are not answered correctly. It is in these situations, when objective measures are preferred and are more reliable as compared to subjective evaluations. Objective measures of anxiety either include physical examination (facial expression [5], eye blink [16]) or physiological measures (galvanic skin response [4], heart rate variability [1], electroencephalography (EEG) [21] and cortisol [7]).

In [6], a study to analyze changes in the EEG signal of a subject recorded in response to watching video clips was presented. The study concluded that individuals in relaxed state had a higher asymmetry index as compared to individuals who were in a state of anxiety. A relationship between features from EEG and photoplethysmogram (PPG) signals and the anxiety level of a person was presented in [21]. It was found that wavelet coefficients of alpha and beta band were significantly correlated with anxiety level of an individual. It was observed that subjects with low mathematical anxiety had an increased cortical activity in the frontocentral and centroparietal brain locations as compared to individuals facing higher mathematical anxiety [11]. An EEG based headband for anxiety alleviation was proposed in [8]. The headband was successful in identifying and reducing the beta band amplitude associated with the anxiety level of a person.

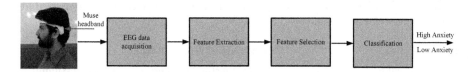

Fig. 1. The proposed machine learning framework for anxiety classification using EEG signals.

Most of the existing studies try to establish the relationship between anxiety level of a person and the physiological signals and have used medical grade EEG devices. To the best of our knowledge, no study for the classification of trait anxiety using a commercially available EEG headset has been proposed. In this study, the STAI questionnaire was filled by participants and the overall score was used for assigning labels. This threshold-based method gave the ground truth for supervised learning. EEG signals of participants were acquired after the filling of the questionnaire. A total of five different time domain feature groups were extracted from the acquired data, which was subjected to a feature selection algorithm for the selection of optimum feature subset. The selected features were classified into low and high level of anxiety using supervised learning. The major contributions of this paper are,

1. A new machine learning framework for the classification of human anxiety using a commercially available EEG headset was proposed.
2. Effect of feature selection algorithm for improvement of classification accuracy and the reduction of feature vector length was analyzed.

The rest of the paper is organized as follows. In Sect. 2, the proposed methodology and experimental setup used to classify the anxiety level is presented. In Sect. 3, experimental results are discussed, followed by conclusion in Sect. 4.

2 Methodology and Experimental Setup

Figure 1 shows the proposed machine learning framework for anxiety classification. It is a four-step process, which includes EEG data acquisition, feature extraction, feature selection, and classification. The details of each step are given in the following subsections.

2.1 EEG Data Acquisition

EEG data of 28 participants (13 males and 15 females) with age ranging from 18 to 40 years were recorded for the experimental study. None of the volunteered participants had any mental disorder and physical illness. The experiment for this study was designed in accordance to the Helsinki declaration. All the participants were having a minimum of 12 years of education. The participants were explained the experimental procedure and an informed consent was signed by

Table 1. Time domain feature groups and their mathematical representation used for human anxiety classification.

Feature group	Mathematical representation
Maximum value	$s_{max} = max(s(t))$, where s_{max} is the maximum value of the signal $s(t)$.
Maximum absolute value (MAV)	$MAV = max(|s(t)|)$
Signal peak-to-peak value (S_{pp})	$s_{pp} = max(s(t)) - min(s(t))$, where $min(s(t))$ is the minimum value of the signal $s(t)$.
Signal sum	$S = \sum_N s(t)$, where N is the total number of samples
Signal energy	$E = \sum_N |s(t)|^2$

them. Participants filled the STAI questionnaire. STAI is a questionnaire developed by the psychologists and is used to measure the state and trait anxiety of an individual. The questionnaire has two parts i.e., first part for measuring the state anxiety, and second part for measuring the trait anxiety. Each part of the questionnaire has 20 questions with an answer ranging from 0 to 4. A value of 0 means that a particular condition does not exist at all and a value of 4 means that a particular feeling is strongly present. The total score of the subject is obtained by the addition of the individual score of each question that can range from 0 to 80. Trait anxiety part of the questionnaire is used in this study.

EEG signal of the participants were recorded for a duration of three minutes in an open eye condition while sitting on a comfortable chair in a noise free and temperature-controlled room. The data acquisition was performed using a four channel Interaxon Muse headband having four electrodes located at $TP9$, $AF7$, $AF8$, and $TP10$. The MuseMonitor mobile application recorded the signals as the headset was connected through a Bluetooth connection. Noise removal of the recorded EEG signal was achieved by an on-board driven right leg feedback circuit between the frontal electrodes and the reference electrode Fpz.

2.2 Feature Extraction

Feature extraction was performed by extracting five time-domain feature groups from the acquired EEG signals. These features included maximum value, maximum absolute value, signal peak to peak value, signal sum, and signal energy. Four feature values from the four channels ($AF7$, $AF8$, $TP9$ and $TP10$) of the EEG headband were obtained for each feature group. A brief description of each feature along with its mathematical description is given in Table 1. A feature vector of dimension 28 × 20 was obtained from the feature extraction process, where 28 represent the number of instances and 20 is the feature vector length.

2.3 Feature Selection

Feature selection was applied to the extracted features for selecting the most appropriate subset of features. The aim of feature selection is to identify a group of features among all extracted features, which have the highest correlation with the class labels. In this study, wrapper method [12] for feature selection was used, which uses best fit search algorithm for searching the optimum set of features [15]. A subset of features was chosen and the machine leaning model was trained on these features. Based on the findings of the previous model, the decision of adding or removing features from the subset is taken. The selection of optimum set of features was formulated as a search problem in which different combination of features were prepared, evaluated and compared to other combinations, thus selecting the subset of features resulting in the highest classification accuracy. Forward selection approach for wrapper method was used in this study, which is an iterative approach with no initial features. The model was iteratively populated with features improving the classification performance, until the point, when adding a new feature does not improve the performance of the algorithm any further.

2.4 Classification

In this study, three different classifiers were used to classify trait anxiety of subjects into two levels using EEG signals. The details of the classifiers are given in the following subsections.

Logistic Regression (LR): Logistic regression is a powerful classification algorithm, which is able to predict the probability of the output classes using a transform called 'logit transform'. LR has been used in a wide range of stress and anxiety classification studies [3]. The algorithm works by finding out a coefficient for each input value, which is plugged into a linear regression model and is transformed via a logistic function. The implementation of the logistic regression classifier in our study used ridge estimator regularization. The regularization method simplified the model by minimizing number of coefficients learned by the model.

Multilayer Perceptron (MLP): Multilayer perceptron is an artificial neural network-based classifier that classifies instances on the basis of back propagation and has been used recently in stress studies [3]. A perceptron is the basis of larger neural networks and is made of inputs and corresponding weights. An activation function takes the input and multiplies them with the corresponding weights to produce an output. A multilayer perceptron is a kind of neural network that consists of at least three nodes which are arranged in input, hidden and output layers. Each of the nodes except the input node is a neuron with a non-linear activation function. The activation function combines the input at a neuron in a weighted manner in addition to bias to produce the output. The activation function for MLP used in our study was the sigmoid function.

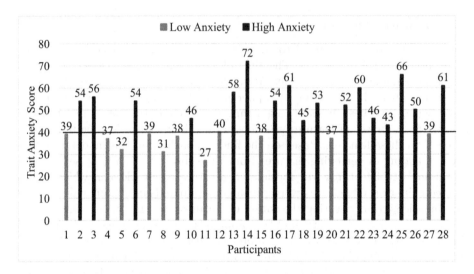

Fig. 2. Participant's labelling into low and high anxiety group based on their trait anxiety score. (Color figure online)

Random Forest (RF): Random forest is a commonly used classifier for both regression and classification tasks and has been explored in different studies for classification of stress condition [10]. As the name suggests, RF create a forest of decision tress in a random manner. It is a supervised machine learning algorithm, which builds multiple decision trees and then merge them together to produce a more accurate and reliable prediction. The hyper parameters of the random forest are same as decision tree or a bagging classifier. Unlike decision tree, while searching for the most important feature in splitting a node, it chooses the best feature among a random set of features which results in a better prediction model.

3   Experiments and Results

3.1   Data Labelling

The participants of the experiment were categorized into low anxiety and high anxiety classes on the basis of trait anxiety score. Subjects having a score ranging from 0–40 were labelled in low anxiety class and scores ranging from 41–80 were labelled in high anxiety class. Figure 2 shows the trait anxiety score of all the participants and are divided into two classes (as shown by the coloured bars). The number of participants in low anxiety and high anxiety class is 11 and 17 respectively. The average trait anxiety score of all the participants is 47.6.

3.2   Evaluation Parameters

A 10-fold cross validation was applied in order to check the classifier performance, which was evaluated in terms of accuracy, precision, recall, F-measure, and kappa statistics. The classification performance in terms of mean absolute error (MAE), root mean square error (RMSE), relative absolute error (RAE) and root relative square error (RRSE) magnitude was also calculated. Accuracy of a classifier is given as the number of correct predictions out of total predictions given by the classifier. Mathematically accuracy is calculated as,

$$Accuracy = \frac{TP + TN}{TP + TN + FP + FN}, \tag{1}$$

where TP, TN, FP, FN depicts true positive, true negative, false positive, and false negative respectively. Precision is defined as the number of correct positive predictions out of the total number of positive predictions. Mathematically it is calculated as,

$$Precision = \frac{TP}{TP + FP}, \tag{2}$$

Recall identifies the number of true positives correctly identified. Mathematically it is calculated as,

$$Recall = \frac{TP}{TP + FN}. \tag{3}$$

F-measure is defined as the harmonic mean of the recall and precision. Mathematically it is given as,

$$F - measure = 2 \times \frac{Precision \times Recall}{Precision + Recall}. \tag{4}$$

Kappa statistics is the measure of how better a classifier is performing when compared to the performance of the classifier that makes a random guess according to the frequency of each class. Mathematically it is calculated as,

$$k = \frac{p_o - p_e}{1 - p_e}, \tag{5}$$

where p_o and p_e are the observed and the expected agreement values. MAE error is the mean value of all the absolute errors. Absolute error was obtained by taking the difference of the actual and the predicted value and then taking the absolute value of the difference. Mathematically it is calculated as,

$$A = \sum_{i=i}^{N} \frac{|O_i - A_i|}{N}, \tag{6}$$

where O_i and A_i are the observed and the actual values, respectively and is the total number of observations. RMSE is the square root of the mean square error (MSE) value. Mathematically RMSE is calculated as,

$$RMSE = \sqrt{\sum_{i=i}^{N} \frac{(O_i - A_i)}{N}}, \tag{7}$$

Table 2. Performance parameters of classification algorithms for anxiety level classification.

Classification algorithm	Correctly classified	Incorrectly classified	Classification accuracy (%)	Kappa statistics	Precision	Recall	F-Measure
MLP	20	8	71.4	0.31	0.80	0.71	0.66
LR	20	8	71.4	0.31	0.80	0.71	0.66
RF	**22**	**6**	**78.5**	**0.52**	**0.81**	**0.78**	**0.77**

RAE of the classifier is calculated as,

$$
RAE = \frac{\sum\limits_{i=i}^{N}|O_i - A_i|}{\sum\limits_{i=i}^{N}|MO_i - A_i|}, \tag{8}
$$

where MO_i and O_i is the mean of the value. RRSE of the classifier is defined as,

$$
RRSE = \frac{\sum\limits_{i=i}^{N}(O_i - A_i)^2}{\sum\limits_{i=i}^{N}(MO_i - A_i)^2}, \tag{9}
$$

In this study, anxiety of a participant was classified using EEG signals acquired with a commercially available headset. A total of 20 features were extracted from the acquired EEG signals and feature selection was applied on the extracted features. The wrapper method algorithm for feature selection gave a feature subset of six features from two different feature groups, which include signal sum and signal energy. Signal sum feature subset included EEG features

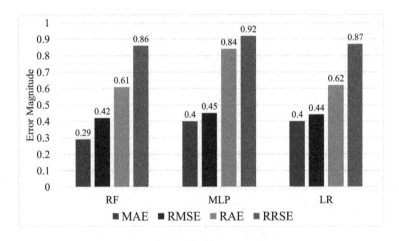

Fig. 3. Error magnitudes of different classification algorithms used.

Table 3. Performance comparison of the proposed scheme with state-of-the-art methods for human anxiety/stress classification.

Method, year	Number of participants	Modality used	Accuracy (classes)	Feature vector length	Classification algorithm
[18], 2017	28	EEG	71.40% (2)	180	Naive Bayes
[21], 2016	20	EEG, PPG	62.5 % (3)	09	PCA-kNN
[19], 2015	28	EEG	71.42% (2)	1440	SVM
Proposed, 2019	28	EEG	78.5% (2)	06	RF

from only three channels i.e., $TP9$, $AF7$ and $AF8$ feature. Whereas, signal energy feature subset included EEG features from only three EEG channels i.e., $AF7$, $AF8$ and $TP9$ features. It was observed that maximum classification accuracy is achieved when this selected subset of features was used for classification. This also resulted in a feature vector length reduction from 20 to 6 and a reduced data matrix of dimension 28 × 6. The selected feature groups were used for classification of anxiety into two levels using three different classifiers.

Table 2 gives the performance comparison of three classifiers used for anxiety classification. Our results show that RF gives the best classification performance, where we achieved an accuracy of 78.5%. In comparison, with MLP and LR the proposed system achieved an accuracy of 71.4% with both classifiers. With RF classifier, we achieved the highest F-measure, precision, recall and kappa statistics value in comparison to other classifiers. The classifiers performance in terms of MAE, RMSE, RAE, and RRSE is shown in Fig. 3. We observed that random forest classifier has the lowest error magnitude for MAE, RMSE, RAE and RRSE as compared to the other two classifiers. This finding is in agreement with the fact that RF classifier has the highest classification accuracy and hence the lowest error magnitudes.

3.3   Discussion

Table 3 presents the performance comparison of the proposed scheme with state-of-the-art methods for the classification of human stress and anxiety. The proposed algorithm was evaluated in terms of the number of participants in the experiment, classification accuracy, feature vector length and the modality used. All studies (Table 3) except [21] used EEG signals, whereas [21] used a combination of EEG and PPG signals for classification of anxiety. Human stress quantification studies using EEG headset is presented in [18] and [19]. A very huge feature vector consisting of 180 and 1440 features is used in [18] and [19], respectively. Study in [21] reduced the feature vector length by using only 9 features for quantification of anxiety at the cost of low classification accuracy. The proposed anxiety classification scheme not only improved the classification accuracy but also reduced the feature vector length, which is the major contribution of the study. Anxiety classification accuracy in the literature using only EEG features have a maximum accuracy of 71.42% and 62.5% for two- and three-class problem respectively, where the three-class problem used both EEG and PPG signals. Whereas, the proposed scheme has a classification accuracy of 78.5% for anxiety classification using a commercially available EEG headset with a significantly reduced feature vector length as compared to the other studies in the literature.

4   Conclusion

In this paper, a machine learning framework to classify human anxiety level using a commercially available EEG headset is presented. Five groups of time domain features namely, maximum, maximum absolute value, signal peak to peak value, signal sum, and signal energy are extracted from the recorded EEG data. Wrapper method for feature selection is applied on the extracted features and three different classification algorithms are used to classify the trait anxiety. It is concluded that RF classifier gives the best classification performance of 78.5% when compared to LR and MLP classifiers. The proposed scheme achieves highest classification accuracy when compared with the methods available in the literature.

References

1. Alvares, G.A., et al.: Reduced heart rate variability in social anxiety disorder: associations with gender and symptom severity. PLoS One **8**(7), e70468 (2013)
2. Arsalan, A., Majid, M., Butt, A.R., Anwar, S.M.: Classification of perceived mental stress using a commercially available EEG headband. IEEE J. Biomed. Health Inform. **23**, 2257–2264 (2019)
3. Asif, A., Majid, M., Anwar, S.M.: Human stress classification using eeg signals in response to music tracks. Comput. Biol. Med. **107**, 182–196 (2019)
4. Bradley, M.M., Silakowski, T., Lang, P.J.: Fear of pain and defensive activation. PAIN® **137**(1), 156–163 (2008)
5. Giannakakis, G., et al.: Stress and anxiety detection using facial cues from videos. Biomed. Signal Process. Control **31**, 89–101 (2017)
6. Giannakakis, G., Grigoriadis, D., Tsiknakis, M.: Detection of stress/anxiety state from EEG features during video watching. In: 2015 37th Annual International Conference of the IEEE Engineering in Medicine and Biology Society (EMBC), pp. 6034–6037. IEEE (2015)
7. Hek, K., et al.: Anxiety disorders and salivary cortisol levels in older adults: a population-based study. Psychoneuroendocrinology **38**(2), 300–305 (2013)
8. Jayakkumar, S., Chong, E., Yeow, C., et al.: A wearable, EEG-based massage headband for anxiety alleviation. In: 2017 39th Annual International Conference of the IEEE Engineering in Medicine and Biology Society (EMBC), pp. 3557–3560. IEEE (2017)
9. Julian, L.J.: Measures of anxiety: state-trait anxiety inventory (STAI), beck anxiety inventory (BAI), and hospital anxiety and depression scale-anxiety (HADS-A). Arthritis Care Res. **63**(S11), S467–S472 (2011)

10. Kalimeri, K., Saitis, C.: Exploring multimodal biosignal features for stress detection during indoor mobility. In: Proceedings of the 18th ACM International Conference on Multimodal Interaction, pp. 53–60. ACM (2016)
11. Klados, M.A., Simos, P., Micheloyannis, S., Margulies, D., Bamidis, P.D.: ERP measures of math anxiety: how math anxiety affects working memory and mental calculation tasks? Front. Behav. Neurosci. **9**, 282 (2015)
12. Kohavi, R., John, G.H.: Wrappers for feature subset selection. Artif. Intell. **97**(1–2), 273–324 (1997)
13. Martin, E.I., Ressler, K.J., Binder, E., Nemeroff, C.B.: The neurobiology of anxiety disorders: brain imaging, genetics, and psychoneuroendocrinology. Psychiatr. Clin. **32**(3), 549–575 (2009)
14. Miller, L.H., Smith, A.D., Rothstein, L.: The Stress Solution: An Action Plan to Manage the Stress in Your Life. Pocket, New York (1994)
15. Pearl, J.: Heuristics: Intelligent Search Strategies for Computer Problem Solving. Addison-Wesley, Reading (1984)
16. Pinkney, V., Wickens, R., Bamford, S., Baldwin, D.S., Garner, M.: Defensive eyeblink startle responses in a human experimental model of anxiety. J. Psychopharmacol. **28**(9), 874–880 (2014)
17. Rector, N.A., Bagby, R.M., Huta, V., Ayearst, L.E.: Examination of the trait facets of the five-factor model in discriminating specific mood and anxiety disorders. Psychiatry Res. **199**(2), 131–139 (2012)
18. Saeed, S.M.U., Anwar, S.M., Majid, M.: Quantification of human stress using commercially available single channel eeg headset. IEICE Trans. Inf. Syst. **100**(9), 2241–2244 (2017)
19. Saeed, S.M.U., Anwar, S.M., Majid, M., Bhatti, A.M.: Psychological stress measurement using low cost single channel EEG headset. In: 2015 IEEE International Symposium on Signal Processing and Information Technology (ISSPIT), pp. 581–585. IEEE (2015)
20. Waters, A.M., Zimmer-Gembeck, M.J., Farrell, L.J.: The relationships of child and parent factors with children's anxiety symptoms: parental anxious rearing as a mediator. J. Anxiety Disord. **26**(7), 737–745 (2012)
21. Zheng, Y., Wong, T.C., Leung, B.H., Poon, C.C.: Unobtrusive and multimodal wearable sensing to quantify anxiety. IEEE Sens. J. **16**(10), 3689–3696 (2016)

Decision Support Systems

A Doctor Recommendation System Using Patient's Satisfaction Analysis

Haseeb Iftikhar[1], Syed Muhammad Anwar[1(✉)],
and Muhammad Majid[2]

[1] Software Engineering, University of Engineering and Technology,
Taxila, Pakistan
s.anwar@uettaxila.edu.pk
[2] Computer Engineering, University of Engineering and Technology,
Taxila, Pakistan

Abstract. The relationship between a patient and doctor is very important in the field of healthcare. It is essential for proper diagnosis and treatment of diseases. There is a substantial effort devoted in devising techniques to identify the key opinion leaders using active surveying methods based on acquiring and integration of secondary and primary data. The results are validated by describing a physician nomination network. A recommender framework has been proposed in various studies for seeking doctors in accordance with a patient characteristic, including their symptoms and preferred choices. The purpose of this study is to identify doctors based on the satisfaction of patients. The data is collected using the patient satisfaction questionnaire (PSQ-3) for subjects located in Pakistan. This data is further analyzed for devising a collaborative filtering-based recommender algorithm using K-nearest neighbor (KNN) similarity measure to recommend doctors to patients in the form of a sorted ranked list.

Keywords: Key opinion leader · Surveys · Doctor performance · Patient preference · Recommender systems · Ranking

1 Introduction

There is a saying "if symptoms persist then consult the doctor" that is commonly heard by health aficionados and this reminder is seen almost on daily basis in commercials, billboards, and pamphlets for medicines and vitamins. One of the most important decisions that a patient must make is which doctor to consult and how to determine whether the doctor is reliable [1]. Pakistan being a developing nation is facing many challenges in digitalizing the healthcare and adoption of new technology. Hence, there are minimal platforms for the patients, where they can find a reliable doctor based on their medical condition and satisfaction [2]. The factors that are part of this problem include low literacy rate, weak socio economic and financial condition, poor medical facilities, attitude of healthcare professionals (HCP), and awareness among patients regarding the symptoms and diseases [3].

© Springer Nature Singapore Pte Ltd. 2020
I. S. Bajwa et al. (Eds.): INTAP 2019, CCIS 1198, pp. 201–209, 2020.
https://doi.org/10.1007/978-981-15-5232-8_18

A recommender system for the identification of doctors for specific diseases is developed using data mining techniques [1]. They have used doctor profiles and academic publications for the collection of data and used unsupervised aggregation approach for integrating ranking features to identify doctors for five gynaecological disease categories. An integrated hybrid framework for recommending doctors to patients based on patient characteristics, illness symptoms, and preferences have been proposed [4]. They have suggested two techniques, one is for user matching model to find similarities between user's consultations and doctor's profiles and the second is for doctor's quality, experience and dynamic user opinions about doctors. A hybrid doctor recommendation algorithm is proposed based on their analysis of the appointment platform, where the doctor performance model is built by analyzing a doctor reception and appointment system. The patient preferences model is built based on the current historical reservation choices. In [5], active surveying methodology is used to address the problem of identifying key opinion leaders in the medical field. They have collected data from primary and secondary sources for describing physician nomination network in which physicians are surveyed to nominate other physicians from whom they will get professional advice and then used this information with secondary data describing publication history (citation and co-authorship), as well as hospital affiliation information.

In [6], a social network named HealthNet is presented in which patients can share their experiences regarding hospitalizations, consultations with doctors and medical histories. They have used this information for suggesting doctors and health facilities to those patients, which match similar medical history and symptoms via a recommender system. A physician ability has been evaluated by using diabetic patient satisfaction, which is rarely observed in public diabetes clinics of Pakistan [7]. The patient satisfaction depends upon the technical expertise of a doctor, interpersonal aspects, communication, consultation time, and access/availability. In [8], the expectations and satisfaction of the patients for the implementation of electronic health record (EHR) system is studied. They have interviewed patients and physicians and found that patients found it very positive to use technology in the consultation and treatment process. The role of patient satisfaction survey as an efficient tool for quality improvement in healthcare organization [9] has studied. They have discussed relationship of dependent and independent attributes in patient satisfaction that helps in the improvement of health care organizations. The impact of gender in medical communication and satisfaction of patient in Japanese context have been studied [10]. Their research shows that communication between patients and doctors is of key importance in delivering quality treatment.

The problem of how to identify reliable doctor based on patient satisfaction has been rarely addressed in Pakistan. A survey was conducted among people from different educational backgrounds and corporate sector in 2 cities, Rawalpindi and Islamabad, under 4 specialties i.e., dermatologist, ears nose and throat (ENT) specialist, eye specialist and urologist to get the satisfaction score for the doctors they have visited. The patient satisfaction survey (PSQ-3) is used for this purpose, which is widely used to measure the satisfaction of patients in chronic diseases [11]. The main contributions of this study are as follows,

- The research in this study focuses on patient satisfaction questionnaire to make patients the key part of doctor finder process. Seven dimensions of patient satisfaction are examined to evaluate the likeness and dislikes of the treatment received by patients.
- Collaborative filtering is used to utilize the satisfaction data and generate doctor predictions based on similar patients.
- This study is the first attempt to the best of our knowledge to find reliable doctor in the south Asia region, based on patient satisfaction.

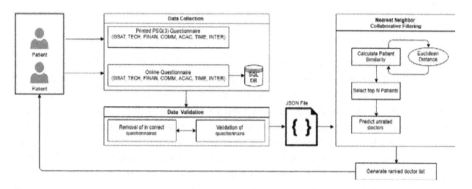

Fig. 1. The proposed doctor recommendation system architecture

2 Proposed Methodology

The proposed system utilizes patient data, satisfaction survey and doctor information to generate a ranked list of recommended doctors for a patient in four specialties i.e., dermatologist, ENT specialist, eye specialist, and urologist. For each specialty, similar patients are identified using K-nearest neighbor algorithm. Figure 1 represents the steps involved in the proposed system. The details are presented in the following subsections.

2.1 Recommendation Process

The heart of collaborative filtering is to find similarity among users, which is used for selecting neighbors. In DRS the interest of a user is to find a reliable doctor based on the satisfaction scores from multiple patients. The user similarity d is calculated based on the Euclidian distance given as,

$$d(p,q) = d(q,p) = \sqrt{(q_1 - p_1)^2 + (q_2 - p_2)^2 + (q_3 - p_3)^2 + \cdots + (q_n - p_n)^2}$$
$$= \sqrt{\sum_{i=1}^{n}(q_i - p_i)^2} \quad (1)$$

where $\mathbf{p} = (p_1, p_2,..., p_n)$ and $\mathbf{q} = (q_1, q_2,..., q_n)$ are two users in the Euclidean n-space. The relationship between $\mathbf{p}$ and $\mathbf{q}$ may involve a direction (for example, from $\mathbf{p}$ to $\mathbf{q}$), so when it does, this relationship can itself be represented by a vector given as,

$$q - p = (q_1 - p_1, q_2 - p_2, \ldots, q_n - p_n) \tag{2}$$

After calculating the similarity score of each person, a weighted satisfaction score by similarity is calculated by multiplying the satisfaction score for each doctor with the similarity score and then all the similarity scores are summed up. After having the similarity sum and total satisfaction score for each doctor, satisfaction score is divided by similarity sum to produce the ranking of each doctor. The final list is sorted in descending order and displayed to the patient as predicted ranked list of reliable doctors based on the other patient's satisfaction.

2.2 Location of the Study

The study was carried out in 2 cities including, Rawalpindi and Islamabad. Satisfaction forms under 4 specialties i.e., Dermatologist, ENT Specialist, Eye Specialist and Urologist were distributed among 200 patients for 20 doctors, where 5 doctors were selected randomly for each specialty. A total of 625 survey forms were filled by the patients. Patient satisfaction questionnaire was distributed among patients containing questions and a Likert scale of 5 to mark their answers from strongly agree to strongly disagree. The study was conducted in 2 phases. In the first phase from November 2017 to March 2018, patients, doctors and medical domain analysts were interviewed to understand the problems faced by patients in accessing the doctor. In the second phase from April 2018 to August 2018, satisfaction forms in both online and printed form were provided to patients to fill out their satisfaction score against their visits to multiple doctors.

2.3 Research Instrument

The PSQ-3 comprising of favorable and unfavorable opinion was adopted [11]. The main variables of research study from PSQ-3 are technical expertise (TECH), interpersonal aspects (INTER), and time spent with doctor (TIME), general satisfaction (GSAT), communication (COMM), access/availability/convenience (ACAC). The questionnaire comprises of 50 questions and patients have provided their answers as "Strongly Agree", "Agree", "Uncertain", "Disagree" and "Strongly Disagree" to evaluate the quality of treatment provided by the doctor. The questionnaire was distributed among patients belonging to different backgrounds. Additional information i.e., age, sex, marital status, education, occupation, location and disease was also obtained.

2.4 Research Scoring and Statistical Analysis

As per specifications from RAND, each item represents a favorable or unfavorable opinion about medical care. All questions were answered on a scale of 5 where

1 = strongly agree and 5 = strongly disagree. The precoding of favorable items was done to achieve higher satisfaction. The responses obtained on printed survey forms and online survey forms were recorded on spreadsheets and then those spreadsheets were analyzed using statistical analysis tool SPSS version © 25.

Correlation test was performed between 7 variables GSAT, TECH, TIME, ACAC, FINAN, INTER and COMM to check if there is a degree of relationship between variables. The significance level (2-tailed) is 0.01, which shows that there is significant positive relationship between variables, which means that as one variable goes up or down so will the other one.

Table 1. Regression analysis for the patient satisfaction questionnaire.

Model summary				
Model	R	R Square	Adjusted R Square	Std. Error of the Estimate
1	.832ᵃ	0.692	0.688	2.610
a. Predictors: (Constant), ACAC, TIME, COMM, INTER, FINAN, TECH				

Regression analysis was performed to understand which independent variables are related to the dependent variables, and to explore the form of these relationships. Regression analysis can be used to infer causal relationships between the independent and dependent variable and the results are presented in Table 1.

The statistic R indicates that there is 83% correlation between dependent and independent variables. The statistic R-square indicates that 69% of the variance in the dependent variable that the independent variables explain collectively. R-squared measures the strength of the relationship between the model and the dependent variable on a convenient 0–100% scale. R-squared is always between 0 and 100%, where 0% represents a model that does not explain any of the variation in the response variable around its mean. The mean of the dependent variable predicts the dependent variable as well as the regression model. On the other hand, 100% represents a model that explains all the variation in the response variable around its mean.

3 Experimental Results

The average score from all 7 parameters GSAT, TECH, TIME, ACAC, FINAN, INTER and COMM was calculated. A group-based rank ranging from 1 to 5 was calculated based on the comparison of average value in 7 groups. Since there were 7 parameters in the questionnaire and maximum value for each parameter was 5 so for this reason 5 groups were created as shown in Table 2.

To calculate the actual recommendations, the group-based rank is normalized further by dividing each rank value to the maximum value in each specialty. The mean

Table 2. Different groups and ranks for the recommendation system.

Groups	Rank
1–7	1
8–14	2
15–21	3
22–28	4
29–35	5

value is calculated in each specialty and compared to the normalized value. If this mean is greater than or equal to the normalized value, the corresponding doctor is recommended and if this is less than the normalized value, then doctor is not recommended

The ranked score for each doctor in each specialty is used in the collaborative filtering-based recommender algorithm. Patient similarity is calculated using KNN classifier and a ranked list of predicted doctors is generated. The predicted score for doctors in each specialty that is ranging from 1.0 to 5.0 is again normalized by dividing each value to the maximum value in each specialty. After that the mean is calculated in each specialty and compared to the normalized value. If the mean is greater or equal to the normalized value, the doctor is marked as recommended and if this is less than the normalized value then the doctor is marked as not recommended.

The recorded values for actual recommendation from satisfaction survey and predicted recommendation from recommender algorithm are used in confusion matrix to evaluate the precision and accuracy of the algorithm and the process. The actual recommendation from survey are compared with the predicted recommendations, which are calculated using the proposed algorithm. The confusion matrix is given in Fig. 2. The performance is evaluated using precision and accuracy, given as,

$$\text{Precision} = \text{TP} / (\text{TP} + \text{FP}) \tag{3}$$

$$\text{Accuracy} = (\text{TP} + \text{TN}) / (\text{P} + \text{N}) \tag{4}$$

where TP, FP, and TN represent the true positive, false positive and true negative respectively. The results are shown in Fig. 2 for various threshold values, where NRCM stands for no recommendation and RCM stands for recommendation. For a threshold of 0.85 the precision and recall are 0.78 and 0.67, respectively. At 0.87 threshold, the precision and accuracy are 0.71 and 0.70, respectively. The performance increases until 0.92 threshold accuracy, where the precision and recall are 0.77 and 0.73, respectively.

A receiver operating characteristic curve (ROC), is a graphical plot that illustrates the diagnostic ability of a binary classifier system as its discrimination threshold is varied. The ROC curve is created by plotting the true positive rate against the false positive rate at various threshold settings. Figure 3 shows the plot of cross tabulation result obtained at various threshold values.

Actual * Predicted Cross tabulation

Threshold 0.85		Actual RCM		
		NRCM	RCM	Total
Predicted RCM	NRCM	90	95	185
	RCM	64	235	299
	Total	154	330	484

Actual * Predicted Cross tabulation

Threshold 0.87		Actual RCM		
		NRCM	RCM	Total
Predicted RCM	NRCM	29	18	47
	RCM	125	312	437
	Total	154	330	484

Actual * Predicted Cross tabulation

Threshold 0.92		Actual RCM		
		NRCM	RCM	Total
Predicted RCM	NRCM	67	45	112
	RCM	87	285	372
	Total	154	330	484

Fig. 2. Confusion matrices for various threshold values.

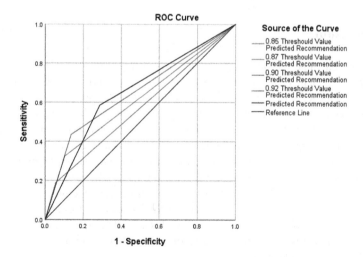

Fig. 3. The ROC performance analysis of the proposed model

4 Discussions

In this paper, we have examined the satisfaction of patients in seven dimensions towards doctors working in public health clinics and hospitals, of 2 cities Rawalpindi and Islamabad located in Pakistan. The variation of patient satisfaction across gender, marital status and age has also been assessed. Correlation analysis shows that all the seven dimensions general satisfaction, technical ability, financial aspects, time, communication, interpersonal aspects and accessibility and convenience are playing their role in determining the satisfaction level. Higher the scores of these variables higher will be the satisfaction. The data presented in this research is consistent with recent study [7], which suggests that patient satisfaction can be used in determining doctor's reliability. For identification of doctor, patient illness symptoms and preferences have been recorded by [4] and proposed user similarity matching model. Surveying methods have also been used by researchers to identify the physician by describing a physician nomination network and co-author citation relationship [5]. The positive a patient's experience is regarding the expertise of a doctor, the higher the level of satisfaction thus help in good identification of doctor [12, 13]. Awareness among patients regarding healthcare is very important as poor and uneducated patients have shown less interest in the survey process. Because of no understanding of the medical terminologies and diseases they responded to questionnaire answers as "Un Certain or Disagree" which affects the satisfaction level [14]. If the sense of vulnerability, privacy can be reduced, and patient's autonomy and patient knowledge can be enhanced then it can lead to improvements in patient satisfaction [15]. We have developed a recommender system that utilizes the satisfaction score of the patient and using collaborative filtering nearest neighbor similarity matching model to generate ranked list of doctors.

5 Conclusion

The study reveals that the doctor identification and recommendation to patients could aid in solving patient health related problems. Recommending a reliable doctor to a patient will help generating positive relationship between both entities. Patient satisfaction can be used as an advanced attribute towards the identification of doctors. The study revealed that satisfaction of the patient in seven dimensions can also help doctors in enhancing their capabilities. The patients only feel dissatisfaction when no specialist doctor is available for consultation, when doctors do not understand the problem of the patient and are unable to diagnose the disease properly. The proposed method using patient satisfaction and the recommender algorithm to generate a ranked list of doctors helps in this process. The future direction in this process is to enhance the recommending capabilities of the algorithm to allow diseases, demographics information like age, sex, marital status, education, occupation and medicines information to refine the results of finding reliable doctor.

References

1. Guo, L., Jin, B., Yao, C., Yang, H., Huang, D., Wang, F.: Which doctor to trust: a recommender system for identifying the right doctors. J. Med. Internet Res. **18**(7), e186 (2016)
2. Ittefaq, M., Iqbal, A.: Digitization of the health sector in Pakistan: challenges and opportunities to online health communication: a case study of MARHAM social and mobile media. Digit. Health **4**, 2055207618789281 (2018)
3. Ahmed, J., Shaikh, B.T.: An all-time low budget for healthcare in Pakistan. J. Coll. Phys. Surg. Pak. **18**, 388 (2008)
4. Jiang, H., Xu, W.: How to find your appropriate doctor: an integrated recommendation framework in big data context. In: 2014 IEEE Symposium on Computational Intelligence in Healthcare and e-health (CICARE), pp. 154–158 (2014)
5. Sharara, H., Getoor, L., Norton, M.: Active surveying: a probabilistic approach for identifying key opinion leaders. In: IJCAI Proceedings-International Joint Conference on Artificial Intelligence, p. 1485 (2011)
6. Narducci, F., Lops, P., Semeraro, G.: Power to the patients: the HealthNetsocial network. Inf. Syst. **71**, 111–122 (2017)
7. Jalil, A., Zakar, R., Zakar, M.Z., Fischer, F.: Patient satisfaction with doctor-patient interactions: a mixed methods study among diabetes mellitus patients in Pakistan. BMC Health Serv. Res. **17**, 155 (2017)
8. Duarte, J.G., Azevedo, R.S.: Electronic health record in the internal medicine clinic of a Brazilian university hospital: expectations and satisfaction of physicians and patients. Int. J. Med. Inform. **102**, 80–86 (2017)
9. Al-Abri, R., Al-Balushi, A.: Patient satisfaction survey as a tool towards quality improvement. Oman Med. J. **29**, 3 (2014)
10. Noro, I., Roter, D.L., Kurosawa, S., Miura, Y., Ishizaki, M.: The impact of gender on medical visit communication and patient satisfaction within the Japanese primary care context. Patient Educ. Couns. **101**, 227–232 (2018)
11. Ware Jr., J.E., Snyder, M.K., Wright, W.R., Davies, A.R.: Defining and measuring patient satisfaction with medical care. Eval. Prog. Plann. **6**, 247–263 (1983)
12. Abioye Kuteyi, E., Bello, I.S., Olaleye, T., Ayeni, I., Amedi, M.: Determinants of patient satisfaction with physician interaction: a cross-sectional survey at the Obafemi Awolowo University Health Centre, Ile-Ife, Nigeria. S. Afr. Family Prac. **52**, 557–562 (2010)
13. Deledda, G., Moretti, F., Rimondini, M., Zimmermann, C.: How patients want their doctor to communicate. a literature review on primary care patients' perspective. Patient Educ. Couns. **90**, 297–306 (2013)
14. Irfan, S., Ijaz, A., Farooq, M.: Patient satisfaction and service quality of public hospitals in Pakistan: an empirical assessment. Middle-East J. Sci. Res. **12**, 870–877 (2012)
15. Rocque, R., Leanza, Y.: A systematic review of patients' experiences in communicating with primary care physicians: intercultural encounters and a balance between vulnerability and integrity. PLoS ONE **10**, e0139577 (2015)

Analysis of White Blood Cells Using Hematology Counts

Syeda Mariyum[✉], Syed Gulfraz, Tayyaba Sultana,
and Khalid Masood

Lahore Garrison University, Lahore, Pakistan
mariyum002@yahoo.com, gulfraz.naqvi@gmail.com,
tayyabaanwar66@gmail.com, kmasoodk@gmail.com

Abstract. This research paper shows the detailed structure of white blood cells in a human body. The complete description includes the cell types, their functions and the importance of white blood cells in human body with the procedure of its calculation. How much amount of WBCs is required to the body and how to calculate them is a very important question. Hematology analyzer analyses the count of blood cells and its types in the human blood. Its usage and types are also discussed in this article. Another important aspect that has been covered in this article is the statically rate of the patients suffering from diseases that happens due to the deficiency of WBCs or due to the access about of WBCs in human blood. These patients are divided in three main categories of child, adult and old age patients. The microscopic images are found from different research laboratories for the better understanding of what happens to the cells when the amount of WBCs increases or decreases from the normal rage in different age groups of a human life.

Keywords: White blood cells · Hematology analyzer · Blood count · Blood cancer · Leukemia

1 Introduction of Complete Blood Count (CBC)

1.1 White Blood Count

Complete blood count or cbc which is extremely common in clinical rotations. It is very commonly ordered lab or blood panel that gives us some good information about the cell types in a patient's blood. And those cell types are divided into three main types:

- White blood cells
- Red blood cells
- Platelets

Here, it is seen that first column is the cell type, the second column is the blood of the patient verses like serum or urine, tissues or something like that [1]. That is the least lab report. The third column is the value for that cell type. The fourth column is giving units. And the last column is reference or normal range. So, this means that the first row

© Springer Nature Singapore Pte Ltd. 2020
I. S. Bajwa et al. (Eds.): INTAP 2019, CCIS 1198, pp. 210–221, 2020.
https://doi.org/10.1007/978-981-15-5232-8_19

represents the total white blood cells taken from the patient's blood. There were 4.6 times ten to the third or in other words 4600 white blood cells per micro liter and the normal range for total white blood cells in the blood is between 4.6 thousand up to 11.03 thousand cells per micro liter. This was the first row and the next five rows are individual cell types or cell lines and all are white blood cells.

Here this article will discuss about White blood cells as shown in Table 1.

Table 1. This table shows the cell types and its ranges.

WBC	Blood	4.6	$X10^3$/mcL	(4.6–11.0)
Neutrophils	Blood	52.1	%	(55–75)
Lymphocytes	Blood	31.8	%	(15–41)
Monocytes	Blood	13.5	%	(1–10)
Eosinophils	Blood	2.2	%	(0–4)
Basophile	Blood	0.4	%	(0–2)

It is clearly shown that the units are given as a percentage. So, of the 4600 white blood cells per micro liter of blood were 52.1% of those. 4600 were neutrophils and 31.8% of those were lymphocytes and so on. If at all those percentages up they should equal to 100% or the total of 4600 white blood cells [2]. The first group of white blood cells is neutrophils [3].

1.2   Neutrophils

The neutrophils alone with the *eosinophils* and *basophils* together makeup the *polymorphonuclear cells, (PMNs)*. They have this name because the nucleus in these cells. The nuclei are multi lobulated which means that instead of having a consolidated circular nucleus the nuclei make little lobules or kind of globs connected together by string like structure that is a thin strands nucleus [4]. The nucleus of a neutrophil has about 2 to 5 of these lobes or labules. Neutrophils are by far the most abundant type of white blood cells that are seen in the blood and play a major part in a reaction to acute inflammation [5].

Mostly inflammation as a result bacterial infection. In fact, the pus that is squeezed out an abscess is mostly neutrophils. Neutrophil part of CBC diagnose the following:

1. Bacterial infections: bacterial infections would cause the neutrophil count to go up. This is called neutrophilia also called neutrocytosis as well but it is not as common.
2. Acute Stress
3. Burns
4. Leukemia
5. Steroid use
6. Rheumatoid arthritis

The kind of diagnosis along with a decreased neutrophil count also called a neutropenia is as followed:

1. Folate/B12 deficiency
2. Aplastic anemia
3. Chemotherapy
4. Chlorampheniol/Sulfonamides

1.3   Eosinophils

These cells are named eosinophils because they stain very well with the dye eosin which is a red dye [6]. These cells are slightly redder than the cells of neutrophils [7]. Some things that might cause the eosinophil count to change up or down these things are as followed:

1. Allergies
2. Parasitic infections
3. Leukemia
4. Polyarteritis nodosa
5. Autoimmune disease

The kind of diagnosis along with a decreased eosinophils count also called eosinopenia is as followed:

1. Nutritional deficiency
2. Glucocorticoids

1.4   Basophils

Basophils are named because the way they take up basic dyes. In this case giving the cells a very blue color [8]. If a basophil is observer under a microscope I looks a lot like a mast cell. But the function is going to be a little bit different. Basophils participate in allergic response and give some of the symptoms that are experienced with an allergic reaction [9]. The causes of basophilia are as followed:

1. Allergic reactions
2. Chronic myelogenous leukemia (CML)
3. Hodgkin's disease
4. Oral contraceptive pills

The kind of diagnosis along with a decreased Basophilia count also called Basopenia is as followed:

1. Nutritional deficiency
2. Gluocorticoids

1.5 Monocytes

Monocytes are the largest of all the white blood cells [10]. That makes then a little bit easier to pick out on a microscope slide. They can approach three times the diameter of red blood cells. So a lot like neutrophils, monocytes are very useful little cells. However unlike neutrophils play more of a role in the chronic inflammation or infection vice the neutrophil which have more of an acute phase cell [11]. Almost half of them are stored in our spleen and are released when an infection is sensed. They are very motile so they are able to get themselves into the tissue, here the inflammation or infection is [12]. They have three important jobs.

1. Phagocytose
2. Antigen presentation
3. Cytokine production

The causes of Monocytosis are as followed:

1. Chronic inflammatory state
2. Stress
3. Cushing's syndrome
4. Viral infection
5. Sarcoidosis

The kind of diagnosis along with a decreased Monocytosis count also called Monocytopenia is as followed:

1. Aplastic Anemia
2. Acute Myeloid Leukemia(AML)
3. Glucocorticoids
4. Myelotoxic drugs

1.6 Lymphocytes

There are three main types of lymphocytes: T-cell: they are further divided into subtypes

1. Helper
2. Cytotoxic
3. Memory

B-cell: they are further divided into subtypes

1. Plasma
2. memory

1.7 Natural Killer Cells (NK)

The causes of Lymphocytosis are as followed:

1. Viral infection
2. Leukemias: CLL, All
3. Adrenal insufficiency

The kind of diagnosis along with a decreased Lymphocytes count also called Lymphocytes is as followed:

1. HIV - destroys T cells (CD4+)
2. Aplasti anemia
3. Gluocorticoids
4. Systemic Lupus Erythematosus (SLE)
5. Rheumatoid Arthritis

2 Procedure of Analysis

2.1 Automated CBC or Hematology Analyzer

Automated CBC or Hematology analyzer is computerized and highly specialized equipment for CBC. CBC or complete blood count which is perhaps the most common routine base line investigation. It analyses the parameters like Red Blood Cells, the white blood cell count, platelets count, hemoglobin level, hematocrit levels (HCT/PCV) [13].

WBC differential Count in percentage and absolute values Platelets indicator like

- Platelets Distribution Width
- Average Volume of Platelets
- Large cell Ratio of Platelets
- Platelet Crit

Automated CBC or Hematology analyzers are of two types based on the type of differential White Cell count. A 3-part differential cell counter can be

- 3-part differential cell counter works on the principal of the electrical impedance to determine the size and volume of the cells
- Differentiates WBC's into neutrophils, lymphocytes and mixed cell counts
- The difference between monocytes, eosinophils and basophils cannot be recognized by this.

A 5-part differential cell counter can be as the rule of flow cytometry and volume conductivity scatter to examine granularity, diameter and inner problems of cells present in human blood is the principle on which 5 part differential cell counter works.

- CBC analyser aspirates the required quantity of blood
- Quantifies
- Classifies
- Describe cell populations using both electrical and optical techniques

There are three main technologies used in CBC or Hematology Analyzers are

- Photometric methods for Hb

RBCs are lysed and Hemoglobin released in converted to a colored measurable compound. A monochromatic light source is then passed through the solution [14]. The absorption of the solution is measured by photosensor in hemoglobin flow cell calculating the hemoglobin concentration.

2.2 Electrical Impedance (Coulter Principle)

The white blood cells, red blood cells and platelets count is done by the principle of electrical impedance. The amplitude of each and the cell volume are directly proportional to each other. The different cell components are depicted in different histograms. As per the size distribution. Histograms are the graphical representation of numerical data of the different cell population counted on the cell counter. The X axis represents the size of the cells in fL which was assessed by the amplitude of the pulse. The smallest cells that is the platelets are represented on the left side of histogram and the largest cells that is red blood cells are represented on the right side. On peripheral smear assess cell size by diameter in mue. Whereas automated analyzer assess volume of cells represented in fL. However mixed cell population of eosinophil, monocytes is seen left of neutrophils on the histogram because of shrinkage of these cells due to stromatolyser effect.

2.3 Flow Cytometry by VCS (Volume Conductivity Scatter)

This is used in 5 part analyser for white blood cell differential counts. This technique is more expansive, due to expansive reagents. It gives detailed information about the morphology of white blood cells. The principle of flo cytometry by VCS, beside using impedance principle, 5 part differential cell counters employ flo cytometric principles. Through hydrodynamic focusing, cells are passed through an aperture in a single file. A laser beam then focuses on these cells as they pass in a single file. The absorbance and scattered light generated by each cell is measured at multiple angles to determine the cell's granularity, diameter, and inner complexity. Based on size, granularity and nuclear structure, the 5 types of white blood cells are separated in three dimensional space and depicted as scattergrams.

2.4 Scattergrams

It is a three dimensional pictorial display of the distribution of WBC based on their size and granularity causing light scatter. In a scattergrams the X axis represents the granularity of cells. And Y axis represents the size of the cells.

2.5 Fluorescent Flow Cytometry

It is used in some instruments where fluorescent reagents are used to identify specific cell populations. The principle is same as that for VCS, and in addition uses fluorescent dyes to revile the nucleus plasma ratio of each stained cell. The added advantage is the analysis of platelets nucleated RBCs and reticulocyte.

3   Comparison Using Histograms and Microscopic Images

3.1   Data of Old Age Patients

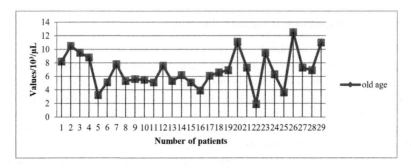

Fig. 1. Old age WBC reports graph

Histogram is the graphical representation of anything. Here is a histogram with a number of old age patients and their rate of platelets in their blood (Fig. 1). There reports are found by CBC test using an analyzer called hematology analyzer. The normal range of white blood cells in the blood of human body is 4–10 ($10^3/\mu L$). Here (a) is the microscopic image that shows normal white blood cells:

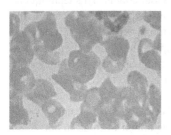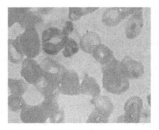

(a) normal white blood cells [15]

The range above this level that is above 10 ($10^3/\mu L$) are the patients of Leukocytosis. The microscopic image below (b) shows the excess amount of white blood cells in the blood:

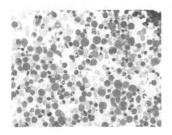

(b) excess amount of white blood cells [15]

Patients below the normal range that is below 4 (10^3/μL) are the patients of leukemia or lymphoma (Fig. 2). Given below (c) is the microscopic image that shows deficiency of white blood cells in blood:

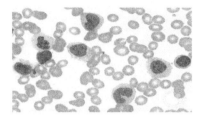

(c) deficiency of white blood cells [15]

3.2   Data for Adult Patients

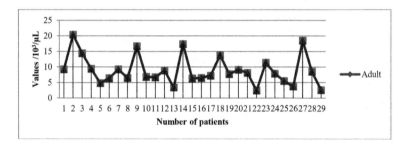

Fig. 2. Adult WBC reports graph

Here is a histogram with a number of adult patients and their rate of white blood cells in their blood. There reports are found by CBC test using an analyzer called hematology analyzer (Fig. 3). The normal range of white blood cells in the blood of human body is 4–15 (10^3/μL). Microscopic image below (d) shows the normal amount of white blood cells in blood:

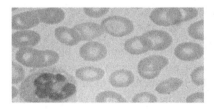

(d) Normal amount of white blood cells [15]

The range above this level that is above 15 $(10^3/\mu L)$ are the patients of Leukocytosis. There is microscopic image (e) that shows excess white blood cells in blood.

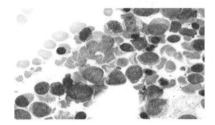

(e) Excess white blood cells [15]

Patients below the normal range that is below 4 $(10^3/\mu L)$ are the patients of leukemia or lymphoma. The microscopic image below shows (f) the deficiency of white blood cells in blood

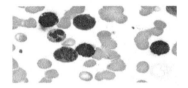

(f) Deficiency of white blood cells [15]

3.3   Data for Infant Patients

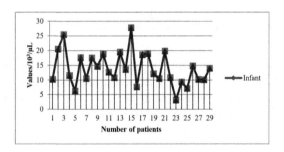

Fig. 3. Infant WBC reports graph

Here is a histogram with a number of infant patients and their rate of white blood cells in their blood. There reports are found by CBC test using an analyzer called hematology analyzer. The normal range of white blood cells in the blood of human body is 10–15 $(10^3/\mu L)$. Here is a microscopic image (g) of normal white blood cells in blood:

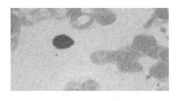 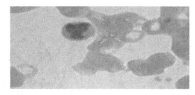

(g) Normal white blood cells [15]

The range above this level that is above 15 ($10^3/\mu L$) are the patients of Leukocytosis. Shown below is the microscopic image (h) of a blood having excess amount of white blood cells:

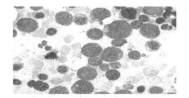

(h) Excess amount of white blood cells [16]

Patients below the normal range that is below 10 ($10^3/\mu L$) are the patients of leukemia or lymphoma. Here is a microscopic image (i) that shows deficiency of white blood cells in the blood:

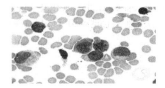

(i) Deficiency of white blood cells [15]

This combined histogram shows the results of old age, adult and infant patients. The rate of white blood cells differs with the age that can be clearly seen in this histogram (Fig. 4).

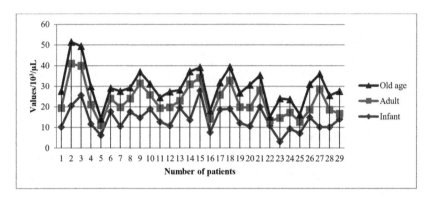

Fig. 4. Combine graph of infant, Adult and old age people WBC reports

4   Conclusions

The presence of WBCs in human blood is very important for the immune system of a body. This article compared three types of patients and the rate of WBCs in their blood. The WBCs rage is not same at different age brackets of life it differs with time. Histogram is the best way of comparing the data and showing the results so for the ease of reader the easiest way has been adopted. The basic research work done in this article is for the microscopic images. The normal and abnormal WBCs in different type of patients are compared and studied. This can be clearly seen in the microscopic images that how different is a cancerous cell from normal cell. This research shows that when body starts suffering the abnormality in WBCs, the cells starts to swell leading to bursting and deforming.

References

1. Diggs, L.W., Sturm, D., Bell, A.: The Morphology of Human Blood Cells. Abbott Laboratories, Abbott Park (1985)
2. Minnich, V.: Immature Cells in the Granulocytic, Monocytic, and Lymphocytic Series. American Society of Clinical Pathologists Press, Chicago (1982)
3. Nilsson, B., Heyden, A.: Model-based segmentation of leukocytes clusters. In: Proceedings of the 16th International Conference on Pattern Recognition
4. Bacus, J.W.: An automate classification of the peripheral blood leukocytes by means of digital image processing. Ph.D. thesis, University of illinois Medical Center, Chicago, Illinois, 19
5. Akenzua, G.I., Hui, Y.T., Milner, R., Zipursky, A.: Neutrophil and band counts in the diagnosis of neonatal infections. Pediatrics **54**, 38 (1974)
6. Rothenberg, M.E., Hogan, S.P.: The eosinophil. Annu. Rev. Immunol. **24**, 147–174 (2006)
7. Wen, T., Mingler, M.K., Blanchard, C., Wahl, B., Pabst, O., Rothenberg, M.E.: The pan-B cell marker CD22 is expressed on gastrointestinal eosinophils and negatively regulates tissue eosinophilia. J. Immunol. **188**, 1075–1082 (2012)

8. Dvorak, H.F., Mihm Jr., M.C.: Basophilic leukocytes in allergic contact dermatitis. J. Exp. Med. **135**, 235–254 (1972)
9. Ito, Y., Satoh, T., Takayama, K., Miyagishi, C., Walls, A.F., Yokozeki, H.: Basophil recruitment and activation in inflammatory skin diseases. Allergy **66**, 1107–1113 (2011)
10. Ingersoll, M.A., et al.: Comparison of gene expression profiles between human and mouse monocyte subsets. Blood **115**(3), e10–e19 (2010)
11. Geissmann, F., Jung, S., Littman, D.R.: Blood monocytes consist of two principal subsets with distinct migratory properties. Immunity **19**(1), 71–82 (2003)
12. Tacke, F., et al.: Monocyte subsets differentially employ CCR2, CCR5, and CX3CR1 to accumulate within atherosclerotic plaques. J. Clin. Invest. **117**(1), 185–194 (2007)
13. Alexander, B.: New hematology analyzers. Clin. Prod. Rev. **3**, 16–23 (1984)
14. Bollinger, P., Drewinko, B.: A quality control program for a computerized, high-volume, automated hematology laboratory. J. Med. Technol. **1**, 633–642 (1983)
15. https://www.hematology.org/

High Performance Simulation of Blood Flow Pattern and Transportation of Magnetic Nanoparticles in Capillaries

Akhtar Ali[1][(⊠)] and Rafaqat Kazmi[2]

[1] Department of Mathematics, Government College University Faisalabad,
Faisalabad, Pakistan
utm.akhtar@gmail.com
[2] Department of Computer Science, The Islamia University of Bahawalpur,
Bahawalpur, Pakistan
rafaqutkazmi@gmail.com

Abstract. In the first place, the paper analyses the blood flow patterns in a capillary during the existence of a uniform external magnetic field by a hybrid CPU/GPU approach. The blood flowing through the capillary is supposed to be Newtonian; while the flow is incompressible and laminar. Magnetic Nanoparticles have been considered as therapeutic agent for the magnetic targeted drug delivery in the defence against cancer. However, the problem is expressed as a boundary value problem containing a system of partial differential equations in order to study the flow field and magnetic Nanoparticles. Finite element discretization is applied to resolve the system of equations which contains a large sparse system of equations requiring high computation. The CPU/GPU method serves as a platform to deal the wide-ranging computations in parallel. Therefore, the solution times can significantly be reduced by this platform as compared to the application of CPU. This allows more effective examination of different mathematical models and their leading parameters. The influence of the magnetic nanoparticle radius R_M, capillary radius R, pressure P, magnetic field intensity H on the velocity profile of blood and magnetic nanoparticles have been investigated in terms of the magnetic field inputs and model. Secondly, the numerical solutions for velocity of blood and velocity of particles are computed along with the observation that an increase in magnetic field leads to increase in the flow pattern. Finally, the simulation concludes that the magnetic parameters have a key role to control the velocity profile.

Keywords: Finite Element Method · CPU-GPU · Parallel computing · Magnetic drug targeting delivery · Magnetic Nanoparticles · MATLAB

1 Introduction

One of the biggest challenges with non-targeted treatment of localized diseases such as cancer is that the therapeutic drug spreads through the circulatory system, leading to low concentrations in the diseased tissue and causing side effects in healthy tissue. While Magnetic Drug Targeting (MDT) is considered a significant proposed technique

© Springer Nature Singapore Pte Ltd. 2020
I. S. Bajwa et al. (Eds.): INTAP 2019, CCIS 1198, pp. 222–236, 2020.
https://doi.org/10.1007/978-981-15-5232-8_20

for handling such problems. MDT aims to solve this problem non-invasively by magnetically guiding the drug particles to the diseased site. An ideal MDT treatment starts with bonding the drug chemically to magnetic particles or inserting magnetic particles in a drug carrier. The magnetic drug particles are injected into the blood stream at a convenient position through this therapy [1]. Unfortunately, this procedure is challenging because, at present, the dynamics of magnetic particles are not well analysed in blood.

Much work has already been contributed to address some of the fundamental questions of magnetic drug targeting. In this context, specific analysis on the up going prospective of the drug targeting through the blood flow by magnetic drug carriers is presented by Cao, Han, Li [2], Shashi Sharma [3], and Katie L. Pitts [4]. Many MDT studies use permanent magnets for steering and capturing of particles owing to their strength, widely availability and cheap price. Both in vitro and in vivo [5] studies have proved that permanent magnets can be very effective in capturing magnetic drug particles if the magnet can be placed close to the target. Other investigations have shown that droplets of Ferrofluid can be controlled in the same way [6]. Some practical works have also been done to optimize the size and orientation of permanent magnets for particle control using a Halbach array [7] and a combination of an externally applied magnetic field with a ferromagnetic wire. Although magnetic particles have been controlled with permanent magnets to some extent, yet there are several disadvantages of their usage. Firstly, the functional range of permanent magnets are short with a narrow region of influence in the circulatory system therefore, the magnetic field cannot control particles deep within the body. Then, physically moving the magnet to change at a certain point in space the only way to fix the magnetic field of a permanent magnet. Then electromagnet field is used through a more flexible technique. By this way, the field can be controlled easily by adjusting the electric current to guide and regulate the particles' flow. It has been proved by experiments that controlling magnetic micro particles is feasible with current electromagnet technology. However, controlling nanoparticles, which are less likely to block micron-sized human capillaries [8, 9] is unrealistic due to overwhelming fluid drag force. Recently, several studies have been published on electromagnet systems specifically designed for MDT that can produce an extremely high magnetic field and gradient in a small region of space [10–13]. For example, Alias N has worked to visualize the growth of tumour based on a large sparse region of space using distributed parallel computing system [14]. Several papers also have been published on CFD simulation of magnetic drug targeting. These include Kenjeres and Stuart Cohen [15] who performed a Lagrangian simulation of magnetic particles in a tube subject to magnetic and drag forces. Yue, Lee, and Afkhani [16] tracked clusters of magnetic particles in Newtonian and shear-thinning fluids, and Kayal and Bandyopadhyay [17] performed a 2D simulation of particles in Newtonian flow with magnetic force applied perpendicularly to the streamwise direction. David, Cole, and Chertok [18] also developed a 2D model for magnetic particle motion, but theirs included hydrodynamic drag, magnetic force, gravity and buoyancy. Cherry et al.

[19] simulated single magnetic particles subject to magnetic force, gravity, stokes drag, and hydrodynamic lift in a straight tube. Finally, Haleh Alimohamadi [20] investigated the Element Simulation. Further, individual forces and fluid properties relevant to magnetic drug targeting have also been analysed by many researchers.

Parallelism has become a new trend in present computations; therefore, scientific problems involve large sparse matrices and complex computation and the microprocessor manufacturers emphasize on enhancing cores rather than increasing single thread performance. Among the many parallel architectures, the most well-known many core architectures are the GPUs and the most common multi core architectures are CPUs [21]. The present trend in scientific computing is to use GPUs for accelerating intensive computations as compared to CPU [22–25]. The GPU market is well established in the computing industry and therefore it is preferred over the other architectures to accelerate the whole or a part of programming code.

A number of researches concentrate completely on porting the FEM subroutines to be executed using GPUs [21, 26]. Other works focus on porting some parts of the FEM program on GPUs. For example numerical integration [27], matrix assembly [28], global FEM matrices and the solution of large sparse linear systems of equation are solved by using GPU [29]. Previous works accelerate the assembly of large sparse FEM matrix [30], such approaches need huge memory of GPU, it means large sized problem needs high capacity of GPUs memory. For this purpose, an expensive GPU with large memory is required. The executed code of hybrid algorithm is compared with its respective serial code executed on CPU to measure the performance of hybrid platform. For this purpose, parallel computing capabilities of hybrid platform using MATLAB 2018 and FEM are analysed in this paper and further the advantage of hybrid platform implementation is observed by using curves.

The comprehensive aim of this study is to explore the dynamics of external force of magnetic particles by simulating their flow through a capillary. The given data address the given problem of trapping magnetic particles in a capillary with steady flow. The parameters of the simulation are chosen to mimic the conditions in a medium-sized capillary where magnetic steering is feasible in a real MDT system. The percentage of particles that could be trapped within the capillary as a function of time is considered a metric of the success of magnetic control. The parameter space of particle injection is varied in order to determine the optimal concentration of particle and flow of blood.

2 Mathematical Model

The mass and momentum conservation equations represent the dynamic of blood flow and particles in the blood vessel. The flow of blood is considered as laminar axisymmetric of a viscous, homogeneous, and incompressible Newtonian fluid in the cylindrical blood vessel as shown in Fig. 1. It is assumed that the flow takes place under the impact of externally applied magnetic field in the direction of x-axis.

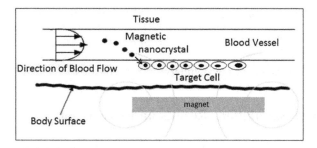

Fig. 1. The mechanism of magnetic nanoparticles that move along with the flow of blood towards the targeted cells.

The flow in the capillary is assumed Hagen-Poiseulle. The electrical conductivity of blood is not considered.

Mass equation

$$m\frac{\partial v}{\partial t} = \mu_0 V_M (M\nabla H)_z + 6\pi\mu R_M (u - v) \tag{1}$$

Momentum equation

$$\rho\frac{\partial u}{\partial t} = -\frac{\partial p}{\partial z} + \mu\left(\frac{\partial^2 u}{\partial r^2} + \frac{1}{r}\frac{\partial u}{\partial r}\right) + \frac{NA}{\rho}(v - u) \tag{2}$$

Where N is number density of suspended nanoparticles and p is the pressure, A is stokes coefficient and ρ is the blood density, m is mass of magnetic nanoparticles and t is time parameter. The dependent variables u and v represent the velocities of blood and magnetic nanoparticles respectively. The pressure gradient is independent on radial coordinate and is defined as in Eq. 3 [31].

$$-\frac{\partial p}{\partial z} = A_0 + A_1 cos\omega t \tag{3}$$

Where A_0 is constant amplitude of pressure gradient, A_1 is the amplitude of the pulsatile component which gives rise to diastolic and systolic pressure.

The initial and boundary conditions are given in Eqs. 4–5 and it is supposed that no flow takes place when system is at rest.

$$u = v = \frac{\partial u}{\partial t} = 0 \quad at\ t = 0 \tag{4}$$

Moreover, the velocity on the capillary wall is taken as:

$$u = v = 0 \quad at \ r = R \tag{5}$$

Where R is the radius of the Capillary.

3 Numerical Simulation, Results and Discussion

Numerical results are presented to explore the effects of different parameters on velocity profile of blood and magnetic nanoparticles in this section. The expression of velocity of blood and nanoparticles are obtained by using Finite Element method and computed data are plotted for different values of time, magnetic field intensity H magnetization M, pressure gradient ∇P and different distances (y) between the magnet and the capillary surface. Some typical values of constants are given in Table 1 [33].

Table 1. Constants and Symbols with their typical values [33]

Variable	Symbol	Units	Value
Kinematic viscosity	υ	m^2s^{-1}	μ/ρ_0
Dynamic viscosity of blood	μ	Kg/ms	$35 * 10^{-3}$
Radius of MNP	R_M	nm	$10 * 10^{-9}$
Radius of capillary	R	m	$3 * 10^{-6}$
Mass of MNP	m	kg	$\rho_p V_M$
Volume of MNP	V_M	m^3	$4/3\pi R_M^3$
Permeability of free space	μ_o	Hm^{-1}	$6\pi * 10^{-7}$
Density of MNP	ρ_p	Kgm^{-3}	$5.1 * 10^3$
Density of blood	ρ	Kgm^{-3}	1060
Magnetization	M	$Nm^{-2}T^{-1}$	$4.5 * 10^3$

In this study the capillary consists of blood with a density $1060\,kg/m^3$ and viscosity value is $3.3 \times 10^{-5}\,Pa.s$. The drug material density value is $5.1 \times 10^2\,kg/m^3$ and viscosity $1 \times 10^{-5}\,Pa.s$. Figure 2 shows velocity profiles of magnetic nanoparticles and blood for different times at different axial positions. The all velocity profiles are same in the sense that they show decrease from their maxima at the axes as one move away from the axis and finally move to zero on the surface of wall. Figure 2 further indicates that velocity of blood and particles show pulsatile dependence with time and reaches the maximum velocity at $t = 0.8$. Simulations demonstrate that shape of blood velocity is concomitant with the graph velocity of magnetic nanoparticles, which is expected as the velocity of blood that brings the magnetic nanoparticles to the targeted site. However, the particles velocity is less as compared to blood due to the drag and other retardation forces. The maximum velocity of blood and particles at the axis is found to be 0.14 and 0.08 respectively. Besides, experiments show that the velocity of blood in capillary varies mainly from 0.05 to 0.15 cm/sec which is agreed with the graphical results as shown in graphs. Finally, graphs show that magnetic nanoparticles offer a much more efficient journey on the site to deliver the drug, along with blood. The radius of capillary and radius of nanoparticles have a key role in velocity profile as shown in Fig. 3. Curves illustrate that flow velocity increases by decreasing capillary radius. It is well experimented that particle preservation rate rises up by increasing the particle diameter and gradient strength of magnetic field. The difference between maximum velocities of magnetic particles is found to be 0.0003 when the capillary radius varies from 3×10^{-4} to 3×10^{-6}. It can be observed that magnetic field can be applied to manage flow rate. The impact of this parameter on velocity of magnetic nanoparticles is demonstrated in Fig. 4. By doubling and triplicating the value of M, as the graph shows, the nanoparticles get rise in velocity up to 0.0013 which is suitable for fatty lump to dissolve in capillary wall. These graphs conclude that by putting on super power magnetic field there is remarkably rise in the velocity. The distance between capillary wall and magnet has a direct impact on velocity profile and is supportive to attract magnetic particles to the blood vessel wall. It is clear from Fig. 5 that lesser the distance between the capillary wall and magnet, greater the velocity of magnetic nanoparticles by which they move backwards to the magnetic region. The variation of particles velocity from distance 2.5 cm to 10 cm is 0.0013340465–0.0013194455. From plots it is clear that velocity profile may be controlled by setting distance between capillary wall and magnet because the magnetic field strength and gradients depend upon the distance between the capillary wall and magnet.

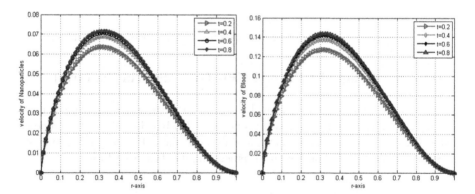

Fig. 2. Velocity profile for blood and magnetic Nano particles for different time.

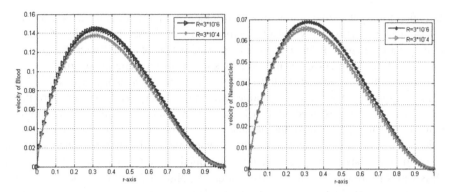

Fig. 3. Effect of the velocity of blood and nanoparticles along radial distance for different values of capillary radius

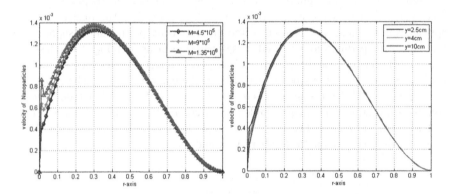

Fig. 4. Variation in velocity of Nanoparticles for different values of magnetization.

4 Implementation of CPU and CPU-GPU (Hybrid Platform)

The main aim in this section is to make a comparison between the computational accuracy and efficiency of GPU-based results and CPU-based results of the proposed model. The programming code is developed using Matlab 2018a. Figure 6 represents the Sequential and parallel algorithm for processing the data using FEM.

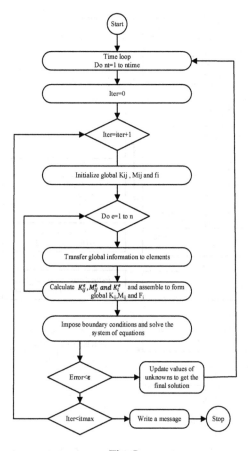

Fig. 5.

Simulations are done on a computer that has 2.10 GHz. Intel(R) Xeon(R) CPU E5-2620 v2, 24 cores and Windows 10, 64-bit operating system. The system has two GPU cards, NVIDIA Quadro K4000, and NVIDIA Tesla K20c. These cards have 3.0 and 3.5 compute capabilities respectively. The CUDA cores of NVIDIA Quadro K4000 and NVIDIA Tesla K20c GPU cards are 768 and 2496 respectively having 3 GB memory. The memory clock rate for both cards is 2808 MHz and 2600 MHz and memory bandwidth is 134 GB/sec.

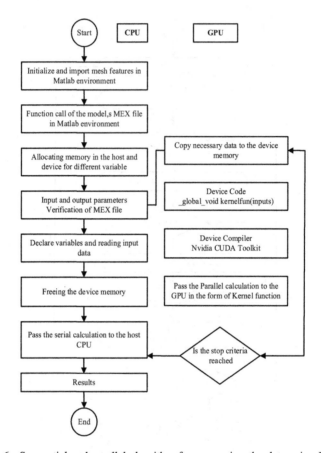

Fig. 6. Sequential and parallel algorithm for processing the data using FEM.

Table 2. Numerical results for sequential performance for a three test cases

Number of elements	Number of unknowns	CPU time	Maximum error	RMSE
1000	20002 * 20002	29143.3258	7.38e−03	5.36e−04
15000	30002 * 30002	33286.7605	4.10e−03	6.57e−04
20000	40002 * 40002	39231.9170	1.46e−01	3.42e−05

Table 2 represents the numerical results of the sequential algorithm for different number of elements. Three test cases are considered to measure the performance evaluation. The first, 2nd and third test case have 1000, 15000 and 20000 number of elements with 20002, 30002 and 40002 unknowns respectively. The Tables 2 also show the direct proportion of matrix size, as the matrix size increases the computational time of CPU also increases.

5   Parallel Results and Discussion

Furthermore, the improvements brought by the GPU acceleration for governing equations are presented in this section. The parallel performance results of numerical schemes for three test cases are shown in Fig. 7. The tests are carried out for large sparse matrices using 1000, 1500 and 2000 number of finite elements. The corresponding number of unknowns are 20002, 30002 and 40002 respectively. The detail solution is generated by storing the time iterations. The initialization and set-up times are also excluded from the time measurements. Thus, the reported execution times represent the computational times spent in solving the model equations. The number of threads per block is taken from 1 to 512 for execution of the kernel.

Figure 7 indicates the execution time for each test case. The execution time decreases as the number of threads per block increases up to 128, subsequently, the execution time increases along the number of threads per block. This happens because of communication overhead process.

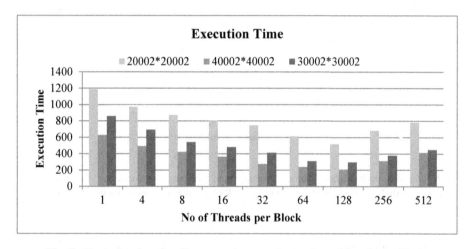

Fig. 7. Execution time for all test cases versus the number of threads per block.

The Speedup and temporal performance are important indicators to measure the performance of any parallel algorithm. The parallel algorithm is considered as the best algorithm if it executes in minimum run time. Temporal performance is measured as the inverse of the run time while the speedup is ratio of CPU time and CPU-GPU time. Speedups and temporal performance are obtained by the GPU w.r.t threads having range from 1 to 512. The performance of numerical method on GPU is presented in terms of speedup and temporal performance in Fig. 8 for three test cases. The speed up for first test case (20002 * 20002), ranges from (32.4499–58.798), for 2nd test case (30002 * 30002), it ranges from (39.2345–74.3203) and for 3rd test case (40002 × 40002), it ranges from (49.5935–85.2950).

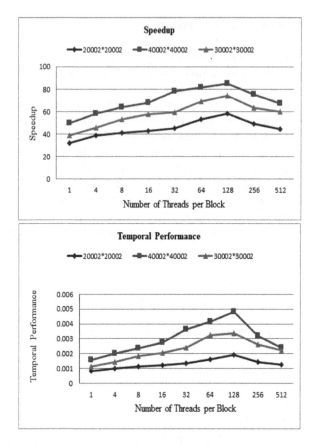

Fig. 8. Parallel performance metric Speedup and temporal performance for number of unknowns 20002 * 20002, 30002 * 30002 and 40002 * 40002 versus number of threads per block.

The speedup is increasing from thread 1 to 128 after that it decreases due to communication overhead (cache ram, register values replacement, bandwidth) in all test cases. The trends of speedup are maximum when a number of threads are 128, later speedup decreases significantly along the number of threads, because of inter-process communication overhead. These increments show the improved parallel performance in terms of speedup. The difference of computational cost also affects the speedup. On the other hand, the temporal performance for 3rd test case is higher as compared to first and 2nd test case. The highest value of temporal performance shows that the computations are calculated in least time. The temporal performance is increasing from thread 1 to 128 after that it decreases due to communication overhead. The high value of temporal performance for large size matrix shows that GPUs are capable to deal large sparse computations.

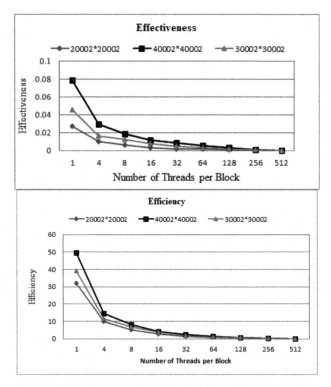

Fig. 9. Parallel performance metric effectiveness and efficiency for number of unknowns 20002 * 20002, 30002 * 30002 and 40002 * 40002 versus number of threads per block.

The effectiveness and efficiency are other important indicators to measure the parallel performance results. The Fig. 9 presents the effectiveness and efficiency of the parallel algorithm for three test cases. The effectiveness in all cases decreases as number of threads increases due to overhead, process congestion and deadlock. In the comparison, the effectiveness for 3rd case is the highest followed by 1st and 2nd case. Additionally, comparing the parallel performance by considering the size of data; the speedup is better when global matrix size is 40002 * 40002 as compared to reduced size 20002 * 20002. This shows that hybrid programs can solve big data more efficiently than CPUs. Other PPIs show good results for large spars systems. Consequently, when the size of data is large the GPU is able to enhance the parallel performance results significantly. These findings confirm the huge potential of using GPUs in large scale computational simulations.

6   Conclusion

In this theoretical paper, an attempt is made to examine various aspects of blood flow and effect of external magnetic field on the magnetic nanoparticles. On the basis of obtained results, it is investigated that the velocity of magnetic nanoparticles and blood may be controlled satisfactorily by the use of external magnetic field. It is also possible to bring down these quantities to any desirable level by increasing or decreasing the magnetic field intensities and other parametric values. The implementation of FEM is done with simplified strategies to achieve results. Other essential solution components are the efficient regeneration of the finite element mesh to solve the time dependent algebraic equations which are obtained by solving space variable. The physical parameters play conspicuous role on the flow in capillary as demonstrated in plots. From the velocity profiles of magnetic nanoparticles, it is observed that a high magnetic field strength is required for targeting a Nano magnetic drug delivery. This requirement is based on decreasing the magnet distance from the capillary as shown in Figs. 5. Since the gradients and strength of magnetic field depend upon the distance between the capillary wall and magnet, therefore, the external magnetic field is more operative for the targets because the body surface is closer to it as compared to the internal parts of the body. In order to control the targeted site more accurately with an aim to get better results of drug transport through blood in capillary, the integrated contribution among theoretical modelling and simulation are useful.

Furthermore, this paper explains our motivation for using GPU accelerators in order to handle computational complexities in the model. We have designed a hybrid CPU/GPU solution for the model solution and obtained satisfactory parallel performance results such as speed ups and temporal performance. The parallel performance results also show that GPU solver is more efficient in large-scale problem simulations. The performance results show significant accelerations by using GPU devices. Thus, numerical experiments show that parallel processing in the finite element allows to reduce time for Simulation. In future research, the present simulation will be used to explore the parameter space of magnetic control and determine whether a stronger or more focused magnetic field gradient would capture magnetic particles more powerfully. Although the GPU is used only in several parts of the algorithm, yet the speed-ups are encouraging which allows us to continue in this direction.

References

1. Derfus, A.M., et al.: Remotely triggered release from magnetic nanoparticles. Adv. Mater. **19**(22), 3932–3936 (2007)
2. Cao, Q., Han, X., Li, L.: Enhancement of the efficiency of magnetic targeting for drug delivery: development and evaluation of magnet system. J. Magn. Magn. Mater. **323**(15), 1919–1924 (2011)
3. Sharma, S., Singh, U., Katiyar, V.: Magnetic field effect on flow parameters of blood along with magnetic particles in a cylindrical tube. J. Magn. Magn. Mater. **377**, 395–401 (2015)
4. Pitts, K.L., Fenech, M.: An analytic study on the effect of alginate on the velocity profiles of blood in rectangular microchannels using microparticle image velocimetry. PLoS ONE **8**(8), e72909 (2013)
5. Mykhaylyk, O., Dudchenko, N., Dudchenko, A.: Doxorubicin magnetic conjugate targeting upon intravenous injection into mice: high gradient magnetic field inhibits the clearance of nanoparticles from the blood. J. Magn. Magn. Mater. **293**(1), 473–482 (2005)

6. Gitter, K., Odenbach, S.: Quantitative targeting maps based on experimental investigations for a branched tube model in magnetic drug targeting. J. Magn. Magn. Mater. **323**(23), 3038–3042 (2011)

7. Sarwar, A., Nemirovski, A., Shapiro, B.: Optimal Halbach permanent magnet designs for maximally pulling and pushing nanoparticles. J. Magn. Magn. Mater. **324**(5), 742–754 (2012)

8. Freund, J., Shapiro, B.: Transport of particles by magnetic forces and cellular blood flow in a model microvessel. Phys. Fluids (1994–Present) **24**(5), 051904 (2012)

9. Saadatmand, M., et al.: Fluid particle diffusion through high-hematocrit blood flow within a capillary tube. J. Biomech. **44**(1), 170–175 (2011)

10. Alexiou, C., et al.: A high field gradient magnet for magnetic drug targeting. IEEE Trans. Appl. Supercond. **16**(2), 1527–1530 (2006)

11. Alexiou, C., et al.: Cancer therapy with drug loaded magnetic nanoparticles—magnetic drug targeting. J. Magn. Magn. Mater. **323**(10), 1404–1407 (2011)

12. Han, X., Cao, Q., Li, L.: Design and evaluation of three-dimensional electromagnetic guide system for magnetic drug delivery. IEEE Trans. Appl. Supercond. **22**(3), 4401404 (2012)

13. Kopcansky, P., et al.: Numerical modeling of magnetic drug targeting. Phys. Part. Nucl. Lett. **8**(5), 502–505 (2011)

14. Alias, N., et al.: The visualization of three dimensional brain tumors' growth on distributed parallel computer systems. J. Appl. Sci. **9**(3), 505–512 (2009)

15. Haverkort, J., Kenjereš, S., Kleijn, C.: Computational simulations of magnetic particle capture in arterial flows. Ann. Biomed. Eng. **37**(12), 2436–2448 (2009)

16. Yue, P., et al.: On the motion of superparamagnetic particles in magnetic drug targeting. Acta Mech. **223**(3), 505–527 (2012)

17. Kayal, S., et al.: The flow of magnetic nanoparticles in magnetic drug targeting. RSC Adv. **1**(2), 238–246 (2011)

18. David, A.E., et al.: A combined theoretical and in vitro modeling approach for predicting the magnetic capture and retention of magnetic nanoparticles in vivo. J. Control. Release **152**(1), 67–75 (2011)

19. Cherry, E.M., Maxim, P.G., Eaton, J.K.: Particle size, magnetic field, and blood velocity effects on particle retention in magnetic drug targeting. Med. Phys. **37**(1), 175–182 (2010)

20. Alimohamadi, H., Imani, M.: Finite element simulation of two-dimensional pulsatile blood flow through a stenosed artery in the presence of external magnetic field. Int. J. Comput. Methods Eng. Sci. Mech. **15**(4), 390–400 (2014)

21. Šimkus, A., Turskienė, S.: Parallel computing for the finite element method in MATLAB. Comput. Sci. Tech. **1**(2), 214–221 (2013)

22. Kirk, D.B., Hwu, W.W.: Programming Massively Parallel Processors: A Hands-on Approach. Newnes, Amsterdam (2012)

23. Alias, N., Sahnoun, R., Malyshkin, V.: High performance computing and communication models for solving the complex interdisciplinary problems on DPCS (2006)

24. Alias, N., Satam, N., Othman, M.S., Che Teh, C.R., Mustaffa, M.N., Saipol, H.F.: High performance nanotechnology software (HPNS) for parameter characterization of nanowire fabrication and nanochip system. In: Fujita, H., Selamat, A. (eds.) SoMeT 2014. CCIS, vol. 513, pp. 251–268. Springer, Cham (2015). https://doi.org/10.1007/978-3-319-17530-0_18

25. Ali, A., Bajwa, I.S., Kazmi, R.: High-performance simulation of drug release model using finite element method with CPU/GPU platform. J. Univers. Comput. Sci. **25**(10), 1261–1278 (2019)

26. Fu, Z., et al.: Architecting the finite element method pipeline for the GPU. J. Comput. Appl. Math. **257**, 195–211 (2014)

27. Knepley, M.G., Terrel, A.R.: Finite element integration on GPUs. ACM Trans. Math. Softw. (TOMS) **39**(2), 10 (2013)
28. Cecka, C., Lew, A.J., Darve, E.: Assembly of finite element methods on graphics processors. Int. J. Numer. Meth. Eng. **85**(5), 640–669 (2011)
29. Ramírez-Gil, F.J., Tsuzuki, M.S.G., Montealegre-Rubio, W.: Global finite element matrix construction based on a CPU-GPU implementation (2015). arXiv preprint arXiv:1501.04784
30. Dziekonski, A., et al.: Generation of large finite-element matrices on multiple graphics processors. Int. J. Numer. Meth. Eng. **94**(2), 204–220 (2013)
31. Burton, A.C.: Physiology and Biophysics of the Circulation: An Introductory Text (1972)
32. Reddy, J.N.: An Introduction to the Finite Element Method, vol. 2. McGraw-Hill, New York (1993)
33. Nacev, A., et al.: Towards control of magnetic fluids in patients: directing therapeutic nanoparticles to disease locations. IEEE Control Syst. **32**(3), 32–74 (2012)

To Explore the Factors that Affect Behavior of Employee Regarding Knowledge Sharing in IT Service Companies

Kiran Naz Abbasi[1], Syed Fakhar Bilal[2], Saqib Ali[3]([⊠]), and Muhammad Naeem[2]

[1] University Institute of Information Technology, PMAS University of Arid Agriculture, Rawalpindi, Pakistan
kiranabbasi91@gmail.com
[2] Federal Urdu University of Arts, Science & Technology, Islamabad, Islamabad, Pakistan
fakhar.bilal39@gmail.com, Naeempk51@gmail.com
[3] Faculty of Information Technology, Beijing University of Technology, Pingleyuan No. 100, Chaoyang District, Beijing, China
Saqibsaleem788@hotmail.com

Abstract. Context: It is vital to investigate that why employees of an organization do or do not prefer to share their acquired knowledge with coworkers and how their perceived barriers and fears influence their knowledge sharing intentions in a working environment. Objective: This study aims to understand significant factors and motives that influence or reduce employee's intention to share knowledge with coworkers in an organization. Method: We planned a field study with 125 employees including HRM and Line managers in an IT service company to test our hypotheses. The structural equation modeling (SEM) approach is employed to test whether our hypotheses are true or not. Results: Results supported the positive effects of ethical leadership, R&R and technology related constructs and showed positive effect of Knowledge Transfer upon employee's knowledge sharing intention. Contribution: This research contributes to concept of Knowledge Sharing and exploring its part in the knowledge seeking and contribution. It will help managers to learn how to promote knowledge sharing intentions between employees by applying knowledge oriented and ethical Leadership, R&R and use of technology.

Keywords: Ethical leadership · Knowledge sharing intentions · R&R · Knowledge Seeking · KMS

1 Introduction

The success of any organization relies on knowledge management and the effectiveness [46] of knowledge management depends on employee's motivation and participation in knowledge distribution activities [22]. Knowledge distribution is defined as "the act of making it sure that knowledge is available to others employees within the organization" [28] has been found necessary for achieving individual level efficiency as well as team

© Springer Nature Singapore Pte Ltd. 2020
I. S. Bajwa et al. (Eds.): INTAP 2019, CCIS 1198, pp. 237–249, 2020.
https://doi.org/10.1007/978-981-15-5232-8_21

level innovation which ultimately leads an organization to success [27], [32] Various scholars hypothesize that employees should willingly contribute in knowledge sharing activities to support organizational interests [3] organizations cannot force employees to share knowledge because unlike other environments, it is a democratic and unconstrained task. Because knowledge is one's rational asset and is enclosed in humans naturally. The reason behind why employees are reluctant to distribute knowledge is, they must have fear of loss of their time and effort [30]. To overcome this hindrance to knowledge distribution, earlier research has featured the numerous factors that influence a person's consent to distribute knowledge from the viewpoint of social exchange theory [7] theory of planned behavior and both theories combined [8, 32].

It is necessary to investigate that why employees of an organization do or do not prefer to share their acquired knowledge with coworkers and how their perceived barriers and fears influence their knowledge sharing intentions in a working environment. This paper investigates the effect of multiple factors that influence the behavior of an employee positively or negatively regarding sharing of acquired skills, experience or thoughts in work settings with coworkers.

1.1   Problem Statement

To Explore the Factors that affects Behavior of Employee Regarding Knowledge Sharing from The Perspectives of Job Characteristics and Technology Usage in IT Service Companies.

This paper is divided into following sections. Section 2 covers background of KM and factors effecting its sharing process. Research Model and Hypotheses formulation is done in Sect. 3. Next; Research Methodology is covered in Sect. 4. Conclusion and future work is given in Sect. 5.

2   Literature Review

This section distinguishes data from information and covers knowledge and its types. Afterwards, importance of knowledge distribution to Strategic Management in organizations is discussed and factors influencing employees' intention to distribute knowledge are explored from literature study.

2.1   Difference Between Data, Information, and Knowledge

The description of "knowledge" is sometimes misinterpreted as either information, data or both [1] depicts features of knowledge based on the extractions of earlier studies [1]. According to [1], data shows ungraded numbers and uncertain facts having no useful meaning. Information is data in processed form and with a meaningful reference frame [51]. From this, we concluded that knowledge is approved, justified and actualized information that includes evidence, practices, conceptions, acquaintance, perception, opinion, investigations and judgments [1].

2.2 Types of Knowledge

Despite of the fact that many scholars have quoted the tacit-explicit division of knowledge, the terminologies implicit and tacit are often used correspondently which is not correct. Figure 1 represents a decision tree to describe the basic differences among explicit, implicit, and tacit knowledge [43].

Explicit knowledge means knowledge that can be delivered, adapted, managed and summarize as visual outcome [1, 10, 43]. This depicts that explicit knowledge is relatively more easy to find and distribute as compared to tacit and implicit knowledge [10]. Tacit knowledge is drawn out from individuals' doing, experiences, and morals [1], it cannot be expressed and codified as accurately as it is known [25, 43].

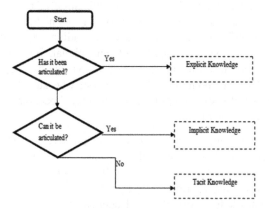

Fig. 1. Decision tree of explicit, implicit and tacit knowledge [43].

2.3 Outcome

Previous studies conclude that an increasing trend has been developed in systemizing individual's contributions to knowledge-oriented artifacts that are meaningful, unique, and reliable. In fact, concentration on resources of this type is encouraged by the Knowledge management, which embody continuation of the Knowledge oriented leadership and is of great value in establishment of the strategies regarding effective knowledge management.

3 Research Methodology

This study investigates substantial factors that prompt knowledge sharing intentions of employees with coworkers in an organization. First of all, we distinguished among data, knowledge and information which further proceeds to the types of knowledge. Hypotheses are developed then to explore key factors of knowledge distribution behavior. Then a theoretical research model is developed that elaborates under what factors employees choose to distribute or not their knowledge with other employees.

We conducted a survey and analyze survey responses using Structural equational Modeling (SEM) technique to check whether our hypothesized factors influence employees' consent to distribute knowledge or not. Based on our results, we concluded that hypothesized factors influence employee's motivation related to knowledge distribution and (1) how intentions of employees are influenced by those factors to distribute their acquired Knowledge with other employees in an IT service Company.

3.1   Research Model and Hypotheses

In this section, hypotheses are formed, and a research model is developed which symbolically interprets that hypothesizes factors positively influence the behavior of employees regarding sharing of their acquired knowledge with their coworkers within an organization. Sharing of knowledge means "utilization of resources to make sure that knowledge is available to others within the organization" [28]. This act needs time and effort and can be influenced by many factors including organizational, behavioral or technical factors. We explored whether Organizational, Behavioral and technical aspects can be an important factor in sharing of knowledge by employees by making some hypotheses. These Hypotheses need to be tested because they provide help in understanding the role of R&R from top management and peers in shaping knowledge sharing behavior and views of employees.

H1. Employees' knowledge sharing behavior is positively influenced by Ethical leadership. Leadership is often described as a basic factor motivating the flow of knowledge among employee in organizations [16, 32, 47]. By taking in account the moral value of knowledge sharing, we hypothesized that leader's ethicality may strongly influence knowledge distribution as leader can pose restriction as well as allow employees to communicate freely. According to [9] ethical leadership is defined as aggregate of morally valuable attributes such as equity, impartiality, and reliability [9] and all these factors are vital constituents that enhance knowledge distribution behavior [5, 28] Ethical and knowledge oriented leaders provide employees with both the favorable circumstances and freedom necessary for distribution of knowledge.

Based on above discussion, we hypothesized that ethical leadership adds to employee knowledge distribution by adorning the bonding of beneficial attachments in the workplace between employees and urging employees' desire for their participation in knowledge distribution and sharing process [29, 35, 37]. Supporting our prediction, earlier studies have also indicated that ethical leadership endorses employees' positive, social and helping behavior towards colleagues [4].

H2. Employee's willingness to share knowledge is influenced by recognition and reward received from management and peers.

It is hypothesized that R&R is needed to boost employees in order to share their knowledge with other [19, 40, 41]. On the basis of such hypothesis, commitment of employees for knowledge distribution is tend to be influenced by recognition and reward offered by management and peer as well as clients [49]. Further, it is noticed that major factor in restraining their knowledge, employees are dissatisfied with the

R&R they get from management and peers seeking an opportunity for alternative as set up their own business to take advantage of their possessed knowledge [19]. This emphasizes the need of R&R as it may be the key factor to influence individual's behavior, yet most current studies have not included this into their research [18] (Fig. 2).

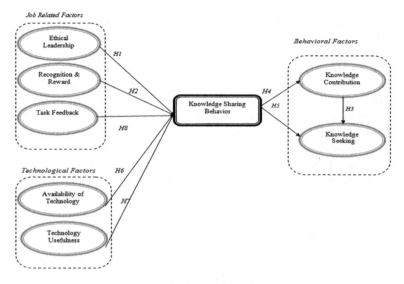

Fig. 2. Research mode

It looks unreal that all members in organization evenly having same approach regarding knowledge and it sharing. To study this, the examination is needed to get insight into employee's perception of the R&R they receive from management and peers for their contribution in knowledge distribution.

H3. Knowledge seeking is positively influenced by knowledge contribution.
H4. Knowledge contribution is positively influenced by Knowledge Sharing.
H5. Knowledge Seeking is positively influenced by Knowledge Sharing.

Knowledge distribution is defined as an exchange of knowledge between a knowledge contributor and knowledge seeker which means the giving and gaining of knowledge [32]. These two behaviors play key role in knowledge distribution process [30]. If either of two is missing, its lack makes the knowledge distribution process inadequate and unendurable [20, 30].

Knowledge sharing depends on employees to intentionally decide if they will contribute in knowledge distribution process or not, because it cannot be forced and is not mandatory act. In accordance with its intentional decision, knowledge sharing process necessitates one who is self-provoked for this act. As for knowledge distribution, an employee makes effort and maintains the time required to transfer knowledge with coworkers [14]. One common factor that employees do not take interest and used to share the acquired knowledge is to escape from any obligation [42]. Therefore, Knowledge contribution seems to be more influencing construct than knowledge seeking in earlier research [12, 33, 36, 50]. Despite of all, more research is needed on relationship of these two behaviors as earlier studies paid less attention in this regard.

H6. Knowledge sharing behavior is positively influenced by Availability of Technology.
H7. Knowledge sharing behavior is positively influenced by Usefulness of Technology.

Availability and the ease of use of technology are pivotal factors in sharing of acquired Knowledge [15]. Ease of use is described as how much usage of a specific system is "free of effort" [15]. Usefulness is described as how much usage of a specific system will enhance his or her job efficiency [15]. That means, how the user takes the particular system to be an effective and helpful in performing the required task(s).

So, conclusion is that use of technology and tools that aid users in sharing their acquired knowledge effectively and easily, enhances knowledge sharing behavior [2]. According to [21, 22] IT tools tend to be considered as empowering technology. Usefulness of shared knowledge is importantly based on employee's effectiveness in terms of performance, and it's worth will enhance individual's motivation to share his/her experience [28]. Therefore, both availability of IT tools and their usefulness will increase an employee's orientation toward the sharing of acquired knowledge with coworkers.

H8. Knowledge sharing behavior is positively affected by Task Feedback.

Task feedback means the magnitude to which an employee receives appreciation about the effectiveness of his or her performance [23]. When employees gain unambiguous information about their efficiency instead of vague and informal, it enhances their interest in job and increases their desire to share their experience regarding that job with other coworkers [26]. A feeling of competency is developed between workers when task feedback is provided to them [5]. From above discussed arguments it is hypothesized that task feedback may also affect behavior of an employee in term of knowledge distribution.

4 Evaluation

In this study, the structural equation modeling (SEM) technique is used to test the proposed hypothesis and relate dependencies between the factors (Ethical leadership, Task feedback, Recognition & Reward, Availability and usefulness of technology, Knowledge Contribution & Knowledge Seeking) and determine the impact of these factors. SEM technique is able to analyze the theoretical network of dependencies among factors and give meaning of enclosed measures.

4.1 Research Setting

The aim of this paper is to relate the impact of Ethical Leadership, Recognition & Reward, Task Feedback, Availability and usefulness of Technology on Knowledge Sharing Behavior of employees' within an organization. Furthermore, this study also describes relationship between knowledge distribution, knowledge seeking and knowledge contribution. A research design of survey is adopted, where data is collected from a sample including employees and managers of the selected company utilizing a survey questionnaire. This type of research setting is selected because IT companies are knowledge demanding and reliance between the knowledge sources & its transfer are significant features in these firms [17, 42].

4.2 Sample Organization

To test the Hypotheses proposed, the opinion of employees who are involved in software development and client services and some line and HR managers in IT Service Company is focused for this study. The firm aims to success by depending on employee's performance and supports all workers in showing their abilities through distribution of their acquired knowledge with coworkers. The KMS is also implemented within organization for better distribution of knowledge among employees. All employees can log in to the system through their accounts to share their views and enhance communicate with other peers. System is secure having many search tools. A task-relevant dictionary clarifies key technical terms in the related business area which assists employees in using this tool efficiently for sharing views and knowledge (Table 1).

Table 1. Profile of survey respondents

Gender	Frequency	%
Male	73	58.4
Female	52	41.6
Position		
HR leaders/managers	09	7.2
Line managers	12	9.6
Software developers	17	13.6
Other	87	69.6
Years served in firm		
0–5 years	34	27.2
6–10 years	65	52.6
11–15 year	19	15.2
Above 16 years	07	5.6

4.3   Data Collection and Analysis

The data collection process continued nearly three months. By the guidance of HRM department of the organization, we arbitrarily selected 125 employees from different units and shared the survey among them. Out of the 125 surveys distributed, 109 fully filled surveys were returned, having a response rate of 87.2%. Most of the participants were male (58.4%) and remaining (41.6%) were female working on different positions (e.g. HR manager, Line manager, Software Developer or others) (Table 2).

Table 2. Types and sources of R&R regarding knowledge sharing determined by % of respondents.

	Formal recognition only	Informal recognition only	Both formal and informal recognition	No recognition
Managers	28	31	25	16.5
Peers	6	57	20	12
Clients	20	29.5	29	22.5
	Financial rewards only	Non-financial rewards only	Both financial and nonfinancial rewards	No rewards
Managers	24	31	20	26.5
Peers	10.5	49	10.5	28.5
Clients	14	31.5	18	30.5

4.4   Results

On this stage, the structural model has to be analyzed for the collinearity problems by checking the value of Variance Inflation Factor (VIF) and tolerance. After that, path coefficient values and standard errors (t-values) are evaluated to determine the significance and relevance of the structural model. Table 3 concludes the result of the collinearity assessment in which values of tolerance are greater than 0.20 and the values of VIF are less than 5. So, VIF and tolerance have cleared the baseline.

Table 3. Result of collinearity assessment

Variable	Tolerance	VIF
EL	0.354	2.847
R&R	0.358	2.105
TF	0.383	2.704
AT	0.721	2.518
UT	0.755	2.201
KC	0.650	2.638
KS	0.898	1.164

As a result, no factor is needed to be exclude from the model as all the factors included in the proposed model are not correlated. The next move is assessment of path coefficients using PLS algorithm for the evaluation of the structural model. The standard value of path coefficient (β) are between -1 and $+1$, in which a value nearer to $+1$ depicts a strong positive association and a value closer to -1 shows a highly negative association.

4.5   Hypotheses Testing

The hypothesis testing in this study is done by following the rules given by [13]. He endorsed that bootstrapping technique can be used to evaluate the path significance by performing t-tests. Typically, t-value > 1.96 refers to significant level (Table 4). Concluded on earlier studies, it is observed that that proposed hypothesis is significant if its p-value < 0.05. The result of bootstrapping technique indicated that Knowledge Sharing Behavior (H2) has a significant effect on knowledge contribution having 18% variance, as well as Knowledge Seeking with 53% variance. Ethical Leadership (H1) and R&R (H2), Availability and usefulness of Technology (H6), (H7), have significant effects on Knowledge Sharing Behavior with 67% variance. We observed an insignificant effect of task feedback (H8) on knowledge sharing behaviors (Fig. 3).

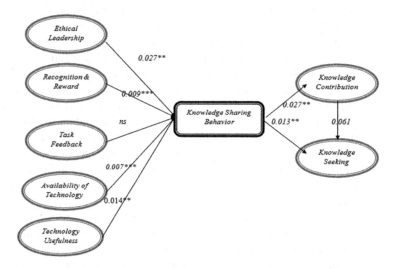

Fig. 3. Hypotheses testing result.

The result of bootstrapping technique indicated that Knowledge Sharing Behavior (H2) has a significant effect on knowledge contribution having 18% variance, as well as Knowledge Seeking with 53% variance. Ethical Leadership (H1) and R&R (H2), Availability and usefulness of Technology (H6), (H7), have significant effects on Knowledge Sharing Behavior with 67% variance. We observed an insignificant effect of task feedback (H8) on knowledge sharing behaviors.

Table 4. Hypothesis testing result

Proposed hypothesis	Relation	Path coefficient	t-value	p-value	Significance level	Results
H1	EL -> KSB	0.140	2.436	0.027	**	Significant
H2	R&R -> KSB	0.153	2.327	0.009	***	Significant
H3	KC -> KSB	0.152	2.523	0.013	**	Significant
H4	KSB -> KC	0.144	2.489	0.027	**	Significant
H5	KSB -> KS	0.629	2.349	0.020	**	Significant
H6	AT -> KSB	0.064	2.097	0.007	***	Significant
H7	UT -> KSB	0.113	2.638	0.014	**	Significant
H8	TF -> KSB	−0.035	0.653	0.061	ns	Not significant

5 Conclusion and Future Work

As organization's success mainly depends on leadership, our research evaluates the part of ethical leadership in provoking employees' intention to take part in knowledge distribution process. Although, earlier scholars have suggested that ethical leadership is considerably related to social behavior among employees but analysis of its impact on employees behavior regarding knowledge distribution is particularly infrequent. Our conclusion is that ethical leadership plays vital role in nurturing employee's behavior regarding knowledge distribution. Further, it is found that to enhance knowledge distribution behavior at work, management should deploy concurrent reward and recognition programs to boost employees and their intentions to take part in knowledge distribution process. Beside this, we found convincing relationships between Knowledge Sharing Behavior and two specific knowledge distribution activities: contribution and seeking. Previous studies also highlighted important factors of knowledge sharing but their perspectives was different in terms of knowledge contribution and knowledge seeking [8, 30]. This study further contributes in finding two significant factors of knowledge sharing behavior in terms of IT tools and technological factors on workplace: Availability and usefulness of IT tools. These two technological factors are still considered as important in personal intentions on implementation of knowledge sharing behavior at workplace [27].

For future directions, our research can be expanded to explore the interaction between individual and collective knowledge in knowledge creation and distribution process at the organizational level. Composite knowledge seems to be a public good as the outcome of shared individual knowledge. Thus, the interchange between individual and composite knowledge is in social crisis. In future research social crisis (i.e. the reluctance of knowledge transfer in the organization by employees) may be examined by employees' uncontrolled social behavior instead of the business point of view and organizational perspective.

References

1. Alavi, M., Leidner, D.E.: Review: knowledge management and knowledge management systems: conceptual foundations and research issues. MIS Q. 107–136 (2001)
2. Amichai-Hamburger, Y., McKenna, K.Y.A., Tal, S.-A.: E-empowerment: empowerment by the Internet. Comput. Hum. Behavior **24**, 1776–1789 (2008)
3. Anand, A., Walsh, I.: Should knowledge be shared generously? Tracing insights from past to present and describing a model. J. Knowl. Manag. **20**(4), 713–730 (2016)
4. Avey, J.B., Wernsing, T.S., Palanski, M.E.: Exploring the process of ethical leadership: the mediating role of employee voice and psychological ownership. J. Bus. Ethics **107**(1), 21–34 (2012)
5. Bandura, A.: Self-Efficacy: The Exercise of Control. W.H. Freeman, New York (1997)
6. Birasnav, M.: Knowledge management and organizational performance in the service industry: the role of transformational leadership beyond the effects of transactional leadership. J. Bus. Res. **67**(8), 1622–1629 (2014)
7. Blau, P.M.: Exchange & Power in Social Life. Wiley, New York (1964)
8. Bock, G.W., Zmud, B., Kim, Y.G., Lee, L.N.: Behavioral intention formation in knowledge sharing: examining the roles of extrinsic motivators, social psychological forces, and organizational climate. MIS Q. **29**, 87–111 (2005)
9. Brown, M.E., Treviño, L.K.: Ethical leadership: a review and future directions. Leadersh. Q. **17**(6), 595–616 (2006)
10. Cabrera, A., Cabrera, E.F.: Knowledge-sharing dilemmas. Organ. Stud. **23**(5), 687–710 (2002)
11. Cegarra-Navarro, J.-G., Soto-Acosta, P., Wensley, A.: Structured knowledge processes and firm performance: the role of organizational agility. J. Bus. Res. **69**(5), 1544–1549 (2016)
12. Chang, H.H., Chung, S.-S.: Social capital and individual motivations on knowledge sharing: participant involvement as a moderator. Inf. Manag. **48**, 9–18 (2011)
13. Chin, W.W.: The partial least squares approach for structural equation modeling (1998)
14. Davenport, T.H., Prusak, L.: Working Knowledge: How Organizations Manage What They Know. Harvard Business School Press, Boston (1998)
15. Davis, F.D.: Perceived usefulness, perceived ease of use, and user acceptance of information technology. MIS Q. **13**, 319–340 (1989)
16. DeTienne, K.B., Dyer, G., Hoopes, C., Harris, S.: Toward a model of effective knowledge management and directions for future research: culture, leadership, and CKOs. J. Leadersh. Organ. Stud. **10**(4), 26–43 (2004)
17. Ejler, N., Poulfelt, F., Czerniawska, F.: Managing the Knowledge Intensive Firm. Routledge, London (2011)
18. Felin, T., Zenger, T.R., Tomsik, J.: The knowledge economy: emerging organizational forms, missing microfoundations, and key considerations for managing human capital. Hum. Resour. Manag. **48**(4), 555–570 (2009)
19. Foss, N.J., Husted, K., Michailova, S.: Governing knowledge sharing in organizations: levels of analysis, governance mechanisms, and research directions. J. Manag. Stud. **47**, 455–482 (2010)
20. Foss, N.J., Minbaeva, D.B., Pedersen, T., Reinholt, M.: Encouraging knowledge sharing among employees: how job design matters. Hum. Resour. Manag. **48**(6), 871–893 (2009)
21. Füller, J., Mühlbacher, H., Matzler, K., Jaweckl, G.: Consumer empowerment through internet-based co-creation. J. Manag. Inf. Syst. **26**, 71e102 (2009)
22. Gagné, M.: A model of knowledge-sharing motivation. Hum. Res. Manag. **48**(4), 571–589 (2009)

23. Hackman, J.R., Oldham, G.R.: Work Redesign. Addison-Wesley, Reading (1980)
24. Hair, J.F., Hult, G.T.M., Ringle, C., Sarstedt, M.: A Primer on Partial Least Squares Structural Equation Modeling (PLS-SEM). Sage Publications (2013)
25. Hislop, D.: Mission impossible? Communicating and sharing knowledge via information technology. J. Inf. Technol. 17(3), 165–177 (2002)
26. Hon, A.H.Y., Rensvold, R.B.: An interactional perspective on perceived empowerment: the role of personal needs and task context. Int. J. Hum. Resour. Manag. 17, 959–982 (2006)
27. Huang, X., Hsieh, J.J., He, W.: Expertise dissimilarity and creativity: the contingent roles of tacit and explicit knowledge sharing. J. Appl. Psychol. 99(5), 816–830 (2014)
28. Ipe, M.: Knowledge sharing in organizations: a conceptual framework. Hum. Resour. Dev. Rev. 2(4), 337–359 (2003)
29. Kacmar, K.M., Andrews, M.C., Harris, K.J., Tepper, B.J.: Ethical leadership and subordinate outcomes: the mediating role of organizational politics and the moderating role of political skill. J. Bus. Ethics 115(1), 33–44 (2013)
30. Kankanhalli, A., Tan, B.C.Y., Wei, K.-K.: Contributing knowledge to electronic knowledge repositories: an empirical investigation. MIS Q. 29, 113–143 (2005b)
31. Kianto, A., Sáenz, J., Aramburu, A.: Knowledge management practices, intellectual capabilities and innovation. J. Bus. Res. 81, 11–20 (2017)
32. Kim, S.L., Yun, S.: The effect of coworker knowledge sharing on performance and its boundary conditions: an interactional perspective. J. Appl. Psychol. 100(2), 575–582 (2015)
33. Koriat, N., Gelbard, R.: Knowledge sharing motivation among IT personnel: integrated model and implications of employment contracts. Int. J. Inf. Manag. 34, 577–591 (2014)
34. Kraimer, M.L., Seibert, S.E., Liden, R.C.: Psychological empowerment as a multidimensional construct: a test of construct validity. Educ. Psychol. Meas. 59, 127–142 (1999)
35. Lam, L.W., Loi, R., Chan, K.W., Liu, Y.: Voice more and stay longer: how ethical leaders influence employee voice and exit intentions. Bus. Ethics Q. 26(03), 277–300 (2016)
36. Lin, S.-W., Lo, L.Y.-S.: Mechanisms to motivate knowledge sharing: integrating the reward systems and social network perspectives. J. Knowl. Manag. 19, 212–235 (2015)
37. Mayer, D.M., Aquino, K., Greenbaum, R.L., Kuenzi, M.: Who displays ethical leadership, and why does it matter? An examination of antecedents and consequences of ethical leadership. Acad. Manag. J. 55(1), 151–171 (2012)
38. Michaelis, B., Wagner, J., Schweizer, L.: Knowledge as a key in the relationship between high-performance work systems and workforce productivity. J. Bus. Res. 68(5), 1035–1044 (2015)
39. Mikalef, P., Pateli, A.: Information technology-enabled dynamic capabilities and their indirect effect on competitive performance: findings from PLS-SEM and fsQCA. J. Bus. Res. 70, 1–16 (2017)
40. Minbaeva, D.: Strategic HRM in building micro-foundations of organizational knowledge-based performance. Hum. Resour. Manag. Rev. 23(4), 378–390 (2013)
41. Minbaeva, D., Mäkelä, K., Rabbiosi, L.: Linking HRM and knowledge transfer via individual-level mechanisms. Hum. Resour. Manag. 51(3), 387–405 (2012)
42. Morabito, J., Sack, I., Bhate, A.: Designing Knowledge Organizations. Wiley, Chichester (2017)
43. Nickols, F.: The knowledge in knowledge management. In: The Knowledge Management Yearbook, 2000–2001 (2000a)
44. Nonaka, I., Toyama, R., Hirata, T.: Managing Flow: A Process Theory of the Knowledge-Based Firm. Palgrave Macmillan, NewYork (2015)
45. Polanyi, M.: The tacit dimension, Chapter 7. In: Laurence, P. (ed.) Knowledge in Organisations, pp. 135e146. Butterworth-Heinemann, Boston (1997)

46. Riege, A.: Three-dozen knowledge-sharing barriers managers must consider. J. Knowl. Manag. **9**(3), 18–35 (2005)
47. Srivastava, A., Bartol, K.M., Locke, E.A.: Empowering leadership in management teams: effects on knowledge sharing, efficacy, and performance. Acad. Manag. J. **49**(6), 1239–1251 (2006)
48. Szulanski, G., Cappetta, R., Jensen, R.J.: When and how trustworthiness matters: knowledge transfer and the moderating effect of causal ambiguity. Organ. Sci. **15**(5), 600–613 (2004)
49. Vroom, V.: Work and motivation. Wiley, New York (1964)
50. Zack, M.H.: Managing codified knowledge. Sloan Manag. Rev. **40**(4), 45–58 (1999)

Decision Support System for Dental Clinics: A Systematic Literature Review Protocol

Muhammad Asim[1(✉)], Muhammad Arif Shah[1,2], Mumtaz Ali[1], and Rashid Naseem[1]

[1] City University of Science and Information Technology, Peshawar, Pakistan
onlyforasiml@gmail.com
[2] Department of Software Engineering, Faculty of Engineering, Universiti Teknologi Malaysia, Johor Bahru, Malaysia

Abstract. Decision Support System (DSS) is a new trend in technology which provides decisions to users based on the information. Nowadays, it is being used in many fields and, it is becoming an essential part of the dental clinic. Many dental diseases are now detecting with the DSS and many treatments for dental diseases are providing through it. Therefore, it becomes an inspiring re-search issue to provide the best solution in sensitive types of data. This paper presents a Protocol for a Systematic Literature Review on DSS for dental diseases. This paper performed a specific documented plan and provides a methodology supportive to perform a Systematic Literature Review (SLR). Five important steps are performed in this review protocol and five research questions in the field of Dental Decision Support System (DDSS) are considered. Important attributes in the field of interest are considered. The expected result of this review will identify the research issues, provide different paths to researchers and it also discussed the importance/requirement of the DDSS. The results of this protocol can be helpful for the researchers, and it will provide a way for researchers to implement SLR more easily and effectively.

Keywords: Decision Support System · Dental diseases · Systematic Literature Review Protocol

1 Introduction

In the field of medical science, data is increasing day by due to advancement in technology. Novel inventions in the form of devices are being developed which produce complex data. Knowledge in the medical field indicates uncertainty, trouble and wisdom and this fact becomes a motivation for the development of decision support system [1]. Information technology is used in the Clinical Decision Support System (CDSS) over a decade ago. CDSS is an application built to help clinical and other health professionals in decision making [2]. Its primary goal is to assist clinical staff for a better treatment plan. In general consensus, the result of treatment can be better with the use of a Decision Support System because it can help the dentist make good decisions [3]. A Dental Decision Support System (DDSS) is used in a way that finds diseases of the teeth by analyzing some sort of input information. Analyzing dental

© Springer Nature Singapore Pte Ltd. 2020
I. S. Bajwa et al. (Eds.): INTAP 2019, CCIS 1198, pp. 250–257, 2020.
https://doi.org/10.1007/978-981-15-5232-8_22

x-ray image to find tooth disease is one of the better methods. For predicting and making a better plan for dental diseases, x-ray images play a significant role [4, 5]. Bokhari and Khan [6] used supervised and unsupervised techniques of data mining to discover the different hidden pattern in the data and find that Tooth Cavity (TC) is the most common problem of dental patients. They find treatment for the TC is "resin-based composite—one surface, Posterior". On the cardiac data, extraction of information, clustering and classification methods are being applied [7]. Based on "The World Oral Health Report", it was found that worldwide estimated 90% of the school children's and other adults effect by dental caries [8]. Based on the above information discussed, most of the literature providing a decision-based system for dental diseases. Different review/survey papers [3, 9] are published in the field of DDSS but no author concentrate on the Decision Support System designed for Dental Diseases. Some questions are arising here that which technique is mostly used in DDSS, which diseases are targeted and what type of datasets are used. These questions let the authors review the published work in the field of DDSS and find the answer to these questions. This paper focuses on the techniques to find the solution for the diseases in the dental decision support system and provides guidelines for Systematic Literature Review for DDSS. Five steps are performed for the Systematic Literature Review Protocol in which five research questions are addressed which will be very beneficial for the researchers working on DDSS. Research Question (RQ) formulation is the first step, in the second step objectives are defined for each RQ, the search string is formulated for searching relevant literature of dental DSS in the different digital libraries. In the fourth step inclusion/exclusion criteria are applied to the downloaded literature and in the last step relevant information from each literature is reviewed and extracted to make an extraction form.

2 Background

2.1 Clinical Decision Support System (CDSS)

A Decision Support System (DSS) is an application developed to help health professionals in decision making in the diagnosing process and treatment plan [2]. Our focus in this Systematic Literature Protocol is only the Clinical Decision Support System developed for dental diseases. Okuda et al. [10] developed a decision support system in 1997 that predicts the location and the risk of dental caries using Artificial Neural Network and a fuzzy inference system. According to Okuda et al. [10], brushing the tooth is only the way to prevent it from tooth decay (dental caries) but if we know the exact location and the risk of tooth decay, we can brush accordingly which is beneficial for us. The Decision support system can be used as a helping tool for the dentist to take a better decision. Mago et al. [11] developed a decision support system for dental caries using Bayesian Network (BN) which helps the dentist to choose a treatment plan according to signs and symptoms. The system was evaluated by 13 different dentists which check the effectiveness of the system.

2.2   Related Works

Many research articles are published in the area of clinical decision support system for dental diseases in various conferences and Journals. There is no Systematic Literature Review Protocol paper published for the Clinical Decision Support System for the Dental Diseases. Son et al. [12] proposed a novel framework for finding dental disease in the x-ray image. For Segmentation, they used segmentation method based on semi-supervised fuzzy clustering. They proposed a new algorithm for clustering called Affinity Propagation Clustering (APC+) and a new decision-making algorithm for finding the final disease from the group of diseases finds in segments of the image. They work on five major diseases namely, missing teeth, decay, include teeth, resorption of periodontal bone and root fracture with an accuracy of their proposed algorithm 92.74%. For segmentation purpose, some of the widely used methods namely edge tracing method, region-based method and integration methods for medical images used by [19–21] simultaneously. Prakash et al. [13] propose a framework for defect analysis in the teeth using different digital image processing techniques. They process the image like dimensional reduction and smoothing, segment the image and extract the features for further processing. The system was trained using tooth images with defects and then input image was given to the system to find defect(s), compare the source image with defect one in the database using Support Vector Machine (SVM) classifier. Park et al. [14] proposed Shared Decision Making (SDM) which enables doctors and patients to communicate dental restorative treatment planning. They use clinical knowledge to generate treatment plans using ontology and Analytical Hierarchy Process (AHP) to construct a strong and reliable hierarchy of preferences which helps in defining treatment priorities. According to Haghanifar et al. [16], 97% of the people effect from dental caries in their life and developed DSS for dental caries. They used Real-Coded Genetic algorithm (RCGA) based Fuzzy Cognitive Map (FCM). The results show that RCGA based FCM performs better than conventional FCM. An effective technique is proposed by El-Barki and Mastarokis [17] with Direct Digital Radiography (DDR) media for dental disease identification. [18] used FIS Tsukamoto using optimization by Swarm Particle Optimization (PSO) for dental disease identification in the DSS and find achieve 88% accuracy. All this literature discussed in this section work on the automation of clinical process especially treatment planning and also on helps the dentist in finding dental disease. It especially enables the dentist to check for the disease nature and select the appropriate treatment plan.

3   Research Method

A systematic literature review is a type of research which identifies and interprets the existing literature to fully understand a specific area of research. It focuses on the literature targeting some defined research questions and tries to answer them. This paper follows the guidelines proposed by Keele [15] and finds it very beneficial.

3.1 Systematic Literature Review Protocol

A good and appropriate systematic literature review protocol is one that follows a properly documented plan for the whole process starting from the searching to the writing of the review paper.

Research Questions. Defining the Research questions for the systematic review is an important step. This review protocol addressed the following research questions:

1. Which techniques are mostly used in the Dental Decision support system? And Why?
2. Which diseases are targeted in the Dental Decision support system? And Why?
3. What type of data sets are used in the Dental Decision support system?
4. What are the benchmarking criteria in the Dental Decision support system?
5. Is a Decision support system in dental clinics required?

Research Objectives. There are some objectives defined in this systematic review protocol to helps the researchers to find their exact area of research and focus on the specific topic. The Research objectives are:

1. To identify frequently used techniques in DSS for dental clinics to help researchers in method selection with accurate results.
2. To know about what type of diseases are treating in dental decision support system to help researchers to work more on the specific disease with specific technique.
3. To know about what kind of data sets are used by researchers for the dental decision support system to help researchers in easy selection of data set.
4. To identify how researchers evaluate their developed DSS.
5. To find out why to use DSS in Dental Clinics

Data Sources. Digital Libraries are used for the Systematic Literature Review; therefore, authors also search for the literature published in the field of Dental Decision Support System for Dental Diseases (Table 1). Each Digital Library returns with the literature according to search query but Google Scholar retrieves some different as well the same literature which was already returned by other Digital Libraries.

Table 1. Database

Database source	URL
ACM Digital Library	https://dl.acm.org/
Science Direct	https://www.sciencedirect.com/
Google Scholar	https://scholar.google.com
IEEE Xplore	https://ieeexplore.ieee.org/
Springer Digital Library	https://link.springer.com/

Search Strategy and Search Strings. The strategy was to search for all relevant literature published in the area of inter- est. After searching for Digital Libraries, the relevant literature was downloaded from 1997 to 2019. Search Strings are very important as all the literatures we search in the digital libraries are return through it. The search strings that used for searching in the digital libraries given in Table 1 is given as:

(DSS or "Decision Support System" or CDSS or "Clinical decision support system" or DDSS or "Dental decision support system") AND ("Dental diseases") AND ("Dental clinics"). We use many types of filters depends upon the database and results in it retrieved.

Study Selection. The research papers for primary studies are selected according to inclusion/exclusion criteria (shown in Table 2). All the downloaded literature was imported to the Endnote database for easier duplication removal and reference insertion. After downloading the papers, first of all, we read the title and abstract of the paper to choose it for further study. Title of the most papers shows the area of the paper while the title of some paper does not depict the area of the study, therefore we read the abstract. After selecting the papers by reading title and abstract, we read full paper to ensure that the paper adheres to inclusion/exclusion criteria. Total of 207 papers were downloaded from electronic databases as shown in Fig. 1. After reading the title and abstract we removed 145 papers because they did not meet the inclusion/exclusion criteria. Five of the papers were found duplicate and removed by End- note and after reading the full text of paper 19 papers were removed as they do not meet the inclusion/exclusion criteria and the remaining 38 papers were selected for analysis as the primary studies for SLR.

Table 2. Inclusion and exclusion criteria

Inclusion criteria	Exclusion criteria
Papers in a decision support system or knowledge-based system for Dental clinics	Decision support system for dental drugs
Papers reviewed by electronic databases	Papers that were not accessible
Papers that describe dental diseases and make decision system using some algorithm	Papers that related to the dental area having no decision support system
A scientific paper	Paper not in the English language

Data Extraction. The search string (Sect. 3.1) was used to search the relevant literature from the digital libraries. The downloaded Literature was arranged in the folders stepwise i.e. Step 1 (all downloaded literature), Step 2 (After applying selection criteria) and studied for inclusion/exclusion criteria.

Data was extracted (Data Item is shown in Table 3) for the selected papers and relevant information was exported to excel database. It was easy to enter, search and maintain an excel file. Data items and Descriptions with relevant research questions used in our systematic literature review process are shown in Table 3.

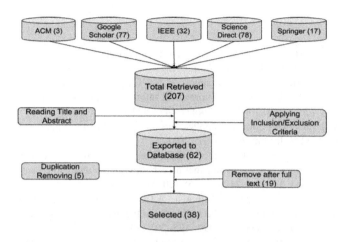

Fig. 1. Study selection

Table 3. Data extraction

Data item	Description	Research questions
Title	Study title name	RQ1
Authors	Study author names	RQ1
Year	Study published year of paper	RQ1
Disease	Diseases targeted in decision support system	RQ2
Techniques	Techniques used in decision support system	RQ1
Data set	Data sets used by authors	RQ3
Benchmark criteria	Evaluation of the results	RQ4

4 Conclusion

Due to the increasing use of the Decision Support System (DSS) in the field of dentistry. Accuracy of the decision and treatment plan for dental disease is an important issue for academic research in dentistry and Artificial Intelligence. To the best of our knowledge, previously no Systematic Literature Review Protocol (SLRP) published in the field of dental decision support system. Therefore, this SLRP gains importance and it provides beneficial information to the researcher in the field of dentistry as general and specific in the Artificial Intelligence and Data Mining. In this protocol, we discussed the important steps for conducting a successful systematic literature review in the field of DDSS. Five important research questions are considered. The predicted results of this review will provide some research paths and will let the researcher select a specific area. This protocol will be beneficial and provide the re- searcher's state of the art decision support system for dental disease in a systematic way. In future, a complete SLR will be performed using this protocol and all answers to RQ's will be discussed in details with evidence.

References

1. Mago, V.K., Bhatia, N., Bhatia, A., Mago, A.: Clinical decision support system for dental treatment. J. Comput. Sci. **3**, 254–261 (2012)
2. Musen, M.A., Middleton, B., Greenes, R.A.: Clinical decision-support systems. In: Shortliffe, E.H., Cimino, J.J. (eds.) Biomedical Informatics, pp. 643–674. Springer, London (2014). https://doi.org/10.1007/978-1-4471-4474-8_22
3. Kaplan, B.: Evaluating informatics applications—clinical decision support systems literature review. Int. J. Med. Inform. **64**, 15–37 (2001)
4. Ines Meurer, M., Caffery, L.J., Bradford, N.K., Smith, A.C.: Accuracy of dental images for the diagnosis of dental caries and enamel defects in children and adolescents: a systematic review. J. Telemed. Telecare **21**, 449–458 (2015)
5. Madoz, L.V., Giuliodori, M.J., Migliorisi, A.L., Jaureguiberry, M., de la Sota, R.L.: Endometrial cytology, biopsy, and bacteriology for the diagnosis of subclinical endometritis in grazing dairy cows. J. Dairy Sci. **97**, 195–201 (2014)
6. Bokhari, A., Khan, S.A.: Applying supervised and unsupervised learning techniques on dental patients' records. In: Chen, L., Kapoor, S., Bhatia, R. (eds.) Emerging Trends and Advanced Technologies for Computational Intelligence. SCI, vol. 647, pp. 83–102. Springer, Cham (2016). https://doi.org/10.1007/978-3-319-33353-3_5
7. Fatima, M., Anjum, A.R., Basharat, I., Khan, S.A.: Biomedical (cardiac) data mining: extraction of significant patterns for predicting heart condition. In: 2014 IEEE Conference on Computational Intelligence in Bioinformatics and Computational Biology, pp. 1–7 (2014)
8. Petersen, P.E.: The World Oral Health Report 2003: continuous improvement of oral health in the 21st century–the approach of the WHO Global Oral Health Pro gramme. Commun. Dent. Oral Epidemiol. **31**, 3–24 (2003)
9. Goh, W.P., Tao, X., Zhang, J., Yong, J.: Decision support systems for adoption in dental clinics: a survey. Knowl.-Based Syst. **104**, 195–206 (2016)
10. Okuda, T., Yoshida, T., Hotta, M.: A dental condition prediction system with artificial neural networks and fuzzy inference systems. In: 1997 IEEE International Conference on Systems, Man, and Cybernetics. Computational Cybernetics and Simulation, pp. 963–968 (1997)
11. Mago, V.K., Prasad, B., Bhatia, A., Mago, A.: A decision making system for the treatment of dental caries. In: Prasad, B. (ed.) Soft Computing Applications in Business. Studies in Fuzziness and Soft Computing, vol. 230, pp. 231–242. Springer, Heidelberg (2008). https://doi.org/10.1007/978-3-540-79005-1_12
12. Son, L.H., et al.: Dental diagnosis from X-Ray images: an expert system based on fuzzy computing. Biomed. Signal Process. Control **39**, 64–73 (2018)
13. Prakash, M., Gowsika, U., Sathiyapriya, S.: An identification of abnormalities in dental with support vector machine using image processing. In: Shetty, N.R., Prasad, N.H., Nalini, N. (eds.) Emerging Research in Computing, Information, Communication and Applications, pp. 29–40. Springer, New Delhi (2015). https://doi.org/10.1007/978-81-322-2550-8_4
14. Park, S.G., Lee, S., Kim, M.-K., Kim, H.-G.: Shared decision support system on dental restoration. Expert Syst. Appl. **39**, 11775–11781 (2012)
15. Keele, S.: Guidelines for performing systematic literature reviews in software engineering. Technical report, Ver. 2.3 EBSE Technical Report. EBSE2007
16. Haghanifar, A., Amirkhani, A., Mosavi, M.R.: Dental caries degree detection based on fuzzy cognitive maps and genetic algorithm. In: Electrical Engineering (ICEE), Iranian Conference on, pp. 976–981. IEEE (2018)

17. El-Bakri, H.M., Mastorakis, N.: An effective method for detecting dental diseases by using fast. In: 8th WSEAS International Conference on Signal, Speech and Image Processing, pp. 144–152 (2008)
18. Fajri, D.M.N., Mahmudy, W.F., Anggodo, Y.P.: Optimization of FIS Tsukamoto using particle swarm optimization for dental disease identification. In: 2017 International Conference on Advanced Computer Science and Information Systems (ICACSIS), pp. 261–268. IEEE (2017)
19. Martelli, A.: An application of heuristic search methods to edge and contour detection. Commun. ACM **19**(2), 73–83 (1976)
20. Hojjatoleslami, S., Kruggel, F.: Segmentation of large brain lesions. IEEE Trans. Med. Imaging **20**(7), 666–669 (2001)
21. Chakraborty, A., Worring, M., Duncan, J.S.: On multi-feature integration for deformable boundary finding. In: 1995 Proceedings Fifth International Conference on Computer Vision, pp. 846–851. IEEE (1995)

Comparison of Localization Algorithms for Unmanned Aerial Vehicles

Imran Qasim$^{(\boxtimes)}$, Nauman Habib, Uzair Habib, Qazi Fakhar Usman, and Mohsin Kamal

National University of Computer and Emerging Sciences, Peshawar, Pakistan
{p156377,p156392,p156061,p156365,mohsin.kamal}@nu.edu.pk

Abstract. Unmanned Aerial Vehicles (UAVs) are experiencing exponential growth these days. UAVs are used for multi purposes such as for security, photography, weather forecasting etc. The increase in number of UAVs are causing compromise to the personal privacy of people as well as threats to the privacy of confidential areas. Determining the exact location of these UAVs is important in many aspects. In this paper, several well-known localization techniques are compared. These techniques include received signal strength (RSS), angle of arrival (AoA), correlative interferometry and Watson-Watt method. These are compared on the basis of different parameters i.e. cost, efficiency, range, accuracy, energy consumption and hardware size. The comparison results show that correlative interferometry is the best available solution for UAV localization. Complexity of each algorithm is also computed. Watson-Watt and AoA has less computational complexities compared to other methods which is computed as $O(n)$ for both algorithms.

Keywords: Localization · UAV · Direction Finding · Angle of arrival · Watson-Watt · Correlative interferometry

1 Introduction

Nowadays, UAVs are getting more popular due to increase in bloggers, photographers and tourism advertisers. It is very helpful in these fields because there most of work is capturing different events, locations and exploring new places that are not easily reachable. Besides that, they are also used for shipping and goods delivery. The use of UAVs has increased due to advancement in technology as well as the affordability of UAV products. This introduced new challenges to the security, safety and privacy of the people. The present UAVs can carry different types of weapons including weapons of mass destruction which can be used for terrorist attacks, smuggling, spy activities and theft of wireless data. They may cause a great threat to commercial airmail as well. It is important to protect many high-risk regions such as prisons, nuclear power plants, demilitarized zones, industrial facilities, embassies, government facilities, concert halls, stadiums, border and no fly zones [11]. Many incidents of criminal and civil offenses related to UAVs have been reported till now [16].

© Springer Nature Singapore Pte Ltd. 2020
I. S. Bajwa et al. (Eds.): INTAP 2019, CCIS 1198, pp. 258–269, 2020.
https://doi.org/10.1007/978-981-15-5232-8_23

UAVs are restricted in many military and industrial areas because of the confidential research and development along with manufacturing processes. The restricted rules and regulations for UAV prompts the user to follow them so that they do not undergo any legal violation. For example, an attacker can leash explosives or other dangerous materials to a UAV for an attack. Criminals can use UAVs to smuggle illegal materials across borders. One can use a UAV with attached camera to spy on inhabitant's private information and to fly over walls. The increasing frequency of such incidents makes it necessary to regulate UAV air traffic [13].

Radio direction finding is needed in various departments especially navigation, military intelligence, geolocation, intelligent communication system and in the tracking field. The importance of radio Direction Finding (DF) is increasing because this information gives location of the enemy units and also provides useful data for jamming the communication network. For the use of such kind of the system, one should investigate the constraints and characteristics of the DF system such as bearing accuracy effects according to DF algorithm, cost, range, energy consumption, hardware size etc. [5].

In this paper, we are investigating these characteristics by analyzing different UAV localization techniques i.e. RSS, AoA, correlative interferometry and Watson-Watt method. After analyzing characteristics of all techniques, best among them is selected. Computational complexity of the algorithms is also computed.

2   Literature Review

Researchers have used several techniques for finding the direction and power of signal using receiver system in the lower ultra-high frequency (UHF) band. Normally, a log-periodic dipole array antenna including a power sensing radio frequency (RF) circuit is used to perform this operation. The receiver system measures RF power [15]. As soon as first RF signal from a source with given RSS threshold is received, source RF localization is initialized. If it is assumed that UAV is circulating around any search area, its center is considered as the first estimation of RF source position [3]. It is not easy to rotate the antenna, so it is achieved by setting a circular antenna array and switching the channel. There is a maximum DOA-Doppler frequency when the switching direction is towards the incident wave. The phase comparison method uses two antennas which receives different phase of signal related to the position of antennas [17].

K-band radar systems are also used for direction finding. Optical fiber is used to increase the transmission speed between the transmitter and receiver [14]. Adcock system using four input multiplexing are also used. The number of antennas can be extended from 8 to 16 for improving the accuracy of detection and increasing the load of processing. If two sensors are used to monitor a selected targeted UAV, then the location of targeted UAV can be determined by triangulation method. It requires angle of the targeted UAV and the distance between sensors [2]. If distributed signals of low intensity are required to be received, optimal antenna characteristics are required in the operating band and the omni-directional beam pattern as well [10]. It is confirmed that the performance of the pilot system is agreed with the result of numerical simulation by using robust Common Intrusion Detection Framework (CIDF) algorithms and fast RF down converter [12]. Time complexity and energy consumption for various scenarios in IoT and advanced metering infrastructure are computed in [7–9]. RSS values are used and processed at node and server level. Various relaying protocols are described in [6]. The decode and forward protocol has outdone all the other protocols in terms of signal to noise ratio.

3   Methodology

In this article, we have comprehensively reviewed some of the commonly used technologies in UAV monitoring and existing anti-UAV systems. Furthermore, we have discussed challenges and open research issues.

3.1   Angle of Arrival

This method is used to find the direction of a RF wave, incident on an antenna array or determined from maximum signal strength during the rotation of antenna. It is also called direction of arrival (DoA). This process finds the target location from multiple pairs of angle direction lines intersecting each other. At the receiving sensors, directional antennas are installed which are adjusted to catch the highest strength signal by antenna array. This helps in measuring the time DoA at individual elements of the antenna. Geometrically, it can measure location when two antennas make an angle and their angle intersects at a point in the range of antenna. For location measuring in two-dimensional plane, at least two receiving sensors are required. This provides improved accuracy because the signals is received at more receiving sensors, comparatively, which is also called triangulation. In its exact form mechanically, agile directional antennas are installed at the receiving sensors to detect the highest signal strength. The position of the antennas can be directly used to resolve the manner of line and approximate the angles formed by θa and θb as shown in Fig. 1. Geometric analysis of AoA technique is presented in Fig. 2.

VHF Omnidirectional Range (VOR) is a system used for navigation of aircraft which have a range of 108.1 to 117.95 MHz. The VOR receiver in an aircraft finds the location of aircraft as it moves towards the VOR beacon. This estimates the AoA with respect to the beacon.

Mathematically,

$$\theta = \cos^{-1} \frac{v_s n}{d f_s}. \tag{1}$$

Where n is the delay in samples, f_s is the sampling frequency, V_s is the time delay and d is distance between two sensors.

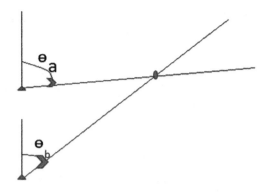

Fig. 1. Direction finding using AoA methodology

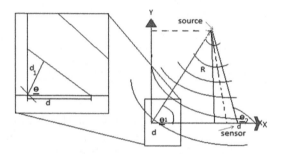

Fig. 2. Geometrical analysis of AoA methodology

3.2 Received Signal Strength

The RSS is a power, which is present in the received radio signal in different communication systems. It is the measure of power of signal on radio link and is express in dBm. RSS is basically used for estimating connectivity of nodes and distance of nodes. First task in designing of any positioning system needs to converts raw RSS signals to the positioning coordinates (valuable information). In Fig. 3, it is shown that several processing steps are needed for finding these coordinates. In the first step of distance estimation, the RSS value is collected from the reference node. Further, these RSS values are used to perform environmental characterization and for finding parameters suitable for that specific region. When the calibration process ends, the environmental parameters are not determined and changed if substantial changes in the region are not occurred.

In positioning system, the next step is to retrieve the consecutive RSS values from the reference node in an online operation. From the distance of RSS, the distance conversion between the target sensor node and the reference node are obtained. Both values of RSS and environmental parameters are used to convert these values of RSS to distances using a path loss model.

$$P_r = \frac{P_{(d_o)}}{(d/d_o)^n},$$ (2)

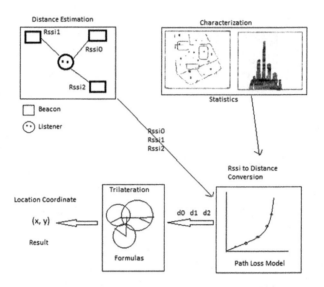

Fig. 3. Block diagram of RSS methodology

where, $P_{(d_o)}$ is the received power measured at the distance d_o. Generally, value of d_o is fixed as constant $d_o = 1$ m. n is the path loss index which is a parameter for characteristics evaluation of environment.

$$P_{r(d)} = P_{r(d_o)} - 10 \times n \times \log_{10}\left(\frac{d}{d_o}\right). \tag{3}$$

After the step of environmental characterization, two main parameters of environment, n and $Pr(d_o)$ are obtained. Therefore, by using Eq. 4, the distance between transceivers can be estimated.

$$d = d_o \exp\left(\frac{P_{r(d_o)} - P_{r(d)}}{10n}\right). \tag{4}$$

3.3   Correlative Interferometry

By triangulation method, information of direction by merging two receiver signals is obtained. The basic principle of the correlative interferometer consists of two steps:

1. Signal received at multiple co-located antennas, find out phase difference.
2. Compare the measured phase differences with a reference data set. DF system reference material known configurations at known transmitter angles. Interpolation can be obtained using lookup table to improve accuracy.

Phase Differences Computation: As illustrated in Fig. 4, difference between the phase depends upon the signal behavior. Consider one antenna as a reference and compare other antennas which are receiving signal phase with reference antenna. Receiver's front end circuitry for n channel converts the amplitude relation (with n channel antenna) into the phase relation for computing the phase difference. After that, the phase difference between any two elements can be easily computed.

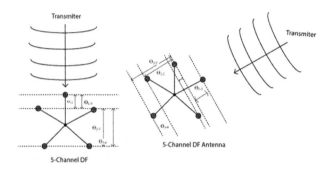

Fig. 4. Phase difference computation using correlative interferometry

FPGA Brute Force Approach: Fast Fourier Transform (FFT) and cordic cores in field-programmable gate array (FPGA) are used for computing the phase difference. Filters are applied to smooth out the results. Phase difference for each FFT is achieved by brute force approach. Phase detecting is difficult at low frequency because apertures are made very large.

3.4   Watson-Watt Method

This DF method is based on two directional antenna pairs and one omni-directional antenna. It consists of three phase-matched receivers and shows angle of arrival in terms of sine and cosine function. After that, the third omni-directional channel is used to solve the quadrant ambiguity.

The aim is to find the DoA of a signal in the range of 2–10 MHz. $\frac{1}{4}$ wavelength antennas are considered for a working frequency of 5 MHz, which means that each antenna is 15 meters long. The antenna separation must be half the wavelength of the maximum frequency. 10 MHz of frequency with a wavelength of 30 m is used and the distance of 15 m is kept between the antennas.

Calculation of the Angle of Arrival: After configuring the array along the E-W and N-S axis, The system starts to receive a signal of interest (SoI). Let ϕ be the angle formed by the waveform in the E-W axis. ϕ is the DoA which is required to be determined. The travel distance is different for each of the antenna, as shown in the Fig. 5. This means that different antennas receive SoI with some phase shifts.

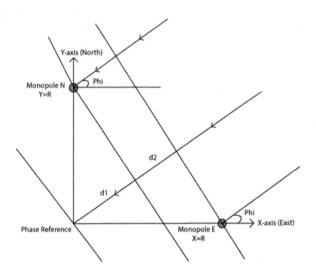

Fig. 5. Wavefront arrival at the Adcock array

Each antenna is placed at a distance R from the origin. The waveform arriving at the N antenna travels d_1 more than the distance to the origin, whereas, the waveform arriving at the E antenna travels a distance equal to the origin along with $d_1 + d_2$. The phase shift of the waveform at both antennas along with the distances $d_1 + d_2$ is obtained as follows:

$$\cos(\phi) = \frac{d_1 + d_2}{R}. \tag{5}$$

The distance d_1 can also be computed by:

$$\cos(90 - \phi) = \frac{d_1}{R}. \tag{6}$$

The following voltages are induced in each of the monopole by the wave front.

$$r_N(t) = m(t) \exp(jkR\sin(\phi)), \tag{7}$$

$$r_S(t) = m(t) \exp(-jkR\sin(\phi)). \tag{8}$$

$m(t)$ is the modulated SoI received and k represents the wave number of the frequency. Subtract the signal from the S antenna with that of the N antenna. k has very low frequencies. The following approximation is made:

$$r_N(t) - r_S(t) \approx m(t)2jkR\sin(\phi) \tag{9}$$

Same procedure is followed at the antennas E and W. The inverse tangent of the quotient of subtractions is calculated to compute the DoA.

$$\arctan \frac{r_N(t) - r_S(t)}{r_E(t) - r_W(t)} = \arctan \frac{\sin(\phi)}{\cos(\phi)} = \phi \tag{10}$$

Solving Ambiguity: The signal received from both the third quadrant SW and first quadrant NE generate the same line. The situation is same for the signals arriving with the same angle but from second and fourth quadrants. It can be solved by inserting a fifth antenna at the center of the Adcock array. Signal received by this antenna is used to modulate the intensity, by plotting the half straight line consistent to the quadrant from where the SoI is arriving. The block diagram is shown in Fig. 6.

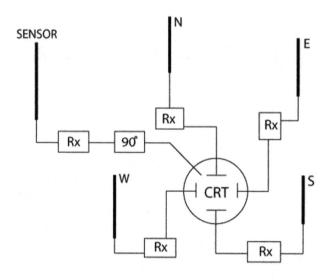

Fig. 6. Block diagram of four element Adcock array with sense antenna

4   Results and Discussions

Results are presented by taking values from various sources. Simulations are done on MATLAB 2016a and LabVIEW 2015 using a 5th generation corei7 machine having 8 GB of RAM. The experimental hardware setup comprises of a Software Defined Radio (SDR) USRP-N200 and a directional antenna. Only one receiving channel of USRP is used. A dual 10 GB/sec Ethernet interface is used to transfer data from USRP to host where signal processing is performed. A receiving directional antenna is placed at a fixed location for capturing the signal. As the transmitter antenna emits single tone signal at 2.4 GHz, the idea is to capture the change in received signal and phase.

It is observed in Fig. 7 that by assigning the center frequency of 2.4 GHz and IQ span of 200 KHz, the USRP can detect the frequency by showing peak value at center.

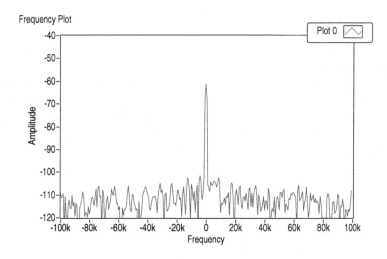

Fig. 7. RF response of receiver

4.1   Comparison of Various Parameters

A study was carried out in order to understand the strengths and weaknesses of four popular direction-finding techniques. From the Table 1, it can be noted that all the above-mentioned methods are based on different techniques which are phase, magnitude, angle along with Tx and Rx power comparison. Correlative Interferometry is found to be the expensive one because of hardware complexity. RSS and Watson-Watt method are less expensive. For achieving the maximum scanning speed through Watson-Watt method, it prefers three-channel and digital scanning. For the limited space, Watson-Watt method is better choice because it is good for the shortwave direction finding [4]. Correlative interferometry and Watson-Watt have better efficiency as compared to other methods. Also, Correlative interferometry has the highest range. For achieving the maximum accuracy and probability of detection, correlative interferometer method is best and if we reduce the scanning speed then it is accepted by the measurements of antenna arrays [1]. Correlative interferometry and Watson-Watt are found to be the accurate ones which shows that they have less SNR value. They are less prone to noise. Correlative interferometry has the largest hardware size as compared to others.

The surveillance technologies are listed in Table 1. It is noted that ranges for detection are obtained from different existing systems and literature review. Also it should be noted that these ranges may vary according to the type of UAVs, the surveillance environments, the corresponding algorithms, and different hardware parameters [13].

Table 1. Comparison of various parameters in direction finding

Parameters	Correlative interferometry	RSS	AoA	Watson-Watt method
Technique	Phase comparison	Powers comparison	Angles comparison	Magnitudes comparison
Cost	High	Low	Medium	Low
Efficiency	High	Medium	Better at outdoor	High
Range	Large	Upto 1 km	Medium	Upto 50 m
Accuracy	High	Medium	Low	High
Hardware size	Large	Small	Small	Small

4.2 Time Complexity

Figure 8 illustrates the Big-O notation graph of time complexity of various DF methods at different number of bits. From Table 2, the Big-O notation of RSS is

Table 2. Big-O notation computed for various algorithms of direction finding

Correlative interferometry	Received signal strength	Angle of arrival	Watson-Watt method
$O(n\log(n))$	$O(n^2)$	$O(n)$	$O(n)$

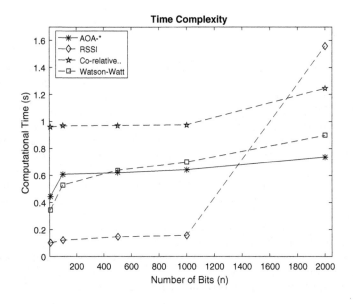

Fig. 8. Time complexity graph

$O(n^2)$ while Correlative Interferometry has $O(n)$. Both Watson-Watt and AoA has Big-O notation of $O(n\log(n))$. Thus, the Correlative Interferometry has the least time complexity. Watson-Watt and AoA shows greater time complexity as compared to others.

5   Conclusion

In this paper, the comparison of four different DF techniques (AoA, Correlative Interferometry, RSS, Watson-Watt) are presented which are used for DF of any RF transceiver. This paper presents the parameters through which the comparison is made. By performance analysis, it is found that the Correlative Interferometry is the best technique among them because in AoA, it works well in situations with line of sight (LoS) but the main problem is that the accuracy and precision decreases when there are multiple paths. Therefore, this method can not be considered as best for indoors. Another problem is that its accuracy also decreases if mobile target moves further from measuring units. Watson-Watt method requires considerable amount of alignment and usually the picked signal is very weak. It is suitable for up to 600 MHz, because at higher frequencies other techniques are found to be superior. Also, elevation calculation is not possible in Watson-Watt method. In the technique of RSS, medium accuracy has multiple propagations, adding effects and bad frontend devices. Therefore, the best of them is only Correlative Interferometry because it has highest accuracy even in inter channel interference, multipath fading and external noise sources for similar antenna diameters. Also its response time is faster than other DF techniques.

References

1. Adewumi, O., Djouani, K., Kurien, A.: RSSI based indoor and outdoor distance estimation for localization in WSN, pp. 1534–1539, February 2013. https://doi.org/10.1109/ICIT.2013.6505900
2. Boddhu, S.K., McCartney, M., Ceccopieri, O., Williams, R.L.: A collaborative smartphone sensing platform for detecting and tracking hostile drones. In: Ground/Air Multisensor Interoperability, Integration, and Networking for Persistent ISR IV, vol. 8742, p. 874211. International Society for Optics and Photonics (2013)
3. Dehghan, S.M.M., Moradi, H.: A new approach for simultaneous localization of UAV and RF sources (SLUS). In: International Conference on Unmanned Aircraft Systems (ICUAS), pp. 744–749. IEEE (2014)
4. Demmel, F., Unselt, U.: Application of DF antennas for direction finders DDF0xS and DDF0xM. NEWS-ROHDE AND SCHWARZ, pp. 22–23 (1998)
5. Ibrahim, M., Kamal, M., Khan, O., Ullah, K.: Analysis of radix-2 decimation in time algorithm for FPGA co-processors. In: 2016 International Conference on Computing, Electronic and Electrical Engineering (ICE Cube), pp. 154–157. IEEE (2016)

6. Kamal, M., Ibrahim, M., Mir, S., Aman, M.N.: Comparison of multihop relaying protocols in cognitive radio networks. In: 2016 Sixth International Conference on Innovative Computing Technology (INTECH), pp. 611–616. IEEE (2016)
7. Kamal, M., Tariq, M.: Light-weight security and blockchain based provenance for advanced metering infrastructure. IEEE Access **7**, 87345–87356 (2019)
8. Kamal, M., Tariq, M.: Light-weight security for advanced metering infrastructure. In: 2019 IEEE 89th Vehicular Technology Conference (VTC2019-Spring), pp. 1–5. IEEE (2019)
9. Kamal, M., et al.: Light-weight security and data provenance for multi-hop Internet of Things. IEEE Access **6**, 34439–34448 (2018)
10. Multerer, T., et al.: Low-cost jamming system against small drones using a 3D MIMO radar based tracking. In: European Radar Conference (EURAD), pp. 299–302. IEEE (2017)
11. Nam, S.Y., Joshi, G.P.: Unmanned aerial vehicle localization using distributed sensors. Int. J. Distrib. Sensor Netw. **13**(9), 1550147717732920 (2017). https://doi.org/10.1177/1550147717732920
12. Park, C.S., Kim, D.Y.: The fast correlative interferometer direction finder using I/Q demodulator. In: Asia-Pacific Conference on Communications (APCC), pp. 1–5. IEEE (2006)
13. Shi, X., Yang, C., Xie, W., Liang, C., Shi, Z., Chen, J.: Anti-drone system with multiple surveillance technologies: architecture, implementation, and challenges. IEEE Commun. Mag. **56**(4), 68–74 (2018)
14. Shin, D.H., Jung, D.H., Kim, D.C., Ham, J.W., Park, S.O.: A distributed FMCW radar system based on fiber-optic links for small drone detection. IEEE Trans. Instrum. Meas. **66**(2), 340–347 (2017)
15. Turgul, V., Dirim, M., Bilgin, S.B., Gok, H.I., Nesimoglu, T.: Broadband signal search and direction finding at UHF frequencies. In: Mediterranean Microwave Symposium (MMS), pp. 288–291. IEEE (2010)
16. Wallace, R.J., Loffi, J.M.: Examining unmanned aerial system threats & defenses: a conceptual analysis. Int. J. Aviat. Aeronaut. Aerosp. **2**(4), 1 (2015)
17. Wan-Jung Chen, I.J.S.: Direction finding of circular correlative interferometer for burst signals. In: Proceedings of Research World International Conference, Seoul, South Korea, pp. 1–5 (2018)

Metaheuristic Algorithms in Industrial Process Optimisation: Performance, Comparison and Recommendations

Tatjana Sibalija[(✉)]

Belgrade Metropolitan University,
Tadeusa Koscuska 63, 11000 Belgrade, Serbia
tsibalija@gmail.com

Abstract. The process parameters design is one of the most demanding tasks in a modern industry, aiming to find optimal process parameters that meet strict requirements for process responses. Various methods have been employed to tackle this problem, including metaheuristic algorithms. The objective of this paper is twofold. Firstly, it presents a review analysis and comparison of metaheuristics' performance in optimising industrial processes as evidenced from the literature, with a particular focus on the most commonly used algorithms: genetic algorithm (GA), simulated annealing (SA), and particle swarm optimisation (PSO). Secondly, an intelligent method for parametric multiresponse process design, based on the soft computing techniques, is presented. GA, SA and PSO are used as an optimisation tool, and comparison of their results in real case studies is performed including two criteria: (i) accuracy of an obtained optimum; (ii) a number of objective function evaluations needed to reach an optimum. Tuning of the algorithms' own parameters is also discussed, which is especially interesting due to a different nature of three algorithms: a single point-based algorithm (SA), a population-based algorithm (GA), and a population-based algorithm with swarm intelligence (PSO). The algorithms' robustness, i.e. sensitivity in respect to the algorithm-specific parameters tuning is studied and introduced as the third criterion in comparing the algorithms' performances. The concluding remarks are drawn from this analysis, followed by the recommendations for an efficient metaheuristics' application in optimising industrial processes.

Keywords: Process parameter design · Metaheuristic algorithms · Genetic Algorithm (GA) · Simulated Annealing (SA) · Particle Swarm Optimisation (PSO)

1 Introduction

The parametric process optimisation is one of the essential issues in industrial processes nowadays. In order to produce outputs from the inputs, the process is controlled by the control factors and negatively affected but the noise factors (Fig. 1). Over the years, optimisation methods have undergone substantial development to address rapid

© Springer Nature Singapore Pte Ltd. 2020
I. S. Bajwa et al. (Eds.): INTAP 2019, CCIS 1198, pp. 270–283, 2020.
https://doi.org/10.1007/978-981-15-5232-8_24

changes especially for new, emerging processes, where the input-output interdependencies are unknown. Modern processes typically involve a large number of control factors and multiple outputs, with very complex and non-linear interdependencies.

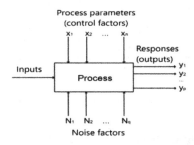

Fig. 1. General model of an industrial process.

The parametric process optimisation aims to find the optimal set of process parameters that simultaneously meets the desired responses mean and minimise the response variation, in a presence of various constraints (the parameter bounds and other constraints):

$$\text{Minimise} \begin{cases} \left|y_1(\mathbf{x}) - y_1^t\right|, \dots, \left|y_p(\mathbf{x}) - y_p^t\right| \\ \sigma_1(\mathbf{x}, \mathbf{n}), \dots, \sigma_p(\mathbf{x}, \mathbf{n}) \end{cases} \text{subject to } \mathbf{l}^l \le \mathbf{x} \le \mathbf{l}^u \text{ and } \mathbf{c}^l \le \mathbf{c} \le \mathbf{c}^u \quad (1)$$

where $\mathbf{x}$ is vector of n process parameters; $\mathbf{n}$ is noise factors vector; $\mathbf{y}$ is process responses vector; $\mathbf{y}^t$ is vector of response target values; σ is vector of response standard deviations; $\mathbf{l}^l$ and $\mathbf{l}^u$ are vectors of lower and upper bounds of process parameters; $\mathbf{c}$ is vector of other constraints, and $\mathbf{c}^l$ and $\mathbf{c}^u$ are vectors of their lower and upper bounds.

Taguchi proposed robust parameter design, based on the signal to noise ratio (SNR), and the quality loss (QL) that shows a loss encountered by the user if the product response deviates from the desired value, even if it is still within tolerance limits [1]:

$$\text{SNR} = \begin{cases} -10\log(\frac{1}{n}\sum_{i=1}^u y_i^2) & \dots & STB \\ 10\log(\frac{\bar{y}^2}{s^2}) & \dots & NTB \\ -10\log(\frac{1}{n}\sum_{i=1}^u \frac{1}{y_i^2}) & \dots & LTB \end{cases}, QL = K \begin{cases} \frac{1}{n}\sum_{i=1}^n y_i^2 & \dots & STB \\ \frac{n-1}{n}s^2 + (\bar{y} - t)^2 & \dots & NTB \\ \frac{1}{n}\sum_{i=1}^n \frac{1}{y_i^2} & \dots & LTB \end{cases} \quad (2)$$

where u is sample size, s^2 is sample variance, and response types are: nominal-the-best (NTB), larger-the-better (LTB), smaller-the-better (STB).

Since the Taguchi method does not address multiple responses, methods based on soft computing techniques have been proposed as an alternative (Fig. 2) [2].

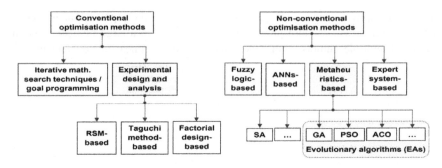

Fig. 2. Methods for parametric process design: general classification.

2 Metaheuristic Algorithms

2.1 Genetic Algorithm

GA is the most frequently used metaheuristic for the parametric process optimisation; it belongs to evolutionary algorithms (EAs). The typical GA procedure [3]:

– It starts with an initial population with n individuals presented as chromosomes. It has to be wide enough to provide enough diversity for the next generations.
– The objective function, i.e. fitness $f(x)$ of each chromosome is evaluated. The better fitness, the higher is probability to be selected for the next generation.
– A new population is formed using the following operations: (i) scaling transforms row fitness values to values suitable for the next operation; (ii) selection of the parent chromosomes is done according to their scaled fitness values; (iii) crossover combines two parents to form a child for the next generation; (iv) mutation implies small random modifications of genes to enhance the search space.
– The worst individuals in one subpopulation are replaced with the best individuals from another subpopulation. Migration is determined by the reproduction option that specified how the algorithm produce children for a new generation. Typically, a certain number of children automatically survives (elite offspring), the next part is produced by crossover, and the remaining part is produced by mutation.
– The objective function, i.e. fitness of chromosomes in new population is assessed.
– The procedure repeats until the termination criterion is met. It typically implies the predefined number of iterations, or the algorithm stops if there is no significant improvement in the objective function over a specified number of iterations.

There are various benefits of GA in comparison to the traditional gradient-based methods. However, it has been criticised for being highly dependent on the algorithm-specific tuning; a premature convergence could occur if they are not properly tuned [3].

2.2 Simulated Annealing

SA is based on the point-to-point search. It mimics the metal annealing process: heating a material to the melting point and then slowly decreasing the temperature to maintain the thermal equilibrium. The common SA procedure is [4]:

– The algorithm starts with an initial point at the initial temperature. New points are randomly produced in a proximity of the old one, at the distance defined by a probability distribution that is dependent on the current temperature. Annealing function is used to generate new points for next iterations.
– Evaluation of the fitness implies decision on whether the new point is better or worse than the current one. The initial temperature determines the probability of accepting a worse solution. It has to be high enough to provide movement to any neighbourhood. If the new point is worse than the current the algorithm accepts it (to decrease the objective function), but the algorithm might accept the superior point to extend the search area and avoid a local minimum. The following probability of acceptance is the most commonly used (Δ is difference between new and old objectives, T_0 is the initial temperature, T is the current temperature):

$$\frac{1}{1 + \exp\left(\frac{\Delta}{maxT}\right)} \tag{3}$$

– As the process proceeds, an annealing schedule controls the temperature decrease with the parameter temperature function. This allows the algorithm to avoid local optimum in the beginning of the search when the temperature is high. A slower temperature reduction is favourable for obtaining the global optimal solution.
– Reannealing is performed after a certain number of points is accepted to prevent being caught at a local solution, which is control by the reannealing interval. Reannealing raises the temperature in each dimension, and the search is resumed.
– The algorithm stops when the termination criterion is met, similarly to GA.

SA is appreciated for its simplicity. It has been statistically proven that with an infinitely slow cooling from high initial temperature and with large number of iterations, the algorithm is almost certain to find the global optimum. The shortcoming refers to dependence on the algorithm-specific parameters tuning and relatively slower convergence. Besides, since it is not population-based, it might not enclose an overall search space, which could jeopardise the capability of performing global optimisation [4, 5].

2.3 Particle Swarm Optimisation

PSO belongs to EAs, and it is a major algorithm in a swarm intelligence subgroup. It mimics the movement of a set of particles (swarm) throughout a multidimensional space in order to obtain the most desired position. The common PSO steps are [6]:

- An initial swarm is initiated, with positions x_i and velocities v_i. It is believed that, contrary to other EAs, PSO is not significantly affected by the initial swarm setting.
- The objective function is computed for all x_i to find the particle best position (*pbest*) and the swarm best position (*gbest*), and their objectives *f(pbest)* and *f(gbest)*.
- The particle velocity is updated based on the previous velocity and inertia weight w (first part of formula), the particle cognition component (the second part), and the social component (the third part of formula), which are controlled by c_1 and c_2 (self-adjustment and social adjustment learning factors):

$$v_i = wv_i + c_1 u_1 (pbest - x_i) + c_c u_2 (gbest - x_i) \tag{4}$$

- The particle positions are updated based on the previous ones and the updated velocities from the previous step. If necessary, the bounds are enforced.
- The objective function is evaluate for all particles. If $f(x_i) < f(pbest)$, then $pbest = x_i$. If $f(x_i) < f(gbest)$, then $f(gbest) = f(x_i)$ and $gbest = x_i$.
- The swarm is updated and procedure reiterated from the second step until the stopping condition is met. The termination criteria are similar as for GA and SA.

It is believed that PSO is less prone to stuck in local solutions and less affected by the algorithm-specific settings (especially regarding the initial swarm) than the other EAs. The major disadvantage refers to a premature convergence if the algorithm-specific parameters are not properly tuned. A larger swarm size and a proper global vs. local search balance (controlled by w and c_1 and c_2) are recommended [7, 8].

3 Intelligent Method for Parametric Process Optimisation

This section presents an intelligent system for multiresponse robust process design (IS-MR-RPD). After designing an experimental plan, performing experiment and collecting experimental results, the pre-processing method is used, as follows [2].

Response values are expressed by QL using formula (2) and normalised ($NQL_i(k) \in [0, 1]$). Since responses are correlated, principal component analysis (PCA) is applied over NQLs to obtain a set of independent components (PCs). The procedure shows the percentages of contribution, i.e. weights, in the total variation for each PC. Details of PCA could be found in [9]. Grey relational analysis (GRA) is applied over PCs to integrate them into a single measure, i.e. grey relational grade, based on their weights from PCA. Therefore, an assessment of a multivariate process is reduced to a grey relational grade (γ) which is adopted as single process performance measure. The higher process performance measure (γ), the better is the process ($\gamma \in [0, 1]$). Details of GRA could be found in [10]. Finally, effects of the control factor on process performance (γ) are computed as the mean of all γ values for each control factor level. The potentially good solution, i.e. potential optimal control factors setting, is obtained by selecting the levels with the maximal effect on γ for all control factors. This solution will serve as a basis to form an initial population or point for metaheuristic algorithms.

Since the process analytical model is unknown, artificial neural networks (ANNs) are employed to model the relation between the process control factors, at the input, and the process performance measure (γ), at the output. The feed forwarded back-propagation network with one hidden layer is used, with the tangent sigmoid and linear functions, for hidden and output neurones, respectively. A smaller learning rate (0.01) and a larger momentum factor (0.9) are adopted to assure a proper training. ANNs with different number of hidden neurones are trained in Matlab (including actual training, validation of generalisation and independent verification), until MSE (mean square error between the original data and the ANN output) of 10^{-3} is achieved. The best ANN is the one with minimal MSE. The coefficient of the correlation between original data and the ANN output is considered to verify a fit (R-value, with the threshold of 0.9).

The adopted neural model serves as an input for metaheuristic algorithms that find optimal process parameters that maximise the process performance (γ). GA, SA and PSO are used and compared according to: (i) quality (accuracy) of the obtained solution; (ii) the convergence speed, i.e. number of iterations needed to reach max. γ; (iii) the algorithm robustness, i.e. dispersion of the results obtained by different algorithm settings: the smaller results dispersion, the better is algorithm robustness.

For GA, the following parameters are used and tested in Matlab environment:

- Population size equal or larger than $5n$ (n is the number of process parameters);
- Initial population seeded with a potentially good solution (pre-processing result);
- Rank scaling function is adopted;
- Three selection types are tested: stochastic uniform, roulette wheel and tournament;
- Three crossover types are tested: single point, two points and arithmetic;
- Adaptive feasible mutation is adopted to accommodate linear parameter bounds;
- Forward migration direction and migration fraction of 0.2 are adopted;
- Termination criterion: 2000 iterations or change in the objective function less than 10^{-9} over 100 iterations, whichever is earlier.

Hence, 9 GAs are run for each optimisation problem. The best GA is the one that found maximal objective (max. γ), and, additionally, that showed a fastest convergence.

SA is implemented using the following algorithm-specific parameters:

- Initial point defined as a potentially good solution (result of pre-processing method);
- Initial temperature: values 10, 100 and 500 are tested;
- Three temperature functions are tested: exponential, fast, and Boltzmann function;
- Annealing function: fast annealing and Boltzmann annealing algorithms are tested;
- Reannealing interval: values 10 and 100 are tested;
- Termination criterion: the same criteria as for GA are adopted.

In total, 36 SA algorithms are run; the best SA is selected at the same way as for GA.

For PSO, the following algorithm-specific parameters are tested in Matlab, so, in total, 30 PSOs with random and 30 PSOs with defined initial swarm are analysed:

- Swarm size: values $2n$, $5n$ and $12n$ are tested (n is the number of process parameters);
- For initial swarm, two options are tested: (i) a random initial swarm, and (ii) initial swarm seeded in a proximity of potentially good solution (result of pre-processing);
- Inertia weight range: values [0.1; 1.1], [0.4; 0.9], [0.5; 2.5], [1.0.; 5.0] are tested;
- Learning factors: $c_1 = c_2 = 0.1$; $c_1 = c_2 = 0.5$; $c_1 = c_2 = 2.0$; $c_1 = c_2 = 5$, and $c_1 = 0.7$, $c_2 = 1.5$;
- Termination criterion: the same criteria as for GA and SA are adopted.

4   Comparison of Metaheuristics in Process Optimisation

4.1   Metaheuristics Comparison Based on IS-MR-RPD Implementation

The proposed IS-MR-RPD was implemented to optimise six manufacturing processes and performance of GAs (9 algorithms with different settings) and SAs (36 algorithms with different settings) were compared (Table 1), in respect to: (i) quality (accuracy) of the obtained solution, expressed by the maximal objective function (process performance γ) and the corresponding optimal process parameters; (ii) convergence speed, expressed by the number of iterations needed to reach max. γ; (iii) algorithm robustness, expressed by the objective function range: less disperse results indicate better robustness. The following conclusions could be drawn from the results presented in Table 1:

- In overall, SA resulted with a better solution quality than GA: it found higher γ value in three cases; in other cases both algorithms found the same max. γ value.
- The convergence speed was almost equal: SA needed less iterations to reach max. γ in three cases, GA was faster in three cases, and in one study they were almost equal.
- SA demonstrated significantly better robustness than GA, since results of SA algorithms were less disperse in all studies, except in study 1 where both algorithms showed very good robustness, and in study 4 where GA showed better robustness but it found significantly lower objective function (max. γ) than SA.

Therefore, it could be concluded that SA overperformed GA within IS-MR-RPD, as proven on six studies (seven cases, since study 3 included two separate experiments and analyses). In the next study 7 (Table 2), PSO was benchmarked with SA.

Table 1. Results of GA and SA applications within IS-MR-RPD in six case studies.

Case study	Results of metaheuristics application	GA	SA
1: Copper (50 μm) wire bonding on bare copper leads - weld side [11]	Objective function (γ) range	0.76724 ÷ 0.76725	0.76724 ÷ 0.76725
	Maximal objective function (max. γ)	0.76725	0.76725
	Optimal set of process parameters	[0; 20; 0; 150; 39; 117; 400; 1; 1]	[0; 20; 0; 150; 39; 117; 400; 1; 1]
	Number of iterations to reach max. γ	3	150
2: Copper (50 μm) wire bonding on Al die pads – bond side [12]	Objective function (γ) range	0.9255 ÷ 0.96870	0.9702 ÷ 0.97054
	Maximal objective function (max. γ)	0.96870	0.97054
	Optimal set of process parameters	[28; 400; 299; 40]	[40; 400; 385; 66]
	Number of iterations to reach max. γ	260	20
3: Gold (70 μm) wire bonding on Al die pads – bond side, for two groups of machines: M1 and M2 [13]	Objective function (γ) range	M1: 0.8807 ÷ 0.8812 M2: 0.7081 ÷ 0.7128	M1: 0.8810 ÷ 0.88120 M2: 0.7578 ÷ 0.75801
	Maximal objective function (max. γ)	M1: 0.88120 M2: 0.71280	M1: 0.88120 M2: 0.75801
	Optimal set of process parameters	M1: [85; 99] M2: [85; 95]	M1: [85; 99] M2: [85, 85]
	Number of iterations to reach max. γ	M1: 8 M2: 710	M1: 21 M2: 3
4: Enamelling process, using historical data from control charts [14]	Objective function (γ) range	0.82114	0.8711 ÷ 0.87285
	Maximal objective function (max. γ)	0.82114	0.87285
	Optimal set of process parameters	[1.70; 11.0; 5.0; 1.71; 11.0; 9.0]	[1.69; 9.5; 5.0; 1.71; 12.0; 9.0]
	Number of iterations to reach max. γ	9	20
5: Laser drilling of Nimonic 263 sheets [15]	Objective function (γ) range	0.7133 ÷ 0.75230	0.7508 ÷ 0.75230
	Maximal objective function (max. γ)	0.75230	0.75230
	Optimal set of process parameters	[7.5; 0.5]	[7.5; 0.5]
	Number of iterations to reach max. γ	4	5
6: Laser shock peening of Nimonic 263 sheets [16]	Objective function (γ) range	0.93044 ÷ 0.93052	0.93045 ÷ 0.93052
	Maximal objective function (max. γ)	0.93052	0.93052
	Optimal set of process parameters	[200; 4; 0.9]	[200; 4; 0.9]
	Number of iterations to reach max. γ	580	5

Table 2. Results of SA and PSO applications within IS-MR-RPD in one case study.

Case study	Results of metaheuristics application	SA	PSO with random initial swarm	PSO with defined initial swarm
7: Laser cutting of Nimonic 263 sheets [17]	Objective function (γ) range	0.890861 ÷ 0.900762	0.894012 ÷ 0.900825	0.893701 ÷ 0.900825
	Maximal objective function (max. γ)	0.900762	0.900825	0.900825
	Optimal set of process parameters	[14; 3; 2039; 4000]	[14; 3; 2034; 4000]	[14; 3; 2034; 4000]
	Number of iterations to reach max. γ	400	30	6

Since it was commented than PSO is less sensitive to initial conditions, both PSO with a random and with the defined initial swarm were tested. PSO showed a remarkable robustness, both with a random and with the defined initial swarm, although the latter group showed a slightly faster convergence. PSO demonstrated a superior solution and a faster convergence speed than SA.

The PSO implementation in the other optimisation problems (the first six studies) and its benchmark with SA is ongoing, to confirm the above conclusions on a large sample. The next steps will include application of cuckoo search (CS) and teaching-learning based algorithm (TLBO) within IS-MR-RPD and their comparison with PSO and SA, since results of an extensive literature review indicated than CS and TLBO showed better performance than PSO (see Sect. 4.2).

Recommendations for Metaheuristics' Settings Based on IS-MR-PRD Application
The following recommendations for the GA settings are drawn:

- Population size equal or larger than $5n$ is recommended.
- Selection: the stochastic uniform and the roulette wheel selection functions showed good results, the tournament selection performed significantly worse.
- Crossover: the single point and the two points crossover functions gave slightly better results that the arithmetic crossover function.

Recommendations for the SA algorithm settings, based on the above seven studies, are:

- Initial temperature: value of 100 showed the best results, followed by the value 500.
- Annealing function: the Boltzmann annealing algorithm performed slightly better that the fast annealing algorithm, so both could be recommended.
- Temperature function: the Boltzmann and the fast temperature function performed very well; the exponential function performed slightly worse.

- Reannealing interval: the interval of 10 in combination with the initial temperature 100 showed the best results, followed by the interval of 10 in combination with initial temperature 500, and the interval of 100 with initial temperatures 100 and 500.

Since PSO has been implemented only in one study, and all algorithms showed very good results, no recommendations for the PSO settings could be drawn at this point.

4.2 Metaheuristics Comparison Based on Extensive Literature Review

The discussion that follows is a consequence of a thorough literature review that included a few hundred of papers published in highly ranked journals from the soft computing, industrial and manufacturing fields [18, 19]. It was focused on the comparison among the most frequent metaheuristic algorithms, based on two criteria: quality of the obtained solution, and the convergence speed. The robustness of algorithms has not been studied in the reviewed papers. The summary of comparisons is as follows:

- GA, SA and PSO: SA and PSO performed better than GA in a vast majority of studies (over 60 studies), especially regarding the solution accuracy. PSO showed better convergence speed than GA in all studies. SA, in average, converged slightly faster than GA. This comparison also included the multiobjective algorithms based on the Pareto front (multiobjective PSO – MOPSO; nondominated sorting GA - NSGA II).
- SA and PSO: PSO found better solution and demonstrated a faster convergence than SA in a vast majority of studies (20 studies were observed).
- SA, PSO and ant colony optimisation (ACO): SA showed inferior performance in comparison to ACO. PSO outperformed ACO in all six studies that were observed.
- SA, PSO and artificial bee colony (ABC): ABC found better solution than SA (five studies). PSO mainly found better solution than ABC (over 10 studies), and it was always faster.
- SA, PSO and Hoopoe heuristic (HH): SA and HH demonstrated, in overall, an equal performance (four studies). PSO outperformed HH in three cases, for both criteria.
- SA, PSO and harmony search (HS): SA and HS showed, in average, equal results (three studies). PSO showed better performance than HS for both criteria.
- PSO and scatter search (SS): PSO found a better solution than SS in all five cases.
- SA, PSO and TLBO: TLBO outperformed SA (seven studies). In six studies, TLBO found a better solution than PSO; the convergence speed was approximately equal.
- SA, PSO and CS: CS found better solution than SA (four studies). CS showed better overall performance than PSO, for both criteria.

Comparisons with the other EAs were reported for a very small number of cases (one or two studies), so the sample is too small to drawn any conclusion.

In overall, PSO clearly outperformed GA and SA in solving process optimisation problems for both criteria, as presented in a large number of studies. Based on a smaller number of studies (three to ten studies), the following conclusions could be drawn:

- PSO clearly outperformed ACO, HS, SS, HH; it showed better performance than ABC (much faster convergence), and worse performance than TLBO and CS.
- SA showed approximately equal performance as HH and HS, and significantly lower performance than ACO, ABC, TLBO and CS, for both criteria.

However, these results should be interpreted conservatively since the sample for comparison was small. Besides, none of the reviewed studies considered the algorithm robustness. As demonstrated in Sect. 4.1, it is necessary to include the algorithm robustness in comparison between algorithms, especially since the repeatability of the metaheuristic results cannot be guaranteed. In some studies subjective benchmarks were performed, to indicate that the proposed algorithm performs better than the others do. These benchmarks typically include only one optimisation problem, without an adequate statistical analysis or considering a scalability of the algorithms application.

Issues in Metaheuristics' Application for the Parametric Process Optimisation

Although metaheuristics were proven effective in solving a variety of optimisation problems, a few issues for parametric process optimisation have been noticed. The analysis considered specifics of single response problems and of multiresponse problems.

For single response problems, the major issue in applying metaheuristic algorithms refers to their own parameters tuning in respect to peculiarities of the observed problem.

Multiresponse studies involve several issues that need to be addressed, as follows.

1. The first problem refers to the assessment of the algorithm robustness, as explained above, which is related to an appropriate tuning of the algorithm-specific parameters.
2. The second problem refers to the objective function formulation. In applying metaheuristics for multiresponse problems, two approaches were adopted:

   - Combination of multiple responses (their models and/or objective functions) into a single objective using the weighted sum approach. In such approaches, allocation of weights to individual responses is based on a subjective judgement (e.g. equal weights for all responses). A subjective weighting affects objectivity of the overall procedure, and, at the end, the results of metaheuristic applications.
   - Development of multiple response models or objective functions, addressed by the Pareto front methods (MOPSO; NSGA II). They can work with two (2D front) or maximum three (3D front) responses simultaneously; they are not convenient in case of a large number of responses. MOPSO implementation for process with four responses (Fig. 3) implies development of two 3D Pareto fronts, each considering three responses. A final solution is found as a subjective trade-off between optimal solutions of two fronts. The future work needs to address applicability of the Pareto front methods for problems with large number of responses.

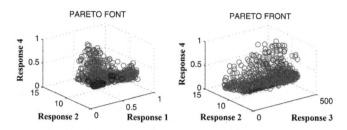

Fig. 3. MOPSO in optimising process with four responses: trade-offs are needed.

3. The third problem refers to an improper application of the parametric optimisation concept. Among a few hundred of reviewed papers, only a smaller part included in both the response mean and variability, mainly by interpreting response values via SNR or QL. This is especially important issue since a main source of problems in real industry is a process variability. Therefore, the results of studies that did not properly addressed the process variability could be useless for industrial practice.

5   Concluding Remarks

An extensive and thorough analysis of the metaheuristics application in parametric process design was presented, focusing on the three major algorithms: GA, SA and PSO.

An intelligent method for parametric design (IS-MR-RPD) was proposed. Its results in solving real industrial problems were listed, comparing the performance of GA, SA and PSO in respect to the solution quality, the convergence speed and the algorithm robustness. In six studies, SA clearly outperformed GA, especially in terms of the algorithm robustness. PSO showed significantly better results than SA in one study, which should be confirmed for the other studies. Settings of the algorithms' own parameters were analysed, and the recommendations for their tunings were drawn.

Findings from a comprehensive literature review were presented, indicating that PSO showed better results than a vast majority of the other metaheuristics, except CS and TLBO. However, since comparison of TLBO and CS with PSO was found in a small number of studies, this has to be confirmed or denied on a large number of studies in a future work. Although metaheuristics have been effective in resolving different optimisation problems, the major issues in applying metaheuristics for the parametric process optimisation were identified and addressed, as follows:

- It is necessary to assess the algorithm robustness in respect to the algorithm-specific parameters tuning, and this should be introduced as the third criteria (beside the solution quality and convergence speed) in evaluating the algorithms' performance. This is especially important due two reasons: a frequent criticism that metaheuristics are highly affected by their own settings, and a fact that the repeatability of the metaheuristic results, even with the same setting of the algorithm, cannot be guaranteed.

- For multiresponse problems, in case of a single objective function formed from multiple responses or their functions, the weights for individual responses or their functions must be assigned in a fully objective manner (e.g. including an appropriate data pre-processing method such as PCA and adopting calculated weights from PCA).
- The Pareto front-based methods can effectively solve problems with maximum three responses. In case of more responses, the final solution implies trade-offs, typically based on a subjective judgement. Therefore, future research should address development of methods to objectively deal with trade-offs among multiple Pareto fronts.
- Since the parametric design relies on the process mean and variability, it is necessary to appropriately address both the response mean and variation in designing an objective function for the metaheuristics. A vast majority of real industrial problems are caused by the process variability, so the importance of a complete understanding of the process parameter design is highlighted, especially in respect to variability.

References

1. Taguchi, G.: Introduction to Quality Engineering. Asian Productivity Organization. UNIPUB, New York (1986)
2. Sibalija, T., Majstorovic, V.: The Advanced Multiresponse Process Optimisation. An Intelligent and Integrated Approach. Springer, Switzerland (2016). https://doi.org/10.1007/978-3-319-19255-0
3. Sivanandam, S.N., Deepa, S.N.: Introduction to Genetic Algorithms. Springer-Verlag, Heidelberg (2008). https://doi.org/10.1007/978-3-540-73190-0
4. Spall, J.: Introduction to Stochastic Search and Optimisation. Wiley, New Jersey (2003)
5. Zandieh, M., Amiri, M., Vahdani, B., Soltani, R.: A robust parameter design for multi-response problems. J. Comput. Appl. Math. **230**(2), 463–476 (2009)
6. Kennedy, J., Eberhart, R.: Particle swarm optimization. In: Proceedings of IEEE International Conference on Neural Networks, pp. 1942–1948. IEEE, Perth (1995)
7. Pant, M., Thangaraj, R., Abraham, A.: Particle swarm optimization: performance tuning and empirical analysis. In: Abraham, A., Hassanien, A.E., Siarry, P., Engelbrecht, A. (eds.) Foundations of Computational Intelligence. Studies in Computational Intelligence, vol. 203, pp. 101–128. Springer, Heidelberg (2009). https://doi.org/10.1007/978-3-642-01085-9_5
8. Li, T.S., Hsu, C.M.: Parameter optimization of sub-35 nm contact-hole fabrication using particle swarm optimization approach. Expert Syst. Appl. **37**, 878–885 (2010)
9. Ramsay, J.O., Silverman, B.W.: Functional Data Analysis. Springer, New York (2005). https://doi.org/10.1007/978-1-4757-7107-7
10. Lu, M., Wevers, K.: Grey system theory and applications: a way forward. J. Grey Syst. **10**(1), 47–54 (2007)
11. Sibalija, T., Majstorovic, V.: Multi-response optimisation of thermosonic copper wire-bonding process with correlated responses. Int. J. Adv. Manuf. Technol. **42**, 363–371 (2009). https://doi.org/10.1007/s00170-008-1595-1
12. Sibalija, T., Majstorovic, V., Miljkovic, Z.: An intelligent approach to robust multi-response process design. Int. J. Prod. Res. **49**, 5079–5097 (2011)

13. Sibalija, T., Majstorovic, V.: Novel approach to multi-response optimisation for correlated responses. FME Trans. **38**, 39–48 (2010)
14. Sibalija, T., Majstorovic, V., Sokovic, M.: Taguchi-based and intelligent optimisation of a multiresponse process using historical data. Strojniski vestnik **57**, 357–365 (2011)
15. Sibalija, T., Petronic, S., Majstorovic, V., Prokic-Cvetkovic, R., Milosavljevic, A.: Multi-response design of Nd:YAG laser drilling of Ni-based superalloy sheets using Taguchi's quality loss function, multivariate statistical methods and artificial intelligence. Int. J. Adv. Manuf. Technol. **54**, 537–552 (2011). https://doi.org/10.1007/s00170-010-2945-3
16. Sibalija, T., Petronic, S., Majstorovic, V., Milosavljevic, A.: Modelling and optimisation of laser shock peening using an integrated simulated annealing-based method. Int. J. Adv. Manuf. Technol. **73**, 1141–1158 (2014). https://doi.org/10.1007/s00170-014-5917-1
17. Sibalija, T., Petronic, S., Milovanovic, D.: Experimental optimization of nimonic 263 laser cutting using a particle swarm approach. Metals **9**, 1147 (2019)
18. Sibalija, T.: Application of simulated annealing in process optimization: a review. In: Scollen, A., Hargraves, T. (eds.) Simulated Annealing: Introduction, Applications and Theory, pp. 1–14. Nova Science Publishers, New York (2018)
19. Sibalija, T.: Particle swarm optimisation in designing parameters of manufacturing processes: a review (2008–2018). Appl. Soft Comput. **84**, 105743 (2019)

Social Media Analytics

Sentimental Content Analysis and Prediction of Text

Ali Haider Khan[1]([⊠]), Muhammad Haroon[2], Osama Altaf[2],
Shahid Mehmood Awan[1], and Aamna Asghar[2]

[1] Department of Computer Science, University of Management & Technology,
Lahore, Pakistan
ali.jiskani@hotmail.com, shahid.awan@umt.edu.pk
[2] National College of Business Administration and Economics, Lahore, Pakistan
mr.harunahmad2014@gmail.com, osamakl80@gmail.com,
aamnaasghar1993@gmail.com

Abstract. In the advancement of technology, the web era revolutionized mankind life; huge amounts of data are available on the internet in the form of articles and blogs. From this huge volume of data opinion mining is an important for extracting the raw data to become useful information. Sentiment analysis provides categorization in opinion mining as positive or negative class for content analysis. English language is considered as a universal language and used almost every part of the word, so classification of opinion is important to get the end meaning of the word phrase and comments. No literature is available for classification of sub opinion in the text mining. SAP of Text through Machine Learning algorithm (KNN) is a three-step technique of opinion mining. In this study, authors have put articles at first removing stop-words, tokenizing the sentence and revamping the tokens, it will calculate the polarity of the sentence, paragraph and text through contributing weighted words by keeping sentiment shifters and intensity clauses in consideration. Secondly, over polarization of sentence is adjusted. Finally, overall trend of the input text on the basis of tokenization and polarization of sentence is predicted with proposed algorithm and compared with KNN. Furthermore, domain specific analysis is a distinct feature of the proposed model where data can be updated according to the required domain to ensure the optimal level of efficiency.

Keywords: Machine learning · Opinion mining · Polarity · Sentiment analysis and training data

1 Introduction

Sentiment content analysis is a recent un-abating research area in text mining. The world of social media has required companies to think about computational ways to extract the behavioral state of the writer or to excerpt the attitude of the customer towards product as well as service to predict customer trend [1]. With rapid improvement in e-commerce, e-blogging, social-media, e-education, and others; a huge amount of data is being produced. This attracted organization to think about techno-logical paths for opinion and emotion mining of the customer, towards entity such as

© Springer Nature Singapore Pte Ltd. 2020
I. S. Bajwa et al. (Eds.): INTAP 2019, CCIS 1198, pp. 287–295, 2020.
https://doi.org/10.1007/978-981-15-5232-8_25

product, service, topic, issue, person and organization. A simple sentence may have individual's viewpoints, opinions, and emotions. However, a sentence that contains either various sentiments or the word that can be referred as sentiment shifter for the same subject or for the various subjects. These different sentiments also take part as sub opinions [2].

Bag of Words (BoW), Supervised Learning and Unsupervised Learning, Rule-based and Using Discourse Information, these are broader grouping of methods which are used for opinion mining [3]. Natural language processing is a field that covers computer understanding and manipulating of human language. Entity extraction, part of speech tagging, sentiment analysis, and word modeling are amongst the most famous NLP algorithms [2].

Work done in this area is based on analysis of simple sentence either by calculating the number of positive or negative words [4], which does not prove to be effective rather it becomes a false choice for complex sentences or by assigning weights to positive/negative words to calculate the polarity of the overall sentence. In contrast to the work presented in [4], complex sentiment can also belong to one of the following three types.

Type 1. Total positive and total negative words are equal, but the sentiment class is not neutral.

Type 2. Total positive words are greater than total negative words, but the sentiment class is negative.

Type 3. Total negative words are greater than total positive words, but the sentiment class is positive.

Table 1. Complex sentiment categorization.

Type	Example	Positive	Negative	Weight polarity	Actual polarity
1	Your efforts are good but not in right direction	1	1	Neutral	Negative
2	Ali is good and fit player, but what of his use, if he cannot win match for Pakistan	2	1	Positive	Negative
3	Never say never	0	2	Negative	Positive

The above complex sentences (Table 1) having sentiment shifters, i.e. negative words or negative-conjunctions, expose the ineffectiveness of the above techniques. Furthermore, the models used so far, categorized the text in simple positive and negative classes. Our model handles the above stated issues through weighted words, intensity words and toggle words and it predicts the text category based on overall weight of the text by applying natural language processing techniques with purposed algorithm to predict the content of the class and compare the predicted results with machine learning algorithm (K Nearest Neighbor) results.

K Nearest Neighbor algorithm is used to compare the predicted results because it is one of the simplest algorithms used for classification even in the small data sets [1].

Sentimental content analysis is divided in two clusters that can be utilized as the basic feature of this paper first is to calculate the total positive and negative words and then calculate the polarity of the sentence using proposed algorithms.

The remainder part of the paper is arranged in Sections, Sect. 2 describes relevant work in literature review and Sect. 3 discusses proposed methodology. Section 4 is organized to describe the proposed cluster. Section 5 presents results of our proposed algorithm. At the end, study is concluded in Sect. 6.

2 Literature Review

This section includes the literature survey related to our proposed methods for a sentiment and used shallow semantic features to classify the sentiment.

Yadollahi et al. [5] discussed the taxonomy of sentiment analysis tasks by dividing into opinion mining and emotion mining and then further categorizing these into subjectivity detection, opinion classification, spam detection and others.

Vo [6] applied machine learning algorithms to introduce a concept of BoS (Bag of Structure) to extract the sentiment and classified the comments of the students.

Abualigah et al. [7] discussed a robust weight scheme naming Length Feature Weight (LFW) based on the occurrence of the features in other documents. He also introduced new dimensionality reduction way to lessen the features to improve efficiency and with K-mean clustering algorithm clusters the documents based on the term frequency features.

Asher et al. [8] discussed the discourse method for opinion and emotion mining and used one-dimensional semantic characteristics to group the opinions or emotions.

Hassan and Shoaib [9] proposed a three-step method to classify the Urdu language text sentiment (i) fragmentation of sentiment using set of hypotheses (ii) calculates the orientation scores of the fragments (iii) as result they estimated the polarity of the sentiment using fragment scores.

Zrin et al. [4] presented a Markov logic-based framework to integrate polarity scores from different sentiment lexicons and neighboring segments. Mukherjee and Bhattacharyya [10] used the discourse relations to target the web-based applications that dealt with noisy, unstructured text, like the tweets.

In contrast to above mentioned related work, our proposed classifier does not require to be trained using dataset to calculate the polarity of complex sentiments.

3 Methodology

The tools and languages used for the approach are C# and Python Programming Language while using a Natural Language Processing Tool Kit and Machine Learning Algorithm (K Nearest Neighbor) to adjust the weights of the sentence & paragraph and to predict the trend of the text.

The framework flow of proposed solution is illustrated below in Fig. 1.

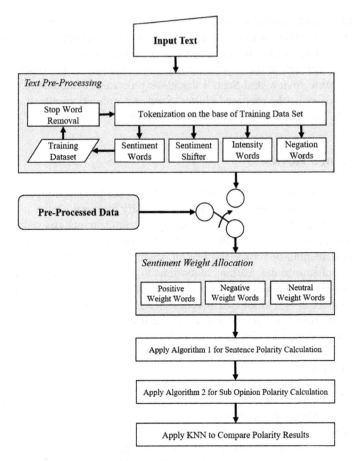

Fig. 1. SAP framework

Figure 1 basically shows the work flow of the proposed model. In this paper, authors have put articles at first removing stop-words, tokenizing the sentence and revamping the tokens, it calculates the polarity of the sentence, paragraph and text through contributing weighted words by keeping sentiment shifters and intensity clauses in consideration.

4 Proposed Classifier

Authors explain the following terms, as these are frequently used in the remaining paper, before discussion of proposed solution. Position: Position of a word tells whether the word contains positive (+1), negative (−1) or neutral (0) thought. Score: Score is an integer value that can be positive, negative or zero.

Dictionary: Dictionary, D is a file that defines the Position and POS tag of words [11]. Position function: Position (w) is a function that finds the Position of w from D and returns +1 or −1 [11].

Polarity function: Let polarity be a function defined as:

$$Polarity\ Score = \begin{cases} positive\ for\ Score > 0 \\ neutral\ for\ Score = 0 \\ negative\ for\ Score < 0 \end{cases} \tag{1}$$

POS function: Let POS (W) is a function that takes a word as input and returns its part-of-speech tag as defined in D. Sentiment: Let S be the input sentiment with n words in linear order as $S = \{W_1, W_2, W_3, \cdots, W_n\}$ and $W_i\ \varepsilon$.

The proposed algorithm classifies the given sentiment S into positive, negative or neutral class. The algorithm involves three steps: sentiment segmentation, polarity score calculation, and sentiment polarity identification.

First, the classifier segments the sentiment S into two fragments S_1 and S_2. The next step calculates the score of both S_1 and S_2. Finally, the algorithm determines the polarity of sentiment S.

Algorithm I: Position Score (S)

```
1     tokens[] = tokenize(S)
2     is Apply Forward Negation = false
3     while (token = tokens.nextToken)
4     {
5         #checking from dictionary
6         tokenPosition = Position(tk)
7         part of Speech Tag = POS(token)
8         if part Of Speech Tag == Adjective then
9         {
10            if is Apply Forward Negation = true
11            token Position = reverse (tokenPosition)
12            stack.push (tokenPostion)
13        }
14        else if part Of Speech Tag == Forward Negation
15            is Apply Forward Negation = true
16        else if part Of Speech Tag == Backward Negation
17        {
18            PreviousPosition = stack.pos()
19            NewPosition = reverse (previousPosition) stack.push(newPosition)
20        }
21    }
22    Score = sum All Position (stack) return score
```

We observed opinions from different social media sites and reached the conclusion that in language, people tend to give a negative opinion at the end of the sentiment or in sub opinion class may change the opinion of complete sentence; In this case polarity of the second opinion dominates the polarity of the overall sentiment.

Let sentiment S holds two sub opinions S_1 and S_2. If the polarity of S_2 is a negative, then the sentiment polarity is also negative. Algorithm 2 is proposed algorithm for Sub Opinion Polarity which calculates the polarity of sentiment based on the sentence with two sub opinion.

Algorithm II: Sentiment Polarity (S)
1   S_1, S_N = sentiment Segmentation(S)
2   if S_1 != null and S_N != null then
3   {
4   score1 = PositionScore (S_1)
5   scoreN = PositionScore (S_N)
6   if scoreN < 0 then
7   {
8   return negative
9   }
10   }
11   score = score1 + score2 + score3 + ... + scoreN
12   return Polarity(score)

Hassan et al. [9] discussed the above algorithm(s) for Urdu text mining and the authors take the above-mentioned algorithm(s), for sub opinion classification to calculate the polarity of words for content analysis.

For training of KNN algorithm authors take (pre-processed) data set of tweets [12] that are labeled as positive negative and neutral. Authors added the sentences to proposed algorithm(s) and KNN for calculating polarity results. After calculation of polarity of words with proposed algorithm, authors compare calculated results with KNN algorithm to check the accuracy of proposed algorithm.

5   Results

The performance of different methods used for opinion mining is evaluated but our results clearly demonstrated the difference.

Example: 1 Afridi is good and fit all-rounder, but what of his use, if he cannot win match for Pakistan.

The above example contains positive word as per BoW but the complete sentence is negative as per our application result.

Example: 2 Although the media criticized Pakistan cricket team all the time, but they gave an excellent performance during Dubai tour.

The above example contains more negative word as per BoW but the complete sentence is positive as per our application result.

In the below Table 2 polarity results demonstrates the actual opinion on the bases of polarity that is not bound on the bases of weighted positive and weighted negative words.

Table 2. Polarity calculation.

Sentence	Positive words	Negative words	Polarity results
1	1	−1	Positive
2	1	−1	Negative
3	5	−6	Positive
4	6	−2	Negative
5	3	−2	Positive
6	2	0	Positive
7	5	−1	Negative
8	3	−3	Negative
9	0	−2	Negative
10	4	−3	Negative

After the calculation of polarity, we add the sentence to KNN and then compare our calculated polarity (of above table) with KNN results, to check the accuracy with our proposed algorithm (Table 3).

Table 3. Comparison of KNN algorithm & polarity results

Sentence	Polarity results	KNN results
1	Positive	Negative
2	Negative	Negative
3	Positive	Positive
4	Negative	Negative
5	Positive	Positive
6	Positive	Positive
7	Negative	Negative
8	Negative	Negative
9	Negative	Negative
10	Negative	Negative

Our proposed algorithm results and KNN results are compared and our proposed algorithm shows 90% accuracy with KNN results. The purposed algorithm will give accurate prediction in opinion mining even if no or less information is available for training or labeling the class. The opinions of compound sentences are calculated on the bases of polarity of the sentences as in [13].

Weibe et al. [14] identified, for each word, the strength of subjectivity clues in the surrounding context. Then, these clues were used to perform opinion recognition.

Thelwall et al. [15] introduced Senti strength algorithm to extract sentiment strength from informal English text. They exploited de facto grammars and spelling styles of cyberspace. Our purposed algorithm also supports all these approaches.

The past few researches like Turnery and Littman [16] that they introduced a method for inferring the semantic orientation of a word from its statistical association with a set of positive and negative paradigm words, this approach is not suitable to classify the sentence on positive or negative category without calculation the our all polarity of the words [17].

6 Discussion and Conclusion

In this paper authors proposed an algorithm that is useful when no data is available for training of machine learning algorithm. Sentimental analysis using ML algorithms needs some datasets for training of algorithm but in this paper our proposed algorithm not required any sort of data for training of algorithm. In this way, author's algorithm saves lot of efforts and resources.

Moreover, it gives almost 90% accuracy results when comparing with KNN algorithm. Sentiment analysis has a wide variety of applications in information systems, including classifying reviews, summarizing review and other real time applications so using this study is helpful in opinion mining.

From the above work it is evident that neither classification model consistently outperforms the other, different types of features have distinct distributions. It is also found that different types of features and classification algorithms are combined in an efficient way in order to overcome their individual drawbacks and benefit from each other's merits, and finally enhance the sentiment classification performance.

The purpose of the study was to extend the capability of BoW based approaches; to classify complex and ambiguous opinions. Sentiment analysis leads to social media mining, brand monitoring, observing the different situation and prediction of possible future turmoil. However, researcher(s) should explore methods other than BoW based approaches; the results encouraged that the sub sentence-level information improved the classification of sentiment. Future research may include identification of complex relationships between sub-opinions and rigorous theory to handle sentiment containing more than two sub opinion.

References

1. Asur, S., Huberman, B.A.: Predicting the future with social media. In: Proceedings of the 2010 IEEE/WIC/ACM International Conference on Web Intelligence and Intelligent Agent Technology. IEEE Computer Society (2010)
2. Kim, N.-R., Kim, K., Lee, J.-H.: Sentiment analysis in microblogs using HMMs with syntactic and sentimental information. Int. J. Fuzzy Log. Intell. Syst. 17(4), 329–336 (2017)

3. Zhang, L., Liu, B.: Sentiment analysis and opinion mining. In: Encyclopedia of Machine Learning and Data Mining, pp. 1–10 (2016)
4. Zirn, C., et al. Fine-grained sentiment analysis with structural features. In: Proceedings of 5th International Joint Conference on Natural Language Processing (2011)
5. Yadollahi, A., Shahraki, A.G., Zaiane, O.R.: Current state of text sentiment analysis from opinion to emotion mining. ACM Comput. Surv. (CSUR) **50**(2), 25 (2017)
6. Vo, H.T., Lam, H.C., Nguyen, D.D., Tuong, N.H.: Topic classification and sentiment analysis for Vietnamese education survey system. Asian J. Comput. Sci. Inf. Technol. **6**, 27–34 (2016)
7. Abualigah, L.M., et al.: Text feature selection with a robust weight scheme and dynamic dimension reduction to text document clustering. Expert Syst. Appl. **84**, 24–36 (2017)
8. Asher, N., Benamara, F., Mathieu, Y.Y.: Appraisal of opinion expressions in discourse. Lingvisticæ Investigationes **32**(2), 279–292 (2009)
9. Hassan, M., Shoaib, M.: Opinion within opinion: segmentation approach for urdu sentiment analysis. Int. Arab. J. Inf. Technol. **15**(1), 21–28 (2018)
10. Mukherjee, S., Bhattacharyya, P.: Sentiment analysis in twitter with lightweight discourse analysis. In: Proceedings of COLING 2012 (2012)
11. Owoputi, O., et al.: Improved part-of-speech tagging for online conversational text with word clusters. In: Proceedings of the 2013 Conference of the North American Chapter of the Association for Computational Linguistics: Human Language Technologies (2013)
12. kaggle: Twitter sentiment analysis (2017). https://www.kaggle.com/c/twitter-sentiment-analysis2. Accessed 01 Jan 2019
13. Vaghela, V.B., Jadav, B.M., Scholar, M.: Analysis of various sentiment classification techniques. Int. J. Comput. Appl. **140**(3), 0975–8887 (2016)
14. Wiebe, J., et al.: Learning subjective language. Comput. Linguist. **30**(3), 277–308 (2004)
15. Thelwall, M., et al.: Sentiment strength detection in short informal text. J. Am. Soc. Inf. Sci. Technol. **61**(12), 2544–2558 (2010)
16. Turney, P.D., Littman, M.L.: Measuring praise and criticism: inference of semantic orientation from association. ACM Trans. Inf. Syst. (TOIS) **21**(4), 315–346 (2003)
17. Ailem, M., et al.: Unsupervised text mining for assessing and augmenting GWAS results. J. Biomed. Inform. **60**, 252–259 (2016)

An Analysis of Depression Detection Techniques from Online Social Networks

Uffaq Bilal[1]([✉]) and Farhan Hassan Khan[2]

[1] Department of Computer Science and Software Engineering,
IIUI, Islamabad, Pakistan
Uffaqbilalll@gmail.com
[2] Knowledge and Data Science Research Centre (KDRC),
College of Electrical and Mechanical Engineering (CEME),
National University of Sciences and Technology (NUST), Islamabad, Pakistan
mrfarhankhan@gmail.com

Abstract. Mental illness is caused by depression which may have a deep negative impact on individuals or on the society as a whole. It is a growing and severe problem which has the tendency to increase with time due to the extensive use of social networking websites such as Facebook, Twitter, Instagram etc. These social networking websites allow users to share images, videos, expressions and emotions. Depression is a form of mental illness. Patients suffering from depression have mood disorders such as low mood, high mood, lack of interest in things, etc. Machine learning techniques on text data and emojis have been applied to automatically classify a user into depressed and non-depressed. State-of-the-art classifiers have been used by the researcher to detect depressed individuals. Benchmark datasets are composed of text and emojis used in the social networking websites where classification is based on four factors Emotional Process, Temporal Process, Linguistic Style and combination of these three factors. In the proposed method, the emotional process is combined with their respective emojis to develop an automatic system for the detection of depressed patients. The features from the emotional process and emojis will be extracted and state-of-the-art classifiers have been proposed to be trained and evaluated using multiple classifiers using different combinations of part-of-speech tags.

Keywords: Depression · Emotion · Sentiment analysis

1 Introduction

Internet provides a communication link for the users to interact with each other and users around the globe. Nowadays there are a number of advance social media platforms such as Facebook, Twitter, Instagram etc. The use of social media applications allow multiple users to communicate electronically and exchange information among each other. Such applications work on text, multimedia content and emojis. Social media is an invisible source of impact on the life of billions people [1]. Large amount of data is stored on social media applications that can be noticed by anyone; however it can be extracted by authorized individual only [2]. Social Network Sites (SNS) contain different tool to categorize the users according to user generated contents (UGC). Mental illness are some situations or states that have impact on the persons emotions like their mood, thinking and feelings. Everyone has different kind of emotions in their lives because they are suffering from different kind of experiences. Most of the times many people suffer from the same situation [3]. Now a day's Mental health poses a serious challenge which is growing day by day especially among youth, 20% of youngsters are globally affected by this problems each year [4]. On social media many people are interacting and communicating online that may have effects on the human behavior and cause mental disorders. Study states that the use of social network sites like Facebook, Twitter etc., can be used to indicate the depression. First study point out that usage of internet performed a significant impact on social affairs and also involved in human life to some extent. Researchers emphasize that more time spent on social media may impact social life that may create the gap between user communication with their friends and family. It may reduce their social circle which may lead towards depression and loneliness. Later many publishers recommended that lot of computer usage may have an impact negatively on youngsters' social development. To calculate output from the input few data was labeled and rest of data leave unlabeled. It consisted of a mixture of supervised and un-supervised techniques [5]. Social media usage increasing day by day specially among young generations due to ease of availability on smarts phones, laptops social network site. By mining the user posts human behavior can be analyzed further which helps us to predict depression. Dataset classification is being used to collect data from UGC and then labeled as either users are depressed or not depressed. In Fig. 1 a block diagram represents the overview to detect the depression using Facebook.

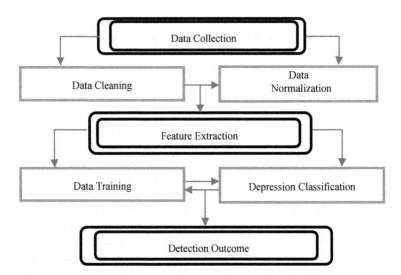

Fig. 1. A methodological overview of Facebook data for depression analysis.

1.1   Motivation

Social media provide a great source to communicate and share your data like post, games, videos with your friends and families by this, can identify the user emotion's and moods regarding their post which is helpful to easily judge the user's behavior. User can use different kind of SNS (social network sites) and nowadays due to technology advancement many different tools and application are available which contain different kind of materials. Some are related to learning aids and some are used for general purposes. Most of the school and colleges enhance the use of Facebook to engaged the student to use it for academic purposes and get their lecture and learning materials from Facebook and to interact with their teachers friends and family through it. These are the positive impacts of these sites on society. On the other hand, there are lot of negative impacts in which most of the student use Facebook and waste their most of time on it. Due to negligence of parents or administration, they get diverted towards the bad social sites which can be harm full for mental health by creating different causes of depression like sadness, loneliness, anxiety and stress. Now a days it is considered as a big challenge.

1.2   Research Contribution

This research has the following contributions:

- Presents a state of art research critical literature review.
- The research gaps have been identified highlighting the limitations of existing techniques.
- A novel framework has been proposed that overcomes the existing limitations.

The rest of paper is organized as follow: Sect. 2 summarized the literature review and in Sect. 3 proposed methodology of depression detection. Finally, Sect. 4 conclude this paper with future work.

2   Literature Review

In [1] focus on four factors on emotional process, temporal process, linguistic style and combined all these factors. Author apply supervised learning machine techniques like Decision Tree, k-Nearest Neighbor and Support Vector Machine. Authors detected the behavior of users by collecting data from face book comments. By using N-Capture tool, analyzing data through LIWC software. Facebook comments data divided into two sets for positive mean yes (the class label is depressed) and for negative means No, (the class label is not depressed). Authors focused time series of using Facebook like AM and PM. Formats. Author wanted to discover the major factors which cause depression using Facebook. KNN, DT, SVM classifiers consists of further multiple sub classifiers. Decision tree gave the highest result as compare to KNN and SVM for precision, recall and F-measures and achieved 60 to 80% accuracy. In future work other techniques can be applied on it. Dig out more different emotional features and applied on different data set. LWIC contain 50 attribute. Author used only 21 attributes, for further research the remaining attributes can be used. In [6] presented a frame work which analyzed the user physiological sates. By using user end reports of the using social media. Author presented the machine learning algorithms such as Naive Bayes to classify the depression level, enhance the accuracy and locate the user towards the doctor. The goal of presenting a frame work is to develop a web application which takes social media posts and survey test as a input and predict output in different ways. Find out depression levels that a user is in stress or not. Author categorized user in two state first is number of stress users and number of non-stress users. Finding presented that 30% students are in stress 50% are not in stress. In [7] has purposed KNN (K-Nearest Neighbor) machine learning technique to identify depression on face book. This paper addressed following two questions.

1. How abstract data of users from Facebook comments?
2. How depression should be detected by using machine learning techniques?

For collecting data Author use N-Capture tool for analyzing qualitative data, KNN technique is used. Author focused on three emotions which are based on Emotional Process, Temporal Process and linguistic analysis. To interpret user comment and to recognize emotions, author used LWIC tool and the data was collected from Bipolar Facebook page. This paper presented following contribution. Firstly discussed the related work which are using some different detection techniques. Secondly, manual classification of the validate data set and apply KNN machine learning techniques to measure who is misery or not from depression. 7145 comments has been taken from Facebook and it can be divided in two sets in the form of YES (Depression) or No (Not depressed) these were justified manually by expert and achieved 58% YES or 42% No. Measurement were conducted using MATLAB. Author applied different KNN classifiers: Fine KNN, Medium KNN, Course KNN, Cosine KNN, Cubic KNN and Weighted KNN. Paper outcomes showed that Course KNN present best result between 60%-70%. In future work different techniques can be applied to extract different kind of emotional features for detecting Depression. In [8] proposed computational models for recognizing disgrace vocabulary in Chinese social media posts. Explored which conditions cause the presence of depression stigma on social media. Author presented three steps strategies followed by this procedure Data collection. Data pre-processing, Data modeling. In first step, data was taken from weibo post which publicly available. Almost 99,925,821 users lie on weibo user pool. This study recognized only active weibo users whose average range is from 2.48 to 40. Posts were downloaded using API. In second step define class labels of stigma or non-stigma on 15,879 webio post. Frame work is used which based on prior stigma detection study. Two researchers were summarized post regarding class by using MS Excel Spread Sheet. To evaluate the frequency of webio post, author used (SCLIWS) Simplified Chinese version of Linguistic Query of Word Count. This study used WEKA tool to construct two groups of classification model. In first classification model labeling of depression stigma or without depressed stigma. In Second for enhancing performance of data model. Author linked three distinct key features Gain Rate Attribute Evaluator (GRAE), Significance Attribute Evaluator (SAE), Chi-squared Attribute Evaluator (CAE). In third for maximizing model performance author used four distinct Classification Algorithms Simple

Logistic Regression (SLR), Multilayer Perceptron Neural Networks (MLPNN), Support Vector Machine (SVM) and Random Forest (RF). The performance was calculated using Precision, recall and F measures. In second group to interpret the classification performance. Author evaluated the Precision, recall and F-measures 75.2%. Result were shown In F-measures among distinct post for Depressed stigma or non-Depressed stigma. F-measure showed different results between three types such as (unpredictable stigma, weakness stigma and false illness stigma) were 86.2% and assessment of F-measure with other related study hold 37–83%. In third to recognize presence of depression stigma linguistic analysis is favorable. At the end author also defined some limitations. Firstly, study targeted only stigma appearance in Chinese Weibo posts. Secondly, it cannot estimate the classification performance due to discrepancy number of post. Thirdly all users were delegate as Chinese. Finally, the method which is used in this study can be continued to discover distinct type of stigmas related mental or heath associated which would be helpful for performance improvement to decline stigma. In [9] has proposed Apriori Algorithm and Associations rule mining to dig out information from different databases. Apriori Algorithm is used to produce common item set and made association rule. It was executed in JAVA language, for testing model 500 individual documents has been taken for forecasting. Author took different appearances of persons as an input. Combining the common factors in graph which are suffering from depression, entered the values in system by user interface. Aim of this paper was exploitation at distinct levels and states and forecasting depression level. Future work can be done at individual level and management with security and providing obstacle techniques. Different mining techniques can be applied for forecasting on different fields. In [10] has proposed DK-LSTM (Domain Knowledge-enhanced Long Short-Term Memory). A novel design which is based on deep learning to recognize the individuals who are suffering from depression and emotions. This proposed model assimilate for both the general knowledge and Domain Knowledge. Performance of DK-LSTM is determined through analysis and through numerous Machine Learning and Deep learning models. Firstly, Researcher constructed general word vectors and domain–lexicon vectors. General word Vector were generated by word 2 vecs and the domain–lexicon vectors were based on LWIC lexicon. To generate word vector, data of size 100 was collected from Wikipedia contents from internet and three steps of pre-processing were performed at the data. First step was, cleaning the data like removing formatting, immaterial words and second step was sub division of sentences into words. In third step, stop words were removed or those words who do not have much information about the process for improving the accuracy of final result. Researcher used Word 2Vec approach that took large text amount as an input and produced output as numeric vector for each word. There are two famous models used in Word 2 Vec, which are CBOW and Skip-gram. For training of words, Skip-gram model was applied. After operating the Word2vec processed each word of the input and expressed as 100-dimentional vector. On the other hand the domain–lexicon based on LWIC lexicon was built on LWIC vector with 71 dimensions. If a word associates with one or more categories in LWIC, the value will be changed with reciprocal elements in the vector to one if not so then vector elements value will be zero. After that it started to encode each input document. There are two sets of vectors used to encode one is general and second is domain demonstrations. These demonstrations accepted to the LSTM layer for investigation. LSTM has a narrow capability to perceive domain-based information. To tackle this problem the DK-LSTM is produced whose aim is to abduct both general and domain information at the same time. There are two LSTM units, one is Genera and second is Domain–lexicon. General LSTM unit was used to analyze semantic and syntactic information. On the other hand, Domain–lexicon LSTM unit helps to detain information to specific domain based on existing knowledge. Researcher divided Word Embedding layer and the LSTM Layer into two parts and then processed independently until Merge layer. Merge layer combined the feature vectors which were produced by the two LSTM units and generated a mixed feature vector. These mixed feature vectors passed to the Dense layer to obtain the final result. Dense Layer used a soft max function to provide outputs. In future, the DK-LSTM design based on Tensor flow Backed may be applied to improve the proposed model's performance. In [11] proposed a machine learning (ML) framework concerning (EEG) signal analysis of anxious members. ML frame work contain EEG feature extraction, feature selection, classification and tenfold cross validation. It detected stress level by performing three analytical cases. In one, every level of stress was related with the primary level of organize. In second case, level of stress was compare with its various level of control. In third, every level of stress was relate with all the other levels of strain. LR classifier was used to form a model and relationship among the decrease set of features and the sub sequent analysis at the end. LR classifier appeared in the form of value of l (x). If l (x) larger than the origin then situation was stated to be tension or else, it was linked with management group. Second categorization model was SVM classifier with linear kernel. Through SVM, it got the maximum categorization accuracy. NB is the third classification model. As a result, framework for two-level identification of stress composed 94.6% accuracy and for several level identification produced 83.4% accuracy. Proposed (Electroencephalogram) EEG-based Machine Learning framework has possibility to measure stress neutrally into multiple levels and help out in establishing a computer-aided symptomatic tool for stress detection. In [12] proposed a self-starting stress process from cress media micro blog data and built a three level framework. First level found the low level characters from tweets and then described abstract center level representation in three conditions, Linguistic attributes, Visual attributes and social attributes. 600 million tweets were taken from Chinese micro blogs. Tweets contain various hash tags, this represent user views about some topics and there mental states. Finally taking the hash tags of 57785 label tweets which are labeled by three persons label considered acceptable only when two person agreed. Total 95% hash tag labels were acceptable among all. Distinct classification model attained same results under the same experiments according to proposed method. CAE based DSNN was compared with SVM, Shallow ANN and DNN with Stacked Auto–Encoder. DSNN is quite beneficial and competent for stress detection. Future work can be done by examining the social interaction mental stress which depend on emotional and art theories. In [13] recognized prediction of depression in persons through Twitter tool. Firstly, gathered Gold Standards according to these label depression, to describe depressive behavior like languages, emotions through proposed social media. Results showed that persons who are suffering from depression, demonstrate lower social life. Superior negative emotions and high self–attention, high medical involvement and contain sensitive appearances of religious speculation. Finally SVM classifier constructed and predicted possibility of individual depression. Through this classifier 70% accuracy achieved. Facebook usage has increased to one billions of peoples around the world, who use it on daily basis. They communicate easily even residing on different places. Due to advancement in tools now it has become more popular, most of the students use it as a learning aid. In [14] designed cross-sectional design and used it for analysis of study population of 76 students Bachelor of Science. Facebook magnitude Scale (FIS) and the Depression Anxiety and Stress Scale were the main appliance, which were used in this study. Questionnaires had three parts which were used in examination, first is detailed information, second is Facebook intensity scale and third is Depression Anxiety and Stress Scale (DASS). First part contain the general information like gender, family. Second part contain 8 questions regarding Facebook activeness. Third one contained 42-item questionnaire which had 3 self-related measurement like harmful emotional states of depression, worry and strain. Study showed that 99% user use FB more than 90 min spending lot of time on FB. It may cause of negative affect on mental health like depression. Facebook still is the foremost social media sites between youth, mostly 99% users are the students, who spend 90 min on Facebook. Present study recognized that the total time spent on social networks linked with expanded depression and uneasiness scores. Spending more time on Facebook may cause depression and anxiety. Stress results indicated some correlation coefficients of 0.11,0.07 and 0.10 between (FIS) Time spend on FB, correlated significantly with depression is (r = 0.233, p = 0.041) and anxiety (r = 0.259, p = 0.023). Moreover, parents and the college administration should guide the children about its usage. In [15] Researcher construct a utilizing layout design science research ideas for outlining common vocabulary around the problem, and resolution design relevant to an intellectual fitness management system. For instance of IT professionals, the established assemble is informed through a social-media primarily based dataset comprising more than 65,000 cells and one hundred attributes probably identifying influencing factors. Researcher tested four Machine Learning classifiers such as Decision trees(DT), K-Nearest Neighbor (KNN), Support Vector Machine (SVM), and Ensemble as mentioned earlier. The experiment was conducted using MATLAB, Machine learning techniques were applied to the dataset to discover new results for this special group. SVM show a best performance model, findings are almost 99%. In future work, researcher will extend the literature in the rising area of 'Mental Health Mining', in certain health related data detection and use further techniques to extract consideration from more types of mental disorder features. It is anticipated that the evaluation pronounced in this find out would make a contribute in developing other electronic health administration structure each for communities and healthcare professionals. In [16] In this paper researcher aim is to detect automatically conceivable online users with SNMDs and propose an (SNMDD) Social Network Mental Disorder Detection framework that discovers several features from data logs of (OSNs) online social networks and another tensor procedure for originating latent features from numerous (OSNs) for SNMD recognition. Work characterizes a community oriented exertion between PC(Personal computer) researchers and mental medicinal services analysts to address developing issues in SNMDs the future plan to study the features derive from mixed media contents by procedures on NLP and PC vision. Study additionally plan to further investigate new issues from the point of view of a social network service worker, e.g., Facebook or Instagram, to improve the well-beings of OSN users without negotiating the user commitment. The methodology is new and creative to the act of SNMD (informal organization mental issue) identification, does not depend on self-uncovering of those psychological elements by means of surveys in Psychology. Rather, Researcher propose a machine learning framework, specifically, Social Network Mental Disorder Detection (SNMDD), that adventures feature extricated from social network data to accurately precisely recognize potential instances of SNMDs. The study likewise abuse multi-source learning in SNMDD and propose another SNMD-based Tensor Model (STM) to improve the precision. To expand the versatility of STM, further improve the productivity with execution ensure. Our system is assessed by means of a user study with 3,126 online social network users. Study direct a component examination, and furthermore apply SNMDD on enormous scale datasets and dissect the attributes of the three SNMD types. The outcomes show that SNMDD is promising for recognizing online social network users with potential SNMDs (Table 1).

Table 1. An overview of State of the art Literature Review for Depression Detection

Ref/Year	Technique	Results	Dataset	Limitations
M Islam et al. [1] (2018)	Decision Tree KNN SVM	Accuracy 60 to 80%	Facebook comments	Takes 21 attributes out of 50. Lack of improvement
Aldarwish and Ahmad [3] (2017)	SVM Naive Bayes	Sentiment, SVM and Naive Bayes Results	Facebook Twitter Live Journal	Lack of different language understanding
Namrata et al. [6] (2018)	Naïve Bayes	Stress 30%. No stress 50%	Facebook posts Questionnaire	Worked on textual data. Algorithm other than Nave Bayes have not been evaluated
Islam et al. [7] (2018)	Proposed KNN	KNN secure accuracy (60%–70%)	Collect data from Bipolar Facebook page	Take specific Facebook page Bipolar
Li et al. [8] (2018)	Proposed computational models	Data Pop was taken from weibo post	Obtain 75.2% accuracy using F-measure	Consider Chinese Weibo posts
Lambodar and Narendra [9] (2014)	Apriori Algorithm	Exploitation of existing model at distinct levels & states	500 document and values Entered in system by user	Not clarify how to identify stress in tweets using Apriori Algorithm

(continued)

Table 1. (*continued*)

Ref/Year	Technique	Results	Dataset	Limitations
Wenwen & Michael [10] (2018)	DK-LSTM architecture	Identify individuals by their posts	Data collected from Wikipedia contents from internet	Lack of domain knowledge for specific tasks Difficult for new user as word embedding methods Only get general syntactic and semantic words
Subhani et al. [11] (2017)	Frame work concerning (EEG) signal study of tense participants	Stress composed 95% accurateness. Multiple level detection produce 83% accuracy	42 subjects were include for this study	(EEG) have possibility to recognize tension levels Multiple levels of strain need further investigation
Lin et al. [12] (2017)	Automatic stress recognition method. Build a three level frame work	Frame work is beneficial. Competent for stress detection	600 million Tweets from Chinese micro blog site	To examine the social interaction mental stress
Choudhury et al. [13] (2017)	Recognized prediction of depression in persons through twitter tool	70% accuracy achieved by SVM classifier	Ground truth data on the presence of MDD crowd sourcing Used for collect labels	Lack of Detecting the disordered persons or those who are in strain Try to get ride from these conditions and prevent from suicide
Labrague et al. [14] (2014)	Discover the Facebook usage effect on teens	Calculated Facebook anxiety depression and stress	Appliance Facebook Intensity Scale (FIS) Depression, Anxiety and Stress Scale	They take users based on time interval of 90 min on Facebook

3 Proposed Approach

Depression is a major issue which is increasing day by day. Millions of people each year suffered from depression. It is a serious medical illness. Previous techniques predict depression mostly worked on Twitter Post and Chinese Web Blogs and text data. Findings of this study may have limited generalizability. To overcome these limitations a framework is proposed. The framework focused on various feature extraction techniques and extracted data from Facebook comments and extracted stress emojis. Presented work focus on part-of-speech tagging (Verb, Adverb, Noun, Adjective). Classify these with different combinations to achieve the better accuracy. The Proposed approach framework based on multiple layers, which represents the detailed description of depression detection by using part-of-speech tagging. There are some components which are written below (Fig. 2).

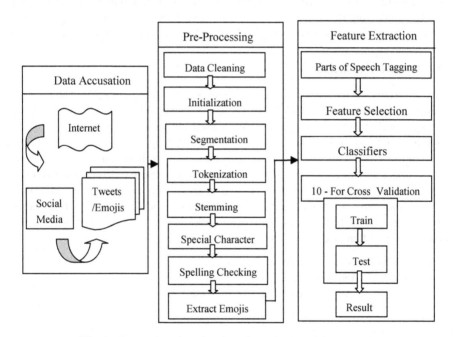

Fig. 2. Depression detection by using POS based frame work.

Major Components are Data Acquisition, Pre-Processing, Feature extraction, Classifier.

3.1 Data Acquisition

One of the methods of assembling and measuring information on variables of interest, systematically, to answer any research query or proposed statement. Following two points should be paid attention while gathering data.

- Quality assurance - activities that take place before data collection begins.
- Quality control - activities that take place during and after data collection.

Collection of (Posts, Comments, Tweets, Emojis) from different Social Media Sites (Facebook) using API.

3.2   Data Pre-processing

The raw data is converted to meaningful information through the process of data processing which give us outcomes to resolve the existing issues. Data cleaning is process of filling the missing values, smoothness of noisy data, identification or removal outliers, and resolve contradictions. Integration of data by using multiple databases, data cubes, or files. Data transformation: normalization and aggregation. Data reduction: produce same results by using reduced volume. Data discretization: part of data reduction, numerical attributes are replaced with nominal ones. In this step, Data Pre-processing should be done by removing stop words, stemming, segmentation, tokenization, grammar and spelling checking and archived depressive (Emojis, Post).

3.3   Feature Extraction

Proposed technique focuses on the various feature extraction techniques. The proposed approach introduces the framework with enhance feature selection, uses of emojis and parts-of-speech tagging. Presented work focused on part- of-speech tagging (Verb, Adverb, Noun, Adjective). Parts of speech tagging help to find out positivity and negativity of sentiments. Among them four Parts of speech including Verb, Adverb, Noun, Adjective will be analyzed in this research. As adjective depicts the maximum level of sentiments, hence it is mostly used in sentiments analysis. Different combination of the above mentioned parts of speech will be made to evaluate whether these combination give us best stress level. Feature selection and classification is done with these possible different combinations:

- Verb, Adverb, Noun, Adjective.
- Verb+Adverb, Verb+Noun, Verb+Adjective.
- Adverb+Noun, Adverb+Adjective, Noun+Adjective.

3.4   Classifier

Multiple supervised machine learning algorithms (SVM, Naïve Bayes, KNN, DT) will be used for classification. However, these are mostly used in classification problems. Proposed work has to implement multiple machine learning algorithms and trying to predict the depression level of social media post. The evaluation of all algorithms using same data set will be carried out and one with the best result. Apply different combinations of part-of-speech tagging (Verb, Adverb Noun, Adjective) and find out results.

4   Conclusions and Future Work

Previous techniques predict depression mostly on Twitter post and Chinese web blog or work with two features *Depressed* or *not Depressed*. The finding of the earlier studies may have limited generalizability. This research work focuses on the various feature extraction techniques. Extract data from face book post comments and also extract stress emojis. The presented work focuses on part-of-speech tagging to find out positivity/negativity of sentiments. Feature selection and classification is done using different POS combinations.

In future work we will use a new technique to dig out more type of features. LWIC contains 50 attributes while we use only 25 attributes, the remaining attributes can further be used in future. This research work is also applicable in interpretation of different languages to manipulate depression. We plan to implement the proposed framework in near future and analyze the results with state of the art comparison.

References

1. Islam, Md.R., Kabir, M.A., Ahmed, A., Kamal, A.R.M., Wang, H., Ulhaq, A.: Depression detection from social network data using machine learning techniques. Health Inf. Sci. Syst. 6(1), 1–12 (2018). https://doi.org/10.1007/s13755-018-0046-0
2. Ardra, B.M.V., Joseph, M.S., Thomas, P.E., Sherly, K.K.: Analyzing the behavior of youth to sociality using social media mining. In: Proceedings of the 2017 International Conference on Intelligent Computing Control and System, ICICCS 2017, vol. 2018–Janua, pp. 1231–1235 (2018)
3. Aldarwish, M.M., Ahmad, H.F.: Predicting depression levels using social media posts. In: Proceedings - 2017 IEEE 13th ISADS 2017, pp. 277–280 (2017)
4. Jenkins, E.K., Bungay, V., Patterson, A., Saewyc, E.M., Johnson, J.L.: Assessing the impacts and outcomes of youth driven mental health promotion: a mixed-methods assessment of the Social Networking Action for Resilience study. J. Adolesc. 67, 1–11 (2018)
5. Toseeb, U., Inkster, B.: Online social networking sites and mental health research. Front Psychiatry 6, 1–4 (2015)
6. Sonawane, N., Padmane, M., Suralkar, V., Wable, S., Date, P.: Predicting depression level using social media posts. Int. J. Innovative Res. Sci. Eng. Technol. 7(5), 6016–6019 (2018)
7. Islam, R., Kamal, A.R.M., Sultana, N., Islam, R., Moni, M.A.: Detecting Depression Using K-Nearest Neighbors (KNN) classification technique. In: 2018 International Conference on Computer, Communication, Chemical, Material and Electronic Engineering, pp. 1–4 (2018)
8. Li, A., Jiao, D., Zhu, T.: Detecting depression stigma on social media: a linguistic analysis. J. Affect. Disord. 232(16), 358–362 (2018)
9. Jena, L., Kamila, N.K.: A model for prediction of human depression using Apriori algorithm, pp. 240–24, (2014)
10. Li, W., Chau, M.: Applying deep learning in depression detection (2018)
11. Subhani, A.R., Mumtaz, W., Naufal, M., Mohamed, B.I.N., Kamel, N., Malik, A.S.: Machine learning framework for the detection of mental stress at multiple levels. IEEE Access 5, 13545–13556 (2017)
12. Lin, H., Jia, J., Qiu, J., Zhang, Y., Shen, G., Xie, L.: Detecting stress based on social interactions in social networks. IEEE Trans. Knowl. Data Eng. 29(9), 1820–1833 (2017)

13. De Choudhury, M., Gamon, M., Counts, S., Horvitz, E.: Predicting depression via social media. In Seventh International AAAI Conference on Weblogs and Social Media, June 2013

14. Labrague, L.J.: Facebook use and adolescents' emotional states of depression, anxiety, and stress. Health Sci. J. **8**(1), 80–89 (2014)

15. Burmeister, O.: A design construct of developing approaches to measure mental health conditions. Australas. J. Inf. Syst. **23**, 1–22 (2019)

16. Shuai, H., Shen, C., Yang, D., Member, S., Lan, Y.C.: A comprehensive study on social network mental disorders detection via online social media mining. IEEE Trans. Knowl. Data Eng. **30**(7), 1212–1225 (2018)

17. https://ori.hhs.gov/education/product/nillinoisu/datamanagement/dctopiic.html. Accessed 29 Nov 2016

18. http://www.cs.ccsu.edu/~markov/ccsucourse/DataMning. Accessed 29 Nov 2018

Classification of Social Media Users Based on Disagreement and Stance Analysis

Farhad Muhammad Riaz[1]([⊠]), Nasir Mahmood Minhas[3]([⊠]),
Sarfraz Bibi[2], and Waqas Ahmed[4]

[1] Department of Computer Science, Sir Syed Science College,
Tipu Road, Rawalpindi, Pakistan
farhad.ssscb.bscs@gmail.com
[2] University Institute of Information Technology, PMAS-AAUR,
Rawalpindi, Pakistan
[3] SERL Sweden, Blekinge Institute of Technology, Karlskrona, Sweden
nasir.mehmood.minhas@bth.se
[4] Foundation University Rawalpindi, New Lalazar, Pakistan

Abstract. Analyzing conversational behavior is a primary task in the field of sentiment analysis. Different researchers have proposed their models to perform the sentiment analysis of social media discussions. Existing approaches mainly studying the conversational behavior based on the text in the conversation. In any discussion, the users could have different viewpoints about the topic of conversation. A user can agree or disagree on the topic of discussion. Agreement of a user to the topic is called a stance, and if the user disagrees to the topic, we refer it as disagreement. The classification of the users based on stance and disagreement is not a well-researched area, and need to be explored further. In this work, we have proposed a computational model to classify the members according to stance or disagreement. The proposed model uses the novel approach, and it is a hybrid of topic modeling and VADER (Valence Aware Dictionary and sEntiment Reasoner). To evaluate the proposed model, we have conducted an experiment, and we did use the WhatsApp group discussion, Facebook comments as a dataset. We also compared the proposed model with two baseline approach, topic modeling, and VADER. From the results, we can conclude that the proposed model can effectively classify social media users based on disagreement and stance.

Keywords: Opinion mining · Sentiment analysis · Stance analysis · Topic modeling · LDA · VADER

1 Introduction

Social media is a powerful platform to express political, educational, business, and other views. Different segments of society, including governments, political parties, business organizations, students, etc. are effectively using social media to achieve their goals [1]. For instance, during the US Presidential Elections (2016), millions of Twitter data were analyzed and classified with different sentiment values (positive, negative,

© Springer Nature Singapore Pte Ltd. 2020
I. S. Bajwa et al. (Eds.): INTAP 2019, CCIS 1198, pp. 309–321, 2020.
https://doi.org/10.1007/978-981-15-5232-8_27

neutral) [38]. During the general elections in India (2019), the sentiment analysis of twitter data played a pivotal role to predict the outcomes of the ongoing elections [39].

Besides, various businesses are heavily depending on the market sentiments gathered from social media discussions. Organizations are using social media data to target and predict potential customers. However, due to the dynamic nature of these platforms, the significant amount of this data is unstructured. The content from Facebook, Twitter, and WhatsApp poses serious challenges. These challenges are because of the amount of data involved and the kind of language used to express the views (sentiments). Many stylists have performed analysis on these discussions [18, 23–27]. Techniques have been proposed to analyze the text form online forum discussions for multiple participants. The analyzed data could be used to determine the role of the participants of the discussions, like the most effective speaker or authoritative participant in the discussion [4, 8–11].

There are two types of posts on social media, text post and images. Friends are invited to make discussions on the posts by using comments. Analysis of the discussion for stance and disagreements is exciting for the researchers in sentiment analysis, and various computational models are available for making sentiment analysis of the user's discussions [16, 28]. However, the classification of users involved in the discussions based on their stance or disagreement is an unaddressed issue. Also, the symbolic conversion still needs to be investigated as very few techniques are available in this domain. These techniques only focus on the text conversation, but the symbolic conversation and simile expression still need to be investigated.

Several options are available to address this obstacle. However, the best one seems to be the classification of these arguments between stance and disagreements. After the classification of the text, the users can be classified in different classes. In this work, we used the method proposed in [28] as a baseline method. The contributions of this work are listed below:

- Discussion on different techniques for the sentiment analysis.
- A new model for the classification of social media users.
- Validating the performance of the proposed model by using different datasets.
- Predication of the user stance or disagreement by using behavior modeling.

The rest of the paper is organized a follow, in Sect. 2, we shall discuss the related work, Sect. 3 contains the problem formulation and proposed framework. Section 4 discusses the experiment and results. Finally, conclusions are presented in Sect. 5.

2   Related Work

Many recent studies documents that the analysis of the text plays a vital role in many applications. In their article [2], the authors proposed that social media sites like Twitter can be used for the prediction in the electoral process. In this study, the limits of social media sites for the prediction of the electoral process has been explored. In [3], the authors demonstrate a very interesting phenomenon for the detection of betrayals. The proposed method has several applications and many domains. They proposed a game for the detection of betrayals. The authors further argue that the sentiment of the discussion can be used for further planning.

In [4], the claim of the authors is that the expression of the user in the discussion can be used for the detection of likeness and dis-likeness of the discussion user. The proposed method has been compared with human judgment. According to [5] the machine learning approach can be applied to the unsupervised learning for conversation and discourse. The proposed method M4 holds good for inter-message structure. The author further compares the proposed model with HMM. The human effort for the analysis of the text can be reduced by using the machine learning approach [6]. The authors of the study [6], proposed a semiautomatic approach called STM (Structural Topic Model) for the analysis of text data. The article further applies this study in survey and experimental base research.

In [7], the authors suggest that discourse can be performed on digital objects. This idea opens the new dimension of discourse analysis and its applications. The authors of [12], proposed a dynamic unsupervised model for style recommendation. They are of the view that the style change in communication plays a key role in verbal communication. Correct recommendation of style during verbal communication is an interesting task.

According to [13, 14], topic modeling approach can be used in online forums and discussion for finding the potential topics and users on the web. Likewise, [15–17] uses the statistical model for the sentiment analysis of the text conversion of web documents. The web users can be divided into subgroups according to their discussions. According to [19–22], many models are available for the subgroup forming by using the positive and negative sentiment analysis of the text. The text can be extracted from online discussions. A technique has been proposed in [33], to extract the information about the topics form the large text. The proposed model used the LDA for the topic extraction for the text documents. LDA is a generation probability model. It could mine the topics through the three-tier Bayesian Model. The multi-granularity has been proposed in [34]. The proposed model has applied to sentiment summary generation. This model used the multi-topic semantic model. The extension of LDA with the name ME-LDA has proposed in [29, 35]. The proposed model combines the topic model with maximum entropy. The extension of LDA with modified LDA has been proposed in [36]. The sentiment analysis by using the machine learning, rule based, Lexicon based and deep learning was proposed in [40–47].

The key advantages of these approaches are the efficiency and accuracy of the classification. These approaches classify the text from different sources with word and sentence level. These approaches produce good results in term of classification. However, these approaches have many limitations, for instance, machine learning based approach needs the domain whereas the rule based approach needs the rule and the last approach need the powerful linguistics features, furthermore the keywords with multiple representation still need to be investigated, also the classification of the users by using their text analysis is still a challenging task. Table 1 shows the summary of different approaches with advantages and disadvantages.

Although the research on the analysis of the text of different web contents exists, the classification users on the basis of stance, disagreement and the analysis of symbolic conversions is still an unaddressed area.

Table 1. Sentiment classification approaches

Approach	Classification method	Features	Limitations
Machine learning	Supervised learning, unsupervised learning	This method is dictionary independent and give the classification with high frequency	Domain dependent. The classifier can work only the domain for which it has trained. This approach cannot be used in multidimensional environment
Rule based	Supervised learning, unsupervised learning	This method demonstrates the high accuracy of classification for instance, 91% for the review based classification and 86% for the sentence level classification The key feature of this classification approach is the sentence level classification. This classification is better than the word level classification	This method can only get the required efficiency and accuracy by using the define rule
Lexicon based	Unsupervised learning	Data is labelled. This approach dos not required the learning as it is the unsupervised learning	Linguistics resources are not available always. The data with ambiguous label cannot be classified

3   Problem Formalization and Proposed Framework

Many approaches have discussed in the literature. All the approaches focus on the classification of the text, existing approaches divide the text corps into three classes called, positive, negative and neutral.

The following scenario elaborates the problem:

Suppose a user x_i belongs to the set of users from set $X = \{x_1, x_2 \ldots \ldots x_n\}$. This user is involved in the social media discussion. We want to classify this user according to the comment or group discussion.

We can predict the class of the current user by using the behavior analysis of the user. That is, the previous discussion could be used to predict the current class of the user without analysis of the current discussion.

To classify the user, we propose a hybrid model. The graphical representation of the proposed model is shown in Fig. 1.

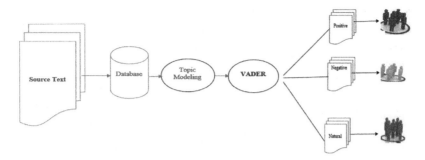

Fig. 1. Proposed framework

3.1 Steps Involved in Proposed Framework

Step 1: In the first step, the media discussion is selected from the given sources (Facebook, WhatsApp).

Step 2: In the second step, the conversation is stored in the database. Each information is stored against the specific user.

Step 3: In the third step, topic modeling is applied, topic modeling approaches are widely used to find the hidden topics from the text document. There are various methods used in topic modeling. In our work, we used the LDA (see Sect. 3.2) as a topic modeling approach. In literature, the LDA shows good results as compared to other approaches. The other reason is that this approach holds well the assign the topics to the symbolic data (Emojis, Slangs, and Emoticons).

Step 4: In the fourth steps, for the sentiment analysis, the selected topics are assigned to the VADER (Sect. 3.3). After extracting the correct topics by using topic modeling, it is easy to classify the topics in positive, negative and natural groups.

Step 5: In the last step on the basis of sentiments produced in the fourth step, each user is assigned a class with the positive, negative or natural label.

3.2 LDA (Latent Dirichlet Allocation)

LDA uses the unsupervised statistical model. This model is used to recommend the words (topics) with positive probabilities [36]. The working principle for both PLSA and LDA are similar but the key difference is the estimation, the LDA uses the Bayes, on the other hand, the PLSA uses the maximum likelihood.

Informal Definition: Let 'M' be the number of documents, in our case the document contains the Facebook comments and WhatsApp group chat, 'α' be the Dirichlet distribution of topics from the given document, 'β' be the vocabulary matrix which conation the all similar topics, and 't' be the topics in a corpus.

The algorithm for the LDA is given below

Procedure
Input: (M, t, β)
Where M is the number of Documents, t is the number of topics and β is the vocabulary matrix
Output: probability distribution of topics for each word in the document

Steps

    i. Choose the α (α is a topic distribution)
   ii. Assign the topic form set of topics t to each word W from a document d.
  iii. For each word, W

- For each topic from t calculate the Probability (Topic t/Document d)
- Calculate probability (W word/ t Topic)

  iv. The selection of the word W for a given topic t depend on the distribution of β

3.3 VADER (Valence Aware Dictionary and sEntiment Reasoner)

VADER (Valence Aware Dictionary and sEntiment Reasoner) is used for the sentiment analysis of social media text. It is a lexicon and rule-based sentiment analysis tool. This tool work with the combination of a list of lexical features called sentiment lexicon, these lexica are generally words or any other symbol which we can use in social media discussion. These lexica are labeled with the semantic orientation, these semantic orientations are either positive or negative [37]. This tool has been found very successful while dealing with social media discussions. The most prominent feature of this tool is that it not only tells about the positive or negative score but also tells how this positive or negative sentiment is. This tool is fully open source.

The reason for using this tool is

- It works well with social media texts and deals with multiple domains
- This tool work with the principle of unsupervised learning so does not need any training data set.
- Work well with the online stream data and does not suffer from speed performance.

While using the VADER we used the **polarity score** () method. This method is used to obtain the polarity for the given text.

The VADER analyses the sentiments on the following points.

1. Punctuation: the exclamation symbol (!), this symbol is used to increase the magnitude of intensity without changing the sentiment orientation
2. Capitalization: the use of the upper case also increases the magnitude of the sentiment intensity.
3. Conjunctions: the use of the conjunctions also change the magnitude of the sentiment intensity.
4. Preceding Tri-gram: negation also flip the polarity of the text.
5. It also deals with **Emojis, Slangs, Emoticons**

4 Experiment and Result Discussion

4.1 Dataset Description

In this work, we have used three different types of dataset. The first dataset contains Facebook posts and comments. Over 2000 Facebook conversations were used in this experiment. The second dataset contains WhatsApp text messages. For this purpose, we use the GitHub for WhatsApp chats. The third dataset is the real-time group discussion. We collect over 500 group chats from three different groups with different nature.

4.2 Preprocessing

For topic modeling, we have performed the standard preprocessing steps of text mining. All irrelevant terms are removed from the dataset. We did not change the case of the text because the case plays an important role in the sentiment analysis. We removed some of the stop words but we did not remove the exclamation mark (!), Emojis, Slangs, and Emoticons, because all these represent the sentiments. In this work, we have performed the sentiment Analysis by using LDA and VADER as a baseline methods. We used the precision and recall in order to measure the performance of the proposed approach and baseline approach.

4.3 Experimental Setup

The code description of VADER is available at Github repository. For installation, we used the command:
> pip install vaderSentiment
after installing the VADER we call the **SentimentIntensityAnalyser** object, the procedure for calling the object is:
from vaderSentiment.vaderSentiment
import SentimentIntensityAnalyzer analyser = SentimentIntensityAnalyzer()

We have used two algorithms for sentiment analysis, in the first step, we worked with the topic modeling by using the LDA [30–32]. All three datasets were used as input, these datasets contain mixed topics (education, business, politics, daily activates, sports and educations). Besides that, the datasets also contain special symbols like Emojis, Slangs, and Emoticons. Figures 2, 3 and 4 show the graphical representation of the topics with frequencies. We extracted interesting topics. We did consider the roman words and the special symbols as specific topics.

In the second step, we have implanted the VADER as a sentiment analyzer. This is an unsupervised learning approach [37]. The primary issue with the VADER is that it cannot classify the topics with ambiguous representation. For instance, it is hard to classify the words with short form and the words with complex structure. We did overcome this limitation with the help of topic modeling by using LDA.

The topics extracted in the first step are given to the VADER as a normalized set. The VADER classifies these topics as positive, negative or natural.

The final task was to classify the users according to positive, negative and natural community. We also predicted the behavior of users according to the posts by using the behavior analysis. In this way, we have classified the user without text analysis.

The main task of this experiment is to find interesting topics from the corpus.

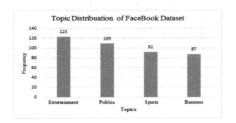

Fig. 2. Topics distribution of Facebook dataset

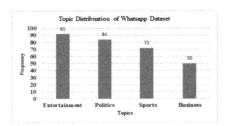

Fig. 3. Topics distribution of WhatsApp dataset

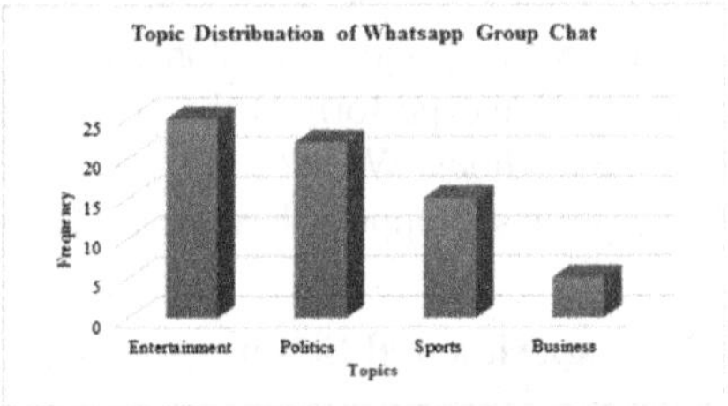

Fig. 4. Topics distribution of WhatsApp group chat

4.4   Results

In our work, we have picked 5, 10, 12 and 15 users from the dataset for community building. The selection of users is random. The dataset contains the users' information with all their posts and chats with relevant topics. The users have the identifier number label with the user id. Our task was to classify the user with relevant class. First of all, the sentiment analysis of the posts with all users have been performed. The users with positive, higher positive, negative or natural are group with each other. These groups are represented in a community.

Table 2, Table 3 and Table 4 shows the results of the LDA, VADER and Proposed Model. We take k = 10, where k indicates the number of users. It is clear from Table 2 that LDA cannot classify some users and label as neutral due to the lack of the understanding of the text. It cannot make the sentiment analysis of symbolic conversion that is why the majority of the user are labeled as neutral due to the high occurrence of the neutral. The community built by the LDA is not the correct representation of the community. The VADER over perform as compared to LDA but it also cannot make correct classification of some users. The reason is that the ambiguous topics and Roman words cannot be included in the analysis so it may be left as neutral or labeled with a wrong label of sentiment due to the ignorance of some important words which plays a role in the analysis.

The proposed model outperforms due to the hybrid model. The LDA makes the topics and VADER uses these topics and its own additional features for the correct sentiment analysis and then build a better community.

Table 2. Classification of users by LDA

No	User id	Label
1	15	Positive
2	10	Neutral
3	14	Neutral
4	19	Positive
5	20	Neutral
6	33	Negative
7	11	Positive
8	05	Neutral
9	01	Negative
10	07	Natural

Table 3. Classification of users by VADER

No	User id	Label
1	15	Negative
2	10	Positive
3	14	Natural
4	19	Neutral
5	20	Positive
6	33	Negative
7	11	Positive
8	05	Neutral
9	01	Negative
10	07	Positive

Table 4. Classification of users by proposed model

No	User id	Label
1	15	Negative
2	10	Positive
3	14	Positive
4	19	Neutral
5	20	Positive
6	33	Negative
7	11	Positive
8	05	Positive
9	01	Negative
10	07	Positive

The experiment compares the influence of different user's number in community building on traditional LDA, VADER and proposed model. The results of the F1 measure are shown in Fig. 5, and the results of precision and recall are shown in Table 5. The results show that the proposed model has a better performance than the LDA and VADER. It is demonstrated in the Table 5, the larger the number of the user better the performance. We get the best performance with precision 0.88, recall 0.84 and F1 measure 0.85 when the number of users is 15.

Table 5. Precision, recall of baseline methods and proposed method

Number of users	LDA		VADER		Proposed model	
	Precision	Recall	Precision	Recall	Precision	Recall
5	0.42	0.41	0.63	0.61	0.84	0.73
10	0.43	0.43	0.64	0.63	0.85	0.79
12	0.54	0.54	0.73	0.86	0.86	0.82
15	0.6	0.6	0.78	0.88	0.88	0.84

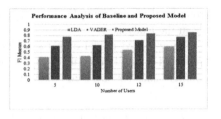

Fig. 5. The Classification Performance of F1- values Using LDA, VADER and Proposed Model with different users.

We also analyzed the prediction of the users on the basis of their previous comment and chat history. The concept of behavioral modeling is used for this purpose. Every user has different behavior on different posts. For instance, a user who likes sports may have positive chat or comment on sports topics and at the same time, this user may also not like politics have a negative sentiment. By using this concept for specifying users and with specific post we predict the class of this user.

5 Conclusion

Sentiment analysis is an important and interesting research area in the field of NLP. This area has a great impact on business, education, and software development process, where decision making is based on user feedback.

In this paper, we have studied two classical methods for sentiment analysis, LDA and VADER. Our aim was to develop a community on the basis of sentiment analysis. We proposed a new model to improve sentiment analysis. As it is believed that, better the sentiment analysis, more effective community. We did test the proposed model with three datasets. Two datasets are publicly available and third dataset is a real-time group discussion. The experiment shows the effectiveness of the proposed model. We also proposed a model for the future recommendation of the specific users on the basis of their previous chat and comment history.

In future, we will test the effectiveness of the newly proposed recommendation on some real-time dataset. We are planning to test this model in others domain as well. We are also interested to test this model for a multi-classification problem.

References

1. Gee, J.: An Introduction to Discourse Analysis: Theory and Method. Routledge, New York (2011). Excerpts
2. Gayo-Avello, D., Metaxas, P., Mustafaraj, E.: Limits of electoral predictions using Twitter. In: Proceedings of the Fifth International AAAI Conference on Weblogs and Social Media (2011)

3. Niculae, V., Kumar, S., Boyd-Graber, J., Danescu-Niculescu-Mizil, C.: Linguistic harbingers of betrayal: a case study on an online strategy game. In: Proceedings of the 53rd Annual Meeting of the Association for Computational Linguistics and the 7th International Joint Conference on Natural Language Processing, Beijing, China (2015)

4. Clavel, C.L.C.: Improving social relationships in face-to-face human-agent interactions: when the agent wants to know user's likes and dislikes. In: Proceedings of the 53rd Annual Meeting of the Association for Computational Linguistics and the 7th International Joint Conference on Natural Language Processing, Beijing, China (2015)

5. Paul, M.: Mixed membership markov models for unsupervised conversation modeling. In: Proceedings of Empirical Methods in Natural Language Processing (2012)

6. Roberts, M., et al.: Structural Topic models for open-ended survey responses. Am. J. Polit. Sci. **58**(4), 1064–1082 (2014). [Note that the code and data are publically available]

7. Jones, R., Chik, A., Hafner, C.: Discourse and Digital Practices: Doing Discourse Analysis in the Digital Age, (Chap. 4). Routledge, London (2015)

8. Bender, E., et al.: Annotating social acts: authority claims and alignment moves in Wikipedia talk pages, In: Proceedings of the HLT-NAACL 2011 Workshop on Language and Social Media (2011)

9. Danscu-Niculescu-Mizil, C., Sudhof, M., Jurafsky, D., Leskovec, J., Potts, C.: A computational approach to politeness with application to social factors. In: Proceedings of the 51st Annual Meeting of the Association for Computational Linguistics, pp. 352–361 (2013)

10. Bak, J., Lin, C., Oh, A.: Self-disclosure topic model for classifying and analyzing Twitter conversations. In: Proceedings of the International Conference on Empirical Methods in Natural Language Processing (EMNLP 2014), Doha, Qatar, 2014 (2014)

11. Danscu-Niculescu, C., Lee, L., Pang, B., Kleinberg, J.: Echoes of power: language effects and power differences in social interaction. In: Proceedings of WWW 2012 (2012)

12. Jain, M., McDonogh, J., Gweon, G., Raj, B., Rosé, C.P.: An unsupervised dynamic bayesian network approach to measuring speech style accommodation. In: EACL 2012 Proceedings of the 13th Conference of the European Association for Computational Linguistics, Avingon, France, April 23–27, 2012, pp. 787–797 (2012)

13. Gweon, G., Jain, M., Mc Donough, J., Raj, B., Rosé, C.P.: Measuring prevalence of other-oriented transactive contributions using an automated measure of speech style accommodation. Int. J. Comput. Supp. Collab. Learn. **8**(2), 245–265 (2013)

14. Tsur, O., Calacci, D., Lazer, D.: A frame of mind: using statistical models for detection of framing and agenda setting campaigns. In: Proceedings of the 53rd Annual Meeting of the Association for Computational Linguistics and the 7th International Joint Conference on Natural Language Processing, Beijing, China (2015)

15. Shutova, E., Teufel, S., Korhonen, A.: Statistical metaphor processing. Comput. Linguist. **39**(2), 301–353 (2013)

16. Riloff, E., Qadir, A., Surve, P., de Silva, L., Gilbert, N., Huang, R.: Sarcasm as contrast between a positive sentiment and negative situation. In: Proceedings of Empirical Methods in Natural Language Processing (2013)

17. Wallace, B., Choe, D., Charniak, E.: Sparse, contextually informed models for irony detection: exploiting user communities, entities and sentiment. In: Proceedings of Empirical Methods in Natural Language Processing (2015)

18. Jang, H., Moon, S., Jo, Y., Rosé, C.: Metaphor detection in discourse. In: Proceedings of SIGDIAL (2015)

19. Piergallini, M., Gadde, P., Dogruoz, S., Rosé, C.P.: Modeling the use of graffiti style features to signal social relations within a multi-domain learning paradigm. In: Proceedings of the European Chapter of the Association for Computational Linguistics (2014)

20. Hassan, A., Abu-Jbara, A., Radev, D.: Detecting subgroups in online discussions by modeling positive and negative relations among participants. In: Proceedings of Empirical Methods in Natural Language Processing (2012)

21. Schwartz, R., Tsur, O., Rappoport, A., Koppel, M.: Authorship attribution of micro-messages In: Proceedings of Empirical Methods in Natural Language Processing (2013)

22. Wen, M., Zheng, Z., Jang, H., Xiang, G., Rosé, C.: Extracting events with informal temporal references in personal histories in online communities. In: ACL 2013 (2013)

23. Huang,T.-H.K.: Social metaphor detection via topical analysis. In: Sixth International Joint Conference on Natural Language Processing, p. 14 (2014)

24. Jang, H., Piergallini, M., Wen, M., Rosé, C.P.: Conversational metaphors in use: exploring the contrast between technical and everyday notions of metaphor. In: ACL 2014, p. 1 (2014)

25. Klebanov, B.B., Leong, C.W., Heilman, M., Flor, M.: Different texts, same metaphors: unigrams and beyond. In: ACL 2014, p. 11 (2014)

26. David Ritchie, S.L.: Metaphor (Key Topics in Semantics and Pragmatics). Cambridge University Press, Cambridge (2013)

27. Wen, M., Zheng, Z., Jang, H., Xiang, G., Rosé, C.P.: Extracting events with informal temporal references in personal histories in online communities. In: ACL, no. 2, pp. 836–842 (2013)

28. Sridhar, D., Foulds, J., Huang, B., Getoor, L., Walker, M.: Joint models of disagreement and stance in online debate. In: Proceedings of the 53rd Annual Meeting of the Association for Computational Linguistics and the 7th International Joint Conference on Natural Language Processing (Volume 1: Long Papers), vol. 1, pp. 116–125 (2015)

29. Li, Y., Zhou, X., Sun, Y., Zhang, H.: Design and implementation of Weibo sentiment analysis based on LDA and dependency parsing. China Commun. 13(11), 91–105 (2016)

30. Cambria, E.: Affective computing and sentiment analysis. IEEE Intell. Syst. 31(2), 102–107 (2016)

31. Guo, A., Yang, T.: Research and improvement of feature words weight based on TFIDF algorithm. In: 2016 IEEE Information Technology, Networking, Electronic and Automation Control Conference, pp. 415–419 (2016)

32. Yeh, J.F., Lee, C.H., Tan, Y.S., Yu, L.C.: Topic model allocation of conversational dialogue records by Latent Dirichlet Allocation. In: Signal and Information Processing Association Annual Summit and Conference (APSIPA), 2014 Asia-Pacific, pp. 1–4. IEEE, December 2014

33. Blei, D.M., Ng, A.Y., Jordan, M.I.: Latent Dirichlet allocation. J. Mach. Learn. Res. 3, 993–1022 (2003)

34. Titov, I., McDonald, R.: Modeling online reviews with multi-grain topic models. In: The 17th International World Wide Web Conference, pp. 111–120 (2008)

35. Zhao, W.X., Jiang, J., Yan, H., Li, X.: Jointly modeling aspects and opinions with a MaxEnt-LDA hybrid. In: Proceedings of the 2010 Conference on Empirical Methods in Natural Language Processing, pp. 56–65 (2010)

36. Ye, J., Jing, X., Li, J.: Sentiment analysis using modified LDA. In: Sun, S., Chen, N., Tian, T. (eds.) ICSINC 2017. LNEE, vol. 473, pp. 205–212. Springer, Singapore (2018). https://doi.org/10.1007/978-981-10-7521-6_25

37. Hutto, C.J., Gilbert, E.: Vader: a parsimonious rule-based model for sentiment analysis of social media text. In: Eighth International AAAI Conference on Weblogs and Social Media, May 2014

38. Yaqub, U., Chun, S., Atluri, V., Vaidya, J.: Sentiment based analysis of tweets during the us presidential elections. In: Proceedings of the 18th Annual International Conference on Digital Government Research, pp. 1–10. ACM, June 2017

39. Chatterjee, S.: Sentiment analysis using deep learning techniques with India elections 2019 —a case study, 19 April 2019. https://towardsdatascience.com/sentiment-analysis-using-deep-learning-techniques-with-india-elections-2019-a-case-study-451549c8eb46
40. Álvarez López, T., Juncal-Martínez, J., Fernández-Gavilanes, M., Costa-Montenegro, E., González-Castaño, F.J.: GTI at SemEval-2016 task 5: SVM and CRF for aspect detection and unsupervised aspect-based sentiment analysis. In: Proceedings of the 10th International Workshop on Semantic Evaluation (SemEval 2016), pp. 306–311. Association for Computational Linguistics, San Diego (2016)
41. Appel, O., Chiclana, F., Carter, J., Fujita, H.: A hybrid approach to the sen- timent analysis problem at the sentence level. Knowl.-Based Syst. **108**, 110–124 (2016)
42. Brun, C., Perez, J., Roux, C.: XRCE at SemEval-2016 task 5: Feedbacked ensemble modeling on syntactico-semantic knowledge for aspect based sentiment analysis. In: Proceedings of the 10th International Workshop on Semantic Evaluation (SemEval 2016), pp. 277–281. Association for Computational Linguistics, San Diego (2016)
43. Çetin, F.S., Yıldırım, E., Özbey, C., Eryiğit, G.: TGB at SemEval-2016 task 5: multi-lingual constraint system for aspect based sentiment analysis. In: Proceedings of the 10th International Workshop on Semantic Evaluation (SemEval 2016), pp. 337–341. Association for Computational Linguistics, San Diego (2016)
44. Chaturvedi, I., Ong, Y.-S., Tsang, I.W., Welsch, R.E., Cambria, E.: Learning word dependencies in text by means of a deep recurrent belief network. Knowl.-Based Syst. **108**, 144–154 (2016)
45. Hercig, T., Brychcín, T., Svoboda, L., Konkol, M.: UWB at SemEval-2016 task 5: aspect based sentiment analysis. In: Proceedings of the 10th International Workshop on Semantic Evaluation (SemEval 2016), pp. 342–349. Association for Computational Linguistic, San Diego (2016)
46. Kumar, A., Kohail, S., Kumar, A., Ekbal, A., Biemann, C.: IIT-TUDA at SemEval-2016 task 5: beyond sentiment lexicon: combining domain dependency and distributional semantics features for aspect based sentiment analysis. In: Proceedings of the 10th International Workshop on Semantic Evaluation (SemEval 2016), pp. 1129–1135. Association for Computational Linguistics, San Diego (2016)
47. Lample, G., Ballesteros, M., Subramanian, S., Kawakami, K., Dyer, C.: Neural architectures for named entity recognition. arXiv preprint arXiv:1603.01360 (2016)

A Framework to Strengthen up Business Interests in Students by Using Matrix Factorization on Web Log

Mehwish Naseer[(✉)], Wu Zhang, and Wenhao Zhu

School of Computer Engineering and Science, Shanghai University,
Shanghai, China
mehwishnaseer@gmail.com

Abstract. Business and entrepreneurship play vital role in economy of a country. Job hunting stress, anxiety and prevailing of criminal thoughts in graduates is common due to unclear mind about their career these days. It is important to shape business skills in students while they are still studying. Internet is great source of motivation and guidance for them. Many students start searching their career goals during their school. At that time, their objectives can be transformed from job seekers to job providers, if they are steered right. In this study we have deliberated web browsing data of students and it is observed that so many of students search for business, finance and entrepreneurship related data while in school. This illustrates deep interest of students in business related activities. Their interest can be evolved and matured with appropriate supervision and direction. So, a two phased approach is demarcated in this paper to strengthen up Business Interests. 1st step involves extracting student's data from the web log who are interested in business activities and matrix factorization (MF) algorithms are applied to recommend them supplementary interrelated knowledge over the internet. Matrix Factorization (MF) techniques, SVD++ and ASVD are applied to appraise the best working one using Root mean squared error. 2nd step is to notify their IP addresses about any business events happening around. This will strengthen up their business interests and they will come up with mature ideas of business after completion of their education.

Keywords: Entrepreneurship · Business ideas · Students analysis · Web log analysis · Recommendation system

1 Introduction

Concept of Entrepreneurship has evolved in past few years, because of increase of unemployment rates among graduates. Stress, anxiety and negative activities are prevailing among educational community because of lack of career counselling. Students face difficulty in deciding what they have to do when they are graduated. This makes them less confident and stressed. No motivation to their own created ideas is given by society and family. Business ideas presented by the new comers need guidance, support and motivation for making it mature. Motivation plays important role in making entrepreneurs. Guidance and support can be given by practitioners of the field and vast

© Springer Nature Singapore Pte Ltd. 2020
I. S. Bajwa et al. (Eds.): INTAP 2019, CCIS 1198, pp. 322–332, 2020.
https://doi.org/10.1007/978-981-15-5232-8_28

study of the respective domain [1, 2]. Good analysis and study lead towards the generation of better idea. Creativity is another important factor that can generate the good idea. This involves thinking in the deeper level and critical study about the basic scheme of work. Business is taught as an important subject in all the schools. However, starting a new business and creating work for others is not only restricted to the business graduates [3]. Anyone can start and run a good business who has the skills and knowledge. At level of a student, encouragement and supervision are significant in moving them in right direction. Basic ideas from students definitely needs improvements and maturity with time. However, generation of idea is something that needs focus, creativity and knowledge. Internet is remarkable source of information and service for students now a days. Inspiration from the people of the field can be great kick to start searching about something that they can do. Intelligence assistance on the internet is foundation of improvement and encouragement that can lead them towards the right direction of quest. Recommendations on the internet is an example of intelligence assistance. But it is required that these recommendations should be directing rather than diverting.

Entrepreneurs have a vital role in mooting the society with regard to financial aspects and human resources [4]. The students of today's generation are vigilant to become supervisors and desire to originate new things. Education system and experts of domain can really motivate young students to become entrepreneurs. Motivation and support from parents are also important facets of student's progress. Entrepreneurship can be defined as a way of thinking. It leads in detecting new prospects and unravelling glitches. It is central to teach entrepreneurship as a basic subject at the schools [5]. But it is not a practice these days. Therefore, if any student wants to learn about it or their mind is leading towards something innovative, there is necessity of means to assist them. Personal maturity is considered as an imperative ability in entrepreneurship skills. This involves personal consciousness, liability and emotional skills.

Internet is one of basic source of knowledge for students. Students search on internet about anything they are interested in or confused about. Browsing behavior is important tool to build interest profiling of its users. Many of researches have used web log to identify multiple prospects of users from their internet usage patterns [6]. This web log data can play important role in construing students. It can be eventually helpful in improving education system. This can progress students learning and grooming process. By observing the browsing data from a server-side web log of a university it is interpreted that large number of students search about business and finance related websites along with computer and technology related websites. This leads towards perceiving that students are certainly interested in business contents and advanced technological methods. Their thought process can be upgraded further with assisting them in their search and moving them deeper into this business knowledge. This knowledge can open up their minds for the new ideas and transmit them towards a defined direction of knowledge about business and new skills of entrepreneur. This strategy can be helpful to settle them in the real business world. To achieve the goal and strengthen up the business interests and knowledge of students, this paper presents a system with the help of Matrix Factorization algorithms. Detailed web log analysis is required to pick the target students that have interest in the business. Comprehensive comparison of MF algorithms will lead in selecting the best algorithm with least error to recommend students related content based upon their profile to enhance their knowledge. Their Ip addresses will be notified about the business events such as any conferences, seminars or discussions that can further lead in strengthening their knowledge and ideas. These events can be a great source of enhancing knowledge about business and entrepreneurship [7].

It is indispensable that entrepreneurial skills should be developed in each and every student to make them successful in various events of their life. Thus, it is compulsory to develop entrepreneurship thinking skills in students. Technology can help in boosting the learning system. The proposed system will help students to make their mind clear about the work ideas. More knowledge about their idea will make them more confident and they will come up with building a practical and impressive approach. At the end this is process of success of educational system and development of healthy and flourished community.

Rest of the paper is organized as follows Sect. 2 explains related work in the proposed domain, Sect. 3 describes research gaps, Sects. 4 presents proposed methodology, Sect. 5 discusses results and Sect. 6 concludes the work.

2 Related Work

Shaping entrepreneurial competencies in students is hot interest now a days. Many researches are discussing means of doing so. [8] discussed role of analytic thinking and emotional competencies for developing entrepreneurial intentions in university students. They discussed that previous models presented that development of entrepreneurial competency in students results in enabling entrepreneurial intelligence. However, they did not find any direct relation among the two and claimed that cognitive experiences are more related in enhancing entrepreneurial intelligence.

[9] revealed the relationship between educational supports, attitudinal factors, and behavioral factors in developing entrepreneurial intention among students. Their research presented that educational support have moderate relationship with entrepreneurial intentions among students. However attitudinal and behavioral factors have weak relationship.

[10] discussed about multiple factors that can hinder students from starting a business while they are studying. They came up with highlighting the most common factors that act as hindrance. Lack of resources, lack of social networking, fear of risk and aversion to stress are among the factors that affect the entrepreneurship intention among the undergraduates.

[5] explained some conditions that impact on education and learning outcomes. Entrepreneur education can be of two types elective and compulsory. Entrepreneurship courses can help in understanding the entrepreneur skills well.

[7] enlightened that there can be diverse purposes of entrepreneur education, depending on the goal there are different means of offering entrepreneur education. In this regard understanding about entrepreneurship can be increased by public channels. Media, Seminars or lectures are great resources. These can direct information to large number of people in short span of time.

[3] claimed that it is important to incorporate entrepreneurship education in non-business disciplines as well. Hence, they presented a set of undergraduate courses that can help in introducing entrepreneurship concepts in students of technical disciplines.

[11, 12] presented that entrepreneurial behavior plays important role in development of new enterprises. Entrepreneurial intentions are one of the most important antecedents in this regard.

[13, 14] explains importance of personality in becoming an entrepreneur. They allied both personality and emotional intelligence in becoming entrepreneur.

[15, 16] Presented importance of entrepreneurship education. With proper education students can start growth-oriented businesses. Entrepreneurship education promotes sense of becoming self-employed. Hence, it is vital in production of desired outcomes.

Recommendation algorithms are being practiced in different new domains. [17] compares the multi label classifiers with recommender systems for the financial services area. They evaluate the performance of classifiers and recommender algorithms Independently and compared the performance results with F measure.

[18] presents the use of recommender strategies in social networking. Location information is an important attribute of social media that can help in making recommendations.

[19] evaluates the performance of multiple recommender strategies for video game platforms.

[20] Higher Education Institutions have obligation to develop entrepreneurship mindset among technical and engineering graduates. Graduates have ability of creative and innovative ideas.

3 Research Gaps

Maturing students' ideas and graduating them with a clear vision about the work they will do is key of successful education these days. Strengthening up the business ideas is one of the thoughts extracted from the demands of today's era. Hence goal of this paper is to present automated assistance method for students to strengthen up business interests. This will make them more knowledgeable hence confident about their work and idea. This system will clear their mind and will be a great source of reducing job hunting stress, anxiety and prevailing of negative and criminal activities among graduates. This paper is presenting comparative analysis among different previous techniques by using a new case study of student's web log. This approach can help students by automatically indulging them in new ideas of business.

4 Proposed Methodology

To strengthen up the business interests among students, this study focusses on presenting an intelligent system that can aid students in searching the business content on the internet and notifying the business and entrepreneurship related events happening around. Figure 1 illustrates the whole process of proposed methodology of the system.

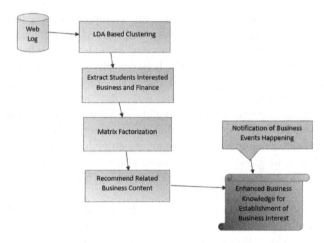

Fig. 1. Proposed system

4.1 Web Log

Web Log is automatically generated text file by web server. It records every hit on the web page against each IP address. Each IP address represent unique user. Proposed system takes web log as input.

4.2 LDA Based Clustering

In Data Analysis LDA (Latent Dirichlet Allocation) possess importance as a significant model for Topic Modeling. By calculation of Dirichlet prior LDA model performs topics distribution [21]. This model assesses the words in documents and generate topics based upon words used in documents. In previous researches this method is used for URL clustering [22]. Results are promising and helpful. LDA based clustering distributes URL into different categories based upon genre. From weblog data set unique URLs are identified. Each record is considered as a separate document. LDA generates set of words from URL. Topic modeling-based clustering will be the final output. This results in similar types of websites in same topic.

Algorithm of LDA for proposed method can be written as,

```
From Set of URLs Sᵢ Extract Unique URLs from them
Extract the URLs in Sᵢ as {U₁, U₂, .............Uₘ}
Extract Topics discovered from by LDA in the URLs in the Sᵢ as Tᵢ = {T₁, T₂,
........Tₓ}
For each URL perform Topic Modeling.
```

A simple tokenization algorithm is used to perform topic modeling for this dataset. LDA can be subtle to the lexis used. Using stop words is prodigious practice The LDA algorithm uses Wordcount weighting structure. Data set is loaded with file path, tokenizer and weighting strategy. K is the number of topics expected to be the outcome of algorithm. Changing the value of K results in different results. Execution of algorithm results in arranging words in each topic. For each word index is followed. Indexes are compared with their coefficient values. This results in generation of multiple topics. Mallet is Java based library that uses the same scheme to perform LDA based topic modeling [23].

4.3   Data Extraction

From the LDA based clusters of web pages, student group having interest in business related web sites is picked up to work further in this study. Data to fed in the next step will contains URLs, IP address, score of URLs. Score of each URL is calculated for each user based upon the number of hits. This format of data is called UIR (User-Item-Rank) format.

4.4   Matrix Factorization

Sparsity is major problem associated with the recommender systems. Matrix factorization algorithms helps to solve the problem of sparsity by decomposing the high dimensional user-item matrix to product of two lower dimensional matrices. User-URL matrix will be a huge matrix, that can lead to high computation cost so MF algorithms are used to solve the problem of sparsity. Cosine similarity is used to build the similarity matrix between student S and Web Page W. Equation 1 represents the calculation scheme for cosine Similarity.

$$Cosine(S, W) = \frac{\sum_{i \in I_{sw}} (r_{si} \cdot r_{wi})}{\sqrt{\sum_{i \varepsilon I_{sw}} (r_{si})^2} \cdot \sqrt{\sum_{i \varepsilon I_{sw}} (r_{wi})^2}} \tag{1}$$

This study evaluates two most commonly used algorithms of matrix factorization.

SVD++. SVD++ computes recommendations by taking implicit interactions into focus. A bias value is used between users and items to compute the final results [24]. Implicit information used in the algorithm is binary information of page access. If a user has accessed a page value is 1 and 0 for the pages that are not accessed. This implicit information improves prediction accuracy. Computation of final predictions by user u to item i is represented in Eq. 2.

$$\overline{r}_{ui} = \mu + b_i + b_u + \sum_{f=0}^{nfactors} H_{u_1 f} W_{f_1 i} \tag{2}$$

Similarity matrix generated by SVD++ is symmetric. H and W are low dimensional matrices generated by decomposing R such that R = H X W. R is users-item matrix. H is matrix containing users latent features. W contains item latent features.

ASVD. Asymmetric SVD algorithm is also matrix factorization algorithm [25]. It replaces latent feature factor matrix with user preferences. Hence for item i predicted ratings by user u can be computed using Eq. 3.

$$\bar{r}_{ui=\mu+b_i+b_u} + \sum_{f=0}^{nfactors} \sum_{j=0}^{nitems} r_{uj}Q_{jf}W_{f_1 i} \tag{3}$$

Q is a matrix that learn user preferences. Q will be different dimensional matrix from W hence resulting similarity matrix will be asymmetric. SVD++ and ASVD algorithms are applied on the data set in two folds and calculation of RMSE (Root mean square algorithms) using Eq. 4 compares the performance.

$$RMSE = \sqrt{\frac{\sum_{i=1}^{n}(p_i - r_i)^2}{n}} \tag{4}$$

P_i is predicted rating of Web Page by the recommendation algorithm.
R_i is actual rating of Web Page.

4.5   Notification of Business Events

To further enhance the interest about the business, students will be notified with the business events happening around through their IP addresses. Events can be any seminar, conference or lecture about entrepreneurship and new business ideas. They may find it interesting and joining such events will further help in making up their minds.

4.6   Enhancement of Business Knowledge

Overall compilation of information from recommended web pages and events notification will result in enhancing the knowledge about business in students. It will motivate them and present a systematic source of getting in depth knowledge about business. This will build their interest and ideas. Exploring further will make them come up with really innovative and mature ideas.

5   Results and Discussion

To explore effectiveness of proposed technique we applied it on a small data chunk of web log of Shanghai University, China, without breaching privacy of students. Users are kept anonymous and IP address is used as identifier. Data set is about information of 104 unique users, who are accessing different business and finance related web pages. There are 42 unique web pages accessed by users. For each page, number of hits by student is considered as score to finally compile the data in UIR format. Computation of SVD++ and ASVD are performed using two folds cross validation. RMSE for each fold is also observed along with average RMSE of each technique. Table 1 signifies the RMSE values of the computations.

Table 1. RMSE computation

	SVD++	ASVD
Fold 1	2.65034555	2.859502299
Fold 2	2.272708657	2.728932992
Average	2.461527105	2.7942176

Results from Table 1 illustrates the effectiveness of SVD++ over ASVD by showing less RMSE (Fig. 2). So, for this case it is experimented that latent features play important role in presenting more accurate predictions. Information about a page accessed or not accessed by a specific student is taken into account with the help of binary data. This evidence contributed in diverting results and making SVD++ more accurate in performance as compared to ASVD. ASVD can work better when working with cold start problem. It evaluates user's preferences that may help is finding ratings about any new users added in the system with no previous log information. Currently we are not dealing with such data.

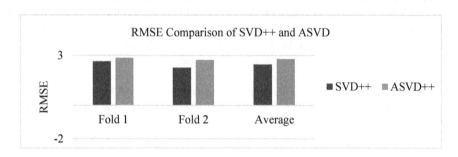

Fig. 2. Comparison of RMSE for ASVD and SVD++

So, this system will work with generating predictions about web pages using SVD++ and notifying events happening around to the IP addresses of students. This will help in more engagement of them in business activities. It will play important contribution in motivating them and strengthening up their interests in business.

Multiple factors are involved in making up business minds of students. Such as Internet help, Participation in related Events, counselling from parents and Instructors, Business courses etc. Here Internet help and events participation are considered as prime attributes to develop entrepreneur's mind set. Effectiveness of the proposed approach can be evaluated once it is applied. This will need recommendation of content for a specific time period. Performance and results can be measured based on the outcomes Results cannot be produced in a shorter period. Developing a mindset towards some effective business idea is not a doddle at all. Performance of approach can be evaluated by applying it practically for a considerable amount of time.

6 Conclusions and Future Work

This paper presents an approach for strengthening up business interests in students. It is substantial to build entrepreneurial intents in students. This study also explains the importance of studying entrepreneurship and business skills in students. A technological framework is proposed to enhance business interests in students by increasing knowledge about the domain. It is collective strategy to recommend related web content and notification of associated events to students. Matrix factorization algorithms SVD++ and ASVD are evaluated on web log data. SVD++ algorithm shows least RMSE. Hence, this approach can be a good source of impetus for students. Web log carries imperative information about browsing habits of students. Patterns extracted from web log are used to scrutinize students who browse business related web content. LDA proved to be a promising technique to perform genre-based clustering of URLs. This approach is great initiative for shaping student's minds as job providers, rather than job seekers. Forte and confidence of students about their creative business ideas will help them to be successful after their graduation. Results will lead in reduction of job-hunting stress, anxiety and negative thoughts among students that occurs due to unemployment and recession. Proposed approach will impact whole society rather than only educational system. In future this technique will be refined further to explore and solve more problems of educational domain. The aim to evaluate the effectiveness of the proposed approach by introducing more parameters and evaluating the performance by practically applying the approach for a longer period of time.

Acknowledgements. The work of this paper is supported by National Natural Science Foundation of china (Nos. 61572434, 91630206 and 61303097) and the National Key R&D Program of China (No. 2017YFB0701501).

References

1. Audretsch, D.B.: From the entrepreneurial university to the university for the entrepreneurial society. J. Technol. Transfer **39**(3), 313–321 (2014)
2. Shah, S.K., Pahnke, E.C.: Parting the ivory curtain: understanding how universities support a diverse set of startups. J. Technol. Transfer **39**(5), 780–792 (2014)
3. Ahmad, F.S., Baharun, R., Rahman, S.H.A.: Interest in entrepreneurship: an exploratory study on engineering and technical students in entrepreneurship education and choosing entrepreneurship as a career. Faculty of Management and Human Resource Development, Universiti Teknologi Malaysia (2004)
4. Audretsch, D.B., Belitski, M.: The missing pillar: the creativity theory of knowledge spillover entrepreneurship. Small Bus. Econ. **41**(4), 819–836 (2013)
5. Hahn, D., Minola, T., Bosio, G., Cassia, L.: The impact of entrepreneurship education on university students' entrepreneurial skills: a family embeddedness perspective. Small Bus. Econ. 1–26 (2019). https://doi.org/10.1007/s11187-019-00143-y
6. Kumar, V., Thakur, R.S.: Web log analysis tools: at a glance. In: Tiwari, B., Tiwari, V., Das, K.C., Mishra, D.K., Bansal, J.C. (eds.) Proceedings of International Conference on Recent Advancement on Computer and Communication. LNNS, vol. 34, pp. 135–142. Springer, Singapore (2018). https://doi.org/10.1007/978-981-10-8198-9_14

7. Hytti, U., O'Gorman, C.: What is "enterprise education"? An analysis of the objectives and methods of enterprise education programmes in four European countries. Educ.+ Train. **46**(1), 11–23 (2004)

8. Fernández-Pérez, V., et al.: Emotional competencies and cognitive antecedents in shaping student's entrepreneurial intention: the moderating role of entrepreneurship education. Int. Entrep. Manag. J. **15**(1), 281–305 (2019)

9. Halim, F.A., Malim, M.R., Hamdan, S.I., Salehan, A., Kamaruzzaman, F.S.: Factors affecting entrepreneurial intention among IKN students. In: Kor, L.-K., Ahmad, A.-R., Idrus, Z., Mansor, K.A. (eds.) Proceedings of the Third International Conference on Computing, Mathematics and Statistics (iCMS2017), pp. 545–554. Springer, Singapore (2019). https://doi.org/10.1007/978-981-13-7279-7_68

10. Patrick, Z.B., Rizal, A.M., Hee, O.C., Mahadi, M., Kamarudin, S.: Factors hindering undergraduate students from starting a business while studying. Int. J. Acad. Res. Bus. Soc. Sci. **9**(1), 455–468 (2019)

11. Liñán, F.: Intention-based models of entrepreneurship education. Piccolla Impresa/Small Bus. **3**(1), 11–35 (2004)

12. Prodan, I., Drnovsek, M.: Conceptualizing academic-entrepreneurial intentions: an empirical test. Technovation **30**(5–6), 332–347 (2010)

13. Shane, S., Venkataraman, S.: The promise of entrepreneurship as a field of research. Acad. Manag. Rev. **25**(1), 217–226 (2000)

14. Rhee, K.S., White, R.J.: The emotional intelligence of entrepreneurs. J. Small Bus. Entrep. **20**(4), 409–425 (2007)

15. Dickson, P.H., Solomon, G.T., Weaver, K.M.: Entrepreneurial selection and success: does education matter? J. Small Bus. Enterp. Dev. **15**(2), 239–258 (2008)

16. Yar Hamidi, D., Wennberg, K., Berglund, H.: Creativity in entrepreneurship education. J. Small Bus. Enterp. Dev. **15**(2), 304–320 (2008)

17. Bai, F., Sadagopan, N., Helmy, A.: IMPORTANT: a framework to systematically analyze the Impact of Mobility on performance of RouTing protocols for Adhoc NeTworks. In: IEEE INFOCOM 2003. Twenty-second Annual Joint Conference of the IEEE Computer and Communications Societies, vol. 2, pp. 825–835. IEEE (2003)

18. Gasparetti, F., Gavalas, D., Ilarri, S., Ricci, F., Yu, Z.: Mining social networks for local search and location-based recommender systems. Pers. Ubiquit. Comput. **23**(2), 179–180 (2019). https://doi.org/10.1007/s00779-019-01241-0

19. Cheuque, G., Guzmán, J., Parra, D.: Recommender systems for online video game platforms: the case of STEAM. In: Companion Proceedings of the 2019 World Wide Web Conference, pp. 763–771. ACM (2019)

20. João, I.M., Silva, J.M.: Exploring students entrepreneurial mindset: Insights to foster entrepreneurship in engineering education. In: IEEE Global Engineering Education Conference (EDUCON), Tenerife, Spain (2018)

21. Momtazi, S., Naumann, F.: Topic modeling for expert finding using latent Dirichlet allocation. Wiley Interdiscip. Rev. Data Min. Knowl. Disc. **3**(5), 346–353 (2013)

22. Leng, B., Liu, J., Pan, H., Zhou, S., Tsinghua, Z.N.: Topic model based behaviour modeling and clustering analysis for wireless network users. In: 2015 21st Asia-Pacific Conference on Communications, APCC 2015, pp. 410–415. IEEE (2015)

23. http://mallet.cs.umass.edu. Accessed 06 Sep 2019
24. Cao, J., et al.: Distributed design and implementation of SVD++ algorithm for e-commerce personalized recommender system. In: Zhang, X., Wu, Z., Sha, X. (eds.) Embedded System Technology. CCIS, vol. 572, pp. 30–44. Springer, Singapore (2015). https://doi.org/10.1007/978-981-10-0421-6_4
25. Pu, L., Faltings, B.: Understanding and improving relational matrix factorization in recommender systems. In: Proceedings of the 7th ACM Conference on Recommender Systems - Rec Sys 2013, pp. 41–48. ACM (2013)

Improving Validity of Disaster Related Information by Identifying Correlation Among Different Social Media Streams

Muhammad Faizan Arshad[1], Bakhtiar Kasi[1(✉)], Riaz Ul-Amin[1(✉)],
and Abdul Sattar Malik[2(✉)]

[1] Balochistan University of Information Technology,
Engineering and Management Sciences, Quetta, Pakistan
{Bakhtiar.Kasi,riaz.ulamin}@buitms.edu.pk
[2] Bahauddin Zakariya University, Multan, Pakistan
maliksattar777@gmail.com

Abstract. Social media has become an important mode for communication and content sharing in this digital world. During large-scale events, a big cluster of data usually posted by the users on social media; in the form of tweets, pictures and videos. The data is informative, but not all the contents which are posted on the social media have reliable information. The existence of spam, fake images and manipulation can reduce the validity of information on social media. To establish trust in information posted on social media, there is a need to identify a mechanism that can recognize and report questionable posts and flag them for scrutiny and verification. This research will provide an approach in assessing and improving the validity of information on social media. The users will able to identify the validity of information along with polarity and subjectivity of tweets and videos.

Keywords: Social media · Validity · Data · Information · Tweets · Videos

1 Introduction

In the age of globalization, social media is becoming the best source of connectivity. Around the world millions of people are using social media networks like Twitter, Youtube and Facebook to express their emotions, opinions, and happiness related to daily lives events [7]. The users on Twitter write short messages for their followers, which are called tweets. In the case of Facebook, they are posts. Apart from it, Youtube has videos for the expression of emotions. From local news to international events, these platforms include several different topics which the people discuss on daily basis [6]. They are good sources to extract public opinions related to serious issues through the collection of data. The information validation is necessary for all the content, which public post on social media related to critical events to reduce the impact of false news propagation.

Social media is becoming an important source for news. The users are getting knowledge about the real-life events of the world by sitting anywhere around the globe [4]. A large portion of social media conversation is directly linked with the headlines of

© Springer Nature Singapore Pte Ltd. 2020
I. S. Bajwa et al. (Eds.): INTAP 2019, CCIS 1198, pp. 333–342, 2020.
https://doi.org/10.1007/978-981-15-5232-8_29

news events. Kwak et al. [10] revealed that 85% of topics of tweets are related to the current news and nearly millions of people are posting their opinions regularly about news focused topics.

For an explanation of this scenario, Lehmann et al. [11] designed a system to extract many important aspects of information about the news. They identified a study pattern related to news management which showed that reporters are able to get many useful informational points related to current events by reading the tweets of different people.

In the disaster situation, the affected people share their situation and others have to gain information about the causalities and damages. The quick humanitarian response and volunteer aids can be started after a complete evaluation of situation [1]. By using the data validation processes, the respective departments and organizations will able to identify the validity of the information.

Unlike the other media outlets, Twitter is the crowd-sourced platform in which the information is present in abundance [12]. On Youtube and Facebook, the situation of data posting is also similar to Twitter because the people are sharing their experiences [3] using posts and videos. During a high impact event, the credibility of the source and validity of information become even more important than before. The data validation is connected with the analysis of posted information related to important events.

In our paper, we focused on finding the best features of information to identify the validation pattern. Along with it, we included the negative and positive polarity of tweets to get major aspects of perception of people related to certain events.

We found the validity of information in online social media, mainly Twitter and Youtube, using the different computational models and functioning systems. The big cluster of data was difficult to handle. In the initial stage, we designed the model for validation and sentimental analysis of social media streams.

2 Literature Review

In the past researches, different methods have been used to perform the validity of information on the online social media streams. The researchers used the supervised and unsupervised machine learning techniques to classify the different aspects of information which were posted on social media during disasters. In order to identify the user's perception about the validity, Morris et al. [12] used the survey-based methodology.

They found a great difference between the features twitter revelated by search engines and the features, which the users considered are relevant to validity. Their results showed that the user did not consider the content of tweets only relevant to the validity. Instead, they are also showed influence by the user-based features, and other aspects to make a validity assessment.

On the other hand, Yang et al. [14] organized the research study on validity indicators and defined their connection with the demographic differences. Message topic, author's gender, username, profile image, location, job role, and cultural differences were mainly included predictor factors. They designed the hypothesis that included indicators to show validity assessment differences between Chinese and American users on Sina Weibo and Twitter respectively.

Castillo et al. [3] designed the automatic method of assessment of validity of Twitter data. They used the feature, which was extracted from the posting and reposting behaviors of the users. They utilized the supervised classification and implanted three-fold cross-validation structure [3]. Their research showed the great influence on features on validity of information.

Similarly, Yang et al. [15] followed the study pattern of Castillo et al. [3] and implemented research on Sina Weibo instead of Twitter. The researcher used the in-build rumor detection system of Sina Weibo and identified the element of validity. Gupta et al. [6] stated the validity of tweets and credibility of data through four options which were labeled as credible, incredible, seems credible or undefined. They used the five categories of features related to tweet meta-data, tweet content, users, linguistics and external resources. They also stated the consideration of the significance of different features and different time frames of occurrence of the event.

Kang et al. [9] proposed the three computational models related to the validity of the information. The social based, hybrid based, and content-based models were included in three models scheme. The authors performed the evaluation on seven topic-based data related to 'Libya' and extracted the tweets through Twitter API. Bobidou et al. [2] extended the work of Gupta et al. [6] by doing analysis on social media activity using the crisis events. They classified the tweets based on validity by using the appropriate classifiers. They achieved nearly 81.25% and 81.38% accuracy respectively in Benston dataset and Hurricane Sandy dataset using J48 and KStar classifier. Duan et al. [5] worked on relevancy techniques to rank tweets, but they did not include the validity aspect mainly.

Moreover, Cheong et al. [4] did the social network analysis (SNA) to identify the connection between Twitter users during the disaster events. They worked on 2010–2011 Australian floods and analyzed the activity of users on online networks. Their research had some secondary aspects to identify the role of local authorities, political personalities, volunteers, media reporters, people belonged to humanitarian groups community services.

Quercia et al. [13] used the Support Vector Machine (SVM) for the topic assigning to profiles and ranking feeds. They described the functionality of L-LDA model for Twitter-based classification. The topics were related to tweets and the profile characteristics of authors. They used data from Twitter's streaming API and collected information from September to December 2010. The topical classification was done related to the profile of different users. The results indicated the procedure effectivity for only a small number of tweets for each profile.

3 Proposed Solution

In this section, we proposed the mechanism to identify the validity of data. In the past researches, the researchers included many different features. But, including other features for our research, we added polarity and subjectivity to extract the biases of tweets and public reviews on videos. Instead of complete system, we developed a model to state the validity factor of data. We used texts and videos with a number of features. We included friends, followers, favorite count and retweeting behavior-based features of Twitter users. Along with it, we included URLs, polarity, subjectivity, words, characters and other features related to content. The location aspect of author and user is also important. We have also decided to add it in our research work, and we are showing it through graphical representation.

For YouTube data, we are using the validity of the source of videos and public reviews with the number of different features including total IDs, users, category, number of views, comments, number of likes and dislikes. We involved polarity and subjectivity to analyze the data deeply.

3.1   Datasets

We collected the datasets related to the Christchurch mosque shootings incident in New Zealand by using Twitter Streaming API and you tube API. They are helpful to extract data in real-time along with specific features. In order to get data related to top trends, we got the help from Trends API. We gathered the tweets and videos until a topic stayed in top trend. In this process, we have included both local and international trending tags in March 2019.

Each tweet is labeled in five levels using the filled starts. We are using the five bases of validity and ranking of tweets. In the case of YouTube, the videos were analyzed on three bases (Table 1).

Table 1. Data validation levels of social media streams

Twitter	Tweet is valid
	Tweet seems valid and includes information
	Tweet has text, but it is not valid
	Tweet has no useful information, but relevant to topic
	Tweet has false information
YouTube	Video has valid source
	Video source seems valid and includes information
	Video source has false information

Including the impact of polarity and subjectivity, we identified the negative and positive aspects of tweets and videos through user's reviews. They are divided with respect to polarity aspect in three groups.

- Negative Polarity
- Positive Polarity
- Neutral

The subjectivity aspect is related to emotions, feelings, and point of views of author. It is significant to state the validity with respect of the author. The objectivity is the opposite term and it included the content-based aspect and generalized idea.

3.2   Selection of Main Events

After the collection of data, we defined events which included one more topic in the trend. The tweets and YouTube videos, which were related to the trending topic were used as the specific sets of events. We selected the random samples of 10,000 tweets and 100 videos. We selected the data related to the English language to simplify the process. They were stated by the users who have pre-defined English in language setting. We skipped the tweets of other languages even if they were related to our selected event. For this research we are using, Christchurch mosque shootings incident 2019 in New Zealand as a disaster event. It was the trending topic on an international scale in March 2019, which affected the public especially the Muslim community from all over the world. The people commented on it and stated their opinions using tweets and videos. We have selected these relevant hashtags; #TheyAreUs #Christchurch #NewZealand #NewZeelandTerrorAttack.

3.3   Ranking Algorithm

We are using SVM ranking model for tweets to state the validity of information. We used the already designed algorithm for SVM-rank of Joachims [8] and performed the operations according to our selected features from extracted API files. It uses the SVM to do pair-wise ranking of available data. The input information changes into pairing order sets. The labeling is done to order the data according to ranking pattern. Based on the learned model, this algorithm helped us to work effectively the ranking pattern and saved the results in a separate file. This field helped us to analyze the patterns of validation.

3.4   Included Features

We included the three basic sets of features related to users, author and content for Twitter as well as Youtube. They helped us in getting the ideas from the tweets and videos. Twitter and Youtube are the useful sources to differentiate the features. They are going to define the pattern of opinions and information related to Christchurch mosque shootings of New Zealand in 2019 (Fig. 1).

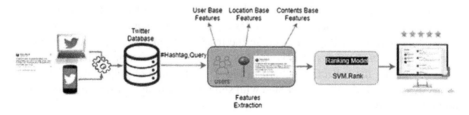

Fig. 1. Proposed solution steps for data validity and sentimental analysis

3.5   Evaluation Setup

The ranking results were not possible without the use of Normalized Discounted Cumulative Gain (NDCG). It helped us to divide the data into multiple grades. We used the transformation of data from 1 to 5 in the form of validity pattern by specifying the value of V. The 5 is representing the most valid tweets, and 1 represents the non-valid tweets. From 5 to 1 the tweets are divided into different stage of validity. The 0 value is related to spam, which has no information and has no validity. The NDGC is basically related to DCG score divided by ideal DCG score. The value of NDGC always stated between 0 and 5. Instead of selecting the above data for processing, we have done random sampling to maintain the effectivity of cross-validation of tweets related to the same events. We wanted to design a pattern which could help us in a more in-depth analysis.

4   Results

4.1   Twitter

We selected the followers-count, friends-count, URL-count, users' names, tweet-content and retweeting behavior as the important features for our project from Twitter API. Along with it, we included the subjectivity and polarity features. We analyzed the results and compared the values of our system with addition of the two new features and without them.

4.2   YouTube

In the case of YouTube, another API file was extracted which provided the features in the form of video id, title, comment count, like count, dislike count and favorite count. We also added the subjectivity and polarity to work on sentimental analysis on viewers reviews on YouTube videos related to the selected event. After putting API file in SVM-rank model and NDCG system, the results were analyzed.

4.3   Polarity and Subjectivity

We analyzed the results and compared the values of our system with addition of the two new features, that are polarity and subjectivity and without them. The results showed the significant improvements in the results of ranking of validation values of tweets. The polarity and subjectivity also have some connection which each other. They are giving the collective pattern in Fig. 2. At the mid of graph, the polarity and subjectivity of values are concentrated with showing gradually a differentiated behavior around the borders.

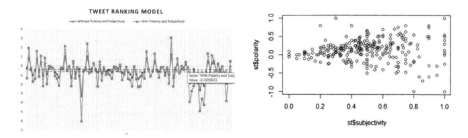

Fig. 2. Impact of polarity and subjectivity features on Twitter data

4.4 Location and Polarity

Including the other aspects, we worked for defining the connection between location and polarity. The process of results in our system showed that the location is impactful to gather the polarity of data. The users also had the same perception that the selected event-based locations related tweets are considered one level more valid than others. We have designed the system and got that the maximum tweets of polarity were related to New Zealand. We have selected Christchurch mosque shootings in 2019 as our main event. So, the location of New Zealand connected areas got positive and negative polarity scores.

4.5 Evaluation of Validity Ranking

We displayed our validity results with the help of graphs. In this part, we are showing the web model having tweets and validity ranking display. We selected the yellow color to fill the stars according to the value of ranking of tweets. The tweets displayed in the form of validity ranking. The yellow filled starts showed the significance of validity of information and less availability of false news. We have tested my system on related tweets and the results were using successful pattern of validity. The displayed showed that the validity of tweets is extracted based on information usefulness and other relevant features.

The validation display results of our selected event of Christchurch mosque shootings 2019 are shown in Fig. 3. The stars are representing the validation ranking. Along with it, we also displayed the subjectivity and polarity in circles. The above circles showed the polarity which could be either positive, negative or neutral. They are our final results. With validity ranking display, it would become easier for users of Twitter to identify the truthfulness of information-based tweets and locate the spams during high impact events.

Fig. 3. Validity display of tweets related to New York 2019 event (Color figure online)

4.6   Comparison of Sentimental Analysis of Social Media Streams

We did the sentimental analysis on the comments of people on Twitter and YouTube. We selected the comments through random selection and investigate the polarity and subjectivity of data. The results are displayed in the graphs of Fig. 4. They are providing a good comparison of sentimental analysis of different social media streams.

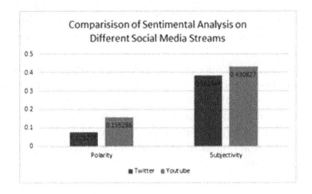

Fig. 4. Comparative analysis of data of YouTube and Twitter

5   Conclusion

The data mining process is helpful to design a system to identify the validity of information. It is very important to identify the trustworthiness of the available data to tackle the problems which arise because of abundance of data after a high impact incident on the national and international scale. The people are connected through social media and they log on to check for the most updated information. We have selected Twitter and YouTube as the influential social media networks. The data sets along with features are extracted to identify the validity of data. By using NDCG and SVM-rank model, we designed the ranking pattern. Along with others, we included polarity and subjectivity features, which improved our results. We have tested our system on selected events. The biggest problem for doing this research work that validity was defined in terms of users and tweets. In the future, a shared database should be developed to give the chance of learning and experience impact of features to new researchers.

References

1. Acar, A., Muraki, Y.: Twitter for crisis communication: lessons learned from Japan's tsunami disaster. Int. J. Web Based Communities **7**(3), 392–402 (2011)
2. Boididou, C., Papadopoulos, S., Kompatsiaris, Y., Schifferes, S., Newman, N.: Challenges of computational verification in social multimedia. In: Proceedings of the 23rd International Conference on World Wide Web, pp. 743–748. ACM (2014)
3. Castillo, C., Mendoza, M., Poblete, B.: Information credibility on Twitter. In: Proceedings of the 20th International Conference on World Wide Web, pp. 675–684. ACM (2011)
4. Cheong, F., Cheong, C.: Social media data mining: a social network analysis of tweets during the 2010-2011 Australian floods. PACIS **11**, 46 (2011)
5. Duan, Y., Jiang, L., Qin, T., Zhou, M., Shum, H.-Y.: An empirical study on learning to rank of tweets. In Proceedings of the 23rd International Conference on Computational Linguistics, pp. 295–303. Association for Computational Linguistics (2010)
6. Gupta, A., Kumaraguru, P., Castillo, C., Meier, P.: TweetCred: real-time credibility assessment of content on Twitter. In: Aiello, L., McFarland, D. (eds.) SocInfo 2014. LNCS, vol. 8851, pp. 228–243. Springer, Cham (2014). https://doi.org/10.1007/978-3-319-13734-6_16
7. Imran, M., Elbassuoni, S., Castillo, C., Diaz, F., Meier, P.: Practical extraction of disaster-relevant information from social media. In Proceedings of the 22nd International Conference on World Wide Web, pp. 1021–1024. ACM (2013)
8. Joachims, T.: Training linear SVMS in linear time. In: Proceedings of the 12th ACM SIGKDD International Conference on Knowledge Discovery and Data Mining, pp. 217–226. ACM (2006)
9. Kang, B., O'Donovan, J., Höllerer, T.: Modeling topic specific credibility on Twitter. In Proceedings of the 2012 ACM International Conference on Intelligent User Interfaces, pp. 179–188. ACM (2012)
10. Kwak, H., Lee, C., Park, H., Moon, S.: What is Twitter, a social network or a news media? In: Proceedings of the 19th International Conference on World Wide Web, pp. 591–600. ACM (2010)

11. Lehmann, J., Castillo, C., Lalmas, M., Zucker-man, E.: Finding news curators in Twitter. In Proceedings of the 22nd International Conference on World Wide Web, pp. 863–870. ACM (2013)
12. Morris, M.R., Counts, S., Roseway, A., Hoff, A., Schwarz, J.: Tweeting is believing? Understanding microblog credibility perceptions. In: Proceedings of the ACM 2012 Conference on Computer Supported Cooperative Work, pp. 441–450. ACM (2012)
13. Quercia, D., Askham, H., Crowcroft, J.: TweetLDA: supervised topic classification and link prediction in Twitter. In Proceedings of the 4th Annual ACM Web Science Conference, pp. 247–250. ACM (2012)
14. Yang, F., Liu, Y., Yu, X., Yang, M.: Automatic detection of rumor on Sina Weibo. In: Proceedings of the ACM SIGKDD Workshop on Mining Data Semantics, p. 13. ACM (2012)
15. Yang, J., Counts, S., Morris, M.R., Hoff, A.: Microblog credibility perceptions: comparing the USA and China. In: Proceedings of the 2013 Conference on Computer Supported Cooperative Work, pp. 575–586. ACM (2013)

An Approach to Map Geography Mark-up Language Data to Resource Description Framework Schema

Ammara Faqir[1]([:envelope:]), Aqsa Mahmood[2], Kiran Qazi[3],
and Saleem Malik[4]

[1] Department of Computer Science and IT, National College of Business
Administration & Economics Lahore, Lahore, Punjab, Pakistan
ammarafaqir99@gmail.com
[2] Department of Computer Science and IT, Government Sadiq College
Women University Bahawalpur, Bahawalpur, Pakistan
aqsa.mahmood@gscwu.edu.pk
[3] Department of Computer Science and IT, The Islamia University
of Bahawalpur, Bahawalpur, Pakistan
kiranaliqazi@gmail.com
[4] Department of Computer Science, Federation University Australia,
Ballarat, VIC, Australia

Abstract. GML serves as premier modeling language used to represent data of geographic information related to geography locations. However, a problem of GML is its ability to integrate with a variety of geographical and GPS applications. Since, GML saves data in coordinates and in topology for the purpose to integrate data with variety of applications on semantic web, data be mapped to Resource Description Framework (RDF) and Resource Description Framework Schema (RDFS). An approach of mapping GML metadata to RDFS is presented in this paper. This study focuses on the methodology to convert GML data in semantics to represent in extended and enriched form such as RDFS as representation in RDF is not sufficient over semantic web. Firstly, we have GML script from case study and parse it using GML parser and get XML file. XML file parse using Java and get text file to extract GML features and then get a graph form of these features. After that we designed methodology of prototype tool to map GML features to RDFS. Tool performed features by features mapping and extracted results are represented in the tabular form of mapping GML metadata to RDFS.

Keywords: Geography markup language · Resource description framework · Resource description framework schema · Mapping · Ontologies

1 Introduction

Geospatial data is the extremely significant information regarding coordinate values of physical entities of our planet which can be represented in the form of numerical value in geospatial system. Geography markup language (GML) is a standard language for

© Springer Nature Singapore Pte Ltd. 2020
I. S. Bajwa et al. (Eds.): INTAP 2019, CCIS 1198, pp. 343–354, 2020.
https://doi.org/10.1007/978-981-15-5232-8_30

storing and transporting geography information to stimulate common policies, principles, framework guidelines and standards for interoperability and inter changeability for geospatial data and services. GML works for geography systems and be responsible for interchanged format for geographic transaction of data on internet. The ontology is the study of classifications of things that occur or may occur in some domain. It mainly deals with generating common terminology for different platforms. It may also be constructed on set of Features like things, events and relations that are specified in some way to create a communal terminology for exchanging information among different platforms. Ontology empower knowledge distribution in a way to facilitate different mindsets for same thing or vice versa.

Semantic web denotes information in well-define meaning, enable computer systems in a better way, and also empower people to work in corporation. Two vital technologies are in exercise to develop semantic web that is Extensible Markup Language (XML) and Resource Description Framework (RDF). In XML every user creates their own tag and it permit users to add random structure to their documents without giving any clue about the structure. Structural meaning is articulated by RDF approach which encodes it in set of triples then writes it in XML tags .RDF document make declaration about particular thing and their properties with certain values.

Resource Description Framework Schema (RDFS) is a semantic extension of RDF which is responsible for providing mechanism to describe the group of related resources, their relationships. RDFS is a basic schema language. RDFS and semantic web technologies permit data created by different teams for different uses at dissimilar times to be connected. RDFS describes classes of objects and inheritance.

Mapping of geography markup language data is to convert it into resource description framework. Only mapping in RDF do not provide comprehensive logic of resources. As geospatial data is accessed by numerous application systems which requires comprehensive description of these resources. So, it has become important to map GML data to RDFS that will describe related resources and their relationships.

We have GML script from case study and parse it using GML parser and get XML file. XML file parse using Java and get text file to extract GML features and then get a graph form of these features. After that we designed methodology of prototype tool to map GML features to RDFS. Tool performed features by features mapping and extracted results are represented in the tabular form of mapping GML metadata to RDFS.

2 Related Work

The related work presented in the era of mapping Geography Markup Language (GML) data to Resource Description Framework Schema (RDFS) to highlight its importance.

Alam and Napoli (2015) presented a study to represent interactive data searching paradigm using pattern structures. It took RDF triples and RDF schema and provided one navigation space resulting from several RDF resources. There is pattern mining algorithms with visualization tool to explore data and identified required patterns. These algorithms are advantageous on small datasets. Iterative process of data exploration was performed on Linked Open Data (LOD). Another approach was presented about deriving of linked data commencing GML data and highlighted its importance to represent GML data in RDF by transforming it from Unified Modeling Language (UML) to Web Ontology Language (OWL) Van den Brink et al. (2013).

Conventional reasoning systems are not appropriate for massive quantity of semantic data due to resource limitations and existing reasoning system are inappropriate for enormous data. A solution was presented by Gu et al. (2015) named as Cichild that considered as proficient reasoning engine, for extensively used RDFS and OWL Horst Rule sets. This engine was based on Spark. It implemented parallel reasoning algorithm with the Spark RDD (Resilient distributed dataset) Programming model. They suggested an optimized parallel RDFS reasoning algorithm. Swift understanding, easy searching and selection of schema and the web document was made possible in a study presented by Troullinou et al. (2015) is a RDF digest, a novel base framework which provide automated summaries of the RDF/S Knowledge Base (KBs). To construct the Graph, algorithm utilizes the semantic, structure of schema and distribution of matching data or instances. Summarized Graphs created by proposed system are used to explore the Semantics of Schema, structure of the RDFS Graph, and distribution of the subsequent data to recognize important elements of ontology.

Linking data object to the dataset URI is presented by Hietanen et al. (2016) using the Vocabulary of Interlinked Datasets (VoID). The dataset is partitioned to the subsets which is given its persistent and specific URI. This permitted the entire dataset to be explored by using web browser and index each object using web crawlers. Another study represented by Zhao et al. (2017) proposed an algorithm to convert RDF query to Web Feature Service (WFS) requests keeping in view that clients can request distributed WFS features as they were RDF instances. The algorithm avoided the cost of changing features to RDF objects while holding the advantages of RDF queries.

The possibility of handling billions of RDF triples on one service machine presented by Corcoglioniti et al. (2015). This made possible by using streaming, sorting techniques, and focus on RDF processing tasks. These tasks are data filtering and transformation RDFS inference OWL that is same as statistics extraction. This paper introduce RDFpro (RDF processor) to handle this. RDFpro is an open source tool which provides streaming and sorting base processor for tasks. Semantic RDF services are become more confronted with many big data issues. In the presence of inference, query processing is one of them. To reduce memory footprint and make simple exchange of huge datasets Cure et al. (2015) presents structured resource identification scheme with help of clever TBox encoding of Features and property hierarchies for the efficient assessment of main and common RDFS entailment rules, while minimizing query rewriting and triple materialization. This paper presents how encoding computed through scalable parallel algorithm.

It becomes difficult for traditional systems to handle enormous data. For better utilization a semantically enriched data representation is required with keep it simple. Malik et al. (2016) provide solution as representation in Resource Description Framework Schema (RDF), introduced by World Wide Web Consortium (W3C). Data that is taken from different sources is formats into the RDF. Improvement is required to handle transition of information between all applications. This paper illustrate transformation of relational database textual data into RDF by using a case study.

To extract geospatial features from various sources Patroumpas et al. (2014) present TripleGeo ETL utility. It transform geospatial data into triples for subsequent loading into RDF Stores. This tool have been tested and validate against OpenStreetMap layers with huge amount of geometries. Spatial information in data formats, schemas, platforms, systems, and web services. This Spatial data remains in databases. Geographic Information Systems (GIS) managed by vendors or by Government agencies. But Open Geo Spatial Consortium (OGC) and the initiatives for constructing Spatial data Infrastructures (SDI) under the EN INSPIRE directive drove path leading towards the Geospatial data Interoperability and distribution.

3 Proposed Methodology

Transformation by means of mapping of GML metadata into RDFS can make it more accessible for other domains of knowledge and can make it more advantageous. Following framework is used to map GML data to RDFS (Fig. 1).

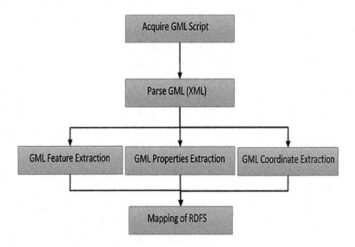

Fig. 1. Proposed architecture for mapping of GML script to RDF schema

3.1 Acquire GML Script

We input GML metadata in this step and will receive XML file of the given GML metadata as a result of this phase. This XML file have the three major types of tags, GML elements is the parent tag have child tag Feature tag, Description tag and Property sets tag.

3.2   Parse GML (XML)

In this phase parsing is performed on XML file that is generated as the output of the first phase. Following figure shows the steps to be performed during parsing of XML file. XML parsing is done in java. Java Programming facilitates to multiple ways to parse XML documents. But we used here DOM parse way and data received in text form (Fig. 2).

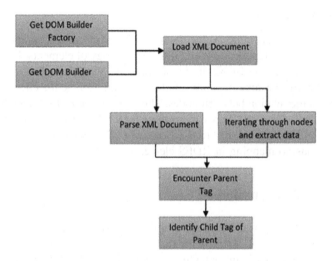

Fig. 2. Proposed methodology to parse GML (XML)

3.3   Extracting GML Features

In this phase, we input the textual data that was output of the previous phase to extract the GML elements. The general elements of GML are Features. Afterwards we apply parsing to distinguish between the noun Feature and Verb Features from the output of the first phase of extracting the Feature.

3.4   Extraction of Feature Property

In this phase parsing is performed on text file in order to extract GML elements. Their noun and verb feature are identified and extracted for further parsing process. Output of this phase is obtained in the form of graph.

3.5   GML Coordinates Extraction

In GML, the Coordinates are among the vital elements besides Features. These Coordinates denote coordinates of geometry instances. In this phase following three elements are used to specify details of a GML coordinate:

- *<gml:coordinates>*
- *<gml:pos>*
- *<gml:posList>*

XML DOM parser provides the complete string instead of individual coordinates. Here, we apply Java string functions to segregate each coordinate value from the resultant string of coordinates.

3.6   Mapping to RDFS

It is the last phase of our proposed methodology, it consists of text graph of RDF and RDFS. In the previous step we received GML terminology of elements. Elements are in two categories: one is Known Features and other is Verb/Facts Feature. In the last phase, noun Features became the node and fact/relation became the edges of the graph that symbolized the relation between nodes. Then our prototype tool map "Features" to "Resources", GML Feature "Property" to the RDFS "Property", "Property Name" to "RDFS:Label", "Description" to "RDFS:Comment" RDFS elements. "Feature Type" GML element has no mapping in RDFS elements.

4   Results and Discussion

We discuss the different features of our tool that included the phases of input, output, and processing of our tool. After it we make experiment by taking a case study to evaluate the performance of our tool. Our prototype tool of RDFS Generated automated transformation of GML statements to RDF and RDFS. Now, we discuss the following Module of our tool in details.

4.1   GML Input to RDF Generator

The Input for our tool is specified in XML file that is generated from GML editor. These GML statements are collected from several case studies. We input the Script rules about features, coordinates and properties of GML file to the editors Shown in Fig. 3. Editor perform processing on GML statements and generate the XML file. Then GML editors again input GML statements and extract vocabulary as GML Noun, Verbs, Fact Types, Object Types, and Quantification etc.

```
<?xml version="1.0" encoding="UTF-8"?>
<wfs:FeatureCollection xmlns:xs="http://www.w3.org/2001/XMLSchema"
  xmlns:ogc="http://www.opengis.net/ogc" xmlns:wfs="http://www.opengis.net/wfs"
  xmlns:ows="http://www.opengis.net/ows" xmlns:xlink="http://www.w3.org/1999/xlink"
  xmlns:gml="http://www.opengis.net/gml" xmlns:gs="http://www.geoserver.org"
  xmlns:xsi="http://www.w3.org/2001/XMLSchema-instance" numberOfFeatures="1"
  timeStamp="2014-08-07T12:22:06.508Z"
  xsi:schemaLocation="http://www.geoserver.org http://localhost:8080/geoserver/gs/wf:
  <gml:featureMembers>
    <gs:CURVES gml:id="CURVES.0">
      <gs:NAME>Arc segment</gs:NAME>
      <gs:GEOMETRY>
        <gml:Curve srsDimension="2" srsName="urn:x-ogc:def:crs:EPSG:32632">
          <gml:segments>
            <gml:ArcString interpolation="circularArc3Points">
              <gml:posList>10.0 15.0 15.0 20.0 20.0 15.0</gml:posList>
            </gml:ArcString>
          </gml:segments>
        </gml:Curve>
      </gs:GEOMETRY>
    </gs:CURVES>
  </gml:featureMembers>
</wfs:FeatureCollection>
```

Fig. 3. Script of rules

4.2   GML Output of RDFS Generator

GML editors generate output in Xml format and separate the noun Feature in tags such as name and terms and verb Feature in tags such as facts where verb show the relation between two nouns. Tagged XML file generated as the output of this phase is shown below (Fig. 4).

```
<xsl:stylesheet version="1.0" ..... >
<xsl:template match="/">
<MapAtlasLab="Cartography"Date="2002-07-25"
xsi:noNamespaceSchemaLocation="E:\Spanaki\GML\XML2GML\MapAtlas_4POINTS.xsd">
  <xsl:for-each select="layer/ROW">
    <MapPoints>
      <xsl:attribute name="STSINM"><xsl:value-of select="STSINM"/></xsl:attribute>
      <xsl:attribute name="OBJECTID"><xsl:value-of select="OBJECTID"/></xsl:attribute>
      <PointsGeometry>
        <gml:coord>
          <gml:X>
            <xsl:apply-templates select="SHAPE/SDO_POINT/X"/>
          </gml:X>
          <gml:Y>
            <xsl:apply-templates select="SHAPE/SDO_POINT/Y"/>
          </gml:Y>
        </gml:coord>
      </PointsGeometry>
    </MapPoints>
  </xsl:for-each>
</MapAtlas>
</xsl:template>
</xsl:stylesheet>
```

Fig. 4.   Generated XML file

4.3   GML/XML Processing

This step of our tool consists of input XML file that is generated from XML editor in previous phase to RDFS generator. Prototype tool parsed it in simple textual format that is the collection of the GML vocabulary. Then Processing is done and vocabulary of GML (Terms, fact type) is extracted. In vocabulary, terms are considered as nouns Features and facts types are considered as verb/ Relation. After extraction phase the vocabulary is written in text file and then text file is input into the graph generator which represent GML vocabulary in graph format as shown in the following figures (Figs. 5 and 6).

```
<rdf:Description rdf:about="#FullSlide">
    <axsvg:GraphicsType>Chart</axsvg:GraphicsType>
    <axsvg:LabelledBy rdf:resource="#BottomLegend"/>
    <axsvg:ChartType>Line</axsvg:ChartType>
</rdf:Description>
<rdf:Description rdf:about="#BottomLegend">
    <axsvg:IsAnchor>true</axsvg:IsAnchor>
</rdf:Description>
```

Fig. 5.   GML vocabulary extraction text file

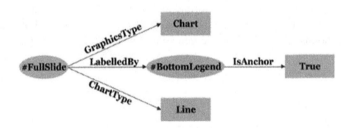

Fig. 6.   GML vocabulary extraction graph

4.4   Output of GML Script to RDFS Script

In this phase we input text file of previous phase that consists of Noun Features and facts type to generate the RDF script in text graph format. In this graph noun Features become the node of RDFS script and facts become the relation between the nodes of RDFS script that is called edges of graph (Fig. 7).

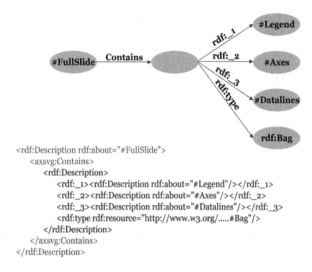

```
<rdf:Description rdf:about="#FullSlide">
    <axsvg:Contains>
        <rdf:Description>
            <rdf:_1><rdf:Description rdf:about="#Legend"/></rdf:_1>
            <rdf:_2><rdf:Description rdf:about="#Axes"/></rdf:_2>
            <rdf:_3><rdf:Description rdf:about="#Datalines"/></rdf:_3>
            <rdf:type rdf:resource="http://www.w3.org/.....#Bag"/>
        </rdf:Description>
    </axsvg:Contains>
</rdf:Description>
```

Fig. 7. Output of GML to RDFS script

4.5 Mapping to RDFS

In the output of previous phase "Legend" is the parent node of the graph, and it has three child node "Axis", "Data lines", "Bag". "Contains" in this word "has" is referent/label of edge of graph similarly "contains" in this word "is in" is the referent of graph. We represent this text graph in mapping of GML elements to RDFS elements where "Feature" element mapped to "Resource" in RDFS, GML element

"Feature Type" not mapped in RDFS, GML" Property" element mapped to "Property" in RDFS, "Property Name" GML element mapped to "RDFS: Label" and "Description" element is mapped to "RDFS: Comment" in the following way (Table 1).

Table 1. Mapping of GML data to RDFS

GML elements	RDF/RDFS elements
Feature	Resource
Feature Type	–
Property	Property
Property Name	RDFS:Label
Description	RDFS:Comment

4.6 Discussion of Results

There were Eight GML rules used in case study problem. The most important reason to select this case study was to test the performance of our tool with the complex GML rules. The correct, incorrect, and missing GML elements/ Rule in Graph using proposed methodology are shown in Table 2.

Table 2. Results of Graph generated from case study

Sr #	Type/metrics	N_{sample}	$N_{correct}$	$N_{missing}$
1	Features	4	3	0
2	Coordinates	8	7	0
3	Properties	14	13	1
	Total	23	21	1

According to our evaluation methodology, table shows sample elements are 23 in which 20 are correct 1 is incorrect and 2 are missing Graph elements (Table 3).

Table 3. Results of recall and precision

Type/metrics	GML features
Nsample	23
Ncorrect	21
Nincorrect	1
Nmissing	1
Recall%	91.30
Precision%	94.45

The results of this primary performance evaluation are extremely promising and supporting both the methodology presented and the capability of this prototype tool in general. There are some other case study that are used to test our prototype tool to achieve the performance results are shown below (Table 4).

Table 4. Evaluation results of various case studies

Input	N_{sample}	$N_{correct}$	$N_{incorrect}$	$N_{missing}$	Recall	Precision	F-value
C1	24	22	1	1	91.16	95.65	93.35
C2	45	40	2	3	88.88	95.23	91.94
C3	33	31	2	0	93.93	93.93	93.93
C4	46	43	1	2	93.47	97.72	95.54
C5	56	45	5	6	80.35	90.00	84.90
Average	40.5	36.2	2.4	Average	89.38	93.88	91.57

5 Conclusion and Limitations

To address the primary objective of this research study we have designed prototype tool to generate RDFS by overcoming GML rule (Generated from English) and Show the relationship between Nouns Feature and Fact type of GML vocabulary in RDFS. GML Generator is capable to parse XML file that is generated from Transaction editors of GML that input the GML rules received from English text. Extract GML vocabulary by using parsed text file which have nouns Features and fact/verb Features of GML, in the last step by using this GML vocabulary our tool generate the RDF and RDFS in text graph form. Then we perform mapping. We apply experiment on different case studies to check the performance of our proposed tool. Hence, the evaluation method proved that our proposed tool performance is satisfactory and work in accurate manner.

The output of our tool can be used to present RDF and RDFS view of GML rules for the better understanding and data interchange. As shown in the results section, the recall (89.38%) and precision (93.88%) results applying on the used case study for software requirements by using our tool are very satisfactory. Similarly, calculated F-value (91.57) is quite encouraging. Generated results also shows that the presented approach is easy and time saving to generate a semantically formal and controlled representation using our automated approach and our prototype tool".

6 Future Work

Keeping an eye towards the future GML and on the possible impact are to be explored. These aspects are discusses below:

- More research can be perform on the approaches based on mapping GML data to RDF and RDFS. Our tool can be expanded towards the skewed area charts (i.e. positive and negative) interpretation.
- Our tool can be expanded towards presenting RDF and RDFS in visual form.
- Implementation of GML in visual graph can be a good pictorial view of GML. Visual graph representation of GML rule by using the object-oriented Programming.

References

Alam, M., Napoli, A.: Interactive exploration over RDF data using formal Feature analysis. In: IEEE International Conference on Data Science and Advanced Analytics (DSAA), 2015, 36678, pp. 1–10. IEEE, October 2015

Van den Brink, L., Janssen, P., Quak, W.: From geo-data to linked data: automated transformation from GML to RDF. In: Linked Open Data-Pilot Linked Open Data Nederland. Deel 2-De Verdieping, Geonovum, pp. 249–261 (2013)

Gu, R., Wang, S., Wang, F., Yuan, C., Huang, Y.: Cichlid: efficient large scale RDFS/OWL reasoning with spark. In: 2015 IEEE International Parallel and Distributed Processing Symposium (IPDPS), pp. 700–709. IEEE, May 2015

Troullinou, G., Kondylakis, H., Daskalaki, E., Plexousakis, D.: RDF digest: efficient summarization of RDF/S KBs. In: Gandon, F., Sabou, M., Sack, H., d'Amato, C., Cudré-Mauroux, P., Zimmermann, A. (eds.) ESWC 2015. LNCS, vol. 9088, pp. 119–134. Springer, Cham (2015). https://doi.org/10.1007/978-3-319-18818-8_8

Hietanen, E., Lehto, L., Latvala, P.: Providing geographic datasets as linked data in SDI. ISPRS-Int. Arch. Photogramm. Remote Sens. Spat. Inf. Sci. **41**, 583–586 (2016)

Zhao, T., Zhang, C., Li, W.: Adaptive and optimized RDF query interface for distributed WFS data. ISPRS Int. J. Geo-Inf. **6**(4), 108 (2017)

Vitolo, C., Elkhatib, Y., Reusser, D., Macleod, C.J., Buytaert, W.: Web technologies for environmental Big Data. Environ. Model Softw. **63**, 185–198 (2015)

Saripalle, R.K., De la Rosa Algarin, A., Ziminski, T.B.: Towards knowledge level privacy and security using RDF/RDFS and RBAC. In: 2015 IEEE International Conference on Semantic Computing (ICSC), pp. 264–267. IEEE, February 2015

Qiu, R., Duan, H., Yu, X., Zheng, L., Cheng, Q.: An ontology matching method for GML application ontology to GeoSPARQL ontology. In: 2015 23rd International Conference on Geoinformatics, pp. 1–5. IEEE, June 2015

Lefrançois, M., Zimmermann, A., Bakerally, N.: Flexible RDF generation from RDF and heterogeneous data sources with SPARQL-generate. In: Ciancarini, P., Poggi, F., Horridge, M., Zhao, J., Groza, T., Suarez-Figueroa, M.C., d'Aquin, M., Presutti, V. (eds.) EKAW 2016. LNCS (LNAI), vol. 10180, pp. 131–135. Springer, Cham (2017). https://doi.org/10.1007/978-3-319-58694-6_16

Hor, A.H., Jadidi, A., Sohn, G.: BIM-GIS integrated geospatial information model using semantic web and RDF graphs. ISPRS Ann. Photogramm. Remote Sens. Spat. Inf. Sci. **3**(4), 73–79 (2016)

Corcoglioniti, F., Rospocher, M., Mostarda, M., Amadori, M.: Processing billions of RDF triples on a single machine using streaming and sorting. In: Proceedings of the 30th Annual ACM Symposium on Applied Computing, pp. 368–375. ACM, April 2015

Cure, O., Naacke, H., Randriamalala, T., Amann, B.: LiteMat: a scalable, cost-efficient inference encoding scheme for large RDF graphs. In: 2015 IEEE International Conference on Big Data (Big Data), pp. 1823–1830. IEEE, October 2015

Malik, K.R., Ahmad, T., Farhan, M., Aslam, M., Jabbar, S., Khalid, S., Kim, M.: Big-data: transformation from heterogeneous data to semantically-enriched simplified data. Multimed. Tools Appl. **75**(20), 12727–12747 (2016)

Patroumpas, K., Alexakis, M., Giannopoulos, G., Athanasiou, S.: TripleGeo: an ETL tool for transforming geospatial data into RDF triples. In: EDBT/ICDT Workshops, pp. 275–278, March 2014

Machine Learning

Multi-aspects Intelligent Requirements Prioritization Technique for Value Based Software Systems

Falak Sher[1], Dayang N. A. Jawawi[1(✉)], Radziah Mohammad[1(✉)],
Muhammad Imran Babar[2(✉)], Rafaqat Kazmi[3(✉)],
and Muhammad Arif Shah[1(✉)]

[1] Faculty of Engineering, School of Computing, Department of Software
Engineering, UTM, 81310 Johor, Malaysia
safalak2@live.utm.my, {dayang, radziahm}@utm.my,
arif.websol@gmail.com
[2] Army Public College of Management and Sciences, Rawalpindi, Pakistan
drimran@apcoms.edu.pk
[3] Department of Computer Science & IT, The Islamia University of Bahawalpur,
Bahawalpur, Pakistan
Rafaqat.Kazmi@iub.edu.pk

Abstract. Requirements engineering (RE) is an important phase of software engineering. During this phase, an important set of activities are carried out to manage requirements elicitation, verification, prioritization and validation. Dimension and dynamics of software development are changing with the passage of time. Economic growth in different sectors is increasing the demand for software development. This enhancement has introduced the concept of Value Base Software (VBS) development. Requirements prioritization is playing a vital role in ordering requirements to support the release planning of the software. A prioritization process is considered as highly complex process and depends on the nature and size of requirements. VBS systems are entirely different from typical software development, and prioritization process for VBS is also very challenging. A need arises from the provision of prioritization techniques to support the technical and business aspects-based prioritization. Existing techniques are not qualified to meet the expectation of the industry for VBS development. Therefore, this research contribution is an effort made, based on an intelligent decision support system for requirements prioritization in the domain of VBS system. Aspects based requirements prioritization is applied to many requirements and results are produced in two clusters. Results are claimed as a prioritized list of requirements for traditional as well as value-based system.

Keywords: Software requirements engineering · Requirements prioritization · VBS · Clustering · Fuzzy C-Means

© Springer Nature Singapore Pte Ltd. 2020
I. S. Bajwa et al. (Eds.): INTAP 2019, CCIS 1198, pp. 357–371, 2020.
https://doi.org/10.1007/978-981-15-5232-8_31

1 Introduction

Software engineering is a combination of different phases, and these phases are followed throughout the software development process. Brooks has said "the hardest single part of building a software system is deciding precisely what to build. Therefore, the most important function that the software builder performs for the client is the iterative extraction and refinement of the product requirements" [1]. According to Zave "requirements engineering is the branch of software engineering concerned with the real-world goals for, functions of, and constraints on software systems. It is also concerned with the relationship of these factors to precise specifications of software behaviour, and to their evolution over time and across software families" [2]. The software development process is mostly influenced by financial and economic factors. This impact of dependency is leading to the growth of VBS (VBS) systems. Activities in RE phase for VBS are carried out by adopting existing approaches. Boehm defined the term VBS engineering (VBSE) as, "the explicit concern with value concerns in the application of science and mathematics by which properties of computer software are made useful to the people" [3].

VBS systems and VBSE are interlinked concepts, where software is evaluated in economic perspective. The value of the VBS system is measured based on its economic worth or market leverage. Traditional software development differs from the VBS development. "The value-based approach to software development integrates value considerations into current and emerging software engineering principles and practices, while developing an overall framework in which these techniques compatible reinforce each other". In VBS development, the key focus is to satisfy and realize the stakeholder with the concept of value delivered from the developed software in the domain of VBS engineering [4]. VBS mainly depends on the key term value, which depends on human services [5]. Software should be developed with the realization of the importance of value. This concept must be followed in current practices and principles in the domain of VBS developed by giving more attention to requirements prioritization, release planning and stakeholders [6].

With the growing age of software development and innovative trends, new challenges are arising in the domain of software development for value-based systems. To address these challenges, requirements engineering techniques are used as a tool to deal with the situation [7]. Requirement engineering phase is treated as the most challenging in the overall success of the software development. Identifying stakeholders, gathering requirements, producing requirements specification, making decision for implementation of requirements are prominent activities performed during requirements engineering phase [8–10].

Software industry depends on data analysis, which is very helpful and significant for the industry to develop quality software [11]. Data analysis is a supporting tool for the industry and it has the largest impact on the processing of large amount of data [12]. Data is described using possible description methods which include cluster visualization, sequential analysis and association of data. Data clustering is a common method used for data description. Its application area covers data mining, pattern recognition, machine learning, bio-informatics and image analysis. Cluster analysis is acknowledged as famous and recognized technique to classify data, where data is classified into clusters based on similarities and differences.

In 1981, Bezdek [13] introduced clustering method known as Fuzzy C-Means clustering. The initial form of clustering is known as hard clustering and extended form is known as Fuzzy C-Means (FCM). Clustering is categorized as supervised and unsupervised and FCM is treated as unsupervised method. There are different domains where clustering is applied, these domains are clustering design, feature analysis and classified design. In many areas FCM is playing its vital role and contributing to humanity in different fields. This list covers the field of agricultural engineering, medical diagnosis, geology, chemistry, image analysis, target recognition and shape analysis [14]. FCM algorithm mainly depends on the theory proposed by Ruspini, Fuzzy clustering, in 1980's. Analysis through the algorithm is performed in a very simple way where the user provides data points in the form of input. Cluster centers are determined for each cluster and then the distance between data points is calculated. This calculation helps in the formation of clusters. Clustering is usually used to cluster data in different groups, FCM is one of the famous techniques which is used to complete the job of clustering. Each data point in the data set has relation to the respective cluster. The impact of this relation is measured as a degree, and this degree is described as high or low. High degree refers to less distance of point to the center of cluster and low degree of relationship mean data point is a faraway place from the center of the cluster.

Software data analysis field is treated as one of the most useful fields and important tool for handling large amount of data. Managing large scale data is rather difficult, but data analysis method has increased the interest of such type of analysis. Different means are used to describe this method which includes an association, clustering visualization and sequential analysis. Data is clustered into different groups for analysis purpose. Data clustering is a method used to cluster data in different groups. Clustering approach is applied and used in different domains like data mining, pattern recognition, bio-informatics, machine learning, and image analysis. Cluster analysis as a clustering technique, and this technique is applied in a way where the data are classified into clusters. For classification of data into different clusters, clustering analysis is declared as important technique. Cluster analysis plays vital role in classification of data, and through this method dataset is divided into different cluster based on similarities within a cluster or differences between different clusters [15].

This paper consists of four major sections. The first part is about research background. Section 2 contains details of existing prioritization techniques and their associated problems. Section 3 deals with the Fuzzy C-Means (FCM) based intelligent Technique for Requirements Prioritization. Section 4 is about experimentation and results based on 2D clustering. At last Sect. 5 contains conclusion and future work.

2 Requirement Prioritization Techniques in Literature

Quality software development depends on the selection of user requirements, and selection process performed with the help of different requirements prioritization techniques. Most prominent techniques highlighted in the literature are the analytical hierarchical process (AHP), cost-value approach, theory W, top ten requirements, Cumulative voting (CV), planning game (PG), Hierarchical Cumulative Voting (HCV), case-based ranking, Value-base Intelligent Requirement (VIRP), priority groups, numerical assignment (NA), bubble sort, PHandler and many other options are added in the list. Existing techniques are compared with each other in term of their reliability one example is bubble sort which is more reliable than AHP, both techniques are not efficient in term of time consumed to prioritize requirements. The implementation of certain techniques becomes complex as more comparison is required, AHP is one example where pairwise comparisons require more time for large number of requirements.

Most of the techniques are not scalable and they are unable to handle large number of requirements. Bubble sort and many other techniques face problem of scalability [16–18]. Nominal, ordinal, rational and interval is most common methods to group assignment. Numerical assignment uses an ordinal scale to method to assign weights to each requirement. Stakeholders are responsible to manage requirements in different groups [19]. The placement of each requirement in a critical group imposes restriction on each requirement to be implemented and this factor reduces the effectiveness of the technique [20]. This technique becomes more complex when all requirements placed in each group have equal priority. This technique is error prone and facing many problems [21].

One of the most common statistical technique used for requirements prioritization is The Analytic Hierarchy Process (AHP) [22]. Key requirements, priority is determined using the AHP method [20]. A simple formula is used to compare requirements where n number of requirements compared $n \times (n - 1)/2$ times. This technique procedures reliable results when it deals with a small number of requirements. Cost-value is another approach used to prioritize requirements [23]. Two factors, cost and value are used to assign weights to each requirement for prioritization. Scaling is the major problem faced and reported with the use of AHP. To overcome the problems of scalability faced in AHP, Karlsson et al. introduced another concept in the form of a technique The Hierarchy AHP (HAHP) [16]. Minimal spanning tree prioritization technique was introduced by Karlsson et al. as a solution to overcome the redundancy problem of AHP [16].

Another name for Cumulative Voting (CV) is the hundred dollar test, this technique depends on discussion [24]. Stakeholders participate in this discussion and each stakeholder is given imaginary units in the form of points or dollars. The final value of each requirement is determined by assigning unit weight by each stakeholder. Results are based on a ratio scale, which provide information about each requirement and its comparison with another requirement. Four techniques, Planning Game, AHP, binary search tree and combination of AHP and planning game are compared with cumulative voting [20]. CV is proved as an efficient and accurate method for requirements prioritization. This technique is suitable for a small number of requirements. Numerical assignment and ranking prioritization techniques depend on an ordinal scale for assigning weights to the requirements [21]. In case 100 requirements to be prioritized, then n will be 100 [25]. This approach is based on some quick sort, bubble sort and binary search tree as acceptable algorithm used for prioritization [2]. Theory W, another name for this technique is Win–Win Model, depends on risk assessment and planning used to prioritize requirements. It depends on two principles, one is 'What values are important?' and the second is 'How is success assured' [26]. This technique is more time consuming and depends on the expert's judgement.

In planning game, customer plays major role to complete the process of prioritization [17]. Planning game is most suitable for extreme development model, as more flexibility is evident from the behaviour of technique. This technique proved more efficient as compared to AHP when an experiment is performed by using 13 requirements [27]. B-Tree prioritize technique is capable of handling requirements change and can handle associated with the change of requirements [28]. Priority groups is the common method used for prioritizing requirements. First, a set of requirements is prepared. Set of requirements is further classified as high, medium and low priority group [16]. Stakeholders are supposed to select the top ten requirements, each time they perform the process of prioritization. They ignore the individual ranking of requirement in the selected group. Again, the main issue with this technique is handling the number of requirements for prioritization, selecting ten requirements each time is a small number. This technique lacks in term of granularity of requirements [19].

The hierarchical cumulative voting (HCV) is one of the technique capable of handling the problem of scalability [29]. Paolo, Angelo present technique known as an interactive genetic algorithm which depends on user knowledge to complete the process of requirements prioritization. According to the technique pairwise comparison is not a suitable and genetic algorithm is applied to reduce the number of comparisons to produce an ordered list of requirements [30, 31]. This technique is also treated as a scalable method of requirements prioritization [32]. The bubble sort prioritization technique depends on the ranking method to assign weights to the requirements [16]. The value-based intelligent requirement prioritization (VIRP) technique's main purpose is to address the problem of scalability [13, 33]. PHandler, is presented to address the problem of scalability. The technique is a combination of value-based intelligent requirement prioritization (VIRP), the Artificial Neural Network (ANN) and AHP approach [34, 35].

The aim of this research paper is to deal with the problem of scalability, consideration of and application of intelligent approach to perform clustering for the large size dataset. Most of the existing techniques are facing following problems.

   I. Most of the techniques are not scalable [27, 33, 36, 37].
  II. They are time consuming and complex [21, 36].
 III. The results achieved are error prone and non-recallable [27, 38].
 IV. Existing techniques are not intelligent [39, 40].
  V. Lacking in term of tool support [41, 42].
 VI. Insufficient evidence for implementation and validation [27, 43].
VII. Lack of consideration of requirements dependencies [44, 45].
VIII. Existing techniques are unable to address properly stakeholders conflicts [46].

The main purpose of this research is to focus on a list of problems. Most of the existing techniques are unable to handle the issue of scalability [47]. An early effort is made to explore different aspects required and those aspects are classified into two major groups [48]. Although some of the technical and business aspects are highlighted in the existing techniques, but there was a need for a compilation of all reported aspects. The suitability of existing technique was not enough to cope the requirements of VBS system. A wide range of business aspects is explored and compiled to manage the issues related to requirements prioritization in the domain of value-base software system.

In this research paper, multi-aspects requirements prioritization technique is applied to calculate the requirement value. A requirement value for each requirement is calculated in two parts. In first part requirement value is calculated based on technical aspects and later same formula is repeated for business aspects. The total value for a requirement is the sum of the value calculated for technical and business aspects. In the second phase exception mechanism is applied to handle the exception in the calculated requirements value. At last intelligent fuzzy c-means is applied to cluster the given set of requirements [49]. FCM is applied to partition the objects (requirements) of a given dataset into clusters and portioning depends on technical and business aspects.

3 Proposed Fuzzy C-Means (FCM) Based Intelligent Technique for Requirements Prioritization

Hard C-Mean clustering is considered as an initial clustering method. Later on, in 1981, Bezdek [13] taken an advantage of introducing Fuzzy C-Means clustering as extended version. Clustering is classified as supervised and unsupervised process. FCM is a part of unsupervised algorithms and it is used to solve problem related to classifier design, clustering and feature analysis. FCM is used as clustering technique to group given dataset into n number of clusters. Each data point establishes relationship with different clusters based on the on the concept of to be in the right place. Soft computing techniques are used to remove biasedness and same is used to remove experts' biasedness in the process of prioritization and this makes requirements prioritization process more effective. Technical and business aspects are used as parameters for requirements prioritization Fuzzy C-Means. FCM is used to make clusters and to choose a most critical cluster of requirements to be included the release planning used for VBS systems.

This research contribution is depending on Fuzzy C-Means (FCM) [50], which was previously used to prioritize requirements in the domain value of based software engineering [39]. FCM is used to compute the position of each data based on calculated distance of each point from a given dataset. Latest versions of FCM are dependent on the fuzzification parameter m and the range of this parameter remains between 1 and n. Parameter m is the base for calculation of degree of belonging to each object (data point), this degree of belonging is classified as high or low. Allocation of data objects (data point) depends on the value of parameter m in each cluster, and most common and acceptable value for m is 2. The process of FCM is initiated with a guess value to calculate the value of centroid (distance means) as a mean distance of each cluster. For efficient multi-aspects requirements prioritization, two metrics are used for requirements as features to be applied in soft computing.

FCM is used to classify the objects in a dataset into different clusters based on the key features or attributes. The FCM computes the right position of an object in the dataset and places it in its respective cluster in the space of two or more clusters. In the improved version of FCM, the fuzzification parameter m is introduced and is in the range of [1, n]. The degree of fuzzification is determined by m, in each cluster. The commonly used value for m is 2. Result in the form of different clusters depends on the threshold value ε. Otherwise the algorithm 1 loop will continue its execution till the time optimal results are achieved for a given problem. This symbol ε in mathematics and especially in calculus is used to represent random small positive value.

Input in this proposed intelligent system is based on weights assigned to each requirement by different experts. The individual requirement weight assigned is multiplied with the aspect's weight to calculate requirement value against technical and business aspects group. FCM parameters are also assigned with variation of values to generalize the results. The input is of two types which are business and technical aspect values as well as fuzzy c-means parameters. Business and technical aspect values are given to the system to determine the total value for weights against each requirement. The computed values for both types of aspects against each requirement is stored in Comma Separated Value (CSV) format and is stored/imported in a database or in a text file. BA reflects the business aspects and TA is referring technical aspect and summation of both aspects is helping to get the total weight value against each requirement. This calculated requirement value is given as data input to the FCM. The second type of input to the system is associated with the fuzzy c-means parameters. The FCM parameters are required number of clusters N, the value of exponent or fuzzification parameter E, I is for the total number.

Figure 1 explains the process adopted for prioritization using two different types of aspects. The interface is a source of input for each requirement, where weights are assigned to individual assignment. Other than weights assignment using interface, one more provision is given for setting parameters for fuzzy C-Mean. Aspects are divided into two subsets, one is technical aspects and the other is business aspects. Technical aspects are a collection of 14 sub-aspects and business aspects cover 19 sub-aspects. Individual and collective value of both aspects is stored in the database. There are two provisions for database handling. One way is to use a spreadsheet template to store weights of requirements or otherwise proper database tool is used to handle values of requirements. Conversion in a text file (CSV) is required of the given database, as a source of the input format is text file FCM.

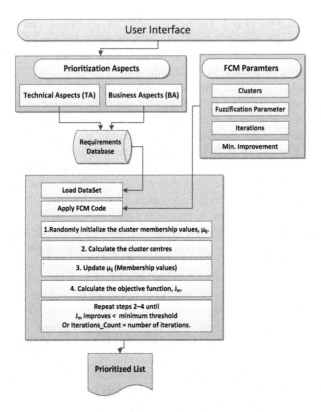

Fig. 1. Intelligent system based on FCM

4 Results

The experiment results depend on FCM parameters. Major parameter includes m (fuzzification value), the number of clusters Requirements data is classified based on aspects classification. Two groups cover aspects related to technical and business aspects. Requirement value is calculated by multiplying aspects weights with requirement weights. The weights assigned to each aspect are decided by software industry experts. Each aspect weight is assigned by experts through survey performed in software industry of Pakistan and Malaysia. A requirement value for each dataset is assigned by stakeholders. There is a chance for fuzzification in the requirements data set based on different possibilities. These possibilities are managed through different exceptions, which are given in detail below.

4.1 Calculating Final Requirements Value

In the Eq. 5, Sr is total score, which is calculated in a very simple way, two parameters are used to calculate the sum value. Each aspect value V_i is assigned during prioritization process and this value is multiplied with its respective weight $W_{r,i}$ assigned by industry experts All types of risks impact negatively so their weights are also given negative values. Final calculation is obtained in the form of net score for all factors in a specific group by subtracting risk value. The net results are derived by dividing net score by 1000. This conversion is performed to address the problem of scaling.

$$\forall r \in \{R\} : Sr = \sum_{i=1}^{n} \left(V_i X W_{r,i}\right) \tag{5}$$

4.2 Calculating Technical Aspects Score and Business Aspects Score for Each Requirement

In Eq. 6, calculation process given in Eq. 5 is further divided into two parts. One part is calculating the sum of value for technical aspects and the second part is calculating results for business aspects. Results calculated individually are summed up to calculate the final score.

$$Sr = \sum_{t=1}^{n} \left(V_t X W_{r,t}\right) + \sum_{b=1}^{n} \left(V_b X W_{r,b}\right) \tag{6}$$

4.3 Preparation of Requirements Dataset

For conducting an experiment, different data sets are available and used by existing research in the domain of requirements engineering and value-base software system [35, 39], [51]. These datasets contain small, medium and large number of requirements. Dataset selected for this experiment is related to enterprise resource planning (ERP) system, United States based organization providing enterprise solutions [52].

Table 1. Technical aspects

Requirements	Risk	Cost	Speed	Effort	Granularity	Time	Sophistication	Sensitivity	Contradictory	Validity	Penalty	Resources	Complexity	Total of all aspects	Technical risk	Net score	Net result
Weights	8	7	6	8	7	8	6	7	6	7	8	8	6		−8		
R1	7	6	5	7	6	8	5	7	5	7	8	8	6	612	5	652	0.652
	…	…	…	…	…	…	…	…	…	…	…	…	…	…	…	…	…
R550	3	4	4	4	4	5	4	3	1	4	5	5	1	341	4	373	0.373

Table 2. Business aspects

Requirements	Sales	Marketing	Competitive	Strategic	Customer retention	Simplicity	Innovative	Depend	Resourceful	Client focused	Friendly	Customer success	Benefit	Value	Performance	Business Growth	Security	Availability	Total of all factors	Business risk	Net score	Net result in points
Weights	7	6	8	9	7	8	7	6	7	9	9	7	7	8	9	7	9	8		−5		
R1	5	5	6	7	5	6	5	4	5	5	5	4	5	6	6	5	1	5	692	3	707	0.707
...	...	...	...	...	...	...	...	...	...	...	...	...	...	...	...	...	...	...	...	...	...	...
R550	4	4	5	5	4	5	4	4	4	4	5	4	4	5	5	5	3	5	609	3	624	0.624

4.4   Experiment

An experiment with 550 requirements is performed to prove the research hypothesis. A range of datasets is reported and used by different researchers [48]. Table 1 and Table 2 contains part of the details for the dataset used in this experiment. The experiment is repeated for different set of parameters required for fuzzy c-mean. Initial results are obtained by setting the number of clusters value equal 2. With two-dimension clustering, value for fuzzification parameter m is changed in descending order from 3.0 to 1.25 to analyze the variation in the results.

4.4.1   Fuzzy C-Means (FCM) Results – 2D Clustering

The data are highly fuzzy due to the unclear scenarios for the selected dataset. It is described in the FCM that a business aspect may have a higher value with a lower value for technical aspects and vice versa. However, it is also observed that some requirements have higher business aspects value and higher technical aspect values and in such cases the decision-making is very difficult. Based on the net value against business and technical aspects, it is very difficult to quantify the requirements due to the induced fuzziness in the data values. Hence, in this research, FCM is used to quantify the requirements based on business and technical aspect values. In my case (Business aspects) β and (technical Aspects) γ are passed as an input to the FCM for making clusters for requirements prioritization. The number of inputs, in the case of FCM, is reduced to two. Hence, the problem has become a 2-D problem. In 2D problem scenario, using a 2D type of clustering, two parameters are required, in this case one parameter is technical aspects and the other is business aspects.

The most common and acceptable value reported in the literature for fuzzification parameter is 2.0. One of the existing experiments made using FCM for clustering of stakeholders is strongly supporting 2.0 as recommendable value for optimized results [53]. With the similar set of parameters, five attempts are made to obtain clustering results for a given set of data. Reason for repeating an experiment with similar parameter and the same data set is to observe the change in the level of objective function that ultimately reflects option of results. These five attempts are reflecting changes in the number of iterations to optimize the results of the clustering, but on the other hand, no major change in the value produced for objective function. Figure 2 representing results of same experiment with multiple repetition. Each attempt has

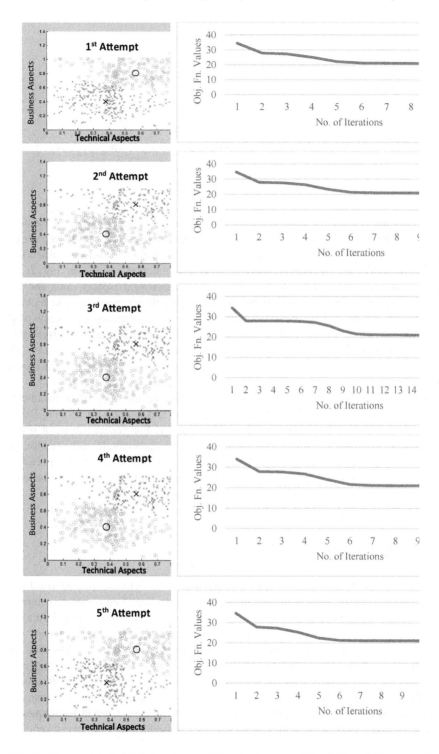

Fig. 2. Exponent (m) = 2.0, iterations = 100, min_improv = 10e−5, No. of Clusters = 2

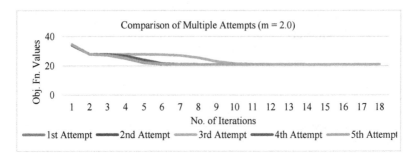

Fig. 2. (*continued*)

shown similar results for clustering and their respective graphs have represented a change in the number of iterations and objective function values. Results represented by each figure are more convincing and optimized due to significant variation in iterations performed for optimization of objective function results. In Fig. 2, two clusters are represented, first cluster represents high technical aspects value and high business aspect value for requirements and the second cluster represents low technical aspects and low business aspects. Both cluster parts are also representing some of the requirements, which are having low technical aspects and business aspects. Highlighted part of clusters is less dense to represent the population of requirements dataset. This problem has led to further distribution of a requirements dataset into a greater number of requirements.

Results are generated with five different attempts with the same set of parameters.

Figure 2 represents results generated using FCM and defined set of data. Results are produced considering two dimensions of clustering. For generalization of results, experiment is revised five times with the same set of parameters. In each attempt, two clusters of requirements are produced based on assigned weights value against each set of aspects. Large set of requirements are allocated between two clusters and these two clusters are helpful in prioritization of requirements. Further results analysis is also possible by adjusting number of clusters and other FCM required parameters.

5   Conclusion

Quality software development directly depends on a set of activities related to software engineering and especially within requirements engineering. Requirements prioritization process being most important phase, is carried on using existing prioritization approaches. Most of the existing techniques are not satisfying experts to meet their expectation in traditional and specially VBS systems. Moreover, Identification and classification of aspects related to technical and business scenarios can change the dynamics of software development. Aspects based requirements prioritization is gaining attention of experts in the industry. Existing techniques are unable to manage a complete range of aspects required for prioritization process. Current techniques are unable to handle large scale requirements datasets. Biasedness of different stakeholders is another issue which affects the quality of decision making in requirements prioritization process. Soft computing introduced intelligent techniques to overcome the problem of biases. This research contribution presents multi-aspect intelligent approach using fuzzy c-mean to resolve issues associated with current requirements prioritization techniques. In future work, more soft computing related approaches can be merged with existing multi-aspects proposed requirements prioritization techniques. Empirical validation of presenting technique on software projects will prove the effectiveness of the techniques of VBS systems and traditional software development. As a part of future work, validation is required by a wide range of datasets from traditional and VBS systems to investigate the weakness and benefits of the proposed technique. A comparative analysis is required to investigate similarities and differences among technique proposed and other intelligence methods available by conducting different case studies in the software industry. For automation of technique, tool support may prove this technique more effective and useful to support the industry experts.

References

1. Brooks, F., Kugler, H.: No silver bullet, April 1987
2. Zave, P.: Classification of research efforts in requirements engineering. ACM Comput. Surv. (CSUR) **29**, 315–321 (1997)
3. Boehm, B.: Value-based software engineering: reinventing. ACM SIGSOFT Softw. Eng. Notes **28**, 3 (2003)
4. Boehm, B., Huang, L.G.: Value-based software engineering: a case study. Computer **36**, 33–41 (2003)
5. Babar, M.I., Ghazali, M., Jawawi, D.N.: Software quality enhancement for value based systems through stakeholders quantification. J. Theor. Appl. Inf. Technol. **55**, 359–371 (2013)
6. Boehm, B.W.: Value-based software engineering: overview and agenda. In: Biffl, S., Aurum, A., Boehm, B., Erdogmus, H., Grünbacher, P. (eds.) Value-Based Software Engineering, pp. 3–14. Springer, Heidelberg (2006). https://doi.org/10.1007/3-540-29263-2_1
7. Grube, P.P., Schmid, K.: Selecting creativity techniques for innovative requirements engineering. In: 2008 Third International Workshop on Multimedia and Enjoyable Requirements Engineering-Beyond Mere Descriptions and with More Fun and Games, MERE 2008, pp. 32–36 (2008)
8. Van Lamsweerde, A.: Requirements engineering in the year 00: a research perspective. In: Proceedings of the 22nd International Conference on Software Engineering, pp. 5–19 (2000)
9. Nuseibeh, B., Easterbrook, S.: Requirements engineering: a roadmap. In: Proceedings of the Conference on the Future of Software Engineering, pp. 35–46 (2000)
10. Hudaib, A., Masadeh, R., Qasem, M.H., Alzaqebah, A.: Requirements prioritization techniques comparison. Mod. Appl. Sci. **12**, 62 (2018)
11. Kitchenham, B.: Procedures for performing systematic reviews. Keele University, Keele, UK, vol. 33, p. 2004 (2004)
12. Chatzipetrou, P., Angelis, L., Rovegard, P., Wohlin, C.: Prioritization of issues and requirements by cumulative voting: a compositional data analysis framework. In: 2010 36th EUROMICRO Conference on Software Engineering and Advanced Applications (SEAA), pp. 361–370 (2010)
13. Bezdek, J.C.: Pattern Recognition with Fuzzy Objective Function Algorithms. AAPR. Springer, Boston (1981). https://doi.org/10.1007/978-1-4757-0450-1

14. Yong, Y., Chongxun, Z., Pan, L.: A novel fuzzy c-means clustering algorithm for image thresholding. Measur. Sci. Rev. **4**, 11–19 (2004)
15. Rao, V.S., Vidyavathi, D.S.: Comparative investigations and performance analysis of FCM and MFPCM algorithms on iris data. Indian J. Comput. Sci. Eng. **1**, 145–151 (2010)
16. Karlsson, J., Wohlin, C., Regnell, B.: An evaluation of methods for prioritizing software requirements. Inf. Softw. Technol. **39**, 939–947 (1998)
17. Laurent, P., Cleland-Huang, J., Duan, C.: Towards automated requirements triage. In: 2007 15th IEEE International Requirements Engineering Conference, RE 2007, pp. 131–140 (2007)
18. Lehtola, L., Kauppinen, M.: Empirical evaluation of two requirements prioritization methods in product development projects. In: Dingsøyr, T. (ed.) EuroSPI 2004. LNCS, vol. 3281, pp. 161–170. Springer, Heidelberg (2004). https://doi.org/10.1007/978-3-540-30181-3_15
19. Khan, K.A.: A systematic review of software requirements prioritization. Unpublished master's thesis, Blekinge Institute of Technology, Ronneby, Sweden (2006)
20. Ahl, V.: An experimental comparison of five prioritization methods. Master's thesis, School of Engineering, Blekinge Institute of Technology, Ronneby, Sweden (2005)
21. Berander, P.: Prioritization of stakeholder needs in software engineering. Understanding and evaluation. Licenciate thesis, Blekinge Institute of Technology, Sweden, Licentiate Series, p. 12 (2004)
22. Saaty, T.L.: The Analytic Hierarchy Process: Planning, Priority Setting. Resources Allocation. McGraw-Hill, New York (1980)
23. Karlsson, J., Ryan, K.: A cost-value approach for prioritizing requirements. Softw. IEEE **14**, 67–74 (1997)
24. Leffingwell, D., Widrig, D.: Managing Software Requirements: A Unified Approach. Addison-Wesley Professional, Boston (2000)
25. Berander, P., Khan, K.A., Lehtola, L.: Towards a research framework on requirements prioritization. SERPS **6**, 18–19 (2006)
26. Boehm, B.W., Ross, R.: Theory-w software project management principles and examples. IEEE Trans. Softw. Eng. **15**, 902–916 (1989)
27. Achimugu, P., Selamat, A., Ibrahim, R., Mahrin, M.N.R.: A systematic literature review of software requirements prioritization research. Inf. Softw. Technol. **56**, 568–585 (2014)
28. Beg, R., Abbas, Q., Verma, R.P.: An approach for requirement prioritization using b-tree. In: 2008 First International Conference on Emerging Trends in Engineering and Technology, ICETET 2008, pp. 1216–1221 (2008)
29. Berander, P., Jönsson, P.: Hierarchical cumulative voting (HCV)—prioritization of requirements in hierarchies. Int. J. Software Eng. Knowl. Eng. **16**, 819–849 (2006)
30. Tonella, P., Susi, A., Palma, F.: Using interactive GA for requirements prioritization. In: Proceedings of the 2nd International Symposium on Search Based Software Engineering (SSBSE 2010), pp. 57–66 (2010)
31. Tonella, P., Susi, A., Palma, F.: Interactive requirements prioritization using a genetic algorithm. Inf. Softw. Technol. **55**, 173–187 (2013)
32. Svensson, R.B., Gorschek, T., Regnell, B., Torkar, R., Shahrokni, A., Feldt, R.: Quality requirements in industrial practice—an extended interview study at eleven companies. IEEE Trans. Software Eng. **38**, 923–935 (2012)
33. Babar, M.I., Ramzan, M., Ghayyur, S.: Challenges and future trends in software requirements prioritization. In: 2011 International Conference on Computer Networks and Information Technology (ICCNIT), pp. 319–324 (2011)
34. Fausett, L., Fausett, L.: Fundamentals of Neural Networks: Architectures, Algorithms, and Applications. Prentice-Hall, Upper Saddle River (1994)

35. Babar, M.I., Ghazali, M., Jawawi, D.N., Shamsuddin, S.M., Ibrahim, N.: PHandler: An expert system for a scalable software requirements prioritization process. Knowl.-Based Syst. **84**, 179–202 (2015)
36. Vestola, M.: A comparison of nine basic techniques for requirements prioritization (2010)
37. Dos Santos, J.R.F., Albuquerque, A.B., Pinheiro, P.R.: Requirements prioritization in market-driven software: a survey based on large numbers of stakeholders and requirements. In: 2016 10th International Conference on the Quality of Information and Communications Technology (QUATIC), pp. 67–72 (2016)
38. Asghar, A.R., Tabassum, A., Bhatti, S.N., Shah, S., Ali, A.: The impact of analytical assessment of requirements prioritization models: an empirical study. Int. J. Adv. Comput. Sci. Appl. **8**, 303–313 (2017)
39. Ramzan, M., Jaffar, M.A., Shahid, A.A.: Value based intelligent requirement prioritization (VIRP): expert driven fuzzy logic based prioritization technique. Int. J. Innov. Comput. Inf. Control (IJICIC) **7**, 1017–1038 (2011)
40. Karlsson, L.: Requirements prioritisation and retrospective analysis for release planning process improvement (2006)
41. Perini, A., Susi, A., Ricca, F., Bazzanella, C.: An empirical study to compare the accuracy of AHP and CBRanking techniques for requirements prioritization. In: 2007 Fifth International Workshop on Comparative Evaluation in Requirements Engineering, CERE 2007, pp. 23–35 (2007)
42. Dabbagh, M., Lee, S.P., Parizi, R.M.: Application of hybrid assessment method for priority assessment of functional and non-functional requirements. In: 2014 International Conference on Information Science and Applications (ICISA), pp. 1–4 (2014)
43. Hujainah, F., Bakar, R.B.A., Abdulgabber, M.A., Zamli, K.Z.: Software requirements prioritisation: a systematic literature review on significance, stakeholders, techniques and challenges. IEEE Access **6**, 71497–71523 (2018)
44. Shao, F., Peng, R., Lai, H., Wang, B.: DRank: a semi-automated requirements prioritization method based on preferences and dependencies. J. Syst. Softw. **126**, 141–156 (2017)
45. Alawneh, L.: Requirements prioritization using hierarchical dependencies. In: Latifi, S. (ed.) Information Technology - New Generations. AISC, vol. 558, pp. 459–464. Springer, Cham (2018). https://doi.org/10.1007/978-3-319-54978-1_59
46. Anand, R.V., Dinakaran, M.: Handling stakeholder conflict by agile requirement prioritization using Apriori technique. Comput. Electr. Eng. **61**, 126–136 (2017)
47. Santos, R., Albuquerque, A., Pinheiro, P.R.: Towards the applied hybrid model in requirements prioritization. Procedia Comput. Sci. **91**, 909–918 (2016)
48. Sher, F., Jawawi, D.N., Mohamad, R., Babar, M.I.: Multi-aspects based requirements priortization technique for value-based software developments. In: 2014 International Conference on Emerging Technologies (ICET), pp. 1–6 (2014)
49. Cannon, R.L., Dave, J.V., Bezdek, J.C.: Efficient implementation of the fuzzy c-means clustering algorithms. IEEE Trans. Pattern Anal. Mach. **2**, 248–255 (1986)
50. Dunn, J.C.:A fuzzy relative of the ISODATA process and its use in detecting compact well-separated clusters (1973)
51. Achimugu, P., Selamat, A., Ibrahim, R.: A clustering based technique for large scale prioritization during requirements elicitation. In: Recent Advances on Soft Computing and Data Mining, Springer, pp. 623–632 (2014)
52. Achimugu, P., Selamat, A., Ibrahim, R.: ReproTizer: A fully implemented software requirements prioritization tool. In: Transactions on Computational Collective Intelligence XXII, Springer, pp. 80–105 (2016)
53. Babar, M.I., Ghazali, M., Jawawi, D.N.: A bi-metric and fuzzy c-means based intelligent stakeholder quantification system for value-based software. SoMeT, pp. 295–309 (2014)

An Intelligent Approach for CRC Models Based Agile Software Requirement Engineering Using SBVR

Hina Afreen[(✉)] and Umer Farooq

The Islamia University of Bahawalpur, Bahawalpur 63100, Pakistan
hinaafreen02@gmail.com, umer.bwnl@gmail.com

Abstract. In requirement engineering (RE) for agile software development, the Class-Responsibility-Collaborator (CRC) models are used as important brainstorming tool. However, manual generation of such CRC models by analyzing the requirements is a difficult and time-consuming task due to ambiguity and informal nature of natural languages-based software requirements. This paper introduces an improved requirement engineering technique based on CRC models that can help in specifying and analyzing software requirements in a better and faster way and curtailing difficulties associated with the traditional RE analysis technique. The proposed technique employs Semantics of Business Vocabulary and Rules (SBVR) to capture and specify software requirements in a controlled natural language. The SBVR representation is processed to extract object-oriented information and map the extracted information to CRC models in both textual and visual form. The proposed approach is implemented as an Eclipse plugin prototype SBVR2CRC as a proof of concept and the results of the experiments validate the effectiveness of the presented approach. Results show that such automated approach not only saves certain time and effort but also assists in generation of better CRC models and simplifies the CRC models based agile software development.

Keywords: Agile modeling · Requirement engineering · CRC models · SBVR

1 Introduction

In recent years, adoption of agile methodologies for software development has resulted in not only a rapid development of high-quality software but also delivering the value to customer [1]. Agile methods are totally different from standard SE process and based on face-to-face communication and iterative development [2]. Agile requirement engineering is a flexible, quicker and modern way of requirements elicitation that helps to make rapid delivery of software [3]. There are different reasons of agile requirements engineering success in software development process. One of the key reasons is face to face communication that makes requirements clearer. Moreover, agile requirement engineering allows customer to freely communicate with team throughout software development process while traditional requirement engineering only allow early stage communication of customer with development team that creates a gigantic gape in requirement understanding.

© Springer Nature Singapore Pte Ltd. 2020
I. S. Bajwa et al. (Eds.): INTAP 2019, CCIS 1198, pp. 372–384, 2020.
https://doi.org/10.1007/978-981-15-5232-8_32

The requirement expert people find requirements elicitation techniques like brainstorming are lengthy and laborious. The Class-Responsibility-Collaborator (CRC) [4, 5] models are typically used brain-storming tool for Agile based requirements elicitation and specification [6]. These days, the agile teams often use CRC models in design of a distinct challenging user story. However, analysis of software requirements and CRC cards based modeling can be a challenging task due to ambiguity and informal natural of natural languages typically used for capturing software requirements. Semantics of Business Vocabulary and Rules (SBVR) [7] has emerged into a widely adopted standard in the recent years, originally introduced by Object Management Group (OMG). SBVR can be useful in capturing and specifying software requirements in a controlled natural language such as Structured English with underlying semantics. In this paper, we present an intelligent and novel approach to generate Class-Responsibility-Collaborator (CRC) models by automatic extraction of object oriented information from SBVR based software requirements and then transform the extracted information into CRC models. CRC cards exhibit an effective way to represent requirement specifications that plays very vital role in software development process.

The rest of this paper is structured into following sections: Sect. 2 provides related work. Section 3 depicts the framework of presented prototype tool, SBVR2CRC. Section 4 explains an experiment and results. Section 5 describes the conclusion and highlights the future work.

2 Related Work

The use of artificial intelligence techniques and methodologies to automate and improve the traditional practices and processes of software engineering is not a new idea. One of the applications of such work is automated generation of class models from natural language text such as Overmyer [8], Harmain [9], Gomes [10], Bajwa [11], Deeptimahanti [12], Sagar [13], Gulia [14], and Arora [15]. Similarly, object oriented analysis of SBVR to generate UML class models has also been partially achieved previously such as SBVR to UML models (Raj [16]), SBVR to class models (Bajwa [17]), SBVR to UML models (Njonko [18]) and extraction of SBVR from class models (Skersys [20]). However, the object-oriented analysis discussed in the mentioned researches is partial and addresses subset of UML models. A few of these above-mentioned works are discussed in the following text to highlight the research gap.

Raj et al. [16] presented an approach to transform SBVR business design into three UML diagrams i.e. activity diagram, sequence diagram and class diagram. Raj's work to generate UML class diagram is at very early stage and reuse some existing transformation rules that are described in official release of SBVR specifications.

Moreover, this approach does not address various object-oriented elements such as methods, interfaces, data types, super lass, sub class etc.

Another automated approach is presented by Bajwa et al. [17] for object-oriented analysis of SBVR based software requirements to generate UML class models. The used approach systematically analyzes SBVR text and then formally transforms object-oriented information into UML class diagrams. However, similar to other approaches, this approach performs partial object-oriented analysis and does not cover extraction of super-class, sub class, categorization, data types, etc.

Another contribution is made by Nemuraite et al. [21] by presenting a tool VeTIS that provides editing facility of SBVR vocabularies and rules and can also partially transforms them to UML and OCL models. Nemuraite's work specifies requirements by using use cases and performs modeling of business process with the help of activities. This tool is integrated with Magic Draw UML case tool.

Another theoretical approach was presented by Awasthi et al. [19] to generate UML class diagram from SBVR based business design. An algorithm was used in presented research to partially extract object-oriented information and VeTIS tool is used to evaluate its results.

One more automated transformation approach was proposed by Bonais et al. [22] to produce the structural design models by defining a subset of SBVR specifications according to the elements of UML class diagram. A formal meta-model of identified SBVR subset is defined and used to generate UML class diagram for the defined subset using a formal transformation. However, this work also generates partial UML class models as the support to extract super-class, sub-class, visibility, multiplicity, interfaces, etc. is not provided.

3   The SBVR2CRC

This section elaborates the presented approach to automatically generate CRC cards from software requirements specification that are described in English text. SBVR2CRC approach consists of two main steps. In first step, SBVR specifications are generated by processing software specifications that are taken as input text. Generated SBVR specifications consist of business vocabulary and business rules. We have only required business vocabulary to generate CRC model. At second step, CRC model is generated using object-oriented information (classes, inheritance, generalization, aggregation etc.) that is extracted from SBVR business vocabulary. Here, we also define transformation rules that transform OO information into CRC model. Remaining part of this section explains all of these steps in detail.

3.1   Generate SBVR Model

To generate SBVR model, SBVR2CRC tool takes English software requirement as input and process these requirements to generate elements of a SBVR model and these elements are further processed to extract SBVR vocabulary and SBVR rules to complete a SBVR model as depicted in Fig. 1.

The processing of software requirements specifications text is divided into three steps like lexical, syntax and semantic analysis to generate SBVR based specifications. Lexical analysis phase starts with the lexical processing of text file that contains software requirements specifications. Lexical processing is process of producing stream of characters and it is referred to as scanning.

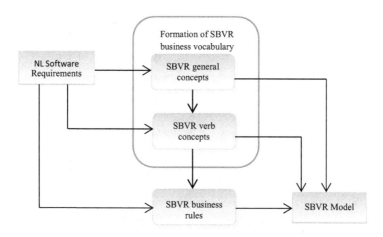

Fig. 1. SBVR model generation from NL text

The lexical analysis phase is further categorized four phases that are sentence splitting, tokenization, POS tagging and lemmatization. After performing lexical analysis, now we want to define the sentence structure of the input text. To accomplish this, we have used Stanford parser [23] that generates a parse tree. After syntactic analysis of text, generated parse tree is further used to perform semantic analysis. Shallow semantic parsing performed in our approach is similar to the Sematic Role Labeling (SRL) [24]. In the used approach, semantic roles are automatically assigned to each token in a sentence with the help of Stanford NER (Named Entity Recognition) also called CRFClassifier [25]. Since, Stanford CRFClassifier provides partial Semantic Role Labelling (SRL); a set of rules are user to identify complete set of semantic roles.

3.2   Transformation of SBVR Model to CRC Model

A complete description of the process starts from taking English software requirements to finally CRC model generation is shown in Fig. 2. The last step is the validation of overall transformation result i.e. CRC model. Validation of CRC model is an optional and during validation stage, one can go back and modify the concepts formed in the preceding stages if necessary.

A CRC card has two sides: front side and back side. The front side of card represents class name, responsibilities and collaborators. The class name represents the name of class for which CRC card is drawn and shown on top of the card. The responsibilities depicts knowing and doing of a class and are shown on left column of a CRC card as depicts in Fig. 3. Each class has some responsibility to fulfil. If a class has sufficient information to perform a responsibility, then it does not need collaborator class. The collaborator classes are needed when a class does not sufficient information to fulfill a job. The collaborators of a class are mentioned on right-hand column of a class [26].

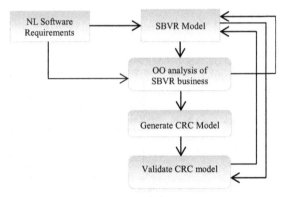

Fig. 2. Transformation of SBVR to CRC model

The backside of CRC card represents attributes and associations. The associations are represented as is - a relationship, aggregation, generalization, etc. It is important to note that consider front side of CRC card as the public information and the back side as encapsulated implementation details.

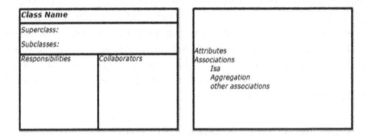

Fig. 3. A template of a CRC card [generated by software ideas modeler]

The NL software requirement has been processed in previous step to generate SBVR vocabulary and rules that define SBVR model. To generate CRC model, there is need to identify SBVR model elements and their corresponding CRC elements as shown in Table 1. After that perform their mapping using transformation rules that are explained in next sub section.

By using the SBVR to CRC mappings given in Table 1, a set of transformation rules are defined that are used to generate metadata of the target CRC model. Each Transformation rule consists of two parts. One is Left-hand-side (LHS) for source pattern and second is Right-Hand-Side (RHS) for target pattern.

Table 1. Mapping of SBVR model elements to CRC model elements

SBVR element	CRC model - front side	CRC model - back side
General noun concept	Class name	–
Verb concept	Responsibility	–
General noun concept	Collaborator	–
Is-property-of or unary verb concept	–	Attribute
Associative verb concept	–	Association
Partitive verb concept	–	Aggregation
Categorization verb concept	Generalization (superclass, subclass)	–

Extracting Class Name: CRC modeling provides a simple, easy and powerful way to identify and organize classes relevant to system requirements. CRC card has been divided into three sections [4]. The top section of CRC card contains class name. A collection of similar objects represents a class. In SBVR vocabulary, all object types are used identify to classes. The Rule1 contains three main parts of CRC card i.e. class name, responsibility and collaboration. To describe each part of CRC card, a transformation rule is needed. So Rule1 consists of three more rules i.e. Rule 2, Rule3 and Rule4. Rule1 explains how CRC card designed is given below:

Extracting Responsibility: Anything that a class knows or does is responsibility. Each class knows about its basic information and functionality that a class can perform. Every class must have some responsibility to be performed. If a class has sufficient information to accomplish assigned responsibility then it does not need any collaborator class otherwise it needs collaboration [27].

Extract Class Attribute: Each class has some basic information. To represent this information, all characteristics or unary verb concept (excluding action verbs) that are extracted from SBVR vocabulary are used.

Extracting Class Methods: A CRC card contains attributes and method of a class. Methods describe basic functionality that a class can perform [27]. There may be some responsibility that a class does not perform and to perform this responsibility class needed collaboration with other class that has ability to perform required functionality. Now, we want to extract methods for a class. In CRC card diagram, left section contains responsibilities that describe what a class knows or does. OO analysis of SBVR vocabulary shows that verb concepts describe actions that all common nouns can perform. So, all the verb concepts (associated to noun concept) are extracted from SBVR vocabulary is mapped to methods of a class.

After identifying the collaborator class, it is necessary to add responsibilities and check whether this class can perform its responsibilities. If identified collaborator class does not fulfill its responsibility then it requires another collaborator class. There are different types of generic relationship between classes that helpful in identification of collaborators.

- Extract is-part-of relationship: There are number of classes that are extracted from software requirements specifications and have some relationship with other classes in terms of functionality. The is-part-of relationship is used to connect all the classes that are part of an aggregate class. This relationship may be a composition or aggregation between classes.
- Find Aggregation: In this type of relationship, a part exists independently of whole and also whole is not especially responsible for parts. Now, we want to express relationship that exist between these classes so that CRC cards effectively show requirements specifications that leads to agile software development. To find relationship between these classes, the categorization verb concepts are mapped to aggregation. The main class is subject part of verb concept while subclass is object part of verb concept.
- Find Composition: If a part is always a part of single whole then it shows composition. The part exists only if the whole exist and whole is responsible for creation of other objects.
- Extract Is-kind-of relationship: Sometimes a class uses attributes and operations of another class additional to its own attributes. And that class does not exist without main class. There exists a relationship of is-kind-of between two classes that identify generalization between these classes.
- Extract Association: Sometimes, there is a more general relationship between classes that is known as association. In association, one class relates to another class. Association creates a links between classes. After performing OO analysis of SBVR based software requirements specifications, we have find that the association is formed from all associative verb concepts.
- Multiplicity: An association can be further elaborated by representing multiplicity. By using OO information that has extracted from software requirements specifica tions, we can represent multiplicity by using quantification with noun concept.

3.3   Drawing CRC Cards

After generating metadata of CRC model in the previous phase, the extracted metadata is used to draw a CRC model. The CRC cards can be generated from the extracted metadata in two ways; by XMI with a professional CASE tool or draw from scratch by using graphics libraries in Java. In our approach, the first way is opted as it generates professional CRC cards in a formal way. The processes of drawing a CRC card starts from a XMI template of an empty CRC card. In our implementation, such XMI template is generated by drawing an empty CRC card in the Visual Paradigm tool and exporting its XMI representation.

4   Experiment and Results

In this section, we have solved an example of library system originally presented by [28]. This example is later solved by Harmain to generate UML class models. Our proposed prototype tool takes software requirements specifications as natural language text and then generates SBVR based software requirements specifications. The SBVR software requirements are further processed to extract business vocabulary as explained in Sect. 3. The SBVR software requirements are further processed to extract business vocabulary and all the extracted SBVR elements from solved example are shown in Table 2.

Table 2. Total number of SBVR elements extracted from the running example

Set no.	SBVR element	Number of entries
1	General noun concepts	42
2	Individual concepts	6
3	Verb concepts	11
4	Associative verb concept	07
5	Partitive verb concept	03
	Total number of entries	69

Following text explains the working of the prototype tool with screen shots. The NLbased software requirements specifications are given as input to the prototype tool SBVR2CRC as shown in Fig. 4.

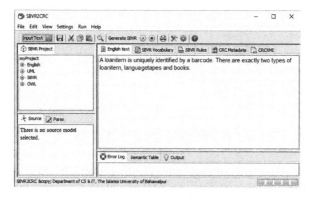

Fig. 4. The input given to the SBVR2CRC tool

When user clicks 'GenerateSBVR' button in menu bar, the SBVR specifications are generated that consists of SBVR vocabulary shown in Fig. 5.

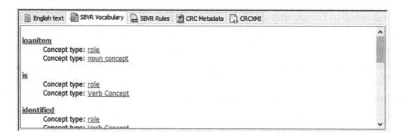

Fig. 5. SBVR vocabulary generated by the SBVR2CRC tool

The proposed prototype tool then automatically extract CRC meta data from SBVR vocabulary and embed this metadata in a XMI of a blank CRC card that have exported from Visual Paradigm tool. We have also generated CRC XMI after embedding the metadata that is shown in Fig. 6.

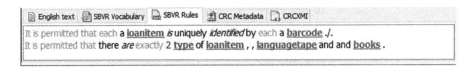

Fig. 6. SBVR rules generated by the SBVR2CRC tool

Our proposed tool has also extracted metadata from given input according to the transformation rules given in Sect. 3. The meatdata that is extracted is also shown in Fig. 7.

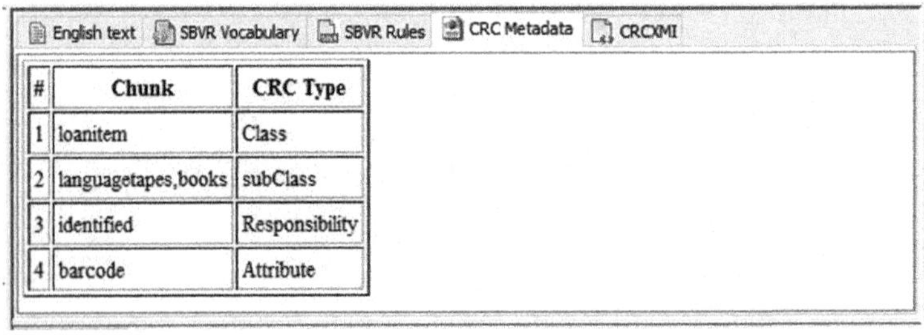

#	Chunk	CRC Type
1	loanitem	Class
2	languagetapes,books	subClass
3	identified	Responsibility
4	barcode	Attribute

Fig. 7. SBVR model mapping to CRC model by the SBVR2CRC tool

The proposed prototype tool then automatically extract CRC meta data from SBVR vocabulary and embed this metadata in a XMI of a blank CRC card that have exported from Visual Paradigm tool. We have also generated CRC XMI after embeding the meatdata.

The CRC XMI consists of information about class name, its attributes, responsibilities and also super classes and sub classes of main class it have. A CRC is generated from the XMI is shown in Fig. 8.

Now, evaluation of proposed tool is performed by using statistical measures precision and recalls. To accomplish this, we compare our presented prototype tool with another tool presented by Harmain et al. [9] because a similar approach was presented to generate class diagram from natural language. To do this comparison, first of all there is needed to identify three sets. The precision and recall measures are defined on the cardinality basis of these three sets is given below. The precision and recall percentage of all CRC elements generated by our transformation and Harmain's transformation is given in Table 3.

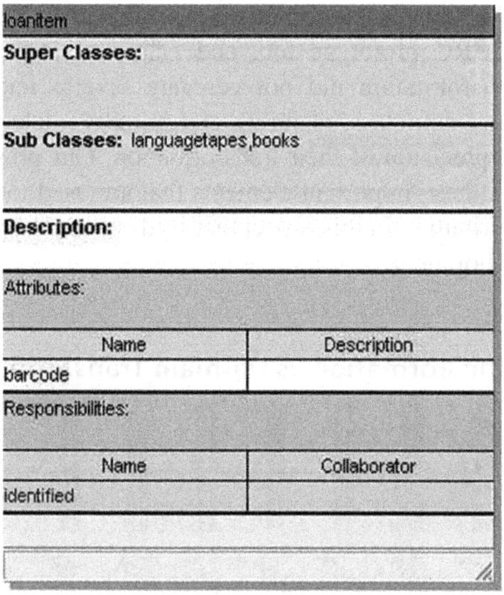

Fig. 8. A CRC card generate from the XMI using Visual Paradigm tool.

Table 3. Precision and recall measures of CRC metadata

CRC element	Expected CRC element	Our Transformation					Harmain's Transformation				
		TP	FN	FP	Precision	Recall	TP	FN	FP	Precision	Recall
Classes	10	10	0	0	100%	100%	10	0	5	0.67	100%
Attributes	10	10	0	0	100%	100%	8	2	5	0.62	100%
Methods	11	11	0	0	100%	100%	9	2	4	0.69	100%
Association	07	07	0	0	100%	100%	5	2	5	0.44	71%
Aggrega-tion	0	0	0	0	100%	100%	0	0	0	0	0
Super class	1	1	0	0	100%	100%	0	1	0	N/A	0
Sub class	2	2	0	0	100%	100%	0	2	0	N/A	0
Visibility	21	19	2	2	95%	95%	0	21	0	N/A	0
Primitive Data Type	17	16	1	1	100%	94%	0	17	0	N/A	0
Composi-tion	02	01	0	1	50%	100%	1	1	1	50%	50%
Overall	**81**	**77**	**3**	**4**	**94.5%**	**96%**	**33**	**48**	**20**	**62%**	**41%**

We have also plotted the clustered column chart that compares values of precision and recall of SBVR2CRC prototype tool and Harmain's transformation shown in Fig. 9. Harmain's transformation did not generate several important elements like aggregation, super class, sub class, visibility and primitive data type that also greatly influenced the overall precision of their transformation. Our presented transformation efficiently identifies all these important elements that are used to generate CRC model and makes a great contribution in this aspect that leads towards generation of quick and accurate software development.

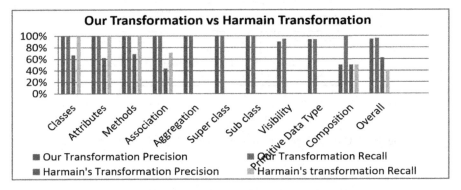

Fig. 9. The precision and recall clustered column chart

5   Conclusion and Future Work

The main objective of paper was to address the challenging aspect of software requirements specifications captured in natural language that are difficult to machine process and produced low quality software. We presented a controlled representation of software requirements that has greatly improved the accuracy of machine processing and generate high quality software in an agile way. Our proposed approach starts from generation of SBVR based requirements specifications. After that perform automatic analysis of SBVR based specifications, CRC metadata like association, super class, subclass, visibility, primitive data type is extracted that all other tools cannot extract. Finally, SBVR2CRC prototype tool maps this extracted information into CRC cards that represent software requirements specifications not only in an efficient way but also improve the accuracy of software as well as faster the development process. Moreover, our automated tool can be helpful for software developers to efficiently represent software requirements specifications that results into agile software development and also increase overall efficiency of development process.

Our presented approach also identifies all CRC elements that are not considered by any other approach. There is not a single approach to generate CRC model of software requirements specification. For the future work, we have planned to extend our approach to handle alias, interface. We expect that our presented approach could play an important role in capturing software requirements specification in the form of CRC model that not only speed up the whole development process but also produce high quality software.

References

1. Sillitti, A., Succi, G.: Requirements engineering for agile methods. In: Aurum, A., Wohlin, C. (eds.) Engineering and Managing Software Requirements, pp. 309–326 (2005)
2. Cao, L., Ramesh, B.: Agile requirements engineering practices: an empirical study. IEEE Softw. **25**(1), 60–67 (2008)
3. Batool, A., Hafees, Y.: Comparative study of traditional requirement engineering and agile requirement engineering. In: 15th International Conference on Advanced Communication Technology (ICACT), pp. 1006–1014 (2013)
4. Beck, K., Cunningham, W.: A laboratory for teaching object-oriented thinking. In: Proceedings of OOPSLA, pp. 1–6 (1989)
5. Wirfs, R., Alan, B.: Object Design: Brief Tour of Responsibility Driven Design. Addison Wesley (2003). book chapter 2, ISBN 0201379430
6. Inayt, I., Salwah, S.: A systematic literature review on agile requirements engineering practices and challenges. Comput. Hum. Behav. **51**, 915–929 (2015)
7. OMG: Semantics of Business Vocabulary and Rules (SBVR) Standard v.1.0. Object Management Group (2008). http://www.omg.org/spec/SBVR/1.0/
8. Overmyer, S.: Conceptual modeling through linguistic analysis using LIDA. In: Proceedings of ICSE 2001 23rd international conference on Software Engineering, pp. 104–410 (2001)
9. Harmain, H.M., Gaizauska, R.: CM-builder: a natural language based CASE tool for object-oriented analysis. Autom. Softw. Eng. **10**(2), 157–181 (2003)
10. Gomes, P., Pereira, F., Paiva, P., Carreiro, P., Ferreira, J.: Reuse of UML class diagrams using case-based composition. In: Proceedings of the Sixteenth International Conference on Software Engineering & Knowledge Engineering (SEKE), pp. 20–24 (2004)
11. Bajwa, S., Mumtaz, S., Samad, A.: Object oriented software modeling using NLP based knowledge extraction. Eur. J. Sci. Res. **32**(3), 613–619 (2009)
12. Deeptimahanti, D., Ali, M.: An automated tool for generating UML models from natural language requirements. In: IEEE/ACM International Conference on Automated Software Engineering (2009)
13. Bhala, R., Sagar, V., Abirami, S.: Conceptual modeling of natural language functional requirements. J. Syst. Softw. **88**, 25–41 (2014)
14. Gulia, S., Choudhury, T.: An efficient automated design to generate UML diagram from Natural Language Specifications. In: 6th International Conference on Cloud System and Big Data Engineering (2016)
15. Arora, A., Sabetzadeh, L., Briand, M., Zimmer, F.: Automated checking of conformance to requirements templates using natural language processing. IEEE Trans. Softw. Eng. **41**(10), 944–968 (2015)
16. Raj, A., Prabhakar, T., Hendryx, S.: Transformation of SBVR business design to UML models. In: Proceedings of 1st Annual India Software Engineering Conference, ISEC, pp. 29–38 (2008)
17. Bajwa, S., I., Afreen, H.: Generating UML class models from SBVR software requirements specifications. In: Artificial Intelligence Conference Belgian/Netherlands (2011)
18. Njonko,: From natural language business requirements to executable models via SBVR. In: International Conference on Systems and Informatics (ICSAI), pp. 2453–2457 (2012)

19. Awasthi, S.: Transformation of SBVR business rules to UML class model. In: Pfeiffer, H.D., Ignatov, D.I., Poelmans, J., Gadiraju, N. (eds.) Conceptual Structures for STEM Research and Education. Lecture Notes in Computer Science (Including Subseries Lecture in AI and Lecture Notes in Bioinformatics), pp. 277–288. Springer, Heidelberg (2013). https://doi.org/10.1007/978-3-642-35786-2_21

20. Skersys, T., Danenas, P.: Extracting SBVR business vocabularies and business rules from UML use case diagram. J. Syst. Sofw. (2018). https://doi.org/10.1016/j.jss.2018.03.061

21. Nemuraite, L.: Vetis tool for editing and transforming SBVR business vocabulary and rules into UML & OCL. Inf. Technol. 377–384 (2010)

22. Bonais, M., Kinh, N., Eric, P., Wenny, R.: Automated generation of structural design models from SBVR specification. Appl. Ontol. **11**, 51–87 (2016)

23. Manning, C.D.: Par-of-speech tagging from 97% to 100%: is it time for some linguistics? In: Proceedings of CICLing, vol. 1, pp. 171–189(2011)

24. Toutanova, K., Klein, G., et al.: Feature-rich part-of-speech tagging with acyclic dependency network. In: Proceedings of HLT-NAACL, pp. 252–259 (2003)

25. Finkel, R.J., Grenager, T., Manning, C.: Incorporating non-local information into extraction systems by Gibbs sampling. In: proceedings of 43rd Annual Meeting of the Association for Computational Linguistics (ACL), pp. 363–370 (2005)

26. Fayad, M., Hamza, H., Sanchez, H.: A pattern for an effective class responsibility collaborator (CRC) cards. In: Proceeding of 5th IEEE Workshop on Mobile Computing Systems and Applications USA, pp. 584–587 (2003)

27. Schach, S.R.: Object-Oriented and Classical Software Engineering. WCB/McGraw-Hill, Boston (2011)

28. Callan, R.E.: Building Object-Oriented Systems: An Introduction from Concepts to Implementation in C++. Computational Mechanics Publications, Southampton (1994)

Automatic RDF, Metadata Generation from Legacy Software Models

Amna Riaz[1(✉)], Imran Sarwar Bajwa[1], and Munsub Ali[2]

[1] Department of Computer Science & IT, The Islamia University of Bahawalpur, Bahawalpur, Pakistan
amna.riaz25@gmail.com
[2] School of Computing, Simon Fraser University, Burnaby, Canada

Abstract. The resource description framework is a method which help us to interchange and reuse of metadata. Early metadata gives a simple method for performing and reporting Data checks. Checks are indicated in an intuitive way to find at which extend we find the relevant data. Moreover, to create vocabularies to handle metadata of larger data sets and to capture the correct relation between the objects we needed some framework that results us reliable. Resource description framework is XML application which follow organize rules to give clear method of explaining semantics. RDF is a data model. It is simple model which have different statement about resources. Resource can be any object. RDF gave metadata of web data and gave structural information. UML data can also be explained in form of RDF that is quite a fruitful in field of RDF. Transformation from UML to RDF, XML help eminently. Metadata of class diagram acquire through XML then Parsing of XML pledge metadata and retinue the RDF rules to change metadata into RDF Triples. Triple include subject, predicate and object. Which transmits a sense of a sentence. Further we store triples in RDF system. This technique helps to keep data useful for many generations.

Keywords: Unified modelling languages · Extensible Markup Language · Extracting metadata · Automatic RDF

1 Introduction

World Wide Web has radically changed the ways of data access, with its present structure, it is reliable and efficient tool for global information access. But the users are in problem of finding relevant information retrieval. A few software tools work with indexes to make a refine search like search tool on web. After that sorting through huge amount of retrieved information to find a relevant one is quite a big issue. Many techniques introduced to refine the search, page-level is also showing its efforts but returned list of pages missed some important information. Manual filters also introduced in this regard. But the Web's current information retrieval Model makes it extremely difficult for users to find and use relevant information. Data available on the Web covers different structures, formats, and content. But lack an easy access to data. To make information access easier, a framework would need, which tell What a Web

© Springer Nature Singapore Pte Ltd. 2020
I. S. Bajwa et al. (Eds.): INTAP 2019, CCIS 1198, pp. 385–397, 2020.
https://doi.org/10.1007/978-981-15-5232-8_33

page actually contains. In other words, such a framework would need to be based on metadata (data about data) that describes content of Web resources.

Many of metadata extracting and ontology generating editor's help to develop the software which make our research effective. Search engines and other information access tools cannot provide highly efficient access to information on the Web. Substantial efforts have been taken to get efficient search results, and a number of frameworks have updated over the years. The most reliable of these is the Resource Description Framework (RDF). RDF provides the developers with a gateway for the description of metadata for the next generation of interoperable Web applications.

Data interoperability is quite impossible before the concept of RDF. RDF can capture and convey the metadata through structured, semi structured and even unstructured data we can frankly said the RDF is a universal solvent. In a common RDF representation, it is easy to create new datasets or new attributes. It is also easy to merge different data sources as if they came from a single source. This enables meaningful composition of data from different applications regardless of format or serialization.

Mapping flexibility points is the immense strengths of RDF in representing diverse schema also help a lot. Lack of RDF created lot of issue but with the help of RDF now we are at a time able to construct vocabularies, can handle large datasets, and can capture virtually any aspect of world or any relation. RDF is an emergent model. It begins as simple "fact" statements of triples that may then be expanded into ever-more complex structures and stories. As an internal, canonical data model, RDF has advantages over any other approach. We can represent, describe, combine, extend and adapt data and their organizational schema flexibly and at will. We can explore and analyse in ways not easily available with other models.

When we find we did worthless search? We keep doing progress in solving a particular task. On completion, we come to know that the data is inconsistent and inaccurate then all our energies are wasted and time we spent is of no worth. Almost 320 million individually accessible object on web but no one is accurate, reliable and up to date. Also find problem in content rating where illicit material is present. After completion of task it is quite difficult to overcome the unreliable data from the whole work done. The search of any mechanism that fixed that problem is first to solve.

Early metadata gives a simple method for performing and reporting Data checks. Checks are indicated in an intuitive way to find at which extend we find the relevant data. Moreover, to create vocabularies to handle metadata of larger data sets and to capture the correct relation between the objects we needed some framework that results us reliable.

2 Related Work

Manual indexing for generating metadata is quite difficult. Many methodologies are working for producing metadata which help in indexing and overcome the manual work load. Methodology works on specific rules of generating metadata from preexisting metadata specified in paper [2].

Using survey approach it was examined to which extend automatic metadata generating application are working on web. Every application tested by its features and functions. With results of 89.27% it founded Metadata generators on web are most available. Pre-existing Analysis tools for Meta tags are 6.34% and 1.46% for those application which get metadata from conversion of digital resource analysis. These results helps in further future work [3].

Metadata tags are entrenched with documents, when formed by the publishing manager. The worth of documents are analysed by detecting these metadata tags through different tools [19].

From article [18] Klarity and DC.dot are two metadata application, proficiencies of these two applications re monitored by research. National institute of environmental health science provide samples of 29 resources, mediate to create a topmost level web page for each resource which was given in to both generators.

Research in [18] shows that Generation of automatic metadata and find out how to integrate FRBR and existing rational. Programmatic research required progresses. For generations of diverse metadata, effectiveness of algorithms should be tested.

Study from Paper [17] illustrated Source of available data has transformed World Wide Web. Retrieval of précised and relevant data become challenging with the presently available structure of foremost search engines.

From [19] we came to know that Advantageous metadata can be generated by using generators. Need of metadata increasing day by day due to growing resources which are foremost challenges for projects of digital library.

In success of RDF compatibility, security and applicable issue is still needed attention to handled. When put a sight on past and upcoming future we have faith web in next generation will be more accessible, searchable and organized that with make data more useful. RDF and semantic web helps in discovering more and more data [15].

3   Used Approach

Resource Description Framework applied to solve ambiguities and many other problems facing in extracting data from different software model. The research described in the previous chapter shows in the modern age how information can be last long useful. RDF have great importance in this aspect. It helps in organizing bulk of data of different format. RDF is a foundation that empowers the encoding, trade and reuse of organized metadata. Here we develop a methodology is used for automatic conversion of UML Class Diagram into RDF. Class Diagram is static Structure diagram. Work is completed in modules. We change Class Diagram in XML. Extensible Markup Language is self-descriptive and was design to store and transport data. We get metadata of UML through its XML parsing. Many parsing techniques help in extracting metadata. We use Dom Parser for extracting metadata in this methodology. Dom Parser defines an interface that enables programs to access and update the style, structure, and contents of XML documents. Extracted Metadata will transform into statements called RDF Triples. It is combination of 3 entities subject, predicate and object. It is then store into RDF system that make the data easy to understand and useful for many generations. RDF emphasizes facilities to enable automated processing of Web resources. RDF metadata can be used in a variety of application areas like in resource discovery to provide better search engine capabilities. The complete framework of software model UML class diagram to RDF is shown in Fig. 1.

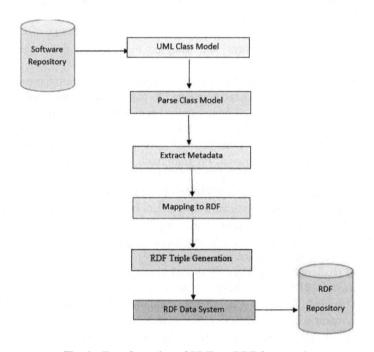

Fig. 1. Transformation of UML to RDF framework

3.1   UML Class Model

First module illustrates the selection of software model from software repository. Selection should be done according to need of work. UML Class Model is taken as input in this approach. It is conceptual modelling technique especially for semantic of application. Class Model has static structure, the structure shows classes, attributes, methods and relationships among objects. By using class diagrams, we easily describe the work road map. Here we make a class model by using ENTERPRISE ARCHITECT which show objects their attributes and different type of relation among different objects.

UML Class Diagram: In this step we simply show the class model of a webinar session. Which have classes like attendance, host, presenter, presentation videos, session, discussion topic and finally question answers. All these classes and related attributes and shown the different relation among them. Every relation have simple Association. Some have one to one relation and some have one to many relationships are shown in Fig. 2.

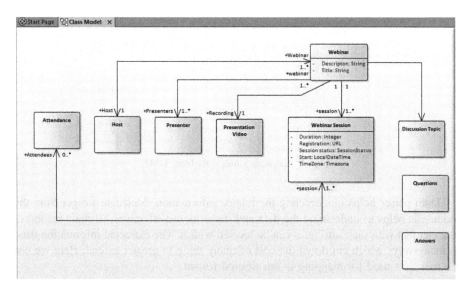

Fig. 2. UML class diagram

3.2 Parse Class Model

Parsing of class model is done in two steps. Firstly we get the XML format of our class model because parsing can't be done on class model. Parsing need some code format to get the metadata and second step include the working of some parser to get the parsing data of XML data format. It need some environment to done with parsing which can gave parse data.

XML is used to outsource data. They are stored in separate XML files. Plain text format is used to store data in XML, we can easily import or export data. Xml makes simply moved much easier. XML of class model which extracted from Enterprise Architect. Parsing is done in Eclipse Environment by using parsing technique of Dom Parser to get metadata of class model. Which further use in next steps. Parsing code is actually displaying the important terms of our model and code using libraries to parse the data.

3.3 Extraction of Metadata

Metadata is actually data about data, which gave all the basic information which code or data have in it, here metadata extraction is a module in which UML or XML file is taken as input and processed it further for results. We used Dom Parser which loads the file either UML or XML with extension of .xml and parse the XML file for extracting related metadata. Each UML have classes, Attributes, methods and relations. XML file have XML tags in it. To extract class information, methods information and parameter information it identified by special tags. By using these tags we extract from XML code. Extracted metadata is classes, methods and attributes. Extraction of metadata shown in Fig. 3.

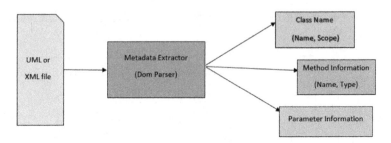

Fig. 3. Extracting metadata from UML

Dom parser helps in extracting the related information. Metadata we get from the module is helps to understand the data and make its use effective. All main resources like element with their attributes can be located with it. The extracted information used in many ways which cut down the cost of many thing to greater extend. Here we use the metadata used for mapping in our desired format.

3.4 Mapping to RDF

All the data get from extraction is mapped with RDF. The RDF friendly XML does not need so much to do, only the RDF parser need to change information into triples.

It's quite easy when XML has no text nodes and elements as similar. It's called as "mixed content". When the element has no mixed content conversion from XML to RDF became easy. When XML file are kind of above mentioned types, conversion task done generically. Otherwise other tasks need so much work to do for conversion as shown in Fig. 4.

Automatic RDF		
UML		RDF
CLASS		RESOURCES
ATTRIBUTES		PPROPERTIES
METHODS		PREDICATES
RELATIONS		TRIPLES

Fig. 4. Mapping chart of UML to RDF

All the above mention entities show the automatic RDF. Which shows the UML to RDF conversion. Class should be public, private and protected in UML modelling are mapped with resources in RDF. Attributes which show the properties in UML are shown as properties in RDF format. Methods which shown how the operations are implemented and methods will be predicate, which is the relationship between subject and object. But in RDF is the value of triple. Relation should be of many type like: association, multiplicity, aggregation, inheritance and composition and the relation in RDF shown as triples. Triples here is the combination of subject, predicate and object.

3.5   RDF Triple Generation

The RDF data model is based on statements to describe and feature resources, in the form of triple that is combination of subject-predicate-object. Subject is a resource. Predicate is the property of resource. Object is value of property that can also be another resource. RDF Model need to know following terms to generate triple. *addproperty:* to add another statement to RDF Model. *listStatemnets ():* is a method which return stmtIterator that is the subtype of java iterator in a model.

StmtIterator: it has method which return next statement nextStatement ( )
Statement: is an interface which gave next method for subject, predicate, object.
To get Subject: Resource subject = stmt.getSubject (); *sTo get Predicate:* Property predicate = stmt.getPredicate (); *To get Object:* RDF Node object = stmt.getObject ()
To get output of subject: System.out.print (subject.toString ());
To get output of predicate: System.out.print (" " + predicate.toString () + " ");
To get output of Object: System.out.print (object.toString ());

3.6   RDF Data System

The Resource Description Framework (RDF) is help in data exchange on web and explain relations between data elements and whole data. It keeps information about metadata which helps about web resources which further explained using graphs.

Representation in RDF: Resource Description Framework show the information in three parts (subject, predicate, object). Resource is described as subject. Predicate show the relation between subject and object or have information about other resources. For example, "Pen has the colour black." In which "Pen" is taken as subject, "has" is predicate and "colour black" is object.

RDF written in XML and its xml prefixes written on top of XML document. We can get metadata from it and then relationship of data shown with the help of graph.

RDF generated in java framework environment like eclipse.

Statement: "The CEO of http://www.google.com is Sundar Pichai".
The subject of the statement above is: http://www.google.com.
The predicate is: CEO.
The object is: Sundar Pichai.

RDF Resource, Property, and Property Value: RDF identifies things using Web identifiers (URIs), and describes resources with properties and property values. Above used example in RDF Resource, Property, and Property value RDF is shown in Fig. 5.

A Resource is something which can have a URI, such as "http://www.google.com"
A Property is a Resource that has a name, such as "CEO"

A Property value is the value of a defined Property, such as "sundar pichai". (A property value can be another resource) like "https://en.wikipedia.org/wiki/Sundar_Pichai"

```
<rdf:RDF
  xmlns:rdf="http://www.w3.org/1999/02/22-rdfsyntax-ns#"
  xmlns:vcard="http://www.w3.org/2001/vcard-rdf/3.0#" >
<rdf:Description rdf:about="http://www.google.com">
  <vcard:N rdf:nodeID="A0"/>
  <vcard:CEO>sundar pichai</vcard:CEO>
</rdf:Description>
<rdf:Description rdf:nodeID="A0">
  <vcard:Family>pichai</vcard:Family>
  <vcard:Given>sundar</vcard:Given>
</rdf:Description>
</rdf:RDF>
```

Fig. 5. RDF data system

- <rdf:RDF>. RDF document is the XML declaration. The XML declaration is done by root element of RDF documents.
- xmlns:rdf is a namespace which shows that elements with the (rdf) prefix are from the given namespace "http://www.w3.org/1999/02/22-rdf-syntax-ns#".
- Vcard is used to add properties of resource that are "given name" and "family name" in the given example.
- <rdf:Description rdf:about> it shows the elements which contains description of the resource.in above example Given shows first name and Family shows the last name.

4   Experiments and Results

In this case study we discuss main objects of a bank system their working and relationship between them. It shows bank facilities to their customers and account management. And how a customer can deposit and withdraw amount using account details. It gave a detail view of a simple bank environment.

We take all the object of a bank as classes which show attributes of each class and their methods which show work done of each object. Here we show the root classes of bank system class model in Fig. 6. Processing show the relationships of classes among themselves.

Bank class: Which have its Id, location and name as attributes. And have association between manager and customer while composition relation with account class.

Account class: Which have account no and customer id as attributes. Account class have further two child classes which have generalization relationship with them. (Checking account, saving account) which have similar properties of account classes.

Manager class: It have id and name as attributes and a manger can perform like open account, close account, issue card and gave information about bank. It has association with bank and account class.

Customer class: Customer has id, account no, name, DOB, address and phone no as attributes and can deposit, withdraw, general inquiry and request for card. It has composition relation with account and association relation with bank class.

It shows the whole class diagram view which show classes and their relationship in Fig. 6.

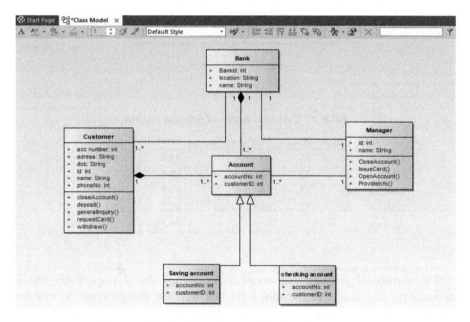

Fig. 6. Class diagram of bank system

RDF Triples form in this way as it is shown in Fig. 7 it shows the working of UML class diagram in form of RDF triples (Table 1).

```
1. [a rdf:Statement;
        rdf:subject :Bank;
        rdf:predicate :has one;
        rdf:object :  manager;
   ]


2. [a rdf:Statement;
        rdf:subject :Bank;
        rdf:predicate :deals many;
        rdf:object :  account;
   ]

3. [a rdf:Statement;
        rdf:subject :Manger;
        rdf:predicate :Manages;
        rdf:object :  account;
   ]


4. [a rdf:Statement;
        rdf:subject :customer;
        rdf:predicate :has one;
        rdf:object :  account;
]
```

Fig. 7. RDF triples

Table 1. Evaluated results of different systems

RDF data	N_{sample}	$N_{correct}$	$N_{incorrect}$	$N_{missing}$	Percision %	Recall %
UML 1	34	25	05	04	83.4	73.5
UML 2	40	32	4	4	88.8	80
UML 3	49	35	5	9	87.5	71.4
UML 4	65	52	09	04	85.2	80
Average					86.2%	76.1%

The average of precision and recall is 86.2% and 76.1% respectively that is encouraging. The results of our tool compared with the manual result to evaluate results. The initial performance evaluation results and result of three more systems is calculated in this table. Which helps us in evaluating and calculating system performance that is encouraging and satisfactory. Figure 8 shows estimation of correct, incorrect and missing RDF components.

Figure 9 emerges the results of Recall and precision which obtained by four different case studies. As per our results system 2 has high Recall and precision. Moreover, system3 has lowest Recall.

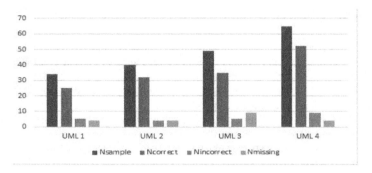

Fig. 8. Evaluation graph of mapping RDF components

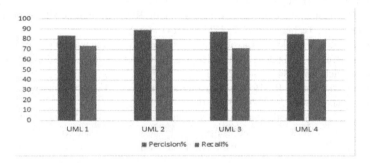

Fig. 9. Precision and recall evaluation

5 Conclusion

In our work we briefly analyse the characteristics of both UML and RDF. Finally, we find approach and implement a tool which transform a class diagram into RDF. We gave UML to RDF full construction steps and discussed them briefly. We also implemented the work in different complete examples then analysed and discussed according to constructed tool. Evaluation of implemented example done through statistical measures and results shows the tool and approach are feasible. This tool gave satisfied correctness recall (76.1%) and precision (86.2%) that was briefly explained in evaluation section. Study for ease of usability explained with purpose of accessible methodology is simple and efficient to produce RDF. Our work is significant link between semantic web and UML applications.

In future we will further mature the work by covering larger scale UML to further evaluate the tool and constructed new tools for other UML diagrams beside class diagram. Some areas of UML class diagram is still more elaborate in RDF form. So, our research will enrich to cover it in more depth. On basis of our work we will go for some related approaches like UML to OWL conversion that will be a big step. Connecting these UML diagrams with RDF on web pages will also a new turn. Moreover, we work for testing of converted diagrams in some suitable environment.

References

1. Purvis, M., Cranefield, S.: UML as an ontology modelling language (1999)
2. Margaritopoulos, M., et al.: Automatic metadata generation by utilising preexisting metadata of related resources. Int. J. Metadata Semant. Ontol. **3**(4), 292–304 (2008)
3. Albassuny, B.M.: Automatic metadata generation applications: a survey study. Int. J. Metadata Semant. Ontol. **3**(4), 260–282 (2008)
4. Jenkins, C., et al.: Automatic RDF metadata generation for resource discovery. Comput. Netw. **31**(11-14), 1305–1320 (1999)
5. Stevens, P.: Small-scale XMI programming: a revolution in UML tool use? Autom. Softw. Eng. **10**(1), 7–21 (2003)
6. Kovse, J., Härder, T.: Generic XMI-based UML model transformations. In: Bellahsène, Z., Patel, D., Rolland, C. (eds.) OOIS 2002. LNCS, vol. 2425, pp. 192–198. Springer, Heidelberg (2002). https://doi.org/10.1007/3-540-46102-7_24
7. Tong, Q., Zhang, F., Cheng, J.: Construction of RDF (S) from UML class diagrams. J. Comput. Inf. Technol. **22**(4), 237–250 (2014)
8. Berners-Lee, T., Hendler, J., Lassila, O.: The semantic web: a new form of web content that is meaningful to computers will unleash a revolution of new possibilities [electronic resource]. Sci. Am. **284**, 34–43 (2001)
9. Erdmann, M., Studer, R.: How to structure and access XML documents with ontologies. Data Knowl. Eng. **36**(3), 317–335 (2001)
10. Berners-Lee, T.: Semantic Web–A Guide to the Future XML Web Services and Knowledge Management. Weaving the Web. Harper San Francisco, San Francisco (1999)
11. Melnik, S.: Bridging the Gap between RDF and XML. 17 (1999). Accessed 26 Feb 2006
12. Scholl, B., Amann, I., Fundulaki, M., Beeri, C., Vercoustre, A.M.: Mapping XML fragments to community web ontologies (2001)
13. Klein, M.: Interpreting XML documents via an RDF schema ontology. In: 2002 13th International Workshop on Database and Expert Systems Applications, Proceedings. IEEE (2002)
14. Thuy, P.T.T., et al.: Transforming valid XML documents into RDF via RDF schema. In: 2007 Third International Conference on Next Generation Web Services Practices, NWeSP 2007. IEEE (2007)
15. Candan, K.S., Liu, H., Suvarna, R.: Resource description framework: metadata and its applications. ACM SIGKDD Explor. Newslett. **3**(1), 6–19 (2001)
16. Forsberg, K., Dannstedt, L.: Extensible use of RDF in a business context. Comput. Netw. **33**(1-6), 347–364 (2000)
17. Dhingra, V., Bhatia, K.K.: Metadata: towards machine-enabled intelligence. Int. J. Web Semant. Technol. **3**(3), 121 (2012)
18. Greenberg, J.: Metadata extraction and harvesting: a comparison of two automatic metadata generation applications. J. Internet Cataloging **6**(4), 59–82 (2004)
19. Noufal, P.P.: Metadata: automatic generation and extraction (2005)
20. Wang, F., Li, J., Homayounfar, H.: A space efficient XML DOM parser. Data Knowl. Eng. **60**(1), 185–207 (2007)
21. Aghaei, S., Nematbakhsh, M.A., Farsani, H.K.: Evolution of the world wide web: from WEB 1.0 TO WEB 4.0. Int. J. Web Semant. Technol. **3**(1), 1 (2012)
22. Lu, W., Chiu, K., Pan, Y.: A parallel approach to XML parsing. In: Proceedings of the 7th IEEE/ACM International Conference on Grid Computing. IEEE Computer Society (2006)
23. Decker, S., et al.: The semantic web: the roles of XML and RDF. IEEE Internet Comput. **4**(5), 63–73 (2000)

24. Cranefield, S.: UML and the semantic web (2001)
25. Jain, A., Farkas, C.: Secure resource description framework: an access control model. In: Proceedings of the Eleventh ACM Symposium on Access Control Models and Technologies. ACM (2006)
26. Corby, O., Dieng, R., Hébert, C.: A conceptual graph model for W3C resource description framework. In: Ganter, B., Mineau, G.W. (eds.) ICCS-ConceptStruct 2000. LNCS (LNAI), vol. 1867, pp. 468–482. Springer, Heidelberg (2000). https://doi.org/10.1007/10722280_32
27. Klein, M.: XML, RDF, and relatives. IEEE Intell. Syst. **16**(2), 26–28 (2001)
28. Miller, E.: An introduction to the resource description framework. Bull. Am. Soc. Inf. Sci. Technol. **25**(1), 15–19 (1998)

An Approach to Measure Functional Parameters for Ball-Screw Drives

Naveed Riaz[(✉)], Syed Irtiza Ali Shah, Faisal Rehman,
Syed Omer Gilani, and Emad-udin

National University of Sciences and Technology (NUST), Islamabad, Pakistan
engrnaveedriaz@gmail.com

Abstract. Linear Ball screw drives are commonly used for precise motion control of different mechanical systems including CNC machine tools, robotics and various aerospace systems. These drives are specifically designed on the basis of required operating performance parameters like output torque, rated power, slew rate, backlash, friction and required efficiency. These desired parameters significantly affect the functionality of ball-screw drive systems. Parameters like torque capability and slew rate should be tested to validate design and ensure safety during operation. Factors like Friction (dead band) and mechanical backlash offers very adverse effect on the repeatability and operation of overall dynamic system; specifically, when precise positioning accuracy is desired under extensive loading. This paper gives an approach to measure performance parameters for ball screw drives. Torque capacity & slew rate are analyzed and evaluated experimentally on a self-designed Hex Twist suspension test setup. Initially, Hex Twist setup was calibrated to find the deflection scale factor. A complete closed loop testing is also performed on the same testing setup to measure the overall functionality of ball screw drive actuator. The results indicate that the developed testing setup is very accurate in measuring open loop and close loop torque and slew rate values.

Keywords: Ball screw drive · Performance factor · Hex Twist bar suspension test setup · Slew rate · Close loop testing

1 Introduction to Ball Screw Drive Functional Parameters

Ball screw drive electro-mechanical actuators work in closed loop system i.e. they take decision based on the feedback from their outputs for further actions. They are one of the most important parts of automation and robotics and are commonly found in position and velocity control of various automated systems and machinery. Ball screw drive actuators should be well analyzed before putting them into the system as they affect its functionality. Performance parameters of ball screw actuators were measured using mathematical tools and then a testing setup was devised based on close simulation to actual system application. Output torque, slew rate, friction & mechanical backlash are the basic parameters which are kept in mind while designing any type of servo actuator [10, 11, 13].

© Springer Nature Singapore Pte Ltd. 2020
I. S. Bajwa et al. (Eds.): INTAP 2019, CCIS 1198, pp. 398–408, 2020.
https://doi.org/10.1007/978-981-15-5232-8_34

A mechanical member, loaded with a moment about its longitudinal axis, is said to be in torsion, and the applied moment is then termed as torque. Torsion produced in the bar directly simulates the amount of applied torque, provided that the metallurgical properties of the bar being kept constant. This property of the bar helps to calculate the required torque, by measuring directly, the amount of twist produced. For this purpose, the bar needs to be calibrated and for this Hex Twist Suspension Test Setup was designed specifically for measuring the twist produced by directly applying the load on a known value of moment arm length. Twist bar jig was adjusted to calibrate the bar at required torque value for testing the actuator [5, 7, 9].

Slew rate is the rate at which servo actuator achieves the desired position at rated torque value. It was calculated by measuring the rise time of actuator output. Friction or dead band is the undesirable parameter in the design of servo actuator, and is required to be kept as minimum as possible to achieve max performance of the actuator. It is the band in the output at which the input changes but the output remains unchanged. Dead band was calculated by generating command voltage and observing the output displacement. The delay was observed that was calculated in open loop at bi-directional operation of actuator [6, 8, 12].

Backlash, another important non-linear parameter, is present inherently in the mechanical systems, and was calculated using both the power and no load condition of actuator by locking the output link and applying a step input [1, 2].

Testing of ball-screw drives ensure their reliable working at system level along with design validation. The testing setup designed in this work takes ball-screw drive as input and measures important functional parameters under medium loading [3, 4].

This work is organized as follows. Section 2 gives the basics on which Hex Twist Suspension setup is based. A calibration method is implemented to find scale factor of testing setup and torque of ball screw drive is calculated at this testing setup. Section 3 gives measurement and calculation of angular slew rate on twist bar setup. Section 4 describes the testing results in both open and close loop on Hex Twist setup. Section 5 gives conclusion of this work.

2   Torque Measurement

Consider a ball screw drive actuator as shown in Fig. 1 below. The actuator is driven by a prime mover (dc motor) accompanied by successive gear reduction and finally recirculation ball-screw assembly. The primary function of ball (bearing) screws is to transfer torque (rotary motion) to thrust (linear motion) and vice versa by maintaining high accuracy, reversibility and efficiency.

Fig. 1. Linear electro-mechanical actuator

The input torque to ball screw gives linear force that the actuator can provide in steady state which is calculated by using governing equations as shown below.

$$T = \frac{F.p_h}{2000.\pi.\eta_p} \tag{1}$$

Where,
T = Input Torque
F = Maximum Load of the cycle
p_h = Lead of ball-screw
η_p = Real direct efficiency

The input torque is calculated by considering motor drive torque and includes common transmission drive torque, friction and pre-load drag torque to the ball screw assembly. For normal operation,

$$T_M = (T_a + T_b + T_d)\frac{N_1}{N_2}$$

Where,
T_M = Motor drive Torque
T_a = Drive torque for common transmission
T_b = Friction torque for supporting bearings
T_d = Preload drag torque
N_1 = No of teeth/speed at driver gear stage
N_2 = No of teeth/speed at driven gear stage

The output torque will be calculated by considering the moment arm length attached with the mechanism where linear actuator will be integrated.

The verification of torque measurement by experimental way was performed by designing a Hex Twist Suspension Test Setup. Consider a straight hexagonal spring steel bar of length 'l'. If we twist this steel bar around the axis resisted by the bar's torsion resistance, the effective bar spring rate can be calculated by the length, diameter and material of the bar. The bar twists about its longitudinal axis and its free end deflects through a twist angle 'θ'. The angular deflection 'θ' due to applied torque is given by torsion equation. The geometry of deformation describes shear strain and the shear angle γ is expressed as:

$$\gamma z_\theta = \frac{\partial}{d_z} = r\frac{d_\theta}{d_z}$$

Where, 'z' defines shearing in the z-plane i.e., the plane normal to z-axis in the θ-direction. Now since material is linear elastic, shear stress is given by:

$$\tau_{z\theta} = G\gamma z_\theta = Gr\frac{d_\theta}{d_z}$$

The summation of all moments constituted by the shear stresses acting on each differential area 'dA' along the cross sectional area must balance the applied moment 'T' as given by:

$$T = \tau_{\theta z}rdA = \int_A Gr\frac{d_\theta}{d_z}rdA = \int_A r^2dA$$

Where the quantity $\int_A r^2dA$ is the polar moment of inertia 'J' which is calculated as:

$$J = \int_{R_i}^{R_o} r^2 2\pi rdr = \frac{\pi\left(R_o^4 - R_i^4\right)}{2}$$

R_o and R_i being outer and inner radii. For solid shafts $R_i = 0$
The quantity $\frac{d_\theta}{d_z}$ can be written as

$$\frac{d_\theta}{d_z} = \frac{T}{GJ} \rightarrow \theta = \int_z \frac{T}{GJ}dz$$

$$\frac{d_\theta}{d_z} = constant = \frac{\theta}{L}$$

The twist θ for a circular shaft acted upon by a torque T along its axis is given by:

$$\theta = \frac{Tl}{JG} \qquad (2)$$

Where;
θ = Twist Angle (in radians).
T = Torque applied (in Nm).
l = length of the bar (in meters).
J = polar area moment of inertia of hexagonal bar.
G = Rigidity Modulus

Equation (2) is the basis for measuring the torque of ball screw actuator. The advantage of designing twist bar jig is that we don't need to calculate J and G of hex bar. These factors are calculated by calibration of twist bar.

2.1   Twist Bar Calibration Method: Theoretical Calculation

Calibration was performed on the loading jig. The loading jig comprises of a twist bar clamped with the wheel of torsion jig assembly. The other end of twist bar remains fixed. The amount of twist produced in the bar while the other end fixed simulates the loading on the steel bar. The amount of twist was measured using feedback poten-tiometer. When the output drive of the servo actuator was clamped with the wheel of the loading jig using link rod attachment, the twist in the bar simulates the loading on the output drive.

Hex Twist bar was calibrated in order to calculate the scale factor i.e. the amount of torque required to twist the bar to 1 degree and to check any permanent deformation produced in the bar and its spring rate. Spring rate, is the torsional resistance of the bar. The amount of twist angle 'θ' in twist bar was calculated by applying known weight at the end of loading arm of length 305 mm clamped with the surface of testing jig. The twist bar experiences twist due to hanged weight. Measure the DC voltage generated by potentiometer due to twist produced. This was the angle 'θ' of torsion jig in terms of voltage at a length 'l' of twist bar setup. From the metallurgical properties and cross section area of twist bar, the amount of twist produced at some particular required length was calculated using Eq. (2), assuming Torque = 1.5 Nm, Length of bar = 305 mm and specific J and G of selected material of bar (spring steel). 'J' was calculated by dividing hexagon bar into 6 equal triangles then calculating the polar moment of inertia of each triangle and then summing it up. The polar moment of inertia of hex bar was found to be 15.75^4 and G = 80.8 GPa where G is the modulus of rigidity of spring steel.

The twist angle 'θ' is;

$$\theta = \frac{1.5 \, \text{Nm} * 0.12 \, \text{m}}{1.575^{-11} * 8.08^{10}}$$

$$\theta = 0.1414 \, \text{radians} = 8.10° \tag{3}$$

Next we try to achieve that angle 'θ' i.e. 8.1° by adjusting the rear plate of the twist bar jig forward or backward (so that to change the effective twist bar length) until a reading of 0.451 ± 0.05 V i.e. equivalent to 8.1° ± 0.8 is obtained. Now lock the plate at this particular position and calculate the twist bar scale factor i.e.

8.10° twist is generated by twist bar at = 1.5 Nm torque.
1° twist is generated by twist bar at = 1.5/8.1 = 0.185 Nm torque.

$$\text{So, twist bar scale factor 'k'} = 0.185 \text{ Nm}/° \tag{4}$$

Ball screw drive actuator is operated at its maximum motor power. The amount of twist produced due to maximum force applied by the actuator is measured by potentiometer; putting it into following equation, yields the maximum torque (Fig. 2);

$$T = k\theta \tag{5}$$

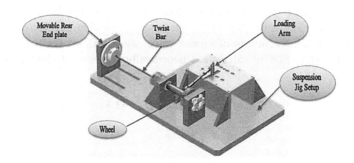

Fig. 2. Hex twist suspension test setup

2.2 Torque Calculation Using Twist Bar Testing Jig

Maximum Torque of ball screw actuator can only be calculated at maximum motor power. Lock the loading arm at zero position (where potentiometer gives 0 V). Mount the actuator on loading jig and connect it to twist bar. Power the actuator so that it rotates the twist bar, which resists due to its torsional resistance, until the actuator applies its maximum power and draws maximum current.

To calculate torque on output arm of the ball screw actuator, measure the voltage on torsion potentiometer;

$$Twist\ Jig\ Pot\ Deflection\ (°) = \frac{Twist\ Jig\ Pot\ (\text{mV})}{55.7(\text{mV}/°)} \tag{6}$$

This value is multiplied with twist bar scale factor i.e. 1.5 Nm/°. This gives the required torque as,

$$Torque = 0.185\ \text{Nm}/° \times \left(\frac{Twist\ Jig\ Pot\ (\text{mV})}{55.7\ \text{mV}/°} \right) \tag{7}$$

The torque on Output Surface is calculated by means of the following formula. *Torque on O/P Surface (N-m) = Twist bar Scale Factor (Nm/°) * Torsion Pot deflection (°)*

The torque on Output arm of ball screw actuator is then calculated by means of the following formula.

$$Torque\ on\ O/P\ arm\ (N{-}m) = Torque\ on\ O/P\ Surface * Arm\ Ratio$$

3 Slew Rate Measurement

Slew rate is basically that constant speed value, which the ball screw actuator can maintain at any load. The input rotary speed of motor is reduced by successive gear reduction. The angular speed input at ball-screw drive is converted into linear speed at ball-screw output. The actuator will be integrated to provide angular movement by attaching with it, a moment arm of known value, which in turn gives angular movement. Angular slew rate is calculated theoretically by using following governing equations.

$$\omega_{BS} = M_S.G_H.\omega_{Gh}.G_T.343.8 \tag{8}$$

$$v_{BS} = \omega_{BS}.r_{BS} \tag{9}$$

$$\omega_{OP} = v_{BS}.r_m \tag{10}$$

Where,

ω_{BS} = Angular Speed at Ball-screw in rad/sec (the constant factor '343.8' gives conversion to rad/sec)

M_S = Motor speed in RPM

G_H = Gearhead ratio included with motor

ω_{Gh} = Gearhead ratio speed limit

G_T = Gear train ratio of actuator

v_{BS} = Linear Speed at ball-nut

r_{BS} = Pitch radius of Ball-screw

ω_{OP} = Output Angular Slew rate

r_m = Output moment arm

3.1 Slew Rate Calculation on Twist Bar Testing Jig

Slew rate depends upon the proportional gain set in the controller that drives the actuator. Slew rate measurement was performed on same twist bar suspension jig setup by mounting the ball screw actuator with twist bar clamped at one end. In this experimentation, oscilloscope was used to measure the twist bar deflection. Twist bar calibration method was repeated and the actuator output drive link was connected with the loading link of twist bar jig. Actuator was also connected with controller/driver circuit. Step input given to actuator generated a slope of deflection that was recorded and displayed on the oscilloscope. Actuator was moved between its end limits. The output step response is the rate at which the deflection signals or output arm reaches the fixed end limit. The rate at which the deflection signals or output arm reached the desired end limit was measured. The rate was calculated by the following relation;

$$Slope/Slew\ Rate, \varphi = \frac{(v_1 - v_0)}{(t_1 - t_0)} \tag{11}$$

Where v_0 and v_1 is the initial and final voltages respectively and t_0 and t_1 is the initial and final time taken to achieve v_1 respectively (Fig. 3).

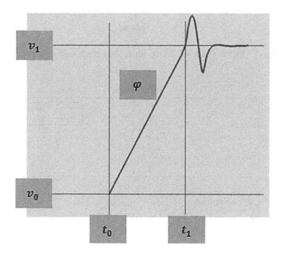

Fig. 3. Slope/Slew rate measurement

3.2 Slew Rate Calculation

Slew rate is calculated for the full load open loop test. In this test loading was applied to the ball screw actuator using twist bar loading mechanism. The load was applied according to the scale factor i.e. 0.185 Nm/°. The slew rate of the actuator was given by the slope of the torsion pot deflection signal. These values were calculated by using the following formula (Figs. 4 and 5).

$$Slew\ Rate\ (using\ Twist\ Jig\ Pot) = \frac{Twist\ Jig\ Pot\ (V/sec)}{0.05547\ (V/°)}$$

$$Slew\ Rate\ (using\ Actuator\ Mechanism\ Pot) = \frac{Actuator\ Pot\ (V/sec)}{0.577\ (V/°)}$$

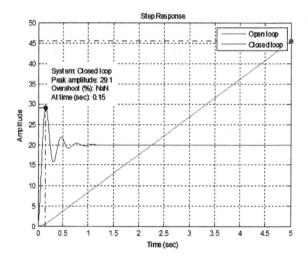

Fig. 4. Open loop vs. close loop step response comparison

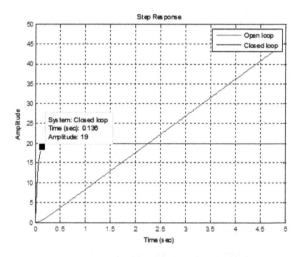

Fig. 5. Open loop vs. close loop servo dynamics

4   Results and Discussion

The important parameters that govern the functionality of ball screw actuator are calculated. These parameters are found in open loop and close loop test on Hex twist setup assembly by mounting ball screw actuator assembly and calculating the test parameters. The twist setup includes mechanical loading setup along with electronics setup to drive actuator assembly and measuring motor command and feedback values. The comparison of open loop and close loop testing is shown in below tables. These tests can be extended for multiple actuators under different loading profiles (Tables 1 and 2).

Table 1. Open loop torque & slew rate test result

Sr	Test parameter	Unit	↓ Limit	↑ Limit	Result
1	Twist bar scale factor 'k'/Stiffness	Nm/°	2.60	2.70	2.64
2	Twist Jig Pot Deflection	mV	100	200	155
3	Power supply current	A	0.9	1.1	1.05
4	Twist Jig Pot Deflection	mV	110	270	215
5	Twist Jig Pot (surface) deflection	°	1.87	4.0	3.5
6	Actuator torque	Nm	30	40	36
7	Twist Jig Pot Deflection	mV	600	750	655
8	Twist Jig Pot (surface) deflection	°	10.2	12.8	11.5
9	Actuator torque	Nm	60	70	65
10	Motor voltage (0.6 A)	V	19.9	20.1	19.9
11	Actuator pot voltage	V	4.5	10	8
12	Act surface deflection	°	13	40	25
13	Twist Jig Pot Voltage	V	3.5	11	8
14	Delta T (slope +ve to −ve)	sec	0.04	0.08	0.06
15	Delta V (slope +ve to −ve)	V	0.1	0.6	0.4
16	Slew rate angular	°/sec	80	100	95
17	Slew rate linear	V/sec	2.5	7.5	6.67

Table 2. Close loop torque & Slew rate test Result

Sr	Test Parameter	Unit	↓ Limit	↑ Limit	Result
1	CMD signal	Vp-p	3.9	4.15	4.05
2	Servo electronics deflection feedback	Vp-p	3.9	4.15	4
3	Surface deflection	°	10	15	14
4	CMD square wave signal @ 0.2 Hz	Vp-p	7.8	8.1	7.9
5	Actuator pot deflection in volts	V	2.0	2.4	2.2
6	Surface deflection	°	12	14	13.5
7	Actuator torque	Nm	60	70	66
8	Actuator slew rate	°/sec	80	100	92
9	Delay b/w CMD & deflection	ms	15	20	15

5   Conclusions and Future Work

This paper describes an effort to measure performance parameters of ball screw drive actuators. Torque capacity and slew rate are the key factors that need to be analyzed while selecting/designing a ball screw actuator. These parameters were analyzed and measured in both open loop testing as well as close loop using designed Hex twist suspension jig setup. Correct measurement of these parameters gives the basics for the acceptance specification of balls screw actuator for use on any critical system/application and increase reliability to meet functional requirements of the system.

This work can be extended to measure important critical parameters like dead-band test, backlash test and frequency response test to evaluate full performance of actuator. Moreover it can also be extended to find performance parameters for different actuators under varying loading profiles which will also verify the overall reliability of designed testing setup.

Acknowledgement. The authors would like to acknowledge their seniors, colleagues, professors, and lab technical staff for their co-operation, suggestions, observations and input regarding this work. We are also thankful to the technical manager and lab supervisor of the concerned organization where we performed our lab/experimental work. We are thankful to everyone for his best wishes.

References

1. Barnett S.: Laboratory test set-up to evaluate electromechanical actuation system for aircraft flight control. Master Dissertation, University of Dayton, USA, 2015 Industrial Devices Corporation "Linear & Rotary positioning systems and controls"
2. Barnett, S.A., Lammers, Z., Razidlo, B., et al.: Test set-up for electromechanical actuation systems for aircraft flight control. SAE paper 2012-01-2203 (2012)
3. Kamerbeek, E.M.H.: On the Theoretical and Experimental Determination of the Torque in Electrical Machines. Philips Tech. Rev. no. Supplement, No. 4 (1970)
4. Li, L.B.: System and method for controlling high side slew rate in a spindle motor driver. Texas Instruments Incorporated. USA, Patent No. US6072289 A
5. Kemper, K., Koepl, D., Hurst, J.: Optimal passive dynamics for torque/force control. In: International Conference on Robotics and Automation (2010)
6. Paul Brian Hvass, D.T.: Condition Based Maintenance for Intelligent Electromechanical Actuators. University of Texas, Austin (2004)
7. Ma, S., Liu, G., Zhou, J., Tong, R.: Optimal design and contact analysis for planetary roller screw. Appl. Mech. Mater. **86**, 361–364 (2011)
8. Varanasi, K.K., Nayfeh, S.A.: Modeling, identification, and control of ballscrew drives. In: American Society for Precision Engineering 16th Annual Meeting, vol. 25, pp. 139–142, Crystal City, Virginia (2001)
9. AbdElhafez, A., Forsyth, A.: A review of more-electric aircraft. In: Thirteenth International Conference on Aerospace Science and Aviation Technology (ASAT-13), 26–28 May 2009, paper no. ASAT-13-EP-01. IEEE, Piscataway
10. Antonelli, M.G., Bucci, G., Ciancetta, F., et al.: Automatic test equipment for avionics Electro-Mechanical Actuators (EMAs). Measurement **57**, 71–84 (2014)
11. Budinger, M., Reysset, A., Halabi, T.E., et al.: Optimal preliminary design of electromechanical actuators. Proc IMechE, Part G: J. Aerosp. Eng. **228**, 1598–1616 (2013)
12. Torabzadeh-Tari, M.: Analysis of electro-mechanical actuator systems in more electric aircraft applications. Ph.D. Dissertation, Royal Institute of Technology, Sweden (2005)
13. Barnett S.: Laboratory test set-up to evaluate electromechanical actuation system for aircraft flight control. Master Dissertation, University of Dayton, USA (2015)

Secure NoSQL Over Cloud Using Data Decomposition and Queryable Encryption

Muhammad Ali Raza[1], Muhammad Usama[2], Waheed Iqbal[1(✉)], and Faisal Bukhari[1]

[1] PUCIT, University of the Punjab, Lahore, Pakistan
{mscsf16m021,waheed.iqbal,faisal.bukhari}@pucit.edu.pk
[2] Bahria University, Karachi Campus, Islamabad, Pakistan
usama@bahria.edu.pk

Abstract. NoSQL-based databases are attractive to store and manage big data, mainly due to high scalability and data modeling flexibility. However, security in NoSQL-based databases is not as compared to the SQL-based relational databases, which raises concerns for users. Specifically, the security of data-at-rest is of serious concern for the users, who deploy their databases on the cloud, because any unauthorized access to the servers will expose the data easily. There have been some efforts to enable encryption for data at rest for NoSQL-based databases. However, most of the existing solutions do not support secure query processing and are difficult to integrate with the applications. In our work, we address the NoSQL data-at-rest security issue by proposing a system which decomposes a given database into two sub-databases. Then encrypt the data, support secure query processing, and enable seamless integration with NoSQL-based databases. The proposed solution for the data at rest is based on a combination of Chaotic Encryption (CE), Order Preserving Encryption (OPE), and Advanced Encryption Standard (AES). The database decomposition into two sub-databases helps to improve data confidentiality while providing comparable performance to the state-of-the-art baseline method.

Keywords: Cloud · NoSQL · Secure Database · Encryption · Data Security

1 Introduction

NoSQL databases are getting traction to manage Big Data mainly due to their schema-less flexibility, horizontal data partitioning, and high scalability features [20, 25]. These databases store the data in flat files instead of tabular relations, which is most common in relational databases. Relational databases are famous due to the ACID (Atomicity, Consistency, Isolation, Durability) properties. However, the performance of relational databases is considerably poor to manage Big Data. NoSQL-based databases offer excellent performance to manage Big Data but do not provide strict data consistency. However, NoSQL

© Springer Nature Singapore Pte Ltd. 2020
I. S. Bajwa et al. (Eds.): INTAP 2019, CCIS 1198, pp. 409–421, 2020.
https://doi.org/10.1007/978-981-15-5232-8_35

databases provide eventual consistency, which ensures to propagate the updates to all machines hosting data eventually, typically in few milliseconds. There are chances that a few read requests might not get the updated data immediately. Many large-scale applications favor NoSQL over traditional relational databases to manage Big Data mainly due to horizontal data partitioning and scaling.

NoSQL stores the data in flat files and deploying over the cloud raises serious concerns as any unauthorized access will get the plain data easily. There have been few efforts to ensure data confidentiality in NoSQL databases [17,18]. However, these solutions do not provide query processing over the encrypted data. Moreover, these do not offer secure query processing over an untrusted communication channel. Most of the techniques, including Hashing (MD5, SHA), and Advanced Encryption Standard (AES) are used to secure the data at rest; however, the data must be decrypted before querying the data. Recently, Ahmadian et al. [1] addressed data confidentiality issues in NoSQL stores. They proposed a solution based on symmetric encryption and a middle-tier proxy server to query encrypted NoSQL database. Their proposed encryption technique is based on AES and OPE. AES is a CPU intensive and time-consuming algorithm, and all the data resides to a single server over the cloud makes the system vulnerable to unauthorized access and security breaches.

A database deployed over the cloud, even encrypted, on a single machine is vulnerable to security threats. In this paper, we propose and evaluate a system to secure NoSQL-based databases over the cloud by splitting the data into multiple partitions, and then apply queryable encryptions. Our proposed approach advocates to split the database into two parts. One part contains the data attributes required to search the data, where another part contains the data against searched attributes. We also propose to deploy these two parts to separate cloud providers to improve the security of the data. We also employ a different type of encryption methods to ensure the security of the data-at-rest while maintaining good performance to query the data. The proposed solution can be integrated seamlessly with any NoSQL database. In this paper, we show the implementation of the proposed system with MongoDB. Moreover, we use OpenEMR [19], an open-source application from the health-care domain, as a benchmark application to evaluate the proposed solution. Our experimental evaluation shows the performance of the proposed system and then compare it with the state-of-the-art baseline method.

The rest of the paper is organized as follows. Related work is discussed in Sect. 2. We explain our proposed methodology to split and secure the NoSQL database over the cloud in Sect. 3. Experimental setup details are given in Sect. 4. Experimental results are presented in Sect. 5. Finally, conclusion and future work are discussed in Sect. 6.

2   Related Work

Cloud computing is widely used by a large number of enterprises, small business, and individual users mainly due to dynamic resource provisioning [10] and pay-as-you-go-features. However, data confidentiality and security for cloud-hosted applications remain challenging [3,13,22]. Chen et al. [6] briefly explained all the vulnerabilities and security loopholes in all phase of the data lifecycle from creation to destruction in cloud environments. This work discussed the data privacy concerns to leak the data into wrong hands if we employ traditional data handling tools in the phase of sharing, storing, transferring, and archiving the data at the cloud. Destruction of data also needs close attention; if this is not done properly data can be retrieved. In [4], authors investigated the cloud security problems from the different perspectives, including cloud architecture, characteristics offered by the cloud, and the cloud service delivery models. Authors conclude that cloud security needs many improvements in almost all areas, including cryptographic keys management, Identity, and access management.

Many researchers point out the lack of security in the NoSQL database. For example, Zahid et al. [28] tested NoSQL databases by security perspective in a different environment like private, cloud, and distributive environments and find out that in the cloud and distributive environment security risk increase dramatically. Many researchers analyses problems in health records management systems. For example, Tang et al. [24] test the security and privacy for most of the Electronic Health Record (EHR) systems and elaborate all the problems in the security of the systems. In another study [27], after analyzing many EHR and EMR authors conclude that the security of health record management systems is inadequate and needs improvement. Many techniques are proposed to overcome this problem like Ahmadian et al. [1], which introduce the concept of a trusted server between user and databases. The paper uses OPE for integer data and AES for string and then to store it in a single database. Whereas, all the encryption and decryption handled by the database proxy.

Jones et al. [12] surveyed all the open-source health information systems. Authors have analyzed the features, security, and technology implementations for different available EHRs. Fabian et al. [9] propose a unique healthcare system using multiple databases. The system proposes that every hospital will have a multi-cloud proxy, and all other types will have their own proxies. The proxy will receive data from the end user, and after authentication using the dual hash system, it will encrypt the document. The encrypted document will be split into many parts, and every part will be stored on a different database. In [7] healthcare management system is proposed especially for accessing the system using the mobile operating system. It provides all the features, but security left unattended. In [14] encryption is recommended as the solution to save the health data of patient from hackers.

In Table 1, we summaries different security features offered by the existing state-of-the-art systems. In this paper, we introduced a new method to secure the EHR system, which decomposes the database into multiple parts and then applied different encryption techniques to improve the confidentiality and security of the data hosted on the cloud environment while maintaining the application performance.

3   Methodology

We build a system for securing NoSQL data over the cloud using data composition and multi encryption methods, which seamlessly integrates with any

Table 1. Security features comparison with the existing state-of-the-art.

Security measures in healthcare systems					
System name	Access control	Encryption	HIPAA compliance	Multi databases security	Multi encryption security
OpenEMR [12]	✓	✓	✓	✗	✗
OSCAR [12]	✓	✓	✗	✗	✗
ClearHealth [12]	✓	✓	✓	✗	✗
Ahmadian [1]	✓	✓	✗	✗	✗
Fabian [9]	✓	✓	✗	✓	✗
Doukas [7]	✗	✗	✗	✗	✗
Shahid [14]	✗	✓	✗	✗	✗
Proposed	✓	✓	✓	✓	✓

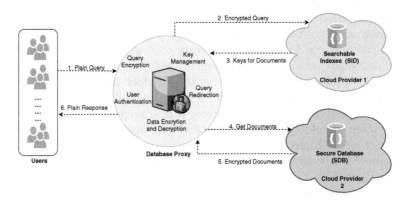

Fig. 1. Proposed system components and query execution flow.

NoSQL system to offer data confidentiality and secure query processing features along with good response time.

Figure 1 illustrates the proposed system workflow and component interactions. The proposed system consists of two NoSQL databases and one database proxy. The database proxy maintains encryption keys and responsible for accepting the query from the users and responding. Two NoSQL databases are used to host the partitioned data into two parts; Searchable Indexes (SID) and Secure Database (SDB) containing primary data for the application. The application developer partition the database into these two parts. SID contains the fields which are searchable by the applications and users, while SDB contains the corresponding documents for the search keys. We employ searchable symmetric encryption on SID using Chaotic Encryption (CE) for text fields and Order Preserving Encryption (OPE) for numeric values in SID. Whereas, AES-256 is applied at SDB to the data for ensuring data confidentiality and security.

The flow of the user query and response through the proposed system works as follows:

1. The database proxy receives plain queries issued by users and applications. The proxy encrypts the query fields, CE for text and OPE for numeric values, and forward the query to the SID.
2. The SID fetches the document/record keys against the issued query and return it to the proxy.
3. The proxy issues the query to get the documents against the keys from SDB. The SDB returns the encrypted documents against the keys.
4. The proxy decrypts the records and send the plain response to the user.

3.1 Database Proxy

Database proxy is a centralized gateway to access the secure data hosted on the cloud environment. It allows end-users and applications to query the database without knowing about the encryption techniques applied to the database because it hides query processing details. It manages the encryption keys, receives the user queries, dynamically encrypt the queries, and retrieve the data from the cloud-hosted NoSQL databases. Whenever a query is received at the proxy, first it encrypts the query, then issue the encrypted query to the SID and obtain the relevant keys for the documents. It releases another query to get the documents from the SDB. Finally, it decrypts the documents and sends the plain response to the user.

3.2 Decomposed NoSQL Databases (SID and SDB)

Data over the cloud requires to be secure for ensuring data privacy and security concerns. Moreover, data storage and retrieval performance should be good, and the data should be easy to integrate with applications. In our proposed solution, we split a given database into two NoSQL databases for storing and managing data. A small portion of data mostly containing searchable attributes are stored in SID, and remaining part of the encrypted data is stored in SDB. Our strategy to split the data into two databases improves the overall system performance and reduce the query processing time. These NoSQL databases can be deployed on a different cloud service providers over the cloud, which adds an extra layer of security to the system. Our proposed solution requires the user to store searchable attributes in SID and then define a mapping through an identical attribute in SDB to retrieve the corresponding data to the searchable attributes.

The purpose of splitting the database into two parts is to obtain excellent performance and also to ensure data security. If one of the databases compromised, the data remains confidential and secure. Because the adversary required to compromise both databases, which is difficult and challenging provided both databases hosted on separate clouds. Moreover, encryptions are CPU intensive, and separating them over two machines helps to gain performance. All user queries go to the SID and retrieve the corresponding document IDs, which then queried from the SDB. The proposed system provides flexibility to the users to select specific data attributed to being added in SID. Further, these data fields are used to query encrypted data in SDB, where all encrypted data stored. However, an extra field is added in SID other than user-defined fields for mapping between SID and SDB.

3.3   Data Encryption Methods

There are several challenges in design and implementation of secure health NoSQL database which may support a wide range of queries on encrypted data and data communication over the cloud. Unlike a simple encrypted data, a NoSQL database should allow performing various queries on encrypted data. Many data encryption algorithms exist to encrypt the data with different strengths and weaknesses depending on security requirements, including encryption and decryption processing efficiency and system integration requirements. Our proposed solution uses AES, CE, and OPE symmetric key encryption algorithms to secure NoSQL databases. In SID, text fields are encrypted using CE, and numeric fields are encrypted using OPE. Whereas, the SDB is encrypted with AES except for the ID field, which is mapping attributed between SID and SDB data. We explain these encryption methods in the following subsections.

Order Preserving Encryption (OPE). OPE [5] is symmetric-key and deterministic encryption. It maps the integer from the range 1 to m to a much bigger range from 1 to n. During the process of mapping, it ensures to preserve the numerical order of the input data. OPE is attractive for data required to serve basic numeric operations including integer matching, sorting, querying a range, and finding comparisons (less than and greater than). The OPE in the proposed system enables the SID to serve numeric operations with good efficiency while ensuring good query execution speed. To determine the order relation between data, we implemented OPE on numeric fields in SID so actual data at cloud remain encrypted while we can easily query it. In OPE, for two numeric values x and y, if $x < y$ then encrypted values must be $OPE(x) < OPE(y)$. Therefore, if a data field is encrypted using OPE, then database engine can query all numeric fields for ranges, minimum, maximum, most significant digit, least significant digit.

Chaotic Encryption. Chaotic Encryption schemes [16,23,26] use chaotic maps to encrypt the text data fields. Chaotic maps are simple and often used in unstable dynamic systems, which are used due to the ability to show sensitivity to control initial conditions as well as parameters. A minor change in initial condition causes a huge deviation in the result which results in long-term forecast untraceable. This feature is highly effective in the cryptography field. Chaotic systems are tested for security, and improvements are suggested in the key selection and parametric values in [15]. We use extended chaotic encryption proposed

Table 2. Sample plain and corresponding encrypted queries used in evaluation.

Query	Plain	SID Query	SDB Query
Equality	db.PatientsData.find({_id:500})	db.PatientsData.find({_id:132156})	db.PatientsData.find({_id:{$in:["Indexes from Ist query"]}})
Comparison	db.PatientsData.find({_id: {$lt:500}})	db.PatientsData.find({_id:132156})	db.PatientsData.find({_id:{$ lt: "Index from query"}})
Range	db.PatientsData.find({_id: {$lt:50200,$gt:50000}})	db.PatientsData.find({_id:{$in: [12865540,12812339]}})	db.PatientsData.find({_id:{$lt:Ist Index ,$gt:2nd Index}})
Logical	db.PatientsData.find({$and: [{lname: "WATKINS"},{ city: "KeyWest" }]})	db.PatientsData.find({$and:[{lname: "eJ/JtTDGFg=="}, {city: "ZLvk3i7tNj8=" }]})	db.PatientsData.find({_id:{$in:["Indexes from Ist query"]}})

in [26] instead of using less secure, traditional single map based encryption. This extended chaotic encryption use six chaotic maps named Logistic, Henon, Tent, Cubic, Sine, and Chebyshev. In our implementation, we used Sine, Tent, and Logistic chaotic maps combination. We use this encryption because of the speed over many other famous encryptions, and it generates the small ciphertext, which is easy to query.

Advance Encryption Standard. Advanced Encryption Standard (AES) [21] is a symmetric block cipher encryption. It is used worldwide to secure the classified information. AES is introduced after Data Encryption Standard (DES) become vulnerable to brute-force attacks, National Institute of Standards and Technology (NIST) developed this as its successor. AES has a block size of 128 bits but the length could 128, 192, 256. For our experiments, we use a 256-bit key for AES. Many people tested it for its security and cost until now it is the most secure and reliable encryption known as tested and explained in [2,8,11]. Our reason for choosing AES is mainly due to its strong security and reliability.

4 Experimental Setup

4.1 Benchmark Application

To test and evaluate the proposed system, we used OpenEMR [19], an opensource electronic health record and patient management system. It has a very complicated schema for SQL databases, and we built a NoSQL implementation for it using two collections on a MongoDB. We deployed one of the collection to the SID and other collection to the SDB. We used *id* field to link SID and SDB databases.

4.2 Testbed Infrastructure

We built a virtualized infrastructure using multiple virtual machines (VMs) to build a testbed environment. Each VM contains Ubuntu 16.04 operating system, 1 GB RAM, 100 GB data storage, and one Intel Core i7 CPU. We use OPE, Chaotic Encryption, and AES encryption to encrypt the records. SID, SDB, and Database Proxy all are deployed on different machines. We compare the performance results with a baseline system [1] that uses only one database and use OPE and AES encryptions. We also compare the performance of the proposed system with databases (SID and SDB) deployed without encryptions.

4.3 Evaluation Queries

We use various different database queries, including `select`, `equality`, `range`, `comparison`, `logical`, and `insert` for test and compare the proposed system. The sample plain and corresponding encrypted queries for SID and SDB using the proposed system are shown in Table 2. We use the same environment for both systems and repeat the experiments three times and then report the average response time.

4.4 Baseline System

Ahmadian et al. [1] presented a solution using the symmetric encryption and a middle-tier proxy server to query encrypted NoSQL database. They used AES encryption for text data fields and OPE for numeric type fields and deployed the database to one machine. We used this implementation as a baseline to compare the proposed method.

5 Experiments Results

We performed two experiments to compare the performance of the proposed system. In first experiment, We evaluates the overall query processing time by the proposed system for a different type of queries and then compare it with the baseline method. In second experiment, we compare the encryption time consumed by the servers using the proposed and baseline methods.

5.1 Performance Evaluation for Query Processing Time

To compare processing time for a different type of queries for the proposed and baseline methods, we log the overall processing time for each query multiple times and then report the average and standard deviation of the queries processing time. Table 3 shows the query processing time (average and standard deviation) for both the proposed and baseline systems. The results show that our system takes slightly high time than the baseline because we are querying two databases as compared to a single, but our system is more secure due to the distribution of data to multiple machines.

Figure 2 shows the increased in query processing time relative to the baseline system. We observed the different queries takes from 0.2x to 0.5x higher execution time compared to the baseline system. The `insert` queries took the highest (0.5x) time, and `equality` shows the lowest (0.2x) overhead.

5.2   Query Encryption Time Comparison

To compare the query encryption overhead for both the proposed and baseline systems, we encrypt different queries and report the average and stand deviation in Table 4. Our proposed system outperforms the baseline system to encrypt the query because the baseline system uses AES encryption to encrypt the queries, while our system used OPE and CE, which are less computationally intensive. We only observe higher encryption time for `insert` queries, because insert queries required to be split into two databases. For each `insert` query, the system applies OPE and CE for part of data to be inserted in SID and then AES encryption.

Figure 3 shows the increase/decreased of encryption time relative to the baseline. We observed that the proposed system significantly reduced the encryption time for a different type of queries for the proposed system. However, we observed 0.4x increased for insertion queries.

Figure 4 compares the overall performance, including query encryption and execution time, for the proposed and baseline methods. We observe comparable performance for using the proposed system for all type of queries except `insert`. Our solution minimizes the proxy overhead compared to the baseline. Furthermore, the proposed system provides more secure deployment as compared to the baseline due to partitioning o of the database and using multiple encryption methods to query the database easily.

Table 3. Processing time of different query types for proposed and baseline.

Query	Results count	Proposed system			Baseline system
		SID	SDB	Total	Total
Equality	1	65 ± 2	33 ± 1	98	67 ± 3
Comparison	500	70 ± 5	48 ± 2	118	100 ± 3
Range	200	80 ± 4	40 ± 1	120	90 ± 2
Logical	12	75 ± 3	55 ± 1	130	105 ± 5
Insert	1	100 ± 4	200 ± 2	300	200 ± 4

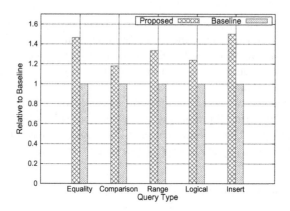

Fig. 2. Query processing time relative to the baseline for different query types.

Table 4. Encryption overhead for different query types.

Query	Proposed system	Baseline system
Equality	4.09 ± 0.27	16.19 ± 3.97
Comparison	4.48 ± 0.28	16.16 ± 2.86
Range	4.21 ± 0.47	16.59 ± 1.70
Logical	2.87 ± 0.40	18.61 ± 3.34
Insert	44.00 ± 12.08	30.00 ± 10.42

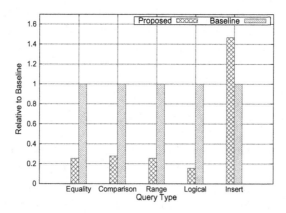

Fig. 3. Query encryption time relative to the baseline for different query types.

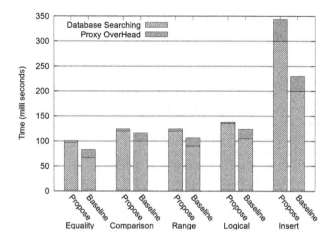

Fig. 4. Overall system performance comparison showing proxy overhead and database searching time for proposed and baseline systems.

6   Conclusion and Future Work

Data confidentiality and security in NoSQL-based databases is a significant concern for the users. In our work, we addressed NoSQL data-at-rest security issue by proposing a system, which decomposes a given database into two sub-databases and then enables queryable encryption on the data while maintaining query execution and encryption performance. In our proposed solution, Chaotic Encryption and Order Preserving Encryption provides the facility to search the encrypted data, whereas Advanced Encryption Standard provide strong data security. The database decomposition into two sub-databases helps to improve data confidentiality while delivering comparable performance to the state-of-the-art baseline method.

Currently, we are extending our work to build a scalable off the shelf service to offer NoSQL data confidentiality and secure query processing to integrate with any NoSQL-based database. For the security, we are planning to evaluate order revealing encryption to improve the data confidentiality further.

References

1. Ahmadian, M., Plochan, F., Roessler, Z., Marinescu, D.C.: SecureNoSQL: an approach for secure search of encrypted NoSQL databases in the public cloud. Int. J. Inf. Manage. **37**(2), 63–74 (2017)
2. Al Hasib, A., Haque, A.A.M.M.: A comparative study of the performance and security issues of AES and RSA cryptography. In: 2008 Third International Conference on Convergence and Hybrid Information Technology, ICCIT 2008, vol. 2, pp. 505–510. IEEE (2008)

3. Alenezi, M., Usama, M., Almustafa, K., Iqbal, W., Raza, M.A., Khan, T.: An efficient, secure, and queryable encryption for NoSQL-based databases hosted on untrusted cloud environments. Int. J. Inf. Secur. Priv. (IJISP) **13**(2), 14–31 (2019)
4. Almorsy, M., Grundy, J., Müller, I.: An analysis of the cloud computing security problem. arXiv preprint arXiv:1609.01107 (2016)
5. Boldyreva, A., Chenette, N., Lee, Y., O'Neill, A.: Order-preserving symmetric encryption. In: Joux, A. (ed.) EUROCRYPT 2009. LNCS, vol. 5479, pp. 224–241. Springer, Heidelberg (2009). https://doi.org/10.1007/978-3-642-01001-9_13
6. Chen, D., Zhao, H.: Data security and privacy protection issues in cloud computing. In: 2012 International Conference on Computer Science and Electronics Engineering (ICCSEE), vol. 1, pp. 647–651. IEEE (2012)
7. Doukas, C., Pliakas, T., Maglogiannis, I.: Mobile healthcare information management utilizing cloud computing and android OS. In: 2010 Annual International Conference of the IEEE Engineering in Medicine and Biology Society (EMBC), pp. 1037–1040. IEEE (2010)
8. Elminaam, D.S.A., Kader, H.M.A., Hadhoud, M.M.: Performance evaluation of symmetric encryption algorithms. IJCSNS Int. J. Comput. Sci. Netw. Secur. **8**(12), 280–286 (2008)
9. Fabian, B., Ermakova, T., Junghanns, P.: Collaborative and secure sharing of healthcare data in multi-clouds. Inf. Syst. **48**, 132–150 (2015)
10. Iqbal, W., Dailey, M.N., Carrera, D., Janecek, P.: Adaptive resource provisioning for read intensive multi-tier applications in the cloud. Future Gener. Comput.Syst. **27**(6), 871–879 (2011)
11. Jeeva, A., Palanisamy, D.V., Kanagaram, K.: Comparative analysis of performance efficiency and security measures of some encryption algorithms. Int. J. Eng. Res. Appl. (IJERA) **2**(3), 3033–3037 (2012)
12. Jones, B., Yuan, X., Nuakoh, E., Ibrahim, K.: Survey of open source health information systems. Health Inform. Int. J. **3**, 23–31 (2014)
13. Kaaniche, N., Laurent, M.: Data security and privacy preservation in cloud storage environments based on cryptographic mechanisms. Comput. Commun. **111**, 120–141 (2017)
14. Khan, S.I., Hoque, A.S.L.: Privacy and security problems of national health data warehouse: a convenient solution for developing countries. In: 2016 International Conference on Networking Systems and Security (NSysS), pp. 1–6. IEEE (2016)
15. Lian, S., Sun, J., Wang, Z.: Security analysis of a chaos-based image encryption algorithm. Physica A Stat. Mech. Appl. **351**(2–4), 645–661 (2005)
16. Makris, G., Antoniou, I.: Cryptography with chaos. In: Proceedings of the 5th Chaotic Modeling and Simulation International Conference, Athens, Greece, pp. 12–15 (2012)
17. Meyer, C., Schwenk., J.: Lessons Learned from Previous SSL/TLS Attacks-A Brief Chronology of Attacks and Weaknesses. IACR Cryptology EPrint Archive, p. 49 (2013)
18. Nafi, K.W., Kar, T.S., Hoque, S.A., Hashem, M.: A newer user authentication, file encryption and distributed server based cloud computing security architecture. arXiv preprint arXiv:1303.0598 (2013)
19. OEMR: Openemr. https://www.open-emr.org/
20. Pokorny, J.: NoSQL databases: a step to database scalability in web environment. Int. J. Web Inf. Syst. **9**(1), 69–82 (2013)
21. Pub NF. 197: Advanced encryption standard (AES). Federal information processing standards publication 197, 441-0311 (2001)

22. Singh, A., Chatterjee, K.: Cloud security issues and challenges: a survey. J. Netw. Comput. Appl. **79**, 88–115 (2017)
23. Sobhy, M.I., Shehata, A.E.: Chaotic algorithms for data encryption. In: 2001 IEEE International Conference on Acoustics, Speech, and Signal Processing, Proceedings (ICASSP 2001), vol. 2, pp. 997–1000. IEEE (2001)
24. Tang, J., Cui, Y., Li, Q., Ren, K., Liu, J., Buyya, R.: Ensuring security and privacy preservation for cloud data services. ACM Comput. Surv. (CSUR) **49**(1), 13 (2016)
25. Tudorica, B.G., Bucur, C.: A comparison between several NoSQL databases with comments and notes. In: 2011 10th Roedunet International Conference (RoE-duNet), pp. 1–5. IEEE (2011)
26. Usama, M., Khan, M.K., Alghathbar, K., Lee, C.: Chaos-based secure satellite imagery cryptosystem. Comput. Math. Appl. **60**(2), 326–337 (2010)
27. Win, K.T.: A review of security of electronic health records. Health Inf. Manage. **34**(1), 13–18 (2005)
28. Zahid, A., Masood, R., Shibli, M.A.: Security of sharded NoSQL databases: a comparative analysis. In: 2014 Conference on Information Assurance and Cyber Security (CIACS), pp. 1–8. IEEE (2014)

Pseudo Transfer Learning by Exploiting Monolingual Corpus: An Experiment on Roman Urdu Transliteration

Muhammad Yaseen Khan and Tafseer Ahmed[✉]

Center for Language Computing, Department of Computer Science,
Mohammad Ali Jinnah University, Karachi, Pakistan
{yaseen.khan, tafseer.ahmed}@jinnah.edu

Abstract. This paper shares two things: an efficient experiment for "pseudo" transfer learning by using huge monolingual (mono-script) dataset in a sequence-to-sequence LSTM model; and application of proposed methodology to improve Roman Urdu transliteration. The research involves echoing monolingual dataset, such that in the pre-training phase, the input and output sequences are ditto, to learn the target language. This process gives target language based initialized weights to the LSTM model before training the network with the original parallel data. The method is beneficial for reducing the requirement of more training data or more computational resources because these are usually not available to many research groups. The experiment is performed for the character-based Romanized Urdu script to standard (i.e., modified Perso-Arabic) Urdu script transliteration. Initially, a sequence-to-sequence encoder-decoder model is trained (echoed) for 100 epochs on 306.9K distinct words in standard Urdu script. Then, the trained model (with the weights tuned by echoing) is used for learning transliteration. At this stage, the parallel corpus comprises 127K pairs of Roman Urdu and standard Urdu tokens. The results are quite impressive, the proposed methodology shows BLEU accuracy of 80.1% in 100 epochs of training parallel data (preceded by echoing the mono-script data for 100 epochs), whereas, the baseline model trained solely on parallel corpus yields ≈76% BLEU accuracy in 200 epochs.

Keywords: Artificial neural network · Deep learning · Transliteration · Transfer learning · Urdu

1 Introduction

Artificial neural networks (ANN) is the bio-inspired computational framework in artificial intelligence (AI) [6, 24], extensively in use nowadays for various machine learning (ML) tasks for resolving diversified problems in different domains like control systems, classifications, machine translation, computer vision etc. [4, 17, 21, 22]. Deep NNs have been proved very successful in many Natural Language Processing (NLP) tasks, from the classification of texts to the machine translations and image captioning, the results of NN are outstanding [31]. Results of different experiments

© Springer Nature Singapore Pte Ltd. 2020
I. S. Bajwa et al. (Eds.): INTAP 2019, CCIS 1198, pp. 422–431, 2020.
https://doi.org/10.1007/978-981-15-5232-8_36

have also shown that the tasks involving sequence-to-sequence translation work better than their classical machine learning counter-parts [16, 33].

In practice, these ANNs and Deep NNs require a lot of training data along with the dire necessity of high computational power [9, 13, 26]. These two requirements are difficult to achieve by the researchers/developers working on low resource languages. The huge training data is usually not available for many of the world languages [25]. Thus, creating massive datasets consisting of annotated or parallel dataset involves not only time and money, but it also needs skillful human resources [32]. Moreover, the researchers working on these languages do not have longer (i.e., for days/weeks) access to the state of art hardware.

The typical assumption in data mining and ML tasks shows the training and testing datasets have to be drawn from the same feature space and distribution [34]. This is, however, not a good idea because, on the occurrence of the change in the domain or the data, we need to rebuild the model based on new data [28]. In this context, knowledge transfer or transfer learning comes as the most beneficial and opportune method which motivates that the ML system should use the knowledge in the same way that inherited knowledge helps people to resolve a new/related problem more efficiently [5].

Urdu is a language that has a moderate level of computational and human resources for developing language-based applications [27]. It is one of the representatives of South Asian languages, most of which have even fewer resources [15, 20, 30]. Urdu is written in a modified Perso-Arabic script [18]; however, a large number of social media users write Urdu in the Roman script using the English keyboard [1, 19]. Transliterating Romanized Urdu in standard Urdu is not a simple character-to-character mapping. In fact it exhibits a many-to-many mapping, for example: the English alphabet s has three candidate alphabets in Urdu, i.e., ث, ص, and س; similarly, the other way round, the Urdu alphabet ی will be mapped on many characters, depending on its position in the word, for instance, b will be used when ی comes in the beginning, whereas, either of ee, i, and y can be used when ی comes at the end of the word. Moreover, some-times the transliteration can produce wrong words, for example, the Romanized Urdu word 'khana' can be transliterated into two semantically different things: کھانا/khana/which means "meal/food", and کھانہ/xana/which means a "cell" (in terms of space).

This paper presents an effective method that handles the limitations, i.e., lack of huge parallel corpus consisting of the source language and target language documents, and ample time to loop too many epochs in experiments. We also show, with an experimental case study of Roman Urdu transliteration, that if the language does not have huge parallel corpus but has a monolingual corpus of considerable size, then the ANN can discover some "pseudo-knowledge" through echoing the monolingual corpus. By echoing, we mean that the input sentences are ditto in output. With this, we can surmise that the ANN has learned the sequence of letters, word formation, and to some extent word segmentation of the target language. Hence, this concept can be termed as "Pseudo Transfer Learning" (PTL) such that other experiments in ANN can take benefit from the pseudo-knowledge if the weights (calibrated through echoing mono-lingual corpus) transferred to them at the step of weight-initialization.

2 Background

This section gives the information of efforts made so far on Urdu transliteration, and related work w.r.t to the work done for this paper. In the end of section, we line out the differences between the existing work and proposed methodology.

In NLP, Sequence to Sequence (Seq2Seq) processing involves tasks that work on a sequence of information (S_i) and produce another sequence (S_t) in result, where S_i and S_t are the source and target sequence respectively, and $S_i \neq S_t$. Machine translation, transliteration, and transcription of a language into any other language/script can be accounted as few examples of Seq2Seq processing [2, 3, 33]. In the recent era, Seq2Seq processing is widely employed with Encoder-Decoder Model (EDM). It refers to the encoding of variable length Si into a fixed-length vector representation (V_e) and decoding V_e to generate S_t [10, 11].

2.1 Review of Roman Urdu Transliteration

Work has been done for both Roman to Urdu (e.g. [35]) and vice versa (e.g. [7, 23]). [1] Lists the major issues of Roman to Urdu script. As the writers in Roman Urdu do not follow any standard, an Urdu word can be written in different ways in Roman Urdu. All of these works need handcrafted rules and algorithms. As a result, the solutions cannot be considered as comprehensive and generic. We find only work on Roman to Urdu transliteration using deep learning. [2] used EDM based Seq2Seq LSTM model for transliteration. The system yielded promising results (quantified with the BLEU accuracy of 48.6); however, its major short-coming was that it was based on a word model. However, the transliteration problem should be modeled by using a character to the character model, which would enable the trained model to deal with out of the vocabulary (OOV) words.

2.2 Related Work

The closest work done in relation with our approach shows the usage of monolingual data in neural machine translation and back-translation for European languages, in particular for English, French, German, Romanian, and Turkish. The work presented in the papers [8, 14] exhibits the coping of monolingual dataset of the target language to generate data such that source and target sequences are identical. The dataset generated through this process is called copied dataset, which in the next step, is mixed with the actual parallel corpus of the source language and target language. Finally, both (of the research works) used the mixed data for the training of ANN. The significant difference between these two works is seen in the data augmentation. [14] used the plain monolingual dataset for copying and later mixing with the parallel corpus, whereas, [8] along with copying the data, also inducted noisy data.

In contrast with the method discussed for Roman Urdu transliteration in the paper [2]; our approach uses the character-based LSTM model, whereas, word-level LSTM model is employed in the work as mentioned earlier. Moreover, the research works [8, 14] which show the usage of monolingual corpus for copying dataset and mixed it with the original parallel corpus for training, clearly appear to be at a different position in comparison to the work done in this paper. The proposed methodology divides the whole process into two parts. In the initial (pre-training) phase monolingual corpus is copied and the network is trained for 100 epochs to tune weights, then in the later phase, these weights are transferred to train the network on the original parallel corpus of Roman Urdu and respective Urdu sequences to achieve transfer learning.

3 Methodology

It is safe to say that the methodology proposed in this paper is simple outright. It consists of two phases: in the pre-training phase, we constructed a source learning model, which is for seeking the weights to initialize the other neural network by transferring. While in the later phase, the system is trained for target learning model (or for the actual experiment), which, in our case, is a transliteration of Romanized Urdu into standard Urdu script. The Fig. 1 gives the overall scheme for the proposed methodology, while the details of these phases are given in Sect. 3.1 and 3.2 respectively; Sects. 3.3 and 3.4 give the detailed insights to the experimental setup and datasets.

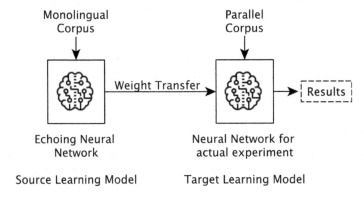

Fig. 1. Illustration of proposed methodology.

3.1 Source Learning Model

Since we know the source language ($\mathcal{L}_s$) of the actual experiment is Romanized Urdu (the representation of running text of Urdu in Latin alphabets (λ)), and the target language ($\mathcal{L}_t$) is Urdu (for standard, which is to be written in the modified Perso-Arabic script (α)). For the knowledge transfer, we need to build a neural network that tasks to generate the sequence in $\mathcal{L}_t$ on any given textual input sequence. For this, we need an expanded parallel corpus showing the eclectic mix of scenarios.

In our course of the experiment, such massive parallel corpus is not available; instead, we have got the huge monolingual (mono-script) corpus in $\mathcal{L}_t$, which comprises over 125M tokens. Thus, we extract the set of unique words ($\mathcal{W}_m$) out from the monolingual corpus, and prepare a dummy parallel corpus ($\mathcal{M}_p$), which can be defined as a set of the pairs of ditto words, $\mathcal{M}_p = \left\{ \left(w_1^\alpha, w_1^\alpha\right), \left(w_2^\alpha, w_2^\alpha\right), \cdots, \left(w_n^\alpha, w_n^\alpha\right) \right\}$, where $w_i^\alpha \in \mathcal{W}_m$ in α script. The $\mathcal{M}_p$ is set for training in an Echoing Neural Network (ENN) for Seq2Seq processing such that, a word given as input will be echoed back in output (identical to the given input). The training has to last until the loss of the ENN is diminished to near zero. We find out that if the $\mathcal{M}_p$ is consisting of 125–150K pairs of words then, 100 epochs are enough for perfecting the weights of echoing network.

Finally, the ENN is ready with the comprehended knowledge of the word's internal representation, for example, word formation, and sequence of letters appearing therein. Since the knowledge is built by employing a monolingual corpus, and the system only knows to echo the words, therefore, we find it appropriate to term this as *pseudo knowledge*. Hence, when the weights of ENN (Ψ) are transferred (at the time of weight initialization) for benefiting any other neural network, we can say the "Pseudo Transfer Learning" happens correspondingly.

3.2   Target Learning Model

In this phase, we have set another neural network for learning the transliteration of $\mathcal{L}_s$ into $\mathcal{L}_t$ (say, Transliteration Neural Network (TNN)). However, the TNN is analogous to the network in the earlier phase. The thing, which makes the basic difference between ENN and TNN, is the parallel corpus ($\mathcal{T}_p$) on which the TNN is trained. We collected 127K distinct pairs of parallel tokens for the development of $\mathcal{T}_p$, mathematically, $\mathcal{T}_p = \left\{ \left(w_1^\lambda, w_1^\alpha\right), \left(w_2^\lambda, w_2^\alpha\right), \cdots, \left(w_n^\lambda, w_n^\alpha\right) \right\}$, where $w_i^\lambda \in \mathcal{L}_s$, $w_i^\alpha \in \mathcal{L}_t$ while w_i^λ is the word in λ and the word w_i^α corresponds to its transliterated copy in α. In next step, the weighs of TNN is initialized with Ψ, and set for the Seq2Seq processing to generate w_i^α on given w_i^λ.

3.3   Experimental Setup

We set a character-level EDM with LSTM, for both neural networks, i.e., ENN and TNN. In this regard, we seek a Python script[1] in Keras [12]. In both phases, the set of input (I) and output (O) characters are formed by the combination of alphabets, punctuation marks, numbers in both scripts, and a symbolic character (Φ) for dealing any unknown/OOV alphabet in future, ($I \equiv O = \{\alpha \cup \lambda \cup \{\Phi\}\}$). Every pair in $\mathcal{M}_p$ and $\mathcal{T}_p$ is transformed into 3D array for one-hot vector representation. Thus, we have three 3D arrays for, encoding input sequence, decoding input sequence, and decoding output sequence, respectively. In following steps, the ENN and TNN are trained (on their respective datasets) with LSTM-based Seq2Seq model for generating target sequence for the given encoded and decoded source sequence. For training, 256 LSTM cells are set as the latent dimensions for encoding and decoding space, and the batch is consisting of 1024 pairs.

In order to make an equitable analysis, we staged two experiments: one–that deals with the basic Seq2Seq learning, such that to get the baseline accuracy of system; and,

---

[1] https://github.com/keras-team/keras/blob/master/examples/lstm_Seq2Seq.py.

secondly Seq2Seq learning with the PTL. Finally, the performance of both experimental systems is evaluated on an unseen parallel corpus.

3.4 Dataset

We have got the massive monolingual (mono-script) corpus ($\mathcal{M}$) of Urdu language that is built from the books, news articles, and the editorial columns available at online news portals, which comprises over 120.7M tokens. However, the 306.9K distinct tokens were yielded from the $\mathcal{M}$. These tokens are employed for the development of $\mathcal{M}_p$.

The parallel corpus of Romanized-Urdu and standard Urdu pairs is constructed through scrapping iJunoon.com[2], where the English-Urdu dictionary facilitates users with the meaning of an English word in standard Urdu script (α) along with its transliterated version in Roman script (λ). For scrapping, we utilized Python scrapping utility BeautifulSoup[3] and the huge list of English words[4] that contains 466.5K distinct English words. The process of scrapping resulted in 284.3K pairs of parallel tokens, which is reduced to 127K distinct pairs of parallel tokens in $\mathcal{T}_p$.

The blind testing corpus ($\mathcal{B}_p$) is consisting of 291 sentences (5K tokens) provided by Conference on Language and Technology, 2014 (CLT14)[5].

4 Results and Evaluation

The results of the experiment are quite impressive. The significant impact observed in the whole experiment is the earlier minimization of loss. Secondly, the BiLingual Evaluation Understudy (BLEU), a well-employed metric, is used for evaluating the result of transliteration [29].

4.1 Effect of Pseudo Transfer Learning

The experiment has shown that on the basic experiment, i.e., about to train a neural network for Seq2Seq processing, 100 epochs are required to minimize loss to $\approx$0.0098 on training data, while $\approx$0.0038 on validation data. What if the network is trained further, will it help to reduce loss anymore? On this viewpoint, we made the network to train a little more, such that; the number of epochs is doubled (i.e., 200). The loss, as we expected, is reduced to $\approx$0.0067 and $\approx$0.0038 on training and validation sets, respectively. The behavior of the basic neural network is subtle, but it does not outperform the results of the proposed methodology. The proposed methodology, i.e., about benefiting a neural network with PTL, we see the loss on the training set is $\approx$0.0048 and $\approx$0.0038 on the validation set, this statistic is secured when the 100 (half) epochs are elapsed. Figure 2 shows the plot of the loss plunging.

---

[2] http://ijunoon.com.

[3] https://www.crummy.com/software/BeautifulSoup/.

[4] https://github.com/dwyl/english-words.

[5] http://crcl.dsu.edu.pk/clt14/shared_call.html.

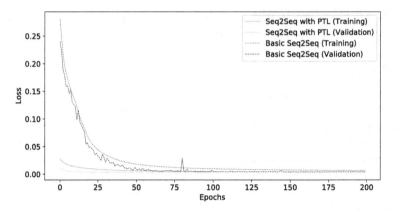

Fig. 2. Comparative plot of loss values along epochs.

4.2   Roman Urdu Transliteration

This section discusses the outcomes, in particular the errors, of the system build on the proposed methodology. However, the magnitude of these errors is very small. We also discuss the points on the proposed methodology builds a sagacious system for Roman Urdu transliteration.

We find out the BLEU score on $\mathcal{B}_p$ is 76% on the basic Seq2Seq processing, whereas, the proposed methodology shows around 4% improvement by securing overall 80.1% BLEU score. In comparison to the results of the experiment discussed in [2] (i.e., word-level Roman Urdu transliteration), the accuracy of basic Seq2Seq learning on character-based transliteration outperformed with the improvement of 27.4%, while, the experiment with PTL shows the most significant result with overall ≈31% improvement.

The errors are mostly with the wrong arrangements of alphabets, but it can be seen that 1–2 alphabets within a word have this issue. Since it is a character-base transliteration, therefore, we did not see any of the out of the vocabulary error.

Table 1 shows the results of transliteration as per the proposed methodology; and symbols (†, ‡, and ○) preceding Urdu words show minute errors in transliteration. Details are given below.

Ordering of alphabets: † as mentioned in row 1 of Table 1 shows the error in the ordering of alphabets in words. The resultant word پرنسل (for the input word 'personal') should be transliterated as پرسنل similarly; the resultant word کران (for the input word 'krna') should have to be کرنا.

Omission or induction of alphabets: ‡ as mentioned in the rows 2, 5, and 6 shows the error of the omission of an alphabet or the induction of a wrong alphabet. The resultant word ہتے and گی (for the input words 'gai', and 'hotay' (see row 2 and 5)) are the omission cases: the expected words should be ہوتے and گئی respectively. Whereas, the resultant word کیا in row 6 shows the case of induction of wrong alphabet ی. We can surmise these errors are happening due to the light vowels, which are often left while writing in Romanized Urdu.

Table 1. Examples of transliteration through PTL.

R.	Input Sequence	Output Sequence
1	is lye kety hain dosro ko apni personal life me bilkul involve nahi krna chahiye	اس لئے کہتے ہیں دوسروں کو اپنی †پرنسل لائف میں بالکل انوالو نہیں †کرنا چاہیے
2	aik bili 30 fut gehre kuen main gir gai hai woh 3 step uper jump kerti hai to 2 step piche a jati hai ab batao k bili kitne dino main bahir nikle gi	ایک بلی تیس فٹ گہرے کنویں میں گر ‡ ‍ی ○ہیں ‡وہ تین سٹیپ اوپر جمپ کرتی ○ہیں تو بو سٹیپ پیچھے آ جاتی ہیں اب بتانو ‡ک بلی کتنے دنوں میں باہر نکلے‌‍گ‍
3	0% bhe pixel nhe phattay but image zoom in main blur ho jata hai	بھی پکسل نہیں پھٹے بٹ امیج زوم ان ہ ں بلر بوجاتا ○ہے
4	Jo duniya ki khidmat karta hai duniya usay apna khadim bana leti hai	جو دنیا کی خدمت ترتا ہے دنیا اسے اپنا خادم بنا لیتی ہے
5	jab bemaar hoon tu yahi reshtay sab se ziyada pershan hotay hain	جب بیمار ہوں تو یہی رشتے سب سے زیادہ پریشان ‡ہتے ہے
6	Fuzul kharchi karne wale shaitan ke bhai hain, aur shaitan apne rab ka bahut na-shukra hai	فضول خرچی کرنے والے شیطان کے بھائی ○ہیں اور شیطان اپنے رب ‡کیا بہت ناشکرا ○ہیں

Confusion of auxiliary verbs: ○ as mentioned in rows 2, 3, and 6 shows the errors with the auxiliary verbs (ہے/he/and ہیں/haĩ/) that are among the most frequent words in the Urdu language; often used to make sense of tense and singularity/plurality of nouns.

Exact English words: One may think of the fact that if the Romanized Urdu is written with Latin alphabets, then many of the English words can be exactly written in Urdu description. Considering this case, the system has performed very well on the words, which are borrowed from the English language. For example, لائف (life) and انوالو (involve) in row 1, سٹیپ (step) and جمپ (jump) in row 2, پکسل (pixel), almost a phrase of 4 words بٹ امیج زوم ان (but image zoom in), and بلر (blur) in row 3 are transliterated with the accuracy of near human-perfection. Nasal alphabets: In general, the writers (in Roman Urdu) omit the alphabet n (since it presents a nasal sound) at the end of the word showing the plurality, specially when the alphabet o is following; for example, the Romanized version of word پھولوں/phu:lõ/is phoolon/phulon (means 'flowers') can be written without the alphabet n in the end. However, for standard Urdu, it is essential to write Urdu alphabet n (Noon-Ghunna) for the correct spelling of the respective word. The result yielded by the system shows the perfect transliteration, as it is seen in row 1 for the words دوسروں/dūsrõ/and نہیں/nahīñ/, and for the word دنوں/ dinõ/in the row 2 for the given input words 'dusro', 'nahi' and 'dino' respectively.

5   Conclusion

Pseudo Transfer Learning helps Seq2Seq processing for deep learning, where a substantial parallel corpus is unavailable. We have shown the monolingual corpus can exhibit some pseudo-knowledge, which can be transferred to other networks. PTL is effective such that it can reduce the efforts by halving the time and data labeling. In the future, we like to use this technique for the neural machine translation and other NLP problems in Indic languages that are written in Perso-Arabic script.

References

1. Ahmed, T.: Roman to Urdu transliteration using wordlist. In: Proceedings of the Conference on Language and Technology, vol. 305, p. 309 (2009)
2. Alam, M., ul Hussain, S.: Sequence to sequence networks for Roman-Urdu to Urdu transliteration. In: 2017 International Multi-Topic Conference (IN-MIC), pp. 1–7. IEEE (2017)
3. Arik, S.Ö., et al.: Deep voice: real-time neural text-to-speech. In: Proceedings of the 34th International Conference on Machine Learning, vol. 70, pp. 195–204. JMLR.org (2017)
4. Bahdanau, D., Cho, K., Bengio, Y.: Neural machine translation by jointly learning to align and translate. arXiv preprint arXiv:1409.0473 (2014)
5. Baxter, J., Caruana, R., Mitchell, T., Pratt, L.Y., Silver, D.L., Thrun, S.: Learning to learn: knowledge consolidation and transfer in inductive systems. In: NIPS Workshop (1995). http://plato.acadiau.ca/courses/comp/dsilver/NIPS95_LTL/transfer.workshop
6. Bishop, C.M., et al.: Neural Networks for Pattern Recognition. Oxford University Press, Oxford (1995)
7. Bögel, T.: Urdu-Roman transliteration via finite state transducers. In: 10th International Workshop on Finite State Methods and Natural Language Processing, FSMNLP 2012, pp. 25–29 (2012)
8. Burlot, F., Yvon, F.: Using monolingual data in neural machine translation: a systematic study. arXiv preprint arXiv:1903.11437 (2019)
9. Canziani, A., Paszke, A., Culurciello, E.: An analysis of deep neural network models for practical applications. arXiv preprint arXiv:1605.07678 (2016)
10. Cho, K., Van Merriënboer, B., Bahdanau, D., Bengio, Y.: On the properties of neural machine translation: encoder-decoder approaches. arXiv preprint arXiv:1409.1259 (2014)
11. Cho, K., et al.: Learning phrase representations using RNN encoder-decoder for statistical machine translation. arXiv preprint arXiv:1406.1078 (2014)
12. Chollet, F., et al.: Keras (2015)
13. Cireşan, D., Meier, U., Schmidhuber, J.: Multi-column deep neural networks for image classification. arXiv preprint arXiv:1202.2745 (2012)
14. Currey, A., Barone, A.V.M., Heafield, K.: Copied monolingual data improves low-resource neural machine translation. In: Proceedings of the Second Conference on Machine Translation, pp. 148–156 (2017)
15. Daud, A., Khan, W., Che, D.: Urdu language processing: a survey. Artif. Intell. Rev. 47(3), 279–311 (2017). https://doi.org/10.1007/s10462-016-9482-x
16. Graves, A.: Generating sequences with recurrent neural networks. arXiv preprint arXiv: 1308.0850 (2013)
17. Hunt, K.J., Sbarbaro, D., Żbikowski, R., Gawthrop, P.J.: Neural networks for control systems – a survey. Automatica 28(6), 1083–1112 (1992)
18. Hussain, S.: Resources for Urdu language processing. In: Proceedings of the 6th Workshop on Asian Language Resources (2008)
19. Javed, I., Afzal, H.: Opinion analysis of bi-lingual event data from social networks. In: ESSEM@ AI* IA, pp. 164–172. Citeseer (2013)

20. Kachru, B.B., Kachru, Y., Sridhar, S.N.: Language in South Asia. Cambridge University Press, Cambridge (2008)
21. Karpathy, A., Fei-Fei, L.: Deep visual-semantic alignments for generating image descriptions. In: Proceedings of the IEEE Conference on Computer Vision and Pattern Recognition, pp. 3128–3137 (2015)
22. Krizhevsky, A., Sutskever, I., Hinton, G.E.: ImageNet classification with deep convolutional neural networks. In: Advances in Neural Information Processing Systems, pp. 1097–1105 (2012)
23. Malik, M.K., et al.: Transliterating Urdu for a broad-coverage Urdu/Hindi LFG grammar. In: Seventh International Conference on Language Resources and Evaluation, LREC 2010, pp. 2921–2927 (2010)
24. McCulloch, W.S., Pitts, W.: A logical calculus of the ideas immanent in nervous activity. Bull. Math. Biophys. 5(4), 115–133 (1943). https://doi.org/10.1007/BF02478259
25. McEnery, T., Baker, P., Burnard, L.: Corpus resources and minority language engineering. In: LREC (2000)
26. Mikolov, T., Karafiát, M., Burget, L., Černocký, J., Khudanpur, S.: Recurrent neural network based language model. In: Eleventh Annual Conference of the International Speech Communication Association (2010)
27. Mukund, S., Ghosh, D., Srihari, R.K.: Using cross-lingual projections to generate semantic role labeled corpus for Urdu: a resource poor language. In: Proceedings of the 23rd International Conference on Computational Linguistics, pp. 797–805. Association for Computational Linguistics (2010)
28. Pan, S.J., Yang, Q.: A survey on transfer learning. IEEE Trans. Knowl. Data Eng. 22(10), 1345–1359 (2009)
29. Papineni, K., Roukos, S., Ward, T., Zhu, W.J.: BLEU: a method for automatic evaluation of machine translation. In: Proceedings of the 40th Annual Meeting on Association for Computational Linguistics, pp. 311–318. Association for Computational Linguistics (2002)
30. Simons, G.F., Fennig, C.D.: Ethnologue: Languages of Asia. SIL International, Dallas (2017)
31. Socher, R., Bengio, Y., Manning, C.D.: Deep learning for NLP (without magic). In: Tutorial Abstracts of ACL 2012, p. 5. Association for Computational Linguistics (2012)
32. Sorokin, A., Forsyth, D.: Utility data annotation with Amazon mechanical turk. In: 2008 IEEE Computer Society Conference on Computer Vision and Pattern Recognition Workshops, pp. 1–8. IEEE (2008)
33. Sutskever, I., Vinyals, O., Le, Q.V.: Sequence to sequence learning with neural networks. In: Advances in Neural Information Processing Systems, pp. 3104–3112 (2014)
34. Weiss, K., Khoshgoftaar, T.M., Wang, D.: A survey of transfer learning. J. Big Data 3(1), 9 (2016)
35. Zahid, M.A., Rao, N.I., Siddiqui, A.M.: English to Urdu transliteration: an application of soundex algorithm. In: 2010 International Conference on Information and Emerging Technologies, pp. 1–5. IEEE (2010)

Classification and Prediction Analysis of Diseases and Other Datasets Using Machine Learning

Junaid Nasir[1], Alishba Ahsan[1], Nadeem Sarwar[1(✉)], Wajid Rafique[2],
Sameer Malik[3], Syed Zeeshan Hussain Shah[4], Sarousha Nasir[1],
and Asma Irshad[5]

[1] Department of Computer Science, Bahria University,
Lahore Campus, Lahore, Pakistan
Junaid.jans@gmail.com, alishbaahsan127@gmail.com,
Nadeem_srwr@yahoo.com, sapisces97@gmail.com
[2] Department of Computer Science and Technology,
Nanjing University, Nanjing, People's Republic of China
rafiqwajid@smail.nju.edu.cn
[3] Department of Computer Science, University of Sialkot, Sialkot, Pakistan
Sameer.malik@uskt.edu.pk
[4] Department of Software Engineering, University of Sialkot, Sialkot, Pakistan
zgellani@gmail.com
[5] Department of Life Science, University of Management & Technology,
Lahore, Pakistan
asmairshad76@yahoo.com

Abstract. Classification is one of the most used machine learning technique especially in the prediction of daily life things. Its first step is grouping, dividing, categorizing, and separation of datasets based on future vectors. Classification procedure has many algorithms, some of them are Random Forest, Naïve Bayes, Decision Tree and Support Vector Machine. Before the implementation of every technique, the model is created and then training of dataset has been made on that model. Learning the algorithm-generated model must be fit for both the input dataset and forecast the records of class label. Many models are available for prediction of a class label from unknown records. In this paper, different classifiers such as Linear SVM, Ensemble, the Decision tree has been applied and their accuracy and time analyzed on different datasets. The Liver Patient, Wine Quality, Breast Cancer and Bupa Liver Disorder datasets are used for calculating the performance and accuracy by using 10 cross-fold validation technique. In the end, all the applied algorithm results have been calculated and compared in the terms of accuracy and execution time.

Keywords: Classification · Naïve Bayes · DT · SVM · CM · Scattered plot

1 Introduction

Data mining is a process of inferring knowledge from datasets [1]. It has three main techniques known as Classification, Clustering and Association Rule Mining. Classification of datasets is one of the most complicated tasks in the present era.

© Springer Nature Singapore Pte Ltd. 2020
I. S. Bajwa et al. (Eds.): INTAP 2019, CCIS 1198, pp. 432–442, 2020.
https://doi.org/10.1007/978-981-15-5232-8_37

Classification of data is done by three phases which are training set, determine class attributes and goal. Taken data is always divided into two parts training set and testing data and for the sake of correct prediction 10 cross fold technique is used mostly [2].

In this paper, we are going to apply classification techniques on different datasets and will measure their accuracy rate along with execution time. For this paper, four different datasets Liver Disorder, Liver Patient Detection, Wine and Breast Cancer has been taken. All these datasets are taken from the UCI Repository. The link of UCI repository is https://archive.ics.uci.edu/ml/datasets.html.

Applied classification algorithms are Decision Tree and it's three sub-algorithms like Support Vector Machine, Fine tree, Coarse tree, Medium tree and Logistic Regression Classifier, and its sub-algorithms like Cubic SVM, Linear SVM, Gaussian SVM, Quadratic SVM, Fine, Coarse SVM and Ensemble Classifier with its sub-algorithms like busted trees and bagged trees (Fig. 1).

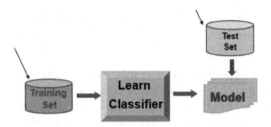

Fig. 1. Illustration of classification technique

After this the second section contains a literature review, third contains the methodology used for four used datasets, section four describes our experimental results and Sect. 5 offers the conclusion and future work.

2 Literature Review

Before discussing the previous work on datasets, let's discuss the used algorithms first.

Decision Tree: Decision tree classification algorithms have major potential for covering and mapping problems and have not been confirmed in detail by the remote identifying public relative to more predictable pattern recognition techniques such as extreme likelihood classification [3].

Logistic Regression Classifier: It is Machine Learning technique used for binary classification problems. Logistic regression is entitled to the function used at the core of the method and the logistic function. It uses the equation as a representation, very much like linear regression [4]. It models the probability of the default class.

Support Vector Machine: It is one of the most talked and used classifier. It was extremely popular around 1990 and people are using it till date [5]. In Fig. 2 SVM is a stimulating control and its ideas are outstandingly batter. A Support Vector Machine (SVM) is a distinctive classifier officially categorized by an isolating hyper-plane.

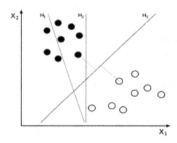

Fig. 2. Support vector machine

This figure is describing the relationship between hyperplanes used in support vector machine. As all hyperplanes are distinguished as H1, H2, and H3 and separated by using lines.

Ensemble Classifier: Combination of at least two than two classifiers is known as outfit classifier. The gathering learning has to expand enthusiasm for the computational training society by producing better quality outcomes when contrasted with the single theory model [6]. Incremental learning calculation has a capacity to gain from the new approaching occurrences even after the classifier is as of now produced. It learns the novel data and pre-serves officially secure information without getting to the officially observed information so far [7]. One of the greatest advantages of a gradual model is it is existence efficient. Be that as it may while preparing it requires the little steady time per test, there ought to be just one example at the time in memory, it fabricates the model by examining the database and safeguard recently acquired information. The upside of utilizing steady ensemble is that it utilizes more than one classifier and different speculations which will be combined by utilizing casting a ballot rule.

For Liver Disease expectation [8] has inferred that these days, the liver is experiencing three noteworthy sicknesses Liver Cancer, Cirrhosis and Hepatitis with particular symptoms. They utilized Naïve Bayes and SVM for malady forecast. Correlation between these two calculations has been done dependent on their order precision measure. From the trial result, they have inferred that SVM is superior to Naïve Bayes as the exactness rate of SVM was 79.66% and for Naïve Bayes precision rate is 61.28%.

Bosom malignant growth is a standout amongst the most well-known diseases among ladies and the reason for ladies passing around the world [9]. Applied Naïve Bayes and J48 calculation on the bosom malignancy dataset for bosom disease forecast in ladies. He has presumed that Naïve Bayes is superior to J48 in light of the fact that the precision of Naïve Bayes was 97.80% and for J48 it was 96.05%.

The interest has been increased in wine from the last few years and people demands quality. To predict the wine quality data mining techniques has been applied to wine dataset by [10]. They applied the SVM and NN technique. From which he concluded that SVM is better than NN because the accuracy rate of SVM was 86.8% while for NN it was 64.3%.

The liver is the biggest internal organ of the human body with 4% of the body weight with a blood flow of 1.5 L per minute. The liver disorder is very common among people nowadays and it is very important to detect this disorder at an early stage. For this purpose [11] applied classification techniques cart and radial algorithm on dataset and concluded that radial algorithm is better than cart because in this specific scenario it was giving 70% accuracy while cart was giving almost 55% accuracy [12–15].

3 Methodology

In this paper, we selected different datasets and classified by using different algorithms as shown in Fig. 3:

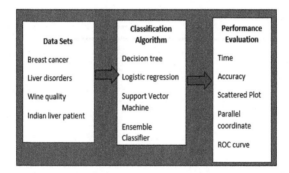

Fig. 3. Evaluation of different datasets using various classification algorithms

The Table 1 is describing that we took four datasets named as breast cancer, liver disorder, wine quality and Indian liver patient on which the classification techniques like trees, logistic regression and SVM has been applied. The evaluation has been done and calculated in the form of accuracy and recalls precision etc. techniques. The datasets are Indian Liver Patient Dataset, Wine Quality, Breast Cancer and Liver Disorder to be classified. Datasets, number of instances, attributes and classes are given as follows:

Table 1. Datasets for classification used

Datasets	No of attributes	No of instances
Breast cancer	11	699
Liver disorders	7	345
Wine quality	12	4989
Indian liver patient	11	416

The sum total of what datasets has been taken from the UCI vault. The connection of UCI vault is https://archive.ics.uci.edu/ml/datasets.html. It is an open-source vault and any-one can download these datasets from here.

4 Results and Discussion

In this paper, we compute the investigational measures by using the performance factors such as the classification accuracy and the execution time. We draw the scattered plots, confusion matrix and ROC curve of every dataset. Let's see the experimental measure of datasets one by one:

4.1 Indian Liver Patient Dataset

The scattered plot (Fig. 4) is a line graph which is used to plot how much one variable is dependent on others. This scatter plot is showing the correlation between two variables known as male and female.

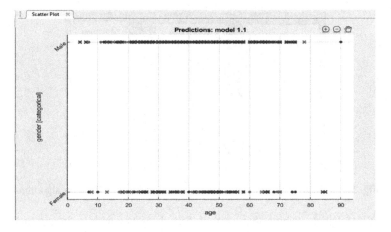

Fig. 4. Scattered plot Indian liver patient

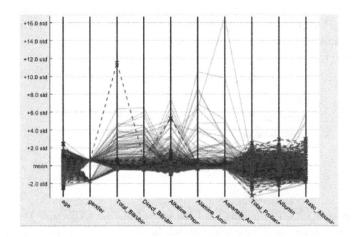

Fig. 5. Parallel coordinate plot Indian liver patient

Model 1.1
(0.30,0.63)
AUC = 0.66
ROC curve
Area under curve (AUC)
Current classifier
True positive rate
False positive rate
0
0.2
0.4
0.6
0.8
1

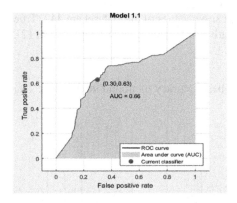

Fig. 6. ROC curve Indian liver patient dataset

Model 1.4
380
36
126
41
True class
Predicted class
1
2

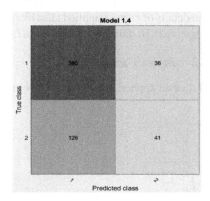

Fig. 7. Confusion matrix Indian liver patient dataset

ROC curve is a measure of usefulness of a test (Fig. 5, 6 and 7). This curve is showing that the range of data is between 0 and 1 and every other thing lies between this [16–18].

As confusion matrix has four components known as True Positive, False Positive, True Negative and False Negative. This confusion matrix shows that the Liver Patient Dataset has 380 TP, 36 TF, 126 FP, and 41 FN values. Out of all applied algorithms, logistic regression gives the best accuracy of 71% (Fig. 8).

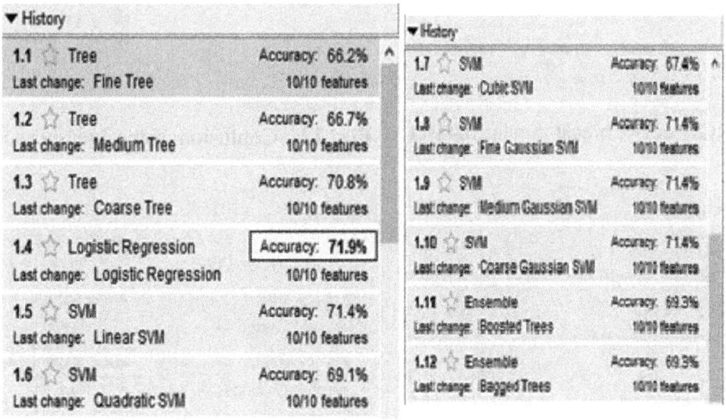

History
1.1 Tree Accuracy: 66.2%
Last change: Fine Tree 10/10 features
1.2 Tree Accuracy: 66.7%
Last change: Medium Tree 10/10 features
1.3 Tree Accuracy: 70.8%
Last change: Coarse Tree 10/10 features
1.4 Logistic Regression Accuracy: 71.9%
Last change: Logistic Regression 10/10 features
1.5 SVM Accuracy: 71.4%
Last change: Linear SVM 10/10 features
1.6 SVM Accuracy: 69.1%
Last change: Quadratic SVM 10/10 features
History
1.7 SVM Accuracy: 67.4%
Last change: Cubic SVM 10/10 features
1.8 SVM Accuracy: 71.4%
Last change: Fine Gaussian SVM 10/10 features
1.9 SVM Accuracy: 71.4%
Last change: Medium Gaussian SVM 10/10 features
1.10 SVM Accuracy: 71.4%
Last change: Coarse Gaussian SVM 10/10 features
1.11 Ensemble Accuracy: 69.3%
Last change: Boosted Trees 10/10 features
1.12 Ensemble Accuracy: 69.3%
Last change: Bagged Trees 10/10 features

Fig. 8. Algorithm results Indian liver patient dataset

This plot (Fig. 9 and 10) shows that all dimensions of the dataset are dependent upon each other.

All data dimensions lie between the range of 0 to 1 where the orange dot represents the details of current applied classifier. True positive values of this dataset are 442, True negative is 16, false positive is 4 and false negative is 237, respectively (Fig. 11 and 12).

4.2 Breast Cancer Dataset

Out of all applied algorithms, KNN gives the best accuracy of around 96.9% (Fig. 13).

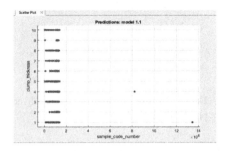

Fig. 9. Scattered plot breast cancer

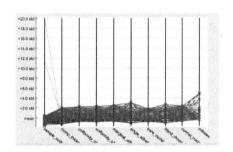

Fig. 10. Parallel coordinate plot breast cancer

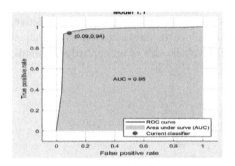

Fig. 11. ROC curve breast cancer dataset

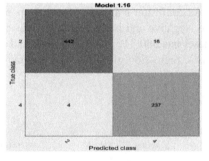

Fig. 12. Confusion matrix breast cancer dataset

▼ History		
1.1 ☆ Tree	Accuracy: 93.1%	
Last change: Complex Tree	10/10 features	
1.2 ☆ Tree	Accuracy: 93.1%	
Last change: Medium Tree	10/10 features	
1.3 ☆ Tree	Accuracy: 94.0%	
Last change: Simple Tree	10/10 features	
1.4 ☆ Linear Discriminant	Accuracy: 95.7%	
Last change: Linear Discriminant	10/10 features	
1.5 ☆ Quadratic Discriminant	Accuracy: 94.7%	
Last change: Quadratic Discriminant	10/10 features	
1.6 ☆ Logistic Regression	Accuracy: 95.7%	
Last change: Logistic Regression	10/10 features	
1.7 ☆ SVM	Accuracy: 96.1%	

▼ History		
Last change: Medium KNN	10/10 features	
1.15 ☆ KNN	Accuracy: 94.7%	
Last change: Coarse KNN	10/10 features	
1.16 ☆ KNN	Accuracy: 96.9%	
Last change: Cosine KNN	10/10 features	
1.17 ☆ KNN	Accuracy: 96.3%	
Last change: Cubic KNN	10/10 features	
1.18 ☆ KNN	Accuracy: 96.4%	
Last change: Weighted KNN	10/10 features	
1.19 ☆ Ensemble	Accuracy: 96.0%	
Last change: Boosted Trees	10/10 features	
1.20 ☆ Ensemble	Accuracy: 96.6%	
Last change: Bagged Trees	10/10 features	

Fig. 13. Result of applied algorithm breast cancer dataset

4.3   Wine Quality

This plot (Fig. 14 and 15) shows that all dimensions are dependent on each other but their correlation is very high so that they are scattered in each other.

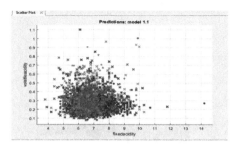

Fig. 14. Scattered plot wine quality dataset

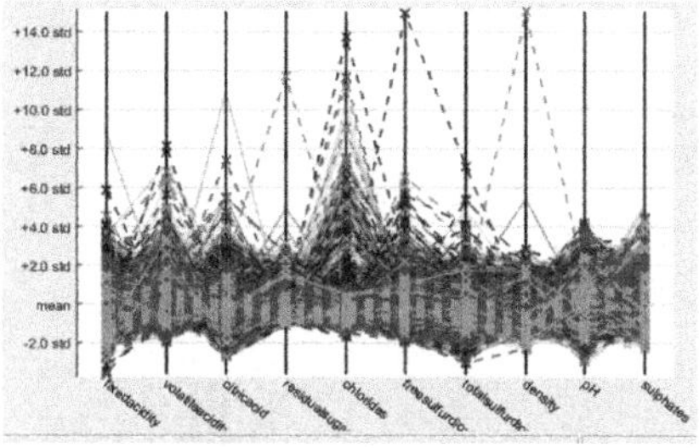

Fig. 15. Parallel   coordinate   plot   wine quality

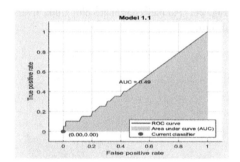

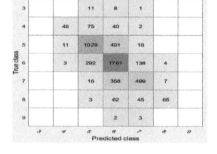

Fig. 16. ROC curve wine quality

Fig. 17. Confusion matrix wine quality

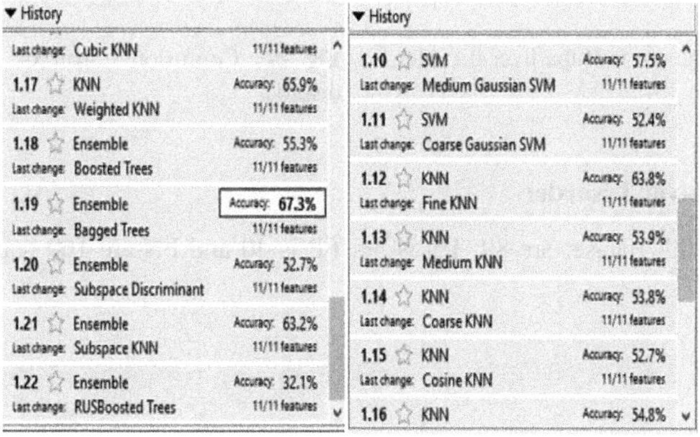

▼ History		▼ History	
Last change: Cubic KNN	11/11 features	1.10 ☆ SVM	Accuracy: 57.5%
1.17 ☆ KNN — Accuracy: 65.9%		Last change: Medium Gaussian SVM	11/11 features
Last change: Weighted KNN	11/11 features	1.11 ☆ SVM	Accuracy: 52.4%
1.18 ☆ Ensemble — Accuracy: 55.3%		Last change: Coarse Gaussian SVM	11/11 features
Last change: Boosted Trees	11/11 features	1.12 ☆ KNN	Accuracy: 63.8%
1.19 ☆ Ensemble — Accuracy: 67.3%		Last change: Fine KNN	11/11 features
Last change: Bagged Trees	11/11 features	1.13 ☆ KNN	Accuracy: 53.9%
1.20 ☆ Ensemble — Accuracy: 52.7%		Last change: Medium KNN	11/11 features
Last change: Subspace Discriminant	11/11 features	1.14 ☆ KNN	Accuracy: 53.8%
1.21 ☆ Ensemble — Accuracy: 63.2%		Last change: Coarse KNN	11/11 features
Last change: Subspace KNN	11/11 features	1.15 ☆ KNN	Accuracy: 52.7%
1.22 ☆ Ensemble — Accuracy: 32.1%		Last change: Cosine KNN	11/11 features
Last change: RUSBoosted Trees	11/11 features	1.16 ☆ KNN	Accuracy: 54.8%

Fig. 18. Result of applied algorithm wine quality dataset

Dimensions of this set also lie between 0 to 1.

As the label classes of this dataset are not binary that's why this confusion matrix is not in its general form. It has more than one TP, TN, FP, and FN classes (Fig. 16 and 17).

Out of all applied algorithms, the ensemble classifier gave its best accuracy at 67.3% (Fig. 18).

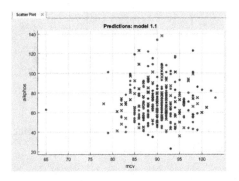

Fig. 19. Scattered plot Bupa liver disorder

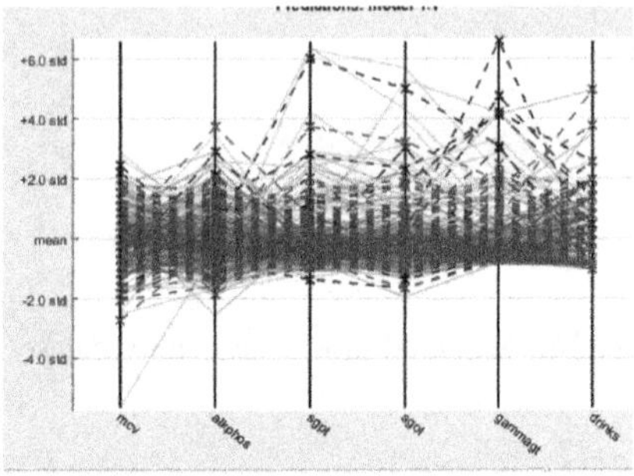

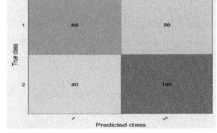

Fig. 20. Parallel coordinate plot Bupa liver disorder

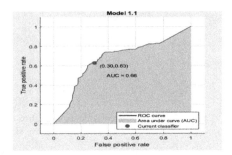

Fig. 21. ROC curve Bupa liver disorder

Fig. 22. Confusion matrix Bupa liver disorder

4.4 Bupa Liver Disorder

TP values of this dataset are 89, TN is 56, FP is 40 and FN are 160 respectively.

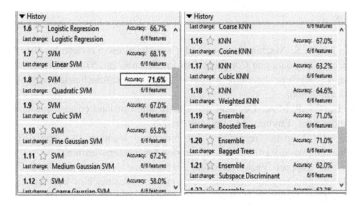

Fig. 23. Result of applied algorithm Bupa liver disorder

Out of all applied algorithms SVM gave its best accuracy at 71.6% (Fig. 19, 20, 21, 22 and 23 and Table 2).

Table 2. Best results given by algorithms on datasets:

Dataset	Best algorithm	Accuracy	Prediction speed	Training time	True positive rate for class 1 & class 2	False negative rate for class 1 & class 2	Positive prediction value for class 1 & class 2	False discovery rate for class 1 & class 2
Indian liver patient dataset	Logistic regression	72.2%	~4500 obs/sec	28.756 s	91%, 25%	9%, 75%	75%, 53%	25%, 47%
Breast cancer dataset	K Nearest Neighbor (KNN)	97.1%	~5100 obs/sec	17.239 s	97%, 98%	3%, 2%	99%, 94%	1%, 6%
Liver disorder	Quadratic SVM	72.2%	~1100 obs/sec	2.179 s	61%, 80%	39%, 20%	69%, 74%	31%, 26%
Wine quality	Bagged tree	69.3%	~7200 obs/sec	294.1 s	Class is not binary for this dataset			

5   Conclusion

In this paper, we analyzed the performance of 12 classifiers, all of them are described above. Performance factors such as classification accuracy and execution time are compared. From the experimental results, it is found that the different algorithms are best for different types of datasets. Like, from all algorithms logistic regression proved best for Indian liver patient dataset, KNN for Breast Cancer Dataset, Quadratic SVM for Liver Disorder and Bagged Tree for Wine Quality. In future various tests like KS, MAE, and RAE, etc. can be applied to these datasets for the sake of more accurate results.

References

1. Ahuja, S., Angra, S.: Machine learning and it's applications: a review. In: 2017 International Conference on Big data and Computational Intelligence, pp. 57–60 (2017)
2. Brownlee, J.: Machine Learning Mastery (2018). https://machinelearningmastery.com/k-fold-cross-validation/
3. Brodley, C., Friedl, M.A.: Decision tree classification of land cover from remotely sensed data. Remote Sens. Environ. **61**, 399–409 (1997)
4. Brownlee, J.: Logistic regression for machine learning, 1 April 2016. https://machinelearningmastery.com/logistic-regression-for-machine-learning/
5. Brownlee, J.: Support Vector machine for machine learning, 20 April 2016. https://machinelearningmastery.com/support-vector-machines-for-machine-learning/
6. Woods, K., Kegelmeyer, W.P., Bowyer, K.: Combination of multiple classifiers using local accuracy estimates. IEEE Trans. Pattern Anal. Mach. Intell. **19**, 405–410 (1997)
7. Lange, S., Zilles, S.: Formal models of incremental learning and their analysis. In: Proceedings of the International Joint Conference on Neural Networks, pp. 2691–2699 (2003)
8. Dhayanand, S., Vijayarani, S.: Liver disease prediction using SVM and Naive Bayes. Int. J. Sci. Eng. Technol. Res. (IJSETR) **4**(4), 816–820 (2015)
9. Borges, L.R.: Analysis of the wisconsin breast cancer dataset and machine learning for breast cancer detection. In: Proceedings of XI Workshop de Visão Computacional 2010, 05th–07th October 2015, pp. 15–19 (2015)
10. Cortez, P., Teixeira, J., Cerdeira, A., Almeida, F., Matos, T., Reis, J.: Using data mining for wine quality assessment. In: Gama, J., Costa, V.S., Jorge, A.M., Brazdil, P.B. (eds.) DS 2009. LNCS (LNAI), vol. 5808, pp. 66–79. Springer, Heidelberg (2009). https://doi.org/10.1007/978-3-642-04747-3_8
11. Olaniyi, E.O., Adnan, K.: Liver disease diagnosis based on neural networks, pp. 48–53 (2015)
12. Ahmed, F., et al.: Wireless mesh network IEEE 802.11 s. Int. J. Comput. Sci. Inf. Secur. **14**(12), 803–809 (2016)
13. Aslam, N., Sarwar, N., Batool, A.: Designing a model for improving CPU scheduling by using machine learning. Int. J. Comput. Sci. Inf. Secur. **14**(10), 201 (2016)
14. Bilal, M., Sarwar, N., Saeed, M.S.: A hybrid test case model for medium scale web based applications. In: 2016 Sixth International Conference on Innovative Computing Technology (INTECH), pp. 632–637 (2016)
15. Bajwa, I.S., Sarwar, N.: Automated generation of express-G models using NLP. Sindh Univ. Res. J.-SURJ (Sci. Ser.) **48**(1), 5–12 (2016)
16. Cheema, S.M., Sarwar, N., Yousaf, F.: Contrastive analysis of bubble & merge sort proposing hybrid approach. In: 2016 Sixth International Conference on Innovative Computing Technology (INTECH), pp. 371–375 (2016)
17. Sarwar, N., Latif, M.S., Aslam, N., Batool, A.: Automated object role model generation. Int. J. Comput. Sci. Inf. Secur. **14**(9), 301–308 (2016)
18. Ibrahim, M., Sarwar, N.: NoSQL database generation using SAT solver. In: 6th International Conference on Innovative Computing Technology, INTECH 2016, no. August 2016, pp. 627–631 (2016)

QoE Analysis of Real-Time Video Streaming over 4G-LTE for UAV-Based Surveillance Applications

Muhammad Naveed[1] and Sameer Qazi[2]

[1] College of Computing and Information Sciences (CoCIS),
PAF Karachi Institute of Economics and Technology Karachi,
Karachi, Pakistan
naveed@pafkiet.edu.pk
[2] College of Engineering (CoE), PAF Karachi Institute of Economics
and Technology Karachi, Karachi, Pakistan
sameer.qazi@pafkiet.edu.pk

Abstract. Drones also known as Unmanned Aerial Vehicles (UAVs) perform an significant role in surveillance at a remote location by streaming real-time video with their attached cameras. A good architecture for such kind of surveillance is required that ensures real-time monitoring at targeted areas. As the streaming video is used in monitoring; it is much important to ensure its quality during transmission so that remote client can view clear insights and could take prompt action on time if required. In this paper, we have proposed a 4G-LTE architecture and examined the effects of different factors in such architecture. We have shown the comparative analysis between two latest codec schemes i.e. H.264 and H.265 (HEVC) in video streaming. Our study is an important step towards exploring the factors that influence the real-time video streaming and degrade the Quality of Experience (QoE) of video viewing in such architecture. To examine the received video quality, two objective metrics, Peak-Signal-to-Noise-Ratio (PSNR) and Structural-Similarity-Index (SSIM) have been considered in this paper. The simulation results are based on the most famous Network simulator in the research community i.e. NS-3. The results have shown that H.265 works better in comparison with H.264 under different circumstances.

Keywords: 4G · LTE · H.264 · HEVC · Video streaming · Surveillance

1 Introduction

Surveillance has always been important to acquire security and safety for human beings; technology plays important role in this context. In modern times, UAV based video surveillance is very much popular and beneficial in prevention of

Supported by PAF-Karachi Institute of Economics and Technology Karachi.

© Springer Nature Singapore Pte Ltd. 2020
I. S. Bajwa et al. (Eds.): INTAP 2019, CCIS 1198, pp. 443–458, 2020.
https://doi.org/10.1007/978-981-15-5232-8_38

crime or any unwanted activity specially at remote site. Camera mounted UAVs not only decline the budget of surveillance but it also safe the human life as UAVs work in place of persons to achieve this objective. UAVs equipped with latest digital equipment are used to stream real-time video across the network in surveillance of monitored zone [16]. There are many surveillance systems proposed based on UAVs [22, 24, 27, 35, 41, 44, 45, 54]. As UAVs mobility supports in surveillance at remote side; there must be a cellular infrastructure that assist UAVs to flight at far distance; otherwise remote control UAVs fly within limited distance are not suitable in monitoring specially for surveillance purpose. For this reason, 4G-LTE networks are considered to be one of the best solution [19, 36, 43, 47]. In this paper, we propose an architecture suitable for 4G-LTE UAV based surveillance applications. This surveillance architecture is designed for monitoring targeted areas inside the buildings where stationary UAVs are responsible to capture the videos and outside the buildings in open space where mobile UAVs capture the videos of interested vantage points for surveillance. These captured video are streaming towards the respective base station of each UAV. From Base station, these videos are streamed to a single command-and-control center where all activities are monitor in real-time to take appropriate action if needed. We investigate different factors that effects the real-time video streaming which degrade the Quality of Experience (QoE) of video viewing in such an architecture. For instance as 4G-LTE supports only hard-handover (which means during flight, UAVs first break the connection from current attached base-station and then establish the connection with new base-station) which crashes the bandwidth suddenly [32], result in poor QoE of video-viewing. We took into consideration such facts and demonstrate their effects on quality of stream video. To examine the quality of video-viewing, we have calculated two objective metrics; the Peak Signal to Noise Ratio (PSNR) and Structural SIMilarity Index (SSIM) [8, 17, 52]. For real-time video streaming we have used two famous codecs i.e. H.264 and H.265. For simulation, we have selected NS-3 to simulate our work. Simulation results revealed how different factors effects the streaming video quality in such an architecture. Simulated results also prove that H.265 performs better than H.264 under different circumstances.

2   Related Work

Recent technology plays an important role in every aspect of life [31]. Surveillance is also a major concern of every modern society [30]. Instead of using fixed cameras for surveillance; it is a nice idea to use drones for this purpose. These drones are also known as Unmanned Aerial Vehicles (UAVs) [26]. These UAVs not only capture the Live video of different vantage points but also stream these captured video towards remote station to check all activities in monitoring zone with low operational cost in minimum span of setup time and effort [9, 39]. Such UAVs can easily fly in an open area and could be tuned-up during flight to capture the important events in monitoring zone [13, 21]. There are several UAV-based surveillance framework proposed to enrich this technology [7, 23, 49]. Two interested survey papers [11,37] for Flying Ad-hoc Networks (FANETs) educate about the fundamental operations of FANETS and their operational behavior in a specific environment. These survey papers also revealed the recent challenges in this technology and provide the solutions of major hurdles in communication among UAVs. Mustaqim et al. [38] evaluate the communication among UAVs during flight in their work. Researchers also examine the UAV to ground communication in FANETs by using antenna arrays. Qazi et al. [42] evaluate the performance of UAVs in different propagation models specially when these UAVs are flying in very low altitude in an surveillance architecture. In another paper Qazi et al. [43] proposed UAV-based framework for surveillance over 4G-LTE network using two tiered architecture by placing stationary UAVs inside the buildings and flying mobile UAVs outside the building. The UAVs transmitted the captured video at remote site in the surveillance framework. Researchers analyzed different factors that effect the streaming of video including losses in shadowing and fading models. Researchers also examine delay, throughput and multi-path propagation-loss over the proposed framework.

3   Surveillance Architecture

For the surveillance architecture, consider the Fig. 1. The basic concept of topology and all concerned terminologies are taken from 3GPP R4-092042 standard. The architecture we have designed have several buildings. There exists certain monitoring targets inside and outside the buildings. Some UAVs are placed inside the buildings are referred as homeUEs while some UAVs are outside the buildings in the air known as macroUEs. In our work, homeUEs are stationary while

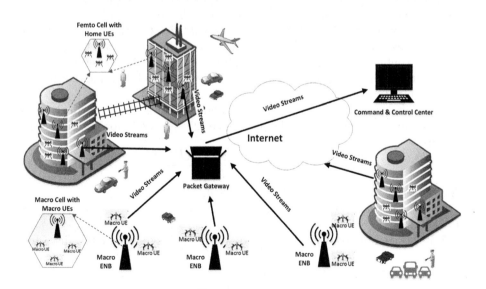

Fig. 1. Proposed surveillance architecture in an urban area

macroUEs are present outside the buildings, flying continuously in the air. Femto cells are inside while macro cells are outside the buildings. HomeUEs are located in femto cells while macroUEs are in macroCells in free space. All UAVs streams their video to their respective base stations. The base stations for homeUEs are known as homeENBs while for macroUEs are known as macroENBs. The base stations are responsible to receive video streams from UAVs and deliver real-time video to the single command and control center located at remote site via legacy internet connection. Such an surveillance architecture not only provide the real-time monitoring of targeted areas but also facilitate to prevent any mishap by taking appropriate action on time.

4   Measuring Metrics Used for QoE of Video

Image quality can be measured in several ways. There are two major categories for the schemes evaluating the image quality i.e. subjective and objective [10]. Subjective schemes are based on human judgment and operate without reference to explicit criteria [46]. Objective methods are based on comparisons using explicit numerical criteria [12,40] and several references are possible such as the ground truth or prior knowledge expressed in terms of statistical parameters and tests [15,33,48].

If we talking about PSNR, it is actually the ratio between extreme-signal's-power and noise-corrupting-power due to which the signal is modified. PSNR represented by means of logarithmic decibels as its bound fluctuates dynamically.

PSNR could be used for a rough approximation of comparative characteristics if types-of-distortions and video-contents remains the same, only the altitude of distortion is changed [50]. Though, dependent upon content of the video and corruption after reception, this is also a reality that the correlation between PSNR and subjective-quality could become very small [25]. For this reason, PSNR considered as an inconsistent approach for measuring the video QoE among dissimilar-contents of the video. Despite all these facts, PSNR is yet considered as a quality-metric. The complexity of PSNR is very low, which is another reason of its popularity [18].

PSNR is derived by applying the Mean-Square-Error (MSE) in relation to the maximum possible value of the luminance ($2^8 - 1 = 255$) for a typical 8 bit value as

$$MSE = \frac{\Sigma_{i=1}^{M} \Sigma_{j=1}^{N} [(f(i,j) - (F(i,j)]^2)}{M.N} \tag{1}$$

Where $f(i,j)$ is the original-signal at pixel (i,j),
$F(i,j)$ is the reconstructed-signal, and
$M.N$ is the picture-size.
MSE is the cumulative-squared-error between the original and the distorted videos.

$$PSNR = 20 \log_{10} \left[\frac{255}{\sqrt{MSE}} \right] \text{dB} \tag{2}$$

The resultant value is a specific digit expressed in decibels. The range of this digit is from 30 dB for medium video quality upto 40 dB for higher video QoE [29]. As depicted in (2), the PSNR and MSE are inversely-proportional to each-other. For the same video, a higher-quality video has a higher PSNR while lower MSE observed and vice-versa.

SSIM is another objective metric which is used to compute the commonality (similarity) between two video frames [29,51]. For measuring the similarity between two pictures, SSIM deals with two pictures in such a way that one picture is taken as error-free and the other picture as erroneous. The major deficit of PSNR is that it could not resolve the irregularities as perceived with human-eyes which is why SSIM has been recommended. SSIM is a quantify-metric between two windows having equal-length. The digit +1 represents the 100% similarity while −1 indicates the 0% similarity in frames.

For calculating the distorted-image quality, correlations in luminance, contrast, and structure are used in comparison locally between the reference and distorted images and averaging these quantities over the entire image. The theme of SSIM scheme is derived from the working of HVS [14]. To gauge the structural similarity between two signals let vector x and y is given below:

$$SSIM(x,y) = (\frac{2\mu_x\mu_y + C_1}{\mu_x^2 + \mu_y^2 + C_1})^\alpha (\frac{2\sigma_x\sigma_y + C_2}{\sigma_x^2 + \sigma_y^2 + C_2})^\beta (\frac{2\sigma_x y + C_3}{\sigma_x^2 + \sigma_y^2 + C_2})^\gamma \qquad (3)$$

where, $x = (x_i), i = 1, 2, 3.... N$

$y = (y_i), i = 1, 2, 3.... N$

$(\frac{2\mu_x\mu_y + C_1}{\mu_x^2 + \mu_y^2 + C_1})^\alpha$ matches the signal-luminance

$(\frac{2\sigma_x\sigma_y + C_2}{\sigma_x^2 + \sigma_y^2 + C_2})^\beta$ matches the signal-contrast

$(\frac{2\sigma_x y + C_3}{\sigma_x^2 + \sigma_y^2 + C_2})^\gamma$ measures the structural-correlation of signal. $\mu_x\mu_y$ are the sample means of x and y respectively,

$\sigma_x\sigma_y$ are the sample standard deviations of x and y respectively,

$\sigma_x y$ indicates the cross co-variance between x and y,

C_1, C_2, C_3 are the constants that are used to stabilize the metric, $\alpha > 0, \beta > 0, \gamma > 0$ are the parameters that are used to adjust the relative importance of the three components.

As α, β, γ should always be greater than one, hence the product should be one, which explains the condition given below

$$(\frac{2\mu_x\mu_y + C_1}{\mu_x^2 + \mu_y^2 + C_1})^\alpha + (\frac{2\sigma_x\sigma_y + C_2}{\sigma_x^2 + \sigma_y^2 + C_2})^\beta + (\frac{2\sigma_{xy} + C_3}{\sigma_x^2 + \sigma_y^2 + C_2})^\gamma = 1 \qquad (4)$$

To obtain the above condition;

$\mu_x = \mu_y \rightarrow$ The mean of two videos must equal

$\sigma_x = \sigma_y = \sigma_{xy} \rightarrow$ The standard deviations of both the videos and their cross covariance must be the same.

A video with extreme bad quality has −1 SSIM value. Such a video represents a strong-negative-correlation and hence a strong-deviation between the frame(s)-of-interest and the original-frame(s).

5   Simulation Settings for Streaming Video

We have captured real video from drone of different events in Intellect 2017, first international conference held on 15–16 Nov 2017 at Pakistan Air Force, Karachi Institute of Economics & Technology (PAFKIET) in Karachi. The captured video converted both into H.264 and H.265 with MP4 format. For the conversion of video in different encoding we have used FFmpeg [2] which offer strong utilities for video conversion even for real-time video-streaming [28].

All the simulation in this work are performed over *Network Simulator-3* commonly known as *NS-3*. *NS-3* is the most popular and trustworthy network simulator among research community. It is mainly designed for research purpose specially to simulate the operations over latest advanced networks. To simulate 4G-LTE in our work, we have used *lena-dual-stripe* package of *NS-3* in the simulation. The simulation parameters set shown in Table 1. For the communication between client/server over 4G-LTE network, we have used *Evalvid*. *Evalvid* is an application developed by GERCOM group [3] which is mainly designed to simulate video-streaming for client/server communication over the network. This application facilitates how user observed video quality on the reception of streaming-video. *Evalvid* uses the trace video file for streaming in the simulation that is derived from *MP4* encoded video. In the original *Evalvid* application Random Waypoint mobility model is applied to simulate the flight pattern of UAVs. In this work, we have changed the mobility model. We have selected Gauss-Markov mobility model which is more realistic flight pattern. The second modification we have applied is to change the streaming direction of video. In the original *Evalvid* application, the video is transmitted from client to the server while in our work, we modify it and the video is streamed from server (which is actually UAV) to remote client (which is static, we refer it as command and control center). All the communications over *Evalvid* application are UDP based. We also preferred UDP for our work as it is suitable protocol for real-time video streaming. For the examination of PSNR and SSIM of streaming video, we go along with the guidelines available at [5] using *Evalvid* binaries required that could be found at [1].

As video captured by UAVs are in uncompressed format hence these are huge videos and take a lot of time to transmit over the network. For this purpose, a good encoding scheme is required that compress the small chunks of captured video before transmission in very short span of time. Now-a-days, for fast and reliable encoding, H.264 is preferred most. H.264 also referred as MPEG AVC is a general-purpose encoding scheme specially designed for mobile low bitrate video applications to high definition video transmission of television. H.264 not only covers the vast range of application but also offers remarkable enhancement in the efficiency of compression has made it the most demanding codec in the industry.

High Efficiency Video Coding (HEVC), also known as H.265 and MPEG-H Part 2, is a video compression standard, designed as a successor to the widely used AVC (H.264 or MPEG-4 Part 10). HEVC provides better compression in comparison with other encoding schemes. It improves the video compression from 25 to 50% for the video with same level of quality at the same bit-rate in comparison with AVC. In comparison with H.264, HEVC or H.265 has low complexity and it is more hardware friendly even in ad-hoc networks [20]. HEVC also provide low delay configuration specially for [53] architecture.

In this study, we compare every instance of result both from H.264 and H.265 video codecs. The objective metrics PSNR and SSIM shows HEVC is much better than H.264. The only drawback is that HEVC taking more encoding time as compare with H.264 [34]. For this reason, high configuration UAVs are required in the surveillance that can faster the encoding process.

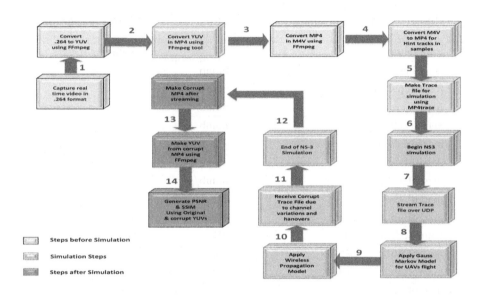

Fig. 2. Complete simulation platform

The complete simulation platform is shown in Fig. 2. The step by step process sequencing from 1 to 14 with directed arrows shows the practical approach for this work. The steps before simulation are labeled with 1 to 5, in which the camera-mounted-UAV captures the video of interested area in the monitored-zone. The captured video used in the simulation in H.264 and H.265 codecs. This captured video then transforms into a YUV-sequence, afterwards in MP4, then in M4V and then finally again to MP4. This MP4 contains the hint-tracks in video samples by using *MP4Box* which is used to insert hint-tracks [4]. *mp4trace* is a tool offered by *EVALVID* which is used to generate trace-file from the hinted MP4 file that transmits over UDP in the networks. Steps during the simulation are labeled from 6 to 11. In the simulation steps, the flying UAVs transmit the captured real-time video towards a static remote client. For wireless medium, a wireless-propagation-model is applied to emulate the wireless-infrastructure.

To mimic the realistic flight pattern of UAVs, we apply Gauss Markov mobility model in the simulation. Corrupt trace file received by the remote client because of frequent handovers and channel variations. Steps after simulation are labeled from 12 to 14 in which the first step is the rebuilding of the streamed video as it is seen by the receiver. To acquire this goal, at the receiver-end, the MP4 and trace files were processed by the *etmp4* tool. This tool produces a possibly corrupt-video file in which the lost-frames are deleted afterwards this corrupted-video then decodes into the YUV-sequence. Finally, the binary file *psnr* offered by *EVALVID* is used to compute the PSNR and SSIM from original and corrupt YUVs which indicates the difference between in original video and the corrupt video.

Table 1. Parameters in simulation adopted from 3GPP R4-092042 specification

Parameter		Values
Buildings	numb	4
Rooms per building	numb	4
Floors	numb	4
Femto cells/building	numb	2–8
macroEnbSites	numb	1–4
Area Margin Factor	numb	0.5
macroUE Density	numb/sq m	0.00002
macroUEs	numb	Upto 20
macroEnb Tx Power	dBm	46
homeENB Tx power	dBm	20
macroEnb DLEARFCN	numb	100
macroEnb ULEARFCN	numb	18100
macroEnb Bandwidth	Resource Blocks	100
homeEnb Bandwidth	Resource Blocks	100
Bearers per UE	numb	1
SRS Periodicity	ms	80
Scheduler	–	Proportional Fair
homeENB deployment ratio	numb	0.2
homeENB activation ratio	numb	0.5
homeUEs to homeENB ratio	numb	1
Line of Sight to Non-Line of Sight ratio	threshold	50

6   Performance Evaluation

We have performed four experiments to analyze the effect of different factors on QoE of video streaming across the network by measuring two objective metrics

PSNR and SSIM. These experiments are based on varying Line of Sight to Non-Line of Sight threshold (LoS2NLoS), varying macroENB sites, varying homeUEs per homeENB ratio and varying internal wall-loss.

Effect of Varying LoS2NLoS Threshold. To consider the impact of Line-of-Sight to Non-Line-of-Sight threshold, we vary it from 200 m towards gradually increasing upto 300 m as shown in Fig. 3 and Fig. 4. Both PSNR and SSIM are showing the rising trend in the graphs and it seems to be obvious as there is no such hurdles or obstacles found within Line-of-Sight range; the minimum losses observed here and hence higher PSNR and SSIM are represented by graphs. For this experiment we have taken all the parameters as mentioned in Table 1 except LoS2NLoS values which are increasing gradually to analyze LoS2NLoS impact over QoE of video.

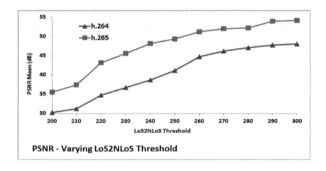

Fig. 3. Effect of LoS2NLoS threshold on PSNR

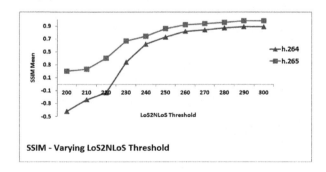

Fig. 4. Effect of LoS2NLoS threshold on SSIM

Table 2. Internal Wall Loss of different materials [6]

Used material	Material thickness (mm)	Internal Wall Loss (dB)
Glass	13	2
Lumber	76	2.8
Brick	267	7
Reinforced concrete	89	27

Effect of Internal Wall Loss of Different Materials. To examine the impact of Internal Wall Loss, we have selected different materials in simulation settings. These material are shown in Table 2 that shows thickness and wall loss of each mentioned material. As the thickness of wall increases because of different type of material, the QoE of video decline that can seen in the Fig. 5 and Fig. 6. The decreasing trend in graph showing lower PSNR and SSIM because of attenuation caused by different materials. Hence it is the fact that the material of the constructed building also effects the QoE of video viewing over the surveillance architecture.

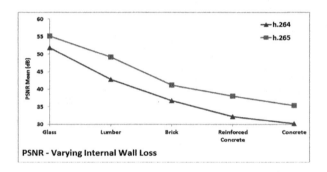

Fig. 5. Effect of internal Wall loss on PSNR

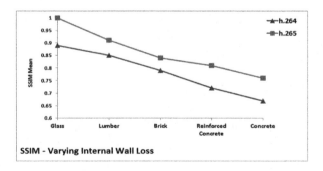

Fig. 6. Effect of internal Wall loss on SSIM

Effect of Varying macroENB Sites. To measure the impact of varying macroENB sites in the surveillance architecture; we increase the number of macroENB sites from 1 to 7. As the number of macroENB sites increases, the QoE of video decreases as depicted by PSNR and SSIM in the Fig. 7 and Fig. 8 respectively. This decline is because of frequent handovers. As we are increasing the number of macroENB sites in limited distance of 500 m, the frequency of handover increases. As 4G-LTE only support hard handover [32], the bandwidth suddenly crashes over each handover, as the result QoE of video degrades; which is why the PSNR and SSIM are showing decline in the graphs.

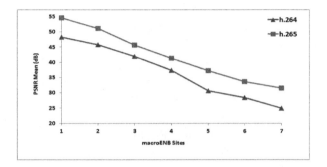

Fig. 7. Effect of macroENB sites on PSNR

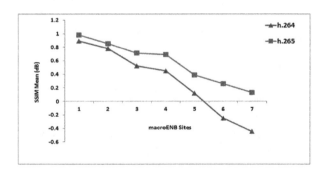

Fig. 8. Effect of macroENB sites on SSIM

Effect of Varying homeUEs per homeENBs Ratio. In this experiment, we allocate homeUEs in random rooms of the buildings. The motive of this placement is to capture different events in different locations of the buildings. The size of such kind of UAVs are very small that nobody could easily recognized these UAVs. We increase the homeUEs to homeENBs ratio gradually from 0.5 to 4 with stepping 0.5. By increasing this ratio we observe decline in QoE of video as depicted in Fig. 9 and Fig. 10. This decreasing trend in PSNR and SSIM in the graphs is because of increasing the burden of homeUEs over homeENBs. This is also the fact that if the burden of homeUEs over homeENBs increases, there are less chances of homeENBs and homeUEs to be in close proximity with each other inside the building. Hence this will introduce higher propagation loss and hence lowers the QoE of streaming video. Therefore, it is suggested to adjust optimal ratio among homeUEs over homeENBs, otherwise poor QoE of video viewing is expected which is of-course not affordable in an surveillance architecture.

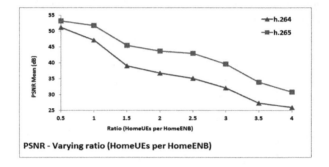

Fig. 9. Effect of HomeUEs/HomeENBs on PSNR

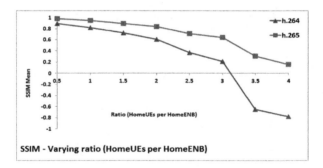

Fig. 10. Effect of HomeUEs/HomeENBs on SSIM

7 Conclusion

In this paper, we proposed an UAV-based surveillance architecture over 4G-LTE network. We have tried to maximize the QoE of video viewing over such an architecture. To examine the QoE of video viewing, we have used two objective metrics i.e. PSNR and SSIM. We consider the impacts of different factors by examine PSNR and SSIM of such an architecture that is helpful in analysis of QoE of streaming video. This study is helpful to evaluate the performance of video streaming over UAV-based surveillance architecture. We have selected NS-3 simulator for all simulations in this work. We have performed several experiments to explore the effects of different factors on the QoE of streaming video over UAV-based surveillance architecture. The experimental results provide useful analysis that could be used to upgrade the QoE of video-monitoring. Two encoding schemes H.264 and H.265 (HEVC) are used for video streaming. The comparative analysis proves that H.265 performs better than H.264 in different scenarios. The only requirement is high configuration UAVs that can compute fastly the complex computation of H.265 scheme to minimize encoding delay.

References

1. EvalVid Binaries for Calculation of PSNR and SSIM. http://www2.tkn.tu-berlin.de/research/evalvid/fw.html
2. FFmpeg. https://ffmpeg.org/
3. GERCOM. http://www.gercom.ufpa.br
4. MP4Box. https://gpac.wp.imt.fr/mp4box/
5. PSNR and SSIM Computation. http://totalgeekout.blogspot.com/2013/04/evalvid-on-ns-3-on-ubuntu-1204.html
6. DIGI Application Note, June 2012. http://ftp1.digi.com/support/images/XST-AN005a-IndoorPathLoss.pdf
7. Alsmirat, M.A., Jararweh, Y., Obaidat, I., Gupta, B.B.: Automated wireless video surveillance: an evaluation framework. J. Real-Time Image Process. **13**(3), 527–546 (2017). https://doi.org/10.1007/s11554-016-0631-x
8. Amirpour, H., Pinheiro, A.M., Pereira, M., Ghanbari, M.: Reliability of the most common objective metrics for light field quality assessment. In: ICASSP 2019–2019 IEEE International Conference on Acoustics, Speech and Signal Processing (ICASSP), pp. 2402–2406. IEEE (2019)
9. Angelov, P., Sadeghi-Tehran, P., Clarke, C.: AURORA: autonomous real-time on-board video analytics. Neural Comput. Appl. **28**(5), 855–865 (2017). https://doi.org/10.1007/s00521-016-2315-7
10. Avcibaş, I., Sankur, B., Sayood, K.: Statistical evaluation of image quality measures. J. Electron. Imaging **11**(2), 206–223 (2002)
11. Bekmezci, I., Sahingoz, O.K., Temel, Ş.: Flying ad-hoc networks (FANETs): a survey. Ad Hoc Netw. **11**(3), 1254–1270 (2013)
12. Cadik, M., Slavik, P.: Evaluation of two principal approaches to objective image quality assessment. In: Proceedings of the Eighth International Conference on Information Visualisation, IV 2004, pp. 513–518. IEEE (2004)
13. Challita, U., Ferdowsi, A., Chen, M., Saad, W.: Artificial intelligence for wireless connectivity and security of cellular-connected UAVs. arXiv preprint arXiv:1804.05348 (2018)
14. Channappayya, S.S., Bovik, A.C., Heath, R.W.: A linear estimator optimized for the structural similarity index and its application to image denoising, October 2006
15. Dosselmann, R., Yang, X.D.: Existing and emerging image quality metrics. In: Canadian Conference on Electrical and Computer Engineering, pp. 1906–1913. IEEE (2005)
16. Hamida, A.B., Koubaa, M., Nicolas, H., Amar, C.B.: Video surveillance system based on a scalable application-oriented architecture. Multimed. Tools Appl. **75**(24), 17187–17213 (2016). https://doi.org/10.1007/s11042-015-2987-5
17. Hore, A., Ziou, D.: Image quality metrics: PSNR vs. SSIM. In: 2010 20th International Conference on Pattern Recognition, pp. 2366–2369. IEEE (2010)

18. Huynh-Thu, Q., Ghanbari, M.: Scope of validity of PSNR in image/video quality assessment. Electron. Lett. **44**(13), 800 (2008)

19. Ivancic, W.D., Kerczewski, R.J., Murawski, R.W., Matheou, K., Downey, A.N.: Flying drones beyond visual line of sight using 4G LTE: issues and concerns. In: 2019 Integrated Communications, Navigation and Surveillance Conference (ICNS), pp. 1–13. IEEE (2019)

20. Jiang, X., Feng, J., Song, T., Katayama, T.: Low-complexity and hardware-friendly H.265/HEVC encoder for vehicular ad-hoc networks. Sensors **19**(8), 1927 (2019)

21. Jung, J., Yoo, S., La, W., Lee, D., Bae, M., Kim, H.: AVSS: airborne video surveillance system. Sensors **18**(6), 1939 (2018)

22. Jung, S., Jo, Y., Kim, Y.J.: Aerial surveillance with low-altitude long-endurance tethered multirotor UAVs using photovoltaic power management system. Energies **12**(7), 1323 (2019)

23. Karaki, H.S.A., Alomari, S.A., Refai, M.H.: A comprehensive survey of the vehicle motion detection and tracking methods for aerial surveillance videos. IJCSNS **19**(1), 93 (2019)

24. Kim, H., Ben-Othman, J.: A collision-free surveillance system using smart UAVs in multi domain IoT. IEEE Commun. Lett. **22**(12), 2587–2590 (2018)

25. Korhonen, J., You, J.: Improving objective video quality assessment with content analysis. In: Proceedings of the International Workshop on Video Processing and Quality Metrics for Consumer Electronics, pp. 1–6 (2010)

26. Kwak, J., Park, J.H., Sung, Y.: Emerging ICT UAV applications and services: design of surveillance UAVs. Int. J. Commun. Syst. e4023 (2019)

27. Lee, S., et al.: Design and development of a DDDAMS-based border surveillance system via UVs and hybrid simulations. Expert Syst. Appl. **128**, 109–123 (2019)

28. Lei, X., Jiang, X., Wang, C.: Design and implementation of a real-time video stream analysis system based on FFmpeg. In: 2013 Fourth World Congress on Software Engineering, pp. 212–216. IEEE (2013)

29. Li, S., Ngan, K.N.: Influence of the smooth region on the structural similarity index. In: Muneesawang, P., Wu, F., Kumazawa, I., Roeksabutr, A., Liao, M., Tang, X. (eds.) PCM 2009. LNCS, vol. 5879, pp. 836–846. Springer, Heidelberg (2009). https://doi.org/10.1007/978-3-642-10467-1_74

30. Lyon, D.: The Electronic Eye: The Rise of Surveillance Society. University of Minnesota Press, Minneapolis (1994)

31. MacKenzie, D., Wajcman, J.: The Social Shaping of Technology. Open University Press, London (1999)

32. Marwat, S.N.K., Meyer, S., Weerawardane, T., Goerg, C.: Congestion-aware handover in LTE systems for load balancing in transport network. ETRI J. **36**(5), 761–771 (2014)

33. Medda, A., DeBrunner, V.: Color image quality index based on the UIQI. In: 2006 IEEE Southwest Symposium on Image Analysis and Interpretation, pp. 213–217. IEEE (2006)

34. Mengzhe, L., Xiuhua, J., Xiaohua, L.: Analysis of H.265/HEVC, H.264 and VP9 coding efficiency based on video content complexity. In: 2015 IEEE International Conference on Computer and Communications (ICCC), pp. 420–424. IEEE (2015)

35. Motlagh, N.H., Bagaa, M., Taleb, T.: UAV-based IoT platform: a crowd surveillance use case. IEEE Commun. Mag. **55**(2), 128–134 (2017)

36. Motlagh, N.H., Bagaa, M., Taleb, T., Song, J.: Connection steering mechanism between mobile networks for reliable UAV's IoT platform. In: 2017 IEEE International Conference on Communications (ICC), pp. 1–6. IEEE (2017)

37. Mukherjee, A., Keshary, V., Pandya, K., Dey, N., Satapathy, S.C.: Flying ad hoc networks: a comprehensive survey. In: Satapathy, S.C., Tavares, J.M.R.S., Bhateja, V., Mohanty, J.R. (eds.) Information and Decision Sciences. AISC, vol. 701, pp. 569–580. Springer, Singapore (2018). https://doi.org/10.1007/978-981-10-7563-6_59

38. Mustaqim, M., Khawaja, B.A., Razzaqi, A.A., Zaidi, S.S.H., Jawed, S.A., Qazi, S.H.: Wideband and high gain antenna arrays for UAV-to-UAV and UAV-to-ground communication in flying ad-hoc networks (FANETs). Microwave Opt. Technol. Lett. **60**(5), 1164–1170 (2018)

39. Najiya, K., Archana, M.: UAV video processing for traffic surveillence with enhanced vehicle detection. In: 2018 Second International Conference on Inventive Communication and Computational Technologies (ICICCT), pp. 662–668. IEEE (2018)

40. Nguyen, T.B., Ziou, D.: Contextual and non-contextual performance evaluation of edge detectors. Pattern Recogn. Lett. **21**(9), 805–816 (2000)

41. Park, J.H., Choi, S.C., Ahn, I.Y., Kim, J.: Multiple UAVs-based surveillance and reconnaissance system utilizing IoT platform. In: 2019 International Conference on Electronics, Information, and Communication (ICEIC), pp. 1–3. IEEE (2019)

42. Qazi, S., Alvi, A., Qureshi, A.M., Khawaja, B.A., Mustaqim, M.: An architecture for real time monitoring aerial adhoc network. In: 2015 13th International Conference on Frontiers of Information Technology (FIT), pp. 154–159. IEEE (2015)

43. Qazi, S., Siddiqui, A.S., Wagan, A.I.: UAV based real time video surveillance over 4G LTE. In: 2015 International Conference on Open Source Systems & Technologies (ICOSST), pp. 141–145. IEEE (2015)

44. Sarkar, S., Totaro, M.W., Elgazzar, K.: Intelligent drone-based surveillance: application to parking lot monitoring and detection. In: Unmanned Systems Technology XXI, vol. 11021, p. 1102104. International Society for Optics and Photonics (2019)

45. Semsch, E., Jakob, M., Pavlicek, D., Pechoucek, M.: Autonomous UAV surveillance in complex urban environments. In: Proceedings of the 2009 IEEE/WIC/ACM International Joint Conference on Web Intelligence and Intelligent Agent Technology-Volume 02, pp. 82–85. IEEE Computer Society (2009)

46. Seshadrinathan, K., Soundararajan, R., Bovik, A.C., Cormack, L.K.: Study of subjective and objective quality assessment of video. IEEE Trans. Image Process. **19**(6), 1427–1441 (2010)

47. Sharma, V., Song, F., You, I., Chao, H.C.: Efficient management and fast handovers in software defined wireless networks using UAVs. IEEE Netw. **31**(6), 78–85 (2017)

48. Sheikh, H.R., Bovik, A.C., De Veciana, G.: An information fidelity criterion for image quality assessment using natural scene statistics. IEEE Trans. Image Process. **14**(12), 2117–2128 (2005)

49. Shin, S.Y., et al.: UAV based search and rescue with honeybee flight behavior in forest. In: Proceedings of the 5th International Conference on Mechatronics and Robotics Engineering, pp. 182–187. ACM (2019)

50. Vijaykumar, M., Rao, S.: A cross-layer frame work for adaptive video streaming over wireless networks, September 2010

51. Wang, Z., Bovik, A.C., Sheikh, H.R., Simoncelli, E.P., et al.: Image quality assessment: from error visibility to structural similarity. IEEE Trans. Image Process. **13**(4), 600–612 (2004)

52. Yan, B., Bare, B., Ma, C., Li, K., Tan, W.: Deep objective quality assessment driven single image super-resolution. IEEE Trans. Multimed. **21**, 2957–2971 (2019)

53. Yang, K., Gong, Y., Ma, M., Wu, H.R.: An efficient rate-distortion optimization method for low-delay configuration in H.265/HEVC based on temporal layer rate and distortion dependency. IEEE Trans. Circuits Syst. Video Technol. **29**, 1230–1236 (2019)
54. Yang, T., Li, Z., Zhang, F., Xie, B., Li, J., Liu, L.: Panoramic UAV surveillance and recycling system based on structure-free camera array. IEEE Access **7**, 25763–25778 (2019)

Natural Language Processing

Urdu Natural Language Processing Issues and Challenges: A Review Study

Usman Khan[1](✉), Maaz Bin Ahmad[1], Farhan Shafiq[2],
and Muhammad Sarim[2]

[1] CoCIS, PAF-KIET, Karachi, Pakistan
usman@pafkiet.edu.pk
[2] Department of Computer Science, FUUAST, Karachi, Pakistan

Abstract. Natural language processing is the technology used to aid computers to understand the human's natural language. However this is not an easy task to teach a machine to understand how humans communicate. This paper provides a summary of information about some speech recognition techniques that are in the literature for new scholars to look into. It also discusses related work along with efficiency comparison for different natural languages. After that, a brief summary of Urdu language and related work done in Urdu language processing issues and challenges is presented. In the last part, future work is proposed for efficient processing of Urdu language along with some useful techniques.

Keywords: Language · Processing · Urdu · Challenges · Review

1 Introduction

Automatic speech recognition (ASR) is basically a well-known issue to be executed by a computer system. Speech production is an interesting process which is attracting a number of researchers especially in the last few decades. Therefore, a number of research and studies have been introduced and several methods and approaches have been conducted in recent years. It all started with Graham Bell when he converted sound waves into electrical impulses, after this speech recognition system was developed by an electric circuit for recognizing phone quality of 10 digits. The receive sound were plot to analyze on x-y axis. Be that as it may, as this is late advancement, the distributed substance in these dialects is still constrained and far falls behind the substance accessible for English, Bengali and some different dialects talked in different nations. More than seven thousands are the languages spoken around the world in which English is the most used one. That's why English language is the most used in this field of research and development [1]. Urdu is spoken all around the Pakistan and also the popular dialects of India have up to 60 million speakers and around 100 million total speakers belonging to 20 nations. Urdu is composed in Nastaliq composing format taking into account Perso-Arabic script. [2] Automatic NLP (Natural Language Processing) has been a advanced area of study in European, English and east Asian languages. [3] Over the last several years, researchers have done so much work for automatic parts of speech tagging in several languages but this study is mainly confined to the Urdu language.

© Springer Nature Singapore Pte Ltd. 2020
I. S. Bajwa et al. (Eds.): INTAP 2019, CCIS 1198, pp. 461–470, 2020.
https://doi.org/10.1007/978-981-15-5232-8_39

2   Approaches in Speech Recognition

There are many different techniques used in Natural Language Processing for speech recognition.

2.1   Acoustic Phonetic Approach

Hughes and Hemdal picked the basic of discovering speech signals and labeling them. They also discussed the existing predetermined total number of individual phonetic sound unit in natural language which is widely differentiate by a group of acoustics real properties changing with respect to time in speech signal. This approach says that the message bearing parts of speech should be classify explicitly with the verification of binary acoustic properties such as, frication, nasality and continuous abilities, ratio of low and high frequencies. However, in case of commercial applications, this approach hasn't showed feasible results. This approach was applied in series of Segmentation and Labeling, Features detection, Spectral analysis [4].

2.2   Pattern Recognition Approach

This approach was first carried out by Itakura and Rabiner and Juang, which showed remarkable support for its acceptance by researchers. This research proved to be the steppingstone for speech recognition in the last 6 decades. The two main pillars of this approach are pattern recognition and pattern training. Importance of Pattern Recognition approach is basically to proper formulate mathematical structure and using that it manages to reliable signal pattern of speech for consistent pattern matching from a group of labeled data [5] e.g. formal training algorithm. Speech pattern depiction usually accepts a speech pattern or a statistical formula that is generally valid to a sound.

2.3   Template Based Approach

The storage of group of ideal speech patterns as position patterns which shows the dictionary of candidate words as version. An unknown spoken speech sound is matched with each of these references of full scale and to select the best matching pattern. In general, it constructs a template for each word. The advantage it provides is that the errors are avoided that are generated because of division or categorization of lesser acoustically greater variable units just like phonemes. According to results, it is necessary that every entry must have its own full reference template.

2.4   Stochastic Approach

Those approaches that makes use of probabilistic models so that incomplete information like confusable sounds, effects and homophones, speaker contextual variability etc. can be dealt with. When we compared stochastic approach with template based approach, HMM modeling is more common and possesses firmer mathematical organization [6].

2.5   Knowledge Based Approach

Knowledge focuses on the mechanization of speech recognition processes in accordance to the way a person applies knowledge in analyzing, characterizing, visualizing and speech based on a group of calculated acoustic capacity. Knowledge based KB approach is considered mixture of pattern recognition approach and acoustic phonetic approach. They need to explore extensive insight into human speech processing by both the template based and approach failed eventually. The loss of both the approaches resulted in generation of knowledge based and error analysis system improvement couldn't get power. Whereas, in traditional knowledge based approach and the rules related to production are created heuristically from observation linguistic knowledge or from the observations from the speech spectrogram [7].

3   Some Relevant Work in Different Natural Languages

Speech is the most fundamental form of human communication. In speech recognition system, a speaker speaks via some source and the computer receives and understands which actually means computer surely tries to convert the speech into a text form [8] Analog signal of voice reorganization rate is more in English. There are many researchers working on different languages around the world. In this paper, we have studied some more popular languages other than English [9].

3.1   Bengali Speech Recognition

We have tried to discuss some of the Bengali STT conversion approaches. The classification was place according to the research topic, approach used in feature extraction and signal analysis approach used in the research. First category is Phonemes in which Hossain et al. [10] basically gives a proper comparison of classification of phones of English and Bengali language based on the formation of phoneme. While Karim et al. specifically focused on Bengali vowels and spoken letters. They experimentally showed recognition of spoken letter; their efficiency rate is 80% [9] Barman gives analysis of the Bengali with English phonemic with reference to similarity measure. [11] There is a limitation for their study because their work is only applicable on phonemic features. In [12], there is a study for comparison of Bengali and English phonemes specifically for the Vowels. Hassan et al. [13] developed Bengali speech recognition system based on phoneme recognizer. Linear Prediction Coding (LPC) by Ali et al. [14] suggested a Bengali recognition system for words which uses Linear Predictive Coding for Bengali speech. They also compared their model graphically showing recognition rate vs. time. Their experiment have accuracy rate of 84% for 100 Bengali words. Mel Frequency Cepstral Coefficient (MFCC) by Rehman et al. [15]

discussed different signal investigation for comparison. This system have 96% accuracy rate when dealing with one speaker and up to 84.24% when there are more than 1 one speakers. Hidden Markov Model (HMM) by Hasnat et al. [16] used Hidden Markov Model for feature extraction and categorization. They also used the static model for some part in scheme for speech to text for Bengali language. Speech Segmentation by Rahman et al. [17] developed a system started with recording the voice signal and classified the continuous signal into distinctively meaningful units. They made a database of 758 words segmentation from 120 sentences. Their accuracy rate is more than 94%. When dealing with acoustical features; more focus was on vowels comparison with consonants. In [13, 15] they used acoustic properties for classification of vowels and consonants.

3.2   Turkish Speech Recognition Approaches

Turkish is one of the orthographically apparent languages [18]. Burcucan et al. [19] presented a system for Speech recognition system for Turkish language. The approach is syllabus-based, where the detection is done by syllabus as speech recognition units. They get an accuracy rate of 65.6% for a large number of vocabularies. While for syllabus boundary algorithm, their accuracy is 44%. Palaz et al. [20] used HMM in the development of TREN- Turkish Speech Recognition Platform. TREN has a high accuracy rate as compared to other Turkish engine. In [21], Ozgul et al. has developed text and audio corpora for Turkish speech recognition tools. The error rate was 29.3% for phoneme recognition.

3.3   Arabic Speech Recognition Approaches

The Arabic language has a standard pronunciation, which basically is the one used to recite the Qur'an. Ettaoui et al. [18] proposed "A hybrid combination of ANN/HMM models for Arabic digit recognition using optimal codebook." In this paper they propose an Arabic numbers recognition system based on hybrid combination of Artificial Neural Network and Hidden Markov Model (ANN/HMM). Their numerical results were more than their expectation and satisfaction. Kuo et al. [22] uses minimum bayes risk discriminative language model for Arabic speech recognition. They found that their DLM is generalized to different conditions. Alotaibi et al. [23] have described how we can use cross language acoustic model for Arabic language. While, A mixture of Artificial Neural Network and Hidden Markov models for Arabic speech recognition with the help of optimal codebook is discussed in [18] by Ettaouil et al. In another study [24], Arabic corpus "NEMLAR" was used to convert Arabic news by different broadcaster. They designed speech recognizer and achieved an accuracy of more than 80%. In [25], authors used Gaussian Copula for spoken Arabic digits only, the accuracy for some words was close to 100% but overall average accuracy was 96.89% (Table 1).

Table 1. Efficiency rate comparison

Language	Related work	Efficiency rate
Bengali	[8]	80%
Bengali	[13]	84%
Bengali	[16]	96% with one speaker 84.24% with more than one
Bengali	[17]	94%
Turkish	[19]	65.6% with large vocabulary
Turkish	[21]	29.3%
Arabic	[18]	Satisfactory
Arabic	[24]	80%
Arabic	[25]	96.89%

4 A Brief Introduction to Urdu Language

Urdu figuring began ahead of schedule, in 1980s, making numerous encodings, so a standard encoding plan was lost around those. Urdu language is used to be written from right to left similar to Arabic and other letters [18]. Word Urdu basically comes from Turkish vocabulary and the meaning is "horde" (Lashkar). It is similar as Hindi Language. Urdu is basically the combination of Persian, Arabic, Turkish, Portuguese and English vocabularies. Pakistan's population is around 200 million and up to 56 different languages are spoken in all over the country [26]. Urdu has an estimated 487 million speakers worldwide [27]. (CRULP) Centre for research in Urdu Language Processing Lahore and (NLA) National Language Authority Islamabad are the most dominant and dedicated research institutes for Urdu language processing in Pakistan [28, 29].

5 Overview of Urdu Speech/Text Related Work in Last a Few Years

Kabir et al. [30] discussed how Urdu text can be converted in to speech in a series of steps. With the help of NLP, steps include are token generation, phonemic stream of tokens and syllabification of words in corpus, primary stress assignments tokens and syllabification of words. This system uses preprocessing module which contains converters for number, date, time, special symbol and graphics to text. This processor takes phonemic signal as input source and produces phonetic stream after applying phonological rules. While Asadullah et al. [31] described a process to develop an Urdu speech recognition system with the help of Hidden Markov Model. Hidden Markov Model is also used in speaker dependent Urdu Speech Recognition by Ashraf et al. [32]. They used an open source speech recognition framework "Sphinx4" and used around 50 most spoken words in Urdu for their speaker independent speech recognition system. So far some small vocabulary speech recognition systems have developed, some are speaker dependent or they don't have higher accuracy rate. The reason for less accuracy is variation in Urdu accents. In [33], two methods were explained by Muhammad Qasim et al. to handle variation in Urdu accents. Accent dependent ASRs and Accent Independent ASR. In [34], Sarmad gives a complete review of Urdu Language resources for processing. He used CRULP research for corpus and lexical data for Urdu. Saira et al. in their paper [34] used neural networks for Urdu isolated words and speech recognition systems. The complete overview of Urdu vocabulary, Urdu text to speech converter and translator of English to Urdu is discussed in [35] by Sarmad in his Urdu localization project. Waqas et al. tried to summarize several linguistic analysis includes POS tagging, name entity detection and parsing. They gave a handy overview of Urdu language and its corpus in [36] and also compared this with other East Asian languages. Humera et al. described an approach i.e. Urdu part of speech tagging (POS). They used ME modeling process, morphological analyzer and stammer for tagging [37]. Simple Urdu text to English text and vice versa have developed in [39] with the help of ISO/IEC 10646 standard Urdu Unicode. They used lexicon rule. Sarmad also in [38] definedan approach for how Urdu letter can be converted in sound/speech. He used different letter to sound conversion rules in his study. So many offline Urdu OCR have been developed in the past years. We give an overview of several offline Urdu OCR and their recognition rate in Table 2.

Table 2. Urdu offline OCR recognition rate comparison

Language	Related work	Recognition rate
Bukhari et al. (2011)	Multi resolution morphology	92% to 96%
Sagheer et al. (2009)	SVM and RBF	98.61%
Shahzad et al. (2009)	Subset of rubine feature	92.8% and 74%
Shamsher et al.	Feed forward neural network	98.3%

6 Proposed Work

As we know, there are many speech to text system (STT) available for speech recognition in the domain of Natural Language Processing such as English, Bengali and Arabic. There are lots of Text to Speech TTS systems available for those languages. When we look around Pakistan regional languages especially Urdu, there is some work for Text to Speech system for Urdu language but as far as Urdu Speech to text system is concerned, there is no Speech to Text system STT available for Urdu language. Speech to text (STT) translator of different languages is there with high accuracy except Urdu and some other languages. The ultimate goal of this survey is to study the natural language processing of different languages and different techniques which can be used in speech recognition. Then, we focused on processing of different languages. From the past time, the study of Automatic Speech Recognition (ASR) has succeeded a lot in the field of complexity reduction. The main goal of such research is to make possible doing more complex recognition tasks using only the restricted capabilities of moveable devices. Speech-to-text-system is a valuable tool for communicating humans with disables properties in terms of hearing impairments e.g. having conferences or interviews. Though, the conversion of speech into written form in actual time needs superior techniques as it must be very quick and approximately 100% correct to be understandable and efficient enough as well. For these tasks, there are many STT systems available all over the world for different languages. We proposed that there can be Speech to text system for Urdu Language in future and researcher can look into it for their future work. We also suggest that neural network can be good choice for this task. The combined study of speech with natural language over neural networks has many advantages. In [39], Bhargab et al. discussed how Assamese isolated words can be classified using Artificial Neural Networks. Their data base consists of 100 frequently used Assamese isolated words. Their experimental accuracy was 99% for speaker dependent recognition system as compared to speaker independent system's accuracy of 93%. While same work for Romanian language isolated word is defined in [36]. They used feed forward Artificial Neural Networks. Their results say that word recognition was higher when the speaker was a female as compared to a male speaker. They used Mean Square Error (MSE) and showed that MSE was better on large data sets. Speech recognition for Malayalam words was defined in [40]. Vimal et al. used 160 samples for five different Malayalam words. They used 4 type of wavelet, recognition rate of 89% was achieved in their approach. Speech recognition system of two English isolated words "yes" and "No" was developed in [41]. They trained two Artificial Neural Networks for both "Yes" and "No". For sample of 25 male they achieved accuracy of 100%. Another work has been done for Malayalam 500 key words in [42]. They used Fast Fourier Transform (FFT) and Discrete Cosine Transform (DCT) for extracting the features and Artificial Neural Networks for classification, their accuracy was 85%. The same team in [43] defined how ANN can be used for recognition of 250 isolated Malayalam query words. The experimental accuracy was 80%. Speech recognition systems have two types: speaker dependent and speaker independent system. Therefor speaker recognition is also important in Speech recognition system. In [44], they recognized speaker and speech using Artificial Neural Networks. They worked on frequency ranges from 12 Hz to 586 Hz of five different speakers. In [45, 46], same work was done by multilayer Neural Network with back propagation. This model is flexible and it can be expendable for hidden layers. In [47], Ning et al. used Fuzzy Neural Network (FNN) for classification. FNN was trained by artificial bee colony (ABC) algorithm. They compared their results with FNN trained by Back Propagation and concluded that FNN by ABC was better and they also compared their result with FNN trained by particle swarm optimization and suggested that there is no difference in both of them. By considering all of above, we can suggest that neural network can be good classifier for speech to text system of Urdu Language.

7 Conclusion

Different techniques for speech recognition along with the related work in processing of different natural languages such as Bengali and Arabic is discussed. Recent work in the field of Urdu Language processing is also analyzed. It seems that there are no proper automatic speech recognition systems for Urdu speech yet, so as a future work we propose that Speech to text converter can be developed with the help of neural networks.

References

1. Olson, H.F., Belar, H.: Phonetic typewriter. J. Acoust. Soc. Am. **28**(6), 1072–1081 (1956)
2. Hussain, S.: Resources for Urdu language processing. In: Proceedings of the 6th Workshop on Asian Language Resources (2019)
3. Ashraf, J., Iqbal, N., Khattak, N.S., Zaidi, A.M.: Speaker independent Urdu speech recognition using HMM. In: Hopfe, Christina J., Rezgui, Y., Métais, E., Preece, A., Li, H. (eds.) NLDB 2010. LNCS, vol. 6177, pp. 140–148. Springer, Heidelberg (2010). https://doi. org/10.1007/978-3-642-13881-2_14
4. Tran, D.T.: Fuzzy Approaches to Speech and Speaker Recognition. A thesis submitted for the degree of Doctor of Philosophy of the university of Canberra (2000)
5. Anusuya, M.A., Katti, S. K.: Speech recognition by machine: a review. Int. J. Comput. Sci. Inf. Secur. (2010)
6. Katagiri, S., et al.: A New hybrid algorithm for speech recognition based on HMM segmentation and learning Vector quantization. IEEE Transactions on Audio Speech and Language processing **1**(4), 421–430 (1993)
7. Shaikh, M.K., Khowaja, H.A., Khan, M.A.: Urdu text translation with natural language processing. In: Student Conference On Engineering, Sciences and Technology, Karachi, Pakistan, pp. 81–85 (2004)
8. Karim, R., Rahman, M.S., Iqbal, M.Z.: Recognition of spoken letters in bangla. In: Proceedings 5th International Conference on Computer and Information Technology (ICCIT02), Dhaka, Bangladesh (2002)
9. Oney, B., Durgunoglu, A.Y.: Learning to read in Turkish: a phonologically transparent orthography. Appl. Psycholinguist. **18**, 1–15 (1997)
10. Tamzida, A., Siddiqui, S.: A synchronic comparison between the vowel phonemes of Bengali & English phonology and its classroom applicability. Stamford J. English **6**, 285–314 (2013)
11. Barman, B.: A contrastive analysis of english and bangla phonemics. Dhaka University J. Linguist. **2**(4), 19–42 (2011)
12. Hossain, S.A., Rahman, M.L., Ahmed, F.: A review on bangla phoneme production and perception for computational approaches. In: 7th WSEAS International Conference on Mathematical Methods and Computational Techniques in Electrical Engineering, pp. 69–89 (2005)
13. Hassan, F., Alam Kotwal, M.R., Rahman, M.M., Nasiruddin, M., Latif, M.A., Nurul Huda, M.: Local feature or mel frequency cepstral coefficients - which one is better for mln-based bangla speech recognition? In: Abraham, A., Lloret Mauri, J., Buford, John F., Suzuki, J., Thampi, Sabu M. (eds.) ACC 2011. CCIS, vol. 191, pp. 154–161. Springer, Heidelberg (2011). https://doi.org/10.1007/978-3-642-22714-1_17
14. Ali, M., Hossain, M., Bhuiyan, M.N., et al.: Automatic speech recognition technique for bangla words. Int. J. Adv. Sci. Technol. **50**, 51–60 (2013)
15. Rahman, M.M., Khatun, F.: Development of isolated speech recognition system for bangla words. Daffodil Int. Univ. J. Sci. Technol. **6**(1), 30–35 (2011)

16. Hasnat, M.A., Mowla, J., Khan, M.: Isolated and continuous bangla speech recognition: implementation, performance and application perspective. In: Center for research on Bangla language processing (CRBLP) (2007)

17. Rahman, M.M., Bhuiyan, M.A.-A.: On segmentation and extraction of features from continuous bangla speech including windowing. Int. J. Appl. Res. Inf. Technol. Comput. 2 (2), 31–40 (2011)

18. Ettaouil, M., Lazaar, M., En-Naimani, Z.: A hybrid ANN/HMM models for arabic speech recognition using optimal codebook. In:2013 8th International Conference on Intelligent Systems: Theories and Applications (SITA), Rabat, pp. 1–5 (2013)

19. Can, B., Artuner, H.: A syllable-based Turkish speech recognition system by using time delay neural networks (TDNNs). Department of Computer Engineering Hacettepe University Ankara, Turkey. IEEE (2013)

20. Palaz, H., Kanak, A., Bicil, Y., Doğan, M.U., İslam, T.: TREN - Turkish speech recognition platform. In: 2005 13th European Signal Processing Conference, Antalya, pp. 1–4 (2005)

21. Salor, O.L., Pellom, B., Çiloglu, T., Hacioglu, K., Demirekler, M.: On developing new text and audio corpora and speech recognition tools for the Turkish language. In: Seventh International Conference on Spoken Language Processing (2002)

22. Kuo, H.J., Arisoy, E., Mangu, L., Saon, G.: Minimum Bayes risk discriminative language models for Arabic speech recognition. In: 2011 IEEE Workshop on Automatic Speech Recognition & Understanding, Waikoloa, HI, pp. 208–213 (2011)

23. Alotaibi, Y., Selouani, S.A., Alghamdi, M., Meftah, A.: Arabic and English speech recognition using cross-language acoustic models. In: 2012 11th International Conference on Information Science, Signal Processing and their Applications, ISSPA, pp. 40–44 (2012). https://doi.org/10.1109/isspa.2012.6310585

24. Bayeh, R., Mokbel, C., Chollet, G.: Broadcast news transcription baseline system using the Nemlar database. In: Proceedings of the 6th International Conference on Language Resources and Evaluation (LREC): the workshop in HLT & NLP within the Arabic world, Marrakech, Morocco (2008)

25. Hammami, N., Bedda, M., Farah, N.: Probabilistic classification based on Gaussian copula for speech recognition: Application to Spoken Arabic digits. In: 2013 Signal Processing: Algorithms, Architectures, Arrangements, and Applications (SPA), Poznan, pp. 312–317 (2013)

26. See http://www.answers.com/topic/urdu

27. Shaikh, S., Strzalkowski, T., Webb, N.: Classification of dialogue acts in Urdu multi- party discourse (2011)

28. Centre for Research in Urdu Language Processing (CRULP). http://www.crulp.org

29. National Language Authority (NLA), Islamabad. http://www.nlauit.gov.pk

30. Kabir, H.: Natural language processing for Urdu TTS system, 58–58 (2002). https://doi.org/10.1109/inmic.2002.1310165

31. Shaukat, A.A., Ali, H., Akram, U.: Automatic Urdu speech recognition using hidden Markov model. In: 2016 International Conference on Image, Vision and Computing (ICIVC), Portsmouth, pp. 135–139 (2016)

32. Anwar, W., Wang, X., Wang, X.: A survey of automatic Urdu language Processing. In: 2006 International Conference on Machine Learning and Cybernetics, Dalian, China, pp. 4489–4494 (2006)

33. Qasim, M., Nawaz, S., Hussain, S., Habib, T.: Urdu speech recognition system for district names of Pakistan: Development, challenges and solutions. In: 2016 Conference of the Oriental Chapter of International Committee for Coordination and Standardization of Speech Databases and Assessment Techniques (O-COCOSDA), Bali, pp. 28–32 (2016)

34. Ali, S., Iqbal, S., Saeed, I.: Voice Controlled Urdu interface using isolated and Continuous speech Recognizer (2012). https://doi.org/10.1109/inmic.2012.6511493
35. Hussain, S.: Urdu localization project **80** (2004). https://doi.org/10.3115/1621804.1621825
36. Oprea, M., Şchiopu, D.: An artificial neural network-based isolated word speech recognition system for the Romanian language. In: 2012 16th International Conference on System Theory, Control and Computing (ICSTCC), Sinaia, pp. 1–6 (2012)
37. Revathi, B., Humera Khanam, B.: Hindi To English part of speech tagger by using Crf method. North Asian Int. Res. J. Sci. Eng. I.T. **2**(1), 2–10 (2016). ISSN: 2454-7514
38. Hussain, S.: Letter-To-sound conversion For Urdu text-to-speech system. Coling (2004)
39. Medhi, B., Talukdar, P.H.: Isolated Assamese speech recognition using artificial neural network. In: 2015 International Symposium on Advanced Computing and Communication (ISACC), Silchar, pp. 141–148 (2015)
40. Krishnan, V.R.V., Jayakumar, A., Babu, A.P.: Speech recognition of isolated Malayalam words using wavelet features and artificial neural network. In:4th IEEE International Symposium on Electronic Design, Test and Applications (delta 2008), Hong Kong, pp. 240–243 (2008)
41. Polur, P.D., Zhou, R., Yang, J., Adnani, F., Hobson, R.S.: Isolated speech recognition using artificial neural networks. In: 2001 Conference Proceedings of the 23rd Annual International Conference of the IEEE Engineering in Medicine and Biology Society, Istanbul, Turkey, vol. 2, pp. 1731–1734 2001
42. Sukumar, R.A., Sukumar, S.A., Shah, F.A., Anto, B.P.: Key-word based query recognition in a speech corpus by using artificial neural networks. In:2010 2nd International Conference on Computational Intelligence, Communication Systems and Networks, Liverpool, pp. 33–36 (2010)
43. Sukumar, A.R., Shah, A.F., Anto, P.B.: Isolated question words recognition from speech queries by using Artificial Neural Networks. In: 2010 Second International conference on Computing, Communication and Networking Technologies, Karur, pp. 1–4 (2010)
44. Dey, N.S., Mohanty, R., Chugh, K.L.: Speech and speaker recognition system using artificial neural networks and hidden markov model. In: 2012 International Conference on Communication Systems and Network Technologies, Rajkot, pp. 311–315 (2012)
45. Hwang, J.-N., Lay, S.-R., Mächler, M., Martin, R.Douglas, Schimert, J.: Regression modeling in back-propagation and projection pursuit learning. IEEE Trans. Neural Netw. **5**, 342–353 (1994). https://doi.org/10.1109/72.286906
46. Vecci, L., Campolucci, P., Piazza, F., Uncini, A.: Approximation capabilities of adaptive spline neural networks **1**, 260-265 (1997). https://doi.org/10.1109/icnn.1997.611675
47. Benvenuto, N., Marchesi, M., Piazza, F., Uncini, A.: A comparison between real and complex valued neural networks in communication applications. In: Teuvo, K., Kai, M., Olli, S., Jari, K. (eds.) Artificial Neural Networks, North-Holland, pp. 1177–1180 (1991)

Urdu Spell Checker: A Scarce Resource Language

Romila Aziz[✉] and Muhammad Waqas Anwar

Department of Computer Science, COMSATS University Islamabad,
Lahore Campus, Lahore, Pakistan
romilaaziz044@gmail.com, waqasanwar@cuilahore.edu.pk

Abstract. In the digital world of computers, several software applications have been developed to ensure spellings of various words. English language is found to have gone far ahead in the development of spell checking applications whilst other languages specifically naming Urdu, lack behind to cherish such technologies. We develop "Urdu Spell Checker" which detects incorrect spellings of a word and provides a list of options containing correct spellings. The spell checker carries correct spellings of words residing inside a predefined lexicon or corpus. It is to ensure whether entered word is correct or not. In case if the input word matches with the corpus words it is considered correct otherwise it is considered as misspelled word. Multiple techniques are used individually as well as a combination these techniques is used to check which set of methods is best in terms of output. By using multiple techniques for error correction, it is observed that Jaro distance provides best results with combination of soundex, shapex and n-gram that is 80.0% precision, 44.87% recall and 57.37% F-Measure.

Keywords: Errors detection · Edit distance · Soundex · Urdu language

1 Introduction

Issue of programmed spell checking is not new in the ranges of Information Retrieval and Language processing. The exploration began as early as 1960s. A wide range of techniques for the discovery and amendment of spelling errors are proposed since last 40 years. Some of these techniques exploit general spelling mistake patterns while others utilize the phonetics of incorrectly spelled word to discover likely correct words. Lately, statistic-based techniques which are not exclusively based on error trends but through training, adjust to error patterns, have gained greater prevalence. Many of these techniques are being utilized with text editors and other context handling and are demonstrating great execution. All things considering the issue of spell checking is as yet thought to be open for additional research and upgrades. There are two reasons behind considering this issue still unsolved; one has to do with the execution of existing methods and other with their scope. For the first reason in Natural Language Processing, it is advanced over the year. The text that is computed is sufficient and errorless. Automated spellcheckers have few choices for replacement. But with human implemented spellchecker we have a plenty of choices and we choose the word accordingly which is actually 100% correct. The second reason for considering the spell checking is that the area of this language is not

© Springer Nature Singapore Pte Ltd. 2020
I. S. Bajwa et al. (Eds.): INTAP 2019, CCIS 1198, pp. 471–483, 2020.
https://doi.org/10.1007/978-981-15-5232-8_40

so vast. As we consider English or Latin languages, much work has been done in these languages. Spellchecker of every language has a boundary in checking other language. In English spellchecker if we want to check the spelling of French, we will fail on the first step because it is outside of the boundary of the system. Therefore, even English which is very vast language is limited in its scope. From the above discussion, it is concluded that for making a new spell checker one has to clearly identify the language specific issues and deeply investigate general spelling error trends of the language, only then a reasonably effective spell checking approach can be proposed.

Urdu is the national language of Pakistan[1]. It is considered as second language in Sri Lanka, Nepal and Bangladesh. Urdu Language follows a Persian script style which is known as Nastalik[2]. It borrows most words from Persian and Arabic to extend its vocabulary. It is used by 100 million speakers who use it during their speech. Urdu is rich morphological language in which many derivations and inflections are derived from one single word. Urdu language does not only contain words that have similar sound but also those which have similar structure. This increases the chance of typing errors. These errors are classified into two main categories that are: cognitive error and typographical error. Typographical error occurs when user enters incorrect word by mistake even though he knows the correct spellings. Cognitive error occurs when user is not aware of correct spellings and gets confused due to homophonic sound.

These types themselves hold errors mentioned by Demarau [1]. According to a study, some data is taken from a newspaper which depicts how Urdu language has chances of error among visually similar and phonetically similar words (Table 1).

Table 1. Single edit distance errors in Urdu

	Total errors	Visually similar	Phonetically similar
Substitution	75	40	12
Deletion	42	4	5
Insertion	21	2	1
Transposition	12	3	0
Total	150	49	18

To handle these kinds of errors, an Urdu Spell Checker is developed which helps the user to check their spelling, highlights the user input and also gives some suggestion for that wrong word. Furthermore, Urdu is also a language which has its own patterns and technique of writing. Therefore, existing techniques will not be applicable on this language without modification. This paper presents the details of a study performed on Urdu language to identify the problem of Urdu spell checking and to test the effectiveness of existing spell-checking techniques on Urdu. So, we have given a hybrid approach for Urdu spelling error correction which uses a combination of more than one existing techniques. These techniques are modified to cater Urdu specific problems and make the spell checker more reliable.

---

[1] https://en.wikipedia.org/wiki/History_of_Hindustani.

[2] https://www.wdl.org/en/item/9700/.

2 Linguistic Issues

2.1 Phonetic Similarity

In currently developed spell checker, phonetic similarity is not under enough consideration with the incorrect word just being highlighted without providing sufficient options to correct it. For example, for the misspelled word "سحت", limited likely corrections like "صحت" and "سحر" are listed in options while "سخت" could also be a possibility [2]. Currently developed applications are hardly flexible to provide users with suggestions of words that have similar sound. The word "لحاض" that has similar sound to word "لحاظ" but spell checkers ignore the fact on basis of correct spellings. This feature enriches our research and takes it a step ahead.

2.2 Space Omission

Now-a-days, Urdu spell checkers are struggling to deal with the issues of space between words. Words like "آپ کا" can be written without space as "آپکا". Such issues are to be considered in the development of proposed spell checker.

2.3 Shape Similarity

While some spell checkers depict only the correct spellings, others only predict words on the basis of shape similarity. Our Spell Checker merges both the concepts of presenting correct spellings for "سحت" i.e. "صحت" as well as provide words like "سحر" and "سخت" which could have been written instead.

3 Literature Review

Spelling mistake is a common phenomenon that occurs while writing text. It needs to be detected and corrected. Hence, spell checking was taken under research consideration with advent of text processing becoming common to users in computer world. Fred J. Damerau [1] provided some basic techniques for the purpose of spell checking. According to Fred J. Damerau [1] spell checking is a process of any input being compared to acceptable terms in a master list. If there is no match found, then input is rejected. Errors that were brought into light by Damerau were (Table 2):

Table 2. Types of errors in Urdu

Error Type	Correct Word	Misspelled Word
Substitution	پاکستان (Pakistan)	پاکصتان (Pakistan)
Insertion	گھر (Home)(Ghar)	گیھر(Ghaer)
Deletion	قبرستان (Graveyard)(Qabrastaan)	قبرستن (Qabrastan)
Transposition	مظبوط (Strong) (Mazboot)	مبظوط(Mabzoot)

There is a lot of work that has been done in English language. English is basically a worldwide international language. Spell checker and Spell predictor are already developed and there is much research work done in this language [3]. Multiple techniques for spell checking have been used over the decades to improve spelling correction process in English. Besides, not only spelling but also grammar checking methods have been developed and implemented for the language.

Oriya Spell Checker successfully takes care of error detection and automatic or manual correction for the misspelled words. Some algorithms have been developed to perform OSC in order to find out more accurate suggestions for a misspelled word. The words are indexed according to their word length in word's database in order for effective searching [4]. It considers following information on the basis of misspelled word. The number of matching Characters, matching Characters in the forward direction, corresponding matching characters in backward direction to give more accurate, suggestive words for the misspelled word. Using these techniques, OSC is successfully running in word processors. Also, Hindi and English spell checkers are developed for word processor. ASCII Format is used to store word files which support Oriya, Hindi and English fonts [4]. Phonetic nature of Turkish language leads it to be adapted to a number of different alphabets. Turkish word development utilizes various phonetic harmony rules. Vowels and consonants change in certain ways when a suffix is added to a root with the goal that such harmony requirements are not damaged [5].

Nadir Durrani [6] discussed word segmentation problem in Urdu. Segmentation issues like space insertion and space omission are discussed. In Urdu spell checking, spelling errors are mostly occurred due to the inconsistent use of space [2]. Different rule based techniques like maximum matching, unigram and bigram etc. are used to solve the problem of space insertion and space deletion. Linguistic information is used to classify the problem and then rule based techniques are applied to solve these problems. Nadir Durrani [6] applied segmentation algorithm to solve the problem of space. Due to rule based techniques 95.8% accuracy is achieved [6]. Wajdi Zaghouani [7] discussed different challenges faced while developing Arabic spell checker. Spelling error is the biggest challenge for Arabic spell checker. In spelling error, character is deleted or substituted by another incorrect character. Another linguistic issue that is being faced while developing Arabic spell checker is morphological issue. This issue arises because of incorrect use of derivation and inflection. For developing spell checker different rules are used [7]. In this paper, web based framework is developed. Then a corpus is designed by using different correction techniques. Error correction algorithm is used for evaluation [7]. Mohammad Sadegh Rasooli [8] developed Persian Spell checker and also discussed the linguistic challenges faced during developing spell checker.

Sadat Iqbal [9] discussed the challenges faced in Urdu spell checking. The first problem is related with space. In Urdu, if space is not given after a joiner character then these characters joins together and cause errors. Morphology is another challenge that is faced in Urdu while developing Spell Checker. Walid Magdy [10] developed Arabic OCR Error Corrector. Walid Magdy [10] also discussed different challenges faced while developing Arabic OCR Error Corrector. Morphological Complexity is the biggest challenge which is faced while developing error corrector. Error correction method is used to solve the problem of spelling error. Language model is also used to correct the spelling errors [10]. Jinhua Xiong [11] developed a framework for the correction of Chinese errors. Jinhua Xiong [11] also discussed some challenges that are faced during the correction of Chinese spelling errors. In Chinese spelling errors are also occurred because of shape similarity. To solve these problems HAN Speller is proposed which detects errors, provides possible suggestions and replaces the word with best candidate. Hidden Markov Model (HMM) approach is used for detecting the errors and correcting those errors [11].

4   Methodology

The spell checking comprises of three phases:

1. Detection of incorrect word.
2. Searching possible matches for the incorrect word.
3. Replacing incorrect word with correct word depending upon match strength.

4.1   Detection of Incorrect Word

The system uses a dictionary that contained the correctly spelled words. The dictionary is used for ensuring that given input word is correct word or misspelled word. For any input to be spell checked, first of all the input is matched with the dictionary, if the input word exists in the dictionary then it is marked as correctly spelled word otherwise it is flagged as misspelled word. So far dictionary is created by tokenizing the corpus (Express news) of 6 Million words and finding 16870 unique words from that corpus. 6 Million words corpus is used for candidate ranking. The words repeat according to their occurrence in sentence in a corpus of 6 Million words. BiGram and Trigram techniques use a corpus of 6 Million words because these two techniques consider frequency of pairs of words which requires structured dataset.

4.2   Techniques for Spelling Error Correction

Three string distance techniques are used in the Urdu spell checker for distance calculation between words.

- Levenshtein Distance – measures distance of difference between two strings.
- Jaro Distance – measures distance of similarity between two strings.
- Hamming Distance – measures distance between strings of same length.

Levenshtein Distance
Levenshtein distance is a way of measuring dissimilarity between two strings by counting the minimum number of operations required to transform one string into the other. It deals with errors of insertion, deletion and substitution[3].

---

[3] https://en.wikipedia.org/wiki/Levenshtein_distance.

$$D = (i,j)min \begin{cases} D(i-1,j)+1 & //insertion \\ D(i,j-1)-1 & //deletion \\ D(i-1,j-1)+ \begin{cases} 2; & (if(X(i) \neq Y(j))//Substitution \\ 0; & if(X(i)=Y(j)) \end{cases} \end{cases}$$

Levenshtein distance returns the distance as a whole number ranging from 0 to a maximum number depending upon dissimilarity between two strings. It is a very popular technique for finding dissimilarity between words of different lengths. The types of errors Levenshtein distance allows are deletion, insertion and substitution.

Jaro Distance

The Jaro distance is a measure of similarity between two strings. The higher the Jaro distance for two strings is, the more similar the strings are. The score is normalized such that 0 equates to no similarity and 1 is an exact match[4]. The Jaro distance of two given strings s1 and s2 is

$$d_j = \begin{cases} 0 & \text{if } m = 0 \\ \frac{1}{3}\left(\frac{m}{|s_1|} + \frac{m}{|s_2|} + \frac{m-t}{m}\right) & \text{otherwise} \end{cases}$$

where **m** is the number of matching characters **t** is half the number of transpositions. As Jaro distance generates distance in decimals therefore, the suggested output is more accurate. Suggestions for incorrect words found using Jaro distance are better than those found using Levenshtein distance.

The types of errors Jaro distance allows are insertion, deletion, substitution and transposition. Jaro Distance has worked best for the words with more similarity than difference. This technique has dealt words with lesser spelling errors more efficiently.

Hamming Distance

Hamming Distance is a technique used to calculate distance between two strings of equal length is the number of positions at which the corresponding symbols are different. In other words, it measures the minimum number of substitutions required to change one string into the other.

$$d^{HAD}(i,j) = \sum_{k=0}^{n-1} [y_{i,k} \neq y_{j,k}]$$

Disadvantage of hamming distance is that it works well for strings of same length which affects the output. It considers strings with equal length. However, in order to improve the technique, changes are made so that it considers extra characters of bigger string as mismatched characters. It has helped to improve results to some extent.

---

[4] https://blogs.sap.com/2013/12/04/jaro-winkler-distance-algorithm/.

The types of errors Hamming distance allows are substitution errors. Hamming distance only allows substitution because it deals with strings of same length. It has produced fine results for such words. It has found the count of different characters at same index of two words. It has helped to know the number of errors made in a single word without any transposition, insertion or deletion.

Example

The three techniques provide different distances for multiple errors.

Table 3. Distances for different types of errors using multiple techniques

Error type	Correct word	Misspelled word	Levenshtein Distance	Jaro Distance	Hamming Distance
Substitution پاکستان(Pakistan)	پاکصتان(Pakistan)		1	0.90476	1
		باقصتان(Bakistaan)	3	0.71429	3
Insertion	گھر (Home) (Ghar)	گپھر(Ghaer)	1	0.91667	-
		گگپھر(Gghair)	2	051111	-
Deletion	قبرستان (Graveyard) (Qabrastaan)	قبرستن (Qabrastaan)	1	0.95238	-
		قبستن(Qabastan)	2	0.90476	-
Transposition مظبوط (Strong) (Mazboot)		مبظوط (Mabzoot)	-	0.93333	-
		مبظطو (Mabzato)	-	0.86667	

The example in Table 3, shows that Jaro distance provides much more precise results for a word for which edit distance generates same output.

4.3   Ranking Techniques

Soundex

We also used Soundex as our ranking approach. Soundex is the first-string matching algorithm which is developed by Odell and it is mainly used for matching names.[5] It does not perform well for spelling error correction. The basic idea behind Soundex is to assign common or same code to the letters of same pronunciation. The length of Soundex code is 4 and the basic form of Soundex code is: letter, digit, digit, digit. We made a Classification of Urdu words on the basis of sounds is as follow (Table 4):

---

[5] https://www.jewishgen.org/InfoFiles/Soundex.html#NARA.

Table 4. Soundex grouping

Group	Case
ث, س, ص,ش	1
ة, ٹ, ط,ت	2
ز, ض, ظ,ذ	3
ج,چ	4
ہ,ح,ه	5
ق,ك,خ	6
د,ڈ	7
ب,پ	8
م,ن,ں	9
گ,غ	A
ڑ,ر	B
ی,ژ	C
ا,آ,ع	D
و,ل,ف	E
ے	F

Example:

Misspelled Word: پاکصتان(Pakistan) => پ D61

Correct Word:پاکستان (Pakistan) => پD61

These two words have same sound and belong to the same group but there is a phonetical error in the spellings of the word پاکصتان(Pakistan).

Shapex: The shape content is intended to be a way of describing shapes that allow for measuring shapes similarity and recovering of point correspondence. Similar to Soundex algorithm, each character or letter in Urdu script is assigned a number or code and all the characters with similar shapes or glyphs are all grouped together with same code so that when the comparison is done, the words with similar shape characters can be matched regardless of minor differences in spelling. We made a Classification of Urdu words on the basis of shape is as follow (Table 5):

Table 5. Shapex grouping

Shapex Grouping	
Group	Case
ث،ف،پ،ب،ٹ،ت	1
س،ش	2
ر،ڑ،ز،ژ	3
ص،ض	4
ج،چ،ح،خ	5
ه،ہ،ۃ	6
د،ڈ،ذ	7
ط،ظ	8
و	9
ق،ن،ں،ل	A
ک،گ	B
م	C
ع،غ	D
ا،آ	E
ی	F
ے	G

Example

Misspelled Word: ابنی (Abni) => l1AF

Correct Word: اپنی (Apni)(Mine)=> ا1AF

N-Gram:

N-gram is used as a ranking approach. Subsequence's of a word are made, and these subsequences' are termed as n-grams, where value of n is either of {1, 2, 3....}. The terms unigram, bigram, trigram is referred to n-gram when n = 1, 2, and 3 respectively.

Bi-Gram: We also used bigram ranking approach for selecting the suitable candidate. In this approach we rank the candidate words based on their previous word, calculates the frequency of candidate words with their previous words and selects the best suitable candidate whose bigram probability is higher.

Example

Misspelled Sentence: "صنعتی شعبوں کے تعان سے"

Correct Sentence: "صنعتی شعبوں کے تعاون سے"

With the cooperation of industrial departments.

In this example word "تعان" (Taan) is marked as misspelled word. After applying edit distance, we obtain the following candidate words of "تعان" (Taan):

Candidate Words: "تعاون(Teavan)(Cooperation)،(appointment)(TaAyun)تعین،(Tune) (Taan)تان،(Tiredness)(Takan)تکان، (a bolt or piece of cloth) (Thaan)تھان, (Smell) (Tafon)".

For ranking these candidate's bigram model is applied which gives us a suggested word "تعاون" (Taawan) (Cooperation).

Tri-Gram: We also used trigram approach which considers three words at a time. This is *trigram;* each three adjacent words create a trigram.
In Urdu

"اسلام میں جہیز لینا منغ ہے"

(In Islam Dowry is strictly forbidden)

Misspelled word is "منغ". After applying edit distance, we get the following candidate words:

Candidate Words: "منح, منی,مرغ, منع, منٹ, من,مند"

We rank candidate words by applying trigram approach which makes pairs of 3 words and finally we select "منع" as our suggested word because it's trigram probability is high.

5   Results and Discussion

The error correction techniques have helped to calculate the values of measurements in order to see which technique provides best output. We used precision, recall and F measure for evaluation (Table 6).

Table 6. Experimental results

Technique	Precision	Recall	F-Measure
Levenshtein Distance			
Levenshtein Distance	69.07	75.28	72.04
Levenshtein Distance + Soundex+ Shapex	69.66	71.26	70.45
Levenshtein Distance + BiGram	59.25	14.67	23.52
Hybrid with Levenshtein Distance	78.57	43.42	55.93
Jaro Distance			
Jaro Distance	68.13	73.56	71.11
Jaro Distance + Soundex + Shapex	69.38	63.80	66.66
Jaro Distance + BiGram	44.44	7.84	13.33
Hybrid with Jaro Distance	80.00	44.87	57.37
Hamming Distance			
Hamming Distance	69.07	75.28	72.04
Hamming Distance + Soundex + Shapex	69.89	73.03	71.42
Hybrid with Hamming Distance	74.62	36.49	49.01

The results provided by hamming distance were not as up to mark as Levenshtein Distance and Jaro Distance.

5.1 Improved Soundex/Shapex

Several spelling checkers have used soundex and Shapex techniques for ranking. However, the improved version consists of more precise grouping of characters with same sound or shape. Although, it has increased the number of cases but codes generated for input and output have also increased the possibility of being matched. Moreover, in order to improve results in case of no exact match for the code of input and candidate word, the 4-digit code from soundex and Shapex is improved by calculating distance between input and candidate word codes through Levenshtein Distance and likewise, through Jaro Distance. This procedure has helped to match the generated code to up to 3 digits and then up to 2 digits in case of no exact match.

Several spelling checkers have used soundex and Shapex techniques for ranking. However, the improved version consists of more precise grouping of characters with same sound or shape. Moreover, in order to improve results in case of no exact match for the code of input and candidate word, the 4-digit code from soundex and Shapex is improved by calculating distance between input and candidate word codes through Levenshtein Distance and likewise, through Jaro Distance. This procedure has helped to match the generated codes upto 3 digits and then upto 2 digits in case of no exact match.

Table 7. Improved distances for different types of errors using multiple techniques

Error type	Misspelled word	Levenshtein		Jaro		Hamming	
		Previous distance	Improved distance	Previous distance	Improved distance	Previous distance	Improved distance
Substitution	باقصتاں	3	0	0.7	1.0	3	1
Insertion	گگپھر	2	2	0.51 11	0.83 333	–	–
Deletion	قیست	3	2	0.85 71	0.83 333	–	–
Transposition	مبظطو	–	–	0.93 33	0.91 667	–	–

Table 7 shows improved distances for misspelled words having different type of errors. The improved distances hence provide a better list of candidate words for misspelled word.

The techniques used separately produced various results however, in case of Jaro Distance precision was observed to be highest with hybrid approach. It was because of the calculation of Jaro distance in decimals which helped to set boundary values higher than Levenshtein distance. Also, combining soundex and shapex with Levenshtein distance and jaro distance twice created more accurate list for suggestions of incorrect word. Previously, the list was long with irrelevant suggestions which were not as close to input as the outputs from improved technique. Even though hybrid approach that was a combination of all methods produced much better results in terms of precision with Jaro distance, it was decided to use an overall hybrid approach including Hybrid Levenshtein distance and Hybrid Jaro distance. This is because suggested list of outputs consisted of more possible options for user than separate techniques. As a result, Urdu Spell Checker consists of Hybrid approach including Levenshtein distance, Jaro distance, Soundex, Shapex and N-Gram (Bi-Gram and TriGram).

6 Conclusion and Future Work

The research is based on an Urdu Spell Checker which helps a user to write error free Urdu text. It provides user the facilities to correct any spelling mistakes. Hybrid approach including Levenshtein distance and Jaro distance with ranking techniques was finally used in order to provide better list of suggestions for misspelled word. Hybrid approach did not contain Hamming distance technique due to its poor results and the fact that it only deals with strings of equal length. Also, it provided same results for substitution as provided by Levenshtien distance therefore, it was discarded. Internet is one of the better way to introduce and provide improved approach of technology to the world. The spell checker that we have developed is limited in terms of platforms. However, in future we plan to come up with its web-based version to augment its use. Also, we intend to merge it as a tool/add on for Microsoft Word to check the spellings. It already has the feature for incorrect English word where it displays the list of related correct words; likewise, the add-on will provide same feature for Urdu language.

References

1. Damerau, F.J.: A technique for computer detection and correction of spelling errors. Commun. ACM **7**(3), 171–176 (1964)
2. Naseem, T., Hussain, S.: A novel approach for ranking spelling error corrections. Lang. Resour. Eval. **41**(2), 117–128 (2007)
3. Naseem, T.: A hybrid approach for Urdu spell checking. Master of Science (Computer Science) thesis at the National University of Computer & Emerging Sciences, pp. 1–87 (2004)
4. Das, M., Borgohain, S., Gogoi, J., Nair, S.B.: Design and implementation of a spell checker for Assamese, pp. 156–162. IEEE (2002)
5. Solak, A., Oflazer, K.: Design and implementation of a spelling checker for Turkish. Literary Linguist. Comput. **8**(3), 113–130 (1993)
6. Durrani, N., Hussain, S.: Urdu word segmentation. In: Human Language Technologies: The 2010 Annual Conference of the North American Chapter of the Association for Computational Linguistics, pp. 528–536 (2010)
7. Zaghouani, W., et al.: Large scale arabic error annotation: guidelines and framework. In: LREC, pp. 2362–2369 (2014)
8. Rasooli, M.S., Kahefi, O., Minaei-Bidgoli, B.: Effect of adaptive spell checking in Persian. In: 2011 7th International Conference on Natural Language Processing and Knowledge Engineering (NLP-KE), pp. 161–164. IEEE (2011)
9. Iqbal, S., Anwar, M.W., Bajwa, U.I., Rehman, Z.: Urdu spell checking: reverse edit distance approach. In: Proceedings of the 4th Workshop on South and Southeast Asian Natural Language Processing, pp. 58–65 (2013)

10. Magdy, W., Darwish, K.: Arabic OCR error correction using character segment correction, language modeling, and shallow morphology. In: Proceedings of the 2006 Conference on Empirical Methods in Natural Language Processing, pp. 408–414 (2006)
11. Zhang, Q., Zhang, S., Hou, J., Cheng, X.: HANSpeller: a unified framework for Chinese spelling correction. Int. J. Comput. Linguist. Chin. Lang. Process. **20**(1), 1–22 (2015)

Maximum Entropy Based Urdu Part of Speech Tagging

Usman Mohy Ud Din[1(✉)], Muhammad Waqas Anwar[1],
and Ghulam Ali Mallah[2]

[1] Department of Computer Science, COMSATS University Islamabad,
Lahore Campus, Lahore, Pakistan
mr.usman76@gmail.com, waqasanwar@cuilahore.edu.pk
[2] Shah Abdul Latif University, Khairpur, Pakistan

Abstract. This paper represents results for a part of speech tagger based on Maximum Entropy model on Urdu corpora. We discussed the specialized features/parameters of the model and their impact on tagger performance. We also discussed the complexity of Urdu language for a tagger to predict correct tag and inconsistencies in corpora found during experiments. For the purpose of detailed experiments, two different corpora are used in this paper. The maximum accuracy recorded for tagger is 93.24% overall and 69.89% on previously unseen data.

Keywords: Entropy · Urdu · Parts of Speech (PoS) tagging

1 Introduction

Urdu is a free-order language which belongs to the Indo-Aryan family of languages. Urdu is developed under the influence of Arabic, Persian, Turkish and Hindi. The word "Urdu" itself is derived from Turkish. Urdu is the national language of Pakistan and one of official language in India and Jammu Kashmir. It is a popular language in other South Asian countries like Bangladesh and Afghanistan. Urdu has almost 104 million speakers around the globe.

Urdu character-set with 38 characters is the super set of Arabic and Persian character-sets with 28 and 32 characters respectively. Usually, characters of Urdu language have four shapes, (1) Isolated, (2) as the First letter of the word, (3) Middle and (4) as the Last letter of the word. Urdu has some interesting characteristics as compared to other languages. Urdu follows SOV (Subject-Object-Verb) structure in a simple sentence. In Urdu, the text is written in right to left manner while digits in sentences are written in left to right. Urdu has additional tenses as compared to English. In Urdu, for example, the past indefinite tense of English language has three sub-types near past, absolute past and distant past [1] (Table 1).

© Springer Nature Singapore Pte Ltd. 2020
I. S. Bajwa et al. (Eds.): INTAP 2019, CCIS 1198, pp. 484–492, 2020.
https://doi.org/10.1007/978-981-15-5232-8_41

Table 1. Urdu Tense sub-types

English	Urdu	
He ate food.	(Near Past)	اس نے کھانا کھایا
	(Absolute Past)	اس نے کھانا کھایا ہے
	(Distant Past)	اس نے کھانا کھایا تھا

There is gender associated with Urdu words like adjectives and verbs. For example, in Urdu literature, table is considered as masculine while chair is considered as feminine. Moreover, verb changes its shape w.r.t subject's gender (male or female) and number (singular or plural) (Table 2).

Table 2. Verb shapes w.r.t subject

English	Urdu
She **eats** food.	وہ کھانا **کھاتی** ہے
He **eats** food	وہ کھانا **کھاتا** ہے
They **eat** food. (male)	وہ کھانا **کھاتے** ہیں
They **eat** food. (female)	وہ کھانا **کھاتی** ہیں

2 Literature Review

Part of speech (POS) is a basic unit in language processing. At some stage, almost every application in language processing demands part of speech tagging for preprocessing or classification of data. Usually, tagging is performed on tokenized data or tokenization is performed on data before tagging. It is quite difficult to assign tags to words as words exist in different forms. Many parts of speech taggers have been developed on different models so far. We will discuss some of them in this literature review.

The first ever automatic parts of speech tagger was built on the rule-based approach in 1963 by Kelin and Simmons [2]. A rule-based approach has the disadvantage to define rules which require prior linguistic knowledge. If we have a large set of rules, say for example 100, then these rules start interacting with each other in a complex way. To identify and modify a faulty rule requires a lot of manual effort and sometimes effects the other rules too. [3] claims 95% success in his transformation based approach for English tag set. It works in two phases. In its initial phase, it assigns tags to words and then on the second stage, it determines which tags should be transformed into other tags. Due to complexities in the Urdu language, discussed in Sect. 6, rule-based and transformation based approaches didn't result on a successful note in regard with Urdu data. [4] used Hidden Markov Model (HMM) based on the stochastic algorithm and analyzed results on Urdu dataset. HMM, based approach did not produce very good results. They used morphological analyzer (MA) and stemmer along with HMM to improve results. They implemented a tagger on both the bigram HMM (first order) and the trigram HMM (second order). Almost 16 extended HMM models were proposed and their performances were analyzed. Maximum accuracy obtained from these models was less than 90% on known data. The performance of their system was not as good as POS taggers available in recent times. [5] analyzed the performance of four state of the art taggers i.e. TnT, TreeTagger, RF Tagger and SVM tool on Urdu tagset. They claimed SVM tool performance better than others with the accuracy of 94-97%. There are five different kinds of model implemented in SVM which differ in terms of feature extraction and selection of examples. [5] used "model 4" of SVM which achieved robustness by simulating unknown words in the learning context. [6] proposed a standalone tagger for the Urdu language. "Model 4" of SVM tool with tagging direction from right-to-left was used to train the tagger. The highest accuracy achieved by the tagger was 88.46%, 54.76% for known and unknown words respectively. [9] developed linear chain conditional random field based part of speech tagging for Urdu language. The proposed approach tested on two different corpora improved the F-measure upto 8.5%. Ensemble methods allow users to integrate semi-supervised/un-supervised methods to integrate with supervised methods to get advantages of both techniques. [10] develop decision tree ensemble part of speech tagger for resource poor languages. In their approach, they integrated semisupervised datamining technique CBL(s) with supervised taggers SVM and CRF where decision tree was implemented using classification and regression trees (CART). The proposed technique showed improvements in terms of oracle accuracy w. r.t baseline results. Training of supervised models heavily depends on proper labelled data which is often unavailable in case of low resource languages like Urdu. [11] presented POS tagging of Indian languages without any label data using feature projection. In proposed methodology, knowledge acquired from the corpus of high resource language is projected to low resource language while assigning tags to words. [12] added character-level supervision in hierarchal recurrent model for part of speech tagging of low resource languages with small amount of data. System tested on different auxiliary tasks like lemmatization, word auto encoding and random string auto encoding performed better generalization of unseen words.

3 Maximum Entropy Model

Maximum Entropy is based on the logistic regression model. Logistic regression is used for prediction of the probability of occurrence of an event. These types of models make it much easier to incorporate a wide range of features. Maximum entropy model takes the decision based on previous tags and the current observation. The model assigns a probability for every tag t in the set of T of possible tags given a word w and its history h.

$$p(h, t) = \pi \mu k \prod j = 1 \ \alpha_j f_i(h, t) \tag{1}$$

The maximum entropy model will choose the probability that maximizes the entropy out of those that satisfies a certain set of conditions. As mentioned by [8], model's probability of a history h together with a tag t is defined as:

Where, π is a normalization constant, $\{\mu, \alpha_1, \alpha_2, \alpha_k\}$ are the positive model parameters and $\{f_1, f_2, ..., f_k\}$ are known features, where $f_j(h, j) \in \{0, 1\}$. Each parameter αj corresponds to a feature fj. In the maximum entropy model, contextual/specialized features are used to predict the correct POS tag. Some of them are window-size, suffixes and prefixes. These features are the subsets of the features explained by [7].

We will try to explain these features w.r.t Urdu data. All these features are used to help tagger to predict the most appropriate tag by analyzing the context and history of the word. Window size (-1, 1) refers that tagger has to check the tag of one word before the current word and one word after the current word in its decision. In Table 3, at position 3, tagger will check tag of one word before that is P and one word after that is NN before assigning any tag to a word at position 3. Similarly, at position 3 with window-size (-2,2), the tagger will consider tags of two words before the current word and tags of two words after the current word before assigning the tag and so on. Table 3 Words with positions

Table 3. Words with positions

Tag:	P	NN	ADJ	P	PN
Position:	5	4	3	2	1
Words:	ہیں	ترقی	معاشی	کی	چین

Prefix refers to, how many characters from the start of the word will be considered during its tagging. Similarly, Suffix refers to how many characters from the end of the word will be considered during its tagging.

In Table 4, we have a word Wi of Urdu language. Wi (1) refers to the first character in case of prefix and for suffix, it refers to the last character of the word. Similarly, Wi (2) refers to the first two characters of the word in prefix and for suffix, it refers to the last two characters of the word and so on.

Table 4. Prefix, Suffix

No. of characters	Prefix	Suffix
$W_i(1)$	ن	ت
$W_i(2)$	نس	ات
$W_i(3)$	نست	یات
$W_i(4)$	نستع	یقات

4 Evaluation and Results

There are a number of taggers available for tagging, based on different machine learning algorithms, some of them have been discussed earlier in the literature review section of this paper. We chose "Stanford Log-linear Part-Of-Speech Tagger"[1] for our experiments. It is based on the maximum entropy model. Proper tagged data is very important in supervised learning. We used two different corpora in this paper and on each corpus, we computed the result of three experiments with a varying set of features.

4.1 First Corpus (C1)

[8] released a monolingual corpus automatically tagged by using three different taggers I.e. SVM tagger, Hum analyzer, and SH parser. It consists of 5.4 million sentences and 95.4 million words. To examine the performance of tagger a portion of this corpus (10,200 sentences). Table 5 shows the characteristics of the corpus (C1) and Table 6 shows the results of the experiments with a specific feature set.

Table 5. Corpus C1 characteristics

Corpus (C1)	Tokens	Types	Unknown tokens
Training	174416	17989	——
Testing	3529	1419	217

Table 6. Corpus C1 results

#	Features (window-size, prefix, suffix)	Overall accuracy	Unknown words accuracy
1	pw2,pw1,cw,nw1,nw2 $|\text{pre}| \leq 6,\ |\text{suff}| \leq 6$	91.15%	63.59%
2	pw4,pw3,pw2,pw1,cw,nw1,nw2, nw3,nw4 $|\text{pre}| \leq 8,\ |\text{suff}| \leq 8$	91.84%	68.20%
3	pw6,..,pw2,pw1,cw,nw1,nw2,..,n w6 $|\text{pre}| \leq 10,\ |\text{suff}| \leq 10$	91.92%	68.20%

During the experiment, we found issues in the corpus (C1) which have affected the tagger's performance. We will discuss those issues in Sect. 6.

4.2 Second Corpus (C2)

Second corpus (C2), a news corpus (www.jang.com.pk), contains approx. 110 k tokens and used by [5]. This corpus is manually tagged and consists of 43 tags. Data is divided

---

[1] https://nlp.stanford.edu/software/tagger.shtml.

into two parts, 90% training corpus, and 10% test corpus. Table 7 shows the characteristics of the corpus (C2) and Table 8 shows the results of the experiments with a specific feature set.

Table 7. Corpus C2 characteristics

Corpus (C2)	Tokens	Types	Unknown tokens
Training	101424	7515	——
Testing	8670	1932	754

Table 8. Corpus C2 results

#	Features (window-size, prefix, suffix)	Overall accuracy	Unknown words accuracy
1	pw2,pw1,cw,nw1,nw2 $\lvert\text{pre}\rvert \leq 6$, $\lvert\text{suff}\rvert \leq 6$	92.25%	64.32%
2	pw4,pw3,pw2,pw1,cw,nw 1,nw2,nw3,nw4 $\lvert\text{pre}\rvert \leq 8$, $\lvert\text{suff}\rvert \leq 8$	93.24%	69.89%
3	pw6,..,pw2,pw1,cw,nw1,n w2,..,nw6 $\lvert\text{pre}\rvert \leq 10$, $\lvert\text{suff}\rvert \leq 10$	93.22%	69.36%

By comparing results Table 6 and Table 8, we can say that C2 results are better C1. We conducted experiments using different combinations of features on two corpora and found that tagger outperformed at the second experiment of Corpus C2 (row#2, Table 6). In Tables 6 and 8, the annotated pw, cw, nw represents the previous word, current word, and the next word respectively. Similarly, pw_i, nw_i represents the previous ith word and next ith word. Pre, suff is the prefix and suffix of a current word. Table 9, presents the confusion matrix of seconds Corpus (C2) results.

Table 9. Most confused pairs

Golden tags	Predicted tags				
	#	NN	PN	ADV	ADJ
	ADJ	71	9	5	—
	ADV	19	4	4	19
	PN	136	—	1	24
	NN	—	52	4	39
	VB	24	2	4	4

5 Discussion on Results

Urdu is rich language when it comes to morphology. A word can be represented in multiple categories like a verb, a noun by using diacritics. During the pre-processing of data, diacritics are removed from the corpus. It becomes very difficult for a tagger to predict correct tag since the removal of diacritic makes them look similar. The tagger has shown the poor accuracy on nouns, proper nouns, adjectives, and verbs. In most of the cases, tagger is confused while predicting correct tag among noun, proper-noun, adjective and verb categories. There are no clear boundaries between a noun and proper noun, proper noun, and adjectives in the Urdu language. Below are some examples where tagger predicts the wrong tag due to these complexities.

- Unlike other languages, Urdu does not follow the rule of capitalizing the first character of a proper noun.
- Words may have only one representation for both singular and plural words. For example, in Urdu word man (singular) and men (plural) both are represented with one word آدمی. Similarly, for word male (singular) and males (plural), the Urdu language uses only one word مرد to represent them. To know the type of such words, we have to analyze the context of the sentence.
- The word حسین (beautiful) is an adjective and حسین (Hussain) is a proper noun in the Urdu language. Without diacritic, they are written in the same way. We found some cases where tagger confused both words.
- The word پاک (PAK) is an abbreviation of word پاکستان (PAKISTAN) which is a proper noun but in Urdu, word پاک (clean) is also used as a noun.
- The word عظیم (Great) is a noun in Urdu while word عظیم (Azeem) is a proper noun. Both words are written and pronounced in the same way.
- The word سونا (sleep) is a verb and word سونا (gold) is a noun. Both are pronounced and written in the same way.
- There are different ways to represent a date in Urdu. These are given as:

    o   306, قبل مسیح
    o 1436 AH o 14 اگست 1947 o
    چودہ اگست انیس سو سنتالیس o

6 Issues in Corpus (C1)

During the analysis of results, we found many cases where a tag assigned to a word is not correct. We attempt to explain some of them.

PN as Adj: There are occurrences of proper nouns where it is marked as an adjective. The word (abbreviation of Pakistan) پاک is a proper noun which is marked as the adjective. Words محمود,مظہر are proper nouns which are tagged as the adjectives. **QW as KP:** In corpus, question word (QW) is marked as Kaf pronoun (KP). The **(what)** کیا word marked as KP.

PN as NN: The Urdu language follows the same rule for proper nouns as any other. During investigation/pre-processing of data, we find many cases in corpus where PN marked as NN.

Incorrect MUL: Below are some cases where the existence of multiplicative (MUL) tag is incorrect.

(1) فکر_NN نہ_NEG کریں_VB اسکے_G لینے_AA_A

ہم_PP کراچی_MUL پہنچ_VB سکتے_TA_A ہیں

(2) انفال_TA کے_P معانی_MUL کیا_KP ہوتے_VB ہیں

U as NN and NN as U: In corpus, the word (square) مربع is marked as NN and word ای میل (Email) is marked as U.

7   Conclusion

We have analyzed the results of maximum entropy based tagger on the different corpus of Urdu language with contextual window size, prefix, and suffix of varying lengths. By using the same corpus C1, our results are better than reported in [5], 54.76% vs 68.20% on unknown data and 88.46% vs 91.92% on known data. Similarly using same corpus C2, this tagger's accuracy with 69.89% on unknown data is better than TreeTagger with 65.92%, RF tagger with 68.08% and TnT tagger with 68.44% as mentioned in [4]. We believe that the accuracy of this tagger can be improved further if the characteristics and complexities of Urdu language, discussed in Sect. 1 and Sect. 5, is considered during the decision making process of a tagger.

References

1. Ahmed, T., Alvi, S.: English to Urdu translation system. Manuscript, University of Karachi (2002)
2. Kelin, S., Simmons, R.: A computational approach to grammatical coding of English words. J. Assoc. Comput. Mach. **10**(3), 334–347 (1963)
3. Bril, E.: A simple rule based part of speech tagging. In: A Treatise on Electricity and Magnetism, 3rd ed., vol. 2, pp. 68–73. Clarendon, Oxford (1892)
4. Khanum, H., Murthy, M.: Part-Of-Speech tagging of Urdu in limited resouce scenario. Int. J. Recent Innov. Trends Comput. Commun., 3280–3285 (2014)
5. Hassan, S., Helmut, S.: Tagging Urdu text with parts of speech tagging: a tagger comparion. In: Proceedings of the 12th conference of the Euorpeon Chapter of the Association for Computationl Linguistics, pp. 692–700 (2009)
6. Jawaid, B., Kamran, A., Bojar, O.: A tagged corpus and a tagger for Urdu. In: Proceedings of the 9th International Conference of language processing and evaluation, LREC 2014, Iceland, pp. 2938–2943 (2014)

7. Ratnaparkhi, A.: A maximum entropy model for part-of-speech tagging. In: Proceeding of the Conferenc on Empirical Methods in Natural Language Processing, University of Pennsylvania (1996)
8. Jawaid, B., Bojar, O.: Tagger voting for Urdu. In: Proceedings of the 3rd Workshop on South and Southeast Asian Natural Language Processing (SANLP), Mumbai, pp. 135–144 (2012)
9. Khan, W., et al.: Urdu part of speech tagging using conditional random fields. Lang. Res. Eval. **53**(3), 331–362 (2018). https://doi.org/10.1007/s10579-018-9439-6
10. Reddy, V.K., Rani, P., Pudi, V., Sharma, D.M.: Decision tree ensemble for parts-of-speech tagging of resource-poor languages. In: Proceedings of the 10th annual meeting of the Forum for Information Retrieval Evaluation, pp. 41–47. ACM (2018)
11. Mishra, P., Mujadia, V., Sharma, D.M.: POS tagging for resource poor indian languages through feature projection (2018)
12. Kann, K., Bjerva, J., Augenstein, I., Plank, B., Søgaard, A.: Character-level supervision for low-resource POS tagging. In: Proceedings of the Workshop on Deep Learning Approaches for Low-Resource NLP, pp. 1–11 (2018)

Towards a Generic Approach for PoS-Tagwise Lexical Similarity of Languages

Muhammad Suffian Nizami[(✉)], Muhammad Yaseen Khan,
and Tafseer Ahmed

Center for Language Computing, Department of Computer Science,
Mohammad Ali Jinnah University, Karachi, Pakistan
{m.suffian,yaseen.khan,tafseer.ahmed}@jinnah.edu

Abstract. The lexical similarity measures of the languages are used to find genetic affinity among them—as the languages come closer in language tree, chances increase to have more cognates in common. In this regard, this paper describes a tool to calculate the lexical similarity between pairs of languages. We used the words present in Universal Dependency (UD) corpora to find lexical similarities of the words. Since, many of languages in the UD corpora share the same scheme of part of speech (PoS) tag-set; we got the lists of words, corresponding to standard set of PoS tags. The tool can compare words of particular PoS tags for two different languages. Hence, we can calculate lexical similarity not only for the whole language but also for the specific PoS or a subset of PoS. Further, a user can compare function-words to find genetic affinity, nouns, and proper nouns to find borrowing or the loan-words. Moreover, this tool is more flexible than using either all of the words or a list (e.g., Swadesh list).

Keywords: Lexical similarity · Part of speech · Language similarity

1 Introduction

Coherent resemblance among the relevant languages generates substantial work for linguistics. Since languages are clustered in different aspects of similarity: like similar in typography [18], shared history, cognate sets, phonetics and phonemic styles, and region [29]; Therefore, the intrinsic coherent relatedness therein can be useful for many purposes, for instance: to identify the loan words, words similarity, the genetic affinity of languages, cognate sets, and in broader perspective for machine translation [23].

The phenomenon of the global village has made a deep-seated necessity of bilingualism [8]. Thus, different languages spoken in the same region borrow words and other linguistic rules [3]. The spread of language prevails on foreign speakers and writers if its linguistic rules are more straightforward and comprehensible. Field linguists have noticed that many languages contain words with some specific features of phonetics and phonemic styles, and their meanings [11]. Researchers have also worked on the cognate sets to describe the genetic similarity of languages [10]. The cognate sets are partially connected when cognate morphemes are identified in words. Partial cognacy occurs in almost every language under language-tree based on proximity/closeness; produces

© Springer Nature Singapore Pte Ltd. 2020
I. S. Bajwa et al. (Eds.): INTAP 2019, CCIS 1198, pp. 493–501, 2020.
https://doi.org/10.1007/978-981-15-5232-8_42

derived morphology [19]. Earlier, many tasks on language similarity measures were done through comparing words, mainly focusing on the Swadesh list, because it has words which are common among them [2].

In this paper, we focus on the lexical similarity through the comparison based on part-of-speech (PoS) tags [25]. The PoS is mainly based on open and closed class words. Thus, for the course of the experiment, we focus the closed class words of the language vocabulary. In general, the open class words carry the contents; hence, it is better to employ and compare the closed class words because functional words (such as pronouns and auxiliaries) are less borrowed in other languages. We have employed the Universal Dependency (UD) treebank data for the targeted languages for similarity. The UD data comes as a standard dataset which contains parallel data for many languages in a uniform format. As we plan to work on word similarity based on the part of speech tags, the tree-banks of UD provide a useful tool for parallel analysis of words [24]. We used word lists and lemma lists of different PoS tags, followed by developing a generalized transcription mechanism through which the words are represented in a uniform orthographic representation for comparative analysis. The generalized transcription scheme was in need due to Buckwalter format of Arabic language, in this format the calculation was not possible, that's conversion applied on Arabic language to get original format/script. Then, words represented into uniform orthographic scheme international phonetic alphabets (IPA) for comparison of words.

The advantages and applications of the proposed tool can be seen in information retrieval, language analysis on PoS tag set, and support in development for a specific system in language translation. Further, the NLP crowd can use this system to work on lexical similarity measures to identify the loan/borrowed words from other languages. The rest of the paper is organized with related work in Sect. 2, methodology in Sect. 3, results in Sect. 4, followed by a conclusion and future work in the end.

2 Background

Johann-Mattis [20] proposed the concept of pair-wise word sequence similarity is checked for all the morphemes of a word in the word-list, by using these similarities they constructed a node network of morphemes and the similarity among them. They used the info-map [28] algorithm, which given the right results to cluster these networks. [13] Inferred the phylogenetic tree of the languages using word-list's. They used the weighted alignment of words into classes, and their algorithm worked more accurate than the un-weighted edit distance between the words. [18] used the historical relatedness of languages, and compute the similarity by using the algorithms from bioinformatics to find the sequence comparison in historical linguistics.

In method [34], two words are matched with their consonant classes to check cognacy. The idea of consonant classes given by [5], in which the sounds of similar frequency mostly occur in related languages and classified into the same classes. In edit distance method [16] the Levenshtein distance is taken of all words with the same meaning and then clustered into the respective cognate sets, this is similar in approach to UPGMA [31] in which its tops when the specific threshold level is achieved. Another edit distance like method is Sound Class Alignment (SCA) in which the same threshold level is used, but the distance is taken of sound class alignment algorithm [18]. There is another algorithm, LexStat [17] in which the word-lists pairs of languages are permuted in a way that words with different meanings are given scores and saved and then these scores are calculated based on the sound correspondences and assigned some clusters. The pipeline for computational linguistics to calculate the similarity between languages is given by [33] and is helpful to process. [4] used the orthographic alignment for cognate detection automatically, their approach requires known cognates with additional information and then suggest cognate pair for language change using machine learning. Rama [26] proposed two statistical methods like Levenshtein distance for cognate detection and the statistical machine translation (SMT) to align the phonemes of semantically equivalent words and then computed the distance of those phonemes. [32] worked on the identification of cognate sets using dictionaries of related languages; their work was on comprehensive feature set including phonetic and semantic similarity. [7] worked on the structured correspondence between the related languages by using minimum description length based algorithm to find the similarity among groups of languages. [27] worked on a method to make a generalized script to teach Spanish to English speakers. The focus was on the linguistic pattern similarities like pronunciation, vocabulary, and grammar alignment between Spanish and English language. [14] used the SVM for phonetic alignment in multilingual word-lists for cognate identification. SVM was trained with these word-pairs, keeping string similarity as feature set, then it predicts the probability of cognacy on the test data between the word-pairs. These probability values then used for clustering of cognates as predicted classes.

3 Methodology

In this section, we describe the methods and materials employed, algorithm devised for the similarity index, word alignment and transcription scheme for different languages with a uniform orthographic representation for computing the similarity index for languages.

3.1 Word Lists Generation

We have extracted word lists (WL) from the UD data sets against each language according to PoS tags. The languages under this study are Arabic, Persian, and Urdu. All of these languages are written in Perso-Arabic script [6] and closer to each other due to similar phonetics rules and loan words [22]. For example, Urdu has many borrowed words from Persian and Arabic [12]. The word lists are extracted based on the PoS tags from the data-sets present at UD web-site[1]. The closed class PoS tags are selected from the Universal PoS. The tags like ADP:Adposition, AUX: auxiliary, CCONJ: coordinating conjunction, DET:determiner, PART:particle, PRON:pronoun and SCONJ: subordinating conjunction word lists are used for the similarity purposes.

---

[1] https://universaldependencies.org/.

Here we represent the set of selected PoS tag-set with symbol Ψ. The UD data was in a standard 'conllu' format. We extracted the required PoS data from this data using python language.

3.2 Orthographic Transcription

In this phase, we developed a generalized mechanism for all languages based on International Phonetic Alphabets (IPA) [1]. The general idea behind it assumes that if languages are similar phonetically, then their IPA will be more analogous for a specific word in two languages. WL transcribed into IPA for Arabic, Urdu, and Persian. During transcription, we faced issues in the Arabic language such that the lemma of Arabic words was in the format of Buckwalter scheme [9]; therefore, we wrote a transliterating algorithm for the conversion of Arabic text into its original format. For example, for the Arabic text أحيانا أشبة يكون (means: "sometimes it is more like") the Buckwalter format is given in the Table 1.

Table 1. Buckwalter representation Arabic word/lemma

Arabic word	Buckwalter format
أحيانا	Hiyn_
يكون	kAn-u1
أشبة	>a$obah2

3.3 Algorithm for Similarity

In literature, many people worked on the similarity of words using different algorithms like (Kondrak, Levenshtein, Lingpy [15, 21, 30]). We will use Levenshtein Distance (LD) for similarity index. Which can be briefly discussed as the string metric for measuring how distant are the words of pair-languages; intuitively, at least how many single-character edits are required to transform the given the word i into any other word j. Further, we know that distance (d), and the similarity (s) is the inversely co-related, $d \propto \frac{1}{s}$, which means the similarity increases as the distance between two things decreases. As a case, the source-language (l^1) and target language as (l^2) with their respective PoS are compared, and the result is stored in the matrix (SM). The overall shape of SM is given below in Eq. 1: in which words of first/source language $\left(w_1^l\right)$ are placed in columns, and in the similar fashion, words for the second/target language $\left(w_2^l\right)$ are placed in rows, where Φ in SM^Φ denotes specific PoS understudy, $\Phi \in \Psi$.

$$SM^\Phi = \begin{vmatrix} w_1^{l1} & w_2^{l1}\dots & w_n^{l1} \\ 0 & 0\dots & 0 \\ 0 & 0\dots & 0 \end{vmatrix} \begin{matrix} w_1^{l2} \\ w_2^{l2} \\ w_n^{l2} \end{matrix} \qquad (1)$$

4 Results

4.1 Similarity Metric

We introduced a formula for calculating the similarity of lists of words. We can consider this as the ratio of similarity between two languages is higher if the number of particular PoS words of one language have lower normalized LD values compared with same PoS words of other language. The LD value is normalized by dividing LD with word length.

Hence, for the generalized formula for calculating similarity, we consider the SM^{Φ} (as presented in Eq. 1); whereas columns and rows we have words of l_1 and l_2 respectively, then:

$$SI = 1 - \frac{\sum \left[\frac{min(SM_{i,j})}{max[w_i, w_j]} \right]}{N}, \forall_i \tag{2}$$

where SI is similarity index, $SM_{i,j}$ shows the LD between i^{th} and j^{th} words in l_1 and l_2 (i.e., source and target language) respectively for the given PoS Φ; and w_i and w_j are the length of corresponding words in l_1 and l_2, and N is the total number of words used for comparison, where LD is found minimum.

4.2 Discussion

One of the primary difference between Arabic and Urdu closed class PoS is of the multiple subtypes of Arabic alphabets in Urdu; for example, the Arabic ة/hā/is also written in Urdu as ہ "Choti he" (see Arabic خطبة and Urdu خطبہ along PRON in Table 2), however, the rendering of these alphabets are subjected to the font under usage. In contrast, we do not see such issues between Persian and Urdu. The most fundamental reason for this can be Urdu-Persian has got more common words than Urdu-Arabic.

Table 2 shows selected words for ADP, PRON, and CCONJ in Arabic-Urdu PoS tag set with their respective IPA. Similarly, Table 3 shows the selected words ADP and CCONJ for Urdu-Persian PoS tag set with respective IPA. However, these are the few selected words out of exhaustive WL residing in UD for the languages mentioned above.

The result has shown in Fig. 1 that the few classes of PoS for compared languages are more similar than others. Like the ADP, DET, CCONJ, and SCONJ classes of PoS of Persian are more similar to Urdu classes. The closed class tagset words are primarily utilized to compute the IPA based similarity.

The detailed quantification of results presented in Fig. 1 is shown in Tables 4 and 5, where the words of one language are compared with the words of second language with respect of PoS lists. The percentage of similarity is calculated using the Eq. 2.

Table 2. IPA-based similarity of Arabic-Urdu Ad-position (ADP), Pronoun (PRON), and coordinating conjunction (CCONJ).

PoS	Arabic				Urdu				LD
	Word	IPA	Roman	Meaning	Word	IPA	Roman	Meaning	
ADP	ضمن	Zmn	ziman	Regard	ضمن	Zmn	ziman	regard	0
	قبل	qbl	qabal	Before	قبل	qbl	qabal	before	0
	ف	f	fe	F	آف	F	of	Of	0
	ب	b	b	With	سب	B	sab	all	1
	لكن	lkn	lekin	But	لگ	Lg	lag	attach	1
	بين	bn	ben	Cry	بنا	bnə	bana	made	1
PRON	فيلم	flm	feelam	Movie	فيلم	flm	film	movie	0
	شينجن	ʃːndʒ	Shenjan	Capital	انجن	nd n	engine	engine	0
	خطبة	xtb	khutbah	Speech	خطب	xtb	khutba	speech	0
	بانک	bon	bank	Bank	بان	bən	baan	poll	1
	ميليس	mls	milis	Measurement	ملے	Mile	miley	meet	1
CCONJ	أن	in	In	–	نے	Ne	ne	–	2
	تي	Tj	Ti	–	تو	tʊ	tu	–	1

Table 3. IPA-based similarity of Persian-Urdu Ad-position (ADP) and coordinating conjunction (CCONJ).

PoS	Arabic				Urdu				LD
	Word	IPA	Roman	Meaning	Word	IPA	Roman	Meaning	
ADP	نزد	nzd	nazd	nearby	نزد	nzd	nizd	nearby	0
	نزدیک	Nzdjk	nazdik	Near	نزدیک	nzdjk	Nazdeek	near	0
	پیش	piʃ	pesh	present	پیش	piʃ	Pesh	present	0
	سمت	smt	simat	Direction	سمت	smt	Simt	direction	0
CCONJ	لكن	lkn	lekun	But	لیکن	lekn	lekin	but	1
	يا	Ja	ya	Or	یا	ja	ya	or	0

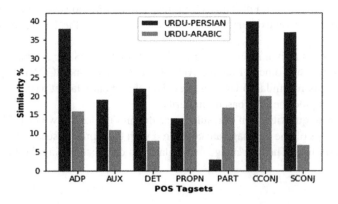

Fig. 1. Languages similarity PoS tag set wise

Table 4. Urdu-Arabic POS tag-wise similarity percentage

Language	Urdu	Arabic	% Similarity
ADP	205	78	16
AUX	78	28	9.3
DET	73	26	7.43
PROPN	3221	1114	24.5
PART	91	37	16.5
CCONJ	21	7	19.49
SCONJ	44	2	7

Table 5. Urdu-Persian POS tag-wise similarity percentage

Language	Urdu	Persian	% Similarity
ADP	205	80	37.4
AUX	78	19	18.6
DET	73	24	22
PROPN	3221	43	14
PART	91	2	3
CCONJ	21	25	39.4
SCONJ	44	52	37

Table 4 and 5 show that Urdu words are more similar to Persian than Arabic. It is comprehensible because of two reasons. Urdu is more closely related with Persian, as both belong to Indo-Iranian family of languages while Arabic is Semitic language. Moreover, Urdu had direct language contact with Persian when Persian was the official language (and language of the elite) of the Indian subcontinent. Hence, we had more chances of cognates and borrowed words from Persian, and the results confirmed this intuition.

5 Conclusion

In this paper, we presented a method to compare lexical similarity of different languages. Our technique uses the corpora created for Universal Dependency (UD). These corpora use the same PoS tagset, hence, we are able to compare PoS tagwise lexical similarity of different corpora. The technique is applied on two language pairs that use same script. However, as the technique converts the words into IPA script, it can be extended to other languages pairs written in different scripts.

Our comparison of lexical similarity between Urdu-Arabic and Urdu-Persian shows that the Urdu is more similar to Persian in terms of ADP, DET, CCONJ, and SCONJ PoS tags. The reason of more similarity of Urdu and Persian is genetic similarity as well as more borrowing due to language contact in the past.

References

1. International Phonetic Association: Handbook of the International Phonetic Association: A Guide to the Use of the International Phonetic Alphabet. Cambridge University Press (1999)
2. Cadora, F.J.: Lexical relationships among arabic dialects and the swadeshlist. Anthropol. Linguist. **18**(6), 237–260 (1976)
3. Calabrese, A., Wetzels, L.: Loan Phonology. John Benjamins Publishing Company, Amsterdam (2009)
4. Ciobanu, A.M., Dinu, L.P.: Automatic detection of cognates using ortho-graphic alignment. In: Proceedings of the 52nd Annual Meeting of the Association for Computational Linguistics (Volume 2: Short Papers), vol. 2, pp. 99–105 (2014)
5. Dolgopolsky, A.B.: Gipoteza drevnejšego rodstva jazykovych semej severnojevrazii s verojatnostej točky zrenija [a probabilistic hypothesis concerning the oldest relationships among the language families of northern eurasia]. Voprosy jazykoznanija **2**, 53–63 (1964)
6. Ferguson, C.A.: Sociolinguistic settings of language planning. In: Language Planning Processes, vol. 21, pp. 9–29 (1977)
7. Fischer, A.K., Vreeken, J., Klakow, D.: Beyond pairwise similarity: quantifying and characterizing linguistic similarity between groups of languages by MDL. Computación y Sistemas **21**(4), 829–839 (2017)
8. Genesee, F.: Dual language in the global village. Bilingual Educ. Bilingualism **66**, 22 (2008)
9. Habash, N., Soudi, A., Buckwalter, T.: On arabic transliteration. In: Soudi, A., Bosch, A., Neumann, G. (eds.) Arabic Computational Morphology. TLTB, vol. 38, pp. 15–22. Springer, Dordrecht (2007). https://doi.org/10.1007/978-1-4020-6046-5_2
10. Hauer, B., Kondrak, G.: Clustering semantically equivalent words into cognate sets in multilingual lists. In: Proceedings of 5th international joint conference on natural language processing, pp. 865–873 (2011)
11. Imai, M., Kita, S.: The sound symbolism bootstrapping hypothesis for language acquisition and language evolution. Philos. Trans. R. Soc. B: Biol. Sci. **369**(1651), 20130298 (2014)
12. Islam, R.A.: The morphology of loanwords in Urdu: the Persian, Arabic and English strands. Ph.D. thesis, Newcastle University (2012)
13. Jäger, G.: Phylogenetic inference from word lists using weighted alignment with empirically determined weights. In: Quantifying Language Dynamics, pp. 155–204. Brill (2014)
14. Jäger, G., List, J.M., Sofroniev, P.: Using support vector machines and state-of-the-art algorithms for phonetic alignment to identify cognates in multi-lingual wordlists. In: Proceedings of the 15th Conference of the European Chapter of the Association for Computational Linguistics: Volume 1, Long Papers, pp. 1205–1216 (2017)
15. Kondrak, G.: N-gram similarity and distance. In: Consens, M., Navarro, G. (eds.) SPIRE 2005. LNCS, vol. 3772, pp. 115–126. Springer, Heidelberg (2005). https://doi.org/10.1007/11575832_13
16. Levenshtein, V.I.: Binary codes with correction for deletions and insertions of the symbol 1. Probl. Peredachi Informatsii **1**(1), 12–25 (1965)
17. List, J.M.: LexStat: automatic detection of cognates in multilingual wordlists. In: Proceedings of the EACL 2012 Joint Workshop of LINGVIS & UNCLH, pp. 117–125. Association for Computational Linguistics (2012)
18. List, J.M.: Sequence comparison in historical linguistics. Ph.D. thesis, Heinrich-Heine-Universität Düsseldorf (2013)
19. List, J.M.: Beyond cognacy: historical relations between words and their implication for phylogenetic reconstruction. J. Lang. Evol. **1**(2), 119–136 (2016)

20. List, J.M., Lopez, P., Bapteste, E.: Using sequence similarity networks to identify partial cognates in multilingual wordlists. In: Proceedings of the 54th Annual Meeting of the Association for Computational Linguistics (Volume 2: Short Papers), vol. 2, pp. 599–605 (2016)

21. List, J.M., Moran, S., Bouda, P., Dellert, J.: Lingpy. Python library for automatic tasks in historical linguistics (2013)

22. Maqsood, B., Saleem, T., Aziz, A., Azam, S.: Grammatical constraints on the borrowing of nouns and verbs in urdu and english. SAGE Open 9(2), 2158244019853469 (2019)

23. Nakov, P., Tiedemann, J.: Combining word-level and character-level models for machine translation between closely-related languages. In: Proceedings of the 50th Annual Meeting of the Association for Computational Linguistics: Short Papers-Volume 2, pp. 301–305. Association for Computational Linguistics (2012)

24. Nivre, J., De Marneffe, M.C., Ginter, F., Goldberg, Y., Hajic, J., Manning, C.D., McDonald, R.T., Petrov, S., Pyysalo, S., Silveira, N., et al.: Universal dependencies v1: a multilingual treebank collection. In: LREC (2016)

25. Petrov, S., Das, D., McDonald, R.: A universal part-of-speech tagset. arXiv preprint arXiv: 1104.2086 (2011)

26. Rama, T., Kolachina, P., Kolachina, S.: Two methods for automatic identification of cognates. In: Proceedings of the 5th QITL Conference, pp. 76–80(2013)

27. Rivera, J.L.: A study conception about language similarities. Open J. Mod. Linguist. 9(2), 47–58 (2019)

28. Rosvall, M., Bergstrom, C.T.: Maps of random walks on complex networks reveal community structure. Proc. Nat. Acad. Sci. 105(4), 1118–1123 (2008)

29. Schepens, J., Dijkstra, T., Grootjen, F., Van Heuven, W.J.: Cross-language distributions of high frequency and phonetically similar cognates. PLoS one 8(5), e63006 (2013)

30. Serva, M., Petroni, F.: Indo-European languages tree by Levenshtein distance. EPL (Europhys. Lett.) 81(6), 68005 (2008)

31. Sokal, R.R.: A statistical method for evaluating systematic relationship. Univ. Kansas Sci. Bull. 28, 1409–1438 (1958)

32. St Arnaud, A., Beck, D., Kondrak, G.: Identifying cognate sets across dictionaries of related languages. In: Proceedings of the 2017 Conference on Empirical Methods in Natural Language Processing, pp. 2519–2528 (2017)

33. Steiner, L., Cysouw, M., Stadler, P.: A pipeline for computational historical linguistics. Lang. Dyn. Change 1(1), 89–127 (2011)

34. List, J.-M.: SCA: phonetic alignment based on sound classes. In: Lassiter, D., Slavkovik, M. (eds.) ESSLLI 2010–2011. LNCS, vol. 7415, pp. 32–51. Springer, Heidelberg (2012). https://doi.org/10.1007/978-3-642-31467-4_3

Preprocessing Techniques in Text Categorization: A Survey

Sayyam Malik$^{(\boxtimes)}$, Sana Ahmad Sani$^{(\boxtimes)}$, Anees Baqir$^{(\boxtimes)}$, Usman Ahmad$^{(\boxtimes)}$, and Faizan ul Mustafa$^{(\boxtimes)}$

Department of Computer Science and IT, University of Lahore, Chenab Campus, Gujrat, Pakistan
sayyamg3@gmail.com, sani.zaheer1@gmail.com, anees.baqir@outlook.com, ahmadusman.se@gmail.com, azson.faizan@gmail.com

Abstract. Text Categorization is a process of categorizing or labeling an unstructured Natural Language (NL) text to related categories with the help of a predefined set. In text categorization, pre-processing is a crucial step which is used for extracting non-trivial, interesting and useful input for further stages of the process of text categorization. As the words in text usually contains a lot of structural variations, so before accessing the information from documents, pre-processing techniques are applied on the data to minimize the size of the data which may increase efficacy of the result and better categorize the text. The main objective of this research is to Survey about the pre-processing techniques like Tokenization, Stop-words removing and Stemming. We'll see how these techniques affect text categorization in good or may be bad ways.

Keywords: Tokenization · Stop Word Removal · Stemming · Pre-processing techniques for text categorization

1 Introduction

In this digital era, advancement of technology is touching skies. People usually work with electronic documents because of which text documents are available in tremendous amount on internet and in databases. As the amount of data increases, the retrieval of useful and required data become tedious. If a user requires date about a specific thing or on a specific topic there should only be relevant data in the result. Text mining is used in various types of research domains like natural language processing, information retrieval, text classification and text clustering.

As mentioned in [1] there are generally two ways to categorize text; one is to do it manually with the help of intellect the other way is by using intelligent software. Manual classification lies under library science and it is time and effort taking process. On the other hand automatic categorization is performed using artificially intelligent software which too takes high level intelligence and effort but once designed, it can save huge amount of time and effort. Automatic text

© Springer Nature Singapore Pte Ltd. 2020
I. S. Bajwa et al. (Eds.): INTAP 2019, CCIS 1198, pp. 502–509, 2020.
https://doi.org/10.1007/978-981-15-5232-8_43

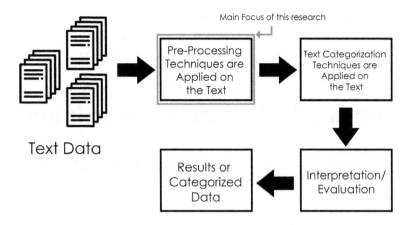

Fig. 1. Text categorization process

categorization classifies the text into one or more predefined categories. Figure 1 shows the steps of text categorizing process in a very simple form:

Text pre-processing is the vital part of text categorization process, since the result of this step is the fundamental unit passed to rest of the processing stages. It consists of many steps in which text is pre-processed and, in these steps, special formats (e.g. dates, numbers & special characters), common words (e.g. pronouns & prepositions) and any other data that cannot help in categorization are eliminated. The main purpose of pre-processing is to convert a raw document not a processed document and to enhance the relevancy between word and document and the relevancy between word and category [2].

Pre-processing techniques consist of Tokenization, Stop Word Removal and Stemming. Their flow is shown in the Fig. 2.

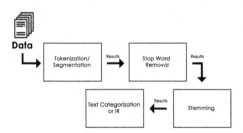

Fig. 2. Flow of tokenization

2   Tokenization

Tokenization sometimes also termed as Extraction, which is the process of converting the stream of text into single unit words. By tokenizing the text we explore the words in the input data. All further processing in text categorization requires the words from the data set or input to categorize it. The main work of tokenization process is to identify each word as token. Figure 3 shows tokenization process.

Fig. 3. Tokenization

Above figure is showing six tokens. This is what simply happens in tokenization process.

2.1 Challenges

Challenges depend on which type of data or language is tokenized. Some languages have white space between each words-pair (e.g. English and French) but some other languages don't have spaces or clear boundaries and referred as unsegmented languages (e.g. Chinese). Additional morphological and lexical information will be required if unsegmented language is under process. Generally, on the basis of structure of a language, it can be divided into following four groups.

- *Isolating:* In which words do not split into smaller units and there are no clear boundaries between morphemes. Example: Thai, Chinese.
- *Agglutinative/Agglutinating:* In which words can be divided into smaller units and have clear boundaries. Example: Japanese, English.
- *Inflectional:* In which boundaries are not clear but unclear in terms of grammatical meaning. Example: Arabic, Latin, Urdu.
- *Polysynthetic:* In which several morphemes are put together which form a complex word that work as a sentence. Example: Chukchi, Inuit [3].

Nevertheless, many other problems are still there rather the language is unsegmented or not; different numbers, time formats, abbreviations and acronyms can create problem which are handled using different techniques.

3   Stop Word Removal

Stop words are those frequently used words in any language which connect useful and important words in a sentence. These are common in all documents and don't help in categorization in any way. These functional words are from a division of natural language which carries no information (i.e. articles, prepositions, pronouns, conjunctions). [2] In a particular text data set 20–30% of the text consists of stop words. [4] If we talk about English language, few examples of stop words are; 'of', 'are', 'the', 'it', 'to'. Due to the high frequency and meaninglessness of these words in the text data, these are just an obstacle in understanding of data and categorization.

Removal of these stop words is the next step of preprocessing. It is considered as a very important step because each and every text document includes stop words which are totally useless for further text data categorization process. Stop words make the data heavier. It will take a lot of time and space if we proceed and apply further techniques without their removal. This step reduces the input text data for further steps and improves the efficiency of system. If we remove stop words from previous example (Fig. 3), the input for next step will not include 'is' and '.', there will be four tokens.

Fig. 4. Tokenization

Smart stop words list can help in the removal process. However, the creation of such stop words list is time taking and difficult. Stop word list can be automatically generated on the basis of frequency of words in huge data. The list of the stop words can also be developed manually by using the dictionary and documents. Stop word list of many languages are available online as well.

Once the list is developed, the words of list are compared with the data under process. When the corresponding match found then that word is removed from the document (Fig. 4).

4 Stemming

Stemming techniques are used to find out the stem of a word. Process of stemming converts inflected or derived words to their stems, which take in a great deal of linguistic knowledge which very language to language. The basic idea behind stemming is that the words having same stem or root which most of the time narrate same or relatively a close concept in text can be conflated to a general or simpler word. Natural language texts typically consist of many different syntactic variants for example corrector (noun), correct, correcting, corrected, correction, correctional, correctly, correctively, corrective, correctness, correctable (adjective), all can be conflated to root word 'correct' [5].

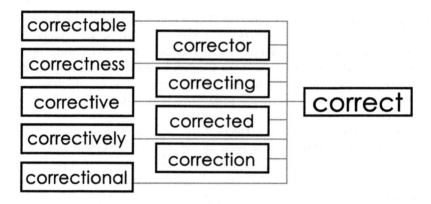

Fig. 5. Stemming

This technique is very extensively used process in text categorization or text processing for information retrieval (IR) (Fig. 5).

4.1 Errors in Stemming

Predominantly two errors can be there in stemming:

- *False Positive:* It occurs when the words with different roots are stemmed to the same root. False positive called as over stemming as well.
- *False Negative:* It occurs when the words that describe the same meaning and should be stemmed to the same root but are not stemmed. False negative is also called as under stemming.

4.2 Principles of Stemming Algorithms

There are basically two principles that are kept in mind and on which stemming algorithms depend; iteration is one and the other is longest match. Algorithms based on these two principles have fewer drawbacks. As stem attaches suffixes in a certain order, there exist order classes. Usually iteration is based on the order classes. A word may or may not be expressed in a certain order class.

- *Last order class:* In which suffix occurs at the very end of the word (e.g. -s, -es, and -ed.).
- *Previous order class:* It is derivational. It occurs when a derivational suffix (e.g -ness) follows an inflectional suffix (e.g. -ed) for example, affectedness relatedness, involvedness.
- *Lowest order class:* It is technically, may be the part of the root (e.g. -ate of relatedness), but for computation purpose it's considered the ending part of the word [6].

Above are the very few examples of order classes. It is a very sophisticated and complicated process to define order classes and endings of words. As it's clear from the name, the iterative algorithm, it is a recursive procedure which eliminates suffixes one by one of each order class. It starts from the end and proceeds towards start of the word leaving the stem behind at the end of process.

In the longest match principle; if more than one class of endings are present in the word, the longest should be eliminated. The algorithm based on longest match principle strictly uses one order class. [6] To process this principle, the algorithm needs all possible affixes ordered on the basis of length. Disadvantages to this method are the compilation of all possible combinations of affixes and the amount of storage space (Table 1).

4.3   Types of Stemming Algorithms

- *Affix Removal Stemmers:* It removes prefix or suffix of the word reducing it to the root. For example removal of the plurals e.g. If a word ends in "ies" but not "aies" or "eies" then "ies" shall be replaced to "y" [4].
- *Table Look-up Approach:* In this method stems and index terms are stored in table. Words of input data then could be stemmed using lookup table, like b-trees or hash tables. These methods are fast, but there are few issues like the domain specific data and the storage overhead.
- *Successor Variety:* Successor variety of the string is the number of various characters that follow the words in some text body. [7] these algorithms are based on the structural linguistics, which determine word and morpheme boundaries with the help of distribution of phonemes in a large text body.
- *N-Gram Stemmers:* It's also known as shared digram method. Pair of consecutive letters is called as digram. Associations between the pairs of terms are calculated on the basis of shared unique digram. Dice coefficient is used to find the similarity measure which is defined as $S = 2C/(A+B)$. In which A is the number of unique digrams in first word; B is the number of unique digrams in second word; and C is the common unique digrams present in both words. Similarity measures are taken for all pairs of terms in the input, resulting into the similarity matrix. After that single link clustering method is used to cluster the terms.

Table 1. Comparison table

Reference	Contributions/Approach	Discussion
[1]	Preprocessing Techniques for Text Mining - An Overview	Efficient pre-processing techniques has been discussed which improves performance of the IR system
[2]	Evaluating Pre-Processing Techniques in Text Categorization	The presented work uses tree important pre-processing techniques namely, stop word removal, stemming and TF/IDF on Reuters dataset
[8]	Tokenization and Sentence Segmentation (Chapter in A Handbook of Natural Language Processing)	Tokenization and Sentence Segmentation has been discussed in detail
[5]	A survey of Stemming Algorithms for Information Retrieval	A variety of stemming methods has been studies and got to know that stemming appreciably increases the Retrieval results for both rule dependent and statistical approach
[7]	Experiments with the Successor Variety Algorithm using the Cutoff and Entropy Methods	Several advantages of the successor variety algorithm can be observed; the most important one is the ability to find a stem without the need to use a dictionary

5   Conclusion

In this research paper we have explaned different pre-processing techniques. Pre-processing is the key components in the typical text classification. It reduces the text data approximately from 60% to 80% and highly improves the efficiency of categorized text results or Information Retrieval (IR) System in terms of both space and time. Though, we can see errors and ambiguity at few steps but the overall affects and results of pre-processing are remarkably good.

References

1. Vijayarani, S., Ilamathi, M.J., Nithya, M.: Preprocessing techniques for text mining-an overview. Int. J. Comput. Sci. Commun. Netw. **5**(1), 7–16 (2015)
2. Srividhya, V., Anitha, R.: Evaluating preprocessing techniques in text categorization. Int. J. Comput. Sci. Appl. **47**(11), 49–51 (2010)
3. Dale, R., Moisl, H., Somers, H.: Handbook of Natural Language Processing. CRC Press, Boca Raton (2000)
4. Gurusamy, V., Kannan, S.: Preprocessing techniques for text mining. In: Conference Paper (2014)

5. Rajput, B.S., NilayKhare, A.: A survey of stemming algorithms for information retrieval. IOSR J. Comput. Eng. **17**(3), 76–80 (2015)
6. Lovins, J.B.: Development of a stemming algorithm. Mech. Translat. Comp. Linguist. **11**(1–2), 22–31 (1968)
7. Al-Shalabi, R., Kannan, G., Hilat, I., Ababneh, A., Al-Zubi, A.: Experiments with the successor variety algorithm using the cutoff and entropy methods. Inf. Technol. J. **4**(1), 55–62 (2005)
8. Palmer, D.D.: Tokenisation and sentence segmentation. In: Handbook of Natural Language Processing, pp. 11–35 (2000)

Educational Data Mining: A Review and Analysis of Student's Academic Performance

Sadia Ijaz[(✉)], Tauqeer Safdar, and Muhammad Sanaullah

Department of Computer Science, Air University Multan Campus,
Multan 6000, Pakistan
engrsachaudhry017@gmail.com

Abstract. Data mining is a technique for extraction of valuable patterns from multiple sources. Data mining plays an important role in marketing, electronic-commerce, business intelligent, healthcare and social network analysis. Advancement in these applications, many researchers show their interest in development of data mining applications in educational context. Educational data mining is a technique defined as a scientific area making inventions within rear types of data that derived from educational surroundings. This Paper reviews different case studies based on data mining educational systems. These systems and mining methods are considered for gathering and analysis of information. Due to huge amount of data in Educational databases, it becomes very challenging to evaluate student performance. Currently in Pakistan, there is dire need to monitor and examine student's academic progress. There are two main causes of why existing systems were not able to analyze performance of students. First, the study on present evaluation methods is still not satisfactory to analyze the appropriate methods for evaluating the progress and performance of students in institutions of Pakistan. Second is because of absence of investigations on parameters; that effects student's success in specific courses. Thus, a comprehensive review is proposed on evaluation of student's performance by using techniques of Data Mining methods to progress student's achievements. The aim of paper is to improve students' academic performance by identifying most suitable attributes by using techniques of EDM.

Keywords: Data mining · Educational datamining · Web mining · Web-based educational mining

1 Introduction

Over last few decades, the advancement of data and information technology in different fields stored data in lots of new formats. The Extraction of data from these different fields require appropriate methods of extraction for making decisions, called data mining [1]. Educational data mining is a rising discipline, which included social network analysis, visual data analytics, information retrieval, psychometrics, recommender systems, cognitive psychology, and many more. Educational data mining comes from numerous disciplines including data mining, machine learning, psychometrics, data visualization

© Springer Nature Singapore Pte Ltd. 2020
I. S. Bajwa et al. (Eds.): INTAP 2019, CCIS 1198, pp. 510–523, 2020.
https://doi.org/10.1007/978-981-15-5232-8_44

and learning theory [2]. Its main purpose is to examine types of information in order to determine educational research issues [3]. EDM is concentrated on development techniques to discover the data in educational context. It examine student's academic performance modeling [35] and find the hidden data, internal and assignment marks [36]. EDM is used to identify priority learning for several groups of students, maximizing graduation-rates, efficiently assessing institutional performance, increasing property resources by finding useful learning information from learning systems and improving teaching processes [37]. Different Educational systems are used such as LMS (learning management system) [35, 38], Traditional Education system [37, 39], ITS and AIWBE [3]. Several techniques such as K-Nearest neighbor, Naïve Bayes, Decision Trees, Statistics and visualization, Neural Networks, and many others are used in EDM.

In higher academic institutions, one of important application is performance evaluation of students. The reason is that, academic performance is one of the essential criteria for good quality and higher ranked university. Many previous researches describe the definition of performance of student prediction. In, author describes that performance of students can be achieved by measuring co-curriculum and knowledge assessments. Usually, many higher education institutions in Pakistan use annual grades to predict performance of students. Recently, there are many methods to evaluate performance of students. The most familiar method to evaluate performance of student is data mining. Data mining would assist the instructors to monitor their class behavior and giving an efficient approach of teaching. Moreover, instructors could also observe progress of their students. The recommended review is to guide the study aims, which are:

1. To learn and find the gaps in present evaluation methods.
2. To learn and find the parameters (and variables) used in evaluating performance of students.
3. To learn the present evaluation methods for evaluating performance of students.

The paper is divided as follows: Second 2 presents reviewed literature in standard framework of educational mining with suitable data evaluation techniques. Section 3 presents methods and objectives in EDM it also describes users, environments with overview of mining tasks along suitable methods. Section 4 describes adopted datamining application and defines parameters to evaluate student academic performance. Section 5 states the implementation and results. Finally, concluding remarks are outlined in forth section.

2   Literature Review

In [3], the authors analyze questions about educational data mining. The authors propose education learning [21], ITSs (intelligent tutoring system) [21], WM (web-based mining) [22, 23] and DM [2, 19, 20] established areas of educational research. It introduces educational data mining and describes educational environment type, the type of data they give, and different groups of users and stakeholders. They also propose techniques of data mining to resolve educational environment issues.

In [41], the authors propose educational data mining to understand better management of class by the teacher. They also give support to understand the academic performance of students [24], based on internal examination plus result and psychological characteristics of a student. The author presents number of issues including training personalization, identifying students in need, prediction of student interaction quality, high rates of drop out. Data mining provide techniques such as decision tree [25, 26], neural networks [27], genetic algorithms [28, 29], nearest neighbor, clustering, regression.

In [40], the authors present the collaboration and communication of two research fields of educational data mining [2] and learning analytics and knowledge [6]. Although these fields are two separate working communities, but formally communicated to contribute for data mining methods in the development service of EDM and LAK fields. The community of EDM discussed in this paper directed at multiple levels: classrooms, unit or lesson levels and student levels. These levels are practiced by many data mining methods combined with learning analytics. The authors suggested that the supervisory fields of educational Data mining (SoLAR), Learning Analytics, and Knowledge (IEDMS) formalize communities for distribution of research and legal community cross ties.

In [37], the author presents the technologies used in EDM that led to the improvement of teaching and learning processes by storage of large amounts of student's data. Author discussed different areas as identifying students at-risk, their academic performance and the learning priorities of group of students [10]. Statistics, visualization [2] and Web mining has received a famous place in theoretical research and discussions in EDM [2, 6]. For all these areas, Baker [10] proposed it by classifying work in prediction, regression, classification (SVM), clustering [11], Sequential pattern mining, association rule mining, correlation mining. They conducted real world experiments in KKU (King Khalid University).

In [38] the authors present the techniques and methods for analyzing the students and predict the better settings for students learning. They conducted real world experiments in SRIEIT (Shree Rayeshwar Institute of Engineering and Information Technology) in Goa (India). They analyzed the student's performance by classifying them in categories (good, average, poor) depending on their marks. Decision tree method was used that helped the weaker students to improve their performance and used for improvising teaching in specific subject. To classify the data, ID3 algorithm of decision tree was practiced by use of greedy search and clustering algorithm conducted by DBSCAN (density based spatial clustering algorithm). They utilized association rule mining [1, 4] and correlation coefficient algorithms [2] to determine the correlation between subjects.

In [39], the authors considered educational data mining as a growing trend in higher education. They discovered large number of students and hidden information from student data repository. They analyze teaching learning problems [16]. The author select the many courses like Bachelors of Science, Bachelors of Arts at Dibrugarh University. Author carried out a relative study on the Three Year Degree (TDC) courses. Major caste wise (or category wise), gender wise and subject wise study was also conducted. The results of experiments visualized through SAS JMP Software with Fit Y by X, Control Chart, Scatterplot3D, Bubble Plot, Run Chart. It may also visualize the results of experiments through SAS JMP Software with Fit Y. The methodology that is used is Bayesian classifiers, regression analysis, and statistical techniques.

In [35], the author focused on the field of education by validating the capabilities of data mining approaches. The author analyses the data upcoming from learning and teaching, policy decision-making and tests theories of learning etc. Disciplines like estimation, categorization (by applying induction algorithms), visualization and classification (supervised and unsupervised) were applied on Educational area [12]. The author analyzed student academic performance [13] and developed a scheme on the bases of data mining methods. These schemes help the institutions to identify and respond to students at-risk [13], course management system [14, 15], and planning and scheduling (engage nontechnical users in data mining tools).

In [36], the author discusses implementation of data mining techniques [30] on educational dataset. It also finds hidden information in mining sectors. The educational datasets include assignments marks. After the analysis of each student's marks, the final semester marks are estimated [32]. The authors make use of different boosting algorithms (in data mining J48 the Java implementation of algorithm C4.5) that estimates the final marks of every student [31].

In [38], author describe educational data mining as the area of scientific inquiry addressed around the growth of methodologies for making findings within the exclusive kinds of information and to better recognize the students [33] and teacher's performance in class. Many types of mining techniques are used to make interaction between entities. In the Sect. 2, various parameters are planned and on the basics of these parameters, their related methodologies are derived. Therefore, during review many techniques and applications of data mining were used to expand the DM applications [3] communication and differences of Learning analytics and data mining [40], such methodologies are out of the scope of this paper and therefore are not included.

3   Educational Data Mining Objectives

According to Yacef and Bakers [30], educational data mining has four major objectives:

3.1   Evaluating Group of Users in EDM

This objective is achieved by observing models that integrate the characteristics of users. It considers behaviors, knowledge and motivation of Users. In Environment, major users are Teachers (Instructors, course developers, learning providers), Students (Pupils, learners), Researchers, Administrators, Organization systems and Institutions [17].

3.2   Reviewing Educational Systems Effect in EDM

This objective is achieved through learning systems in EDM. Learning systems are Traditional classrooms, LCM (Learning Content Management), AIWBES (Adaptive and intelligent web-based education), distance education and web based courses.

Traditional Classrooms: Traditional classrooms are centered on face-to-face communication between teachers and pupils organized by lecturers. This system is most widely used in Educational data mining. Traditional environments contain many subtypes like primary and elementary education, public and private education, academic and tertiary education, special education, adult and higher education system etc. [32]. In traditional classroom educators use data about class schedule, course information, attendance information of students, information about traditional databases and multimedia databases etc. [33].

Adaptive and Intelligent Web Based Educational System. It gives an alternative environment to the traditional classroom's environment [34] in the advancement of educational environments. Adaptive hypermedia system (AHS) and intelligent tutoring systems (ITS) are jointly evaluated and are resulted in AIWBES (Adaptive and Intelligent web based educational system). The data in this system are semantically better and can lead to more investigating than from traditional classrooms [35]. This system is more suitable to interact contextual data with model of students. This interaction of students can be investigated at numerous granularity layers like sessions, constraints, problems, course and attempts [36]. Data mining methods can be used in IAWBES to find the solutions of different problems: to achieve the level to success of learners [37], wrong statement of feedback [36], to share individual learning activities for pupils [38].

Learning Content Management. LCM are systems that offers number of different channels to give facility of communication and sharing of information between applicants in a course, prepare content material, let teachers to give information to learners, make **tests** and assignments [39]. LCM system records all student actions like: taking tests, writing, reading and performing different tasks in virtual and real environment. They also make available a database that contains all information about user's profile, contact data of users, academic results etc. In this context, Data mining can be practiced to analyze, visualize and explore information to find useful designs or patterns [3].

Distance Learning. Distance learning (Distance education) contains systems and approaches give access to programs of education for pupils who are separated by space and time from educators. This learning system not have face-to-face communication, it lack **relationship** between pupils and lecturers. Well-known form of distance learning is Web-based learning. It contains diverse types of web-based systems like open and closed corpus, collaborative and non-collaborative, asynchronous and synchronous, etc. It contains web logs to record student's accesses [40].

Web Based Courseware. Standard HyperText Markup Language is used in this specific web-based courseware. Instructors may predict their performance in EDM. They desire to find what educational experience are more beneficial to overall educational experience, why one class performance varies on performance of other same cluster of pupils. **Zykow** and Sanjeev [41] stated the first contribution in EDM, they focus on statement "P pattern holds for information in R Range" and applied knowledge discovery on it.

Adaptive Environment and Users in EDM. Data mining is integrating multiple areas, which provide coverage to users and Educational Systems in number of recent Case studies. Table 1 provides a comparison of all objectives in Recent Case studies.

Table 1. Comparison of all users and environment in recent case studies.

Authors	Users/Stakeholders	Educational system	Case study
Cristobal Romero and Sebastian Ventura [3]	Learners, Educators and course developers, organization, system administrator	Traditional education LCM, ITS, AIWBE system, web-based course Ventura	Cordoba University
Falguni Ranadvie and Dhaval Mehta [41]	Students, Educational researchers, learning providers	Traditional education	Educational Classrooms
George Siemens and Ryan Baker [40]	Research Communities, tool developers, analytics practitioners	Learning analytic and Knowledge	Society for Learning analytic and International data mining society knowledge (SoLAR & IEDMS)
Algarni [37]	Students and course developers	Traditional education, LMS	KKU (King Khalid University)
Nikhil Rajadhyax and Shirwaikar [38]	Students, Teachers	Learning Content Management System	Shree Rayeshwar Institute of Engineering & IT) SRIEIT
Sadiq and Hazarika [39]	Administrators, Students, Teachers	Learning Content Management System	Dibrugarh University
Jiechao Cheng [35]	Learners, teachers, researchers, institutions	Learning Content Management System, web-based system	International school of software Wahan Universidad National de Colombia
Kalaivani, Priyadharshini and Selva [36]	Administrators, Students	Web based system	Universidad National de Colombia

Educational systems are used as LMS [38] learning management system [3, 35], LAK [40], Traditional Education system [37, 39], ITS, AIWBE [3]. Different mining algorithms used in various places; different case studies are mentioned here.

3.3   Determining and Refining Mining Models

Models for EDM [9] are drawn from literatures, including areas of statistics, machine learning, computational modeling, data mining, data visualization and psychometrics. EDM work is divided into following classes:

- Clustering
- Relationship Mining
  - Correlation
  - Association Rule Mining
  - Causal data mining
  - Sequential pattern mining
- Prediction rules
  - Density estimation
  - Regression
  - Classification

The three types of prediction rules would seems to be similar in other data mining research. These categories are drawn directly from Moore's data mining methods. Another viewpoint in EDM is stated by Ventura and Romero [31], which is categorizes as (Fig. 1):

- Web mining
  - Text mining
  - Outlier detection, classification and Clustering
  - Sequential pattern mining and Association rule mining
- Visualization and Statistics.

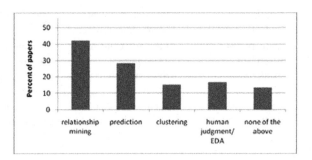

Fig. 1. The quantity of papers including each type of EDM method. Note that papers can use numerous methods, and thus some papers can be found in many types.

In Educational Data Mining, web data is focused on applications that accord with history of research field. These we mining methods are very promoted in others educational data types.

3.4   Progressing Scientific Awareness About Learners and Learning

In EDM research field, by making and integrating student's models, numerous software's and technology are used.

Adaptive Models and Objectives in EDM. This review going to describe grouped by tasks to some application of data mining and educational web based systems. Authors of different papers discussed that, visualization and statistic [3, 40] is mining technique make multidimensional student data collected from web-based systems or learning content management. Association rules [37] is very common mining method (this associate more than one attributes data with one another). Several other clustering [37], classification [40], regression [39] and decision trees [38] are two most familiar mining technique [41]. Table 2 gives a comparison of all methods and objectives in EDM.

Table 2. Comparison of all methods and objects adapted in EDM.

Authors	Mining tasks	Methodology	Objective
Cristobal Romero and Sebastian Ventura [3]	Visualization, Statistics	Swarm optimization (SBACPSO) algorithm, genetic algorithm, ARTMAP algorithm	Analysis and Visualization of data, providing feedback for supporting instructor, recommendations for students, detecting undesirable student behavior
Falguni Ranadvie and Dhaval Mehta [41]	Decision trees, Visualization and Clustering	Genetic algorithms, K-means, Visualization	Analyze training personalization, Predication of student interaction, high rates of dropout
George Siemens and Ryan Baker [40]	Visualization, Classification	Visualization algorithms	Collaboration and communication of two research fields & Learning analytic of knowledge
Algarni [37]	Statistics, Visualization	Association Rules	Identifying student at risk, their academic performance and learning priorities, optimizing subject syllabus renewal and graduate rates
Nikhil Rajadhyax and Shirwaikar [38]	Decision tree, Clustering	ID3 algorithm & Clustering algorithms	Analyzing the student's performance, better settings for learning, also for Improvising teaching in specific subject
Sadiq and Hazarika [39]	Bayesian classifiers, statistics, regression analysis	Charts, Scatterplot3D, Bubble plot, Run charts (SAS JMP software), fit Y by X, control	Analyze teaching learning problems, Major caste wise gender wise and subject wise study conducted

(continued)

Table 2. (*continued*)

Authors	Mining tasks	Methodology	Objective
Jiechao Cheng [35]	Prediction, Clustering, Outlier detection	Induction Algorithm	Analyses the data upcoming from learning and teaching, policy decision making and tests theories of learning
Kalaivani, Priyadharshini and Selva [36]	Decision Stump	Adaboost, J48 C4.5 algorithm	Analysis of each student's marks is estimated by use of assignments marks

4 Adopted Application of Data Mining in EDM

Many applications of data mining are described in EDM. Baker describes list of applications like Visualization and analysis of data, Students Profiling evaluation, Cheating Detection in online examination, Syllabus Organization, Scheduling and planning, courses Evaluation, Students recommendation system, Detection of undesirable behavior, improving teacher's behavior [18] etc. Due to huge amount of data in Educational databases, it becomes very challenging to evaluate student performance. Currently there is a dire need to monitor and examine students' academic progress.

4.1 Predicting Student Academic Performance

This objective is achieved by estimating unidentified value of variable that defines the student. Usually the values like knowledge, performance, academic scores, semester results, grades, evaluate performance. These values can be classification task (discrete or categorical) and Regression task (continuous or numerical value). Evaluating performance of student is most familiar and older application in data mining, that is evaluated by using different methods like rule-based methods, correlation method, regression, neural networks and Bayesian networks. The focus of this review is to evaluate student's best outcomes by selecting suitable parameters or variables with perfect corresponding EDM methods or Techniques. There are list of Parameters to evaluate student performance (see Fig. 2).

Description of Parameters, Their Variables and Domain. The parameters described in Fig. 2 are use classification and association rules to evaluate performance of students. All these parameters are used to collect dataset. These Parameters are explained as description of parameter, variables/attribute and Possible Values for each parameter respectively; all these parameters are as follows:

Medium of study (MED). Urdu, English.
Student family status (FStat). Joint Individual
Annual Income (ANN). BPL, High, Low, Medium
Residence (RES). Rural, Urban
Student Living Location (LL). Hostel, Home
Age (AGE). <18, 18–20, >20

Father's Qualification (FQual). No education, elementary, secondary, UG, PG, Ph. D. NA

Mother's Qualification (MQual). No education, elementary, secondary, UG, PG, Ph.D., NA.

Father's Occupation (FOcc). Service, Business, Agriculture, Retired, NA

Mother's Occupation (MOcc). House wife, Service, Retired, NA

Student Health (Hlth). Current Status of Student health.

Student Attendance (Std Attd). =100%, >65%, <65%

Study Hours (SHR). <1 h, 2_3 h, 4_5 h, >6 h.

Tution (TU). Whether student take private coaching or not

Family Size (FSize). 1, 2, 3, >3

Nutrition (NTRN). Whether student takes Healthy food or take meal on time.

Higher School Grade (HSG). O-90%_100%, A-80%_89%, B-70%_79%, C-60% _69%, D-50%_59%, E-40%_49%, F-<40%.

Travel Time (TTm). <15 min, 15–3 min, <1 h, 2_3 h, 4_5 h, >6 h.

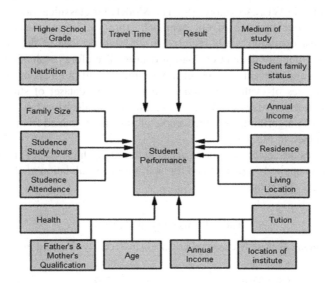

Fig. 2. The framework (key parameters/variables) to predict performance of student

5   Implementation of Mining Methods and Results

Weka is a tool that implements various machine learning techniques and broadly used in applications of Data mining [5, 7]. Based on all described parameters dataset .arff document was created. The arff file is uploaded into Weka explorer. In classification panel, user will be able to apply regression and classification algorithms to resulting dataset, to evaluate the accuracy of resulting predictive model and to visualize the model itself.

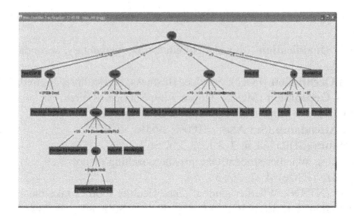

Fig. 3. C4.5 algorithm rules

There are approximately more than 16 decision tree models like J48, ID3, and ADT etc. implemented in WEKA explorer [8]. The Models for classifications is like CART, ID3, and C4.5. For analyses of our approach cross validation of about 10-fold is selected for Test operations. It is required to get realistic idea of the general model because there is not any distinct evaluation dataset. Therefore, evaluation model provide different ways to evaluate whether a new student will progress or not. There are three decision trees of evaluation models obtained from dataset of student by algorithms of machine learning like CART algorithms, ID3 decision tree algorithm and C4.5 decision tree algorithm. Here the sample of outcome is gained from C4.5 decision tree algorithm (see in Fig. 3).

Table 3 gives the accuracy of three decision tree algorithms: CART, ID3, and C4.5, for classification applied on dataset and for analyses cross validation of about 10-fold is selected for Test operations.

Table 3. Accuracy of classifiers

Algorithm	Accurately classified instances	Inaccurately classified instances
CART	63.3333%	38.8889%
ID3	63.3333%	27.7778%
C4.5	68.8889%	33.3333%

Displayed Table 3 shows that C4.5 algorithm has largest accuracy of 68.8889% as compared to other decision tree algorithms.

Table 4 displays the three decision tree algorithms: CART, ID3, and C4.5, which produce predictive models with better accuracy.

Table 4. Accuracy of classifiers

Algorithm	Class	FP Rate	TP rate
CART	Promoted	0.19	0.32
	Pass	0.350	0.810
	Fail	0.106	0.644
ID3	Promoted	0.233	0.626
	Pass	0.185	0.715
	Fail	0.062	0.787
C4.5	Promoted	0.214	0.518
	Pass	0.210	0.746
	Fail	0.093	0.787

6 Conclusion

This paper reviews the most important and relevant objectives in Educational data mining. The review describes the methods and objectives of data mining in EDM. Each study describes different data mining techniques, approaches and methodologies, further classified by the data types and the academic tasks and problems that they solve. It provides optimized key settings and best learning environments for students. This research work focus on the blooming of data mining methods so that it is helpful for learners to evaluate their academic progress. The data mining methods i.e. Regression and Classification is motivating topics as it classifies the data accurately. In this paper, decision tree classifiers are discussed to find the students' academic performance. From accuracy of classifiers, it is clear that TP (true positive) rate of the model for "Fail" class is 0.787 for C4.5 and ID3 decision trees. This TP value shows that model is accurately classifying the students who are fail. These class of students can be considered for proper guidance to improve their academic performance. Among the several classification algorithms, C4.5 decision tree method can acquire efficient predictive model for evaluating students' performance.

References

1. Han, J., Pei, J., Kamber, M.: Data Mining: Concepts and Techniques. Elsevier, Amsterdam (2011)
2. Baker, R.S., Yacef, K.: The state of educational data mining in 2009: a review and future visions. JEDM J. Educ. Data Min. **1**(1), 3–17 (2009)
3. Romero, C., Ventura, S.: Educational data mining: a review of the state of the art. IEEE Trans. Syst. Man Cybern. Part C (Appl. Rev.) **40**(6), 601–618 (2010)
4. Abdel-Basset, M., Mohamed, M., Smarandache, F., Chang, V.: Neutrosophic association rule mining algorithm for big data analysis. Symmetry **10**(4), 106 (2018)
5. Bakhshinategh, B., Zaiane, O.R., ElAtia, S., Ipperciel, D.: Educational data mining applications and tasks: a survey of the last 10 years. Educ. Inf. Technol. **23**(1), 537–553 (2018)

6. Long, P.: Proceedings of the 1st International Conference on Learning Analytics and Knowledge. ACM (2011)
7. Kiranmai, S.A., Laxmi, A.J.: Data mining for classification of power quality problems using WEKA and the effect of attributes on classification accuracy. Prot. Control Modern Power Syst. **3**(1), 29 (2018)
8. Asanbe, M., Olagunju, M.: Data mining technique as a tool for instructors' performance evaluation in higher educational institution. Villanova J. Sci. Technol. Manag. **1**(1) (2019)
9. Nithya, P., Umamaheswari, B., Umadevi, A.: A survey on educational data mining in field of education. Int. J. Adv. Res. Comput. Eng. Technol. (IJARCET) **5**(1), 69–78 (2016)
10. Mohamad, S.K., Tasir, Z.: Educational data mining: a review. Procedia Soc. Behav. Sci. **97**, 320–324 (2013)
11. Dutt, A., Aghabozrgi, S., Ismail, M.A., Mahroeian, H.: Clustering algorithms applied in educational data mining. Int. J. Inf. Electron. Eng. **5**(2), 112 (2015)
12. Baker, R.S.: Data mining for education. Int. Encycl. Educ. **7**(3), 112–118 (2010)
13. Chacon, F., Spicer, D., Valbuena, A.: Analytics in support of student retention and success 1–9. Res. Bull. (2012)
14. Huebner, RA.: A survey of educational data-mining research. Res. High. Educ. J. **19** (2013)
15. Wang, Y.H., Liao, H.C.: Data mining for adaptive learning in a TESL-based e-learning system. Expert Syst. Appl. **38**(6), 6480–6485 (2011)
16. Pandey, U.K., Saurabh, P.: Data mining: a prediction of performer or underperformer using classification. arXiv:1104.4163, arXiv preprint (2011)
17. Kaur, P., Singh, M., Josan, G.S.: Classification and prediction based data mining algorithms to predict slow learners in education sector. Procedia Comput. Sci. **57**, 500–508 (2015)
18. Hemantkumar, M.S., Modi, N.I.: A study on educational data mining: applications and tools. Int. J. Sci. Res. **8**(8) (2019)
19. Rao, H., Zhi, Z., Ai-ping, L.: Research on personalized referral service and big data mining for e-commerce with machine learning. In: 2018 4th International Conference on Computer and Technology Applications (ICCTA), pp. 35–38 (2018)
20. Altunan, B., Arslan, E.D., Seyis, M., Birer, M., Üney-Yüksektepe, F.: A data mining approach to predict e-commerce customer behaviour. In: Durakbasa, N.M., Gencyilmaz, M. G. (eds.) ISPR 2018, pp. 29–43. Springer, Cham (2019). https://doi.org/10.1007/978-3-319-92267-6_3
21. Rajendran, R., Anabil, M., Mona, E., Gautam, B.: A temporal model of learner behaviors in OELEs using process mining. In: Proceedings of ICCE, pp. 276–285 (2018)
22. Srivastava, M., Rakhi, G., Mishra, P.K.: Analysis of data extraction and data cleaning in web usage mining. In: Proceedings of the 2015 International Conference on Advanced Research in Computer Science Engineering & Technology, ICARCSET 2015, p. 13. ACM (2015)
23. Jagan, S., Rajagopalan, S.P.: A survey on web personalization of web usage mining. Int. Res. J. Eng. Technol. **2**(1), 6–12 (2015)
24. El-Halees, A.M.: Mining students' data to analyze e-Learning behavior: a case study. In: Mining Students' Data to Analyze E-Learning Behavior: A Case Study, vol. 29 (2009)
25. Masci, C., Johnes, G., Agasisti, T.: Student and school performance across countries: a machine learning approach. Eur. J. Oper. Res. **269**(3), 1072–1085 (2018)
26. Chakraborty, T., Chattopadhyay, S., Chakraborty, A.K.: A novel hybridization of classification trees and artificial neural networks for selection of students in a business school. Opsearch **55**(2), 434–446 (2018)
27. Mason, C., Twomey, J., Wright, D., Whitman, L.: Predicting engineering student attrition risk using a probabilistic neural network and comparing results with a backpropagation neural network and logistic regression. Res. High. Educ. **59**(3), 382–400 (2018)

28. Nayak, J., Naik, B., Kanungo, D.P., Behera, H.S.: A hybrid elicit teaching learning based optimization with fuzzy c-means (ETLBO-FCM) algorithm for data clustering. Ain Shams Eng. J. **9**(3), 379–393 (2018)

29. Marappan, R., Sethumadhavan, G.: Solving channel allocation problem using new genetic algorithm with clique partitioning method. In: 2016 IEEE International Conference on Computational Intelligence and Computing Research (ICCIC), pp. 1–4. IEEE (2016)

30. Chalaris, M., Gritzalis, S., Maragoudakis, M., Sgouropoulou, C., Tsolakidis, A.: Improving quality of educational processes providing new knowledge using data mining techniques. Procedia Soc. Behav. Sci. **25**(147), 390–397 (2014)

31. Jishan, S.T., Rashu, R.I., Haque, N., Rahman, R.M.: Improving accuracy of students' final grade prediction model using optimal equal width binning and synthetic minority over-sampling technique. Decis. Anal. **2**(1), 1 (2015)

32. Meier, Y., Xu, J., Atan, O., Van der Schaar, M.: Predicting grades. IEEE Trans. Signal Process. **64**(4), 959–972 (2016)

33. Onah, D., Jane, S.: Massive open online courses: an adaptive learning framework. In: 9th International Technology, Education and Development Conference, pp. 2–4 (2015)

34. Fatahi, S.: An experimental study on an adaptive e-learning environment based on learner's personality and emotion. Educ. Inf. Technol. **24**(4), 2225–2241 (2019). https://doi.org/10.1007/s10639-019-09868-5

35. Cheng, J.: Data-Mining Research in Education. arXiv preprint arXiv:1703.10117 (2017)

36. Almasri, A., Erbug, C., Rami, S.A.: EMT: ensemble meta-based tree model for predicting student performance. Sci. Programm. **2019**, 13 (2019)

37. Algarni, A.: Data mining in education. Int. J. Adv. Comput. Sci. Appl. **7**(6), 456–461 (2016)

38. Shirwaikar, PR., Rajadhyax, N.: Data Mining on Educational Domain. arxiv preprint arXiv: 1207.1535, 6 July 2012

39. Hussain, S., Hazarika, G.C.: Educational data mining using JMP. arXiv preprint arXiv:1411.2081 (2014)

40. Siemens, G., Baker, R.S.: Learning analytics and educational data mining: towards communication and collaboration. In: Proceedings of the 2nd International Conference on Learning Analytics and Knowledge, pp. 252–254. ACM (2012)

41. Ranadive, F., Mehta, D.: Improving Students' Performance using Educational Data Mining (2011)

Multi Agents Based System Architecture for Market Research in E-Business

Amna Ashraf[✉], Muhammad Aslam, and Nayab Tasneem Bari

Department of Computer Science, University of Engineering and Technology,
Lahore, Pakistan
amnace39@gmail.com, maslam@uet.edu.pk

Abstract. Companies and organizations in today's business especially online business are found in dire need of hiring employees for market research. They pay handsome compensations for the services of such employees in return. In addition, market research deals with loads of internet surfing, spending time on studying potential markets and tapping potential customers. Few existing market research tools/platforms are able to generate potential clients and assist to run marketing campaigns; but, these also require prepared data sets that need to be mapped as per the software's own requirements and capacities. Our idea is to employ Multi Agent System (MAS) to search particular markets and provide an efficient route to gather business opportunities that are incessantly created in the fast paced world today. Two basic methodologies for MASs are complementary to each other; one is iterative on each stage of development while the other one is a cyclic process of analysis and design. Amalgamation of these two, is used for designing our desired multi agent system for Market Research in E-Business (MREB). In order to make a prototype, we used Netbeans, JADE FIPA-compliant with SQL Server 5.7. It equips any company using this platform with an opportunity to get a huge list of suitable projects according to its product base and/or services expertise. We have achieved considerable results by our system MREB with some new features.

Keywords: E-Business · Multi-agents · Organizations · Online business

1 Introduction

Electronic business (e-Business) is a market Internet search to buy and deliver any kind of products. Thus E-Business empowers business processes, managerial communication, and collaboration within an organization and with customers [1]. Market research is the basic component of any business strategy [2] and its main concern is with markets [3].

A company within e-business can be considered as a service provider in a consistently changing environment. The company can be roughly modeled in according to a set of its interacting departments, which are commonly classified in four categories. HR: These people help their organization in achieving its objectives of becoming a socially and environmentally responsible firm. Finance: The employees from this department keep record for the financial consequences of organizational activities.

© Springer Nature Singapore Pte Ltd. 2020
I. S. Bajwa et al. (Eds.): INTAP 2019, CCIS 1198, pp. 524–536, 2020.
https://doi.org/10.1007/978-981-15-5232-8_45

Development: It's the department whose employees actually develop products for client; requirements for these collected firstly and then proceed with them and Market Research Executive (MRE) that has the duty to help company in capturing market share.

MRE is expected to gather business for companies by building upon market research and finding customers for the company. MRE searches for businesses online potential customers to fill electronic surveys, launches inquiries to assess interests, and accordingly with these interests suggests customized yet effective solutions to scale up the company's overall performance efficiency. MRE is also involved in tasks to advertise the companies across multiple social media and web-based platforms. MRE also performs the functionalities to tap business opportunities that are continuously being created in today's fast paced world. These business prospects, may they be as results of financial institutions, mergers, investments to expand some company's service lines, acquisitions of companies in same or diverse fields, are prodigious profit deals for software houses. These opportunities are detailed promptly for establishing quick contacts with such potential business leads and thus prove their (software house's) role as a solution provider in time of need.

Many online platforms for market search are available, e.g., Communities247 (formally known as e-Communities) DigitalMR [4]; another is the Market Search World [5] that its site is visited by 900 users on daily basis, making it the largest market research resource portal on Web.

In general, we find market research agents associated to e-business. Although agent-based learning environment exists to help entrepreneurs learning market research strategies within new businesses [8], but the direct use of these agents to find potential market is never seen. Thus, we study how multi-agent systems.

(MAS) can support the market research and how human dependency can be minimized for this market research executive post in software houses.

The rest of the paper is organized as follows: Sect. 2 describes a review about some methodologies for MAS design. Section 3 explains our approach. Section 4 discuss our testing prototype and analyzes obtained results. Section 5 presents conclusions and future work.

2   Literature Review

MAS is a system consist of autonomous agents which perform a series of acts to achieve some specified goals [21]. Basically, there exist three main methodologies for MAS development: GAIA, MaSE, and MAS-CommonKADS. Three methodologies overlap each other in many aspect of the implementation and present some differences. GAIA and MaSE methodologies use an iterative process at each stage of the system development and thus lack at tracing risks and errors. On the other hand, MAS-CommonKADS based on a cyclical process, allows that the two phases analysis and design to perform in a progressive manner. All the three methodologies provide models to develop MAS. GAIA use cases to develop roles, instead of sequence diagrams. MaSE and MAS-CommonKADS use cases. Thus any methodology is enough for the development of MAS. Therefore, we decided to use the three methodologies together for our system design. Let's have a review for each methodology.

GAIA has analysis and design stages. The former defines roles corresponding to individuals, organizations, and the corresponding departments. Protocols associated to these roles are identified so that they can interact with each other in the system. By using these protocols, roles model is defined and the three stages then iterate. The Design stage, the Agent model is created first by aggregating roles into different agent types. So that agent hierarchy is formed by instances of all agent types. Service model is created by considering the characteristics of activities, protocols and roles. Then Acquaintance Model is developed from the interaction model and agent model [6].

MaSE also has analysis and design phase. Analysis phase defines goals based on user requirements, constructing a hierarchy. Roles and communication paths are created, based on the use cases and sequence diagrams. Then goals are transformed into set of roles. The identification of roles and associated tasks imply the creation of a role model. Finally, the set of roles is defined by concurrent task model for each task [7].

The MAS-CommonKADS methodology provides a framework of reusable knowledge models which can be used according with the frequently performed tasks [8]. Five phases are defined [9]: i).- *Conceptualization* describes the problem by means of use case diagrams to better understand the system. ii).- Analysis phase determines a set of functional requirements of the system and develops models. iii). Design phase uses the developed components to create new ones. iv).- Model implementation takes the obtained models of the Analysis previous phase as input and progresses into the design models, in order to implement them. v).- Development and testing phase is related to the deployment of code and test agents based on the tasks associated to agents. The Operation phase is related to the system maintenance and also its functionalities.

Business process modeling found multi-agent system helpful for its modeling architecture. In this regard, process mining techniques can also be used to exploitation in business process modeling [19]. The use of intelligent agent technique in Food Supply Chain Management(FSCM) by specifically gathering information, contacting, requisitioning and intelligence is another clue to enhance business gains [20].

3   Market Research in E-Business

The functionality and working of our proposed system is demonstrated by specifying concepts, modeling, and implementation. Different models for MREB from MASCommonKADS methodology are illustrated. MAS Conceptualization.

By using CommonKADS methodology [8], actors are specified and described (first step) based on user requirements and needs of the system. The use case technique allows us to manage user demands for the system and also to generate and inspect the test cases. In our system MREB, the actors are company, employee, researcher, operator, and technical-marketing.

3.1   MAS Analysis

There are software engineering techniques required for agents to be realized. Some years ago, the only existing techniques were the object-oriented analysis and design [10, 11], which were not tailored to agents. The reason was the basic mismatch between object-oriented concepts and the agent-oriented view [12, 13]. Then the methodology GAIA was introduced to capture properly self-determining and problem-solving behavior of agent. GAIA defines a set of organized roles and their interactions i.e., an agent-based society [14]. MAS-CommonKADS is another technique which defines some additional models to GAIA methodology. All the components of the system are made generic for the re-usability purpose.

The key role in a system is defined as a **role model**. A role can be visualized as an entity expected function. Our MREB system defines the roles such as company, employee, researcher, operator and technical-marketing. They communicate with each other through their relations with each other. These roles or actors are defined according to their objectives, responsibilities and their skills. These roles are distinguished by two types of attributes: Permissions and responsibilities of the role. **Agent Modeling** is basically from the concepts of MAS-CommonKADS methodology and it is a link between the remaining models of this methodology. There are certain techniques that can be combined or used individually to figure out agents of a given problem. We have used two of them. We analyzed the actors of the use cases from conceptualization phase. This helped us in finding the external agents of our system. Many roles are mapped onto one agent to keep problem simplify and for efficiency purpose [15]. To analyze the initial tasks and expertise model for agent's discovery is the second strategy we find useful for our problem. So from the roles defined in role model, the agents considered are operator, researcher, and company.

Task model is part of MAS-CommonKADS methodology, that describes minor and major assignments, and thus gives a complete sequence of activities to achieve the target. A task is identified by a name, it defines preconditions, destination, input and output description, activity structure, and pre-requirements such as capabilities of actor. The main purpose of the model is to document the changes in activities of an organization before and after implementation of MAS to some organization. This information later helps in maintenance and managements of activities and further changes can be made easy. Tasks can be performed either sequentially or in parallel pattern. To achieve goal of market research, we use the sequential hierarchy of sub tasks. The main sub tasks are Request MR, Design MR, Evaluate MR, Analyze MR, and Report MR.

Experiment and Knowledge model is also adapted from MAS-CommonKADS methodology and can be interpreted as a reasoning model, because it presents the reasoning mechanism for agents actions, as knowledge model. Since it determines the knowledge of agents, which they use to progress with the desired goal. The reasoning of the agent is modeled as a problem-solving technique to achieve particular goals, similarly the modeling of the conjecture of environment, i.e., how an agent can handle the situation, due to other agents or the external world. Firstly variables are defined and hypothesis is formulated.

These variables are evaluated along with the hypothesis. When they are suitable then methodological design proposal came into existence. This design is tested to get approved. If so then data analysis phase started and if not, changes have been made in methodological design. After data analysis phase market behavior is checked and potential market is searched. On finding some potential market niche, a contract is tried to be made for further progress in business. If it comes to be fruitful, then the information is stored in company's profile.

Basically, **coordination model** represents the interaction among different agents of the system. The agents interaction is launched when some target must be achieved. The interaction follows predefined communication protocols and the decisions are stored. A company can enter in the environment of our system by registering itself. This is done particularly by the operator agent of that company. To find a potential market niche a researcher agent made an effort to hypothesis along with the variables which are approved by the company. Then method selection process is initiated by researcher agent and approved by the centralized system connected to all the companies exist in this circle. Data analysis phase begins then and potential market niche is being searched by researcher agent. After finding the company tries to contact them and make a contract. If this contract is established successfully, then the details of contract are record in company's profile.

Human-machine interaction (HMI) is necessary to operate a system according to our desire. HMI is based on a **communication model**, adopted by the MASCommonKADS methodology.

Coordination model shows dynamic relationship and the **organization model** represents the static relationships between agents. Any human organization or MAS society can be modeled by the organization model from MASCommonKADS organization model. The agents relationships in a system is analyzed via a group perspective. The organization in this model is represented in terms of related suborganizations to better perceive the structure of system [16]. Few hierarchies exist in our MREB organization. Both operator and researcher belong to the company. So the company and the other two have the 'Has' relationship between them. In order to carry out the desired goals all companies have horizontal relationships and cooperate with each other.

3.2   MAS Design

MAS design phase contains two models: Service and Design whose details are described as follows.

The properties or details of all services provided by agents are specified in **service model**. These services are actually agents actions to accomplish mission of the system. Thus, the activities previously mentioned in analysis phase, are supposed to be the services accordingly, in the model. Services were introduced in 2011 [8] and further explained in 2013 [17]. These are following: variables and hypothesis generation suggest methodologies, budget analysis, identifying potential market and record it.

Design model converts the abstract models from the analysis phase into adequately low level of abstraction that can be implemented easily. This model is part of both the methodologies GAIA [14] and MAS-CommonKADS [18]. This model scripts the requirements of MAS that should be fulfilled for its technical implementation aspects.

The MREB components, communication, access to other systems, and the Internet repository is shown in Fig. 1.

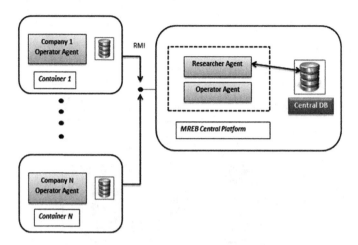

Fig. 1. MREB's component diagram

The AUML diagram in Fig. 1 shows three modules, the main host_1 contains the Jade central platform. It has the JADE specific main container and agents: Operator and Researcher agents.

Operator Agent has to keep record of the company's projects or work processed by the employees. This record is further used for searching the other projects for company to extend the business. Operator Agent takes the information about recent projects launched by a company through a suitable screen. A human operator has to put in all the information. *Researcher Agent:* This agent has to search for projects from internet repository based on what operator agent has record in for company's profile. This search is carried out on the basis of category of projects. For example, suppose a company has a background in banking projects or finance, thus the Researcher agent figures out projects only related to banking. The list of these projects thus can be downloaded from a excel file. This excel file is very precious to the company as it helps in business to the company.

The other two modules contain the secondary JADE containers, which each one has the other company Operator agent. All the other company's operator agents can communicate with host_1 using the RMI protocol, used by JADE to call remotely their agents. The researcher agent has access to system DB through JDBC compliant. We have used MySQL Server 5.5.8 along with FIPA-compliant. Mandrill API is used to send mail to contact with other companies. A template is made for initial contact mail.

3.3 MREB's Architecture

The system's architecture is also adopted from the design phase of MAS CommonKADS methodology. It utilizes the previous models of this methodology and claims the suitable architecture for all the agents required for the system. Figure 2 shows the clear distribution of components of the system and the agent's distribution into different containers/nodes.

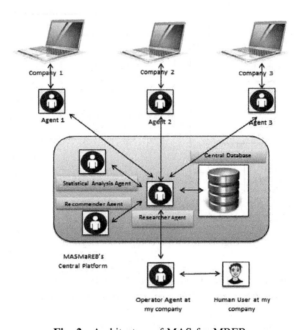

Fig. 2. Architecture of MAS for MREB

The highlighted node is the central platform of our MREB system. while others are the secondary nodes representing different companies entered in the circle. Nodes can be continue adding into the system as many different companies entered into the system.

3.4   MREB: Decision Making Process

The whole implementation of the system has four stages of the decision making process, that insure the market research strategy to be implemented. The main stages of this system are as follows.

Evaluating and Suggesting Market Research Variables: The variables on which Market Research would be carried out are decided in this stage. This is done by our operator agent which actually keeps record of a company's profile, i.e., all the information of projects ever done by this company. In which category they fall such as banking, finance, web development, Java, PHP, etc. So the operator agent has the information of category as well of its company's projects. The analysis of these variables is send to the researcher agent. This agent is incharge of searching new projects from the central database in which other company's projects are available to be done. The resulting market research is analyzed by recommender agent to suggest or discard it on the basis of previously done projects by the company and their budget. A recommender agent can be trained with some simple functions of mathematics, such as to discard the project with minimum cost in the list of suggested projects or to give priority to a high budget project. After that the selection of project is done by company and company tries to contact them via email.

Evaluating and Suggesting Market Research Hypothesis: The aim of this stage is to guide the company in formulating hypothesis. The formulation of hypothesis involves the variables which our operator agent finalizes in previous stage. Several agents are involved in this whole process of formulation of hypothesis. Researcher agent can asks recommender agent to suggest hypothesis from the market research previously done. The hypothesis is then sent to the statistical analysis agent who analyzes the hypothesis and its assumptions. The useful information is extracted to provide it to the company. The company receives information and can reject the hypothesis which was initially qualified by our MAS system MREB.

Evaluating and Suggesting Methodological Designs: In this stage, the selection of methodological designs to be used, takes place. The selection depends upon the population that assumed to utilize this methodological design. With all these dependencies, the system makes suggestions about methodological designs, considering ad-vantages and disadvantages of implementation of each of these designs. MAS system MREB gives methodological designs which can be distinguished by their qualitative and quantitative suggestions. Qualitative way of research methods is used to maximize objectivity, for generalization of findings and typically to predict outcome. Whereas quantitative research methodology consists of material practices that make the world visible. This can be done by transforming the world into series of representations, demos, photographs and recordings [18].

Evaluating the Budget and Suggesting Potential Market Niche: This stage evaluates the budget and makes the project done with the client. All this depend upon the methodological design selected by the company and approved by the researcher agent. This selection process competes after the series of communication between client and operator agent. This negotiation results into the formulation of a contract. If the contract is signed between the client and the company, it means that the project is owned by the company and the relevant information about the project, its budget and the company is stored by the operator agent for further references to the work done by company. From this, the system provides opportunity to finalize an appropriate cost for a particular project with a client, which is also a company who enter in the circle of our system MREB for business in Market Research perspective.

4 Prototype Implementation, Validation, and Results

We have started working with NetBeans as it provides the facility to work with MySQL in the IDE's Database Explorer by creating new databases and tables. The results are satisfactory. JADE (Java Agent Development Environment) is used to create agents and to interact them. Figure 3 (a) and (b) shows the basic screen to create agents.

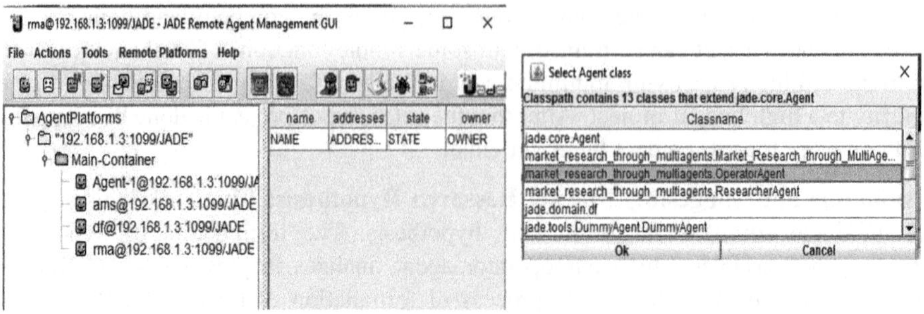

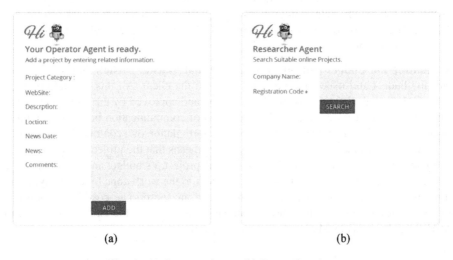

Fig. 3. (a) JADE RAM GUI, (b) Agent selection screen

A company is entered in the system by registering itself through official site of MREB. In response to registration, Operator Agent is created through series of action performed on these screens. Once an operator agent of a company is created, company can start updating its profile by entering details of projects done so far.

It means that company is ready to enjoy market research service. Whenever this company starts a new project, the details of that project are entered too into the company's record. A screen is designed for this purpose Fig. 4(a). This screen triggers by the operator agent.

Fig. 4. (a) Operator Agent, (b) Researcher Agent

Another important agent is the researcher agent Fig. 4(b). This agent will search projects for a company from central database, depending upon that company's record. The company's record is the same that is maintained by the operator agent of that company. For experimentation, we have considered our central database as the internet repository and for our convenience we have loaded it with some dummy data. For future we will work to load it with actual internet repository (Table 1).

Table 1. Comparison between existing MR systems

Software	Technology	Generates survey	Online reach-out	Results	Data analysis	Keyword search
Creative Research Systems	Java applet	Automatic	N.A	Feedback Reports	N.A	Non functionality
Question Pro	Not found	Automatic	Distributes online	Survey feedback reports	Provides analytics	N.A
Questback	Integrated business technology	Automatic	Distributes online through admin features	Feedback report	Export Data files only	N.A
FreeLunch	Moody's analytics' technology	N.A	N.A	N.A	Economic, Demographic & Financial Data Analysis	N.A
Soovle	Uses multiple search engines	N.A	N.A	N.A	N.A	Empowered search
Google Trends	Google Search & AI Technology	N.A	N.A	N.A	Shows graphic trends	Keyword search enabled on Internet
Social Mention	Not found	N.A	N.A	N.A	Latest industry insights on social media	Empowered search on social media
Salesforce	Apex	N.A	Distributes to email IDs only	N.A	N.A	Only for searching company details
ActOn	Java	N.A	Distributes to email IDs only	Tracks data & generates visitor reports	N.A	N.A
MREB	JADE Java framework	N.A	Distributes to email IDs only	Prepare list of suitable projects	N.A	N.A

5   Comparison of MREB with Existing MR Platforms

As per the research conducted on the existing market research and marketing automation software most widely used in the corporate sector of today, including the company under consideration, a number of findings have been concluded. Most of these systems offer limited number of functionalities, i.e., online surveys and feedback systems, or keyword searches for scaling up advertising efficacy or running self-configured marketing campaigns. According to an article "Market Research methods" research is of two types: primary and secondary [18]. Primary research deals with observation, surveys and interviews while secondary deals with the information available at other sources like Internet. These types are used to define the parameters for comparison.

Most companies do not offer the generation of customized surveys according to different sets of consumers' needs and wants. However, those that do they offer some form of tailoring it is with limited capacities of customer on-line reach out. And only one company namely QuestionPro offers social-media reach out for its potential customers. Others in this domain only offer emailing capacities and that also without being directly linked to a comprehensive customers database, with only one exception Salesforce. However, Salesforce does not offer any comprehensive results for the online project search.

6   Conclusion Remarks

In this paper, we have took a step forward towards building an optimistic approach for market researchers in today's business. An online Market Research Platform is presented that provides diverse functionalities to assist business seekers or the companies providing online services to E-businesses in the market research business. Using this system, they may acquire new projects, expand their clientele, research about latest developments in an industry and ultimately grow their businesses as a whole with unmatchable swiftness. A prototype is developed to elaborate on concurrent working of operator and researcher agents. The platform if implemented at an organization shall eliminate the requirement of large numbers of human resources engagement in the extensive market research field and offer high cost-effectiveness for the executed research. Moreover, the challenge of privacy and security has been targeted throughout the span of this research. It is resolved by developing a database that holds companies, entered in the system only after going through a complete authentication process of its registration. So, there remains no chance of cumulating garbage data that usually a market researcher finds while working on this job without using any platform like MREB.

In the future, it is proposed that the MREB platform be enhanced so it is able to target business for tangible products as well. Operator and researcher agents' interfaces shall be changed in this case, as product's information requirements are different as compared to online projects.

References

1. Sharma, B.A.: "E-Business" sem. Mechanical Engineering Bhilai Institute of Technology Durg (C.G.), 20 August 2010
2. McQuarrie, E.: The market research toolbox: a concise guide for beginners, 2nd edn. SAGE (2005). ISBN 978-1-4129-1319-5
3. McDonald, M.: Marketing Plans, 6th edn. Butterworth-Heinemann, Oxford (2007). ISBN 978-0-7506-8386-9
4. Michael, M.A.: communities247 now available to marketing and market research agencies in selected markets, 27 June 2013
5. http://www.marketresearchworld.net/. Last visited 29 April 2016
6. Wooldridge, M., Jennings, N.R., Kinny, D.: The GAIA methodology for agent oriented analysis and design. Auton. Agent. Multi-Agent Syst. **3**, 285–312 (2000)
7. DeLoach, S.A., Wood, M.F., Sparkman, C.H.: Multiagent systems engineering. Int. J. Software Eng. Knowl. Eng. **11**(03), 231–258 (2001)
8. Arias, A.V., et al.: Agent-based market research learning environment for new entrepreneurs. Respuestas **17**(1), 11–19 (2012)
9. Iglesias, C.A., Garijo, M.: The agent-oriented methodology MASCommonKADS. In: Intelligent Information Technologies: Concepts, Methodologies, Tools, and Applications. IGI Global, pp. 445–468 (2008)
10. Booch, G.: Object-Oriented Analysis and Design, 2nd edn. AddisonWesley, Reading (1994)
11. Coleman, D., et al.: Object-Oriented Development: The FUSION Method. PrenticeHall International, Hemel Hempstead (1994)
12. Wooldridge, M.: Agent-based software engineering. IEEE Proc. Softw. Eng. **144**(1), 26–37 (1997)
13. Wooldridge, M., Jennings, N.R.: Pitfalls of agent oriented development. In: Proceedings of the Second International Conference on Autonomous Agents, Agents 98, pp. 385–391. Minneapolis, St Paul (1998)
14. Wooldridge, M., Jennings, N.R., Kinny, D.: The GAIA methodology for agentoriented analysis and design. Auton. Agents Multi Agent Syst. **3**, 285–312 (2000). Repeated
15. The Agent-Oriented Methodology MAS-CommonKADS by Carlos A. Iglesias, Mercedes Garijo (2005)
16. Iglesias Fernández, C.A.: Definición de una Metodología para el Desarrollo de Sistemas Multiagente (1998)
17. Valencia, A., Salazar, O., Ovalle, D.: Improving the entrepreneur's market research strategies learning process using the MaREMAS environment. In: Corchado, J.M., et al. (eds.) PAAMS 2013. CCIS, vol. 365, pp. 363–374. Springer, Heidelberg (2013). https://doi.org/10.1007/978-3-642-38061-7_34
18. Harwell, M.R.: Research design in qualitative/quantitative/mixed methods. In: Conrad, C.F., Serlin, R.C. (eds.) The SAGE Handbook for Research in Education: Pursuing Ideas as the Keystone of Exemplary Inquiry, 2ª Edn., pp. 147–163. SAGE Publications, Thousand Oaks (2011)
19. Website Title: Business Queensland, Article Title: Market research methods, Last Updated, June 2017. https://www.business.qld.gov.au/startingbusiness/planning/market-customer-research/basics/methods
20. Ito, S., et al.: Process mining of a multi-agent business simulator. Comput. Math. Organ. Theor., 1–32 (2018)

21. Alsetoohy, O., Ayoun, B.: Intelligent agent technology: The relationships with hotel food procurement practices and performance. J. Hospitality Tourism Technol. **9**(1), 109–124 (2018). https://doi.org/10.1108/JHTT-04-2017-0028
22. Memon, Q.A. (ed.): Distributed Networks: Intelligence, Security, and Applications. CRC Press (2017)

Image Processing and Analysis

An Investigation on Ability of Pre-trained Convolutional Neural Networks Trained on ImageNet to Classify Melanoma Images Without Re-training

S. S. Tirumala[1(✉)], Noreen Jamil[2], and Bahman A. Sassani[3]

[1] ATMC NZ, Auckland, New Zealand
ssremath@aut.ac.nz
[2] Fast University, Islamabad, Pakistan
[3] Unitec Institute of Technology, Auckland, New Zealand

Abstract. Deep learning, particularly with Convolutional Neural Network based implementations for medical diagnostics using images is widely acclaimed for assisting doctors. Medical image processing serves as a second opinion for doctors particularly for diseases like Meleroma. Several deep learning paradigms have proved their ability and advantages interns of reducing the training time which is crucial for medical image processing. Using a pre-trained deep architecture is always advantages and one such successful and widely used CNN based deep learning architecture is ResNet50.

This paper tries to explore the ability of ResNet for classification of Melodrama images to articulate the possibility using pre-trained deep architectures in healthcare decision making systems. The dataset used in this paper is provided by International Skin Imaging Collaboration, as part of ISIC challenge 2019.

Experiments are performed using pre-trained ResNet50 with and without retraining and using multiple sets of test data with different sample sizes. The experiment results shows that by a simple retraining with a small number of samples, the classification accuracies can be improved which is 13.41% for the set of experiment conducted using a sample size of 6000 images. Further, it is noteworthy to observe that ResNet was able to provide a classification accuracy of 61.39% without any re-training.

Keywords: Residual deep learning · Melanoma images · Convolutional Neural Networks · ResNet

1 Introduction

Deep structural learning or simple deep learning is widely accepted as the most successful among all artificial intelligence and machine learning paradigms. The extensive application of deep learning in various image processing applications,

I. S. Bajwa et al. (Eds.): INTAP 2019, CCIS 1198, pp. 539–548, 2020.
https://doi.org/10.1007/978-981-15-5232-8_46

attracted research to apply deep learning for medicinal image classification and prediction [4,15]. Among various deep learning architectures, convolutional neural networks or simply CNNs are widely used for image processing and classification without any exclusion for medical images [5,6].

The implementation of deep learning requires large amount of data which may not be an issue at this time. However, the one aspect of deep learning that is seeking a continues attention is slow training. The question of 'how to improve the learning aspect of deep architectures is completely overtaken by the question of how to make the deep architectures learn faster and quicker? Several transfer learning approaches were proposed and were successfully implemented [19,21] along with evolutionary strategies [23] for optimising training time for CNNs.

However, due to the availability of open-source resources and implementations, pre-trained deep architectures have gained popularity and are widely used in classification irrespective of type of domains. One such network is ResNet, a 50-layered residual CNN that is trained using over a million images of ImageNET dataset [11]. ResNet since its initial success in 2015, is acclaimed as one of the fastest CNN deep architectures on image datasets [31]. Since ResNet is trained on generic images, it will be interesting to see how ResNet can be used on a specific task based image dataset with and without additional training.

This paper try articulate the ability of ResNet50 using (skin cancer) melanoma dataset provided as a part International Skin Imaging Collaboration, ISIC Challenge 2019. This will be a preliminary investigation towards achieving an accurate classification for the ISIC 2019 dataset. The novelty of this research is that a pre-trained network on one problem is used to test the on a different dataset without re-training it.

The paper is presented as follows. Section 2 presents a brief detail on melanoma detection using image analysis followed by Sect. 3 with the background of ResNet50 and its abilities. Section 4 details the experiment setup for the proposed implementation and dataset. This is followed by experiment results and discussion as Sect. 5 and conclusion and future work as Sect. 6.

2   Melanoma Detection Using Image Analysis

Image analysis has been critical in recent times particularly with medical diagnostics. Simple deep neural networks approaches have attained tremendous success classification of images with in visible and invisible marking with shapes and sizes [28]. Melanoma's primary indication is a visible spore on the skin. However, not all the spores are melanoma which makes it challenging to differentiate positive and negative cases of melanoma. The initial work on melanoma diagnosis from color images using neural networks dates back to 1994 [2]. This study is primarily based on size and the authors were able to attain over 80% of accuracy with the limited dataset. Since then, there were notable works using similar approaches typically on smaller medical imaging datasets [1,7].

Recent success of deep learning enabled to train and obtain considerable success on large-scale datasets particularly with CNNs [20]. The ability of deep learning has provided the dermatologist level classification of melanoma [3] as well as variant of melanoma lie eye-melanoma [15]. Apart from melanoma, deep learning implementations for other skin diseases have produced efficient results; for instance one such implementation for 12 types of skin diseases has produced over 96% of results [10].

However, it is interesting to see the performance of deep learning against human diagnostic testing which was implemented in [9]. A competition between the dermatologist and CNN network for melanoma detection is resulted in AI based system out performing the humans for the first time.

3 Residual Neural Network - ResNet

Deep architectural learning or simply deep learning attained state of the art results in majority of artificial intelligence applications. The are three variants of deep architectures namely that are considered as the primary implementations of deep learning.

- Deep Belief Networks or DBNs,
- Convolutional Neural Networks or CNNs
- Stacked Autoencoders or Deep autoencoder networks

A simple feedforward artificial neural network with enough 'depth' is also be considered as deep neural network or simply DNNs. Apart from these standard types, there are some unconventional architectures that have attained considerable success [25]. Due to slow training, initial deep learning implementations are confined to classification tasks. Several optimisation approaches were adopted to improve the training process including implementing evolutionary strategies [24,27]. Transfer learning, sometimes referred as deep transfer learning (DTS) has been another choice for reducing training time by transferring trained network or layers or in some cases simply features [8,18]. These transfer learning implementations are evaluated in all three types of deep architectures [14,17,21,26].

The two strategies, optimisation and transfer learning, for speeding up the training process of deep architectures involve retraining which is again time consuming based on the problem and implementations. Considering the fact, it is quite expensive to adopt these two strategies of optimisation and transfer learning for CNNs particularly for large datasets explicitly for image datasets. The transfer learning process is also complicated considering the fact that the transfer or layers, parameters or both is complicated particularly for pooling layers of CNNs.

An innovative idea of using pertained architectures was first proposed in 2012 with AlexNet [16]. AlexNet is a CNN based deep architecture and was widely acclaimed for its success in image classification. AlexNet is a 8 layered CNN which attained 15.3% of error rate in NIPS completion and was lowest at that time.

In 2015, a new Deep Residual Neural Network (ResNet) was proposed which was able to speedup the training process with better accuracies for imageNet dataset with an error rate of only 3.57% [11]. ResNet is a form of CNNs designed with 50 layers and further demonstrated its ability to train a 100 layer to 1000 layer networks on CIFAR-10 dataset.

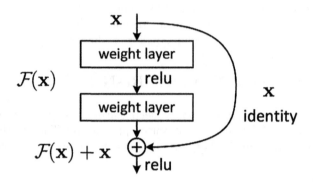

Fig. 1. The first two sections of a residual block of Deep ResNet proposed by citehe2016deep

ResNet is based on deep residual framework that dictates the flow of connections from one layer to another in a deep neural network. Increasing number of layers may not be always efficient, and it is widely accepted that the high number of layers will produce the vanishing gradient problem. Though the vanishing gradient was tackled by optimising initialisation procedure, the higher number of layers creates degradation which result in reducing the efficiency [11].

Further, all the layers in the deep architectures may not be useful which bringup an idea of skipping one or more layers based on some criteria. ResNet demonstrates the principle of skipping layers based on an underlying residual mapping [11]. The depth of deep architectures evades some intermediate layers which are simply used for mapping to the next layer. By skipping these layers, the training process could be improved which was demonstrated by ResNet. A simple illustration of ResNet is pressed in Fig. 1 as proposed in [11]. ResNet termed this a shortcut connections which was an improved version of highway networks proposed prior to ResNet [22]. So, A highway net is built on a set of ResNets. However, ResNet attained better results than the highway networks in spite of being build on same principle.

ResNet produce state of art results for on imageNet, CIFAR and COCO detection. ResNet50 is simple yet powerful as it is trained on one million images of ImageNet and is widely used along with other variants of ensemble ResNets [29] and stochastic deep networks [13], ResNetxt [30], Densely connected CNN [12].

4   Experiment Setup and Dataset

The primary objective of this work is to understand how much we can utilise a pre-trained CNN architecture trained on a different dataset to perform classification on an entirely different dataset. As mentioned earlier, ResNet50 is trained on ImageNet dataset and it is interesting to see what level of accuracy it can produce to classify melenoma dataset.

First section of ResNet-50

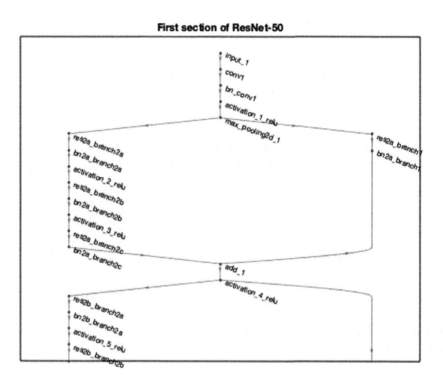

Fig. 2. Representation of ResNet - First section of the ResNet50 with input, Convnets and propagation

The ResNet is trained using Scale gradient Descent with Momentum (SGDM) algorithm and the retraining is also followed the same parameters. The structural representation of the first section of ResNet is presented in Fig. 2. The values of various parameters used are presented Table 1.

International Skin Imaging Collaboration (ISIC) has been conduction ISIC challenge for image classification for few years. Every year ISIC provides a comprehensive melanoma dataset with a separate training and testing images. For 2019, the training dataset consists of 25,331 images with 8 different categories

Table 1. Technical details and parameters of the deep autoencoder network used for the experiments

Parameter name	Value
Training algorithm	SGDM
Number of layers	50
Input size	[224 224 3]
Normalisation	Zerocenter
Classes	1000x1 categorical
LossFunction	Crossentropyex
MaxEpochs	80
Training/Testing ratio	70%/30%
miniBatchSize	10 to 100

and the testing dataset which not labelled consists of 8240 images. A sample image of melanoma and non melanora cases is presented in Fig. 3.

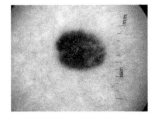 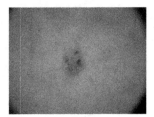

Fig. 3. Sample images of Melanoma (Left) and non Melanoma (Right) cases from the ISIC 2019 dataset.

5   Experiment Results and Discussion

For this work, the experiments are divided into two types. The first set of experiments are conducted without retraining the ResNet50 whereas the second set of experiments are conducted with retraining. The experiments are carried out using 3 different sample sizes of images with equal number of images from positive and negative cases of the melanoma.

The three samples sizes chosen are 200, 2000 and 6000 images out of which 70% are randomly selected from the labelled training images and 30% from the testing samples. Since this is an initial investigation, it is noteworthy to mention that the experiments are designed to understand the ability of ResNet50 with and without training rather then training to achieve highest classification accuracies. The experiment results for proposed scenarios and sample sizes is presented in Table 2.

Table 2. Experiment results: classification accuracies for two strategies with different sample sizes

No.	Sample size	Classification without re-training	Classification with re-training	Error rate false positive	Error rate false negative
1	200	45.00	57.83	0.39	0.5143
2	2000	56.21	63.12	0.1572	0.3650
3	6000	61.39	74.8	0.1514	0.2629

The results presented in Table 2, represents the three sample sizes and the classification accuracies attained with and without training along with the false positive and false negative error rates. The classification accuracies have improved with increasing sample size as well as training which is expected in case of deep learning. It is important to note that the false positive and false negative rates are reduced inline with the improving accuracies. The experiment results are quite positive considering that the ResNet is training on a different dataset and the retraining is performed only with a small dataset and training time and the complexity of the dataset. However, the ResNet50 was able to achieve better results with a difference of around 16% when tested on the test dataset of sample size of 6000 compared with a sample size of 200. This aspect needs further investigation which in turn will enable to provide an understanding on importance of trained weights.

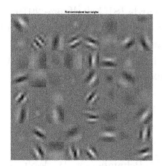 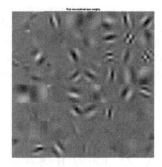

Fig. 4. Representation of weights in the first convolution layer without and with re-training for the sample size 3 (6000 images). ResNet50 weights visualisation without re-training is presented in the left side and with retraining is presented in the right side of the figure.

The visualisation of weights from the initial convolution layer of ResNet50 with and without re-training on the sample size 3 (6000 images) is presented in Fig. 4. The ResNet50 weights without training are presented in the left size and the visualisation of weights with re-training is presented in the right side of the

Fig. 4. It is evident that with a minimum, the ResNet50 was able to learn better (discrete representations) which resulted in an improved accuracy of 13.41%. The retraining time evaluated since there is no initial training time recorded for this dataset which is part of future implementations. However, for these sets of experiments, the re-training time was quite less which reassertions the ability of ResNet and its reputation of being quick to train. It is noteworthy to observe that the sample size is also very important for with and without retraining scenarios as there is a considerable difference in terms of classification accuracies.

6   Conclusion and Future Prospects

Melanoma diagnostics with deep learning are helpful and at the same time challenging considering the complexity of the image processing. The prediction needs to be accurate and at the same time quick enough to serve as a second opinion of the doctor. This paper presented the experimental evaluation of a pretrained convolutional neural network architecture ResNet50 for classification of melanoma images using complex ISIC dataset.

Th experimental results shows that ResNet50 which is trained on an entirely different dataset was able to achieve an accuracies of 45.0%, 56.21% and 61.39% for three different sample sizes of 200, 2000 and 6000 images without any retraining. However, the classification accuracy is improved to 57.83%, 63.12% and 74.8% for the sample sizes of 200.200 and 6000 respectively with a small amount of re-training. The experiment results reiterate the ability of ResNet50 and shows that re-training ResNet50 could provide an improvement as high as 13.41% for a sample size of 6000 images.

This work is a preliminary investigation towards ISIC challenge 2019. Future work includes the redesign and full training of ResNet with different number of layers and testing the full ISIC dataset. Further, it would be interesting to evaluate and present a comparative study between ResNet50 and other pre-trained deep learning architectures like GoogleNet, AlexNet and other deep architectures trained on image datasets.

References

1. Binder, M., Kittler, H., Seeber, A., Steiner, A., Pehamberger, H., Wolff, K.: Epiluminescence microscopy-based classification of pigmented skin lesions using computerized image analysis and an artificial neural network. Melanoma Res. **8**(3), 261–266 (1998)
2. Ercal, F., Chawla, A., Stoecker, W.V., Lee, H.C., Moss, R.H.: Neural network diagnosis of malignant melanoma from color images. IEEE Trans. Biomed. Eng. **41**(9), 837–845 (1994)
3. Esteva, A., et al.: Dermatologist-level classification of skin cancer with deep neural networks. Nature **542**(7639), 115 (2017)
4. Esteva, A., et al.: A guide to deep learning in healthcare. Nat. Med. **25**(1), 24 (2019)

5. Frid-Adar, M., Diamant, I., Klang, E., Amitai, M., Goldberger, J., Greenspan, H.: Gan-based synthetic medical image augmentation for increased cnn performance in liver lesion classification. Neurocomputing **321**, 321–331 (2018)
6. Fu, G.S., Levin-Schwartz, Y., Lin, Q.H., Zhang, D.: Machine learning for medical imaging. J. Healthc. Eng. **2019** (2019)
7. Ganster, H., Pinz, P., Rohrer, R., Wildling, E., Binder, M., Kittler, H.: Automated melanoma recognition. IEEE Trans. Med. Imaging **20**(3), 233–239 (2001)
8. Geng, M., Wang, Y., Xiang, T., Tian, Y.: Deep transfer learning for person re-identification. arXiv preprint arXiv:1611.05244 (2016)
9. Haenssle, H.A., et al.: Man against machine: diagnostic performance of a deep learning convolutional neural network for dermoscopic melanoma recognition in comparison to 58 dermatologists. Ann. Oncol. **29**(8), 1836–1842 (2018)
10. Han, S.S., Kim, M.S., Lim, W., Park, G.H., Park, I., Chang, S.E.: Classification of the clinical images for benign and malignant cutaneous tumors using a deep learning algorithm. J. Invest. Dermatol. **138**(7), 1529–1538 (2018)
11. He, K., Zhang, X., Ren, S., Sun, J.: Deep residual learning for image recognition. In: Proceedings of the IEEE Conference on Computer Vision and Pattern Recognition, pp. 770–778 (2016)
12. Huang, G., Liu, Z., Van Der Maaten, L., Weinberger, K.Q.: Densely connected convolutional networks. In: Proceedings of the IEEE Conference on Computer Vision and Pattern Recognition, pp. 4700–4708 (2017)
13. Huang, G., Sun, Y., Liu, Z., Sedra, D., Weinberger, K.Q.: Deep networks with stochastic depth. In: Leibe, B., Matas, J., Sebe, N., Welling, M. (eds.) ECCV 2016. LNCS, vol. 9908, pp. 646–661. Springer, Cham (2016). https://doi.org/10.1007/978-3-319-46493-0_39
14. Huang, J.T., Li, J., Yu, D., Deng, L., Gong, Y.: Cross-language knowledge transfer using multilingual deep neural network with shared hidden layers. In: 2013 IEEE International Conference on Acoustics, Speech and Signal Processing, pp. 7304–7308. IEEE (2013)
15. Kermany, D.S., et al.: Identifying medical diagnoses and treatable diseases by image-based deep learning. Cell **172**(5), 1122–1131 (2018)
16. Krizhevsky, A., Sutskever, I., Hinton, G.E.: ImageNet classification with deep convolutional neural networks. In: Advances in Neural Information Processing Systems, pp. 1097–1105 (2012)
17. Lee, H., Grosse, R., Ranganath, R., Ng, A.Y.: Convolutional deep belief networks for scalable unsupervised learning of hierarchical representations. In: Proceedings of the 26th Annual International Conference on Machine Learning, pp. 609–616. ACM (2009)
18. Long, M., Cao, Y., Wang, J., Jordan, M.I.: Learning transferable features with deep adaptation networks. arXiv preprint arXiv:1502.02791 (2015)
19. Molchanov, P., Tyree, S., Karras, T., Aila, T., Kautz, J.: Pruning convolutional neural networks for resource efficient transfer learning. arXiv preprint arXiv:1611.06440 3 (2016)
20. Nasr-Esfahani, E., et al.: Melanoma detection by analysis of clinical images using convolutional neural network. In: 2016 38th Annual International Conference of the IEEE Engineering in Medicine and Biology Society (EMBC), pp. 1373–1376. IEEE (2016)
21. Oquab, M., Bottou, L., Laptev, I., Sivic, J.: Learning and transferring mid-level image representations using convolutional neural networks. In: Proceedings of the IEEE Conference on Computer Vision and Pattern Recognition, pp. 1717–1724 (2014)

22. Srivastava, R.K., Greff, K., Schmidhuber, J.: Training very deep networks. In: Advances in Neural Information Processing Systems, pp. 2377–2385 (2015)
23. Sun, Y., Xue, B., Zhang, M., Yen, G.G.: Evolving deep convolutional neural networks for image classification. IEEE Trans. Evol. Comput. (2019)
24. Tirumala, S.S.: Implementation of evolutionary algorithms for deep architectures. In: CEUR Workshop Proceedings (2014)
25. Tirumala, S.S.: Deep learning using unconventional paradigms. Int. J. Comput. Res. **23**(3), 295 (2016)
26. Tirumala, S.S.: A deep autoencoder-based knowledge transfer approach. In: Chaki, N., Cortesi, A., Devarakonda, N. (eds.) Proceedings of International Conference on Computational Intelligence and Data Engineering. LNDECT, vol. 9, pp. 277–284. Springer, Singapore (2018). https://doi.org/10.1007/978-981-10-6319-0_23
27. Tirumala, S.S., Ali, S., Ramesh, C.P.: Evolving deep neural networks: a new prospect. In: 2016 12th International Conference on Natural Computation, Fuzzy Systems and Knowledge Discovery (ICNC-FSKD), pp. 69–74. IEEE (2016)
28. Tirumala, S.S., Jamil, N., Malik, M.G.A.: A deep neural network approach for classification of watermarked and non-watermarked images. In: Bajwa, I.S., Kamareddine, F., Costa, A. (eds.) INTAP 2018. CCIS, vol. 932, pp. 779–784. Springer, Singapore (2019). https://doi.org/10.1007/978-981-13-6052-7_67
29. Veit, A., Wilber, M.J., Belongie, S.: Residual networks behave like ensembles of relatively shallow networks. In: Advances in Neural Information Processing Systems, pp. 550–558 (2016)
30. Xie, S., Girshick, R., Dollár, P., Tu, Z., He, K.: Aggregated residual transformations for deep neural networks. In: Proceedings of the IEEE Conference on Computer Vision and Pattern Recognition, pp. 1492–1500 (2017)
31. Yamazaki, M., et al.: Yet another accelerated SGD: ResNet-50 training on ImageNet in 74.7 seconds. arXiv preprint arXiv:1903.12650 (2019)

Effect of Laplacian Smoothing Stochastic Gradient Descent with Angular Margin Softmax Loss on Face Recognition

Mansoor Iqbal[1(✉)], Muhammad Awais Rehman[2], Naveed Iqbal[3], and Zaheer Iqbal[4]

[1] Department of Electronic Engineering and Information Science,
University of Science and Technology of China,
Hefei, People's Republic of China
man2017@mail.ustc.edu.cn
[2] Department of Electrical and Computer Engineering,
Air University, Islamabad, Pakistan
awais.rehman@mail.au.edu.pk
[3] Mathematics Department, Faculty of Science, University of Hail,
Hail, Kingdom of Saudi Arabia
naveediqball1989@yahoo.com
[4] School of Sciences, Tianjin University TJU,
Tianjin, People's Republic of China
z.iqbaal@gmail.com

Abstract. An important task in deep learning for face recognition is to use proper loss functions and optimization technique. Several loss functions have been proposed using stochastic gradient descent for this task. The main purpose of this work is to propose the strategy to use the Laplacian smoothing stochastic gradient descent with combination of multiplicative angular margin to enhance the performance of angularly discriminative features of angular margin softmax loss for face recognition. The model is trained on a most popular face recognition dataset CASIA-WebFace and it achieves the state-of-the-art performance on several academic benchmark datasets such as Labeled Face in the Wild (LFW), YouTube Faces (YTF), VGGFace1 and VGGFace2. Our method achieves a new record accuracy of 99.54% on LFW dataset. On YTF dataset it achieves 95.53% accuracy.

Keywords: Face recognition · Loss function · Angular margin · Additive margin · Face dataset · LSSGD · SGD

1 Introduction

Deep Face Recognition (FR) has achieved remarkable progress and is one of the contemporary research direction in the past few years because of having too many real-world applications. Convolution Neural Network (CNN) supervised by softmax loss is addressed in DeepID [1] and DeepFace [2] for multi-class classification problem (open-set FR) and learning features on large dataset (multi-identities). Inspired by triplet loss,

© Springer Nature Singapore Pte Ltd. 2020
I. S. Bajwa et al. (Eds.): INTAP 2019, CCIS 1198, pp. 549–561, 2020.
https://doi.org/10.1007/978-981-15-5232-8_47

unified face embedding [3] used Euclidean space embedding, triplet loss and 200 million face image to achieve FR accuracy. For enhancing the performance with feature embedding, DeepID2 [4] combined softmax loss and contrastive loss in order to mutually supervise the CNN training for identification and verification. [5] explained center loss for CNNs by linear discriminant analysis and obtained an appreciable performance. Advanced network structures for feature extraction is explored in DeepID2+ [6] and DeepID3 [7] for recognition accuracy. Recently, well-performing CNNs in FR are either build on triplet loss or contrastive loss. Different approaches also offer a significant performance by upgrading on FR deep CNNs [8, 9]. All the researches has been conducted with the idea for increasing discriminating capability [5, 10–13] (maximizing and minimizing inter-class and intra-class variance respectively). [5] proposed the minimization of intra-class variance and ignores the inter-class variance.

Face Recognition (who is this person) and face verification (is this the same person) both need to solve in three stages: face detection, feature extraction and classification. Deep CNN is famous for the extraction of clean high-level features which avails relatively simple classifier to differentiate. However, recent work [5, 14] explored that traditional softmax loss has less relegation power for feature discrimination.

For solving large scale deep and machine learning problems, stochastic gradient descent (SGD) has been one of the tool. Quality algorithms are born to make the training of Deep CNNs practical, which somehow smooths the implicitly of loss functions. Many researches have been conducted to generalize the Deep CNNs by searching flat minima [28–30]. Uniform Stability is one of the alternative theory to view more potential of SGD.

By Adding Noise in SGD, slow down the convergence of regular gradient descent but has great advantage to reach the local minima and generalize at its best. Somehow to recover the linear convex function and variance reduction different algorithms are also introduced e.g. SVRG [31] and SAGA [32]. But for training of Deep CNNs none of them are suitable.

In this paper, we have combined some multiplicative angular margin α_1 with Laplacian Smoothing Stochastic Gradient Descent (LSSGD) which has carefully designed positive definite matrix to smooth the stochastic and general gradient descent. LSSGD reduce noise in SGD and improve training of Deep CNNs. We are using this LSSGD on face recognition problem to explore how different smoothing algorithms helps to optimize the maximum likelihood of the softmax regression. By optimizing the explained angular margin softmax loss with LSSGD, it enlarges the inter-class margin and compresses the intra-class angular distribution with more clear decision region.

The major contribution is coalescing both the multiplicative angular margin and LSSGD, which learns feature discrimination on hypersphere manifold. We train our model on relatively small dataset CASIA WebFace [15] and achieved competitive and appreciable results on several academic benchmarks, including Labeled Face in the Wild (LFW) [16], YouTube Faces (YTF) [17], VGGFace1 [18] and VGGFace2 [19]. However, [25, 26] has great age, intensity and pose variation.

Rest of the paper is organized as follows: In Sect. 2, we present review of Related work. Softmax are explained in Sect. 3. Laplacian Smoothing Stochastic Gradient Descent is formulated and presented in Sect. 4. Results, dataset details and experimental techniques along with CNN architecture is demonstrated in Sect. 5. In Sect. 6, we draw the conclusion.

2 Related Work

Face recognition (FR) has been the prominent biometric technique for identity authentication and has been widely used in military, finance, public security and daily life. Due to its nonintrusive characteristics, FR has been great research topic in the CVPR community. Early 1990s, FR study became popular with the introduction of the historical Eigenface approach [38]. The holistic approaches derive the low-dimensional representation through certain distribution assumptions, such as sparse representation [41], linear subspace [38] and manifold [42]. However, these theoretically holistic methods fail to address the uncontrolled facial changes. So, this problem gave rise to local-feature-based FR. LBP [39] and Gabor [40] achieved robust performance through some invariant properties of local filtering.

Learning-based local descriptors were introduced in early 2010s to the FR community [36, 37], where local filters are learned for better distinctive features, and for better compactness encoding codebook is learned. However, certain limitation to these shallow representations are still a competitive task like robustness against the complex nonlinear facial appearance variations. Traditionally, FR problem attempted to solve by one or two-layer representation (filtering responses or histogram). To improve the FR accuracy, researchers intensively studied to separately enhance the preprocessing, local descriptors, and feature transformation. After decade, some methods only improve the accuracy of the LFW benchmark to about 95% [35], which clear portray that the methods are insufficient to extract stable identity feature against unconstrained facial variations.

Great concepts have changed in 2012 when AlexNet won the ImageNet competition by a large margin using a technique called deep learning [34]. Convolutional neural networks in deep learning uses a cascade of multiple layers of processing units for feature extraction and transformation. System learn multiple levels of representations which leads the problem to tackle different levels of abstraction. After that, FR problem leads to the levels of hierarchy concepts, showing strong invariance to the face pose, lighting, and expression.

From 2014, [1–9] achieved the state-of-the-art accuracy on the LFW benchmark dataset [16], approaching human performance on the unconstrained condition for the first time. Since then, focus of FR research community has shifted to deep learning, and the accuracy was drastically boosted in just five years. Deep learning technique has reshaped the research field of face recognition in almost all aspects such as algorithms, learning, datasets, and evaluation parameters.

3 Softmax Loss

Keeping the decision criteria in mind, we can rewrite the softmax loss [20]. Posterior probabilities obtained from softmax loss in the binary-classes case are

$$P_{p1} = \frac{e^{\left(W_1^T x + b_1\right)}}{e^{\left(W_1^T x + b_1\right)} + e^{\left(W_2^T x + b_2\right)}}$$

$$P_{p2} = \frac{e^{\left(W_2^T x + b_2\right)}}{e^{\left(W_1^T x + b_1\right)} + e^{\left(W_2^T x + b_2\right)}}$$

where x is the feature vector. W_1 and W_2 are the weights of the D_1 and D_2 class. Bias of fully connected layer of each class is denoted as b_1 and b_2 respectively. The labels to each class can be predicted the way that it is D_1 if $P_{p1} > P_{p2}$ or D_2 if $P_{p1} < P_{p2}$. By comparing the posterior probability P_{p1} and P_{p2}, one can easily see that $\left(W_1^T x + b_1\right)$ and $\left(W_2^T x + b_2\right)$ determine the classification results. From that decision boundary will define as $(W_1 - W_2)^T x + b_1 - b_2 = 0$. By simplifying, we can get $\left(W_j^T x + b_j\right)$ which leads to $\left\|W_j^T\right\| \|x\| \cos(\theta_j) + b_j$, where θ_j is the angle between weights vector W_j and feature vector or learned (L2 norm) feature vector x. If we want our final result to be only dependent on angle θ_1 and θ_2, we have to normalize the weights and zero the biases $(\|W_j\| = 1, b_j = 0)$, as both P_{p1} and P_{p2} have common learned features. The posterior probabilities P_{p1} and P_{p2} depends on $\|x\| \cos(\theta_1)$ and $\|x\| \cos(\theta_2)$ respectively. $\cos(\theta_1) - \cos(\theta_2) = 0$ will be the updated decision boundary. Keeping the above discussion in mind, we can now generalize the softmax loss for multi-class case. The modified softmax loss $(\|W_j\| = 1, b_j = 0)$ encourages features from each class to have small angle θ_j, which makes angles between W_j and feature x a reliable metric for classification. By defining input features x_i and output (label) y_i, original softmax loss can be written as

$$L_{original} = -\frac{1}{S} \sum_{i=1}^{S} \log\left(\frac{e^{\tau_{y_i}}}{\sum_j e^{\tau_j}}\right),$$

Where S is the total number of samples used for training. τ_j denotes the j-th element $(j \in [1, D], D$ is the class number) of the class score vector τ. As $\tau_j = W_j^T x_i + b_j$ and $\tau_{y_i} = W_{y_i}^T x_i + b_{y_i}$, where x_i is the i-th training sample, W_j and W_{y_i} are the j-th and y_i-th column of W respectively. By redefining original softmax loss we obtain,

$$L_{original} = -\frac{1}{S} \sum_{i=1}^{S} \log\left(\frac{e^{\left(W_{y_i}^T x_i + b_{y_i}\right)}}{\sum_j e^{\left(W_j^T x_i + b_j\right)}}\right)$$

$$= -\frac{1}{S} \sum_{i=1}^{S} \log\left(\frac{e^{\left(\|W_{y_i}\| \|x_i\| \cos(\theta_{y_i,i}) + b_{y_i}\right)}}{\sum_j e^{\left(\|W_j\| \|x_i\| \cos(\theta_{j,i}) + b_j\right)}}\right)$$

where $\theta_{j,i} \left(0 \leq \theta_{j,i} \leq \pi \right)$ is the angle between vector W_j and x_i. By examining the above equation, we have to normalize weights $\left(\|W_j\| = 1, \forall j \right)$ in each iteration and zero the biases. By doing so, we get the modified softmax loss:

$$L_{modified} = -\frac{1}{S} \sum_{i=1}^{S} \log \frac{e^{\|x_i\| \cos\left(\theta_{y_i,i}\right)}}{\sum_j e^{\|x_i\| \cos\left(\theta_{j,i}\right)}},$$

In order to enhance the discriminative power for feature classification, we use angles as distance metric with an angular margin. As angular margin is necessary for discrimination, we explained different angular margin and also combines for better classification results.

3.1 Multiplicative Angular Margin to Softmax Loss

The multiplicative angular margin is introduced in [20]. Modified softmax loss then reformulated as:

$$L = -\frac{1}{S} \sum_{i=1}^{S} \log \frac{e^{\|x_i\| \cos\left(\alpha_1 \theta_{y_i,i}\right)}}{e^{\|x_i\| \cos\left(\alpha_1 \theta_{y_i,i}\right)} + \sum_{j \neq y_i} e^{\|x_i\| \cos\left(\theta_{j,i}\right)}},$$

where α_1 in is angular margin and $\theta_{y_i} \in [0, \pi/\alpha_1]$. For making it optimizable in CNN, we generalize it to monotonically decreasing angle function. Meanwhile, when $\alpha_1 = 1$, it becomes the modified softmax loss. In our case, we are choosing $\alpha_1 = 4$ as [17] explained that system get maximum convergence.

4 Laplacian Smoothing Stochastic Gradient Descent

For the explanation of Laplacian Smoothing Stochastic Gradient Descent some basic idea about Convexification and Hamilton-Jacobi PDEs must be highlighted first hand.

4.1 Convexification and Hamilton-Jacobi PDEs

Machine learning and deep learning problems are generally formulated as the extraction of optimal parameters w of a function $y = h(x, w)$, where x is an input and y is possible accurate output. Empirical risk function $f(X, Y, w) = f(w)$ is minimized to obtain optimal w, where $\{X, Y\}$ is the given training data. HJ-PDE with $f(w)$ as initial condition has introduced to find global or relatively flat minima [27]. The gradient smoothing has done by evaluating tri-diagonal linear system with original gradient on right hand side. Pre-multiply gradient for some positive constant $\sigma \geq 0$ with the inverse tri-diagonal circular matrix. Consider, positive matric $A_\sigma = I - \sigma L$, where I is the identity matrix, and L is the discrete one-dimensional Laplacian which acts on indices.

$$\begin{cases} u_t + \frac{1}{2}\nabla_w u, A_\sigma^{-1}\nabla_w u = 0, & (w,t) \in \Omega \times [0,\infty) \\ u(w,0) = f(w) & w \in \Omega \end{cases}$$

The viscosity solution to that problem has represented by Hopf-Lax formula [33]

$$u(w,t) = \inf_v \left\{ f(v) + \frac{1}{2t}\langle v - w, A_\sigma(v - w)\rangle \right\}$$

Local maxima gets down while wide minima retain its position by $u(w,t)$ viscosity solution which makes $f(w)$ more convex. Reaching global or flat minima of the original nonconvex function $f(w)$ with the proper step size on the function $u(w,t)$ gives you smoothing GD.

4.2 Laplacian Smoothing Stochastic Gradient Descent

Consider the finite-sum optimization setting for stochastic gradient decent SGD

$$\min_w F(w) = \frac{1}{S}\sum_{i=1}^{S} f_i(w),$$

where $f_i(w) = f(w, x_i, y_i)$ is the loss of machine learning model on the training data. Presented finite-sum formula is the main key of machine learning models. General optimization of SGD gives

$$w^{k+1} = w^k - \mu_k \nabla f_{ik}(w^k)$$

Where μ_k is the step size and i_k is the random sample. [27] proposed to replace the stochastic gradient $\nabla f_{ik}(w^k)$ by the Laplacian smoothing surrogate, which is written as

$$w^{k+1} = w^k - \mu_k A_\sigma^{-1} \nabla f_{ik}(w^k)$$

By doing so it smooths the gradient by an elliptic smoothing operator meanwhile entries gradient preserves the mean. Fast Fourier Transform FFT is fueled to get $A_\sigma^{-1}\nabla f(w^k)$. From $d = A_\sigma^{-1}g$, smoothed vector d can be extracted. So, vector $g = d - \sigma d * d$, where $v = [-2, 1, 0, \ldots, 0, 1]^T$ and $*$ is the convolution operator.

$$d = \text{ifft}\left(\frac{\text{fft}(g)}{1 - \sigma.\text{fft}(v)}\right)$$

Here fft and ifft are the FFT and inverse FFT respectively. To verify the improved convexity, we are using the Laplacian smoothing stochastic gradient descent on the face recognition problem which shows that LSSGD helps to speed up the convergence with some acceleration technique (learning rate and momentum etc.). Performance, loss and training accuracy of above explained algorithms are shown in the next section using FR problem.

5   Experiments

5.1   Experimental Settings

Preprocessing. General preprocessing steps on face images are done by arranging the data for training and testing purpose. MTCNN [21] is polished to extract the facial landmarks of all images of training and tests datasets discretely. Two eyes, nose, two mouth corner points some general used reference points are employed to execute similarity transformation for face cropping. Each pixel ([0; 255]) in RGB images is normalized at the initial level by subtracting each pixel to 127.5 and then dividing it by 128.

Training Data. For fair comparison to the existing results, we use publicly available web-collected training dataset name CASIA-WebFace [15] is used to train our CNN models. Number of both the images and identities of all the datasets used for this work is shown in Table 1. Note that the scale of our training data (0.49M) is relatively small, especially compared to other private datasets used in DeepFace (4M) [2], Range Loss (5M) [22], Marginal Loss (3.8M) [23] and FaceNet (200M) [3]. In [24], residual learning is utilized and all the comparison techniques are operated on same CNN architecture. CNN architecture of depth 20 is used to evaluate the method. 20 layer CNN architecture setting is shown in Table 2. Due to less number of resources, it is hard for us to increase the depth of CNN architecture. Fully connected layer and angular margin softmax loss is used at the end of CNN architecture as shown in Fig. 1. For LSSGD, the weight decay is set to 5×104. The learning rate begins with 0.1 and is divided by 10 at the 8.8K, 17.7K and 26.6K iterations and training finishes at 45K iterations.

Table 1. Statistics of publicly available academic benchmark datasets.

Datasets	Purpose	No. of identities	No. of images
CASIA [15]	Training	10,575	494,414
LFW [16]	Testing	5,749	13,233
YTF [17]	Testing	1,595	3,425 videos
VGGFace1 [18]	Testing	2,621	33,436
VGGFace2 [19]	Testing	500	169,396

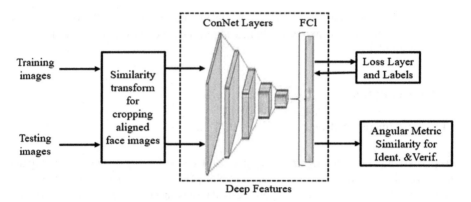

Fig. 1. Cropping aligned face images using similarity transform for both training and testing face images. The discriminative face features are learned in the training phase with proposed method. The testing data is fed into model to extract face features for performing face verification and identification using cosine similarity from angular matric.

Table 2. Our 20-layers CNN architecture with different convolutional layers. Multiplicative term denotes cascaded convolutional layer with respective filters of size 3×3.

Layer	20 Layers CNN [In-channel, Out-channel, stride, padding]
Con1.x	$[Input\ channel, 64, 2, 1]$. $[64, 64, 1, 1] \times 2$
Con2.x	$[64, 128, 2, 1]$. $[128, 128, 1, 1] \times 4$
Con3.x	$[128, 256, 2, 1]$. $[256, 256, 1, 1] \times 8$
Con4.x	$[256, 512, 2, 1]$. $[512, 512, 1, 1] \times 2$
Fully connected layer	

Testing. Firstly, we extract the deep features from the output of the FC1 layer. For all testing experiments, the final testing face image is obtained by concatenating its horizontally flipped features with original face features. The cosine distance helps to compute the score of two features. At the end, the thresholding and Nearest Neighbor (NN) classifier are hired for face identification and verification, respectively. We test our proposed models on popular public available face datasets LFW, YTF, VGGFace1 and VGGFace2. Statistics of used datasets along with respective purpose are shown in Table 1.

5.2   Exploratory Experiments

We have performed different experiments which clearly portray the performance improvement of LSSGD with angular margin softmax. As [17] explained that the system get maximum convergence when $\alpha_1 = 4$, so we are choosing the same value of angular margin in softmax loss for the comparison of SGD and LSSGD. Face recognition is performed on several academic benchmarks, including LFW [16], YTF [17], VGGFace1 [18] and VGGFace2 [19] have training dataset of CASIA WebFace [15].

To clearly demonstrate the effect of LSSGD over SGD training loss has shown in Fig. 2. However, graph distinctly shows that LSSGD has comparative less loss at every point from SGD.

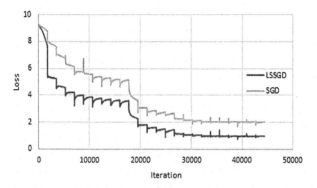

Fig. 2. Loss of training on CASIA face images by SGD and LSSGD with angular margin softmax loss.

As in machine learning it is difficult to maintain the training accuracy as the loss decreases. Figure 2 and 3 are supporting each other in a way that LSSGD loss decreases drastically, meanwhile keeping the training accuracy of LSSGD higher. One can simply judge that the angular margin softmax loss performance becomes better by using LSSGD optimizer, which comprehensibly propel the system to stronger discriminative power. For limited number of resources, we can only afford 20-layer CNN.

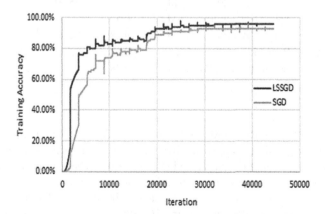

Fig. 3. Training accuracy of CASIA face images by SGD and LSSGD with angular margin softmax loss.

5.3   Experimental Results

Evaluation on LFW and YTF. LFW [16] and YTF [17] are standard testing datasets for face verification. LFW dataset includes 13,233 face images of 5,749 subjects and YTF dataset contains 3,422 videos of 1,595 subjects collected from the website and YouTube respectively. Both the datasets have a large variation of pose, illumination and expression in face images. Evaluation protocols of unrestricted with labeled outside data [16] is followed with 6000 pairs of testing images from LFW and 5000 pairs of testing videos from YTF. Results are exhibited in Table 3. In comparison with all state-of-the-art methods, we have used 20-layers CNN architecture and the rest have shared the same 64-layers CNN architecture. Huge data for training the model is used by all the competitors. We have used publically available CASIA-WebFace dataset for training which is quite small and noisy as compared to private training datasets. Our proposed approach has achieved state-of-the-art results of 99.54% accuracy on LFW which is highest among all the methods. Results on YTF dataset have reached to 95.53% which is runner-up in the set of aforementioned models. One should notice that our YTF performance is worse than [21] only which is trained on 3.8M private dataset with more computation power along with 64-layer CNN.

Table 3. Verification accuracy (%) of different methods on LFW and YTF.

Methods	Train data	LFW [16]	YTF [17]
DeepID [1]	0.2M	99.47	93.20
Deep Face [2]	4.4M	97.35	91.40
FaceNet [3]	200M	99.63	95.10
Baidu [25]	1.3M	99.13	–
SphereFace [20]	0.5M	99.42	95.00
SphereFace+ [26]	0.5M	99.47	–
Center Loss [5]	0.7M	99.28	94.90
Range Loss [22]	5M	99.52	93.70
Marginal Loss [23]	3.8M	99.48	95.98
Proposed approach	0.5M	**99.54**	**95.53**

Evaluation on VGGFace1 and VGGFace2. VGGFace1 [18] is standard dataset usually used for training purpose in face verification problem. On the other hand VGGFace2 [19] has both the training and testing dataset. The reason for choosing these datasets to test our model because of massive variation on age, pose, expression and illumination in face images. VGGFace1 dataset includes 33,436 images of 2,621 identities and VGGFace2 dataset contains 169,396 images of 500 identities collected from websites and slightly modified for testing. CASIA-Webface is used for training. 6000 pairs of testing images have been prepared from each dataset individually. Our proposed approach has successfully achieved the state-of-the-art results of 86.93% and 93.72% accuracy on VGGFace1 and VGGFace2 dataset respectively. Results are given in Table 4.

Table 4. Verification accuracy (%) of proposed approach on VGGFace1 and VGGFace2 (large scale of age and pose variation).

Method	Train data	VGGFace1 [18]	VGGFace2 [19]
Proposed approach	0.5M	86.93	93.72

6   Conclusion

In this paper, we have proposed a novel approach of combining multiplicative angular margin and Laplacian Smoothing Stochastic Gradient Descent in softmax loss which greatly enhances the discriminative power of feature classification learned by Deep CNN for face recognition. Competitive results are taken on several academic benchmark datasets. We strongly desire that our effort will copiously benefit the face recognition community around the globe. We will additionally be encouraging researchers to use this enhanced softmax loss to some other practical problems such as action recognition, expression and pose estimation, age prediction, object detection, etc. For future, combine some heuristic base approach with SGD or Newton or Barrier method to increase the efficiency.

References

1. Sun, Y., Wang, X., Tang, X.: Deep learning face representation from predicting 10,000 classes. In: IEEE Conference on Computer Vision and Pattern Recognition (2014)
2. Taigman, Y., Yang, M., Ranzato, M., Wolf, L.: DeepFace: closing the gap to human-level performance in face verification. In: IEEE Conference on Computer Vision and Pattern Recognition (2014)
3. Schroff, F., Kalenichenko, D., Philbin, J.: FaceNet: a unified embedding for face recognition and clustering. In: IEEE Conference on Computer Vision and Pattern Recognition (CVPR) (2015)
4. Sun, Y., Chen, Y., Wang, X., Tang, X.: Deep learning face representation by joint identification-verification. Adv. Neural. Inf. Process. Syst. **27**, 1988–1996 (2014)
5. Wen, Y., Zhang, K., Li, Z., Qiao, Yu.: A discriminative feature learning approach for deep face recognition. In: Leibe, B., Matas, J., Sebe, N., Welling, M. (eds.) ECCV 2016. LNCS, vol. 9911, pp. 499–515. Springer, Cham (2016). https://doi.org/10.1007/978-3-319-46478-7_31
6. Sun, Y., Wang, X., Tang, X.: Deeply learned face representations are sparse, selective, and robust. In: IEEE Conference on Computer Vision and Pattern Recognition (CVPR) (2015)
7. Sun, Y., Liang, D., Wang, X., Tang, X.: DeepID3: face recognition with very deep neural networks. arXiv preprint arXiv:1502.00873 (2015)
8. Wang, Z., He, K., Fu, Y., Feng, R., Jiang, Y.-G., Xue, X.: Multi-task deep neural network for joint face recognition and facial attribute prediction. In: ACM on International Conference on Multimedia Retrieval, New York, NY, USA (2017)
9. Hu, G., et al.: When face recognition meets with deep learning: an evaluation of convolutional neural networks for face recognition. In: IEEE International Conference on Computer Vision Workshop (ICCVW) (2015)

10. Chopra, S., Hadsell, R., LeCun, Y.: Learning a similarity metric discriminatively, with application to face verification. In: IEEE Computer Society Conference on Computer Vision and Pattern Recognition (CVPR) (2005)
11. Hadsell, R., Chopra, S., LeCun, Y.: Dimensionality reduction by learning an invariant mapping. In: IEEE Computer Society Conference on Computer Vision and Pattern Recognition (CVPR) (2006)
12. Hoffer, E., Ailon, N.: Deep metric learning using triplet network. In: Feragen, A., Pelillo, M., Loog, M. (eds.) SIMBAD 2015. LNCS, vol. 9370, pp. 84–92. Springer, Cham (2015). https://doi.org/10.1007/978-3-319-24261-3_7
13. Wang, J., et al.: Learning fine-grained image similarity with deep ranking. In: IEEE Conference on Computer Vision and Pattern Recognition (CVPR) (2014)
14. Liu, W., Wen, Y., Yu, Z., Yang, M.: Large-margin softmax loss for convolutional neural networks. In: Proceedings of the 33rd International Conference on Machine Learning, New York, NY, USA (2016)
15. Yi, D., Lei, Z., Liao, S., Li, S.Z.: Learning face representation from scratch. arXiv preprint arXiv:1411.7923 (2014)
16. Huang, G.B., Mattar, M., Berg, T., Learned-Miller, E.: Labeled faces in the wild: a database for studying face recognition in unconstrained environments. In: Workshop on Faces in 'Real-Life' Images: Detection, Alignment, and Recognition, Marseille (2008)
17. Wolf, L., Hassner, T., Maoz, I.: Face recognition in unconstrained videos with matched background similarity. In: IEEE Conference on Computer Vision and Pattern Recognition (CVPR) (2011)
18. Cao, Q., Shen, L., Xie, W., Parkhi, O.M., Zisserman, A.: VGGFace2: a dataset for recognising faces across pose and age. In: 13th IEEE International Conference on Automatic Face Gesture Recognition (FG) (2018)
19. Zhang, K., Zhang, Z., Li, Z., Qiao, Y.: Joint face detection and alignment using multitask cascaded convolutional networks. IEEE Signal Process. Lett. **23**, 1499–1503 (2016)
20. Liu, W., Wen, Y., Yu, Z., Li, M., Raj, B., Song, L.: SphereFace: deep hypersphere embedding for face recognition. In: IEEE Conference on Computer Vision and Pattern Recognition (CVPR) (2017)
21. Zhang, X., Fang, Z., Wen, Y., Li, Z., Qiao, Y.: Range loss for deep face recognition with long-tailed training data. In: IEEE International Conference on Computer Vision (ICCV) (2017)
22. Deng, J., Zhou, Y., Zafeiriou, S.: Marginal loss for deep face recognition. In: IEEE Conference on Computer Vision and Pattern Recognition (CVPR) Workshops (2017)
23. Parkhi, O.M., Vedaldi, A., Zisserman, A.: Deep face recognition. In: Proceedings of the British Machine Vision Conference (BMVC) (2015)
24. He, K., Zhang, X., Ren, S., Sun, J.: Deep residual learning for image recognition. In: IEEE Conference on Computer Vision and Pattern Recognition (CVPR) (2016)
25. Liu, J., Deng, Y., Bai, T., Huang, C.: Targeting ultimate accuracy: face recognition via deep embedding. arXiv preprint arXiv:1506.07310 (2015)
26. Liu, W., et al.: Learning towards minimum hyperspherical energy. arXiv preprint arXiv:1805.09298 (2018)
27. Osher, S., Wang, B., Yin, P., Luo, X., Pham, M., Lin, A.: Laplacian smoothing gradient descent. arXiv preprint arXiv:1806.06317 (2018)
28. Keskar, N.S., Mudigere, D., Nocedal, J., Smelyanskiy, M., Tang, P.T.P.: On large-batch training for deep learning: generalization gap and sharp minima. arXiv preprint arXiv:1609.04836 (2016)

29. Chaudhari, P., Oberman, A., Osher, S., Soatto, S., Carlier, G.: Deep relaxation: partial differential equations for optimizing deep neural networks. Res. Math. Sci. **5**(3), 1–30 (2018). https://doi.org/10.1007/s40687-018-0148-y
30. Chaudhari, P., et al.: Entropy-SGD: biasing gradient descent into wide valleys. arXiv preprint arXiv:1611.01838 (2016)
31. Johnson, R., Zhang, T.: Accelerating stochastic gradient descent using predictive variance reduction. In: Advances in Neural Information Processing Systems (2013)
32. Defazio, A., Bach, F., Lacoste-Julien, S.: SAGA: a fast incremental gradient method with support for non-strongly convex composite objectives. In Advances in Neural Information Processing Systems (2014)
33. Arjovsky, M., Chintala, S., Bottou, L.: Wasserstein generative adversarial networks. In: International Conference on Machine Learning (2017)
34. Krizhevsky, A., Sutskever, I., Hinton, G.E.: ImageNet classification with deep convolutional neural networks. In: NIPS, pp. 1097–1105 (2012)
35. Chen, D., Cao, X., Wen, F., Sun, J.: Blessing of dimensionality: high-dimensional feature and its efficient compression for face verification. In: CVPR, pp. 3025–3032 (2013)
36. Cao, Z., Yin, Q., Tang, X., Sun, J.: Face recognition with learning-based descriptor. In: CVPR, pp. 2707–2714. IEEE (2010)
37. Chan, T.-H., Jia, K., Gao, S., Lu, J., Zeng, Z., Ma, Y.: PCANet: a simple deep learning baseline for image classification? IEEE Trans. Image Process. **24**(12), 5017–5032 (2015)
38. Turk, M., Pentland, A.: Eigenfaces for recognition. J. Cogn. Neurosci. **3**(1), 71–86 (1991)
39. Ahonen, T., Hadid, A., Pietikainen, M.: Face description with local binary patterns: application to face recognition. IEEE Trans. Pattern Anal. Machine Intell. **28**(12), 2037–2041 (2006)
40. Liu, C., Wechsler, H.: Gabor feature based classification using the enhanced Fisher linear discriminant model for face recognition. IEEE Trans. Image Process. **11**(4), 467–476 (2002)
41. Wright, J., Yang, A., Ganesh, A., Sastry, S., Ma, Y.: Robust face recognition via sparse representation. IEEE Trans. Pattern Anal. Machine Intell. **31**(2), 210–227 (2009)
42. He, X., Yan, S., Hu, Y., Niyogi, P., Zhang, H.-J.: Face recognition using Laplacianfaces. IEEE Trans. Pattern Anal. Mach. Intell. **27**(3), 328–340 (2005)

Brain Tumor Localization and Segmentation Based on Pixel-Based Thresholding with Morphological Operation

Muhammad Yousuf[1]([⊠]), Khan Bahadar Khan[2],
Muhammad Adeel Azam[1], and Muhammad Aqeel[1]

[1] Department of Electronic Engineering, UCET,
The Islamia University of Bahawalpur, Bahawalpur, Pakistan
myousufee@yahoo.com
[2] Department of Telecommunication Engineering, UCET, The Islamia
University of Bahawalpur, Bahawalpur, Pakistan
kb.khattak@gmail.com

Abstract. Brain tumor localization and segmentation from MRI of the brain is a significant task in medical image processing. Diagnosis of brain tumors at early stages play a vital role in successful treatment and raise the survival percentage of the patients. Manual separation of brain tumors from huge quantity of MRI images is a challenging and time taking task. There is need for an automatic efficient technique for brain tumor localization and segmentation from MRI images of brain. Some years ago, improper filtration and segmentation techniques was used for brain tumor detection, which gives almost inaccurate detection of tumor in MRI images. The proposed technique is mainly based on the preprocessing step for de-noising input MRI, thresholding, and morphological operation and calculating performance parameters for validation. Firstly, anisotropic diffusion filter is applied for removal of noise because input MRI images are mostly noisy and inhomogeneous contrast. Secondly, MRI pre-processed brain image is segmented into binary using thresholding technique. Thirdly, the region-based morphological operation is used for separation of tumorous part from segmented image. At the end, Root mean square error (RMSE), peak signal to noise ratio (PSNR), tumorous area in pixels and centimeters, system similarity index measurement (SSIM), area under curve (AUC), accuracy, sensitivity and specificity are the parameters used for evaluation of the proposed methodology. Visual and parametric results of proposed method are compared with the existing literature.

Keywords: MRI · Brain tumor segmentation · Region-based morphological operation

1 Introduction

Currently, the brain tumor localization and segmentation from MRI of brain images is interesting and stimulating task in medical imaging. Different techniques are developed to distinguish the tumorous and non-tumorous part of brain MRI image. The different

© Springer Nature Singapore Pte Ltd. 2020
I. S. Bajwa et al. (Eds.): INTAP 2019, CCIS 1198, pp. 562–572, 2020.
https://doi.org/10.1007/978-981-15-5232-8_48

image modalities are frequently used for segmentation, but the MRI image gives more detailed information on tumor size, shape and location. Thousands of people in the world are suffering from different stages of brain tumor. Brain tumor is very painful disease and disturbed many lives of peoples. Medical imaging techniques are used to find the presence of brain tumor. Many methods of image processing are used for localization of brain tumors. The image processing techniques for brain tumor localization are still challenged tasks according results of accurate size, shape, and position of tumor in brain [1].

Tumor can be defined as scarce, partition and unrestrained growth of the body cells. The amount of anomalous development of cells in the brain is called brain tumor. It is also one of the most fatal and not very common cancer. Our skull is very hard and rigid that surrounds our brain safely. Abnormal cells growing inside the skull can cause complications. Brain cancer can be benign or malignant. When benign or malignant tumors grow, they cause pressure inside our skull. This can cause brain problems like headaches, brain cells damaging, and it can be life-threatening [2]. Brain tumor is unusual and deceased numerous breaths. According to international agency for research on cancer (IARC) of biomedical image processing, 126000 people are suffering from dangerous brain tumor disease. To reduce this disease, scientists are using multi-disciplinary method. These methods are including knowledge in computer science, mathematics and medicine for more actual treatment methods and find better solution to the disease [3].

Biomedical imaging modalities such as Ultrasound, X-rays, Computed Tomography (CT) scan and MRI are used for diagnoses of various diseases. Many authors proposed diagnose brain tumor techniques using symptom of diseases for sure the presence of disease in patients. MRI machine uses strong magnetic field inside it to take the picture of interior organisms of the body. When MRI image is captured, then the size, position, and location of the tumor help for selecting the types of biopsy. Precise discovery of the type of brain abnormality is very important for treatment scheduling. Before treating any therapy, segmentation of MRI is critical for tumor detection in order to protect healthy brain tissues while abolishing and destroying tumor cells during therapy. The position, size, grade, and nature of a tumor in the brain is detected first, then biopsy technique is used to remove abnormal cells present in the brain. Some of the biopsy techniques are listed here [4].

- Surgery
- Laser interstitial thermal
- Radiation therapy
- Chemotherapy

2   Literature Review

This section consists of related works about brain tumor localization from MRI of brain and criticism of the earlier algorithms utilized for brain tumor localization and segmentation from MRI of the brain. The image segmentation is a method which can be applied in numerous applications like image investigation, detection of diseases and many more. Digital image is separated into specific regions for separation of cancerous part from non-cancerous with help of different operations used on it.

Maksoud et al. [4], used cross segmentation algorithm for tumor detection. K-Means segmentation and detection algorithm was combined with FCM segmentation algorithm. This method gives output with efficient brain tumor detection. The output results are due to the K-Mean clustering algorithm for features of least calculation time and the benefits of FCM features for efficiency. K-Means clustering algorithm is identified more rapidly than FCM. But FCM gives information of cells precisely. Melegy et al. [5], worked on the segmentation of brain tumor detection using fuzzy method. This method was applicable for segmentation of regular and pathological brain from MRI pictures. Also, this method was established on FCM process. PIGFCM segmentation process segmented the brain tissues as cerebrospinal fluid, white matter grey matter. Previous information based on knowledge was used for tissue segmentation. Pathological brain had some additional classes like unusual tissues such as necrosis and edema. Authors have worked on both simulated and real images.

Huang et al. [6], offered a process to segment the tumor as a classification problem. Brain tumor segmentation is still an interesting job, high variety in tumor presence, uncertainty in tumor limitations. To solve this problem authors proposed an automatic segmentation and tumor detection method for MRI image. LIPC classification-based method was implemented to categories each tumorous part of the brain tumor into different classes. LIPC divide data into different class model. LIPC used a local independent plan for organization model. The authors estimated the proposed technique using both artificial and openly offered MRI image datasets. Makropoulos et al. [7], proposed a probability boosting procedure for the automatic segmentation of neonatal brain. This method is robust and tested on neonatal brain images aging. Hamamci et al. [8], proved cellular machines based seeded method that used T1 weighted magnetic images. The cellular automata method used to find a straight path in graph theory. It is recognized for the segmentation. Then, to use the complex parameter it becomes reputable for heterogeneous brain tumor segmentation. The authors tested their technique on synthetic, clinical and actual datasets. Tumor-cut segmentation method is then used for separating the tumor tissues into different parts and enhancing them.

3   Proposed Methodology

This section explains the working flow of the proposed model including pre-processing stage, pixel-based thresholding, morphological operation, and validation. The proposed technique is mainly based on the preprocessing step for de-noising input MRI, thresholding for conversion of input image into binary format, morphological operation for tumor separation and performance parameters for comparing proposed method with existing literature. First, anisotropic filter is applied for removal of noise because input MRI images are mostly noisy and inhomogeneous contrast. Then, MRI pre-processed brain image is segmented using thresholding algorithm. The region-based morphological operation is used for separation of tumorous part from segmented image. RMSE, PSNR, tumorous area in pixels and centimeters, SSIM, AUC, accuracy, sensitivity, and specificity are the parameters used for evaluation of the proposed methodology. Visual and parametric results of proposed method are compared with the existing literature (Fig. 1).

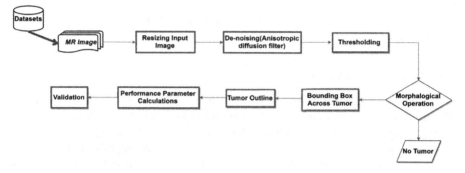

Fig. 1. Flowchart of the proposed methodology.

3.1 Image Acquisition

MRI brain images with abnormal and normal cases are collected from three different resources. For experimental purposes, 25 cases of brain tumor patients are selected from Kaggle resource [9]. Kaggle web dataset consists of total 253 images with 155 tumor cases and 98 with normal brain. 15 cases are selected from BraTS 2015 [10] datasets, which are all tumorous. 5 cases are selected from local Bahawalpur Victoria Hospital (BVH) in which 4 cases are tumorous and 1 case is normal. All these selected scanned images are saved as JPEG format.

3.2 Preprocessing Stage

In this stage, noise elimination, resizing and normalization of the images are performed for further processing. Different types of noises are present in the MRI brain images. Noise is basically a mixture of white and gray color in one pixel. MRI images which are used for preprocessing are digital images which are in the form of 0 and 1. Pixels in input image must be white or black. The noise elimination and contrast enhancement comparisons of an average filter, wiener filter, median filter, and the proposed anisotropic diffusion filter is shown in Fig. 2.

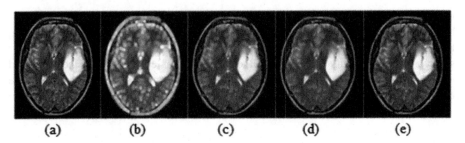

Fig. 2. Filter comparison a) Input image b) Average filter c) Wiener filter d) Median filter e) Anisotropic diffusion filter.

3.3   Image Segmentation

In biomedical engineering, image segmentation is the technique used for tumor detection and many other diseases detection such as lung cancer, skin cancer, bone and joint disorder, breast cancer, vision problems etc. There are three main segmentations of images used for the detection of many diseases. These are segmentation of images based on borders, regions, and pixels. Edge-based segmentation is used for the detection of active edges and contours. Region-based segmentation is mainly used for graph cutting and merging and splitting images from based image or into base images. Pixel-based segmentation is separated into two class's thresholding and clustering. Thresholding and clustering are the efficient and simplest methods of image segmentation. Pixel-based thresholding is used in proposed method. In pixel-based thresholding, thresholding level value is selected as average if all the pixels in the MRI image. It can also be select as fix number that gives inaccurate segmentation where MRI images are not homogeneous or noisy [11]. All the image pixel converts selected as 0 and 1 comparing each of present value with the thresholding value.

3.4   Morphological Operation

The morphological operation is a large set of image processing operations that process images based on size and shapes. In a morphological operation, each pixel in the image is adjusted based on the value of other nearby pixels. By choosing the size and shape of the neighborhood, it is possible to build a morphological operation sensitive to specific shapes in the input image. Dilation and erosion are two basic morphological operation commands that helps to perform various operations in image processing [12]. Morphological operations with region property are applied to the segmented image to separate tumorous part of the image from the preprocessed image. The tumorous part in the MRI image of brain is high dense area, the intensity of the tumor portion is high than a normal healthy brain. Each pixel carries value 0 or 1. The decision about tumor is taken at values of each pixel. Output visual and performance results of proposed method are shown in Fig. 3.

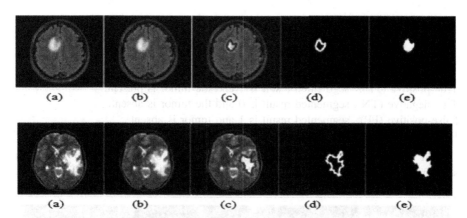

Fig. 3. Output results of the proposed method a) Input image b) Filtered image c) Segmented tumor d) Tumor outline e) Tumor alone.

4 Results and Discussions

This section deliberates and analyzed the experimental results and critical discussion on output results of table and figure. The success of the proposed method of tumor localization is validated by performance parameters like accuracy, specificity, sensitivity, dice and mean square error. Automated segmentation and tumor detection of the proposed method is nearly same with manual segmentation of tumor. By comparing segmented and answer images, four basic parameters true negative (TN), false negative (FN), true positive (TP) and false positive (FP) are calculated for measurement of area under curve (AUC), specificity, sensitivity, accuracy and dice. All these four parameters give information about segmented results comparing with answer image. TP means segmented results in image is 1 and answer image for that's pixels also 1 or simple tumor is present. TN means segmented results in image is 0 and answer image for that's pixels is 0 or simple tumor is absent for that pixels. FP means segmented results in image is 1 and answer image for that's pixels is 0 or simple tumor is absent for that pixels. FN means segmented results in image is 0 and answer image for that's pixels 1 or simple tumor is present for that pixels. Performance parameters for the proposed system can be computed as follows.

$$Dice = \frac{(2 * TP)}{((TP + FP) * (TP + FN))} \tag{1}$$

$$Accuracy = \frac{(TP + TN)}{(TP + TN + FP + FN)} \tag{2}$$

$$Sensitivity = \frac{TP}{(TP + FN)} \tag{3}$$

$$Specificity = \frac{TN}{(TN + FP)} \tag{4}$$

True positive (TP): segmented result is 1 and the tumor is present.
True negative (TN): segmented result is 0 and the tumor is absent.
False-positive (FP): segmented result is 1 and tumor is absent.
False-negative (FN): segmented result is zero and tumor is present.

The output visual results of our proposed method are compared with the manual segmented image for different cases of MRI of brain are given in Fig. 4.

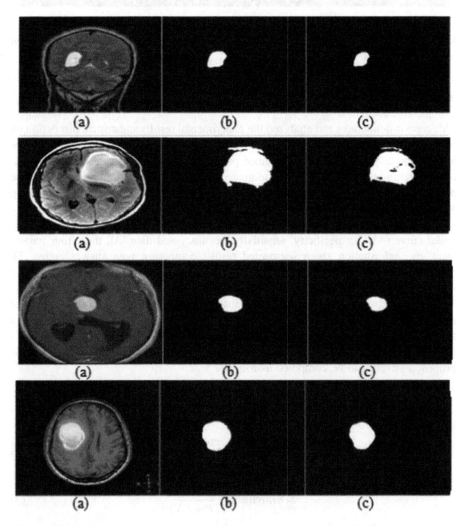

Fig. 4. Output visual results of our proposed method a) Input image b) Manual segmented image c) Proposed method results.

Table 1. Table average performance parameters of the proposed method on Kaggle and BraTS datasets.

Dataset	Accuracy	Sensitivity	Specificity	AUC	SSIM
BraTS	98.89	84.04	99.83	91.94	0.998
Kaggle	98.83	95.41	99.42	97.42	0.991

Table 2. Comparison of performance parameters of our proposed method with existing literature.

Ref	Year	Accuracy	Sensitivity	Specificity	AUC
[13]	2004	95.6	-	-	-
[14]	2008	-	78	79	78.5
[15]	2009	-	92	100	96
[16]	2010	-	91.02	87.8	89.41
[17]	2011	93.6	-	-	-
[18]	2011	93.9	-	-	-
[19]	2012	85	89	84	86.5
[20]	2014	-	69.66	-	-
[21]	2015	-	77.66	-	-
[22]	2015	79.3	77.2	81.3	79.25
[23]	2015	98.98	95.90	94.10	95.50
[24]	2017	99.18	98.05	97.95	98.00
[25]	2017	-	82	78	80
[26]	2017	-	82.5	76.66	79.56
[27]	2017	96.51	97.72	94.2	95.96
[28]	2017	-	88.68	93.9	91.29
[29]	2018	-	91.50	96.81	94.15
[30]	2019	98.81	97.75	98.88	98.32
[31]	2019	-	95.10	99.8	97.45
Proposed method	2019	98.83	95.41	99.42	97.42

Table 1 shows the average performance parameters of our proposed method on Kaggle and BraTS datasets and Table 2 shows the comparison of performance parameters of our proposed method with existing literature. The (-) sign given in Table 2 shows that the literature paper doesn't consist of that performance parameter. The accuracy, sensitivity, and specificity of any method show their performance comparison with existing literature. These performance parameters should be nearest to 100% for any proposed method. For any automated and efficient system, these parameters should be 100%.

5 Conclusions and Future Work

This section summarized the conclusion and future work of the proposed model. In this paper, brain tumor localization and segmentation based on pixel-based thresholding with morphological operation is done. The performance parameters and graphical outcomes of the proposed methodology are superior to existing literature. The proposed method provides a competent and precise detection of the tumor portion of the brain from MRI of all modalities in all three views of brain MRI. The visual and parametric outcomes of the proposed method are compared with the existing literature. The proposed method accuracy for BraTS dataset is 98.89% and for Kaggle web dataset is 98.83%. The sensitivity and specificity of the BraTS dataset are 84.03% and 98.43% respectively, for Kaggle web dataset is 95.41% and 99.41% respectively.

This research will pay attention to a greater efficiency of the proposed method to tackle a greater amount of segmentation problems by enlightening the excellence of segmentation and greater precision in a minimum implementation time. Future work of the proposed method is the 3D evaluation of brain tumor detection will be performed using a 3D slice. The detection and segmentation of brain tumors from MRI are not used clinically, it will be necessary to apply this approach for clinical purposes, which will be useful in automated CAD biopsy techniques.

References

1. Bahadure, N.B., Ray, A.K., Thethi, H.P.: Image analysis for MRI based brain tumor detection and feature extraction using biologically inspired BWT and SVM. Hindawi Int. J. Biomed. Imaging (2017). Article ID 9749108, 12 pages
2. Devkotaa, B., Alsadoona, A., Prasad, P.W.C.: Image segmentation for early stage brain tumor detection using mathematical morphological reconstruction. Procedia Comput. Sci. **125**, 115–123 (2018)
3. Mustaqeem, A., Javed, A., Fatima, T.: An efficient brain tumor detection algorithm using watershed & thresholding based segmentation. Int. J. Image Graph. Sig. Process. **4**(10), 34–39 (2012)
4. Maksoud, E.A., Elmogy, M., Al-Awadi, R.: Brain tumor segmentation based on a hybrid clustering technique. Egypt. Inform. J. **16**(1), 71–81 (2015)
5. El-Melegy, M.T., Mokhtar, H.M.: Tumor segmentation in brain MRI using a fuzzy approach with class center priors. EURASIP J. Image Video Process. **2014**(1), 1–14 (2014). https://doi.org/10.1186/1687-5281-2014-21
6. Huang, M., Yang, W., Wu, Y., Jiang, J., Chen, W.: Brain tumor segmentation based on local independent projection-based classification. IEEE Trans. Biomed. Eng. **61**(10), 2633–2645 (2014)
7. Makropoulos, A., et al.: Automatic whole brain MRI segmentation of the developing neonatal brain. IEEE Trans. Med. Imaging **33**(9), 1818–1831 (2014)
8. Hamamci, A., Kucuk, N., Karaman, K., Engin, K., Unal, G.: Tumor-cut: segmentation of brain tumors on contrast enhanced MR images for radiosurgery applications. IEEE Trans. Med. Imaging **31**(3), 790–804 (2012)
9. LNCS Homepage. https://www.kaggle.com/navoneel/brain-mri-images-for-brain-tumor-detection

10. LNCS Homepage. https://www.smir.ch/BRATS/Start2015
11. Shanthi, K.J., Kumar, M.S.: Skull stripping and automatic segmentation of brain MRI using seed growth and threshold techniques. In: 2007 International Conference on Intelligent and Advanced Systems, pp. 22–426. IEEE (2007)
12. Somasundaram, K., Kalaiselvi, T.: Automatic brain extraction methods for T1 magnetic resonance images using region labeling and morphological operations. Comput. Biol. Med. **41**(8), 16–25 (2011)
13. Lukas, L., et al.: Brain tumor classification based on long echo proton MRS signals. Artif. Intell. Med. **31**(1), 73–89 (2004)
14. Lee, M.C., Nelson, S.J.: Supervised pattern recognition for the prediction of contrast-enhancement appearance in brain tumors from multivariate magnetic resonance imaging and spectroscopy. Artif. Intell. Med. **43**(1), 61–74 (2008)
15. Wang, S., et al.: Differentiation between glioblastomas and solitary brain metastases using diffusion tensor imaging. Neuroimage **44**(3), 653–660 (2009)
16. Song, Y., Liò, P.: A new approach for epileptic seizure detection: sample entropy-based feature extraction and extreme learning machine. J. Biomed. Sci. Eng. **3**(6), 556–567 (2010)
17. Hemanth, D.J., Vijila, C.K.S., Selvakumar, A.I., Anitha, J.: Performance enhanced hybrid Kohonen-Hopfield neural network for abnormal brain image classification. In: Kim, T., Adeli, H., Ramos, C., Kang, B.-H. (eds.) SIP 2011. CCIS, vol. 260, pp. 356–365. Springer, Heidelberg (2011). https://doi.org/10.1007/978-3-642-27183-0_38
18. Blanchet, L., et al.: Discrimination between metastasis and glioblastoma multiforme based on morphometric analysis of MR images. Am. J. Neuroradiol. **32**(1), 67–73 (2011)
19. Zöllner, F.G., Emblem, K.E., Schad, L.R.: SVM-based glioma grading: optimization by feature reduction analysis. J. Med. Phys. **22**(3), 205–214 (2012)
20. Axel, D., et al.: Brain tumor segmentation with deep neural networks. In: Proceedings MICCAI-BRATS, pp. 01–05 (2014)
21. Pereira, S., Pinto, A., Alves, V., Silva, C.A.: Deep convolutional neural networks for the segmentation of gliomas in multi-sequence MRI. In: Proceedings MICCAI-BRATS, pp. 52–55 (2015)
22. Nabizadeh, N., Kubat, M.: Brain tumors detection and segmentation in MR images: Gabor wavelet vs. statistical features. Comput. Electr. Eng. **45**, 286–301 (2015)
23. Abdel-Maksoud, E., Elmogy, M.: Brain tumor segmentation based on hybrid clustering techniques. Egypt. Inform. J. (2015)
24. Lahmiri, S.: Glioma detection based on multi-fractal features of segmented brain by particle swarm segmentation technique. Biomed. Signal Process. Control **31**, 48–155 (2017)
25. Havaei, M., et al.: Brain tumor segmentation with deep neural networks. Med. Image Anal. **35**, 18–31 (2017)
26. Mohsin, H., El-Dahshan, E.S.A.: Classification with deep neural networks for brain tumor segmentation. Future Comput. Inform. J. **3**, 68–71 (2018)
27. Bahadure, N.B., Ray, A.K., Thethi, H.P.: MRI based brain tumor detection and feature extraction using biologically inspired BWT and SVM. Hindawi Int. J. Biomed. Imaging (2017)
28. Filho, P.P.R., Cortez, P.C., da Silva Barros, A.C., Albuquerque, V.H.C., Tavares, J.M.R.S.: Novel and powerful 3D adaptive crisp active contour method applied in the segmentation of CT lung images. Med. Image Anal. **35**, 503–516 (2017)
29. Rodrigues, M.B., et al.: Health of things algorithms for malignancy level classification of lung nodules. IEEE Access **6**, 18592–18601 (2018)

30. Bousselham, A., Bouattane, O., Youssf, M.: Towards reinforced brain tumor segmentation on MRI images based on temperature changes on pathologic area. Hindawi Int. J. Biomed. Imaging (2019)
31. Shakeel, P.M., Tobely, T.E.E., Al-Feel, H.: Neural network based brain tumor detection using wireless infrared imaging sensor. Special Section on New Trends in Brain Signal Processing and Analysis (2019)

Classification of Breast Lesions in Combination with Metamorphic Segmentation and Saliency Feature Block

Bushra Mughal[(⊠)], Faheem Mushtaq, and Attaullah Buriro

Department of Computer Science and IT,
Khawaja Fareed University of Engineering and IT, Rahim Yar Khan, Pakistan
{bushra.mughal,attaullah.buriro}@kfueit.edu.pk,
faheem.mushtaq88@gmail.com

Abstract. Breast cancer is leading disease of females and every year death rate is increased gradually due to the breast cancer. Early diagnosis and treatment of breast cancer is an effective way to reduce the death rate of women. The development of the CAD systems improved the mortality rate by reducing false assumptions. This proposed work presents a computer-aided diagnosis (CAD) system for early detection of tumor in digitized mammograms. A novel classification method for breast lesions is proposed using transformative segmentation and saliency feature block. Experimental results show that proposed methods outperformed the existing method and provide timely diagnosis which greatly reduces the mortality rate in medical informatics.

Keywords: Benign · Malignant · Computer-aided diagnosis system · Mammography · Breast lesion

1 Introduction

Breast cancer is familiar disease in female and every year death rate is increasing gradually due to the breast cancer however, timely diagnosis can save lives [1]. The World Health Organization (WHO) estimates that death rate is about 400,000 women per year from this disease [2, 3]. Breast cancer is serious malady in the female, especially who belong to the age group of 40 to 55 years. The latest imaging techniques for detection of breast tumor have developed over the past several years [4–6] yet, there is still inadequate data on these novel techniques to modify the recent practices [7]. A mammogram is an x-ray of breast that can expose the abnormalities (benign or malignant). The insignificant rate of change in x-ray attenuation between normal and malignant tissues causes the mammography, a poorly contrasted imaging modality. Mammograms can be used for both screening and diagnostic purpose [8]. Mammography has low sensitivity rate in younger women or women having dense breast tissue. Breast density is a significant feature that affects the performance of mammography and sensitivity rate in mammography decreases with high breast density [9, 10]. The performance of mammography abnormality identification approaches is based on the breast tissue types either dense or non-dense and classification [14]. Computer-aided-

© Springer Nature Singapore Pte Ltd. 2020
I. S. Bajwa et al. (Eds.): INTAP 2019, CCIS 1198, pp. 573–580, 2020.
https://doi.org/10.1007/978-981-15-5232-8_49

diagnosis system [19] is considered as efficient system for breast cancer detection by highlighting suspicious masses and micro-calcification on mammograms. However, due to many causes which include dense breast tissues and pectoral muscle, these automated systems may cause high rate of false positives. So, these systems are not yet reliable as an independent reader. Automated detection system should be improved for exact pathological assessment to aid the radiologists or a surgeon in the health care environment.

Initially preprocessing technique are used which are usually involved contrast enhancement techniques like histogram equalization and filtering techniques etc. The second step is the segmentation of mammogram for extraction of affected area. The most commonly used region growing segmentation techniques is used. The segmentation process further proceeded towards feature extraction and various types of features like texture feature, statistical and morphological features are extracted from the segmented region. These features are further used by the classification model. Various classifiers like SVM, weighted KNN are trained on these features set and obtained results from the purposed work shows the improved performance of CAD system.

2   Proposed Methodology

The purpose of this research effort is to positively contribute to a reduction in the death rate of women attributable to breast cancer by detecting the small hidden abnormal cells very early before they start to grow. This issue is more common in dense breast. For this purpose, we have to increase the visibility of hidden masses and micro-calcifications by improving the performance of an automated detection system. This attempt will make tumor detection system consistent to check and find tumor region; its size, shape, nature, stage of tumor and other relevant parameters. Image processing techniques in combination with machine learning prove to be a great mean for early detection and classification of different breast tumor types, like benign and malignant. In order to minimize the erroneous pathological decisions in a CAD system, there is a need to classify the normal and malignant tumor with higher classification accuracy using pectoral muscle removal, segmentation, and feature extraction and classification techniques. An elaborate procedure, implementing (a) enhancement for increasing the visibility of tiny abnormal cells without adding any noise and artifacts, (b) segmentation for extraction of breast region (c) descriptor mining and (d) classification method for mammogram will be pursued. It will be then tested and employed for a promising diagnosis as an integral part of computer aided system aimed at detection of breast tumor and its associated maladies.

2.1   Image Acquisition

Mammographic Image Analysis Dataset: Most of mammography databases are not open access. However, MIAS database is one of the most famous publicly available databases used by the researcher [20, 21].

2.2   Preprocessing

Contrast Enhancement and Noise Removal: As the noise and poor contrast makes the image blurs and hide details that may cause misdiagnoses of disease. Denoising and enhancement of mammograms are very important for both the manual inspection stage and for the computer aided second reading stage. In proposed method we make use various contrast enhancement and noise removal technique however after the comparison of the PSNR and error rate of these techniques, we make use of median filter in combination with top hat filter to improve the quality of mammogram.

2.3   Metamorphic Segmentation

The mammographic images used in proposed work are taken from MIAS dataset that contains some patches with highest intensity value at the top. Patches around Breast region are manually extracted to segment the abnormal areas from the remaining of the image, considered as background.

Transformation of Mammograms: Mammograms are the textured images. Mesh of transformation techniques highlights obscured salient texture descriptions which can improve performance of classification model. Transformation of gray scale image into colored images improve the visual quality of mammograms and achieved high accuracy in splitting regions with different temperature which is further used in screening applications and can reduce false positive rate. The main purpose of this work is to reduce the false decisions in computer aided diagnosis. Patches around Breast region are manually extracted to segment the abnormal areas from the remaining of the image, considered as background. We use the color-size histogram (in Lab color space) to build a region filtering to screen out most of irrelevant regions and images.

Region growing segmentation method is implemented on transformed image to refine the segmentation process. Region growing is a region-based method starting with seed points in the image. Here seed point is the highest intensity pixel in Lab color space. Seeds propagate until the specified stop criterion is satisfied. Different steps of region growing are presented as the following:

   i. Input image = ROI; (x, y) = maximum intensity in ROI; t = produced seed point using trained ANN; mean of region = $I(x, y)$;
  ii. Start region growing until the distance between the region intensity mean and new pixels intensity mean become higher than the threshold t.
 iii. Add new 4-neighbors pixels.
  iv. Add neighbor if inside and not already part of the segmented area.
   v. Add pixel with intensity nearest to the mean of the region, to the region.
  vi. Calculate the new mean of the region.
 vii. Save the x and y coordinates of the pixel (for the neighbor add process) (Figs. 1 and 2).

Return 2

- Seed pixel (high intensity)
- Growth Direction
- Grown Pixel
- Pixel being considered

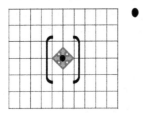
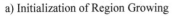
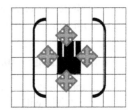

a) Initialization of Region Growing   b) Growing Process after some Iteration

Fig. 1. Region growing method

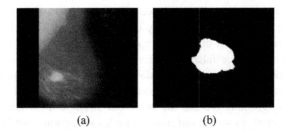

(a)   (b)

Fig. 2. Metamorphic segmentation process (a) Orignal Mammogram (b) Segmented Mammogram

2.4   Feature Extraction

In typical CAD systems, segmentation of ROIs and feature extraction for generated ROI are prerequisite steps prior to performing classification of ROIs. In our study feature subspace are classified into three sets texture based feature, intensity and shape or morphological. A description of these features are given in Table 1, Table 2, and Table 3.

Table 1. GLCM based features

Dataset	Feature_Name
MIAS & DDSM	Energy
MIAS & DDSM	Homogeneity
MIAS & DDSM	Contrast
MIAS & DDSM	Correlation

Table 2. Region based feature

Dataset	Feature_Name
MIAS & DDSM	Area
MIAS & DDSM	Major Axis length
MIAS & DDSM	Minor Axis length
MIAS & DDSM	Convex Area
MIAS & DDSM	Eccentricity
MIAS & DDSM	Diameter
MIAS & DDSM	Diameter
MIAS & DDSM	Solidity
MIAS & DDSM	Orientations
MIAS & DDSM	Perimeter
MIAS & DDSM	Extent
MIAS & DDSM	Spiculated
MIAS & DDSM	Skeleton
MIAS & DDSM	Circularity

Table 3. Intensity based features

Dataset	Feature_Name
MIAS & DDSM	Mean
MIAS & DDSM	Variance
MIAS & DDSM	Kurtosis
MIAS & DDSM	Skewness

3   Experimental Results and Discussion

The proposed method is implemented on two state-of-the-art dataset named as MIAS and DDSM. The classification results of breast lesion detection are described in Table 4 and Table 5 respectively. These results show that proposed method show significant results on SVM classifier as compared to other state-of the art classifiers (Table 6).

Table 4. Classification results on MIAS datasets using different classifier

Dataset	Imaging modality	Classifier	Sensitivity	Specificity	Accuracy
MIAS	Mammography	Ensemble classifier	86.15%	88.23%	87.5%
MIAS	Mammography	KNN	90.7%	89.42%	90.05%
MIAS	Mammography	SVM (linear)	96.15%	98.23%	97.50%
MIAS	Mammography	SVM (quadratic)	97.25%	97%	98.75%
MIAS	Mammography	Adaboost	85.21%	87.23%	87.01%
MIAS	Mammography	Decision tree	78%	80%	79.75%

Table 5. Classification results on DDSM datasets using different classifier

Dataset	Imaging modality	Classifier	Sensitivity	Specificity	Accuracy
MIAS	Mammography	Ensemble	84.15%	86.23%	86.05%
MIAS	Mammography	KNN	90.5%	89%	88.75%
MIAS	Mammography	SVM (linear)	96.25%	98.75%	98%
MIAS	Mammography	SVM (quadratic)	96.25%	98%	97.50%
MIAS	Mammography	Adaboost	86.21%	87.35%	86.75%
MIAS	Mammography	Decision Tree	78%	79%	78.75%

Table 6. Comparison of proposed technique with different State-of the-art methods

Algorithm	Year	Datasets	Imaging modality	Techniques	Sensitivity	Specificity	Accuracy
Gedik et al. [15]	2016	MIAS, DDSM	Mammography	Wave-atom transform, KNN	–	–	91.18%
Wang et al. [23]	2016	Hospital Images	Mammography	Fused feature model	88%	90%	87%
Rouhi et al. [25]	2015	DDSM, MIAS	Mammography	MLP	96.87, 96.25	95.94, 93.78	96.47, 95.01
Elangeeran et al. [26]	2014	DDSM	Mammography	Wavelet transform CC-ELM	–	–	96.19%
Tabalvandani [27]	2014	DDSM	Mammography	Ensemble	–	–	92%
Liu et al. [28]	2013	DDSM	Mammography	SVM	92.00	93.00	93%
Proposed Method		MIAS	Mammography	SVM (quadratic)	97.25%	97%	98.75%
Proposed		DDSM	Mammography	SVM (linear)	98.75%	98%	96.25%

4 Conclusion

A more precise breast lesion classification scheme with transformed segmentation scheme and multi-saliency feature block is introduced. This scheme is helpful in extraction of ROI and salient descriptors which improve the performance of automated breast lesion detection system. The proposed method shows highest accuracy rate of about 98.75% on MIAS datasets and 96.25% on DDSM.

References

1. Jalalian, A., et al.: Computer-aided detection/diagnosis of breast cancer in mammography and ultrasound: a review. Clin. Imaging 37(3), 420–426 (2013)
2. DeSantis, C.E., et al.: International variation in female breast cancer incidence and mortality rates. Cancer Epidemiol. Biomark. Prev. 24(10), 1495–1506 (2015)

3. Eltoukhy, M.M.M., Faye, I., Samir, B.B.: Using curvelet transform to detect breast cancer in digital mammogram. In: 5th International Colloquium on Signal Processing & its Applications. CSPA 2009. IEEE (2009)

4. Starikov, A., et al.: 2D mammography, digital breast tomosynthesis, and ultrasound: which should be used for the different breast densities in breast cancer screening? Clin. Imaging **40**(1), 68–71 (2016)

5. Deng, S., et al.: Radiolabeled cyclic arginine-glycine-aspartic (RGD)-conjugated iron oxide nanoparticles as single-photon emission computed tomography (SPECT) and magnetic resonance imaging (MRI) dual-modality agents for imaging of breast cancer. J. Nanopart. Res. **17**(1), 1–11 (2015)

6. Hildebrandt, M.G., et al.: [18F] Fluorodeoxyglucose (FDG)-Positron Emission Tomography (PET)/Computed Tomography (CT) in Suspected Recurrent Breast Cancer: a prospective comparative study of dual-time-point FDG-PET/CT, contrast-enhanced CT, and bone scintigraphy. J. Clin. Oncol. **34**(16), JCO635185 (2016)

7. McGuire, A., et al.: Effects of age on the detection and management of breast cancer. Cancers **7**(2), 908–929 (2015)

8. Shanmugavadivu, P., Sivakumar, V., Sudhir, R.: Fractal dimension-bound spatio-temporal analysis of digital mammograms. Eur. Phys. J. Spec. Top. **225**(1), 137–146 (2016)

9. Lehman, C.D., et al.: Cancer yield of mammography, MR, and US in high-risk women: prospective multi-institution breast cancer screening study 1. Radiology **244**(2), 381–388 (2007)

10. Oliver, A., et al.: A statistical approach for breast density segmentation. J. Digit. Imaging **23**(5), 527–537 (2010)

11. Oliver, A., et al.: A novel breast tissue density classification methodology. IEEE Trans. Inf Technol. Biomed. **12**(1), 55–65 (2008)

12. Nithya, R., Santhi, B.: Computer aided diagnosis system for mammogram analysis: a survey. J. Med. Imaging Health Informatics **5**(4), 653–674 (2015)

13. Kwok, S.M., et al.: Automatic pectoral muscle segmentation on mediolateral oblique view mammograms. IEEE Trans. Med. Imaging **23**(9), 1129–1140 (2004)

14. Saraswathi, D., Srinivasan, E.: An ensemble approach to diagnose breast cancer using fully complex-valued relaxation neural network classifier. Int. J. Biomed. Eng. Technol. **15**(3), 243–260 (2014)

15. Gedik, N., Atasoy, A., Sevim, Y.: Investigation of wave atom transform by using the classification of mammograms. Appl. Soft Comput. **43**, 546–552 (2016)

16. Wang, Z., et al.: Breast tumor detection in double views mammography based on extreme learning machine. Neural Comput. Appl. **27**(1), 227–240 (2016)

17. Rouhi, R., et al.: Benign and malignant breast tumors classification based on region growing and CNN segmentation. Expert Syst. Appl. **42**(3), 990–1002 (2015)

18. Elangeeran, M., Ramasamy, S., Arumugam, K.: A novel method for benign and malignant characterization of mammographic microcalcifications employing waveatom features and circular complex valued—Extreme Learning Machine. In: 2014 IEEE Ninth International Conference on Intelligent Sensors, Sensor Networks and Information Processing (ISSNIP). IEEE (2014)

19. Tabalvandani, N.S. and K. Faez. Multiple classifier systems for breast mass classification. In: 2014 22nd Iranian Conference on Electrical Engineering (ICEE). IEEE (2014)

20. Liu, X., Tang, J.: Mass classification in mammograms using selected geometry and texture features, and a new SVM-based feature selection method. IEEE Syst. J. **8**(3), 910–920 (2014)

21. Saki, F., et al.: Fast opposite weight learning rules with application in breast cancer diagnosis. Comput. Biol. Med. **43**(1), 32–41 (2013)

22. Tiedeu, A., et al.: Texture-based analysis of clustered microcalcifications detected on mammograms. Digit. Signal Proc. **22**(1), 124–132 (2012)
23. Zhang, Y., et al.: Building an ensemble system for diagnosing masses in mammograms. Int. J. Comput. Assist. Radiol. Surg. **7**(2), 323–329 (2012)

Analysis of the MIDAS and OASIS Biomedical Databases for the Application of Multimodal Image Processing

Muhammad Adeel Azam[1(✉)], Khan Bahadar Khan[2],
Muhammad Aqeel[1], Abdul Rehman Chishti[2],
and Muhammad Nawaz Abbasi[2]

[1] Department of Electronic Engineering, UCET,
The Islamia University of Bahawalpur, Bahawalpur, Pakistan
adeelazam70@gmail.com
[2] Department of Telecommunication Engineering, UCET,
The Islamia University of Bahawalpur, Bahawalpur, Pakistan
kb.khattak@gmail.com

Abstract. In the last two decades, significant advancement occurs related to medical imaging modalities and image processing techniques. In biomedical imaging, the accuracy of a diagnosed area of interest can be increased using a multimodal dataset of patients. A lot of research and techniques are proposed for processing and analysis of multimodal imaging, which requires datasets for benchmarking and validation of their performances. In this connection, two important databases: MIDAS and OASIS are selected and evaluated for the guidance of the researcher to perform their results in the field of multimodal imaging. The associated diseases to these datasets and open issues in the field of multimodal imaging are also discussed. The main objective of this article is to discuss the current interest of the researcher and open platforms for future research in multimodal medical imaging. We originate some statistical results of graphs and charts using the online Web Analysis tool "SIMILIARWEB" to show public interest on these databases and also arranged these datasets according to various modalities, body scanned areas, disease-based and classification of images to motivate researchers working in multimodal medical areas. The significance of these databases in the field of multimodal image processing is encapsulated by graphical charts and statistical results.

Keywords: Multimodal imaging · Biomedical image databases · MIDAS dataset · OASIS dataset

1 Introduction

Single modality images frequently can't give enough data to specialists in real clinical circumstances. It is generally important to merge various modalities to get progressively exhaustive informative data on ailing tissue or organs [1]. In multimodal medical imaging, it is very difficult for researchers to diagnosed disease and effective region of interest when there is no multimodal dataset available. Open databases are valuable

© Springer Nature Singapore Pte Ltd. 2020
I. S. Bajwa et al. (Eds.): INTAP 2019, CCIS 1198, pp. 581–592, 2020.
https://doi.org/10.1007/978-981-15-5232-8_50

instruments for scientists. They are used to gather essential information on various diseases to test new techniques and to take into account quantitative correlations between various methodologies. Decencière et al. proposed one database called MESSIDOR for medical imaging and also described the public interest in this database, but the MESSIDOR database contains only eye fundus images [2]. Müller et al. proposed some large scale and small scale size multimodal and mono-modal datasets for multi-modal retrieval and included some important multimodal databases like "Alzheimer's Disease Neuroimaging Initiative" (ADNI), "National Cancer Imaging Archive" (NCIA), "Open Access Series of Imaging Studies" (OASIS), etc. but did not mention any current public interest on these datasets to motivate researchers working on this multimodal filed [3].

To perform different techniques on multimodal images, we suggest two common databases and their current significant role by showing public interest. The MIDAS and OASIS are two important databases among other popular databases. Other databases are also publicly available for researchers working on multimodal medical imaging. The first and main problem comes in biomedical imaging to gather some useful datasets for validation of different techniques. This article provides insight into the researchers to understand and utilize these datasets. Some important multimodal research areas are the detection of a region of interest, segmentation, fusion, and registration [4]. Precise image segmentation of multimodal images can be performed by deep learning techniques [5]. Researchers can also work on different techniques of fusion related to multimodal imaging [6]. Segmentation, registration, and fusion of multimodal images become more challenging when we don't have a multimodal dataset of the same patient. Dr. Michael Fitzpatrick provided a multimodal 3D medical images dataset named "Retrospective Image Registration Evaluation" (RIRE), which is a combination of 3D Computed Tomography (CT) and Magnetic Resonance Imaging (MRI) images [7]. This dataset becomes freely available as a part of the MIDAS database. Many other databases deal with multimodal medical imaging like ADNI which required formal approval to access datasets and is limited to brain imaging only and Harvard medical school which is restricted to only on the brain and available only in one standard image format. The reason for choosing MIDAS and OASIS databases due to their broad availability of dataset. MIDAS having different scanned body areas with different image formats and various modalities while OASIS has the latest brain datasets, OASIS-3 related to brain multimodal medical modalities for future research in this area. To show the growing research interest in the utilization of biomedical databases, we summarized some statistical and graphical information. This information provides the interest of researchers targeting these datasets on a daily or monthly basis from all over the world. We displayed three months of user's data of accessing and downloading these databases. The statistical results are collected using the SIMILARWEB application [8], which is an online web-based tool for analyzing information about the visitors targeting any specific website. To use this tool, first, we create an account by giving some basic information. All the results of these databases are collected from SIMILARWEB. The main target of these statistical results is to motivate researchers working in the field of multimodality and other image processing areas.

The rest of this paper can be summarized in the following section. Section 2 explains the overview of these two biomedical databases and discussed their nature of datasets and the arrangement of datasets according to modalities, body organs, and classification of images wise. In Sect. 3 we described the current interests of researchers to access these databases by showing some statistical and graphical results related to the public interest. In Sect. 4 we discuss our results and discussion. The Sect. 5 describe conclusion of this paper and further more described some future research and direction in this filed.

2   The MIDAS and OASIS Database

The MIDAS dataset is a collection of server, client and standalone tools for data archiving, analysis, accessing and it contains a collection of biomedical multimodal images. These images are available in DICOM format and it also contains metadata images. MIDAS support 20 types of different format images related to medical and non-medical images. By using the MIDAS database, researchers can work in the area of biomedical multimodal imaging which includes image segmentation, registration, computer-aided diagnosis methods, and fusion techniques. This dataset can be accessed by using the web-link [9].

The OASIS (Open Access Series of Imaging Studies) database is an open-access database of neuroimaging and provided detailed imaging information which can be used in the research of neuroimaging, clinical and psychological analysis on normal aging and cognitive decline. All versions of this dataset can be accessed by using a web-link [10]. OASIS-3 is the most recent release of the OASIS neuroimaging dataset which is freely accessible to the researcher's community to encourage future discoveries in essential and clinical neuroscience. Previously released data for OASIS-1 is cross-sectional [11] and OASIS-2 is longitudinal [12] have been used for the improvement of neuroanatomical atlases and development of segmentation algorithms. OASIS-3 is a longitudinal neuroimaging, clinical and biomarker dataset for ordinary aging and Alzheimer's disease. OASIS-3 is an assemblage of information and data for greater than 1000 members that were gathered over a few continuous projects through the WUSTL Knight ADRC throughout 30 years. Members incorporate 609 subjectively normal adults and 489 people at different phases of intellectual decrease going in age from 42–95 years. The dataset contains more than 2000 MR sessions, which incorporate T1w, T2w, SWI, ASL, FLAIR, time of flight, resting-state BOLD, and DTI arrangements 42–95 years.

The MIDAS and OASIS databases are compared in Table 1 by adding information based on the projects for acquiring data, year of acquisition, organs of the body, modality used, dataset arrangement and image format. It is observed that the OASIS dataset is latest and advanced than the MIDAS database. An addition of OASIS-3 release to the OASIS database makes it advanced while in MIDAS you can search many datasets of different body parts and modalities. The OASIS database only deals with neuroimaging. An overview of the comparison between datasets is described in Table 1. We also collected some sample biomedical images from both databases and classified them upon different modalities and body parts.

Table 1. Comparison between MIDAS and OASIS databases.

Database	Project name	Year	Scanned area	Modality	Classification of images	Format
MIDAS	CTK	2010	Cardiac	MRI	Six different direction images (AP, IS, LR, PA, RL, SI)	Dicom
	CREATIS	2011	Bones	CT	Images of bones classified by synchrotron radiation	Raw and Mhd
	KITWARE	2010	Brain	CT	Segmentation of brain	hdr/img and byu
	KITWARE	2010	Liver	MRI	Normal liver scan include contrast enhanced images	Dicom and Mha
	NAMIC	2010	Brain	MRI, DTI, fMRI	20 cases: Ten are normal controls and ten are Schizophrenic	nrd/nhdr
	RIRE	2009	Head	MRI, CT and PET	18 patient datasets including one training dataset	mhd
OASIS	OASIS-3	2018	Brain	MRI and PET	2000 MR sessions (T1, T2, Flair, SWI, ASL) PET images from 3 different tracers	Nifti
	OASIS-2	2010	Brain	MRI	Total 150 subjects from aged between 60 to 96 72 subjects are nondemented, 64 as demented, 51 are Alzheimer's disease, 14 are nondemented	Nifti
	OASIS-1	2007	Brain	MRI	416 subjects from aged 18 to 96 100 subjects with over aged 60 have Alzheimer's disease, 20 non-demented subjects	Nifti

In Fig. 1 we collected images from the OASIS database of MRI brain images and classified these images into different AD (Alzheimer's disease) Stages from a Healthy control brain image. MIDAS database contains biomedical images of different modalities, different body parts, and organs. We arranged some of these sample images upon the modality of source images and isolate different body parts of the human body. In Fig. 2 datasets of MIDAS sample images are shown. These images included a CT scan of the liver and MRI scan of Cardiac phantom images obtained from six different directions (AP, IS, LR, PA, RL, SI). The dataset obtained from MIDAS was in a different format we use Dicomconverter and Dicomviewer software to display such types of files and convert from one format to another.

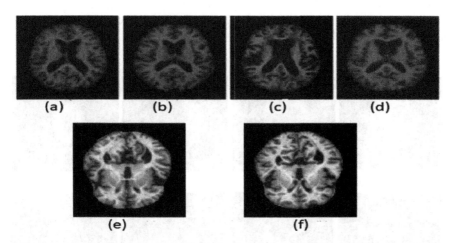

Fig. 1. OASIS dataset of MRI brain sample medical images: (a) Nondemented [20], (b) very mild dementia [20], (c) mild dementia [20], (d) moderate dementia [20], (e) Alzheimer's Disease brain image (AD) [21], (f) Healthy Control (HC) brain image [21].

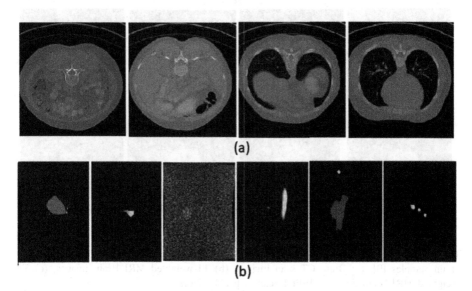

Fig. 2. MIDAS dataset of CT Liver and MRI Cardiac phantom sample medical images [9]: (a) Liver CT scan sample images, (b) Cardiac phantom MRI scans. The same phantom was scanned from 6 different sides (AP, IS, LR, PA, RL, SI).

We also collected some multimodal biomedical images of the same patient from the MIDAS database shown in Fig. 3. These images contain three different modalities of brain images included CT scan of the brain, MRI scan (T1 and T2 weighted sample images) and PET scan of the brain. In MIDAS dataset named rigid multimodality of head scan under the project of Retrospective Image Registration Evaluation (RIRE) contain many patients' brain images of different modalities. We have shown only one patient CT, MRI and PET sample images.

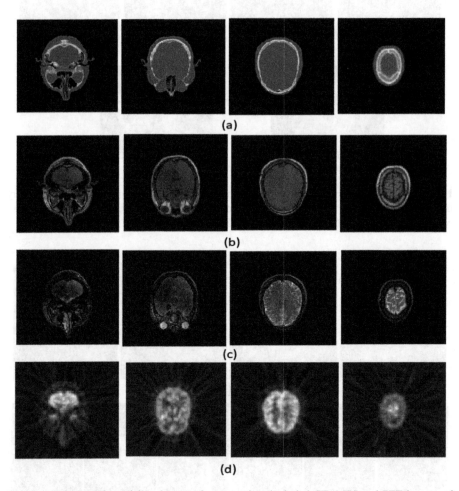

Fig. 3. MIDAS Multimodality dataset of same patient included CT, MRI and PET images of Brain samples [9]: (a) Brain CT scan images, (b) T1-weighted MRI Brain images, (c) T2-weighted MRI Brain images, (d) PET scan of Brain images.

3   Public Interest on MIDAS and OASIS Database

This section consists of the statistics and graphical results on the MIDAS and OASIS databases. All the results collected from the online SIMILARWEB application are summarized. The SIMILARWEB is a website that provides website analytics services founded in 2007. We compared the accessing URL of these databases to show the current interest of researchers. The number of visitors increases day-by-day. The rank of these two databases based on global, country-wise and category-wise is shown in Fig. 4. This figure describes the ranking of these two websites in the observed time duration from February to April 2019.

Fig. 4. Global, country and education based ranking of the MIDAS and OASIS databases.

The significance of these two databases is also observed from the estimation of the total visitors and researcher approaches to these websites from February to April 2019. It is noticed that the researcher is more likely to visit the OASIS database as this database is more concern with neuroimaging diseases. The total number of visitors is shown in Fig. 5.

Fig. 5. Total number of visitors using the datasets: MIDAS and OASIS.

The number of visitors varies over the specified time duration. The variation of visitors is shown in Fig. 6. The OASIS database attracts more visitors than the MIDAS database and has a high bounce rate of visitors. Results are analyzed in the interval from February to April 2019.

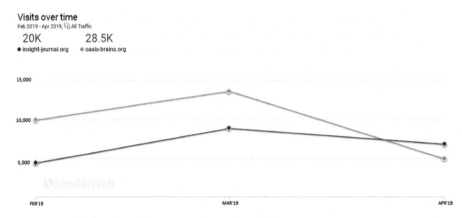

Fig. 6. Graph of the visitors of the MIDAS and OASIS database.

These two databases play a significant role in current research and researcher all around the world utilize it for validation and testing of their algorithms. The topmost countries which visit these databases are United State, India, China, Germany, and France. It is clear from the statistical result that the OASIS database is more targeting from recent three months because this database has a most recent dataset of neuroimaging OASIS-3 on which researchers and scientists can perform multimodal advanced research methods. The top five countries searching these databases are shown in Fig. 7.

Fig. 7. The top five countries searched these databases in the specified time interval.

To determine how many visitors are interested in these datasets, we focused on top keywords that are used within the specified time duration. Figure 8 showed that researchers mostly searched the OASIS brain dataset by using it as a keyword. MIDAS database is present as a subdomain in the domain of [13], so the more search term datasets of MIDAS is not significant appears in our result using statistical analyzing tools.

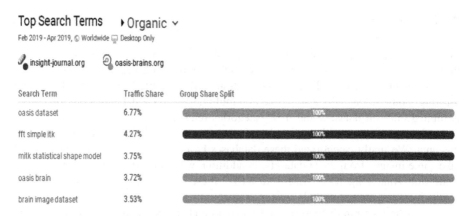

Fig. 8. Keywords used by researchers to access these databases.

The above discussion is not enough to identify the researcher's community targeting these databases. To evaluate the importance of these databases, we gather information on recent research papers utilizing these databases for medical image processing. Among these research articles, the highest citation score is recorded by using the OASIS-1 dataset. The number of citations using OASIS and MIDAS databases is summarized in Fig. 9.

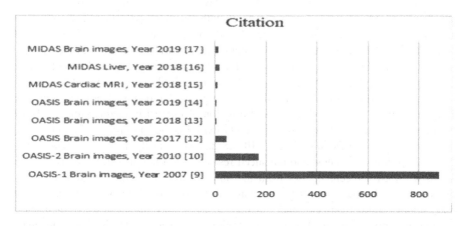

Fig. 9. Citation scores of the MIDAS and OASIS database related to research articles.

Figure 9 describes the importance of these databases in the scientific community of biomedical research. We mentioned some important citation that cited in a couple of recent years. There are many other citations of these databases but we describe some significant citation of these databases.

4 Discussion

In our paper we suggested two databases MIDAS and OASIS, the reason for choosing these databases is that these are freely available, having multiple scanned body images from different medical modalities combinations, different file format, and latest brain imaging. Some researchers also worked on multimodal image databases but their work is limited only on datasets and their categories related to multimodal imaging, these researchers give no intension toward statistical results and show no current interest in this area. We firstly categorized these databases based upon some useful features and take some images from these datasets, in addition, we obtained some graphical results from web Analyzing tool "SIMILARWEB" these results showed some significant results including daily, monthly visitors, top countries accessing these datasets, the top key term search and in the end we make a citation chart score. All these results proved the significance of the multimodal medical field.

5 Conclusion

The MIDAS and OASIS databases have been publicly distributed their datasets. The researcher can utilize these databases, working in the field of multimodal medical imaging, classification of the healthy and Alzheimer's patient using MRI images of OASIS dataset, image registration, and fusion. We have demonstrated the importance of the biomedical multimodal field by displaying the total number of researchers accessing and downloading theses databases within a specified period. The analysis of various researchers from numerous developed countries utilizing these databases validates the importance of the biomedical field. The researcher can work in the future in the field of multimodal image processing includes fusion, combining different sources in medical data, deep learning with inputs from multiple sources of data, advanced registration methods for multimodality imaging, cross-modality learning techniques and many other automatic detections of a region of interest in medical images. Based on the statistical analysis, we observed that OASIS-3 is the latest release for performing multimodal image processing. In the MIDAS database mostly dataset are published in 2010. To perform the latest and advanced research on different various body scanned areas, we need a recent dataset from the latest source of biomedical modality. The proposed two databases encourage researchers to work on different body organs cardiac, bones, brain, liver, etc. and can help to accurately diagnose different diseases through multimodal medical image registration and fusion methods. There are many diseases like Astrocytoma Disease, neoplastic tumor, Alzheimer's disease (AD) in the brain and Coronary Artery Disease that occur in the heart that cannot be sometime diagnosed form single modalities. The researcher can work in these areas to diagnose these medical issues using effective and some progressive techniques by using our proposed two databases for benchmarking their results.

References

1. Rajalingam, B., Priya, D.R.: Hybrid multimodality medical image fusion technique for feature enhancement in medical diagnosis. Int. J. Eng. Sci. Invention (IJESI) **2**, 52–60 (2018)
2. Decencière, E., et al.: Feedback on a publicly distributed image database: the Messidor database. Image Anal. Stereology **33**(3), 231–234 (2014)
3. Müller, H., Unay, D.: Retrieval from and understanding of large-scale multi-modal medical datasets: a review. IEEE Trans. Multimedia **19**(9), 2093–2104 (2017)
4. Alam, F., Rahman, S.U.: Challenges and solutions in multimodal medical image subregion detection and registration. J. Med. Imaging Radiat. Sci. **50**(1), 24–30 (2018)
5. Guo, Z., Li, X., Huang, H., Guo, N., Li, Q.: Deep learning-based image segmentation on multimodal medical imaging. IEEE Trans. Radiat. Plasma Med. Sci. **3**(2), 162–169 (2019)
6. Rajalingam, B., Priya, R.: Review of multimodality medical image fusion using combined transform techniques for clinical application. Int. J. Sci. Res. Comput. Sci. Appl. Manage. Stud. **7**(3) (2018)
7. https://www.mathworks.com/help/images/registering-multimodal-3-d-medical-images.html; jsessionid=31c7560af3783f25ea02367456c4
8. https://www.similarweb.com/
9. https://www.insight-journal.org/midas/
10. www.oasis-brains.org
11. Marcus, D.S., Wang, T.H., Parker, J., Csernansky, J.G., Morris, J.C., Buckner, R.L.: Open Access Series of Imaging Studies (OASIS): cross-sectional MRI data in young, middle aged, nondemented, and demented older adults. J. Cogn. Neurosci. **19**(9), 1498–1507 (2007)
12. Marcus, D.S., Fotenos, A.F., Csernansky, J.G., Morris, J.C., Buckner, R.L.: Open access series of imaging studies: longitudinal MRI data in nondemented and demented older adults. J. Cogn. Neurosci. **22**(12), 2677–2684 (2010)
13. www.insight-journel.org
14. Salehi, S.S., Erdogmus, D., Gholipour, A.: Auto-context convolutional neural network (auto-net) for brain extraction in magnetic resonance imaging. IEEE Trans. Med. Imaging **36**(11), 2319–2330 (2017)
15. Pang, S., Orgun, M.A., Yu, Z.: A novel biomedical image indexing and retrieval system via deep preference learning. Comput. Methods Programs Biomed. **158**, 53–69 (2018)
16. Pang, S., Du, A., Orgun, M.A., Yu, Z.: A novel fused convolutional neural network for biomedical image classification. Med. Biol. Eng. Comput. **57**(1), 107–121 (2019)
17. Mahapatra, D., Antony, B., Sedai, S., Garnavi, R.: Deformable medical image registration using generative adversarial networks. In: 2018 IEEE 15th International Symposium on Biomedical Imaging (ISBI), Washington, DC, USA, pp. 1449–1453. IEEE (2018)
18. Moghbel, M., Mashohor, S., Mahmud, R., Saripan, M.I.: Review of liver segmentation and computer assisted detection/diagnosis methods in computed tomography. Artif. Intell. Rev. **50**(4), 497–537 (2018)
19. Dar, S., Yurt, M., Karacan, L., Erdem, A., Erdem, E., Çukur, T.: Image synthesis in multi-contrast MRI with conditional generative adversarial networks. IEEE Trans. Med. Imaging **38**(10), 2375–2388 (2019)

20. Islam, J., Zhang, Y.: A novel deep learning based multi-class classification method for Alzheimer's disease detection using brain MRI data. In: Zeng, Y., et al. (eds.) BI 2017. LNCS (LNAI), vol. 10654, pp. 213–222. Springer, Cham (2017). https://doi.org/10.1007/978-3-319-70772-3_20

21. Hon, M., Khan, NM.: Towards Alzheimer's disease classification through transfer learning. In: 2017 IEEE International Conference on Bioinformatics and Biomedicine (BIBM), Kansas City, MO, USA, pp. 1166–1169. IEEE (2017)

Image Quality Assessment Using a Combination of Hand-Crafted and Deep Features

Nisar Ahmed[1]($\boxtimes$), Hafiz Muhammad Shahzad Asif[1],
and Hassan Khalid[2]

[1] Department of Computer Science and Engineering,
UET Lahore, Lahore, Pakistan
nisarahmedrana@yahoo.com
[2] Pakistan Space and Upper Atmosphere Research Commission,
Karachi, Pakistan

Abstract. No-reference image quality assessment is an important area of research and has gained significant interest over the past years. Full-reference image quality assessment is not feasible in some scenarios where the reference image is not available. Hand-crafted features are statistics of natural scene images which are used to train a regression algorithm. Deep learning based approaches learn discriminatory features from images. This paper proposes a hybrid method to Image Quality Assessment (IQA) which uses combination of hand-crafted and deep features. The hand-crafted features are extracted in multi-scale and color space configuration in order to capture greater details. Deep features are extracted using transfer learning of Vgg19. Dimensionality reduction is achieved using principal component analysis and features with 95% variance are retained and a final feature set of 102 transformed features is obtained. Gaussian process regression using the squared exponential kernel is used for modeling. The final model is tested on seven benchmark databases for correlation of estimated image quality and mean of subjective score. A comparison with twelve state-of-the-art methods is performed and superior performance is achieved.

Keywords: Image quality · No-reference image quality assessment · Gaussian process regression · Deep features

1 Introduction

The rapid development of digital multimedia technologies has transformed human life significantly. Video broadcasting, video surveillance, high-definition TV, telemedicine, tele-education, video-on-demand, and other such applications are part of daily life. Digital image acquisition devices have deeply proliferated human life due to availability of cheaper and better technologies. Availability of cameras in smartphones and other mobile devices have not been so popular and easy few years ago. These applications produce a large amount of digital content and therefore require the attention of the research community. Distortion and artifacts in the process of image acquisition and

© Springer Nature Singapore Pte Ltd. 2020
I. S. Bajwa et al. (Eds.): INTAP 2019, CCIS 1198, pp. 593–605, 2020.
https://doi.org/10.1007/978-981-15-5232-8_51

storage are common especially in mobile devices due to cheaper hardware, processing limitations and inexperienced users [1]. The processing, transmission, and compression of multimedia content introduce additional distortions and artifacts which resultantly affect human visual experience [2]. Better algorithms for processing and acquisition of multimedia content may reduce the occurrence of these artifacts and distortions but assessment and quantification of the amount of distortion is paramount to the improvement of human visual experience.

Two approaches for the assessment of image quality are: no-reference, where reference image is absent and full-reference, where the reference image is available for analysis [3]. The approaches which require reference are categorized to full-reference and reduced reference methods (which use some information extracted from reference image). The approaches which require reference information actually measure the difference in the distorted image and pristine image. The approaches which do not require reference image are called no-reference or blind and measure only the perceptual quality of images experienced by humans. This makes the Blind Image Quality Assessment (BIQA) a complex problem and requires the modeling of human visual system in order to produce assessment which can correlate well with human judgment. The goal of the NR-IQA is to provide a human visual understanding based quality of the image also referred to as perceptual quality of the image. There are basically two approaches in order to address the problem. The first approach is referred to as subjective image quality assessment that directly involves humans. A group of humans under the same luminance, screen resolution, and room conditions are requested to provide perceptual quality of the image on a predefined scale. Mean opinion score for each of the image is computed by averaging the score. This is the optimal way of acquiring perceptual image quality but it is expensive and time-consuming and cannot be applied in every scenario. The second approach is objective image quality assessment which is independent of these limitations but pose additional challenges. The approach is based on an algorithm which can mimic the behavior of human subjective assessment. The goal is fulfilled by training a supervised learning algorithm with subjective scores commonly known as Mean Opinion Score (MOS) or Differential Mean Opinion Score (DMOS).

The training of supervised algorithms follows two methods: one is hand-crafted features and the other use learned features. In hand-crafted features, Natural Scene Statistics (NSS) and other statistical and structural measures of the image which affect human visual perception are calculated and provided to the training algorithm. This approach requires expert knowledge of human visual system in order to completely model the IQA process whereas the human visual system is yet a naively understood area. Moreover, addition of more statistical and structural features result in improvement of quality assessment performance as demonstrated in [4] but obtaining a reliable no-reference image quality assessment method is still a challenge. The learning based approaches automatically learn discriminative features and the best approach in this category is Convolutional Neural Networks (CNN). CNN requires a large number of training images with MOS to accurately model the human perceptual behavior whereas the currently available image databases with MOS have smaller number of images. The principal reason for this limitation is the availability of a large number of humans for subjective evaluation and the number of images a human can evaluate in a single session without affecting the credibility of the experiment. The scoring of image quality in multiple session cause additional complications and session alignment protocols for subjective quality assessment are sometime employed.

Training of a deep CNN requires a large number of training images due to larger number of learnable parameters. Some of the approaches in the literature has used a pre-trained CNN such as AlexNet, GoogleNet or VggNet and modified its last layers from classification to regression. These networks were originally trained for classification task on ImageNet database. The training images are either resized to fit the input layer size of the network or cropped for transfer learning. The image quality score is obtained by performing non-overlapping cropping and averaging the quality score obtained over multiple cropped image regions. Additionally, data-augmentation using quality invariant distortions can be used to increase the training dataset size which improve the performance of transfer learning.

Another approach to CNN training for small image quality databases is to construct comparatively shallow CNN with specialized architectures to perform the task of IQA. These approaches train CNN with one or two convolutional layers with feature pooling and they provide intermediary performance. The problem with such networks is that they are unable to learn complex features as opposed to deeper CNN and the quality estimates are based on lines strokes and simple textures.

In this work, we have followed a hybrid approach to BIQA. The approach uses a carefully crafted set of features which have demonstrated performance in the area of blind image quality assessment. These features are extracted at three different scales as it has been demonstrated that scale has strong effect on human visual perception [5]. Moreover, feature extraction is performed in different color spaces as opposed to literature and it has provided better performance. Feature analysis is performed to select a suitable subset of features having good correlation with subjective score. This feature set is consolidated with deep features to form a final feature set. The deep features are extracted by pre-trained CNN (Vgg19), originally trained for ImageNet classification task. Then the different layers of CNN are explored to obtain activations which are treated as deep features. This combined feature set is used for training a Gaussian process regression for BIQA.

2 Related Work

2.1 Full-Reference Image Quality Assessment

Mean Squared Error (MSE) is the simplest and intuitive image quality assessment metric in the category of full-reference IQA methods. It measures the squared average of the difference between the absolute pixel values of pristine and distorted images. Although simple and intuitive it fails to correlate well with the perceived image quality by humans [6]. Peak Signal-to-Noise Ratio (PSNR) is a comparatively better measure then MSE as it works by dividing the maximum pixel value (255 in case of an 8-bit image) with MSE and taking the logarithm of the signal. It has been most widely used quality metric to assess the amount of distortion in an image until recently. It was observed that although it is better than MSE it doesn't have a very good correlation with human perceived visual quality. Zhou et al. [2] proposed another measure which is based on the idea that perception of visual quality is principally related to structure, contrast and luminance changes of the image. Therefore, they proposed a metric Structural Similarity Index Metric (SSIM) which computes three terms, namely structural similarity, contrast similarity, and luminance similarity. This metric has gained popularity as it provided better performance than PSNR and several variants of this metric having better correlation with perceived visual quality are proposed.

Another variant of SSIM is MS-SSIM [5]. In MS-SSIM the methodology of computation of features from the original and distorted images remain the same, however, the concept has been extended to multi-scale in order to achieve better performance. DeepSim [7] is based on pre-trained CNN for the image recognition problem, it has been proposed that features obtained from the image recognition are also very valuable in the determination of the perceived quality of the images. The Difference of Gaussian (DOG)-SSIM [8] is based on the Contrast Sensitivity Function (CSF). The approach emulates the bands of frequencies of the CSF by utilizing the channel decomposition methodology. The channel-wise quality has been calculated by using SSIM. In the last, a regression model is used in order to have an overall estimate i.e. the quality of the image. HaarPSI [9] is a wavelet based full-reference image quality evaluator. Haar Wavelet is used for decomposition and an inexpensive approach for statistics extraction is used to calculate the similarity between the reference and distorted image.

There, are a number of FR-IQA algorithms and can be useful with success in compression scenarios. However, in image enhancement, noise reduction, super resolution and other such scenarios they provide poor performance or are unusable so BIQA or no-reference image quality assessment methods are desired.

2.2   No-Reference Image Quality Assessment

The basic no-reference IQA approach is the determination of the impairments or artifacts introduced within the natural or pristine images in the absence of reference image.

One of the most famous approaches based on the above-mentioned principle is DIIVINE [10]. It is basically a two-stage approach the first stage determines the type of the distortion while the second stage determines the quality. Two supervised learning algorithms are used in this approach. Support Vector Machine (SVM) based classifier is used for the determination of the distortion type while Support Vector Regression (SVR) is used for the determination of the quality of the image. BIQI [11] follows similar methodology of performing blind image quality assessment in two stages.

BLIINDS-II [12] is generalized Gaussian distribution fitted DCT coefficients based approach. BRISQUE [13] is an approach the is based on the asymmetric Gaussian distribution model fitted to the features extracted in the spatial domain. NIQE [14] is an unsupervised learning based approach. It is based on multivariate Gaussian distribution. FRIQUEE [15] is a 4-layers neural network-based approach. Handcrafted features are given as an input to the neural network and the features in the modified form are collected from the last layer and then are used with SVR for the image quality prediction. CORNIA [16] is a k-mean clustering and SVR based approach. A codebook is designed based on the contrast normalized and luminance images patches clustering based on the k-mean algorithm. The distance between the visual codewords and distorted images patches are used as a feature to train the SVR which is then used for the image quality prediction. QAF [17] is just like CORNIA as it also computes the codewords. It is based on the sparse learning based on the Log-Gabor filter responses on the images. A convolution neural network based image quality estimator is proposed in [18]. The approach uses the shallow network with one layer in the convolution and the pooling layers while 2 in the fully-connected layers that results in the production of a block performing the feature extraction and regression. BIECON [19] is another approach based on the deep convolution neural network. It is a two-stage approach where the first stage mimics the FR-IQM but within the no-reference format, it consists of two pooling and convolution layers and 5 fully-connected layers. In the second stage, a perceptron with the one hidden layer is used to regress the standard deviations and mean of the patch-wise images into the quality of the image.

CORNIA [20] is a local feature aggregation based image quality assessment method which propose an efficient codebook construction method and then train an SVR for quality prediction. DeepBIQ [21] explored the use of pre-trained CNN and fine-tuned CNN for quality estimation task and then used a shallow CNN with multiple crops followed by feature pooling for quality estimation. dipIQ [22] presents an opinion-unaware blind IQA method. They have used learning-to-rank method to generate discriminable image pairs for un-supervised training. GM-LOG [23] presents a local contrast based image quality evaluator. The proposed method use gradient magnitude and Laplacian of Gaussian for statistics extraction followed by adaptive normalization method to train an SVR. ILNIQE [24] is an opinion-unaware quality assessment method which work in un-supervised configuration. A multivariate Gaussian model is used for statistics extraction from multiple image patches. Average-pooling is used to obtain the final quality score. HOSA [25] is a high-order statistical aggregation approach which extract local statistics from several normalized overlapping image patches and construct a codeword through k-means clustering. An SVR is trained to estimate the quality score.

3 Materials

Training of supervised no-reference image quality assessment algorithms requires images with subjective scores in the form of MOS or DMOS. It is, however, difficult to get a large number of images with subjective scores. According to ITU recommendations [26] 4–40 human are required to rate an image quality for subjective experiment. The length of a subjective experiment is also important as it will create boredom and tiredness and will affect the outcome of experiment. Multiple scoring sessions pose additional challenges. However, some benchmark databases are released by various research groups having a varying number of images and distortions and are mentioned in Table 1.

The first three databases have similar scoring, the only difference is the number and type of distortions used to generated distorted images. The scoring in these databases is Differential Mean Opinion Score (DMOS) i.e. the score is a difference between the

Table 1. Benchmark databases for image quality assessment

#	Database	Ref.	Dist.	Type	Scoring	Range
1	LIVE-I	29	460	Synthetic	DMOS	0–100
2	LIVE-II	29	982	Synthetic	DMOS	0–100
3	Live MD	15	480	Synthetic	DMOS	0–100
4	TID2008	25	1700	Synthetic	MOS	1–10
5	TID2013	25	3000	Synthetic	MOS	1–10
6	CSIQ	30	900	Synthetic	DMOS	0–1
7	Toyama	24	196	Synthetic	RAW	1–5

mean opinion of the pristine image and distorted image. The obtained score is scaled from 0 to 100, zero being the lowest quality image and 100 being the highest quality. The databases at serial number 4–5 use similar scoring and the images are assigned MOS with 0 having lowest quality and 10 having highest quality. The scoring in the database at serial number six is DMOS with 0 quality score having lowest quality and vice versa. We have scaled the scores in CSIQ database to 0–100 range so it can be combined and cross-validated with first three databases. The dataset at serial seven has provided RAW scores and we have processed it to obtain DMOS and then scaled it to 0–100 range. At the end we are left with two sets of databases: the first set contains LIVE release I, LIVE release II, Live Multiply Distorted, CSIQ and Toyama database having DMOS scores, scaled in the range of 0–100 and the second set contains TID2008 and TID2013 databases having MOS scores with 0–10 range (not-scaled).

4   Methodology

As explained earlier there are two categories of BIQA algorithms: hand-crafted features based and learning based. The first category use carefully crafted NSS based feature to train a regression algorithm for IQA. The second category use learning based methods to automatically learn discriminatory features from images and therefore require no-expert knowledge. Human visual system is a poorly understood system and therefore hand-crafted features cannot fully model it and therefore there is always a room for improvement. On the other hand, learning-based algorithms such as CNN require a good number of images to successfully learn the discriminatory features. We have 3018 images in one set of databases and 4700 images in the other set which is a limited number for successful training of a deep CNN. We have therefore adopted a hybrid approach, containing both hand-crafted as well as learned deep features. This hybrid feature set is used to train Gaussian process regression which is the most suitable regression algorithm for image quality assessment.

We have extracted gradient statistics [27] which includes gradient magnitude, relative gradient magnitude, and relative gradient orientation. Statistics of mean subtracted and contrast normalized products and statistics of standardized luminance [13, 14]. The feature extraction is done at multiple scale as human visual perception is strongly affected by scale [5]. Moreover, chrominance and luminance layers of YCbCr color space and Hue and Saturation layers of HIS color space represent image information differently than RGB layers or grayscale image so the features are extracted in these layers as well. It was observed experimentally that some of these features, extracted in other color space have better prediction performance towards image quality. The final feature set is formed by consolidating all these feature and using ReliefF for feature selection. ReliefF is a filter based feature selection method and has demonstrated performance.

For the extraction of deep features, we experimented with different pre-trained CNN and observed that Vgg19 has optimized performance in terms of feature quality and computational performance. The last softmax layer and classification layers are replaced with fully connected layer with one neuron and regression layer. This network is then trained through transfer learning on image quality database with data-augmentation. Horizontal and vertical translation, slight right or left rotation and horizontal reflection are used as data-augmentation strategies as they didn't affect the perceptual quality of an image. The network is then used to obtain activations at different convolutional and fully connected layer for analysis. These activations are treated as features and training and cross-validation of their performance is performed. It was observed that fc8 layer of Vgg19 provides a compromise in terms of performance and computational complexity. The final feature set is constructed by concatenating the hand-crafted and deep features acting as hybrid feature set. Figure 1 provides the workflow of feature extraction and consolidation.

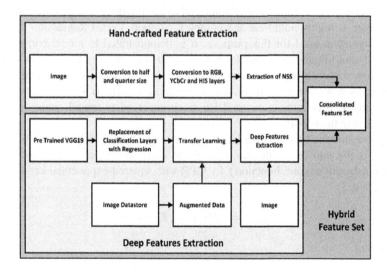

Fig. 1. Feature extraction workflow

4.1 Dimensionality Reduction

Keeping in view the large feature set, it seems understandable to use dimensionality reduction. There are two approaches to dimensionality reduction: feature subset selection and orthogonalization. There are three types of algorithms in the first category i.e. filter based, wrapper based and hybrid.

We have opted orthogonalization using Principal Component Analysis (PCA) [28] which is a popular approach which can effectively eliminate redundancy in feature set. We opted to retain 95% explained variance and the feature set is reduced to 102 features ($f: x^{1297} \rightarrow x^{102}$ where x is the feature vector and the superscript denote the dimension). Although the new data have reduced dimensionality and somewhat less variance but the learned trained model provided less RMSE and better R-squared measure. The training time on the same machine reduced from ~ 756 s to ~ 157 s.

4.2   Quality Prediction

There are several different sources of distortions in natural images and the databases under consideration utilize some of these distortions with varying degrees of intensity. Prediction of perceptual image quality is a complex process which involves modeling of HVS. A suitable feature set with discriminatory features combined with an efficient learning algorithm can provide encouraging results. Let $x = \{feat_i\}_{i=1}^{1297}$ is the concatenated hybrid feature vector. The quality of image can be predicted using Eq. 1:

$$Q = f(x) \tag{1}$$

Where f is a function which calculate the quality score from the elements of S. Direct modeling of the function f is nontrivial as the interface between the features and quality score is highly nonlinear and complex. Support Vector Regression (SVR) is a popular algorithm used for this purpose. It is demonstrated to model complex, non-linear and multidimensional problems [43]. Gaussian Process Regression (GPR) is another approach which has not gained so much popularity in this domain. GPR automatically learn the regularization and kernel parameters as well as feature rank. It delivers probabilistic predictions and has been observed to model quality prediction problem better than SVR.

Suppose that the training data $\{(feat_1, y_1), \cdots, (feat_N, y_N)\}$ is provided to the GPR, where N is the number of images, $feat_i$ is the extracted feature vector and y_i is the averaged subjective score. Function f for GPR with squared-exponential kernel is given in Eq. 2 and 3.

$$f(x) = GPR\{\mu(x), K(x, x')\} \tag{2}$$

Whereas

$$K(x, x') = \sigma_0^2 \exp\left[-\frac{1}{2}\left(\frac{x - x'}{\lambda}\right)^2\right] \tag{3}$$

Here σ_0 is the maximum allowed variance and λ is length-scale are learnable hyper-parameters. The network training is done with hyper-parameter optimization to select the values of learnable parameters using Bayes optimization. Figure 2 highlights the steps followed for model construction and evaluation.

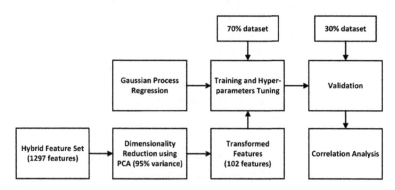

Fig. 2. Model construction

4.3   Evaluation Measures

Evaluation of performance of image quality assessment system is important and it involves the measurement of correlation between the predicted quality values and subjective evaluation scores by a human. The correlation with human subjective evaluation is important as the human are the ultimate recipient of the most image processing systems. It is to be noted that the coefficient of determination (R-squared) and Root Mean Squared Error are calculated during model tuning and are reported to indicate the error and fit of the model. We have incorporated two measure of correlation: Pearson Linear Correlation Coefficient (PLCC) which measure the linear relation with the predicted quality score and the subjective score and Spearman Rank Order Correlation Coefficient (SROCC) which measure the monotonicity of the relationship between the predicted score and the subjective score.

5   Performance Evaluation

The performance of the proposed approach is evaluated on seven benchmark databases which are widely used in the literature. The databases provide a comprehensive ground for evaluation as they contain diverse distortion and scene types. The experiment is done by training the model with 70% data and tuning the hyper-parameters. The trained model is evaluated on 30% data and the results are reported in Table 2.

The results in Table 2 demonstrate the performance of the proposed approach. It is evident that the Proposed Approach is an efficient method to model the HVS behavior for images distorted using synthetic distortions. The consistency of performance with different databases indicate that the approach is well suited to the problem of image quality as it is trained on a comprehensive set of hybrid features. The choice of training algorithm is particularly important as different regression algorithms are tried on the same feature set and the chosen algorithm provided the best performance. GPR

Table 2. Performance of Proposed Approach on seven benchmark databases

Sr.	Database	R^2	RMSE	PLCC	SROCC
1	LIVE-I	0.9692	4.1532	0.9824	0.9614
2	LIVE-II	0.9428	3.4127	0.9813	0.9781
3	Live MD	0.9212	5.1294	0.9642	0.9628
4	TID2008	0.8618	0.4701	0.9678	0.9667
5	TID2013	0.8807	0.4212	0.9738	0.9761
6	CSIQ	0.9522	0.2524	0.9784	0.9748
7	Toyama	0.9718	0.6854	0.9928	0.9874

provided better performance as the subjective scores followed a Gaussian distribution and it seems intuitive to model it using Gaussian process regression.

5.1 Comparison with Existing Approaches

There are several approaches to image quality as reported in Sect. 2, however, some of these approaches has gained particular importance in the research community. We have selected 12 such approaches and the comparison of the proposed approach with the state-of-the art approaches is reported in Table 3. It is to be noted that Proposed Approach has provided best values for correlation coefficients PLCC and SROCC which indicates that the proposed scheme has good linear relation with subjective scores and good monotonicity. Likewise HOSA [25] has provided lowest RMSE for three dataset and it has comparable performances with the Proposed Approach. DeepBIQ [21] is a deep learning based approach which has also provided comparable performance with the Proposed Approach. The proposed approach has provided lowest performance in the case of LIVE multiply distorted database as it has smaller database size with multiple distortions per image.

5.2 Cross-dataset Testing

The generalizability of the proposed method is tested by splitting the datasets into two categories. The first category contains TID2008 and TID2013 datasets and the experiment use combination of these two for training and validation. The second category contains LIVE-I, LIVE-II, LIVE-MD, CSIQ, and Toyama datasets and the experiment use its train/test split for training and validation. The results of the experiments are reported in Table 4 to demonstrate cross-dataset performance. It is remarkable to note that there is performance gap between the two database combinations. The reason for this difference is that the first database combination contains two databases collected by the same research group under the same subjective experimental conditions. The second database combination contains more diversity and the realignment of scores in case of CSIQ and Toyama database lead to slight decrease in the resulting performance.

Table 3. Performance comparison of Proposed Approach with existing approaches

Database	Evaluation measures	BIQI [11]	BLIINDS-II [12]	BRISQUE [13]	CORNIA-10K [20]	DeepBIQ [21]	DIIVINE [10]	dipIQ [22]	GM-LOG [23]	HaarPSI [9]	HOSA [25]	ILNIQE [24]	NIQE [14]	Proposed approach
LIVE	SROCC	0.8642	0.9302	0.9409	0.9417	0.98	0.9162	0.958	0.9503	0.9683	0.9504	0.9020	0.9135	**0.9722**
	PLCC	0.8722	0.9357	0.945	0.9434	0.97	0.9172	0.957	0.9539	–	0.9527	0.9085	0.9147	**0.9784**
	RMSE	13.285	9.6189	8.9048	9.0204	–	10.810	–	8.1723	–	8.2858	11.4007	–	**3.2146**
Live MD	SROCC	0.5722	0.2548	0.5017	0.906	–	0.6563	–	–	–	–	–	0.7785	**0.9628**
	PLCC	–	0.3574	0.5485	0.913	–	0.7183	–	–	–	–	–	0.8370	**0.9642**
	RMSE	–	17.663	15.813	–	–	13.157	–	–	–	–	–	10.329	**5.1294**
TID2008	SROCC	0.8438	0.8982	0.9357	0.899	0.95	0.893	–	–	0.9097	0.917	–	0.6503	**0.9667**
	PLCC	0.8704	0.9219	0.9391	0.9347	0.95	0.9039	–	0.9269	–	0.899	–	0.7409	**0.9678**
	RMSE	8.4704	1.1389	1.1329	–	–	–	–	–	–	–	–	1.144	**0.4701**
TID2013	SROCC	0.8191	0.8786	0.8917	0.8998	0.96	0.8753	0.894	0.9282	0.8732	0.9521	0.8871	0.317	**0.9716**
	PLCC	0.8407	0.9053	0.9176	0.9277	0.96	0.8859	0.877	0.9439	–	0.9592	0.9030	0.426	**0.9738**
	RMSE	0.7569	0.5921	0.5534	0.5239	–	0.6474	–	0.4629	–	**0.3941**	0.6020	–	0.4212
CSIQ	SROCC	0.8115	0.914	0.9099	0.893	0.96	0.876	0.949	0.9228	0.9604	0.9298	0.8885	0.8829	**0.9748**
	PLCC	0.8476	0.9323	0.9278	0.9175	0.97	0.8983	0.93	0.9408	–	0.9480	0.9173	0.9345	**0.9784**
	RMSE	0.1491	0.101	0.1044	0.1123	–	0.122	–	0.0950	–	**0.0887**	0.1098	0.1089	0.2523
Toyama	SROCC	0.5949	0.7995	0.85	0.8565	–	0.8198	–	0.8551	–	0.9066	0.7772	–	**0.9874**
	PLCC	0.5948	0.7672	0.8269	0.8434	–	0.7915	–	0.8371	–	0.8999	0.7798	–	**0.9928**
	RMSE	1.0039	0.7914	0.7099	0.6781	–	0.772	–	0.6897	–	**0.5409**	0.7759	–	0.6854

Table 4. Performance of Proposed Approach with combined databases

Evaluation measure	TID2008 and TID2013	LIVE-I, LIVE-II, LIVE-MD, CSIQ, and Toyama
RMSE	1.2727	8.7431
PLCC	0.9860	0.8712
SROCC	0.9847	0.8676

6 Conclusion

Image quality assessment in no-reference scenario is a complex problem and require modeling of the human visual system for prediction of image quality without any reference information. The proposed approach is based on a hybrid feature set which is a combination of hand-crafted features and deep features. The hand-crafted features are scene statistics calculated in multi-scale and different color spaces. The training algorithm is Gaussian process regression with a squared exponential kernel which is an efficient probabilistic algorithm. The result of correlation analysis and RMSE demonstrate that the Proposed Approach has good correlation with subjective scores and provide low RMSE. The performance of the proposed method is also calculated by combining multiple databases to demonstrate generalizability and encouraging results are achieved. The comparison of the proposed model is done with twelve state-of-the-art methods and it has been observed that the Proposed Approach has provided competitive or better performance.

The model can be further improved by training on a large image set with synthetic scores to learn the peculiarities of image quality and then retraining on smaller benchmark database with subjective scores. Deep features extracted using this approach can be more discriminatory and can provide better performance. Moreover, the set of hand-crafted features can be further improved by adding more quality aware features. An ensemble approach can be adopted to further improve the correlation with human judgment and decrease generalization error.

References

1. Ghadiyaram, D., et al.: Subjective and objective quality assessment of mobile videos with in-capture distortions. In: IEEE International Conference on Acoustics, Speech and Signal Processing (2017)
2. Wang, Z., et al.: Image quality assessment: from error visibility to structural similarity. IEEE Trans. Image Process. **13**(4), 600–612 (2004)
3. Bosse, S., et al.: Deep neural networks for no-reference and full-reference image quality assessment. IEEE Trans. Image Process. **27**(1), 206–219 (2017)
4. Ghadiyaram, D., Bovik, A.C.: Perceptual quality prediction on authentically distorted images using a bag of features approach. J. Vis. **17**(1), 32 (2017)
5. Wang, Z., Simoncelli, E.P., Bovik, A.C.: Multiscale structural similarity for image quality assessment. In: The Thirty-Seventh Asilomar Conference on Signals, Systems & Computers, 2003. IEEE (2003)
6. Girod, B.: What's wrong with mean-squared error? In: Watson, A.B. (ed.) Digital Images and Human Vision, pp. 207–220. MIT Press, Cambridge (1993)
7. Gao, F., et al.: DeepSim: deep similarity for image quality assessment. Neurocomputing **257**, 104–114 (2017)
8. Pei, S.-C., Chen, L.-H.: Image quality assessment using human visual DOG model fused with random forest. IEEE Trans. Image Process. **24**(11), 3282–3292 (2015)
9. Reisenhofer, R., et al.: A Haar wavelet-based perceptual similarity index for image quality assessment. Signal Process. Image Commun. **61**, 33–43 (2018)
10. Moorthy, A.K., Bovik, A.C.: Blind image quality assessment: from natural scene statistics to perceptual quality. IEEE Trans. Image Process. **20**(12), 3350–3364 (2011)
11. Moorthy, A.K., Bovik, A.C.: A two-step framework for constructing blind image quality indices. IEEE Signal Process. Lett. **17**(5), 513–516 (2010)
12. Saad, M.A., Bovik, A.C., Charrier, C.: Blind image quality assessment: a natural scene statistics approach in the DCT domain. IEEE Trans. Image Process. **21**(8), 3339–3352 (2012)
13. Mittal, A., Moorthy, A.K., Bovik, A.C.: No-reference image quality assessment in the spatial domain. IEEE Trans. Image Process. **21**(12), 4695–4708 (2012)
14. Mittal, A., Soundararajan, R., Bovik, A.C.: Making a "completely blind" image quality analyzer. IEEE Signal Process. Lett. **20**(3), 209–212 (2013)
15. Ghadiyaram, D., Bovik, A.C.: Feature maps driven no-reference image quality prediction of authentically distorted images. In: Human Vision and Electronic Imaging XX. International Society for Optics and Photonics (2015)
16. Ye, P., Doermann, D.: No-reference image quality assessment using visual codebooks. IEEE Trans. Image Process. **21**(7), 3129–3138 (2012)
17. Zhang, L., et al.: Training quality-aware filters for no-reference image quality assessment. IEEE Multimedia **21**(4), 67–75 (2014)
18. Kang, L., et al.: Convolutional neural networks for no-reference image quality assessment. In: Proceedings of the IEEE Conference on Computer Vision and Pattern Recognition (2014)

19. Kim, J., Lee, S.: Fully deep blind image quality predictor. IEEE J. Sel. Top. Sign. Process. **11**(1), 206–220 (2017)
20. Xu, J., et al.: Local feature aggregation for blind image quality assessment. In: Visual Communications and Image Processing (VCIP), 2015. IEEE (2015)
21. Bianco, S., et al.: On the use of deep learning for blind image quality assessment. SIViP **12** (2), 355–362 (2018)
22. Ma, K., et al.: dipIQ: blind image quality assessment by learning-to-rank discriminable image pairs. IEEE Trans. Image Process. **26**(8), 3951–3964 (2017)
23. Xue, W., et al.: Blind image quality assessment using joint statistics of gradient magnitude and Laplacian features. IEEE Trans. Image Process. **23**(11), 4850–4862 (2014)
24. Zhang, L., Zhang, L., Bovik, A.C.: A feature-enriched completely blind image quality evaluator. IEEE Trans. Image Process. **24**(8), 2579–2591 (2015)
25. Xu, J., et al.: Blind image quality assessment based on high order statistics aggregation. IEEE Trans. Image Process. **25**(9), 4444–4457 (2016)
26. ITU-T RECOMMENDATION P. Subjective video quality assessment methods for multimedia applications. International telecommunication union (1999)
27. Liu, L., et al.: Blind image quality assessment by relative gradient statistics and AdaBoosting neural network. Signal Process. Image Commun. **40**, 1–15 (2016)
28. Shlens, J.: A tutorial on principal component analysis. arXiv preprint arXiv:1404.1100 (2014)

An Ensemble Classification-Based Methodology Applied to MRI Brain Images for Tumor Detection and Segmentation

Abuzar Qureshi[1(✉)], Khan Bahadar Khan[1], Hamza Ali Haider[1], Rameez Khawaja[1], and Muhammad Yousuf[2]

[1] Department of Telecommunication Engineering, Faculty of Engineering,
The Islamia University of Bahawalpur, Bahawalpur, Pakistan
{abuxar.coresh,kb.khattak,hamza.ali51214,
rameezkhawaja}@ieee.org
[2] Department of Electronic Engineering, Faculty of Engineering,
The Islamia University of Bahawalpur, Bahawalpur, Pakistan
myousufee@yahoo.com

Abstract. Automated brain tumor detection is an important application in the medical field. There is a lot of methods developed for this task. In this paper, we have implemented an algorithm which detects the type of brain tumor from MRI image using supervised classification techniques. The major part of the work includes feature extraction using DWT and then reduction of features by using PCA. These reduced features are submitted to different classifiers like SVM, k-NN, Naïve Bayes and LDA. The results from each classifier are then submitted to a voting algorithm that chooses the most frequent result. The dataset for training contains 160 MRI images. The algorithm is processed on 200 * 200 images to reduce processing time. This method is tested and found to be much beneficial and rapid. It could be utilized in the field of MRI classification and can assist doctors to detect the tumor type and diagnose about patient abnormality level.

Keywords: Image segmentation · MRI classification · MATLAB · Image processing · Tumor detection · Feature extraction · Feature reduction

1 Introduction

Nowadays, image processing is a key tool for biomedical engineering. We can use it for examination of different medical images. The most important one is brain tumor detection. The brain tumor is of two types. One which doesn't spread over time called Benign tumor and other which spread with the passage of time is called Malignant tumor.

Image processing techniques are applied for enhancement of the image or to acquire some valuable information from it. Image processing is also used for image segmentation which deals with the extraction of different features of the image. The image segmentation has a vast scope in biomedical engineering. One of the most crucial parts of the biomedical image processing is MRI classification.

© Springer Nature Singapore Pte Ltd. 2020
I. S. Bajwa et al. (Eds.): INTAP 2019, CCIS 1198, pp. 606–615, 2020.
https://doi.org/10.1007/978-981-15-5232-8_52

The MRI stands for Magnetic Resonance Imaging. It is the imaging technique that produces the high-definition images of anatomical structures of any part of human body, especially in brain. It provides unparalleled view inside human body for clinical decision and biomedical field research. In this algorithm, we use discrete wavelet transform (DWT) [1] to extract features of MRI images. But due to the large storage requirement of wavelet transform, the principal component analysis (PCA) [2] is used. It reduces the dimensionality of the data and reduce computational costs.

Now, the PCA is used to reduce the dimension to get the important features of the MRI image, but we need to classify the data extracted. A lot of techniques are proposed by researchers for the classification of MRI images. These can be described by two classes; one is supervised classification while other is unsupervised. The supervised classification has some superiority over the unsupervised in terms of accuracy. Each approach had achieved good results, but the supervised classification performs better than all in terms of classification accuracy.

In this algorithm, we use two supervised classifiers and two unsupervised classifiers to inspect the accuracy and other parameters between them. In supervised classification, we used the support vector machine (SVM) [3] with linear and Gaussian Radial Based Function (RBF) parameter. The other supervised classifier used is K-nearest neighbor (K-NN) [4]. These both are the popular classification methods based on machine learning basics. The second approach is unsupervised classification in which we use Naïve Bayes (NB) [5] algorithm and Linear Discriminant Analysis (LDA) [6]. These both are the most used unsupervised classification algorithms for biomedical image classification.

Moreover, we use kernel SVMs instead of conventional SVMs. These SVMs are different from conventional SVMs only in terms of the dot product form. All of these classifiers are recommended individually by the researchers and have a very high percentage of accuracy. To make the algorithm more accurate, we use voting method on the results from all the classifiers and chooses the option with more repetition.

We apply segmentation techniques like Otsu Binarization to acquire the segmented image, which is then preprocessed to extract the features. The classification results are subjected to a voting algorithm to select the option with the maximum number of occurrences. We also compared the results of all classifiers to inspect the accuracy of each classifier.

2   Literature Review

Zhang et al. [3], proposed a method for MR brain image classification in which DWT and PCA techniques are employed for feature extraction and reduction. These features are classified using kernel SVM. The purposed method addresses common brain diseases. The input data set is 160 MR brain images with 20 normal and 140 abnormal. The accuracy achieved by RBF kernel comes out to be 99.38% while the linear kernel gives 95% accuracy. So, it is observed that the accuracy rate is high with RBF kernel as compared to linear kernels.

El-Sayed et al. [7], presents a hybrid technique for brain MRI classification. For feature extraction and reduction, DWT and PCA are used respectively. For classification, two classifiers are used. The first classifier based on feed-forward back-propagation artificial neural network (FP-ANN) and the second is based on k-nearest neighbor (k-NN). The success rate of FP-ANN and k-NN is 97% and 98% respectively. Andrés et al. [8], proposed the SOM-FCM based method for MRI segmentation. Features are extracted from GLCM and histogram of the 3-D image. SOM training with fuzzy clustering is employed to classify the input data. The input data contain T1 MR Images with ages between 7 to 71 years old. The results of SOM-FCM classification provide high accuracy.

Saritha et al. [9], proposed the classification method for MR brain images using combined wavelet entropy-based spider web plots and probabilistic neural networks. The wavelet entropy-based spider web is used to extract the features and the probabilistic neural network classifies the MR images. This classification accuracy of this algorithm found out to be 100%. Chandra et al. [10], presented the brain MR images classification with SVM classifier and compared it with another classifier AdaBoost. The input dataset contains 86 abnormal and 48 normal images. The dataset is used for MRI training and then classified by SVM as well as AdaBoost. The accuracy of SVM and AdaBoost comes out to be 92.71% and 89.31% respectively.

3   Proposed Model

Classification of brain MR images is mostly used to detect the type of tumor in the brain. Our model to identify the tumor is shown in Fig. 1. The model has two major parts; pre-processing and classification. Pre-processing includes two blocks of feature extraction and feature reduction. The segmented image is subjected to DWT for feature extraction and PCA is employed for feature reduction. In classification, we have employed four classifiers to individually classify the data.

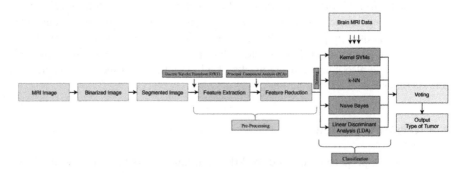

Fig. 1. Block diagram of the proposed model

SVM and k-NN classifier belong to supervised classification while Naïve Bayes and LDA belongs to unsupervised classification. Then the individual results of all classifiers are subjected to voting algorithm which selects the option with maximum numbers of occurrence.

3.1 Feature Extraction (DWT)

For feature extraction, we use a discrete wavelet transform (DWT), which is given by

$$W_\psi(a, b) = \int\limits_{-\infty}^{\infty} x(t)\psi_{a,b}(t)dt$$

In the case of 2D images, the DWT individually apply on each dimension causes the result to be 4 sub-bands (LL, LH, HH, HL).

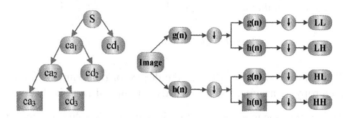

Fig. 2. Two-dimensional wavelet transform tree [3]

Thus, we use a 3-level wavelet decomposition tree. 2D DWT results in 4 sub-bands (LL, LH, HH, HL) and the sub-band LL is used for next DWT. The right portion of Fig. 2 [3] represents the 4 sub-bands obtained as the result. This LL sub-band is regarded as approximation component of the image while the other three sub-bands are regarded as detailed component of the image. So, the approximation component is again subjected to 2D DWT to repeat the process. Thus, the wavelet transform provided us the hierarchal framework to interpret the details of image.

3.2 Features Reduction (PCA)

Excessive feature increases the computational time and requires more storage. The classification and decision become more complicated with large number of features. Therefore, it slows down the executing process. This complication refers to the curse of dimensionality.

To reduce features, we use principal component analysis (PCA) which is a useful tool to reduce the dimensions of the dataset having a large number of unrelated variables. It is done by transformation of the dataset to new variables in terms of their significance. The PCA technique has three stages; first, it performs orthogonality method on the components of the input vector to make them uncorrelated with each other. Second, it creates the order of resulting orthogonal component with the first largest variation. Third, it removes the components of vector whose contribution is least to the dataset.

The features after extraction and reduction are:

Mean: The mean value presents the contribution of pixel intensity to the whole image. For benign tumors, the mean is less than that of malignant. As an image is basically a matrix with rows and column vectors. So, the mean can be calculated by

$$Mean\ of\ Matrix = \frac{Sum\ of\ all\ elements\ of\ matrix}{Total\ number\ of\ elements}$$

Standard Deviation: It is the measure of variation and dispersion in an image. It can be simply calculated as the square root of the variance of the Matrix.

$$Standard\ Daviation = \sqrt{Variance}$$

Entropy: The entropy is the measure of the degree of randomness and disorder in an image. The entropy of an image can be easily interpreted from its histogram.

RMS: RMS is a root-mean-squared value. It is the RMS value of each row for each column.

Variance: The matrix obtained from subtracting its mean from its each element has another mean which is called variance of the matrix. Generally, it is the measure of how far a data set is spread out. In image processing, it is used to find that how every individual pixel varies from the center pixel as well as neighbor pixels.

Smoothness: It is the measure of the average value of an image with noise removed. It is often used to reduce the noise in the image.

$$Smoothness\ of\ Image = 1 - \frac{1}{1 + (sum\ of\ elements)}$$

Kurtosis: Kurtosis is the measure of the highest peaks in the image. In other words, it can be described as the measure of heaviness and thickness of the given data. It determines the noise in the image with respect to resolution.

Skewness: Skewness is the measure of symmetry in distribution which tells us about the glossiness and darkening of the image surface. The dataset is symmetric when it looks same from left and right side of the center point.

IDM: Stands for Inverse Difference Movement.
　　It is a type of image textural feature which deals with the discontinuities in image.

Contrast: Contrast is the difference in luminance or color that makes an object distinguishable. It is the difference in color and brightness of the objects lying in same field of view.

Correlation: Correlation is the process of moving the filter mask on the screen and taking the largest magnitude value.

Energy: Energy can be calculated by the square root of uniformity which is the summation of each element of the image's matrix. It is the mean squared value of image.

Homogeneity: It refers to the surface of images having similar characteristics.

3.3 Ensemble Classification

Classification of the biomedical images can be done by employing either supervised or unsupervised classification techniques [11]. In supervised classification, the user can provide the custom sample pixels for decision, but in unsupervised classification, the results only based on software analysis. In this proposed model we have implemented four different classifiers to compare their results. The two classifiers are from supervised classification class while the other two are from unsupervised class.

Support Vector Machine (SVM): SVM is a support vector machine, whose introduction is the landmark in the field of machine learning. It belongs to supervised classification class. The major benefits of SVM are mathematical tractability, high accuracy, and direct geometry decision. There are a lot of SVMs, but the best among them is kernel SVM. In the proposed model, we use kernel SVM with two different parameters; linear and RBF. Traditional SVM uses hyperplane to classify the data. In kernel SVM, the algorithm is almost same but each dot product between vectors is replaced by non-linear kernel function.

K-Nearest Neighbor (k-NN): k-NN is one of the trusted algorithms for classification and belongs to the supervised classification class. Its work based on the minimum distance of query instance to the training samples. It provides a variety of distance measuring techniques like Euclidian or Hamming distance.

Naïve Bayes Classifier: Naïve Bayes algorithm works on conditional probability. Its working is based on the Bayes theorem on conditional probability, which is given as:

$$P(H|E) = \frac{P(E|H) * P(H)}{P(E)}$$

So, this classifier predicts the data on the basis of the predicted class. It belongs to unsupervised classification class. The major advantages of this classifier are high scalability, less use of training data and easy to implement.

Linear Discriminant Analysis (LDA): Linear Discriminant Analysis (LDA) can be used as a classifier as it makes the assumption about the input data. It makes assumption that whether the data is Gaussian or not. And the variance of each attribute of the acquired set of features. It also falls in the unsupervised classification class.

4 Results and Discussion

In this study, we have developed the algorithm for tumor detection using DWT+PCA+ Classifiers. We apply different image processing techniques including grayscale of the image, OTSU binarization of the image and then filtration of the image to get the segmented image. The results are shown in Fig. 3.

Next, we compute the DWT of the segmented image to extract the features. The three-level DWT technique makes the feature vector of 1024 values. These extra features are reduced using the PCA technique. The results of feature reduction are shown in Fig. 3 and Table 1.

Next, these features are classified by different classifiers and the results shown in Table 2. After the detection of tumor type, all results are subjected to a voting algorithm to choose the right option. The results of all classifiers are stored in a 1D array. The voting algorithm inspects that array and chooses the option with more occurrences.

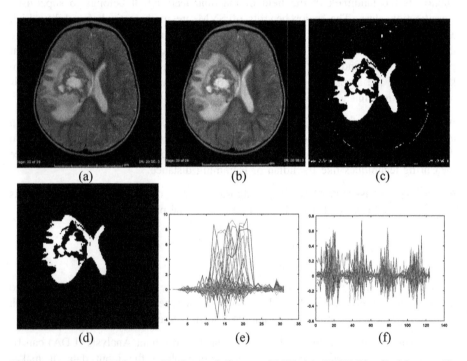

Fig. 3. (a). Brain MRI image, (b). Grayscale image of MRI, (c). OTSU Binarized Image, (d). Segmented Image, (e). Extracted features from DWT, (f). Reduced feature using PCA.

Figure 3 represents the image processing steps on the MR images of the brain. Figure 3 (d) represents the segmented image from which we extract the features. After extraction of features, Fig. 3 (e) shows the plot of the extracted features which are then reduced and shown in Fig. 3 (f). So, the reduction in features is approximately about 92%.

Table 1. Some useful extracted features

MRI image	Type of tumor	Entropy	Kurtosis	Correlation	Smoothness	RMS	Energy
IMG001	Benign	3.17346	7.32819	0.199005	0.920457	0.0898	0.7621
IMG002	Benign	3.26983	7.95668	0.093089	0.897422	0.0898	0.7685
IMG003	Benign	3.07565	7.7971	0.089525	0.904047	0.0898	0.7556
IMG004	Benign	2.74648	10.9703	0.097650	0.718636	0.0898	0.7861
IMG005	Malignant	3.67005	5.62099	0.076926	0.918462	0.0898	0.7577
IMG006	Malignant	3.52392	6.52204	0.073405	0.928384	0.0898	0.7402
IMG007	Malignant	3.62834	5.32384	0.095075	0.913222	0.0898	0.7378
IMG008	Malignant	3.19429	9.73182	0.142678	0.951576	0.0898	0.7604

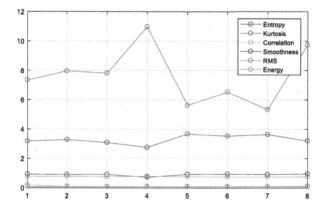

Fig. 4. Graphical representation of Table 1.

Table 1 and Fig. 4 represents the different feature values for some MR images samples. This shows the trend of values difference between Benign and Malignant tumors. For example, we can see that the entropy for Benign tumor is always less as compared to Malignant tumor. As the Entropy is the measure of randomness in image, it is less for Benign tumors.

Table 2 represents the results of all the classifiers. This provides the data of 8 images in which 4 are Benign and 4 are malignant tumors. From the table, we can infer that the Linear SVM and LDA classifier are the most accurate. Moreover, k-NN is also more accurate as compared to Naïve Bayes.

Table 2. Classification results

MRI image	Type of tumor	Results of classifiers		k-NN	Naïve Bayes	LDA
		SVMs				
		Linear	RBF			
IMG001	Benign	Benign	Malignant	Benign	Benign	Benign
IMG002	Benign	Benign	Malignant	Benign	Benign	Benign
IMG003	Benign	Benign	Benign	Benign	Benign	Benign
IMG004	Benign	Benign	Malignant	Benign	Malignant	Benign
IMG005	Malignant	Malignant	Malignant	Malignant	Malignant	Malignant
IMG006	Malignant	Malignant	Malignant	Benign	Benign	Malignant
IMG007	Malignant	Malignant	Benign	Malignant	Benign	Malignant
IMG008	Malignant	Malignant	Malignant	Malignant	Malignant	Malignant

5 Conclusion and Future Work

A hybrid model is proposed to detect the type of tumor from the MR images of the brain. This shows accurate results and reduces human efforts as well. The proposed model employees DWT and PCA for feature extraction and reduction from MRI of brain. On basis of features, the type of tumor is detected using different classifiers. For more accuracy, voting algorithm is used. From the results, we see that the Linear SVM and LDA classifiers detect the accurate type of tumor. k-NN classifier is also accurate in most of the cases. And the RBF SVM has the least accuracy for the given dataset. In future, we can use other methods for feature extraction and feature reduction and compare their results with the existing ones. More advancements can be made to make the model more integrated and accurate.

References

1. Tufekci, Z., Gowdy, J.N.: Feature extraction using discrete wavelet transform for speech recognition. In: Proceedings of the IEEE SoutheastCon (2000)
2. Kambhatla, N., Leen, T.K.: Dimension reduction by local principal component analysis. Neural Comput. **9**(7), 1493–1516 (1997)
3. Zhang, Y., Wu, L.: An MR brain images classifier via principal component analysis and kernel support vector machine. School of Information Science and Engineering, Southeast University, Nanjing, China (2012)
4. Cocosco, C.A., Zijdenbos, A.P., Evans, A.C.: A fully automatic and robust brain MRI tissue classification method. Med. Image Anal. **8**(1), 93–94 (2004)
5. Zhou, X., et al.: Detection of pathological brain in MRI scanning based on wavelet-entropy and Naïve Bayes classifier. In: International Conference on Bioinformatics and Biomedical Engineering (2015)
6. Gladis Pushpa Rathi, V.P., Palani, S.: Brain tumor MRI image classification with feature selection and extraction using linear discriminant analysis. In: Computer Vision and Pattern Recognition (2012)

7. El-Dahshana, E.-S.A., Hosny, T., Salem, A.-B.M.: Hybrid intelligent techniques for MRI brain images classification. Dig. Sig. Process. **20**(2), 433–441(2010)

8. Ortiz, A., Palacio, A.A., Górriz, J.M., Ramírez, J., Salas-González, D.: Segmentation of brain MRI using SOM-FCM-based method and 3D statistical descriptors. Communications Engineering Department, University of Malaga, 29004 Malaga, Spain (2013)

9. Saritha, M., Paul Joseph, K., Abraham,Mathew, T.: Classification of MRI brain images using combined wavelet entropy based spider web plots and probabilistic neural network. Pattern Recogn. Lett. **34**(16), 2151–2156 (2013)

10. Chandra, S., Bhat, R., Singh, H., Chauhan, D.S.: Detection of brain tumors from MRI using Gaussian RBF kernel based support vector machine. Department of CSE & IT, Jaypee University of IT, Solan, HP, India (2009)

11. Ozer, S., et al.: Supervised and unsupervised methods for prostate cancer segmentation with multispectral MRI. Int. J. Med. Phys. Res. Pract. **37**(4), 1873–1883 (2010)

Efficient PatchMatch Algorithm to Detect False Crowd in Digitally Forged Images

Rakhshanda Javid[1]([✉])[ID], M. Mohsin Riaz[2], Abdul Ghafoor[1],
and Naveed Iqbal[1]

[1] College of Signal, National University of Sciences and Technology NUST,
Islamabad, Pakistan
`rjavaid.phdcs@students.mcs.edu.pk`, `abdulghafoor-mcs@nust.edu.pk`,
`naveedi@mcs.edu.pk`
[2] COMSATS University, Islamabad, Pakistan
`mohsin.riaz@comsats.edu.pk`

Abstract. The authenticity and reliability of digital images have become one of the major concerns recently due to the ease in manipulating and modifying these images. Similar manipulation in crowded images gives rise to the false crowd, where a person or group of persons is copied and pasted in the same image. Thus, the detection of such false crowds is the focus of current research. In this paper, false crowd detection in forged images is carried out using modified and improved PatchMatch algorithm which can even detect multiple copies of the same instance. To seperate humans from non-human objects a human detection algorithm is used in the post-processing phase. A benchmark database consisting of false crowd images has also been developed. Experimental results confirm that the technique is capable of detecting the false crowds successfully and even robust for multiple cloning problem.

Keywords: False crowd · Crowd behavior analysis · Image forgery · Dense field

1 Introduction

Digital image tampering has become an easier task because of the advancement in digital imaging devices and photo editing tools. These advance softwares have made the manipulation of digital images easier without degrading the quality. In addition, enormous data is shared over social media through the internet on daily basis. These digital images can be easily altered, misrepresenting their content with malicious intentions. Thus the authenticity of digital images has become very important and focus of the current research communities.

Different objects that are present in the digital image are manipulated with the intention to tamper the image. The most common form of forgery or image tampering for images consisting of a human crowd is when a person and/or a group of persons is copied from the image and then pasted once or more times in

© Springer Nature Singapore Pte Ltd. 2020
I. S. Bajwa et al. (Eds.): INTAP 2019, CCIS 1198, pp. 616–626, 2020.
https://doi.org/10.1007/978-981-15-5232-8_53

Fig. 1. False crowd examples

the same digital image. This copy-pasted crowd will be called a false crowd (see Fig. 1). So, a false crowd or forged crowd is the part of the image where a person or a group of persons from a crowd is copied and pasted in the same image. These false crowd images can be used to misrepresent the actual count of people in any ceremony, meeting, or protest. The detection of false crowd manipulation can be formulated as a copy-move forgery detection problem followed by a human detection algorithm.

Copy-move forgery detection for digital images is extensively studied in the literature [7–9]. All the proposed algorithms follow a common set of operations which include feature extraction, matching and post-processing [9]. These techniques can be categorized as dense field and key-point based techniques. In dense field based techniques all these steps are performed on each pixel of the image while in key-point based techniques, only a set of selected points undergo the whole process. Thus suggesting that later technique is faster than the dense field ones. Many robust key-point based techniques have been developed that use well-known descriptors like Scale Invariant Feature Transform (SIFT) [2,3], Speeded-up Robust Features (SURF) [4] , DAISY [5], Harris corners points [6]. Some of the variants have also been proposed in the literature dealing with multiple duplicated regions [31]. A detailed evaluation of these techniques has been provided in different survey papers [7–9].

These methods though faster are unfortunately less accurate than the dense field ones, evaluated in the paper [7]. This derives our focus to dense field approach. The only issue associated with the approach is the complexity. This can be solved by selecting features as short and simple as possible. In literature some transforms have been used to extract the features like DCT [10,11], wavelet [12,13], SVD [14]. But these transforms fail in the presence of scaling and rotation. This diverted the researchers to look for features that are invariant to these issues. Several invariant features have been tested in the literature including Zernike Moments [15], Fourier-Mellin Transform (FMT) [17], polar cosine transform (PCT) [16]. Many researchers have focused on a faster matching phase in order to deal with the problem of speed for dense fields. The use of kd trees [18] and similarly hashing techniques [15] have been used. All these techniques have been tested for different publicly available datasets.

These techniques detect the forged area in an image but to detect false crowd in an image, a human detection algorithm is required. A person or a group of persons in a digital image is copied and tampered to symbolize the crowd. This tampering does not necessarily involve the full human figure (e.g. human face, upper body). This will involve different recognition techniques related to face and behavior detection in order to identify the manipulated and tampered regions. A lot of sophisticated techniques are available in the literature [19]. Different features like Haar wavelet [22], Histogram of oriented gradients [23], edge templates [24], Adaptive contour features [25] have been used with varying results. While classification has been successfully performed using support vector machine (SVM) [23,26], and cascade structure boosting based classifiers [27,28]. However, all these techniques can detect humans in an image but they can not be directly applied for our false crowd detection problem.

Another major aspect of copy-move forgeries is multiple copies of the same instance. It may happen that a copied part is pasted more than once in the image, which is very common in false crowd manipulations. Most of the techniques discussed do not address the multiple copies problem. However, Amerini [31] proposed a generalized 2NN approach based on key points.

Some of the observations in false crowd images are listed below.

- Single or a group of persons is copied from the image and then pasted in the same image.
- The copied part can be scaled and pasted. Very small rotation is applied since a larger rotation will show non-human behavior.
- Multiple copies of an instance are possible, which is the case is many crowd-based forged images

These observations are the core of the proposed work. A simple and efficient technique is proposed to detect false crowd, which is also robust against different transformations and multiple copies. The general work flow of copy-move forgery detection is followed as in [7] but proposed a modified and improved patch match algorithm that can solve the multiple copies problem. Efficiency is also pursued in post-processing where the human detection algorithm is applied to the detected forged regions instead of applying to the whole image. Thus achieving the speed as fast as key-point based methods. The use of scale and rotation invariant features also result in more robustness and dense fields helps in achieving more accuracy.

The contributions of our proposed technique are outlined below,

- The development of effective dense field PatchMatch Algorithm to detect false crowds and is able to deal with resizing and rotation.
- A new dataset is developed which comprises of different scenarios for false crowd.
- The proposed algorithm can deal with multiple copies of an instance.

The rest of the paper discusses the proposed version of the PatchMatch algorithm in Sect. 2. Section 3 carries out a detailed discussion of experimental results. Conclusion of the proposed work is given in the last section.

2 Proposed Methodology

The paper develops an algorithm to detect false crowd regions in terms of copy-move forgery detection in images based on a modified patch match algorithm with a pre-trained SVM for person detection.

A modified patch match algorithm, using invariant features for dense fields, will ensure the detection of multiple copies of the same region, while a pre-trained SVM is used to further classify the detected regions into human and non-human objects. Thus only the false crowd which is copied once or multiple times is detected.

2.1 Improved PatchMatch Algorithm

The basic patch match algorithm [20] is a key-point based method and follows a three-step procedure i.e. initialization, propagation and random search. The method is extended for dense field to achieve more accuracy in case of multiple replication. Let A be an image defined over a rectangular grid Ω and is given as

$$A = \{A(x,y) \in \Re^2, (x,y) \in \Omega\} \tag{1}$$

For simplicity, let z denote a pixel (x,y). Then $f(z)$ is the associated feature vector of patch P centered at z. The goal is to find the nearest neighbor $z' \in \Omega$ where $z' \neq z$. Instead of looking for the exact nearest neighbor field (NNF), which is computationally complex, the equivalent offset field is considered and is given as

$$z' = z + \Delta(z) \tag{2}$$

The NNF minimizes a suitable distance measure D so the equivalent offset field is given as

$$\Delta(z) = \underset{\phi:z+\phi\in\Omega}{\arg\min} D(f(z), f(z + \phi)) \tag{3}$$

In the initialization phase, the offset field is initialized randomly. Only those offsets are considered that are relatively far. That is why the offsets which are smaller from a given threshold are not included. Now the remaining offsets may not all be optimal but it is very likely that a few of them are optimal. Thus the algorithm quickly propagates these good offsets and updates the offset field simultaneously. For the propagation step, the image is scanned. The scanning is performed for each pixel and is carried out from top to down and left to right updating the offset field given in 1.

$$\Delta(z) = \underset{\phi\in\Delta^s(z)}{\arg\min} D(f(z), f(z + \phi)) \tag{4}$$

here $\Delta^s(z) = \{\Delta(z), \Delta^r(z), \Delta^c(z)\}$ corresponds to the scanning order which is performed for rows and columns respectively. As a result, if z has correct mapping then all the region below and to the right will be filled. The scanning process is reversed in order to avoid any biases. The random search phase helps to minimize and reduce the risk of being stuck within a local minima.

This basic algorithm does not solve the scale and rotation changes. These changes are very common in false crowd tampered images. Different solutions have been devised to solve the problem. One of which has been provided in [21] in which a $4d$ space is considered. It is a straight forward approach in which scaling α and rotation θ are included making a $4d$ search space. The main problem with this is that with the increase in dimension, the computational complexity also increasses. One of the solution is to use invariant features [9]. Some of the features work better for scaling and some for rotation so a tradeoff or a combination has to be considered. Another modification given in [29] uses first order predictors along with zero order predictors to compare a current offset. In this case the computational complexity remains almost similar to the basic version.

Even though most of the problems have already been addressed in the literature but one of the major problems in false crowd copy-move forgeries is that a certain instance is copied more than once in the image. It is a common practice in manipulated crowded images to copy a person or a group of persons more than once in an image leading to a misrepresentation of the crowd with wrong intentions e.g. faking the density of the crowd.

To solve the multiple copies problem [31] proposed a key point based generalized 2NN (g2NN) approach. They used a generalized version of the algorithm 2NN proposed in [30]. The g2NN algorithm works on the observation that the key-points which has similar features are at low distances as compared to others. Basically the 2NN works on the idea of calculating the ratio of the distance between candidate and second nearest neighbor. This idea is iterated for k number of nearest neighbors in g2NN, where k is determined on the ratio until it is greater from some threshold. So if k is the value where the algorithm halts then these key-points with distances $\{d_1, \ldots, d_k\}$ will be considered as a match for the keypoint under inspection.

The same idea is extended for the patch match algorithm. The Eq. 4 does not manage multiple offsets matching for a single point z. In other words, it only finds a single best matching offset. Now in order to cater to the problem of multiple copies of the same features, we extend the g2NN and propose a patch-based g2NN (p2NN). In p2NN the idea is to consider all the candidate offsets for a point z in patch P that satisfies the condition

$$d_i/d_{i+1} < \tau \tag{5}$$

where d_i is the current offset field and $d_i i + 1$ is the next nearest neighbor. If the distance measure of features for two offsets is less than τ it suggests that these two offsets can be candidate offsets for the propagation phase. The process is repeated for k times.

The process is further explained in Fig. 2 in which different offsets for point z are shown and the selected ones are shown with a green line, which fully explains the algorithm's ability to detect multiple copies.

Fig. 2. Good offsets versus bad offsets (Color figure online)

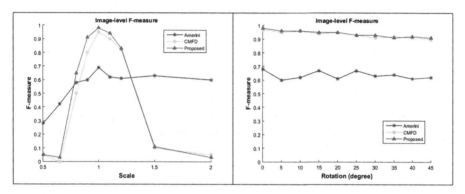

Fig. 3. Image-level F-measure curves

Instead of taking a single best offset field all the offsets that satisfy the condition in Eq. 5 are considered and propagation is performed accordingly. With this explanation now $\Delta(z)$ is a set of offset fields and is updated as

$$\Delta(z) = \operatorname*{arg\,min}_{\phi_i \in \Delta^s(z), i=1,..k} D_i(f(z), f(z + \phi_i)) \tag{6}$$

and k is the number of offset fields considered. By keeping a strict τ the false alarms and extra overload of wrong offset fields can b avoided (Fig. 3).

As a result the offset field obtained is chaotic with some smooth regions. Some post-processing is applied to remove any false alarms. There can still be non-human objects segmented by the above-outlined algorithm for this purpose a human detection algorithm is applied. The segmented regions consist of forged parts of the image. These forged parts are classified as human or non-human. Since the scenario here is too simple and no complex computation is required so to classify an object as human or non-human a pre-trained SVM classifier is used based on HOG features. Once a region is identified as human all its copies are also classified as human.

3   Experimental Results

The details about the developed database are given along with quantitative and qualitative analysis in this section. For performance comparison the proposed

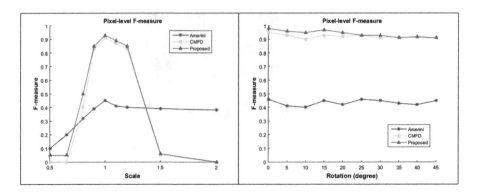

Fig. 4. Pixel-level F-measure curves

approach is compared against recently proposed CMFD [29], which is closest to our approach, and Amerini et al. [31]. The comparison is performed for only these techniques because the issue addressed can not directly compared with other techniques (Fig. 4).

3.1   False Crowd Database (FCD)

One of our contributions is the development of the false crowd images database. A database consisting of 45 images is prepared with realistic copy-move of the crowd along with their ground truth, some of which are shown in Fig. 1. Different types of forgeries have been incorporated in order to deal with rotation, scaling and multiple cloning. Figure 1 shows some example images. This new database will be called FCD from now on.

3.2   Quantitative Results

The proposed technique is evaluated for both pixel and image level. The evaluation metric that is used to compile results is F-measure and is given as follows.

$$F = \frac{2TP}{2TP + FN + FP} \tag{7}$$

where TP = true positive is the number of detected forged images, FN = false negative is the number of undetected forged images and FP = False positive is the wrongly detected genuine images.

The same definitions hold for pixel-level evaluation. By definition it can be seen that evaluation at image level measures the system's ability to classify the image either original or forged correctly, while evaluation at pixel level also accounts for the accuracy in localization.

The SIFT-base Amerini [31] gives the most stable results under most of the conditions. Clearly showing the significance of keypoints. Even the results

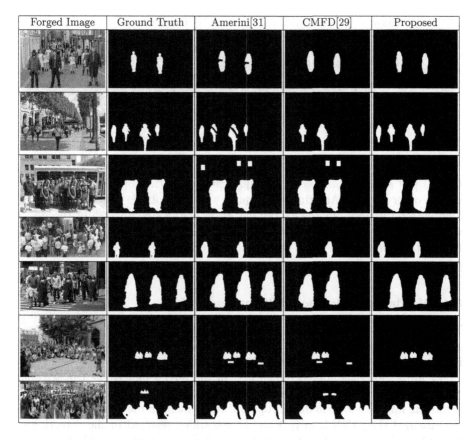

Forged Image	Ground Truth	Amerini[31]	CMFD[29]	Proposed

Fig. 5. Qualitative comparison between proposed and state-of-the-art techniques. First and second columns show the forged and ground truth images respectively. Third, fourth and fifth columns shows the results of CMFD [29,31] and Proposed Methodology.

are somewhat stable under large scaling and rotation. Unfortunately the overall results here show impaired performance because algorithm fails to detect forgeries for smooth regions.

The proposed method performs better than both Amerini [31] and CMFD [29], this is because the algorithm's ability to detect multiple clones making it more robust. Similarly, the use of dense field accounts for its high accuracy under small transformations.

3.3 Qualitative Results

For qualitative comparison, the results of the proposed methodology and state-of-the art techniques are compared. The methodologies chosen for comparison are closely related to the proposed technique in Fig. 5. The first column shows example images, the second column contains the ground truth for corresponding images.

Forged Image	PatchMatch	PatchMatch+g2NN	Proposed

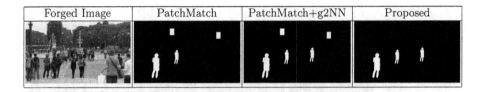

Fig. 6. Contribution of each component of proposed algorithm

In the light of results presented in Fig. 5 we can conclude that Amerini [31], CMFD [29] and the proposed technique can detect the copied regions. But it can be observed that Amerini works quite well for multiple copy detection and high entropy images but misses the detection of the smooth area of the image which fully explains the main issue with keypoint based techniques. CMFD fails for multiple detections while the proposed technique detects all the forgeries robustly.

3.4   Validation of Proposed Technique

To understand and evaluate the contribution of each component in the proposed algorithm, the results of each phase are shown in Fig. 6 . The results of a single image are shown to better understand the contribution of each phase.

Figure 6 shows the forged image left. In the forged imaged we can see that a person is copied multiple times and an object is also copied. The PatchMatch algorithm fails to detect multiple copies of the person. In the proposed algorithm we extended the g2NN idea to PatchMatch which resulted in the detection of multiple copies as well. Now to sperate human from non-human object, we have further applied a pre-trained SVM and the results are shown in the last column. The false crowd is detected successfully.

4   Conclusion

The authenticity of digital images nowadays is highly questionable due to the advancement in digital media and softwares. Manipulating images is becoming more and more easy and is very common. However, detecting them can be very challenging. Key-point based techniques are quite fast but they are not accurate like dense field based techniques.

The proposed technique based on dense field uses a modified and improved version of the PatchMatch algorithm which is combined with a generalized 2NN approach to make it more robust. Thus the proposed algorithm can detect multiple cloning. Further, the detected regions are classified as human figure/person or non-human figure using HOG features which are then classified using a pretrained SVM classifier. The human detection is kept simple so as to keep the speed of the algorithm faster.

Experimental results show satisfactory results and the robustness of the proposed algorithm. Nonetheless, there is still much room for further improvements. The advantages of both dense field and keypoint based techniques can be utilized by fusing them. The use of a convolution neural network or deep learning methods is also one of our focus for future experimentations. Similarly with time the size of the images is increasing day by day and may develop a need for faster algorithms in the near future. Future directions also include the expansion of the FCD dataset.

References

1. Raje, N., Dinakar, C.: Overview of immunodeficiency disorders. Immunol. Allergy Clin. **35**, 599–623 (2015)
2. Pan, X., Lyu, S.: Detecting image region duplication using SIFT features. In: IEEE International Conference on Acoustics, Speech and Signal Processing, pp. 1706–1709 (2010)
3. Pan, X., Lyu, S.: Region duplication detection using image feature matching. In: IEEE Transactions on Information Forensics and Security, pp. 857–867 (2010)
4. Shivakumar, B.L., Baboo, S.S.: Detection of region duplication forgery in digital images using SURF. Int. J. Comput. Sci. Issues (IJCSI) **8**, 199 (2011)
5. Guo, J.M., Liu, Y.F., Wu, Z.J.: Duplication forgery detection using improved DAISY descriptor. Expert Syst. Appl. **40**, 707–714 (2013)
6. Chen, L., Lu, W., Ni, J., Sun, W., Huang, J.: Region duplication detection based on Harris corner points and step sector statistics. J. Vis. Commun. Image Representation **24**, 244–254 (2013)
7. Christlein, V., Riess, C., Jordan, J., Riess, C., Angelopoulou, E.: An evaluation of popular copy-move forgery detection approaches. IEEE Trans. Inf. Forensics Secur. **7**, 1841–1854 (2012)
8. Qazi, T., et al.: Survey on blind image forgery detection. IET Image Process. **7**, 660–670 (2013)
9. Warif, N.B., et al.: Copy-move forgery detection: survey, challenges and future directions. J. Netw. Comput. Appl. **75**, 259–278 (2016)
10. Huang, Y., Lu, W., Sun, W., Long, D.: Improved DCT-based detection of copy-move forgery in images. Forensic Sci. Int. **206**, 178–184 (2011)
11. Cao, Y., Gao, T., Fan, L., Yang, Q.: A robust detection algorithm for copy-move forgery in digital images. Forensic Sci. Int. **214**, 33–43 (2012)
12. Muhammad, G., Hussain, M., Bebis, G.: Passive copy move image forgery detection using undecimated dyadic wavelet transform. Dig. Investigat. **9**, 49–57 (2012)
13. Hashmi, M.F., Anand, V., Keskar, A.G.: Copy-move image forgery detection using an efficient and robust method combining un-decimated wavelet transform and scale invariant feature transform. Aasri Procedia **9**, 84–91 (2014)
14. Zhao, J., Guo, J.: Passive forensics for copy-move image forgery using a method based on DCT and SVD. Forensic Sci. Int. **233**, 158–166 (2013)
15. Ryu, S.J., Kirchner, M., Lee, M.J., Lee, H.K.: Rotation invariant localization of duplicated image regions based on Zernike moments. IEEE Trans. Inf. Forensics Secur. **8**, 1355–1370 (2013)
16. Li, Y.: Image copy-move forgery detection based on polar cosine transform and approximate nearest neighbor searching. Forensic Sci. Int. **224**, 59–67 (2013)

17. Wu, Q., Wang, S., Zhang, X.: Log-polar based scheme for revealing duplicated regions in digital images. IEEE Signal Process. Lett. **18**, 559–562 (2011)

18. Christlein, V., Riess, C., Angelopoulou, E.: On rotation invariance in copy-move forgery detection. In: 2010 IEEE International Workshop on Information Forensics and Security, pp. 1–6 (2010)

19. Nguyen, D.T., Li, W., Ogunbona, P.O.: Human detection from images and videos: a survey. Patt. Recogn. **51**, 148–175 (2016)

20. Barnes, C., Shechtman, E., Finkelstein, A., Goldman, D.B.: PatchMatch: a randomized correspondence algorithm for structural image editing. ACM Trans. Graph. (ToG) **1**, 24 (2009)

21. Barnes, C., Shechtman, E., Goldman, D.B., Finkelstein, A.: The generalized patchmatch correspondence algorithm. In European Conference on Computer Vision, pp. 29–43 (2010)

22. Papageorgiou, C., Poggio, T.: A trainable system for object detection. Int. J. Comput. Vis. **38**, 15–33 (2000)

23. Dalal, N., Triggs, B.: Histograms of oriented gradients for human detection. In: International Conference on Computer Vision and Pattern Recognition (CVPR 2005), pp. 886–893 (2005)

24. Gavrila, D.M.: A bayesian exemplar-based approach to hierarchical shape matching. IEEE Trans. Pattern Anal. Mach. Intell. **29**, 8 (2007)

25. Gao, W., Ai, H., Lao, S.: Adaptive contour features in oriented granular space for human detection and segmentation. In: 2009 IEEE Conference on Computer Vision and Pattern Recognition, pp. 1786–1793 (2009)

26. Maji, S., Berg, A.C., Malik, J.: Efficient classification for additive kernel SVMs. IEEE Trans. Pattern Anal. Mach. Intell. **35**, 66–77 (2013)

27. Dollár, P., Babenko, B., Belongie, S., Perona, P., Tu, Z.: Multiple component learning for object detection. In European Conference on Computer Vision, pp. 211–224 (2008)

28. Dollár, P., Belongie, S.J., Perona, P.: The fastest pedestrian detector in the west. In: BMVC, p. 7 (2010)

29. Cozzolino, D., Poggi, G., Verdoliva, L.: Efficient dense-field copy-move forgery detection. IEEE Trans. Inf. Forensics Secur. **10**, 2284–2297 (2015)

30. Lowe, D.G.: Distinctive image features from scale-invariant keypoints. Int. J. Comput. Vis. **60**, 91–110 (2004)

31. Amerini, I., Ballan, L., Caldelli, R., Del Bimbo, A., Serra, G.: A sift-based forensic method for copy-move attack detection and transformation recovery. IEEE Trans. Inf. Forensics Secur. **6**, 1099–1110 (2011)

Analysis of the Lifetime and Energy Consumption of WSN Routing Protocols: LEACH, EAMMH and SEP

Muhammad Yasir Farooq[1], Khan Bahadar Khan[2],
Ghulam Mohayy ud din[1(✉)], Eid Rehman[3], and Sundus Amin[4]

[1] Department of Electronic Engineering,
UCET, The Islamia University of Bahawalpur, Bahawalpur, Pakistan
yasirgill1616@gmail.com,
ghulammohayyuddin6471@gmail.com
[2] Department of Telecommunication Engineering,
The Islamia University of Bahawalpur, Bahawalpur, Pakistan
kb.khattak@gmail.com
[3] Department of Computer Science, International Islamic University Islamabad,
Islamabad, Pakistan
eidrehmanktk@gmail.com
[4] Department of Computer Science, COMSATS University Islamabad,
Islamabad, Pakistan
sundusramey.7@gmail.com

Abstract. The lifetime of Wireless Sensor Network (WSN) is based on the energy of each sensor. Therefore, numerous routing protocols have been introduced such as SEP (Stable Election Protocol), LEACH (Low energy adaptive clustering hierarchy) and EAMMH (Energy Aware Multi-hop Multi-path Hierarchical routing protocol) to stable the lifetime of WSN by efficient utilization of energy of the sensors. In WSN networks data is collected and forwarded wirelessly to the base stations. Routing protocols in WSN provide an efficient path for multi-hop communication because the transmission range and battery power storage of nodes is limited. As nodes are usually deployed in remote areas so, they face challenges of long lifetime, network architecture, security issues, and network coverage. Many routing protocols have been developed to increase the efficiency of networks. Out of these clustering algorithms are the best choice to increase the lifetime of the nodes. Each protocol has its limitations in different scenarios. In this paper, we discussed and compared the performance of LEACH, EAMMH and SEP. SEP is an efficient algorithm due to its weighted cluster head (CH) selection method. Simulation results are obtained using MATLAB. Design metrics of energy consumption and network lifetime are under consideration in this research work.

Keywords: WSN · Multi-hop · CH · LEACH · EAMMH · SEP · Nodes · Lifetime

© Springer Nature Singapore Pte Ltd. 2020
I. S. Bajwa et al. (Eds.): INTAP 2019, CCIS 1198, pp. 627–637, 2020.
https://doi.org/10.1007/978-981-15-5232-8_54

1 Introduction

WSN consist of hundreds of sensor nodes that are distant in connection. Sensor nodes are connected wirelessly with each other. These nodes contain transceiver, embedded electronic circuits, and battery storage. They collect data, process it and send it to base stations. The problem of energy, security, lifetime, coverage, data collection, deployment techniques, and network architecture may arise due to the poor networking algorithm according to the environment conditions [1]. Due to multi-hop indirect communication between sink node and sensor nodes, routing is necessary to take a suitable path for communication, which is the responsibility of the network layer. Wireless nodes have limitations in storage, onboard energy, capacity, and transmission energy according to the desired applications. Clustering is one of the efficient techniques to increase lifetime and processing and transmitting data correctly to the base station. In clustering, the nodes are divided into groups. In each group of clusters, one node is assigned the task to process and transmit the evaluated data to the base station which is CH. Other nodes of the group send the sensed and collected data to CH and are called member nodes [2]. The clustering in WSN is shown in Fig. 1.

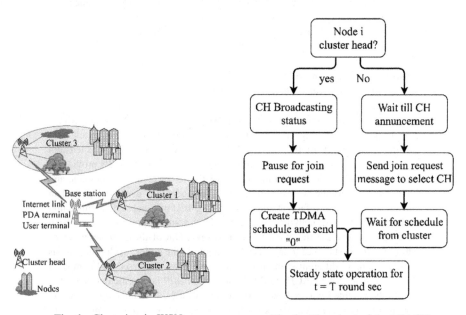

Fig. 1. Clustering in WSN   **Fig. 2.** Flowchart of the LEACH

Inter-cluster routing is communication between different clusters. It may be either single-hop or multi-hop. CH transfers data directly to the base station in single-hop. In multi-hop clustering CH transfer data indirectly through different intermediate CH's. Intra-cluster routing is communication within the cluster between CH and member nodes. In this type also clustering can be single-hop and multi-hop but it is limited within the cluster, which is between member nodes and CH of that particular cluster. In clustering, CH's require more energy than member nodes due to their more responsibilities of data processing [12, 11].

With the advancement in technology, the size of the electronic components is decreasing and their functionality is increasing. Wireless communication and WSNs have become hot areas of research. Wireless control of systems in this modern era reduced the complexity of the network. Nodes of the WSN are used to measure and control physical and environmental changes. Parameters like temperature, pressure, humidity, motion, and sound are measured by sensors. The nodes of WSN can either be homogeneous or heterogeneous Nodes are deployed according to the relevant applications. WSN's are applicable mostly in hazardous and remote environments. WSN's role in non-reachable places such as sea, mountains, and forest is its key advantage. Flexibility, less cost, and multi-functionality attracts designers to WSN [3]. But security issues still exist. Applications of WSN involve tracking, monitoring and controlling in defense, process management, healthcare, natural disaster prevention, environment analysis, and industries.

2 Routing Protocols in WSN

In this section LEACH, EAMMH and SEP routing protocols are presented elaborately with their equations and schematic diagrams.

2.1 LEACH

LEACH [13] is the first proposed clustering protocol for WSN with reduced energy consumption. It aims to increase the lifetime of the network by distributing the energy consumption among all nodes. In any cluster, nodes continue to rotate their CH randomly to give chance to all sensor nodes to become CH. Data aggregation is done to minimize the communication cost. All member nodes communicate with CH with single-hop communication [14].

In LEACH, first the network is distributed into clusters by setup phase and then processing, data aggregation, and transmission to sink is done by steady-state phase [4]. Each node produces a random number between 0 and 1 during the CH selection process. If the produced number value of the sensor node is less than the threshold value, then that node act as CH. Threshold value T(si) is found from the following equation [7].

$$T(si) = \begin{cases} \dfrac{P}{1 - P * \left(r \, mod \frac{1}{P}\right)} & if \; i \varepsilon G \\ 0 & otherwise \end{cases} \tag{1}$$

Where, P = percentage of cluster head nodes, r = round numbers and G = those nodes which are not selected as a CH in the last (1/P) rounds. Clusters are made dynamically according to the given Fig. 2 [5].

Leach has limitations when there is a large network and an extraordinary number of nodes because single-hop routing is used and each node communicates with a CH directly. So for, a large network, it is a tough job to transmit data correctly with less energy consumption.

2.2   EAMMH

EAMMH [15] routing protocol has energy aware and multi-hop intra-cluster routing characteristics. In this algorithm, the energy level of sensor nodes as well as their location in the cluster and neighbor clusters is under consideration. When nodes of the network are deployed at a far distance, the cost of communication increases, so more energy is required for surviving the nodes. In this case, efficient routing and clustering can minimize the cost of communication and thus energy consumption [14]. EAMMH routing protocol of WSN is one of the solutions in this condition that works in rounds. The following step by step diagram in Fig. 3 explains the working of the EAMMH protocol [6].

In the beginning, the number of nodes is given, then the random location of each node is generated. After deploying the nodes, each node checks its neighbor nodes, then CHs are determined. The Routing table has information about efficient routing which is updated. CH collects and processes data from multiple nodes using the DRAND (Distributed Randomized) algorithm and sends the data in different time slots to the base station [6]. Heuristic equation describe the best path for routing which is given by

$$h = k\left(\frac{Eav}{hmin * t}\right) \tag{2}$$

Where k is a constant, Eav is the average energy of the current path, hmin is the minimum hop count in the current path, and t is traffic in the path. The highest heuristic function value path is chosen. When the minimum energy of this path is greater than a threshold, that path will be elected as the best routing path. Else the next highest heuristic value path will be chosen [7]. The minimum energy is calculated by using the equation that is given below.

$$E_{min} = \frac{Eav}{constant} \tag{3}$$

If the minimum energy Emin of any sensor node is not greater than the threshold value, then the node with the highest Emin will be selected.

2.3   SEP

Each protocol aims to increase the efficiency of the WSN. Each protocol uses a different strategy to make WSN extra efficient. SEP [14] is a routing protocol with high throughput and it tries to distribute energy evenly among all nodes. It is a heterogeneous protocol that enhances the time to die the first node. In LEACH, the selection of cluster head is random but in SEP selection of CH is weighted. All the sensor nodes are divided into two categories: one of high energy and other low energy. Nodes with high energy are called advance nodes and nodes of low energy are called normal nodes. After the division in two categories, mostly advance nodes will be elected as CH and normal node will not be able to become the CH. Here, the CH is selected through proper planning. As more energy is consumed by the CHs and here the node with high energy is made CH, that's why this strategy makes our network more reliable [13]. It increases the stability of the network but decreases the life duration of the network after the failure of the first node. The given Eq. (4) tells the possibility of node to become the CH. In this equation $T(si)$ = Threshold probability, si = node, Pi = Probability to become cluster head, G = the arrangements of those nodes that are not selected as cluster head in every round, r = round number.

$$T(si) = \begin{cases} \dfrac{P}{1 - P*(r \bmod \frac{1}{P})} & \text{if } i \in G \\ 0 & \text{otherwise} \end{cases} \tag{4}$$

The probability of advance nodes and normal nodes is calculated. The energy of the node at its initial conditions decides whether it is an advance node or a normal node. After knowing the energy of the node, the CH is decided. The probability of advance nodes and normal nodes is calculated. The energy of the node at its initial conditions decides whether it is an advance node or normal node. After knowing the energy of the node, the CH is decided.

$$Pnrm = \frac{P}{1 + \alpha.m} \tag{5}$$

$$Padv = \frac{P}{1 + \alpha.m} \times (1 + \alpha) \tag{6}$$

Here, $Popt$ = Optimal probability of every node to become cluster head in the network, $Pnrm$ = Probability of becoming a normal node, $Padv$ = Probability of becoming advance nodes [8].

$$T(Snrm) = \begin{cases} \dfrac{Pnrm}{1 - Pnrm * (r \bmod \frac{1}{Pnrm})} & \text{if } Snrm \in G \\ 0 & \text{otherwise} \end{cases} \tag{7}$$

$$T(Sadv) = \begin{cases} \dfrac{Padv}{1 - Padv * (r \bmod \frac{1}{Padv})} & \text{if } Sadv \in G \\ 0 & \text{otherwise} \end{cases} \tag{8}$$

The threshold values of normal and advanced nodes are calculated with the help of above Eqs. 7 and 8 respectively [7]. Here m = fraction of total nodes, n = total number of nodes, a = Energy factor and **T(Snrm)** = Threshold probability of the normal nodes and **T(Sadv)** = Threshold probability of the advance nodes [13].

The process of selection of clusters in SEP can be seen from the flowchart. At the start the protocol checks the nodes whether they are alive or dead, only alive nodes take part in network. In the second stage, normal and advanced nodes are determined, and pass through the same process until CH selection. The working flow of the SEP is shown in Fig. 4 [9].

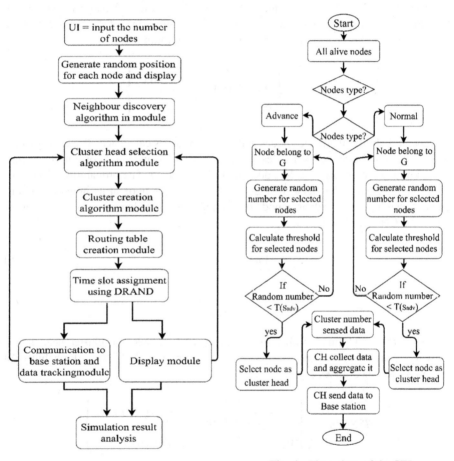

Fig. 3. Flowchart of the EAMMH   **Fig. 4.** Flow chart of the SEP

3 Comparisons and Simulation Results

MATLAB codes of the LEACH, EAMMH, and SEP routing protocols are developed according to the details of the simulation environment given in Table 1. Lifetime and energy consumption of the network is observed and compared using the simulation. First, LEACH is compared with EAMMH by altering the number of nodes and probability. Probability here refers to the chances for a particular node to become CH. Then LEACH and SEP are compared by altering the probability and number of nodes [10]. From simulation results, we can analyze which one is better. The following results are gained under considering the following parameters.

1- Round Number with respect to Number of Dead Nodes (with variation of probability and number of nodes)
2- Round Number with respect to Average Energy of Each node (with variation of probability and number of nodes)

As in real-time implementation, WSN depends on different variable parameters but in a simulation, it is difficult to take all these variable parameters so we simulate on some fixed value of parameters. Different parameters that are necessary for the simulation environment are taken into consideration in the MATLAB code. These are described in Table 1.

Table 1. List of parameters for creating simulation environment

No.	Parameters	Values
1	Number of nodes in the space	n = 100, 150
2	Initial energy	Eo = 0.1
3	Field dimensions - x and y co-ordinates maximum (in meters)	xm = 100, ym = 100 (100,100)
4	x and y Coordinates of the Sink	x = 1.5*xm, y = 0.5*ym, (150,50)
5	Optimal Election Probability for CH selection	P = 0.05, 0.1
6	Energy of Transmission Energy of Reception	ETX = 50*0.000000001 ERX = 50*0.000000001
7	Transmit Amplifier	Efs = 10*0.000000000001 Emp = 0.0013*0.000000000001
8	Data Aggregation Energy	EDA = 5*0.000000001
9	Heterogeneity parameters for LEACH vs. EAMMH	m = 0.0, a = 1
10	Heterogeneity parameters for LEACH vs. SEP	m = 0.2, a = 1

3.1 Comparison of the LEACH and EAMMH

From the analysis, it is clear that LEACH is better than EAMMH for small networks when the number of nodes is less than 50. This simulation result shows that as the number of nodes increases the performance of EAMMH is increased while the performance of LEACH is decreased. EAMMH is the best choice for a large number of nodes. Figures 5, 6, 7 and 8 describe the simulation results.

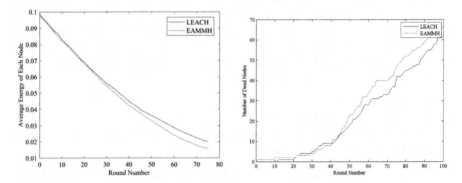

Fig. 5. Comparison of the LEACH and EAMMH with probability of 0.05 of 100 nodes.

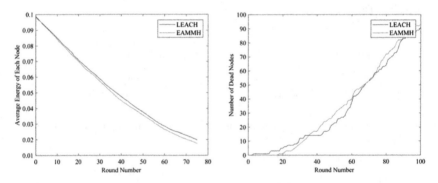

Fig. 6. Comparison of the LEACH and EAMMH with probability of 0.05 of 150 nodes.

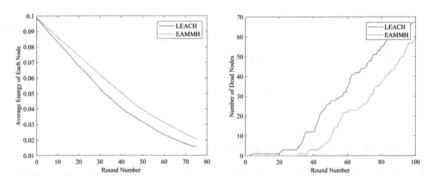

Fig. 7. Comparison of the LEACH and EAMMH with probability of 0.1 of 100 nodes.

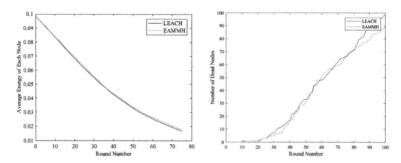

Fig. 8. Comparison of the LEACH and EAMMH with probability of 0.1 of 150 nodes.

3.2 Comparison of the LEACH and SEP

From the analysis, it is clear that SEP performs better than the LEACH which is due to the CH selection method in SEP. In SEP each node consumes energy equally, the initial energy of advanced nodes becomes efficient so they take a long time to die. In LEACH CH selection is random. It doesn't care about the energy of node that's why nodes die in less time. It can be analyzed from Figs. 9, 10, 11 and 12 that the performance of SEP is better than LEACH.

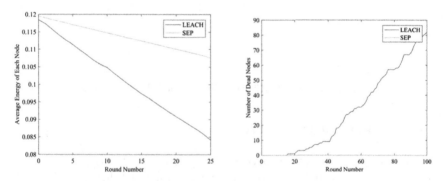

Fig. 9. Comparison of the LEACH and SEP with probability of 0.05 of 150 nodes.

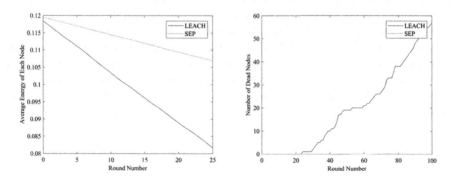

Fig. 10. Comparison of the LEACH and SEP with probability of 0.1 of 100 nodes.

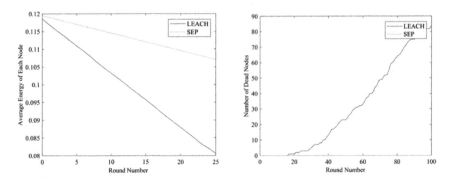

Fig. 11. Comparison of the LEACH and SEP with probability of 0.1 of 150 nodes.

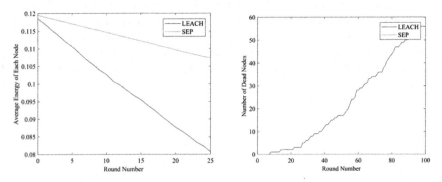

Fig. 12. Comparison of the LEACH and SEP with probability of 0.05 of 100 nodes.

4 Conclusion and Future Work

In this research paper, the performance of WSN protocols EAMMH, LEACH and SEP is compared. First LEACH is compared with EAMMH and then with the SEP by varying the number of nodes and probability to become CH. The importance of the routing protocols in WSN is described. EAMMH performance is better as compared to LEACH. In SEP, the first node takes a long time to die, but after this dead node, a lot of nodes lose their energy in short time. It is concluded from the comparison that LEACH is suitable for smaller networks and EAMMH is good for larger networks where heuristic probability of CH selection becomes more. Due to advanced nodes that have high initial energy, SEP is the best choice. To improve these routing protocols space still exists. Useful work can be done on network security to prolong the lifetime of networks.

References

1. Pinar, Y., et al.: Wireless Sensor Networks (WSNs). In: 2016 IEEE Long Island Systems, Applications and Technology Conference (LISAT). IEEE (2016)
2. Mahajan, S., Dhiman, P.K.: Clustering in WSN: a review. Int. J. Adv. Res. Comput. Sci. **7**(3) (2016)
3. Tiwari, P., et al.: Wireless sensor networks: introduction, advantages, applications and research challenges. HCTL Open Int. J. Technol. Innovat. Res. (IJTIR) **14** (2015)
4. Mundada, M.R., et al.: Clustering in wireless sensor networks: performance comparison of EAMMH and LEACH protocols using MATLAB. In: Advanced Materials Research, vol. 705. Trans Tech Publications (2013)
5. Kaur, H., Kaur, N., Waraich, S.: Comparative analysis of clustering protocols for wireless sensor networks. Int. J. Comput. Appl. **115**(1), 35–43 (2015)
6. Hussain, R.: Comparison the performance of two wireless sensor networks protocols (LEACH and EAMMH). Univ. Thi-Qar J. Sci. **5**(3) (2015)
7. Abedin, Z., et al.: Selection of energy efficient routing protocol for irrigation enabled by wireless sensor network. In: 2017 IEEE 42nd Conference on Local Computer Networks Workshops (LCN Workshops). IEEE (2017)
8. Juwaied, A., Jackowska-Strumitto, L.: Analysis of cluster heads positions in stable election protocol for Wireless Sensor Network. In: 2018 International Interdisciplinary Ph.D. Workshop (IIPhDW). IEEE (2018)
9. Iqbal, S., et al.: Performance analysis of stable election protocol and its extensions in WSN. In: 2014 IEEE International Conference on Advanced Communications, Control and Computing Technologies. IEEE (2014)
10. Jain, N., Mannan, M.: Comparative performance analysis of teen sep leach eammh and pegasis routing protocols. IEEE Proc. IRJET. **3**(3), 983–987 (2016)
11. Karakaya, A., Akleylek, S.: A survey on security threats and authentication approaches in wireless sensor networks. In: 2018 6th International Symposium on Digital Forensic and Security (ISDFS). IEEE (2018)
12. Singla, A., Sachdeva, R.: Review on security issues and attacks in wireless sensor networks. Int. J. Adv. Res. Comput. Sci. Software Eng. **3**(4) (2013)
13. Ayoob, M., et al.: Research of improvement on LEACH and SEP routing protocols in wireless sensor networks. In: 2016 IEEE International Conference on Control and Robotics Engineering (ICCRE). IEEE (2016)
14. Singh, O., Rishiwal, V.: On the scalability of routing protocols in WSN. In: 2017 3rd International Conference on Advances in Computing, Communication & Automation (ICACCA) (Fall). IEEE (2017)
15. Lv, L.: An energy aware multipath routing algorithm for wireless sensor networks. Int. J. Online Eng. **13**(4) (2017)

Intelligent Environments

Crash-Resilient Synthesizer in Logic Optimization Paradigm for Sustainable Hardware Design of ASIC and Digital Systems

Noor-ul-Qamar$^{(\boxtimes)}$, Muhammad Habib$^{(\boxtimes)}$, Waseem Ahmad$^{(\boxtimes)}$,
and Taimoor Hassan$^{(\boxtimes)}$

Department of Computer Science, Lahore Garrison University, Lahore, Pakistan
noorulqamar@lgu.edu.pk, ch.muhammadhabib@gmail.com,
mogli302@gmail.com, taimoorhassan9@yahoo.com

Abstract. Fault detection and its recovery has always been a major concern in research. Both hardware and software level faults of a system are required to be dealt with for any liable fault-tolerant framework. Self-sustainable systems play an important role in diagnosing such problems in systems through an automatic response. ASIC (Application Specific Integrated Circuit) is a latest technology whose fabrication level designing and coding, utilizing logic synthesis phase can be a source of relief from multiple faults at hardware level. Various existing repair techniques for self-healing systems have been discussed in this research. An algorithm along with a flow model is further explained that is helpful to cater with physical, logical and electrical faults possibly occurring at chip and gate level for improving reliability and efficiency in upcoming self-sustainable systems.

Keywords: Self-sustainable systems · Logic synthesis · Fault hypothesis · Field-programmable gate arrays · Pro-filing · Application Specific Integrated Circuit (ASIC)

1 Introduction

Combination of software and hardware that is capable of detecting various problems, errors and that also removes these inefficiencies is referred as self-sustaining systems. Example of such failure can be like if there is a distributed environment in which the data flow changes after some time. For instance, if there is a chance that a specific information structure is prone to a regular repair, it may be corresponded with this data flow which may endure any damage. Several advancements in technology, today, have led to the possibility of dealing with problems in systems at advance levels.

A self-sustaining system is one that can modify its behavior based on its observation and detection mechanism and is self-aware of the environment in which it must operate. A current practice in high quality frameworks, particularly in telecom programming, embedded systems and real time environment is in progress, which utilizes check pointing, resource estimation and rollback among different strategies to guarantee legitimate operations. Most programs are intended for running (right) calculations

© Springer Nature Singapore Pte Ltd. 2020
I. S. Bajwa et al. (Eds.): INTAP 2019, CCIS 1198, pp. 641–650, 2020.
https://doi.org/10.1007/978-981-15-5232-8_55

shaped in right projects. This can become possible in opposition to the requirements of a few sections of self-supporting frameworks, which must have the capacity to express the perception of running projects and modify their running conduct. They should therefore have the power of detection and must be tolerant of mistakes on their own.

In self-healing systems particularly, there is a need of a reliable fault model that can be trusted and that is always self-aware of the conditions under which it must perform its services. The concept of automatic recovery arises from Autonomous Nervous System and is therefore very interesting to deal with the real time problems in systems just like in body. This research discusses in detail the aspects of dealing with various faults at fabrication level of chip designing and provides solution at logic synthesis phase of ASIC for troubleshooting incoming faults and generating reliable outputs for smooth running of the systems. It also discusses the importance of this phase through an algorithm considering the existing repair plans of healing and their impact on systems.

2   Aspects of Dealing with the Faults for Self-sustainable Systems

As a fault hypothesis must deal with all the possible conditions that can lead to fault occurrence the self-healing systems in this regard need to have effective research to diagnose both the hardware and software threat posing problems. In this case more work must be done in the following three major aspects for more understanding of the faults.

2.1   Fault Detection

The ability to detect faults is one of the major factors that has become a constraint in the development and advancement of the self-healing systems. So, the ways to effectively deal with the fault detection keeping in view the computational cost and the lower memory is of great importance for the systems and the users.

A way to proceed with this issue is to show concerns towards researching in hardware features and collection of nodes. These two things can help to not only improve the fault detection mechanism but also will help to perform responsively towards the attack cure through the collaborative use of fault-occurrence information and profiling as last specified in 2006. It will raise the urge to handle significant issues despite of the natural diversity of the monocultures. The self-healing mechanisms of defense also need to have a detailed analysis on the application behavior combined with the code analysis techniques. Application profiling enable the self-healing systems to ought and learn about the common behavior by further detecting the semantic in contrast to the opposite faults. The best approach in this case is to employ integrity and reliability policies that enable anomalies and error detection by specifying application-specific values for the runtime state internally.

A research suggests the need of more techniques to identify the performance bugs as they take long time to get detected and the aid by the profilers is also limited in this area of research (Stojnić and Schuldt 2012).

2.2   Fault Recovery/Mitigation

After detection the recovery of the fault is also essential, and it requires proper ways in self-healing systems to cope up with. The fault masking techniques of error virtualization and failure-oblivious computing, data structure repair has already been briefed in this research; most of the today's systems are dependent towards this snapshot combined with input filtering. However, on a large scale the technical success of the self-healing systems id most probably relying on their self-ability to get recovered from the issues being diagnosed while ensuring system reliability and availability.

The need is to pay more attention towards additional mitigation, fault-recovery techniques that can superbly deal with the various semantic levels of faults. Two high level approaches can be kept in notice in this regard; one is to use application-specific recovery policies and second is to use applications pro-filing to identify more appropriate ways to get recovery, like fault detection (Arulraj et al. 2013).

As the techniques applied for fault detection will need corresponding ways for their recovery as well. Some suitable repair plans in this notice are also kept in view to make the fault model more convenient as shown in Fig. 1.

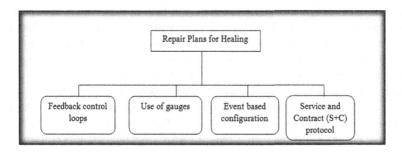

Fig. 1. Repair plans for healing

Once the detection and recovery ways are acknowledged it is important to validate these techniques and make sure that the real world could get benefit of it. A reasonable and notified level of assurance is also a must for the self-healing systems to prevail and flourish. This is the biggest challenge being faced by several automated defense systems. It is not humanly possible to satisfy each user expectation, but autonomic computing is somehow close to this factor as well. Assurance of the systems needs to build this trust that there will be no further damage to the application or any system component and that they can fight with other adversary attacks. They also need to assure that they are way much better than the available secured systems; this requires meeting the higher standards of the associated privileges that they have to operate.

For this purpose, there are some measures that can make the self-healing systems most trustworthy and demandable systems for the operators. Undo functionality, transparency of the specific operations, capabilities of reporting, reaction speed, response time, human supervision are all these necessary measures for the self-healing system to be assuredly successful and loyal.

3 Problem Statement

One of the crucial precepts of trustworthy processing is that a fault model must be indicated for any fault tolerant framework, satisfying errors.

3.1 Analysis on the Problem Statement

The goal of achieving and creating self-healing systems to reduce human intervention allowing machines to decide and make decisions for fault incurred situations is kept in regard while working for this research. The solution can be taken in two perspectives either at hardware or at a software level. This analysis primarily focuses on the hardware side to know that what possible conditions can help in building a fault tolerant framework and what factors it has to notice to not only work against faults but to also authenticate that it can manage everything logically as well leaving the users with comfort and security.

3.2 Application Specific Integrated Circuit (ASIC)

ASIC with their design and implementation can help in determining the specific and variant aspects of a fault model along with the constraints that must be satisfied. It is an integrated circuit that is made for specific and customized uses rather than for general purposes like a chip to be used in a digital voice recorder. The complexity growth in ASIC has reached from 5000 to over 100 million gates with improving designs, modern ASICs involve entire blocks of memory like RAM, ROM referred to as an SOC or system-on-chip however for lower volumes of production FPGAs (Field-programmable gate arrays) (Averbouch et al. 2016) are used in many applications being more cost-effective, they are similar to ASICs but they are less efficient and are reprogrammable used in development or research operations. The ASIC chips are intended to satisfy more application required or intended narrow tasks in a particular industry, so they are mostly designed by applying a standard-cell technique using basic functions of both IP core or cell library to fulfill the primary functions of a chip. For this purpose, the designers need not only to map the logic design, but they are also required to work with the physical component design for appropriate functionality. ASSPs on the other hand serve as the intermediate between the industry standard ICs like 4000 series and ASICs. Figure 2 gives this explanation below.

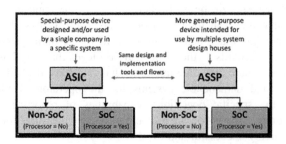

Fig. 2. ASIC and ASSP description

3.3   ASIC Modeling Language

In the basic design flow of the ASIC a code in specific language is being submitted to the design entry level where it becomes the basis of the whole chip to be developed. ASIC modeling is dependent primarily on the selection of these languages in which the hardware and software designing is performed. All the necessities for the chip to accomplish and present are kept in mind while coding at the design entry phase in these languages mentioned below with their brief descriptions.

3.4   VHDL and HDL

In order to describe the functionalities of ASICs the designers mostly use HDL (Hardware Description Language) such as Verilog or VHDL (VHSIC Hardware Description Language). HDL includes description of operators, statements, inputs, expressions and outputs. HDL compilers supply a gate map which is then downloaded for getting an understanding of the operations for the circuit. HDL is used for designing all circuit types as standardized by IEEE 1364 consisting of modules for dataflow, structural description and it has emerged to satisfy the need of a language used in both hardware and software code designing in 1970. HDL has eased the task of circuit designing by letting separate modules to serve various purposes and provide benefits of achieving goals like power, area consumption and functionality etc. as compared to C language HDL supports timing information for the designs.

VHDL type of HDL is generally a language that has been implied in the automation designs of the electronics to describe mixed and digital signal systems like ICs and FPGA. It can also be used in general purpose parallel programming languages. It is commonly applied to write models that could possibly describe a logic circuit and these models are processed by some synthesis programs (Deschamps et al. 2017). VHDL is not case-sensitive and the operations which are commonly used in hardware are represented in VHDL by implying several features. Like to represent sets of Boolean operators including NOR and NAND. Being valuable for text processing this language can also serve for input and output file capabilities. It can also serve to write a test-bench (collection of simulation models) to check the functionality of the logic design matching with the fault model simulation by comparing the results of the expected values. In order to develop a proper test-bench for a VHDL code there is a need of defining appropriate inputs first like a loop process is required for a clock input.

When a VHDL code is translated into wires and gates they are then applied to a logic device for example FPGA and then the steps to form the actual hardware to be used is started and configured. It is a dataflow language and so it allows the concurrent systems to be described and benefited instead of the other procedural languages of computer like C to run sequentially. A VHDL project once formed can be utilized in other projects and is portable for several element bases. One major benefit of VHDL is that it allows behavior of a required system to be modeled and simulated or verified beforehand it can get translated into the real hardware in form of wires or gates by the synthesis tools.

The VHDL comprises of combinational circuits and registers but has no implicit finite machines, timing delays and multidimensional arrays support. VHDL code that describes that how the data is changed as it passes from one register to the other is referred as RTL (register transfer level) and this transformation is usually done by the combinational logic existing between these registers (Adya et al. 2016).

4 Logic Synthesis

After the phase of design entry, the stage of logic synthesis comes in the general design flow of the ASIC; an aspect of electronic designs automation in terms of electronics. It provides a way of communication among the code in HDL and the netlist like the way the C compiler helps establishing a link between the C and machine language. The process of logic synthesis is complex as it involves using subsets of VHDL or Verilog, it becomes necessary to have knowledge of the hardware while working with logic synthesis tools in HDL as they must produce the net list and that has to be anticipated in advance. Logic synthesis can be considered basically as a process that can transform a circuit behavior at RTL level into an implemented design of logic gates (Yang and Marek-Sadowska 2016).

The synthesis tools in this case develop bit streams for logic devices like FPGAs. An HDL behavioral model gets completed once it has state diagrams, truth tables and other such graphical templates as it does not have any logic cells references. After this a cell library (with various logic cells like NAND gates) and a logic synthesizer (for documentation and software) is required to further simulate the model in order to determine that the created design satisfies the needs so that the synthesizer can work with generating the structural model for establishing references to the logic cells (Huang et al. 2017). There is no such standard format used by the logic synthesis however EDIF is mostly used. With this the design as a result is simulated again and then compared with the earlier simulations helping to focus on the layout of any particular type of ASIC. Talking about the design of logic synthesis representing the functional design of a circuit is changed into the use of several operations like arithmetic and logical ones using high-level synthesis (ESL synthesis) tools. These tools using high-level languages like C++ have emerged in the commercial use. This whole thing can be seen with the help of Fig. 3.

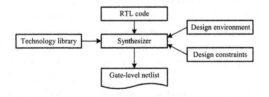

Fig. 3. Logic synthesis flow

4.1 Phases of Logic Synthesis

The mechanism followed in logic synthesis can be described by means of two basic phases which depicts the working at both the front and the back end. These phases are:

1. In the 1st phase the translation of HDL into an ideal and generic logic description allowing the verification of various functional operators by generating logic expressions.
2. The 2nd phase brings this design to the resultant physical device considering all the speed, complexity, delays and power constraints. This helps in simulating the further physical operation of the device.

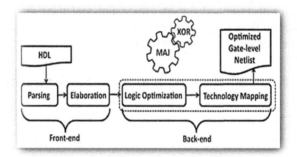

Fig. 4. Front-end and back-end phases in logic synthesis

The process of these phases operating at backend and front-end can be diagrammatically understood in Fig. 4, the logic optimization can be however technology independent or technology dependent.

4.2 Proposed Design

As in self-healing systems there is a need of an effective fault tolerant framework that can automatically respond to faults and brings the system back to its normal state the logic synthesis phase is most important. This research is concerned to determine the influences of faults at hardware level (Maier and Kleeberger 2016) and has not gone in deep to the software level discussion, so keeping in view the basic design flow of ASIC it suggests ensuring a mean of security from any kind of threats by making the synthesis level strong. If the logic is faulty the rest of the system has to deal with the arrival and suspicious interference of the errors.

Several algorithms have been implied in this case to find out the best way to deal with troubleshooting (Warnquist and Kvarnström 2016). Keeping them in mind at logic synthesis level the algorithm that can be applied needs to be the one that fulfills all the criteria's and constraints that can deal possibly with the incurred faults at the hardware level.

4.3   Algorithm

A generic algorithm to explain the flow of this fault incurring situation and remaining in a safe state at the phase of logic synthesis can be proposed as:

begin
1. write the RTL HDL code
2. present it for simulation
3. if (simulation==OK) then synthesize the HDL code to logic gates for further implementation
4. else go to step 1 to 3 and then go to step 5
5. perform the logic synthesis considering the area and timing constraints
6. if (Constraints==OK) then go to the next phase of designing
7. else perform analysis and consider the major violations made and repeat the algorithm starting from step 1 to step 6.
8. if no major violations are found then go to step 6
end

The Design flow of this algorithm can be well understood with the help of Fig. 5 given.

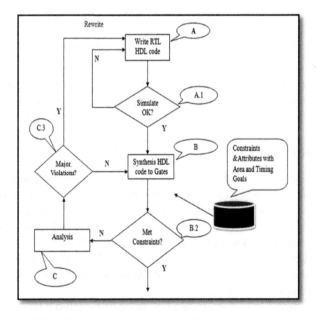

Fig. 5. Design flow of the logic synthesis operations

Figure above explains the whole process of logic synthesis starting from the level of writing the code to its implementation and analysis in an electrical form with the use of logic gates. An indicates electrical faults, B shows the possibility of physical faults and C refers to the logical faults. These are the three major faults that can possibly occur at the fabrication level of the chip at this phase (Ngo et al. 2016; Sahoo et al. 2016).

5 Conclusion

In case of fault tolerance framework if this design is taken into consideration then it is possible to minimize the chances of faults disturbing the system functionality and presents a way of solving these faults at hardware level as a machine effort without much human intervention. Once a developed code is applied to a machine a to a logical fault model it has to satisfy all needs and make sure that it considers every possible state of fault and its solutions. This can be managed best through certain goals which are set initially in order to produce an effective fault tolerance framework. Every fault model has its own specifications which make it different from the others, these demands, and approaches depend primarily on the type of machine and its level for which the model has been designed. The goal of logic synthesis has already been discussed so in order to work on that criteria it has to make sure first that the simulation is made in accordance to the code written. If at this initial stage it faces problem, then it must re check that which areas are creating issues in its way and improve the code again. Just like when a code is written in any language to get a desirable result and it generates any syntax errors which are not identifiable for the compiler of that language and so it does not produce the required output unless those errors are fixed. Similarly, after resolving not only the machine demanding or model capability-based require-ments the synthesis phase must make sure that it gets a proper simulation before it proceeds to its actual task.

After the simulation is done appropriately the next step is to transform the code by means of various operators used in logic gates like AND, OR, NOR, XOR, BUFFER etc. to describe the relationship among input, output and the next possible state. These Boolean expressions and truth tables are then mapped into a technology of gates (Lee et al. 2016). Likewise, the code sometimes does not generate correct outputs even when there are no syntax errors because of logical errors. Therefore, all these possible errors are kept in mind while designing chip at each level.

In self-healing systems this analysis can be considered in terms of having an effective fault tolerance framework, keeping in view the logic synthesis phase and its design. There is a need of strong fault detection models in systems that in state of incurred faults can take appropriate decisions of dealing with these faults of different types and levels. These systems also need to take alternative actions in case of any problem and to deal with the faults in such a manner that the system can get back to its normal position with very less human involvement.

References

Arulraj, J., Chang, P.C., Jin, G., Lu, S.: Production-run software failure diagnosis via hardware performance counters. ACM SIGARCH Comput. Architect. News **41**(1), 101–112 (2013)

Warnquist, H., Kvarnström, J.: A modeling framework for troubleshooting automotive systems. Appl. Artif. Intell. **30**(3), 257–296 (2016)

Averbouch, I., Margalit, O., Nahir, A., Naveh, Y.: Solving constraint satisfaction problems using a field programmable gate array. U.S. Patent No. 9,337,845. Google Patents (2016)

Deschamps, J.P., Valderrama, E., Terés, L.: Design methods. Digital Systems, pp. 171–177. Springer, Cham (2017). https://doi.org/10.1007/978-3-319-41198-9_6

Lee, N.Z., Kuo, H.Y., Lai, Y.H.: Scalable synthesis of PCHB–WCHB hybrid quasi-delay insensitive circuits. IEEE Trans. Comput. Aided Des. Integr. Circuits Syst. **35**(11), 1797–1810 (2016)

Yang, P.L., Marek-Sadowska, M.: Majority-inverter graph a new paradigm for logic optimization. IEEE Trans. Comput. Aided Des. Integr. Circuits Syst. **35**(5), 806–819 (2016)

Maier, P.R., Kleeberger, V.B.: Embedded software reliability testing by unit-level fault injection. In: 21st Asia and South Pacific Design Automation Conference (ASP-DAC), pp. 410–416. IEEE (2016)

Stojnić, N., Schuldt, H.: Osiris-sr: a safety ring for self-healing distributed composite service execution. In: Proceedings of the 7th International Symposium on Software Engineering for Adaptive and Self-Managing Systems, pp. 21–26. IEEE, June 2012

Adya, S., McElvain, K.S., Paul, G.: Circuit design and optimization. U.S. Patent Application No. 15/063,479, Google Patents (2016)

Sahoo, S.S., Veeravalli, B., Kumar, A.: Defect and fault tolerance in VLSI and nanotechnology systems (DFT). In: IEEE International Symposium, pp. 63–68. IEEE (2016)

Ngo, X.T., Najm, Z., Bhasin, S., Guilley, S., Danger, J.-L.: Method taking into account process dispersion to detect hardware Trojan Horse by side-channel analysis. J. Cryptogr. Eng. **6**(3), 239–247 (2016). https://doi.org/10.1007/s13389-016-0129-2

Huang, Z., Wei, X., Zgheib, G., Li, W., Lin, Y., Jiang, Z.: NAND-NOR: a compact, fast, and delay balanced FPGA logic element. In: Proceedings of the 2017 ACM/SIGDA International Symposium on Field-Programmable Gate Arrays, pp. 135–140. ACM (2017)

An Improved Ensemble Based Machine Learning Technique for Efficient Malware Classification

Farwa Maqbool Hussain[1(✉)] and Farhan Hassan Khan[2]

[1] Department of Computer Science and Software Engineering, IIUI,
Islamabad, Pakistan
frwamaqbool@gmail.com
[2] Knowledge and Data Science Research Centre (KDRC),
College of Electrical and Mechanical Engineering (CEME),
National University of Sciences and Technology (NUST), Islamabad, Pakistan
mrfarhankhan@gmail.com

Abstract. Android smartphones have become an emerging technology due to widespread adoption. The widely used Android devices allow installation of apps and grant privileges to access confidential information from the phone which resulted in being targeted by malware developers. The dramatic rise in the number of attacks, develop an interest to make a robust system that automatically identifies the presence of malicious behavior in Android applications. The previous malware detection studies comprised of static and dynamic analysis techniques, extreme learning machine and virtual machine introspection that have few shortcomings in detection of data outflow such as high computational and performance cost, low accuracy, high false positive rates, etc. The proposed approach overcomes the problems of static and dynamic techniques in malware detection. The novel classification approach senses all kinds of source-code and application behaviors. The proposed technique scans the keywords of manifest. xml files for malicious items. By the enhancement of manifest.xml feature the proposed technique can reduce apps scan time as compared to previous proposed malware detection frameworks. This technique also improves the security of Android users.

Keywords: Android · Malware detection · Machine learning

1 Introduction

Malware, malicious software, disrupts computer operations, collect sensitive information and get access to private computer systems [1]. Now a day, the software development has been seen to move toward mobile applications. *Android*, most popular smart phone operating system (OS), organized with pre-installed applications by the device manufacture. The software running on smartphone enhance the phone functionality and provide interaction with end users. It provides diverse services such as short messages service (SMS), email, internet surfing, social networking, map, GPS and mobile payment applications [2]. However, the android smartphone increasingly

© Springer Nature Singapore Pte Ltd. 2020
I. S. Bajwa et al. (Eds.): INTAP 2019, CCIS 1198, pp. 651–662, 2020.
https://doi.org/10.1007/978-981-15-5232-8_56

targeted by cybercriminals and infected by malicious applications. Android malware have increased dramatically, and stole stored sensitive privacy data such as by making premium calls, send an SMS, advertisement span without user knowledge and location information [3]. Recent studies introduced several types of Android malware and decided that the most dominant is privacy violation, which hacked the personal privacy information [4]. Moreover, many harmful attacks such as: botnet, this malicious perform distributed denial of services (DDoS) attack, steal data, spam and permit the attackers to access the device and its connection [5]. Fraud phishing and identity theft utilize the personal and financial data that fraudulently obtained from smartphone for taxpayer identity and financial assists [6].

To allow the installation of applications from unreliable third-party market can easily attacked android platform through the distributed applications with malware [7]. MacAfee security report [8], in first quarter of 2018, the range of mobile malware reaches more than 6 billion. There is need for effective an efficient malware exposure technique for avoiding explosion of malware applications. The Android platform offers many security mechanisms that overcome the presence of malware, Android permission control mechanism. Applications explicitly affirm the permissions they need to accomplish certain sensitive operations such as obtained contact information and users consent. However, both, developers must follow the latest privileged set principal to agree upon requested permission and users should know risks of giving permission. As a result, the permission control mechanism can limit the circulation of malicious applications [9].

Machine learning technique automatically assumed the application behavioral properties when associate with program analysis techniques, which identify the mainstream of malicious applications. The program analysis techniques comprise of static approaches and dynamic approaches. Li et al. [10] perform the static analysis to extract behavior characteristics such as, requested permissions, API calls (Application Program Interface), determined types and network addresses from applications. Static analysis is valuable to quickly scan and check the malicious applications. In contrast, dynamic analysis is better suitable for obfuscation because it monitors run-time behaviors such as API calls, system calls, and hidden icon operation and combine supervised learning algorithm to effectively detect the malware. It is computationally expensive, while testing might not see the malicious behavior.

Machine learning utilize two techniques for malware detection, namely: classification and clustering. Classification is supervised machine learning technique, which can be categories data into a given number of classes. An algorithm used that maps the input data into specific category that are: Support Vector Machine (SVM), Random Forest (RF), Naïve Bayes, C4.5 Decision tree, JRIP and AdaBoost. Clustering is an unsupervised machine learning technique that grouping similar entities together and used K-means, Farthest First and Expectation Maximization (EM) to evaluate the performance.

The rest of paper is organized as follow: Sect. 2 summarized the literature review, Sect. 3 provide proposed malware detection technique. Section 4 explains experimental results and discussion. Finally, Sect. 5 briefly conclude this paper and outlines future work.

2   Literature Review

In [11] author, proposed a classification of app permission that rely on machine learning model for the detection of malware. The proposed technique is lightweights and systematically low-cost and installed on numerous mobile devices. The results indicate performance: 89% malicious applications detected by permission-based technique whereas 95% through source code. The accuracy rate was 95.1% by use of SVM that maps the input with high dimension features space. The classification of source code more expensive and takes more than 10 s on one application. So, practically used in scanning Google play store apps. In [12], dynamic analysis, Android application detected for malware after finishing installation. It is not a secure to detect malware because user grants all access permission during installations. Before installing application, proposed model used installed APK file strings for comparison in malware string. If APK file string and malware strings not matched each other then consider malicious applications otherwise legitimate. The highest accuracy achieved by SVM was 85.5%. In [13], author propose static dataflow analysis technology applied on machine leaning model that provide efficient data analysis and classification to detect sensitive transmission of data in Android. The results indicate that 97.66% accuracy was achieved. The overhead in term of time reduced by almost 40% in static privacy leakage analysis. In [14], proposed ELM detects distributed data of Apache Spark that is a scalable data processing framework. In form of NetFlow data accessed through system and stored in HDFS. In additional, processed on NetFlow data to extract features to calculate model parameter that utilized in NIDS that run on machine learning model. The results reveal that NetFlow analysis based on ELM classifier give efficient and consistent system for the detection of incidents.

In [15], VMI security model work on VMM or hypervisor to inspect disloyal guest on OS. In proposed work introduced advanced VMM based on A-IntExt system. The VMI occasionally detect the status of VM by used of MFA and machine learning model. In A-IntExt system applied an ICVA process to noticed hidden, distinguish, dead of data on VMI and find out the malware indicators through the TIT technique. By 10 fold cross attained 0.004 FPR and 99.55% accuracy of A-IntExt system. Periodic introspection, A-IntExt not consider the malware explosion in kernel method. The proposed scheme [16] repeatedly takes label data and update model to make prediction of a new sample. The proposed CASANDRA handle the volume of malware populations. 89.92% accuracy was attained on ITW dataset. On large experimental values, CASANDRA takes only 28.23 ms to detect label sample. [17] proposed EnDroid analysis framework that consequently used dynamic behavior based features to detect malware families. In [18] Author proposed permission pattern that detect difference between malicious and clean applications. The efficient mining techniques provide contract authorized design that distinct legitimate from malicious applications. The mining technique that used pattern related to contrast permission to determine the permission activity that used in malware tasks. Although, proposed technique not support indirect inherent permissions, basically helps to measure the permission patterns. Since, the obfuscation pattern not applied on Android permission and generated permission sets applied for differentiate clan and malicious apps.

In [19] the author proposed IagoDroid technique that generate the mislabel malware samples by triage procedure to detect potential models of malware. IagoDroid main purpose to validate, the attacks that impose on classification of Android malware become possible to achievable by manipulating on original model while secure of its semantic model. As compared to RevealDroid choose IagoDroid that commonly used open source classifier relies on various static features. The proposed IagoDroid have the capability to search out evasive folder with less time and 100% evasive achieved in generation 4. Hence, the potential evasive detected by IagroDroid in between 90% and 99%, depending upon the introduced modifications and detect the potential original families for malware. The countermeasure has some limitations of evasion methods. In addition, limitation in the variant of final generation, in current version needed the human intervention for transforming recommended changes vector to authentic modified.

In [20] author proposed Malytic approach to distinguish the malware families. The proposed approach makes differentiate between benign and Android application through the static features get from binary files. The proposed technique divides on three categorized: abstraction of features, classification and resemblance measurement. The categorized steps applied on two hidden and one outer layers of neural network. The tf-simhashing used in extraction of features that resembled to ELM first layer of neural net. The ELM output layer used to enhance the proposed scheme performance. For measurement of similarity accomplish through RBF kernel. The Malytic technique with distinct state of art perform better as compared to DexShare, and PEShare. Malytic performance on imbalanced datasets. Malytic robust and resilient in addressing zero-day malware sample and it showed 97.21% and 99.45% of F1-score respectively. The speed and reliability of Malytic demonstrate the promising result for large-scale data. The limitation that consider in proposed Malytic technique that consume a lot of memory to accumulate all input sample data and output layer weight of big data. Malytic has all hashes fie that merged into one vector, not consider good for binary file which partially targeted by malicious families.

In [21] author proposed MADAM, A host-based malware detection system that not only examines but also correlates features. MADAM composed itself with help of 2,800 applications taken from 125 different families. This technique simultaneously improved the detection rate from 93–96% and balanced CPU performance from 7–1.4%. On other side, while run time not discovered the botnet class. In [22] author proposed a system for Android that detect behaviors of applications and categorize known and unknown malwares. The dataset used by proposed technique identified 150 benign and 104 malware applications. The accuracy attained while identifications of malware applications is 88.2%. Dynamic method generally used tools that are custom automated to trigger the events and might usage users themselves trigger events. Thus, to analyses large number of applications took a lot of times. In [23] author offered Androidetect capture instantaneous attacks by analyzing affiliation between system function calls, sensitive permission and interface of sensitive application programming. The proposed technique detects 102 benign and 219 malicious samples. The technique has good result in FPR that noted 7%, likewise has 87% lower TPR.

3 Proposed Approach

The proposed technique overcome the static and dynamic approaches problems in detection of malware. A novel robust approach combination of static and dynamic techniques that capable of detecting all kinds of malware presence through machine learning model. Static analysis scans all the application code and recognize the malicious behavior without executing it. In static analysis, static features (requested hardware elements, application elements (service, receiver, content provider), intent filters, suspicious API calls and restricted API calls) take out using Android Asset Packaging Tool and Baksmali tool. While in phase of dynamic analysis, system installs application on the real Android device and analyze run time behavior and monitored dynamically loaded and decrypted code. Dynamic feature analyze the system call to know the behavior of application in real time. The malicious applications raise specific application call more regularly than legitimate application. The frequently occurrence of system call (open, ioctl, brk, read, write, close, sendto, sendmsg, recvfrom, recvmsg) represent the malware application behavior. The main components of proposed approach are explained below:

3.1 Data Collection

The method involves of running applications on a device and identify the behavior of applications using dynamic and static analysis.

App Archive .APK. The APK files are types of archive file that used by Android operating system to download any phone apps. An APK file contains on programs codes, resources, constant string and manifest file. hence, the constant string of downloaded APK method relate to the malware application of constant string and then manifest.xml file application to determine either the application malware or nor. By this way, the proposed scheme detected the malware pattern before installing into an Android phone.

Decompressing. After downloaded the APK file, the static features extracted from it. The Android package decompressed by Android Asset Packaging Tool. This component unpacks the manifest.xml and provide outputs of classes.dex file. the manifest file extracted all the requested permission, application components, filtered intents and hardware features that used by applications. Baksmali tool, used for assembling and disassembling of applications. In this module classes.dex application code disassemble, output generated the smali files. The smali files hold java code of Android application in samli language. The smali code files help to extracted out of suspicious API calls and restricted API calls.

3.2   Feature Extraction

To make a robust Android malware detection model need some representative features for analysis that are: user permission, provider and receiver information, process name, intent filter and binaries taken out by reverse engineering. The APK file convert into java code format then after modifications turn it back to APK file. The feature that extracted while reverse engineering from Android manifest.xml file and constant string are: binaries and permission, providers, receiver, intent filter and process. After reverse engineering of APK file the binaries are the form of constant string located in the folder. The attacker attempt attacks to constant string and make change by reverse engineering the applications. Like that, the source code of application attained form decompiling of APK file, attacker may also attempt attack into source code of constant string by execution changes into it [const-string v1, 'Device Not Rooted'] and can upload it into google play store. Hence, every Android app have manifest.xml file that contained requested permissions. So, users must accept the requested permissions before installation apps. During constant strings, keyword (manifest feature) also taken out from application that help in malware detection and have some specific purpose like 'Read SMS' mean received the sent message and read. 'Read Phone State' the user phone number is read. These keywords also found in malicious applications. So, to detect the malicious and legitimate file compares all the manifest extracted feature to the proposed keyword. After that, to calculate the malignancy score of applications by threshold values and then applied machine learning algorithms.

In proposed technique keywords of manifest files used to find out more keywords of manifext.xml files of malicious. So, by enhancing the keywords of manifest feature got higher accuracy than previous proposed malware detection framework. This technique works better in searching out of malicious applications and on other side improve the security of Android to users.

3.3   Behavior Analysis

First, gathered the dataset of Android applications after that through the constant string and manifest.xml file extracted feature for benign and malicious apps. The binaries have the built constant string, API calls and system calls. Likewise, keywords have broadcast receiver, then made training and testing of proposed model to achieve the required results. Through the attainable sample performed the classification and evaluations of algorithm by utilizing the 10-fold cross validation. In 10-fold cross validation the sample divided into subsamples and from each sample 9 used for training and 1 for testing. After testing the sample validation is done to check out the issues. permission, intent filter, provide and process name. The constant strings collected through benign and malware apps and manifext.xml collected by sample of malware analysis. From the manifest.xml applications of Android, database was created by the collections of searching services, broadcast, activities and broadcast receivers. The data structure created by analyzing previous existing malware sample and frequent keywords.

Machine Learning Classifier. In machine learning classifier phase the classifiers output is produced. According to result determines the optimum machine learning classifier for detection of malware. This section elaborate the description of selected classifiers that applied to determine the behavior of malicious and benign apps.

KNN. K nearest neighbor is a clustering algorithm [24] that simply belongs to a K data points in training set which nearest to the test set of data points, and then shows fraction of members that have its place in specific class.

SVM. Support vector machine is a supervised machine learning binary classification model to analyze sparse data and high dimensional data and identify patterns [25]. The classification problem comprise of two stages: training and prediction. In training dataset the SVM classifier maps input to the high dimensional feature space. In prediction phase, separately each sample classify by testing dataset.

RF. Random forest is an ensemble classification algorithm that evade over-adjustment with a least cost [26]. The forest built by using bootstraps methods. The main purpose of bootstrapping is to combine all the decision trees and provides the mode of specific decision by decision tree.

Naïve Bayes. Naïve Bayes is a simple probabilistic machine learning classification algorithm that built on Bayes theorem [27]. This classifier perform surprisingly well on Bayes theorem data that assumed conditionally independent between features.

3.4   Detection Model

In proposed technique more keywords extracted using manifest files to improve accuracy results than previous proposed malware detection technique. The previous technique utilized four list of features and in proposed techniques extended it to eight like permission, intent-filter (action), intent filter (category), process name, provider, intent-filter (scheme), receiver, intent-filter (priority). With the enhancement of manifest keyword got high accuracy with well malware application detection. Furthermore, proposed machine learning model also upgraded security to Android users.

Benign and Malicious App Classification. Firstly, randomly extracted the features of malicious and benign applications from Android dataset. The binaries and manifest files also extracted from the benign and malicious applications. The binaries built in files consist on constant string, API calls and system calls while permissions, broadcast receiver, intent filter, provider and process name are combined in keywords. The constant string gather from benign and malicious applications and Android manifest file (keywords) collected by analysis of malware samples. To analyze malware sample created database by searching services, activities, broadcast, and broadcast receiver from manifest.xml file of Android applications. The data structure created by analyzing most frequent occurrence of malicious keywords in malware models.

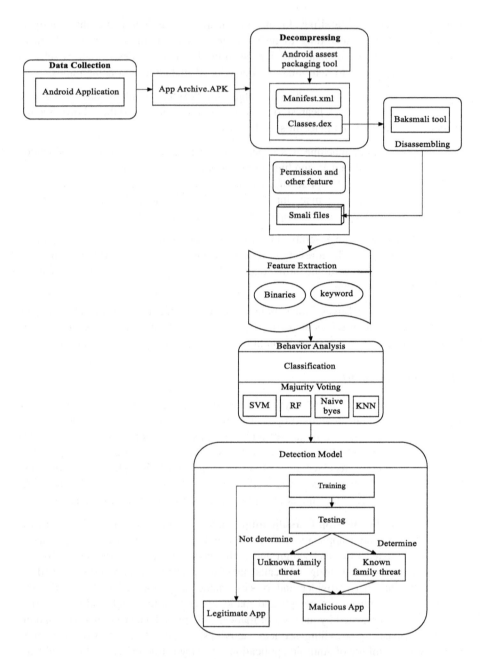

Various parameters and ensemble algorithms applied in the proposed model to get accurate malware detection system. The F-measure, Euclidian distance inner product similarity, constant similarity and Kernel Euclidean distance were used for better accuracy. Although cosine similarity work well with malware detection model and attained high rate of accuracy. Similarly, used the automatic sampling technique for training and testing in 10-fold cross validation. The stratified sampling used in automatic sampling, if it not available then used shuffles sample in the threshold. After setting out parameters and implemented of supervised algorithms on machine learning model then made training and testing of proposed model to achieve the required results.

Through the attainable sample performed the classification and evaluations of algorithm by utilizing the 10-fold cross validation. In 10-fold cross validation the sample divided into subsamples and from each sample K-1 used for training and one part for testing. The data split into three ways: training, testing and validation. After testing data the validation performed to check the over fitting problems. The over fitting issues reduced by implementing algorithms and validation is achieved. The main benefit of overfitting is that each part of data used for both training and testing.

4 Comparison and Discussion

In the following, to further explain the significances of our novel approach, this paper summarized the pros and cons of existing state-of-art malware detection technique based on efficient malware classification. As show in Table 1, Milosevic et al. [11] analyzed machine learning aided approaches and attained 95.1% accuracy by use of SVM. Rehman et al. [12] used hybrid machine learning framework that detect different types of malwares and accuracy 85.5% was finally achieved by SVM. Wu et al. [13] used dataflow analysis technology on machine learning mode and results indicate that the accuracy was achieved till 97.66% and consider overhead in term of time reduced almost 40% in static privacy leakage analysis. Kozik [14] analyzed extreme machine learning that detect distributed data of Apache spark that is a scalable data processing framework and CTU dataset was used that comprise on cyber-attacks and botnet types. Ajay et al. [15] extracted the VMI security features from VM and hypervisor to attain 0.004 FPR and 99% accuracy. Narayanan et al. [16] analyzed online learning framework, 89.92% accuracy achieved and it took only 28.23 ms to detect label sample.

Feng et al. [17] used EnDroid framework that consequently used dynamic behavior based features to detect malware families. The experimental result denote that stacking obtained well performance in classification of malware detection. Moonsamy et al. [18] extracted permission pattern that find difference between malicious and benign applications. Based on experimental result that several permissions not appeared on required permission set but exist on used permission set. Calleja et al. [19] used IagoDroid technique that generate the mislabel malware samples by triage procedure to detect potential model of malware. IagoDroid detect potential evasion in between 90% to 99% depending upon the introduced modifications and detect original malware families. Yousefi-Azar [20] analyzed Malytic approach to distinguish malware families. The dex file work well to compete the previous work. Saracino et al. [21] analyzed MADAM, A host based malware detection system which analyze correlate features and 93 to 96% detection improved. Sun et al. [22] used a system that analyzed a behaviors of Android applications and identify known and unknown malware. The accuracy of malware application identification was 88.2%. Wei et al. [23] used Androidetect which capture instantaneous attacks by analyzing relationship between function, sensitive permission, and sensitive programming interface. Androidetect system has a better detection result in FPR(7%).

Table 1. An Overview of State of the art Research

Ref/Year	Technique	Dataset	Results	Limitations
Milosevic et al. [11] (2017)	SVM	MODROID	Accuracy rate was 95.1% using	Takes more than 10 s on one application
Rehman et al. [12] (2018)	Hybrid machine learning framework	MODROID	Accuracy 85.5%	Take 3 s second to scan applications
Wu et al. [13] (2016)	Static dataflow analysis with machine leaning	VirusShare apps benign 1160 malware 1050	Achieved 97% accuracy	Static privacy leakage analysis
Ajay et al. [15] (2017)	Advanced VMM based on A-IntExt system	VMM benchmark dataset.	0.004 FPR and 99.55% accuracy	Not consider the malware explosion in kernel method
Narayanan et al. [16] (2017)	Online learning framework	DREBIN 5560 malware 179 families	89.92% accuracy	28.23 ms to detect label sample
Feng et al. [17] (2018)	EnDroid analysis framework that consequently used dynamic behavior based features to detect malware families	M1 dataset 8806 legitimate 5213 malicious M2 dataset 5000 benign 5000 malicious	Stacking outperformed in classification of malware detection	MokeyRunner and DroidBox may fail to trigger malicious behaviours of malware due to lacking of necessary UI operations
Calleja et al. [19] (2018)	Triage procedure to detect potential models of malware	RevealDroid DREBIN 1919 malware 29 variant malware families	Between 90% and 99%, depending upon the introduced modifications	Comprehensive evaluation missing
Azar et al. [20] (2018)	Malytic approach to distinguish the malware families	Drebin, DexShare, PEShare dataset		Human intervention for transforming recommended changes
Saracino et al. [21] (2018)	MADAM, host-based malware detection which analyses & correlates features	2,800 apps coming from 125 different families	Detection rate from 93% to 96%	The botnet class not discovered by MADAM at run-time
Sun et al. [22] (2018)	Detect behaviours of applications and categorize known/unknown malware	150 benign and 104 malware apps	Accuracy is 88.2%	To analyse large number of apps took a lot of time
Wei et al. [23] (2017)	Affiliations in system function calls, sensitive permissions	102 benign 219 malicious samples	FPR noted 7%	Lower TPR

5   Conclusions and Future Work

Although, Ensemble based machine learning has demonstrated its ability to provides high detection accuracy with binaries and manifext.xml files, but it has some inevitable limitations. Firstly, the source code based classification consider computationally expensive because it needs de-compilation of files preceding to analysis. Secondly, proposed technique only detect source code based malware, but it failed to detect structural features that encode method instruction order to fight obfuscated code. There are several issues remaining to be solved. In our future work, we will conduct experiments and publish results. We aim to extend the proposed framework to update the intended data structure of malicious keywords for detection of recently created malware. Another research focus is to combine the string features and structural features into a uniform feature space, they can treat into learning algorithm.

References

1. Wu, W., Hung, S.: DroidDolphin: a dynamic android malware detection framework using big data and machine learning. In; RACS 2014, 5–8 October 2014, Towson, MD, USA, pp. 247–253 (2014)
2. Talha, A., Alper, D.I., Aydin, C.: APK Auditor: permission-based Android malware detection system. Digit. Investig. **13**, 1–14 (2015)
3. Damodaran, A., Troia, F.D., Visaggio, C.A., Austin, T.H., Stamp, M.: A comparison of static, dynamic, and hybrid analysis for malware detection. J. Comput. Virol. Hack. Tech. **13**(1), 1–12 (2015). https://doi.org/10.1007/s11416-015-0261-z
4. Fan, M., et al.: Android malware familial classification and representative sample selection via frequent subgraph analysis. IEEE Trans. Inf. Forensics Secur. **13**(8), 1890–1906 (2018)
5. Idrees, F., Rajarajan, M., Conti, M., Chen, T.M., Rahulamathavan, Y.: PIndroid: a novel android malware detection system using ensemble learning methods. Comp. Secur. **68**, 36–46 (2017)
6. Narudin, F.A., Feizollah, A., Anuar, N.B., Gani, A.: Evaluation of machine learning classifiers for mobile malware detection. Soft Comput. **20**(1), 343–357 (2014). https://doi.org/10.1007/s00500-014-1511-6
7. Kabakus, A.T., Dogru, I.A.: An in-depth analysis of Android malware using hybrid techniques. Digit. Investig. **24**, 25–33 (2018)
8. Wang, W., Gao, Z., Zhao, M., Li, Y., Liu, J., Zhang, X.: DroidEnsemble: detecting Android malicious applications with ensemble of string and structural static features. IEEE Access **6**, 31798–31807 (2018)
9. Chen, S., et al.: Automated poisoning attacks and defenses in malware detection systems: an adversarial machine learning approach. Comput. Secur. **73**, 326–344 (2018)
10. Li, J., Sun, L., Yan, Q., Li, Z., Srisa-an, W., Ye, H.: Significant permission identification for machine-learning-based Android malware detection. IEEE Trans. Industr. Inf. **14**(7), 3216–3225 (2018)
11. Milosevic, N., Dehghantanha, A., Choo, K.R.: Machine learning aided Android malware classification. Comput. Electr. Eng. **61**, 266–274 (2017)
12. Rehman, Z., et al.: Machine learning-assisted signature and heuristic-based detection of malwares in Android devices. Comput. Electr. Eng. **69**, 828–841 (2018)

13. Wu, S., Wang, P., Li, X., Zhang, Y.: Effective detection of Android malware based on the usage of data flow APIs and machine learning. Inf. Soft. Technol. **75**, 17–25 (2016)
14. Kozik, R.: Distributing extreme learning machines with Apache Spark for NetFlow-based malware activity detection. Pattern Recognit. Lett. **101**, 14–20 (2018)
15. Ajay Kumara, M.A., Jaidhar, C.D.: Leveraging virtual machine introspection with memory forensics to detect and characterize unknown malware using machine learning techniques at hypervisor. Digit. Investig. **23**, 99–123 (2017)
16. Narayanan, A., Chandramohan, M., Chen, L., Liu, Y.: Context-aware, adaptive, and scalable Android malware detection through online learning. IEEE Trans. Emerg. Top. Comput. Intell. **1**(3), 157–176 (2017)
17. Feng, P., Ma, J., Sun, C., Xu, X., Ma, Y.: A novel dynamic Android malware detection system with ensemble learning. IEEE Access **6**, 30996–31011 (2018)
18. Moonsamy, V., Rong, J., Liu, S.: Mining permission patterns for contrasting clean and malicious Android applications. Future Gener. Comput. Syst. **36**, 122–132 (2014)
19. Calleja, A., Martín, A., Menéndez, H.D., Tapiador, J., Clark, D.: Picking on the family: disrupting Android malware triage by forcing misclassification. Expert Syst. Appl. **95**, 113–126 (2018)
20. Yousefi-Azar, M., Hamey, L.G.C., Varadharajan, V., Chen, S.: Malytics: a malware detection scheme. IEEE Access **6**, 49418–49431 (2018)
21. Saracino, A., Sgandurra, D., Dini, G., Martinelli, F.: Madam: effective and efficient behavior-based Android malware detection and prevention. IEEE Trans. Dependable Secure Comput. **15**(1), 83–97 (2018)
22. Sun, S., et al.: Real-time behavior analysis and identification for Android application. IEEE Access **6**, 38041–38051 (2018)
23. Wei, L., et al.: Machine learning-based malicious application detection of Android. IEEE Access **5**, 25591–25601 (2017). Special Section Internet-of-Things (IoT) Big Data Trust Management
24. Zhang, F., Coble, J.: Multilayer data-driven cyber-attack detection system for industrial control systems based on network, system, and process data. IEEE Trans. Industr. Inf. **15**(7), 4362–4370 (2019)
25. Du, D., Sun, Y., Ma, Y., Xiao, F.: A novel approach to detect malware variants based on classified behaviors. IEEE Access **7**, 81770–81782 (2019)
26. Domenick Morales-Molina, C., Santamaria-Guerrero, D., Sanchez-Perez, G., Toscano-Medina, K., Perez-Meana, H., Hernandez-Suarez, A.: Methodology for malware classification using a random forest classifier. In: IEEE International Autumn Meeting on Power, Electronics and Computing, ROPEC 2018 Ixtapa Mexico, pp. 1–6 (2018)
27. Kumar, R., Zhang, X., Wang, W., Khan, R., Kumar, J., Sharif, A.: A multimodal malware detection technique for Android IoT devices using various features. IEEE Access **7**, 64411–64421 (2019)

Green Computing: A Contribution Towards Better Future

Khawar Saleem[1](✉), Nadia Rasheed[1], Muhammad Zonain[1],
Salman Muneer[1], Abdul Rauf Bhatti[2], and Muhammad Amjad[1]

[1] University College of Engineering and Technology,
The Islamia University of Bahawalpur, Bahawalpur 63100, Pakistan
khawar.ks@gmail.com, nadia.rashid@iub.edu.pk
[2] Department of Electrical Engineering,
Government College University Faisalabad (GCUF), Faisalabad, Pakistan

Abstract. Energy efficiency has become one of the momentous factors in the development of computer systems. Increasingly, processors and memory subsystem hankering after power have reinforced the need for audacious power management. Green computing allude to environmentally viable computing by paring down the use of electricity as well as energy consumption, hence making the environment more eco-friendly. Perceptibly a practice of utilizing reckoning resources available to us in a very optimistic way. Data and Information, during transmission, from one system to another must be secure, also making sure that it does not compromise on green computational factors. Though many modern techniques with different experiments have been carried out to minimize hazardous environmental affects since vacuum tubes. Dynamic Voltage Scaling (DVS) has become an important consideration for designing dynamic and energy efficient processors yet not compromising over system performance, efficiency and low-cost maintainability. Moreover managing energy consumption of RAM has also become censorious, ranging from small portable devices to VLSI based systems. As applications are becoming more database-centric, pressurizing memory systems and subsystem, in very fast-pace and competitive environments. This paper discusses about comparison of Intel and AMD processors with power consumption factors, emphasizing DVS to achieve next level of energy-efficient CPUs for computing.

Keywords: DVS · Latency · Virgin resources · Green IT · Cryptography
E-waste · Benchmark

1 Introduction

Green computing is a term that is used in computer technologies i.e. environmentally responsible use of computers systems and its resources. It is also called Green Information Technology (Green IT) [1]. It began over couple of decades ago, when IT vendors and manufacturers started using green products and eco-friendly equipment's. With the passage of time, the strength of internet and IT equipment's usage is increased for this purpose. Green IT is defined as "the study and practice of designing,

© Springer Nature Singapore Pte Ltd. 2020
I. S. Bajwa et al. (Eds.): INTAP 2019, CCIS 1198, pp. 663–674, 2020.
https://doi.org/10.1007/978-981-15-5232-8_57

manufacturing, using disposing of monitors, printer storage devices and network and system efficiency and effectively with minimal or no impact on environment" [2].

As we have become more and more aware of the threats posed by the substances outlined on the Green Manufacturing Industries and footprints that our advancements in technologies are leaving on the environment, organizations have emerged that strive to educate the public and promote the use of less hazardous materials and better energy efficiency.

In this paper, a comparative study has been presented for Intel and AMD processors through environmentally monitored benchmark simulations to give insightful view of their power consumption factors. As well as, DVS has been discussed in reference of the requirements for next level energy efficient CPUs.

The paper is structured according to the sections as follows: Sect. 2 reviews briefly about some of the important and popular companies and agencies, which initiated Green Computing standards. Subsequently, DVS related studies and techniques are discussed for Intel and AMD manufacturers. In Sect. 3, benchmarked simulations are presented regarding power consumption factors of Intel and AMD processors. Discussion in Sect. 4 and paper ends in Sect. 5 with concluding remarks.

2 Relevant Literature

From the ancient times societies have been working hard to develop and improve life standards. Discovering new, fast, safe and effective technologies and to control everything on the Earth and beyond in eco-friendly way. Many advancement in IT technology have evolved in our daily lives, gradually becoming essentials of our life styles, hence leaving almost impossible to ignore environmental consequences.

Energy star is a labeling program which was one of the earliest initiatives launched by United States, in 1992, by Environmental Protection Agency (EPA) [3]. It began to promote all types of hardware of energy potency, additionally climate management instruments, and different technologies. Energy Star Computers are designed to consume less energy than standard computers and have already helped Americans, saving over 3.5T kWh of electricity since 1992, all through voluntary actions [3].

Another collaborative effort by Google and Intel in 2007, was a non-profit organization Climate Savers Computing Initiative (CSCI), comprised of various businesses and organizations who have committed to produce products that meet a set of efficiency specifications, with their stated mission to reduce energy consumption by computers by 50%, leading to a reduction in energy costs of over $5.5 billion [4].

Electronic Product Environmental Assessment Tool (EPEAT) on the other hand, "is a system that helps purchasers evaluate, compare, and select electronic products based on their environmental attributes" [5]. HP with the release of their rp5700 Business Desktop PC, in 2007, was the first company to receive a gold rating by meeting all 23 of the essential criteria. This model boasts an 80% efficient power supply, and 95% recyclable materials.

Regulations are currently in place to proscribe the use of common perilous substances such as mercury, cadmium, lead and chromium, or replacing them with safer alternatives, also promoting proper disposal of electrical equipment [6]. This is being accomplished by Restriction of Hazardous Substances (RoHs) directives under WEEE including but not limited to mobiles, old TV-sets, microwave ovens, personal computers, fridges and other consumer electronics i.e. fastest growing waste streams and expected to grow over 12 million tonnes by 2020 in EU [7, 8].

2.1 Intel and AMD Contribution

Generally, processor is an electronic chip which is used as brain of the computer to compute and enhance the overall system performance, management of power distribution throughout the infrastructure connected and simultaneous processing of multiple tasks via digitally embedded control lines, are core functionalities of CPU. Microchip implanted within a single CPU contains billions of transistors that processes instructions sent to it by application or system software programs operated by the user. Sizes of latest processors are becoming small and no. of transistors per processor are increasing vastly influenced by latest and 3-D technologies. They come in a number of sizes manufactured by different companies such as Intel and AMD.

The Intel processors are the next generation high-performance processors, fully compatible with the Multi cores CPU. They are Superscalar implementation of the x86 as well as x64 instruction sets. Techniques used to achieve this level of performance are tested comprehensively, focusing mainly over cryptographic ability, arithmetic and floating point operations, cache and memory latency and power management technologies.

AMD on the other hand comprises of multiple cores not limited to the odd numbers as Intel uses either dual, quad or octal-cores etc. AMD processors are also cost effective but compromises in terms of performance, power consumption, availability and temperature to which the CPU operates, have to be dealt with. AMD's performance lags up to a significant level as compared to Intel's processors.

2.2 Green Computing Correspondence

Complex tradeoffs are to be considered while taking into account of reducing power consumption, ultimately going towards green computing. There are multiple factors to which energy efficiency mostly depends upon while operating any computer system or laptop machine including CPU power dissipation, undervolting, program execution speed, DFS (Dynamic Frequency Scaling), temperature at which system operates and caveats etc. Those factors depend upon the particular system, load presented to it, power management goals and techniques implemented. When quick responses are needed, clocks and voltages might be raised together. Otherwise, to maximize saving they may both be kept low.

The contribution of ICT (Information and Communication Technology) industry to GHG emission is expected to reach about 9% globally, estimated by smart 2020 report [9]. Which means that controlling carbon footprints at production level is also important for the achievement of green computing. However this paper emphasizes over one approach i.e. Dynamic Voltage Scaling for Power Management.

2.3   DVS

Dynamic Voltage Scaling is widely used as part of strategies to manage switching power, specially in battery powered devices such as PDA's, cell phones and laptops. Low voltage modes are used in conjunction with lowered clock frequencies to minimize consumption associated with components such as CPUs and DSPs i.e. the frequency and voltage be raised only when significant computational power is needed.

Another crucial factor in terms of power consumption is leakage current, chips are often designed so that portions of them can be powered completely off. This is not usually viewed under DVS, because it is not limpid to the software. When idle constituents of main board can be turned off to save energy the efficiency of distinct voltage regulators start decreasing with increase in temperature, causing thermal increase in voltage-frequency pair, subsequently it may increase system power demands even faster than usual [10].

2.4   Previous DVS Implementations

DVS being one of the major aspect in designing and development of any computer system, researchers from all around the world have been taking under consideration the techniques to improve it by any means.

R. P. Martins and Seng-Pan U proposed a fully integrated DC to DC converter ring with over 100 phases. The design consists mainly of switch-based step down capacitor which is designed with a fast DVS feature for the microprocessor. The square ring design has 31 phases on each of the edge except on top where it has 30 phases [11].

However actual implementation of any of the proposed design comes with its own practical limitations. Researchers, Robert. W. Brodersen and Thomas D. Burd from University of California, Berkeley, proposed a momentous study containing most common but essential factors i.e. reducing capacitance, circuit delay variations, transition power dissipation, circuit design constraints and many more, affecting DVS design process practically vulnerable to some extent [12].

Another approach for designing a DVS based system is to stop CPU operation in transitory state abruptly. However the downside to this approach would be the augmentation in latency interrupt and as a result potentially applicable CPU clock cycles might be discarded [13].

2.5   DVS by Intel and AMD

Latest technological advancements are being carried out while it comes to improve the overall computer system efficiency by taking into consideration almost every aspect of the system. Specially, in laptop machines sizes are getting thinner and thinner while performance has to be up to the mark whether it is being used in routine office work or being run by a professional pro gamer. Both Intel and AMD have been pushing their limits to overcome high performance hence not compromising over system power efficiency.

Enhanced Intel SpeedStep Technology (EIST) is one of the marvelous effort by Intel focusing over power and thermal management, in their Core branded processors. EIST reduces the latency inherent with changing the voltage-frequency pair, thus allowing those transitions to occur more frequently. This allows for more granular, demand-based switching and can optimize the power-to-performance balance, based on the demands of the applications [14].

Mostly, the CPU in our laptops has a standardized clock which moderately determines how quickly it performs. In order to conserve power, the stated clock speed is the fastest unless we decide to over-clock. However, Intel's new Core i5 and Core i7 processors have ultra-low voltage demand as a way of improving battery life because of another feature called Turbo Boost. It has the ability of dynamically scaling up/down the clock speed of a processor depending upon the thermal headroom available, apart from being a great feature it is also the reason why Intel's latest processors are often superior to those from AMD [15].

The fact is also seconded as AMD cloned their first microprocessor Am286 by reverse engineering Intel's 80 × 86 architecture, with the help of database registers received as a result of "Technology Exchange Agreement" back in 1981 [16].

Unlike SpeedStep, AMD introduced PowerNow technology which is designed particularly for considerable power savings and enhanced battery life for end users. "PowerNow goes beyond simply ramping down to a lower processing speed when the unit is unplugged, hence limiting almost 75% of the power dissipation [17]. It actively monitors the system resources and programs being run to perform dynamic voltage/frequency transitions to a number of processing speeds," said AMD director Gary Baum, during a demonstration of the technology.

With the release of AMD K10 micro-architecture enhanced version of PowerNow with two main features was introduced by AMD, Dual Dynamic Power Management (DDPM) and Independent Dynamic Core Technology (IDCT) [18]. Latter deals specifically with individual core frequencies depending on their usage and access time. Cool'n'Quiet is yet another technology that allows the system to select the CPU speed automatically, also monitoring the power combination that matches instantaneous user performance needs, however it is only platform dependent and will work only with the dedicated hardware infrastructure built and defined within the system motherboard and BIOS respectively [19].

3   Benchmarking Methodology

Firstly, a detailed review and market survey was carried out by professional PC users to identify the available resources, state-of-the-art technology and architecture manufacturers for careful selection of hardware infrastructure for benchmarking. Out of IBM, Intel, Fujitsu, Mediatek, Nvidia, AMD, Qualcom and Samsung; Intel and AMD were selected for experimentation, powering Dell Vostro 14 and HP Elitebook 745 respectively. As most of the popular laptop manufacturers like Samsung, Lenovo, Dell and HP, were either using Intel or AMD's microprocessors within their machines.

Comparison between Intel core I7 7th generation (running 7500U processor with 14 nm technology built with cache level up to 3, and level 1 having separate Data and Instruction channel) and AMD A8 Pro (built with 28 nm microprocessor technology having cache up to level 2 of 2 MB), has been carried out measuring multiple aspects of the connected infrastructure.

We setup two laptops and installed multiple benchmarking softwares including PCMark 10, CPU-Z, Speccy, HW Monitor, Fraps and Sandra Lite Titanium on each laptop in order to run and test different parameters under constrained environment [20–24].

Technical specification for both of laptop hardware can be seen in the following Table 1 and 2.

Table 1. Dell Vostro 14 laptop specifications

HP Elite Book 745 laptop hardware specifications	
Parameter	Description
OS name	Miscrosoft Window 7 Ultimate
Version	6.1.7601 Service Pack 1 Build 7601
System manufacturing	Hewlett-Packard
System model	HP EliteBook 745 G2
System type	x64 based PC
BIOS version/date	Hewlett-Packard M84 Ver.01.08, 7/22/2015
SMBIOS version	2.7
Motherboard model	221C
Hardware abstraction layers	Version = "6.1.7601.17514"
Install physical memory (RAM)	4.00 GBs
Total virtual memory	6.89 GB
Page file space	3.45 GB

Table 2. HP Elite Book 745 laptop specifications

INTEL CORE i7 7500U 7th Gen. processor parameters		
Parameter	Description	
Max. TDP (POWER)	15.0 W	
Technology	14 nm	
Core VID	0.706 V	
Memory	8 Gb DDR3	
Cache		
Level 1 data	2 × 32 KB (8-way)	
Level 1 instruction	2 × 32 KB (8-way)	
Level 2	2 × 256 KB (16-way)	
Level 3	4 MB (16-way)	
Processor	Max. value	Normal value
CPU Core 00	100%	4%
CPU Core 01	100%	4%
CPU Core 02	100%	9%
CPU Core 03	98%	1%
Core temperature	82 °C	73 °C

The process of benchmarking was carried out under careful observation at 22 °C room temperature. Our first test system had built in Intel and other AMD microprocessor chip. Both of them were placed over rigid flat and ventilated surface having enough space to provide proper air intake for the processor to work through heavy load. While on stand-by, core voltage readings were 0.706 V for system 1 and 0.812 V for system 2, with initial core temperatures 73.0 °C and 88.0 °C respectively. Slight increment in voltage reading and notable temperature increment was observed as soon as CPU's were hit by maximum load operation.

However, these readings were observed with dummy load over processor generated by CPUID-CPUZ tool and scenario would definitely be different while working with power-hungry applications. A summary of our benchmarking simulation machines with minimum and maximum load over all the connected cores and their respective voltage readings along with other physical parameters appears in Table 3.

Table 3. Intel Core i7 7500U 7th Gen. processer parameters

AMD A8 Pro processor parameters		
Parameter	Description	
Max. TDP (POWER)	19.0 W	
Technology	28 nm	
Core VID	0.812 V	
Memory	4 Gb DDR3	
Cache		
Level 1 data	4 × 16 KB (4-way)	
Level 1 instruction	4 × 96 KB (3-way)	
Level 2	2 × 2 MB (16-way)	
Processor cores	Max. value	Normal value
CPU Core 00	100%	17%
CPU Core 01	100%	12%
CPU Core 02	100%	14%
CPU Core 03	100%	9%
Core temperature	100.4 °C	88.0 °C

For over 5 min this test was run, maximum temperature observed was 82 °C for Intel and 100.4 °C for AMD. No significant increment in voltage reading was seen during, or even after 10 min of releasing the maximum load.

3.1 Power Management

Efficiency in case of power management includes two factors, which is Power consumed by processor and ALU Integer Power Efficiency, measured in GIPS (Giga Instructions Per Second) [25].

This benchmark test is specifically designed to measure the efficiency of the Power Management Technologies employed by processors. Anyhow this does not test the efficiency of other infrastructure connected. Also, during the test system consumes maximum power by switching into high-performance state, hence testing the machine to its limits.

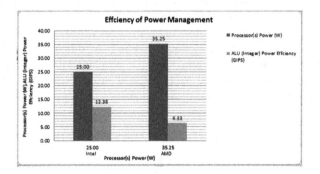

Fig. 1. Power management and ALU power efficiency

As a result, higher power consumption by AMD can clearly be seen in Fig. 1, as well as half the efficiency of the Integer ALU with respect to the Intel Processor.

3.2 Cryptographic Performance

When it comes to test the limits of any processor cryptographic ability is what really tests the system to its limits [26]. As shown in Fig. 2, system running Intel processor performed just right, measuring 3.594 Gb/s utilizing all 4 core units at 25 W power consumption factor, whereas system 2 went out of range consuming way more power (35.25 W) than prior and resulting 1.235 Gb/s cryptographic performance.

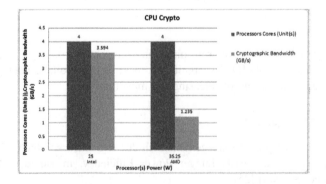

Fig. 2. Cryptographic bandwidth measurement

3.3 Access Time of Cache and Memory

Architectural parameters of the system decide the total amount of memory that can be added to a computer. In this section, we've described briefly the behavior of Intel and AMD processors and their ability to access cache-memory cycles.

In our test, system 1 and 2 are equipped with 8 Gb and 4 Gb physical memory. While accessing data to or from the cache and memory, smaller the time better the performance of the chip. Figure 3 explains clearly that, It took 129.8 ns at 31.03 W of chipset power for AMD and 24.8 ns at 12.04 W for Intel chipset to perform this very operation. Though installed physical memory of system one is twice still the consumed energy is almost 2/3rd and access time ratio is about 1:5, which is a bigger disappointment at AMD's side.

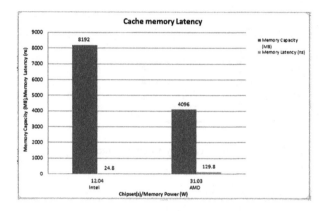

Fig. 3. Cache memory latency

3.4 Arithmetic and Floating Operations

This test includes the performance of processors regarding arithmetic and floating point operations. Readings are measured in Aggregate Native Performance [27], GOPS (Giga Operations Per Second) as shown in the Fig. 4, Intel again beats AMD with remarkable Integer and Floating Point calculations, maintaining the power consumption to minimum.

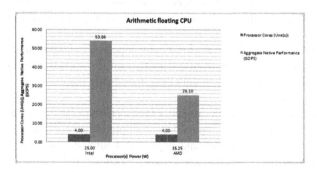

Fig. 4. Arithmetic floating CPU

3.5   Memory Latency

RAM latency refers to the delay that occurs during data transmission while moving to and from the processor. It describes the amount of time for the processor to retrieve data from RAM and it takes more time to fetch data from RAM than it takes to retrieve it from cache memory [28]. Overall memory score is taken in unit kPT (1 GPT = 1000 MPT, 1 MPT = 1000 kPT, 1 kPT = 1000 PT). Through comparison, though installed RAM capacity of Intel was twice, the overall memory performance was over 3 times better than AMD as shown in Fig. 5.

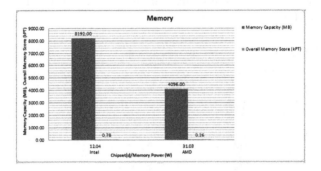

Fig. 5. Memory capacity vs chipset memory power

4   Discussion and Analysis

In terms of Hardware infrastructure there are different kinds of microprocessors, motherboard manufacturers globally in ICT industry. However not everywhere has access to the state-of-the-art of the technology as AMD's latest "Ryzen Threadripper 2990WX" is claimed to be world's first 32-cores processor chip while Intel's latest 9th generation processor which according to Intel is "The most powerful generation of Intel Core Desktop Processors" [29, 30]. Whereas hands-on availability throughout the middle east is "Ax series" and "7th Generation" for AMD and Intel respectively.

As far as benchmarking methodology is concerned the same problem is risen with up to the mark tools, specifically designed to test the hardware limits and performance thresholds while installed infrastructure does not even supports such heavy tools to be tested on such machines.

This study focuses mainly over already developed ICT equipment, processors to be specific, and their ability to perform efficiently and eco-friendly. In this way, Green Computing making a difference to anticipate worldwide warming that caused to devastate common atmosphere.

The limited resources result limited experimentation, in future the findings of research can be extended by comparing multiple processors including Qualcom, Mediatek, Nvidia, IBM, Samsung and Fujitsu, not limited to Intel and AMD manufacturers only. Also more discrete and intense benchmarking with heaviest and latest tools would result more detailed analysis. In addition to DVS, techniques like DVFS

(Dynamic Voltage and Frequency Scaling), PDP (Power-Delay Product), DFS (Dynamic Frequency Scaling), EDP (Energy-Delay Product), PMM (Power Measurement Module) and E-Waste management altogether would incorporate maximize energy saving resulting Green Computing as well as Carbon free Environment.

5 Conclusion

The concept of Green responsible computing is emerging gradually in our daily lives as technology advances. It not only reduces environmental impact (less e-waste fewer virgin resources needed for mass production) but also improves device's longevity. However the available resources of disposing e-waste off properly, to a common person are none to very few, leaving the waste off the roads. Governments, from all around the globe has to play their role vitally focusing mainly over safety of our environment by all the means necessary.

When it comes to industrial manufacturing and mass production of IT resources, Dynamic strategies needs to be adopted, making sure off safest end devices production. Up to date research and development programs needs to be considered while designing and manufacturing Computer Systems and mobile devices.

Though Intel has brought many technological advancements lately, some of them are already implemented in their 9th generation core processors, but still there's always room for more perfection. Unlike AMD which seems to divert their focus from basic computing to Gamers specific domain i.e. Graphic Cards. As tested intensely, AMD lacked by many factors, including but not limited to Cryptographic performance, temperature variations, access times of cache/memory and power management etc.

References

1. Loeser, F., Erek, K., Loeser, F.: Aligning Green IT with environmental strategies : development of a conceptual framework that leverages sustainability and firm competitiveness. In: Proceedings Of AMCIS (Americas Conference On Information Systems, Detroit, Michigan, vol. 7, August 2011
2. Murugesan, S.: Harnessing Green IT : principles and practices. IT Prof. 10(1), 24–33 (2008)
3. Hoffman, J.: Energy star overview. https://www.energystar.gov/about Accessed 03 Dec 2018
4. ENERGY STAR: Climate Savers Computing Initiative White Paper Issued by Govt. of America with the Collaboration of Google and Intel in July, p. 1, (2008)
5. Green Electronics Council: Electronic product environmental assessment tool (EPEAT). https://www.epa.gov/greenerproducts/electronic-product-environmental-assessment-tool-epeat. Accessed 13 Jan 2019
6. European Union: Official Journal of the European Union, Legislative Acts Under Regulation (Eu) 2017/2101 of the European Parliament as Regards Information Exchange On, and an Early Warning System and Risk Assessment Procedure for New Psychoactive Substances, by EU Govt., vol. 12 (2017)
7. European Commission: The Rohs directives (2017). http://ec.europa.eu/environment/waste/rohs_eee/index_en.htm. Accessed 09 Feb 2019

8. European Commission: Waste Electrical & Electronic Equipment (WEEE). http://ec.europa.eu/environment/waste/weee/index_en.htm. Accessed 14 Feb 2019
9. Smarr, L.: Project greenlight optimizing cyber-infrastructure for a carbon-constrained world. Computer **43**, 22–27 (2010)
10. Bi, M.: Optimizing processor and memory for Green computing, Published By UMI Dissertations Publishing, The University Of Arizona, pp. 21–22 (2011)
11. Jiang, J., Martins, R.P., Lu, Y., Ki, W., Yue, C.P., Sin, S.: ISSCC 2015/Session 20/Energy harvesting and SC power conversion/20.4 with Fast-Dvs for microprocessors. In: IEEE International Solid-State Circuits Conference, pp. 364–366 (2015)
12. Burd, T.D., Brodersen, R.W.: Design issues for dynamic voltage scaling. In: Proceedings of International Symposium on Low Power Electronics and Design, University Of California, Barkeley, pp. 9–14, July 2000
13. Semião, J., IST INESC-ID: Dynamic voltage and frequency scaling for long-term and fail-safe operation. In: The Finale Workshop on Manufacturable and Dependable Multicore Architectures at Nanoscale (MEDIAN Finale 2015), Tallinn, Estonia, pp. 1–6, November 2015
14. Intel: Enhanced Intel® Speedstep® Technology for the Intel® Pentium® M Processor. Official White Paper, no. 3, p. 4, March 2004
15. Intel: Intel® Turbo Boost Max Technology (TBMT) 3.0. Production version 1.1 Release Notes, no. 5, pp. 1–10, May 2018
16. Quindara, H.: History of AMD — Advanced MICRO DEVICES, Inc. (2017). https://medium.com/dotmachines/history-of-amd-advanced-micro-devices-inc-c4e6bfa35a24. Accessed 09 May 2019
17. AMD PowerNow! TM Technology: Dynamically Manages Power and Performance. Informational White Paper, no. 11, p. 8. November 2000
18. Shvets, G.: AMD Enhanced PowerNOW! technology. http://www.cpu-world.com/glossary/e/enhanced_powernow_technology.html. Accessed 23 Feb 2019
19. AMD'S Cool'n'Quiet Software. Release Notes For Version 1.0.8.1, p. 1. September 2005
20. UL Benchmarks: PCMARK 10 benchmarking software. https://benchmarks.ul.com/pcmark10. Accessed 05 Nov 2018
21. CPUID: CPUID-CPUZ benchmarking tool. https://www.cpuid.com/softwares/cpu-z.html. Accessed 10 Nov 2018
22. CCleaner: Speccy HW information tool. https://www.ccleaner.com/speccy. Accessed 10 Nov 2018
23. Fraps: Benchmarking software. http://www.fraps.com/. Accessed: 05 Nov 2018
24. Sandra: Sandra Titanium. Sisoftware, UK (2018). https://www.sisoftware.co.uk/. Accessed 05 Nov 2018
25. Agrawal, V.D., Nelson, V.P.: Computer architecture and design performance of a computer (Chapter 4). ELEC5200-001/6200-001 performance lecture. Department Of Electrical and Computer Engineering, Auburn University, Auburn, no. 4 (2013)
26. Gaspar, L.: Crypto-processor – architecture, programming and evaluation of the security. Ph. D. thesis Presented to obtain doctor degree. Université Jean Monnet - Saint-Etienne, France, p. 38 (2012)
27. Marklogic Server: Aggregate Functions. Search Developer's Guide Provided By Marklogic Corporation, Singapore Pte. Ltd., pp. 468–470 (2017)
28. Webopedia: Ram latency. https://www.webopedia.com/term/r/ram_latency.html. Accessed 10 May 2019
29. AMD: AMD Ryzentm Threadrippert 2990WX. https://www.amd.com/en/products/cpu/amd-ryzen-threadripper-2990wx. Accessed 08 Sep 2019
30. B Intel: 9 Generation Intel® Core TM Desktop Processors, pp. 1–6

An Intelligent Approach to Detect Actuator Signal Errors Based on Remnant Filter

Naveed Riaz[✉], Syed Irtiza Ali Shah, Faisal Rehman,
Syed Omer Gilani, and Emad-udin

National University of Sciences and Technology (NUST), Islamabad, Pakistan
engrnaveedriaz@gmail.com

Abstract. Linear electro-mechanical actuators are commonly found in a variety of critical dynamic systems including hazardous robotic applications and various aerospace applications, and are specifically designed on the basis of required operating functional parameters. The performance of electro-mechanical actuators significantly affects the performance of overall system. This paper works to improve the reliability of linear electro-mechanical actuators through analytical redundancy for critical applications. A fault diagnostic algorithm is designed based on dynamic mathematical model and a remnant filter is implemented to detect actuator faults. The remnant filter generates residual signal proportional to the induced fault. Fault detection thresholds are set and decision logic is established to compare residual signal with the lower and upper threshold constants. This designed diagnostic filter is tested experimentally on a fault diagnostic testing setup and results of designed model have been validated.

Keywords: Linear electro-mechanical actuator · Analytical redundancy · Model-based fault detection · Remnant filter · Fault diagnostic algorithm

1 Introduction

The reliability of critical dynamic systems that operate in severe environments including robotic UGV's for safety applications as well as aerospace systems need additional consideration in order to ensure their safe operation. In case of aerospace systems, commercial aircrafts or UAV's are required to meet two major reliability requirements i.e., no single disastrous failure per 109 flight hours and no single point failure [1, 2]. For large aircrafts, these critical reliability requirements are achieved through the use of redundancy in hardware. In case of Boeing 777, triple redundant flight computer architecture and multiple redundant actuators are deployed [2]. For small aircrafts as well as critical ground vehicle systems, redundancy in hardware is unaffordable especially where there is a weight, volume, cost or power constraints. This paper discusses the use of analytical redundancy as a substitute but effective way of improving the reliability of critical systems. Specifically, this work uses mathematical model-based approach and defines a model-based algorithm to detect faults for linear electro-mechanical actuators.

Analytical redundancy can be provided through a model-based fault finding and fixing (FFF) filter. This FFF filter, also known as a diagnostic filter, creates residuals

© Springer Nature Singapore Pte Ltd. 2020
I. S. Bajwa et al. (Eds.): INTAP 2019, CCIS 1198, pp. 675–683, 2020.
https://doi.org/10.1007/978-981-15-5232-8_58

which allow the reliable identification in case a fault occurs. Thus, the residuals should approach to zero in no fault situation for all control signal, external disturbance and noise signal inputs. In the case of presence of a fault, the residual should generate amplitude oscillation proportional to the extent of fault induced. Various methodologies for dealing with fault diagnosis and fixing filter design problems and providing their solutions are available in the literature work [3, 4] and [5].

Analytical redundancy can be effectively applied for small aerospace systems either at the system or part level. The system level approaches, like the one used in [6, 7] and [8] combines aircraft system dynamics models with different inertial (position) measurements (linear and angular). The system level approach becomes quite challenging as it requires accurate and precise models of the flight system dynamics which are usually not available for low power and low cost UAV system [9, 10]. On the other hand, fault diagnosis and isolation algorithms can be developed at the critical elements level like at sensor or electro-mechanical actuator level.

Electro-mechanical actuators' faults can be identified by using fault detection filters, which investigates the actuator input and output signals. This approach was previously used for hydraulic actuation system for big military or passenger aircrafts [11, 12]. This part or subassembly level analysis requires some additional sensing elements to measure the response of actual actuator output position without the need of accurate flight dynamics models [13, 14].

This paper suggests an approach to design critical component-level failure diagnosis algorithm for servo-actuators that impart and control desired motion to control surfaces and thus serve a vital position in the overall system for low power and cost UAV systems. The fault detection architecture, described in Sect. 2 below, requires actuator model along with corresponding sensor to measure and analyze actual servo actuator output position [15, 18, 22]. The actuator fault detection model along with remnant filter design is developed in Sect. 3 and in the end; the developed algorithm is validated on experimental testing setup developed using both no-fault and faulty actuator as discussed in Sect. 4.

2 Servo Actuator Fault Detection: Design Architecture

A complex dynamic electro-mechanical system like an unmanned airplane may undergo failure in different ways. Timely detection of upcoming faults and the knowledge of the cause of these faults may save dangerous failure. Any breakdown in electro-mechanical actuators severely disturb the entire system which may lead to loss of planned mission and loss of system control. In this section we present a description of the types of actuator failure modes encountered on the aircraft. An overview of the fault detection approach to address aircraft actuator failures is also presented here.

2.1 UAV Actuator Failure Modes

There are a number of different failure modes that may occur in a UAV electro-mechanical linear actuator during its operation [17]. All these modes of failure may be classified as being catastrophic (most severe), critical (more severe), significant (severe), or minor (least severe), according to the flight standards defined by NASA Failure Modes Analysis Cell (FMEC). In this paper we deal with the following two modes of failure that may encounter in flight tests:

Critical Fault Mode: These faults may be catastrophic in nature and may occur due to any damage in the actuator output linkage or drive shaft or due to any misaligned or unbalanced surface. This fault may lead to mission or control loss and may severely damage the system.

Uncertain Fault Mode: These faults may occur due to any sudden damage to output shaft, gears or any other mechanical linkage under loading. These may also occur due to slippage of gears or any other member. This may lead to unexpected loss of mission.

2.2 Fault Detection Structure

Figure 1 below shows basics of fault detection structure developed in this paper. In this architecture, the operator sends instructions through the flight computer to the servo actuator resulting in desired motion control of actuating surface. The performance parameters of electro-mechanical actuator are examined by keeping record of the input-output data. This recorded actuator data is then given to the remnant filter which generates a residual signal based on the mode of failure. The remnant filter is basically a mathematical model based fault diagnosis filter which includes a precise model of the servo actuator. This model, after analysis gives an estimation of the actuator true position output. Decision logic is finally applied to declare the existence of induced fault. Further details on the FFF design are discussed in Sect. 3.

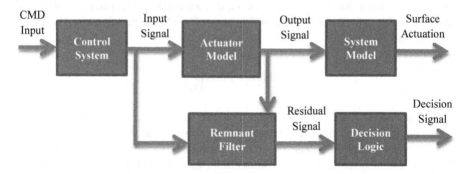

Fig. 1. Actuator fault diagnosis architecture block diagram

3 Servo Actuator Fault Detection: Model Design

This section discusses the approach to define servo actuator fault detection model. For fault diagnosis, remnant filter is implemented to detect actuator faults. The fault diagnosis based on model is explained in [3] as the diagnosis of faults of a system from the comparison of measured system parameters with preceding information charac-terized by the system's developed mathematical model through the analysis of generated residual quantities. The identified actuator model shown in Sect. 2 gives this preceding information, while the input and output signals are the known and desired system measurements. The fault detection filter based on this resultant model uses system parameters measurements as required inputs to generate residual signal which is likely to undergo faults.

The design of fault diagnostic filter for the servo actuator should work to:

1) Uncouple the input signal from the output
2) Couple the fault signal with the residual, and
3) Should be stable and accurate.

Various methodologies to solve this filter design problem based on observer-based approaches or similarity space calculations are available in literature. The work [16, 19, 20] describes in detail the design problems that are directly resolvable and all these approaches generate the same fault diagnostic filter. These design problems are directly solvable since no unknown inputs are needed to be decoupled from the system. The methodology used in this paper to solve the remnant filter design problem for linear actuator design model is based on simple void space calculations like the work given in [21]. This method involves fundamental arithmetical operations and offers the designer with the choice to directly select filter poles.

Modeling servo actuator faults in addition to other inputs, the input output form is given by the relation:

$$x(s) = H_{ft}(s) . \{v(s) + f(s)\} \tag{1}$$

Where, $x(s)f(s)$ and $v(s)$ are the Laplace transformed quantities of input servo position $x(t)$, the input fault (t) and the input command $v(t)$ respectively. The fault detection problem for the system defined in above Eq. (1) can be solved by designing a remnant filter.

$$rem(s) = T(s) . \begin{bmatrix} x_s \\ v_s \end{bmatrix} \tag{2}$$

Where, $rem(s)$ is the Laplace transformed quantity of the residual signal $rem(t)$ and $T(s)$ being the remnant filter. The remnant filter takes in to account the command input signal v available and the actuator position x measured to generate residual signal **rem**. The idea of void space approach becomes clearer by merging Eqs. (1) and (2) resulting in

$$rem(s) = T(s) . \begin{bmatrix} H_{ft}(s) \\ 1 \end{bmatrix} v(s) + T(s) . \begin{bmatrix} H_{ft}(s) \\ 0 \end{bmatrix} f(s) \tag{3}$$

The residual signal **r** will be zero in no- fault scenario and non-zero if any fault occurs. Moreover, the residual signal may also be zero in case of no-fault ($f(s) = 0$) only if input $u(s)$ is decoupled. Thus, the remnant filter $T(s)$ must assure

$$T(s) \cdot \begin{bmatrix} H_{fi}(s) \\ 1 \end{bmatrix} = 0 \tag{4}$$

It implies that remnant filter $T(s)$ associates with the left void space of $H_{fi}(s)$. This filter creates the residual signal r as a difference between measured actuator position x and its estimate $x^{\wedge} = H_{fi}$. The impact of input signal u when decoupled from the residual signal r leaves only fault signal f

$$rem(s) = H_{fi}(s)f(s) \tag{5}$$

The above equation allows the detection of fault signal. Filter designed via the calculation of vectors-polynomial basis for the required void space approach gives the designer with maximum freedom of design.

The detection of a fault involves a decision logic that compares the generated residual signal r with the lower and upper lower threshold constant τ. The constant i termed as decision variable is defined by the equation

$$i = \begin{pmatrix} 0 \;\; if \;\; \tau > r > \; -\tau \\ 1 \;\; otherwise \end{pmatrix}$$

The above relation indicates the absence of fault ($i = 0$) or presence of a fault in the system ($i = 1$). The designed fault diagnostic filter and its connected decision logic can be applied to the servo actuator system to validate the results of designed model.

4   Servo Actuator Fault Detection: Model Validation and Results

This section shows time and frequency domain results to justify the developed model and validate its accuracy. Frequency domain techniques were applied using MATLAB to detect the actuator fault detection model. A fast Fourier transformation (FFT) of the input-output signal was analyzed and observed frequency response and transfer functions were found. The MATLAB function *"spa"* was applied to get smooth frequency response. This function measures frequency response using spectral analysis with constant frequency resolution. To give smooth estimation and minimize bias, optimum window width was selected.

Figure 2 and 3 shows frequency response magnitude and phase variation whereas Fig. 4 demonstrates the model fit transfer function frequency response compared with the smoothed frequency response of servo actuator.

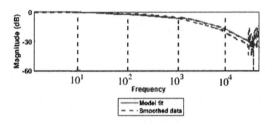

Fig. 2. Frequency response - magnitude

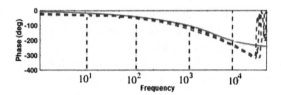

Fig. 3. Frequency response - phase

The normalized magnitude error is shown in figure below.

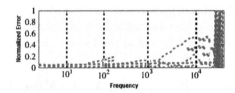

Fig. 4. Model fit normalized magnitude errors

Figure 5 shows time-domain results validation executed using test data. Actuator commands are used as input signal to the servo control at a sample rate of 200 Hz. The output signal obtained from the actuator model designed above gives the actuator response with good accuracy. The error between actual output of actuator and the simulated value in terms of standard deviation was found to be about 0.3°. It is important to recognize that all these actuator signal measurements are in unloaded condition. There may be a significant difference when actual flight data will be used of output actuation surfaces.

4.1 Fault Diagnostic Test Setup

Figure 6 below describes the fundamental components of fault diagnostic test setup used for actuator study. The purpose of this setup is to achieve lab level investigation of servo actuator used in actual flight for prototype modeling and fault detection. The control circuit based on microcontroller is used to control the Servo actuator. Servo actuator motor and feedback device is given power through a DC battery source. A common ground is established between microcontroller, servo actuator motor and

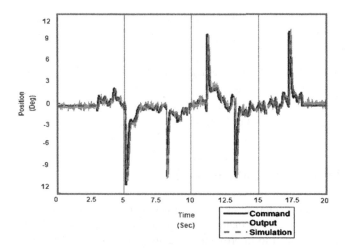

Fig. 5. Servo actual output vs. simulated output

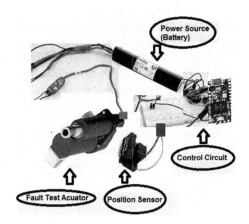

Fig. 6. Diagnostic test setup

feedback. Servo actuator motor is connected with PWM drive. An external position sensor is attached to this setup for output position measurement of the fault test servo actuator. Before testing, all feedback device measurements are calibrated.

The actuator model as verified above can now be considered as the true estimated output of the actuator. Later if the actuator undergoes any fault, this output would be considered as reference to reflect the presence of fault. Based on the technique described above, fault diagnosis can be done to avoid any failure. Upon careful measurement and analysis, it was found that the scheme devised in this work is highly helpful for the desired purpose. To confirm the repeatability of this overall system, multiple experiments can be conducted with different actuators under different loading profiles (Table 1).

Table 1. Servo actuator test result

Parameter	Value
Bandwidth	32.3 rad/s
Response time	0.09 s
Rise time	0.18 s
Slew rate	85°/s
Transfer function	$\dfrac{1.58 \times 10^5}{s^2 + 435s + 1.1 \times 10^5}$

5   Conclusions and Future Work

This work focused on modeling of servo actuator system and development of fault diagnostic filter for servo actuators. A remnant filter-based fault diagnostic methodology was implemented to improve the reliability of actuators. The focus of this work was to identify any undesirable behavior of servo actuator. A lab level testing setup was built to investigate difference in servo actuator response. The results of a fault free actuator were considered as a reference to identify faults of faulty actuators.

The technique developed and the experiment performed currently does not cater the effect of impact loading and aerodynamic loading that the actuator undergoes during operational working. For future work, the model designed and the experimental setup can be upgraded to consider effect of these types of loading. Improvement in the testing setup can be helpful in developing more precise simulations and models.

Acknowledgement. The authors would like to acknowledge their seniors, colleagues, professors, and lab technical staff for their co-operation, suggestions, observations and input regarding this work. We are also thankful to the technical manager and lab supervisor of the concerned organization where we performed our lab/experimental work. We are thankful to everyone for his best wishes.

References

1. Collinson, R.: Introduction to Avionics Systems. Springer, Boston (2003). https://doi.org/10.1007/978-1-4419-7466-2
2. Yeh, Y.: Triple-triple redundant 777 primary flight computer. In: Proceedings on the 1996 Aerospace Applications Conference, pp. 293–307 (1996)
3. Chen, J., Patton, R.: Robust Model-Based Fault Diagnosis for Dynamic Systems. Kluwer academic Publishers, Boston (1999)
4. Gertler, J.: Fault Detection and Diagnosis in Engineering Systems. Marcel Dekker Inc., New York (1998)
5. Frank, P.: Fault diagnosis in dynamic systems using analytical and knowledge-based redundancy-a survey and some new results. Automatica **26**(3), 459–474 (1990)
6. Pandita, R., Bokor, J., Balas, G.: Closed-loop performance metrics for fault detection and isolation filter and controller interaction. Int. J. Robust Nonlinear Control **23**, 419–438 (2013)

7. Freeman, P., Pandita, R., Srivatsava, N., Balas, G.: Model-based and data-driven fault detection performance for a small UAV. IEEE/ASME Trans. Mechatron. **18**, 1300–1309 (2013)
8. Ma, L., Zhang, Y.: DUKF-based GTM UAV fault detection and diagnosis with nonlinear and LPV models. In: IEEE/ASME International Conference on Mechatronics and Embedded Systems and Applications (MESA), pp. 375–380 (2010)
9. Bateman, F., Noura, H., Ouladsine, M.: Actuators fault diagnosis and tolerant control for an unmanned aerial vehicle. In: 16th IEEE International Conference on Control Applications (2007)
10. Yang, X., Warren, M., Arain, B., Upcroft, B., Gonzalez, F., Mejias, L.: A UKF-based estimation strategy for actuator fault detection of UASs. In: 2013 International Conference on Unmanned Aircraft Systems (ICUAS), USA, pp. 516–525 (2013)
11. Zolghadri, A.: The challenge of advanced model-based FDIR techniques for aerospace systems: the 2011 situation. In: Proceedings of 4th European Conference for Aerospace Sciences (2011)
12. Goupil, P.: AIRBUS state of the art and practices on FDI and FTC. Control Eng. Pract. **19**, 524–539 (2011)
13. Vanek, B., Edelmayer, A., Szab, Z., Bokor, J.: Bridging the gap between theory and practice in LPV fault detection for flight control actuators. Control Eng. Pract. **31**, 171–182 (2014)
14. Varga, A., Ossmann, D.: LPV-techniques based robust diagnosis of flight actuator faults. Control Eng. Pract. **31**, 135–147 (2014)
15. Reti, I., Lukatsi, M., Vanek, B., Gozse, I., Bakos, A., Bokor, J.: Smart mini actuators for safety critical unmanned aerial vehicles. In: Proceedings of 2nd Conference on Control and Fault-Tolerant Systems (SysTol 2013), pp. 474–479 (2013)
16. Lie, F., Dorobantu, A., Taylor, B., Gebre-Egziabher, D., Seiler, P., Balas, G.: An airborne experimental test platform: from theory to flight (part 2). In: InsideGNSS, pp. 40–47, May/June 2014
17. Freeman, P., Balas, G.: Actuation failure modes and effects analysis for a small UAV. In: American Control Conference (ACC), pp. 1292–1297 (2014)
18. Owens, D., Cox, D., Morelli, E.: Development of a low-cost sub-scale aircraft for flight research: the FASER project. In: 25th AIAA Aerodynamic Measurement Technology and Ground Testing Conference, June 2006
19. Lie, F., Dorobantu, A., Taylor, B., Gebre-Egziabher, D., Seiler, P., Balas, G.: An airborne experimental test platform: from theory to flight (part 1). In: InsideGNSS, pp. 44–58, March/April 2014
20. Gertler, J.: Analytical redundancy methods in fault detection and isolation. In: IFAC/IMACS Symposium on Fault Detection, Supervision and Safety for Technical Processes SAFEPROCESS, pp. 9–21 (1991)
21. Amos, J., Bergquist, E., Cole, J., Phillips, J., Reimann, S., Shuster, S.: UAV for reliability, December 2013. http://www.aem.umn.edu/ ~ SeilerControl/Papers/SeilerAll.html
22. Frisk, E., Nyberg, M.: A minimal polynomial basis solution to residual generation for fault diagnosis in linear systems. Automatica **37**, 1417–1424 (2001)

Driving Activity Recognition of Motorcyclists Using Smartphone Sensor

Aasim Raheel, Muhammad Ehatisham-ul-Haq, Anees Iqbal, Hanan Ali,
and Muhammad Majid[✉]

Department of Computer Engineering,
University of Engineering and Technology Taxila, Taxila, Pakistan
{asim.raheel,m.majid}@uettaxila.edu.pk

Abstract. Smartphone sensors ubiquitously provide an unobtrusive opportunity to develop solutions for road anomaly detection, driving behavior analysis, and activity recognition. Driver's activity recognition is important for monitoring streets and narrow lanes where employed vehicles cannot get along. In this paper, smartphone sensor is used to monitor driving activity of motorcyclists. Motorcyclists are asked to follow a predefined path and gyroscope data is recorded from the phone, which is placed in motorcyclist pocket. Features are selected from twelve extracted statistical features from the recorded gyroscope data to classify four driving activities i.e., left turn, right turn, U-turn, and a straight path. Three different classifiers i.e., Bayes Net, random forest, and support vector machine are used to classify four motorcyclists driving activities. It is evident that the random forest classifies four motorcyclist driving activities with the highest accuracy of 86.51%.

Keywords: Motorcyclist driving activity · Smartphone · Gyroscope · Feature extraction · Machine learning

1 Introduction

World population is increasing day by day, which results in the number of vehicles and road networks. Road navigation and safety have become more persistent and complex with the passage of time throughout the world, especially in under-developed countries [17]. In the last decade, worldwide road traffic accidents, injuries, and deaths have become unacceptably high [19]. Due to increase in usage of smartphones, ubiquitous sensing provides a cost-effective solution and paves the way towards monitoring road anomalies, provide navigation, routing, and traffic analysis. The road accidents can be associated with a range of factors, including road anomalies such as bumps, potholes, and driving behavior. Road anomalies not only affect the driving behavior of the user while driving, but also affect the condition of the vehicle. It is also a challenging task to monitor narrow lanes for navigation where large vehicles cannot be driven. In the last few years, many vehicle manufacturing companies have developed solutions for vehicle monitoring and driving behavior analysis. However, these solutions are only available

© Springer Nature Singapore Pte Ltd. 2020
I. S. Bajwa et al. (Eds.): INTAP 2019, CCIS 1198, pp. 684–694, 2020.
https://doi.org/10.1007/978-981-15-5232-8_59

in certain models of the vehicle and are very costly. Few studies have also shown interest in developing automated methods for collecting information about road pavement using image analysis [2,4,6]. However, these camera-based methods are computationally extensive and costly because of the utilization of complex computer vision algorithms. Moreover, lighting conditions, shadow effects, and camera positioning also degrades the results of vision based algorithms.

Due to advancement and innovation in sensing technologies, smartphones are now equipped with motion sensors such as accelerometer, gyroscope, and magnetometer. The ubiquitous presence of these smartphones along with their embedded sensors provides an unobtrusive opportunity to develop viable solutions for road anomaly detection and recognition, vehicle monitoring, navigation, and driving behavior analysis. Researchers have put a lot of attention towards studying smartphone sensor based methods for analyzing road pavements [11,16,21], detecting road anomalies [18], and analyzing the road surface quality [3,5,7,10,15,20]. A few research studies have also focused to monitor driving behavior and detecting abnormal driving events using smartphone sensors [12,22].

In [16], smartphone-embedded gyroscope is used for identifying road swerves and turn. A clustering algorithm is used for differentiating a straight road, road swerve, and a road turn. The experiments are carried out using multiple types of cars. In [1], a smartphone-based method is proposed for detecting abnormal driving activities i.e., weaving, turning, swerving, side-slipping, high speed U-turn, and emergency braking. In [13], a system is proposed that can detect vehicle i.e., car, bus, motorcycle, bicycle, walking and then recognize the driving activity i.e., braking, following straight path, turning left, and turning right based on smartphone sensors. Moreover, different set of feature (time, frequency, and Hjorth features) are used to compare performance in vehicle activity detection experiments. In [22], a fine-grained approach is proposed for detecting and monitoring abnormal behavior of car drivers. Support vector machine and neuron network (NN) classifiers are used to identify U-turn, sideslipping, braking, swerving, turning, and weaving as abnormal driving activities by extracting time domain features from smartphone sensors. Threshold based techniques have also been utilized for detection and identification of driving events. In [9], an approach is proposed for detecting dangerous driving activity for a car and bus driver using smartphone sensors. Accelerometer, gyroscope, global positioning system (GPS), and microphone sensors are used to detect irregular lane change, increase and decrease of vehicle speed. However, the major drawback of thresholding-based scheme is that it cannot be extended or modified to identify driving activities of motorcyclists, which nowadays is becoming critical for the society.

Most of the existing methods primarily utilized cars as a vehicle to detect and assess the road surface quality or road anomalies. A major limitation of these systems is that they cannot be used to monitor narrow streets or bicycle lanes. It hinders many potential applications that are related to pedestrians and motorcyclists. The main contribution of this paper is to recognize motorcyclist driving activities based on smartphone sensor to monitor narrow lanes and driving behavior. Four different driving activities i.e., going straight (ST), left turn (LT), right turn (RT), and U-turn (UT) are recognized based on time domain features using gyroscope data of smartphone. Three classifiers including Bayes network (BN), support vector machine (SVM), and random forest (RF) are used for activity classification. The rest of the paper is organized as follows. The proposed methodology for motorcyclist driving activity recognition using smartphone sensor is described in Section 2. Section 3 deals with the experimental results followed by conclusion in Section 4.

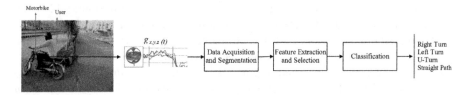

Fig. 1. Proposed methodology for motorcyclist driving activity recognition system using smartphone sensor.

2   Proposed Methodology

The proposed methodology of motorcyclist driving activity recognition system using smartphone sensor is shown in Fig. 1. The detail of each stage is given as follows:

2.1   Data Acquisition

In the first stage, data is acquired using smartphone sensor while driving a motorcycle. This study involves 12 healthy participants having age in the range of 18–22 years (average = 21.8 years). All participants have driving license and fit for driving. They were informed about the scope of the study and gave written consent. A path is selected consisting of two right, two left, and two U-turns as shown in Fig. 2. Right and left turns were at angle $90° \pm 10°$, whereas, U-turn was at an angle of $180°$. Straight path is followed for 150 m. Gyroscope data is acquired by asking the participants to follow predefined path on motorcycle. An application on Samsung android phone is used to acquire data at a sampling rate of 100 Hz. Smartphone is placed in the right-side pocket of the motorcyclists.

2.2   Segmentation

The acquired data is segmented into different segments. An additional participant is involved in the study to add checkpoints for labelling the start and end points of each right, left, and U-turn. The acquired data is segmented based on those checkpoints. The number of total instances are $12 \times 4 \times 2 = 96$. Analysis is performed on 89 instances whereas, remaining are not analyzed due to technical difficulties and unfinished data collection.

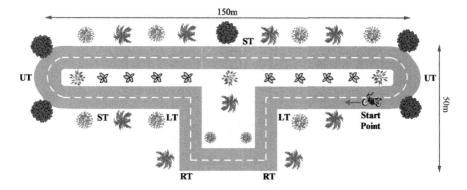

Fig. 2. Map of path followed for motorcyclist driving activity recognition.

2.3   Feature Extraction and Selection

In this paper, twelve time domain features are extracted from the acquired gyroscope data and are calculated as follows:

1. Maximum Amplitude:
$$g_{d_{max}} = max\, g_d[n],\tag{1}$$

where, d represents the dimension x, y, and z.

2. Minimum Amplitude:
$$g_{d_{min}} = min[g_d[n]],\tag{2}$$

3. Absolute Latency to Amplitude Ratio (ALAR):
$$ALAR = |\frac{t_c}{g_{d_{max}}}|,\tag{3}$$

where $t_{g_{max}}$ is latency.

4. Mean (μ_{g_d}):
$$\mu_{g_d} = \frac{1}{N}\sum_{i=1}^{N} g_d(i),\tag{4}$$

where N is the total number of samples in the signal.

5. Peak-to-peak value (g_{pp}):
$$g_{pp} = g_{d_{max}} - g_{d_{min}}.\tag{5}$$

6. Mean of absolute values of first difference (δ_{g_d}):
$$\delta_{g_d} = \frac{1}{N-1}\sum_{i=1}^{N-1} |g_d[i+1] - g_d[i]|.\tag{6}$$

7. Mean of absolute values of second difference (γ_{g_d}):

$$\gamma_{g_d} = \frac{1}{N-2} \sum_{i=1}^{i=N-2} |g_d[i+2] - g_d[i]|. \tag{7}$$

8. Entropy ($H(g_d[n])$):

$$H(g_d[n]) = -\sum_i P(g_d[n])logP(g_d[n]), \tag{8}$$

where, $P(g_d[n])$ represents probability.

9. Energy (E):

$$E = \sum_{i=1}^{N} |s[i]|^2. \tag{9}$$

10. Variance ($\sigma_{g_d}^2$):

$$\sigma_{g_d}^2 = E[(g_d[i] - \mu)^2]. \tag{10}$$

where, E is the expected value.

11. Kurtosis (K):

$$K = \frac{m_4}{\sigma_{g_d}^2}, \tag{11}$$

where m_4 is the fourth moment.

12. Skewness (S):

$$S = \frac{m_3}{m_3^{3/2}}, \tag{12}$$

where m_3 is the third moment.

These features are extracted by utilizing the z-axis of the gyroscope data as it represents the turn or change in the lane [14]. Thus, the feature vector length against each instance is 12. After extracting twelve time domain features from the z-gyroscope, a supervised feature selection method is applied for minimizing the classification cost. Wrapper subset evaluation (WrapperSubsetEval) based method is used to evaluate the importance of a subset of features. It uses the induction method to search for an optimal set of features [8]. These selected features include mean, kurtosis, skewness, energy, absolute mean of second difference, and entropy, which results in a final feature vector length of 6.

2.4   Classification

The final stage is the motorcyclist activity classification based on selected features. Following classifiers are used in this paper for motorcyclist driving activity recognition.

Bayes Network (BN). Bayes Network or Bayes Net is a probabilistic machine classifier, which is based on Baye's theorem. The test data is assigned to multiple classes using probabilistic models that work by learning the probability distribution on pre-defined classes. It predicts a class based on the probability of each action class relating to testing feature.

Support Vector Machine (SVM). SVM is a classifier that reduces the generalization error by maximizing the distance between the hyper planes separating different classes. A hyperplane or a decision plane is capable of separating a set of objects associated with different classes using support vectors. Poly kernel-based algorithm is used for classification in this study.

Random Forest (RF). Random forest is an ensemble classification and regression algorithm that constructs multitude of decision trees while training of the model. Trees are popular methods for machine learning based models that are grown to train in case of irregular patterns.

3   Experimental Results

In this study, three different classifiers are used to detect motorcyclists driving activity i.e., RT, LT, UT, and ST using gyroscope sensor of smartphone. Total instances for RT, LT, UT, and ST are 24, 23, 21, and 21 respectively. The results of three classifiers are compared in terms of accuracy, kappa statistics values, mean absolute error (MAE), root absolute error (RAE), root mean squared error (RMSE), and root relative squared error (RRSE). Results are discussed in two stages i.e., classifiers performance and comparison with existing techniques.

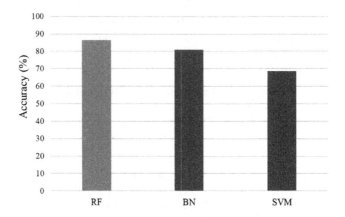

Fig. 3. Accuracy of three different classifiers used to classify motorcyclist driving activities using smartphone gyroscope data.

3.1   Classifier Performance

For analyzing the performance of classifiers, 10-fold cross validation scheme is used. In this scheme, nine instances are used for training whereas, one instance is used for testing purpose. The average classifier accuracy of RF, BN, and SVM using gyroscope is shown in Fig. 3. It is evident that the RF classifies driving activities more accurately as compared to BN and SVM. RF achieves highest accuracy of 86.51% for four driving activities. Comparing in terms of kappa, RMSE, MAE, RRSE, and RAE as shown in Table 1, RF has kappa value closer to 1 and less mean and absolute error rates as compared to BN and SVM classifier. This shows that test data is in more agreement with the ground truth and has less error rate for classification of driving activities as compared to BN and SVM. Correctly classified and misclassified instances of each class are represented in terms of confusion matrix. The confusion matrices for RT, LT, UT, and ST for RF, BN, and SVM classifiers are shown in Table 2, Table 3, and Table 4 respectively. It is evident that the instances of LT and ST are classified more accurately by RF as compared to BN and SVM. Classifiers performance is also compared in terms of precision, recall, and F-measure, which are shown in Fig. 4. It is evident that the motorcyclists driving activity recognition using smartphone gyroscope sensor has the highest precision, recall, and F-measure using RF as compared to BN and SVM, whereas, SVM has least values as compared to BN and RF classifiers.

Table 1. Overall performance comparison of RF, BN, and SVM classifier based on Kappa, MAE, RAE, RMSE, and RRSE using gyroscope for motorcyclist driving activity recognition.

Classifier	Kappa	MAE	RMSE	RAE	RRSE
RF	0.819	0.128	0.228	34.21%	52.73%
BN	0.745	0.150	0.292	40.04%	67.60%
SVM	0.578	0.288	0.367	76.90%	84.89%

Table 2. Confusion matrix for RF classifier

Instance	Classified as			
	RT	LT	UT	ST
RT	20	3	0	1
LT	2	20	1	0
UT	0	0	20	1
ST	2	2	0	17

Table 3. Confusion matrix for BN classifier

Instance	Classified as			
	RT	LT	UT	ST
RT	19	2	3	0
LT	0	18	4	1
UT	0	1	20	0
ST	0	3	3	15

Table 4. Confusion matrix for SVM classifier

Instance	Classified as			
	RT	LT	UT	ST
RT	20	1	2	1
LT	0	19	4	0
UT	3	1	17	0
ST	3	13	0	5

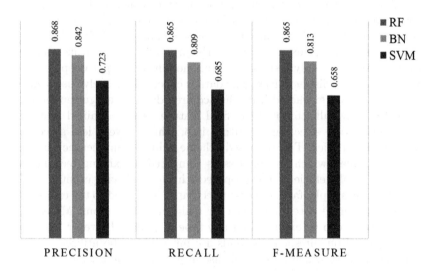

Fig. 4. Comparison in terms of precision, recall, and F-measure for motorcyclists driving activity recognition based on smartphone gyroscope sensor using RF, BN, and SVM classifiers

3.2 Performance Comparison

Table 5 summarizes a performance comparison of the proposed scheme with the existing studies. In [13], three smartphone sensors i.e., accelerometer, gyroscope, and magnetometer are used for recognizing four motorbike driving events i.e., stopping, moving straight, right turn, and left turn by collecting data from three users.

Table 5. Performance comparison of the proposed scheme with existing studies.

Method	Driving activities	Vehicle/ subjects	Sensors	Classifier	Features (length)	Results
[22]	Side-slipping, u-turn, weaving, turning, swerving, braking	Car/2	Orientation, accelerometer	SVM, NN	Time (152)	Accuracy 96.88%
[13]	Stopping, straight, left turn, right turn	Motorbike/20	Gyroscope, Accelerometer, magnetometer	RF, SVM, KNN, NB, decision tree	Time, frequency (41)	Accuracy 88.85%
[14]	Accelerating, change of direction, deaccelerating	Car/–	Gyroscope, gps accelerometer, microphone	Thresholding	(100)	Precision 93.95%
Proposed	Straight, right turn, left turn, u-turn	Motorbike/12	Gyroscope	RF, BN, SVM	Time (6)	Accuracy 86.51%

They extracted features from both time and frequency domain, having an overall feature vector length of 41. Different classifiers are applied to recognize the driving activity and the best accuracy of 88.85% is achieved. The research work in [22] utilized accelerometer and orientation sensor to recognize six car driving events using SVM and NN classifiers. The best accuracy rate achieved is 96.88% with a feature vector length of 152. In [9], thresholding scheme for recognizing abnormal car driving events is used, which achieves an overall precision of 93.95%.

In comparison to the existing studies, the proposed scheme utilizes motorbike as a vehicle and used only a single smartphone sensor i.e., gyroscope, for recognizing four motorcyclist activities. The data is collected for twelve users and time domain features are extracted from the acquired data to recognize motorcyclist activities. The overall length of the final feature vector obtained after applying wrapper feature selection algorithm is 6, which is very less as compared to the existing studies. The proposed scheme achieves an accuracy of 86.51% using RF classifier, which is a bit less as compared to existing techniques but yet computationally efficient. The proposed scheme for driving event detection is computationally simple, fast, and cost-effective as compared to the existing techniques, which can be potentially used for real-time applications. Moreover, the proposed scheme can be extended for any type of vehicle. However, the existing techniques based on threshold methods are infeasible to be utilized in all type of carrying vehicles, which limits their use in practical applications.

4   Conclusion

A cost-effective solution for driving behavior analysis involves utilizing the embedded smartphone sensors. In this work four driving activities of motorcyclist are recognized using gyroscope data of smartphone. Twelve time domain features are extracted from the acquired data which is reduced to six by applying wrapper-based feature subset selection algorithm. In this paper, motorcyclist driving activities are classified using Bayes net, random forest, and support vector machine classifiers. Random forest achieves best classification accuracy of

86.51% for motorcycle driving activity recognition using gyroscope sensor. It is also evident that RF has highest precision, recall, and F-measure as compared to BN and SVM classifiers. The proposed method achieves comparable classification performance with minimum feature vector length when compared with existing techniques.

References

1. Chen, Z., Yu, J., Zhu, Y., Chen, Y., Li, M.: D 3: abnormal driving behaviors detection and identification using smartphone sensors. In: 2015 12th Annual IEEE International Conference on Sensing, Communication, and Networking (SECON), pp. 524–532. IEEE (2015)
2. Coenen, T.B., Golroo, A.: A review on automated pavement distress detection methods. Cogent Eng. **4**(1), 1374822 (2017)
3. Douangphachanh, V., Oneyama, H.: A model for the estimation of road roughness condition from sensor data collected by android smartphones. J JSCE, Ser. D3 (Infrastr. Plann. Manage.) **70**(5), I_103–I_111 (2014)
4. Doycheva, K., Koch, C., König, M.: GPU-enabled pavement distress image classification in real time. J. Comput. Civ. Eng. **31**(3), 04016061 (2016)
5. Gawad, S.M.A., El Mougy, A., El-Meligy, M.A.: Dynamic mapping of road conditions using smartphone sensors and machine learning techniques. In: 2016 IEEE 84th Vehicular Technology Conference (VTC-Fall), pp. 1–5. IEEE (2016)
6. Gopalakrishnan, K.: Deep learning in data-driven pavement image analysis and automated distress detection: a review. Data **3**(3), 28 (2018)
7. Harikrishnan, P., Gopi, V.P.: Vehicle vibration signal processing for road surface monitoring. IEEE Sens. J. **17**(16), 5192–5197 (2017)
8. Kohavi, R., Sommerfield, D.: Feature subset selection using the wrapper method: overfitting and dynamic search space topology. In: KDD, pp. 192–197 (1995)
9. Li, F., Zhang, H., Che, H., Qiu, X.: Dangerous driving behavior detection using smartphone sensors. In: 2016 IEEE 19th International Conference on Intelligent Transportation Systems (ITSC), pp. 1902–1907. IEEE (2016)
10. Li, X., Goldberg, D.W.: Toward a mobile crowdsensing system for road surface assessment. Comput. Environ. Urban Syst. **69**, 51–62 (2018)
11. Lima, L.C., Amorim, V.J.P., Pereira, I.M., Ribeiro, F.N., Oliveira, R.A.R.: Using crowdsourcing techniques and mobile devices for asphaltic pavement quality recognition. In: 2016 VI Brazilian Symposium on Computing Systems Engineering (SBESC), pp. 144–149. IEEE (2016)
12. Lu, D.-N., Ngo, T.-T.-T., Le, H.-Q., Tran, T.-T.-H., Nguyen, M.-H.: MDBR: mobile driving behavior recognition using smartphone sensors. In: Nguyen, N.T., Papadopoulos, G.A., Jędrzejowicz, P., Trawiński, B., Vossen, G. (eds.) ICCCI 2017. LNCS (LNAI), vol. 10449, pp. 22–31. Springer, Cham (2017). https://doi.org/10.1007/978-3-319-67077-5_3
13. Lu, D.N., Nguyen, D.N., Nguyen, T.H., Nguyen, H.N.: Vehicle mode and driving activity detection based on analyzing sensor data of smartphones. Sensors **18**(4), 1036 (2018)
14. Ma, C., Dai, X., Zhu, J., Liu, N., Sun, H., Liu, M.: DrivingSense: dangerous driving behavior identification based on smartphone autocalibration. Mob. Inf. Syst. **2017** (2017)

15. Ma, X., Wang, H., Xue, B., Zhou, M., Ji, B., Li, Y.: Depth-based human fall detection via shape features and improved extreme learning machine. IEEE J. Biomed. Health Inf. **18**(6), 1915–1922 (2014)
16. Seraj, F., Zhang, K., Turkes, O., Meratnia, N., Havinga, P.J.: A smartphone based method to enhance road pavement anomaly detection by analyzing the driver behavior. In: Adjunct Proceedings of the 2015 ACM International Joint Conference on Pervasive and Ubiquitous Computing and Proceedings of the 2015 ACM International Symposium on Wearable Computers, pp. 1169–1177. ACM (2015)
17. Silva, N., Shah, V., Soares, J., Rodrigues, H.: Road anomalies detection system evaluation. Sensors **18**(7), 1984 (2018)
18. Silva, N., Soares, J., Shah, V., Santos, M.Y., Rodrigues, H.: Anomaly detection in roads with a data mining approach. Proc. Comput. Sci. **121**, 415–422 (2017)
19. Singh, G., Bansal, D., Sofat, S., Aggarwal, N.: Smart patrolling: an efficient road surface monitoring using smartphone sensors and crowdsourcing. Perv. Mob. Comput. **40**, 71–88 (2017)
20. Vlahogianni, E.I., Barmpounakis, E.N.: Driving analytics using smartphones: algorithms, comparisons and challenges. Transp. Res. Part C: Emerg. Technol. **79**, 196–206 (2017)
21. Yi, C.W., Chuang, Y.T., Nian, C.S.: Toward crowdsourcing-based road pavement monitoring by mobile sensing technologies. IEEE Trans. Intell. Transp. Syst. **16**(4), 1905–1917 (2015)
22. Yu, J., Chen, Z., Zhu, Y., Chen, Y.J., Kong, L., Li, M.: Fine-grained abnormal driving behaviors detection and identification with smartphones. IEEE Trans. Mob. Comput. **16**(8), 2198–2212 (2016)

PARK MY RIDE: Your True Parking Companion

Muhammad Rizwan[1], Muhammad Asif[2($\boxtimes$)], Maaz Bin Ahmad[3],
and Khalid Masood[2]

[1] Department of Computer Science, Lahore Lead University, Lahore, Pakistan
`rizix99@gmail.com`
[2] Department of Computer Science, Lahore Garrison University, Lahore, Pakistan
`astz786@yahoo.com, khalid.masood@lgu.edu.pk`
[3] PAF Karachi Institute of Economics and Technology, Karachi, Pakistan
`maaz@pafkiet.edu.pk`

Abstract. Due to the increase in population and the number of vehicles, the parking issue is getting worst day by day in many big and crowded cities of the world. People have to spend more money and time to find safe parking for their vehicles. The street and roadside parking causes various troubles like fines and damages to the vehicles. In this paper, an optimum solution is proposed to find available parking slots in near by parking areas and to manage them efficiently. A mobile application is designed that helps users in a number of ways, find nearest parking areas, search for available parking slots and allow real time reservation of these slots. Moreover, a complete navigation map is provided that help users to reach the designated parking slot. The additional feature of this application is administrator panel, that allow parking owners to manage parking and collect the respective parking fee. With this application not only the time is saved but the safety of the vehicle is also ensured.

Keywords: Android application · Parking issues · Pakistan · Mobile application · Simulation

1 Introduction

All around the world, one of the main challenges facing by the people in many big and crowded cities is to find vacant spaces for parking vehicles [1]. According to the statistics provided by the global vehicle ownership and vehicle production, the number of vehicles are rapidly growing in the world and this number is expected to exceed 1 billion before 2020 [2]. This increase in number of vehicles will further boost the problem of finding free parking slots [3]. To address this issue, numerous countries are working for the development of smart parking systems [4].

Similar to the rest of the world, Pakistan mega cities are overcrowded due to the huge influx of human population who want to settle in these cities for better

© Springer Nature Singapore Pte Ltd. 2020
I. S. Bajwa et al. (Eds.): INTAP 2019, CCIS 1198, pp. 695–708, 2020.
https://doi.org/10.1007/978-981-15-5232-8_60

employment opportunities, quality education and up to date medical facilities. The increase in the population of cities raises numerous challenges. The parking of the vehicle is one of the primary challenge as most of the old residential areas, hospitals, universities, colleges, schools, public places, and commercial areas have narrow roads and lesser parking facility [5, 6].

It is reported that the number of total licensed vehicles was 4,701,600 in year 2000 [7]. In only 15 years this number has been risen up to 17,317,600 an increase of almost four times. Figure 1 shows the number of registered vehicles in 2000 and 2015.

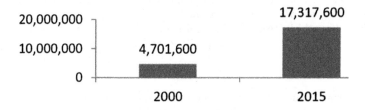

Fig. 1. Total registered vehicles in 2000 and 2015 [7]

Keeping 2000 as the base year to measure the progress in the number of registered motor vehicles, from 2000 to 2015, there has been a 439% increase in the number of registered motorcycle, 413% increase in the number of registered auto rickshaws, 114% increase in the number of registered motor cars (Jeep, Wagon etc.), 95% increase in the motor cabs (where Karachi holds the highest numbers of cabs in the world), 48% increase in the number of registered buses, 73% increase in the number of registered trucks, 88% increase in the number of other registered vehicles and 268% increase in total number of registered vehicles [7]. Due to large volume of traffic it is inferred that parking is one of the greatest challenges that need to be addressed. Figure 2 illustrates the percentage change in number of registered vehicles from year 2000 to 2015.

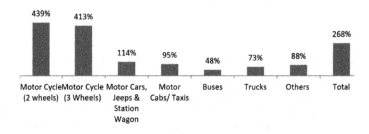

Fig. 2. Percentage change in number of registered vehicles (2000–2015) [7]

The existing parking lots are overcrowded and mismanaged as shown in Fig. 3. People are bound to look around and find a better and safe place for their vehicles whether it is a residential area, shopping mall, hospital or a well-established institute. It is roughly estimated that the car runs on an average of 400 h only out of 8,760 h in a year, leaving 8,360 h when it is parked [8]. Every user wants to park his vehicle nearest to his destination but to find the empty parking slot is a real challenge. The situation is more critical for visitor or newcomer.

Fig. 3. Parking place

In this era, where the technology has flourished, the every day life has become more comfortable and convenient. There are new products, new tech gadgets that are being invented daily to facilitate the human beings. Smartphone is not only used for communication and entertainment purpose but it also raises the standard of living. In recent times, many real world problems have been addressed using smartphone applications.

In this work, a smart phone application is introduced to solves the parking issues. The proposed system is a web-based Android application. This application will help it's users to see parking spots in near to them and will also navigate people to that parking lot with maps activity. This application is beneficial not only for the people living in the cities but also for the visitors.

The proposed application has the following main features:

- Find the nearest parking locations for its users.
- Show space availability of those parking lots.
- Parking owner's can manage the entries of vehicles to keep their parking lots updated.

- Save time to find the allotted parking slot.
- Dual login functionality in the application for both parking owner and end-user.

The rest of the paper is organized as follows. Section 2 covers the previous works that have been done in this area. The proposed application is presented in Sect. 3. Section 4 describes the main attributes and working flow of the proposed solution. Section 5 comprises the comparative analysis and discussion. Finally, the conclusion is drawn in Sect. 6.

2   Literature Review

In literature, several studies have been performed to address the parking issues. Kianpisheh et al. [9] suggested a smart parking system (SPS) that assist the drivers to find the vacant parking space in parking lot and to detect improper parking. The system is based on ultrasonic sensors that are fixed in the ceiling above each parking space. The driver is guided about the vacant space and their by a LED display board.

Srikanth et al. [10] has proposed a Wireless Sensor Network (WSN) technology based parking system named as SPARK. The system has the ability to manage and monitor each parking space and provides a parking space reservation service to the users. Moreover, SPARK uses light sensors for detecting vehicles and the parking slot. The data collected from the sensors is transmitted to a sink subsystem using radio frequency (RF) that is stored in a local server for further processing.

Wang and He [11] have presented a system that sends parking information and provides a reservation service to the users. A sensor network using ZigBee modules for real time monitoring of the occupancy status of the parking spaces. Each module consist of luminosity and a vibration sensors in order to detect the vehicle. There is also a bluetooth module which is responsible for communicating with the user's smartphone and validate his identity. The user can also reserve a parking space through smartphone. Based on the occupancy status, the system can determine the parking price and notify the users about the cost.

Anderson et al. [12] has evaluated the reliability of the Smart Parking using an empirical analysis. The outcomes contains, number of errors in a certain period of time, the error and success rates and the most frequent error. In [13], a computer vision algorithm is proposed that identifies available parking slots using three different Convolutional Neural Network (CNN) models. Using a picture of a parking area occupied slots are labeled and empty slots are identified. The proposed system was tested on three data sets and 99.94% classification accuracy was achieved.

Junhuai et al. [14] has proposed smartphone-based car-searching methods in large parking areas. The car-searching algorithm is based on QR code to find the available parking spots. The smartphone built-in sensors are used to navigate the path. The Quick Response (QR) codes consist of parking lot number, floor number and parking location. Pedometer is used for tracking the vehicle in the proposed system. The flaw of this system is that it is not flexible and portable to other parking areas.

The Sharjah Parking app works in United Arab Emirates to book parking lots for a specific period of time [15]. The application is based on Short Messaging Service (SMS) where a user can be notified with a text message on the standard career network. Parking.sg is another application that guides its user to the selected parking lot through maps navigation and calculates parking charges at the end of the trip [16]. The user will be able to pay bills through smartphone application.

Most of the existing solutions provide information about location of parking areas and the number of vacant spaces in that parking area. The major flow in these techniques is that it cannot identify the exact location of the vacant slots. However, in a recent study [9] vacant slots have also been identified but still a complete management solution has not been proposed. In proposed system, not only nearest parking areas are navigated but also vacant slots are also identified. Moreover, it also provides a complete parking management system.

3   Proposed Solution

The proposed application consists of three modules which are Administrator (admin) Panel, End-User Application, and Database.

3.1   Administrator Panel

In this work, the .NET framework is used to build the admin panel of application. The Model-View-Controller (MVC) application design model is used to shape the admin panel. The following are the main features of the admin panel:

- Managing Admin Features
- Authorization of new parking lot
- Managing parking lots
- Creating a separate panel for every parking owner so he/ she can track their records
- Managing users

In this work, seven different types of controllers are used that will help to manage the admin panel. These controllers are:

- Admin Controller.
- Booking Controller.
- History Controller.
- Login Controller.
- Parking Controller.
- Parking Owner Controller.
- Home Controller.

Every controller has the list that contains various tasks and features. There are two master pages for each controller. One master page is linked to the admin side and the other page is for the parking owner. Figure 4 shows the admin panel.

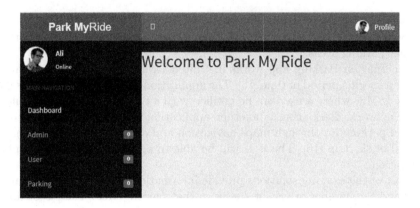

Fig. 4. Administrator panel

3.2 End-User Application

The end-user application is developed in android. The main functionality of the android application is demonstrated in Fig. 5. A login page is restricted to allow only valid users. For using the application the users have to register with a valid email address.

Duplicate registration is not allowed i.e, an email address can be used only once. The admin panel is only for administrator and parking owners. The end user would not be able to access the admin panel. The login mechanism is smart to distinguish between parking owners and end users through emails addresses registered/stored in SQL database. If the email belongs to a parking owner, it will redirect it to the parking owner page. This page consists of details of the vehicles that are currently parked. If it is an end user, the system will redirect it to features that are built for the end user in this android application. The user will be seeing (P shaped) Blue parking markers on his/her screen that are actually nearest parking areas. When a user clicks on the marker, information for available sots is shown in the application. When a user wants to park the vehicle in the nearest selected parking, by clicking on navigation, he is directed to the nearest parking location and Google Maps API will select the best an optimum route that will take him to the available parking spot. The user will reach the exact parking location using the navigator and will park his/her vehicle in that parking lot. When a user has parked the vehicle, the number of available slots will be decreased by one. The owner of the parking area can also get the information about number of vehicles currently parked and the other necessary information such as License Plate Number, Parking in/out time, vehicles type (Car, Bike) and parking charges.

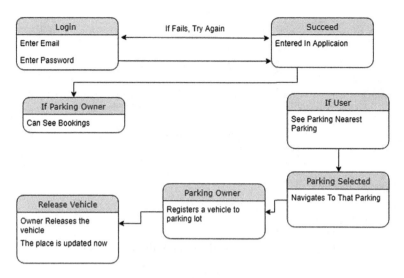

Fig. 5. User end functionality

3.3 Database

To maintain the user record and to check the validity of the user an SQL database system is connected to both admin panel end users application. This SQL database consists of four records containing Booking, History, Parking, and User details. A few validations are added on top of the existing email strings and parking owners/users that will enhance the validity of the users or parking owners. Tables are connected to each other's via primary and foreign keys relations as it is a relational database. The entity relation diagram of the database system is shown in Fig. 6.

4 Main Attributes and Working Flow

4.1 Login and Registration

The login page of the application is the same for both the user and parking owner. The distinction between user and parking owner is made on user ID. The parking owner can only view the booking details. The login page of the proposed application is shown in Fig. 7.

4.2 Location Accessibility

Location accessibility options are helpful for customers to get the exact location on the maps. It is a good practice for using maps as GPS are tuned at high accuracy that attains the best user experience for the application that supports and facilitates maps navigation. The application always notifies users before

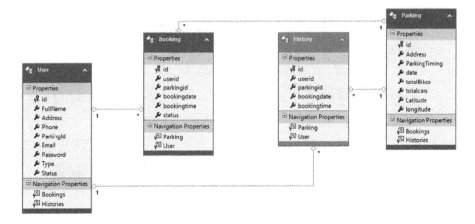

Fig. 6. Entity relation diagram of database system

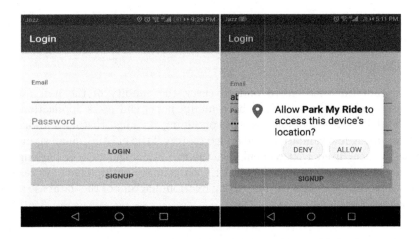

Fig. 7. Login page

using maps to enable location tab as it's up to the user to set GPS accuracy from device settings. Figure 8 shows device setting to allow the application get user location. The user can enter its location manually.

4.3 Parking Area Searching, Space Availability and Navigation

In order to search the parking area, the user presses the search parking area button. The application shows the nearest parking areas. The "P" markers on the maps in left screen in the Fig. 9 shows available parking lots in its vicinity.

The middle screen shows space availability feature that shows the number of available vacant slots in the parking area. The right screen shows the Google maps activity to navigate the user to it is selected parking space by finding the

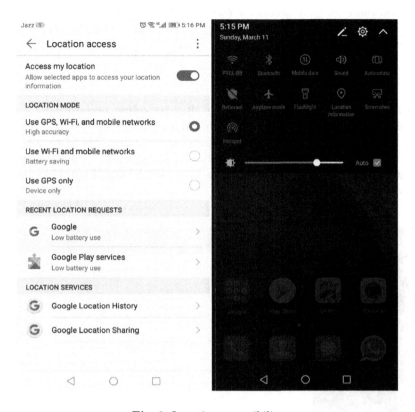

Fig. 8. Location accessibility

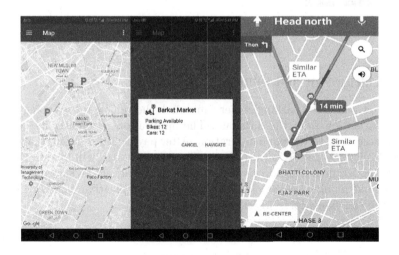

Fig. 9. Parking areas, space availability and navigation

optimum route for easy access for the parking in the minimum available time. The maps activity also provides alternate routes that a user can select to reach his selected parking lot.

4.4   Parking Spot Reservation

The user can reserve a parking space after providing necessary information including vehicle type and registration number. The acquired information is stored into the SQL database to manage users record. This feature is linked with space availability feature. So, whenever a reservation is made for a user, the number of available parking slot is decreased by one. Figure 10 shows the reservation page.

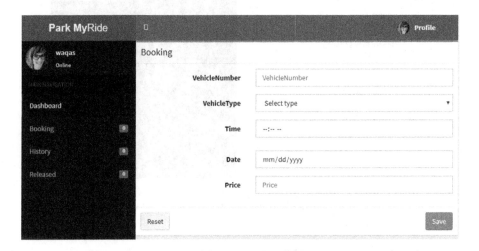

Fig. 10. Reservation page

4.5   Vehicles Exit and Billing

At the exit point, the parking owner can search the vehicle record using number plate information from the database. The application automatically generates the bill according to the parked duration. After payment of the bill, the status of vehicle is changed to the release status. The release status will update the space availability features in the record and maps. The parking owner can also view the updated number of vehicles on his Android application as well. Figure 11 shows the exit panel for vehicles.

Fig. 11. Exit panel

4.6 Working Flow

The following is the working flow of the proposed system:

- The user login the application after turning on wifi and location.
- The application automatically gets its current location. The user can also enter its location manually.
- After that the user presses the search parking area button. The application shows the nearest parking areas.
- The user can check the free space in any parking area by selecting it.
- The user can choose one of the parking area and reserve the available slot after providing the necessary information.
- The application navigates the user to the selected parking area using Google map.
- At the exit point, the application automatically generates the bill according to the duration.
- After bill payment, the status of vehicle is changed to the release status and all the records are updated.

5   Comparative Analysis and Discussion

To evaluate the performance of the proposed system, data of numerous parking areas of the Lahore city (e.g. DHA parking area, Lahore Leads University, Lahore Garrison University, LUMS University Lahore, and etc.) is gathered and testing is performed. The experimental results show that the proposed solution functions well as intended.

The comparison between the proposed system and existing solutions is made on the basis of following five features:

- F1: Parking area searching
- F2: Navigation to parking area
- F3: Parking area management (available parking slots, search vacant space in parking area, vehicle searching in parking lot, detect improper parking)
- F4: Reservation
- F5: Billing system.

These are the most common features reported in number of studies and the comparison is based on a single criterion that which technique is offering more features. Table 1 gives the comparison of proposed solution and existing system with respect to the provided features.

Table 1. Comparison of proposed solution with existing systems (✓: Present and ✗: Missing)

Technique	F1	F2	F3	F4	F5
Kianpisheh et al. [9]	✗	✗	✗	✓	✓
Srikanth et al. [10]	✗	✗	✓	✗	✗
Wang and He [11]	✗	✗	✗	✓	✗
Junhuai et al. [14]	✗	✗	✓	✗	✗
Sharjah Parking [15]	✗	✗	✗	✗	✓
Parking.sg [16]	✓	✓	✗	✗	✓
Proposed system	✓	✓	✓	✓	✓

Figure 12 illustrates that most of the existing techniques provide a single feature only whereas the proposed system offers all the main features. Based on the comparative analysis, it can be concluded that proposed system outperform the existing solutions as it incorporates the maximum number of features.

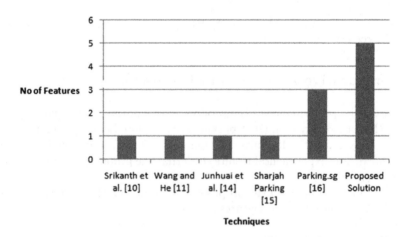

Fig. 12. Techniques vs number of features provided

6   Conclusion

An efficient car parking solution is proposed that maintains the convenience and safety for its users. The proposed system reduces the stress of parking in the developed and congested cities of our country. It is very simple and a user friendly application. The map feature is especially helpful for new users that struggle to find a parking area. The proposed application not only assists users in parking but it also maintains the security of vehicles and parking areas.

References

1. Lookmuang, R., Nambut, K., Usanavasin, S.: Smart parking using IoT technology. In: 5th IEEE 5th International Conference on Business and Industrial Research (ICBIR), Thailand (2018)
2. Natarajan, P.B., Ghosh, S.K.: Design and implementation of smart car parking system using lab view. Int. J. Pure Appl. Math. **120**(6), 329–338 (2018)
3. Alam, M., et al.: Real-time smart parking systems integration in distributed ITS for smart cities. Hindawi J. Adv. Transp. **2018**, 1–18 (2018)
4. Lee, S., Yoon, D., Ghosh, A.: Intelligent parking lot application using wireless sensor networks. In: International Symposium on Collaborative Technologies and Systems, pp. 329–338 (2008)
5. Chowdhury, I.H., Abida, A., Muaz, Md.M.H.: Automated vehicle parking system and unauthorized parking detector. In: 20th IEEE International Conference on Advanced Communication Technology (ICACT), South Korea (2018)
6. Masood, M.T., Khan, A., Naqvi, H.A.: Transportation problems in developing countries Pakistan: a case-in-point. Int. J. Bus. Manage. **6**(11), 256–266 (2011)
7. Short Round on Transport Infrastructure in Pakistan Year 2000–2015, Gallup Pakistan Big Data Analysis Edition 2, November 2, (2016). http://gallup.com.pk/wp-content/uploads/2016/11/Gallup-Pakistan-Big-Data-Analysis-Series-Edition-2-on-Transportation-Infrastructure-in-Pakistan-2000-to-20151.pdf. Accessed 17 Sept 2019
8. Patel, V., Patil, P., Shah, S., Ahirrao, H., Shinde, V., Patil, R.: Parking problems in central business district (CBD) area of vadodara: a detailed survey. Int. J. Eng. Sci. Comput. **7**(6), 12970–1293 (2017)
9. Kianpisheh, A., Limtrairut, P., Keikhosrokiani, P.: Smart parking system (SPS) architecture using ultrasonic detector. Int. J. Softw. Eng. Appl. **6**(3), 51–58 (2012)
10. Srikanth, S., Pramod, P., Dileep, K., Tapas, S., Patil, M.U., Babu, S.C.: Design and implementation of a prototype smart parking (SPARK) system using wireless sensor networks. In: IEEE International Conference on Advanced Information Networking and Applications Workshops, pp. 401–406 (2009)
11. Wang, H., He, W.: A reservation-based smart parking system. In: IEEE Conference on Computer Communications Workshops (INFOCOM WKSHPS), pp. 690–695 (2011)
12. Araújo, A., Kalebe, R., Giraõ, G., Filho, I., Goncalves , K.: Reliability analysis of an IoT-based smart parking application for smart cities. In: IEEE International Conference on Big Data (BIGDATA) (2017)
13. Mauro, D.D., Moltisanti, M., Patane, G., Battiato, S., Farinella, G.M.: Park smart. In: IEEE/AVSS International Workshop on Traffic and Street Surveillance for Safety and Security (2017)

14. Li, J., An, Y. Fei, R., Wang, H.: Smartphone based car searching system for large parking lot. In: IEEE 11th Conference on Industrial Electronics and Applications (ICIEA) (2016)
15. mParking Sharjah. https://play.google.com/store/apps/details?id=com.mparking. app&hl=en. Accessed 17 Sept 2019
16. Parking.SG. https://www.parking.sg/. Accessed 17 Sept 2019
17. Corneille, N.: Online vehicle parking reservation system a case study: people's park Kyeban. Kampala Uganda, May 2016. https://doi.org/10.13140/RG.2.2.12134. 32325

Cloud and Data Systems

Edge Caching Framework in Fog Based Radio Access Networks Through AI in Quantum Regime

Tayyabah Hassan[(✉)], Wajiha Ajmal Khan, Fahad Ahmad,
Muhammad Rizwan, and Rabia Rehman

Department of Computer Science, Kinnaird College for Women,
Lahore, Pakistan
tabbyhassan14@gmail.com

Abstract. Fog Computing based Radio Access Networks are a promising paradigm for 5th Generation wireless communication technology (5G) having edge devices endowed with some caching and storage capacity, as a key component for reducing caching burden on the cloud server and providing fast access and retrieval at F-UEs in a scenario where IoT based devices requiring ultra-low latency will be used extensively. The amount of static as well as dynamic data requests generated by these real-time applications will be unpredictable and unmanageable shortly causing fronthaul congestion. In order to avoid performance degradation of F-RANs in near future, cache resource allocation strategies to increase cache hit ratio, must be redefined in a further better way. Quantum computing, on the other hand, seems to be the future for every kind of classical computing problem having non-linearity and exponential growth of computation and memory with a linear increase in Quantum bits due to its parallelism. In this paper, AI has been engaged in an attempt to enhance the caching capability in F-APs by updating caching content intelligently in quantum regime, accelerating computational speed and facilitating limited storage concerns. To validate our proposed framework, certain simulations are carried out in MATLAB. The results show an inevitable outcomes for F-RANs performance up gradation.

Keywords: Fog Computing based Radio Access Networks (F-RANs) · Edge caching · F-AP (fog-access point) · Adaptive Neuro-Fuzzy Inference System (ANFIS) · Quantum computing

1 Introduction

1.1 Fog Computing and Edge Caching

Fog computing is a new paradigm which is a further enhancement to the cloud computing that extends storage, processing and communication control at the edge of the network (user end) instead of centralized cloud storage and utilization [1, 2]. Furthermore, with the increasing number of smart IoT devices ultra-low latency applications have gained attention of many in the IT industry. IoT networks can cause

© Springer Nature Singapore Pte Ltd. 2020
I. S. Bajwa et al. (Eds.): INTAP 2019, CCIS 1198, pp. 711–722, 2020.
https://doi.org/10.1007/978-981-15-5232-8_61

considerable burden on the backhaul resulting in unfavorable circumstances for delay-sensitive applications. Fog computing seems to be the solution for such issues by distributing computing and communication services from cloud servers to the edge of the network known as Edge Computing, which means that part of control and other processing functions are carried out through edge caching in local baseband units or even Remote Radio Heads (RRHs) other than centralized BBU pool [3]. This idea was named as Fog Computing based Radio Access Networks (F-RANs) and was proposed in Next Generation Mobile Network (NGMN) in June 2014.

In order to associate edge devices with fog computing, conventional RRHs are further improved to become fog computing based access points (F-APs) by implementing certain caching, CRSP (Collaboration Radio Signal Processing) and CRRM (Cooperative Radio Resource Management) capabilities in them [4]. To support or integrate additional smart UEs (F-UEs) CRRM is used, whereas, CRSP can not only be executed in centralized BBU pool but also in F-APs and F-UEs causing a relief for the fronthaul [5]. Basic architecture of F-RANs is shown below in Fig. 1.

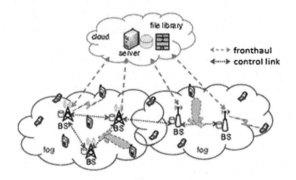

Fig. 1. Basic F-RAN architecture

Talking particularly about media requirements, there are certain challenges edge caching seems to cater, keeping in view poor user experiences including buffering, poor quality playback, hitting bandwidth caps, etc. At times, in terms of size, audio and video content is heavier than the encyclopaedias requiring higher hardware and network capacities. Edge caching can support such kind of throughput at scale results. Moreover, scalability of streaming servers during live events, which require special provisioning of these servers, can also be catered.

1.2 Quantum Computing

Now, coming to an entirely different regime in computing world, i.e. Quantum computers, which are based upon laws of Quantum Mechanics, claim to solve many of the problems at atomic or sub-atomic level, that are intractable for traditional computers. Quantum parallelism, based on superposition and entanglement, is the basic feature of these computers which offers exponential speed up over classical computers making them extremely fast [6]. A traditional computer composed of n bits will have 2n possible states. Such a system can store and process a single state at any given moment. Whereas, a quantum computer having n qubits can store and process all 2n possible classical states at the same time by combining them in an unusual way known as superposition, described as:

$$|\Psi\rangle = \alpha_0|0\ldots00\rangle + \alpha_1|0\ldots01\rangle + \ldots + \alpha_{2^n-1}|1\ldots11\rangle \tag{1}$$

Where $\alpha_i \epsilon$ complex numbers and $\sum|\alpha_i|2 = 1$.

Due to quantum No-cloning theorem, it is not possible to regenerate copies of data as in classical systems, so the data itself needs to be moved from source to destination. Quantum information processing makes use of electrons or photons encoded with some information (qubits) in coherent state and passing this information to another qubit via a quantum bus accessible to large number of qubits in a system, accelerating the speed of computation in contrast with the classical computing [7, 8]. Few of the quantum computing hardware architectures which are yet being investigated in well-equipped laboratories are: Trapped Ion architecture, Quantum Computing using Superconducting Qubits and Quantum Computing with Nitrogen Vacancy Center in Diamonds [9].

Quantum information processing is way different from classical information processing. Quantum systems suffer fragility due to the decoherency issue, i.e. the information stored in qubits can be lost if interacted with the environment, causing error rate. However, these systems can be protected by quantum error correction (QEC) and fault tolerant computations (FTC) [10]. Due to these facts all the studies and works are yet theoretical but as soon as these computers are widely available in the market, they can cause breakthroughs in every field of computing.

Further details are given in the coming sections of this article. Problem Statement for our work has been defined in detail in Sect. 2. In Sect. 3, the literature review has been discussed in which different attempts of authors have been studied. Section 4 proposes the main idea of our research work in detail along with the proposed model. To validate our proposed work, results have been verified and discussed in Sect. 5 of this article, followed by the conclusion in Sect. 6.

2 Problem Statement

Although F-RANs seem to be promising to cater all the challenges encountered by Cloud Radio Access Networks or Heterogeneous Cloud-RANs (including geo-distribution, heterogeneity, low end-to-end latency, location awareness, etc. for real-time applications), there still have some shortcomings which need to be dealt with, for performance up gradation of F-RANs and avoiding fronthaul congestion. One such issue that needs to be addressed is the edge catching and limited storage capacity in RRHs (considered as F-APs) [11]. Few essential interests of edge caching in F-RANs are: to reduce the load on fronthaul, backhaul or even backbone, dealing with end-to-end latency, implementation of content-aware techniques dynamically to improve performance.

The caching capacity at each F-AP is relatively very limited as compared to the execution of centralized caching operations in C-RANs or H-CRANs largely because of the limited memory. However, increasing cache size in Base Stations seems to have a trade-off between increased throughput and network's spectral efficiency (SE) [12]. Therefore, this caching technique, including caching policies and cache resource allocation strategies, needs to be handled intelligently in order to improve performance of F-RANs.

This article proposes an intelligent edge caching framework in Quantum regime for Post-Quantum era making use of quantum information processing in an attempt to optimize the performance of F-RANs.

3 Related Work

In this section, different proposed works for edge caching in classical regime have been analysed in attempt to upgrade the performance of F-RANs which have proved to be the great source of guidance for us to come up with our idea. One such attempt is proposed in [3] in which two learning based edge caching architectures have been designed. The main aim of this work is to predict content popularity in terms of space and time, for particular regional users, for both online and offline user preferences. Content popularity prediction algorithm has also been proposed using online gradient descent (OGD) and Follow the Regularized Leader (FTRL-Proximal) methods.

Another approach to optimize the cache performance is to use fog computing with ICN (Information-centric Networks) architecture [14]. ICN approach involves the Content Store (CN) feature in which users retrieve data from adjacent nodes rather than remote server. This hybrid approach use ICN as global network and fog computing as a medieval layer to provide the content-aware ability and its calculation capacity making better use of routers by providing in-network caching on appropriate time. Fog computing supports data processing to classify data into dynamic or static data form and thus decides whether this data should be kept in cache or not with the assigned label. Then the Content store with cache policies verify the label of the data packet. In case of false flag, data packet will not be cached according to cache policy and permits the forwarding process to occur.

The F-RANs incorporate RRHs and UEs that strongly demand bandwidth dissipation issues of RANs and fronthaul. So the Markov-chain-based model is presented in [15] to handle edge caching to examine the influence of Mobile Social Networks (MSNs) on the F-RANs. This model works on the content diffusion by considering the social perspective for the reduction of bandwidth consumption, power dissipation and the edge caching between RRHs and UEs by calculating the expectation of bandwidth consumption. This approach contains a lot of parametric statistics to compute and much knowledge is required to achieve edge optimization.

The information-theoretical analysis is also proposed in [16] which focuses on the use of Normalized Delivery Time metric for the delivery delay up to a worse rate with respect to interference free system in the high SNR (signal-to-noise ratio), enabling the measurement of edge caching performance. Number of edge nodes and users are utilized to know trade-off between NDT and caching resources, revealing the outcomes which demonstrate the optimized edge caching policies.

Coded and Uncoded schemes are used in [17] to analyse the performance of multilayer-edge caching in terms of energy efficiency through calculating backhaul and access throughput of equal sized caches and base stations containing content delivery. These outputs are then used as a derived function for the optimization as it contains the closed-form expression for calculating the delivery time. In Coded scheme the requested files are encoded by the data center intelligently in the beginning and Uncoded scheme sends parts of the requested files to each user independently. Both Coding and Uncoding schemes inquire the cache placement time delivery phases to fulfil the varying demands of user preferences.

CachinMobile scheme is used in [18] for the social networks in which edge node is responsible for providing the requested content from the end users using device-to-device communication. In case of not receiving the requested content in neighboring edge nodes then it refers to other edge nodes for that content and in this way it proceeds its functioning and thus a content placement strategy is used using this approach causing optimization in edge caching. But it also incurs some other challenges like dynamic mobility, interference management and bandwidth resource scheduling which should be focused on.

The work on optimization for edge content caching for mobile streaming is emerging incredibly as it demands the improvements in caching. The methods are analysed by incorporating datasets that involves 50 million trace items of 2 million users, viewing videos, using mobile devices and examining the performance of edge caching in Wi-Fi and cellular-based systems. Thus, a Geo-collaborative caching strategy has been proposed in [19] for optimization.

Optimization through Proactive caching is also proposed in [20] that includes content-awareness and social networks. Caching at base stations and users' devices is done by proactively serving expected user requirements. Two case studies are proposed-First one include the backhaul congestion detection in which least demanded files are cached proactively which are focused on file recognition and pattern. Second one describes the prediction by the set of significant users to (proactively) cache strategic contents and publicize them to their social ties via device-to-device communications.

4   Proposed Work

In this section, our proposed work has been described in detail. Better edge caching revolves around three basic features: caching content management, fast computation and greater storage capacity. The cache size cannot be increased due to certain good reasons but the issues can be catered by efficiently and intelligently managing the caching content through Fuzzy Inference System which sets the priorities of the requested content as high, medium and low. The highly prioritized and medium prioritized data is then sent to the two quantum repositories separately by exploiting Two-Level Spin quantum phenomenon of quantum particles, ensuring efficient content placement within the limited memory and opening gates for fast computation and maximum storage in limited size. Quantum computers are yet not available in the market but the time is not so far when they will be widely available. So, making use of quantum phenomena opens up new doors in edge caching.

4.1   Proposed Model for Edge Caching in Quantum Regime

In this model, we have assumed that the monitoring cycle is initialized by BBU pool where the centralized cloud servers reside. Once the cycle is initialized, following steps are repeatedly carried out in scenarios where innumerable amount of user requests are generated every moment. The process is shown in flow diagram in Fig. 2.

1. A regional user set has been defined for a particular time and for particular F-AP, through synchronization and inter F-APs information sharing.
2. If the requested content is locally available, serve the user request for that particular region. If that content is not present in the local F-AP cache, it must be updated intelligently and efficiently.
3. After the content is being updated through AI and two-level spin phenomenon in the quantum memory module, it needs to be sent back to facilitate synchronization and cooperation among neighbouring F-APs for being cached.
4. This time, the requested content may be served through some other F-AP in the same region or other to support the mobility of users and the cycle goes on like this.

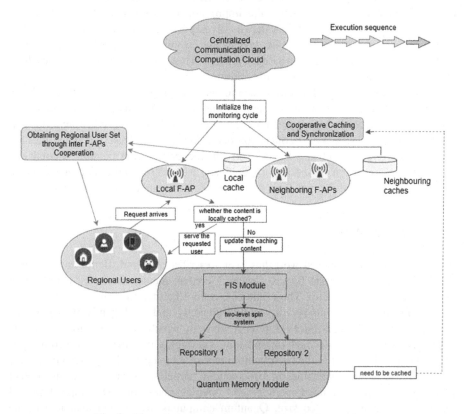

Fig. 2. Flow diagram of edge caching in quantum regime

Working of Quantum Memory Module. The Quantum Memory Module is the most significant part of this model in which data is stored and manipulated in the form of quantum particles. The Adaptive Neuro-Fuzzy Inference System prioritizes the requests for the content placement in memory by setting priorities as low, medium and high. The content with medium and high priorities is then stored in the two quantum repositories separately and can be cached to serve the user request. The content with the low priority will have minimum likelihood to be placed in cache so it will be expired.

FIS Module for Cache Resource Management. We targeted media content particularly for our research. The Adaptive Neuro-Fuzzy Inference System for cache resource management in Quantum Memory Module prioritizes the content logically as high, medium and low for the content placement in memory according to certain parameters. We have collected Youtube's dataset for Trending Youtube Videos Statistics from Kaggle, which includes statistics of videos which are trending in US and UK each day. To meet our requirements we carefully selected 5 input variables namely, video_elapsed_time, video_size, views, likes and downloads which are suitable to represent certain parameters required for edge caching, like content popularity, content size, user's preferences, service response time, etc.

To generate our results, three triangular membership functions has been used in Sugeno inferencing technique in MATLAB which can be mathematically written as piece-wise functions defining different ranges for each MF between 0 and 1, as given below.

$$\mu_{low}(x) = \begin{cases} 0 & x \leq 0 \\ \frac{x-0}{0.17-0} & 0 \leq x \leq 0.17 \\ \frac{0.34-x}{0.34-0.17} & 0.17 \leq x \leq 0.34 \\ 0 & x \geq 0.34 \end{cases} \tag{2}$$

$$\mu_{medium}(x) = \begin{cases} 0 & x \leq 0.17 \\ \frac{x-0.17}{0.17-0.34} & 0.17 \leq x \leq 0.34 \\ \frac{0.66-x}{0.66-0.34} & 0.34 \leq x \leq 0.66 \\ 0 & x \geq 0.66 \end{cases} \tag{3}$$

$$\mu_{high}(x) = \begin{cases} 0 & x \leq 0.34 \\ \frac{x-0.34}{0.17-0} & 0.34 \leq x \leq 0.66 \\ \frac{1-x}{1-0.66} & 0.66 \leq x \leq 1 \\ 0 & x \geq 1 \end{cases} \tag{4}$$

These piece-wise functions are being defined for fuzzification of low, medium and high content priorities for each variable. As there are five input variables so fifteen such functions will be used. The Adaptive Neuro-Fuzzy structure is shown in Fig. 3 below.

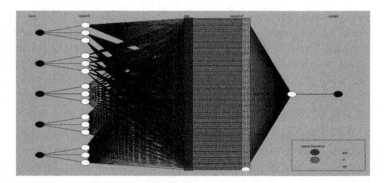

Fig. 3. ANFIS structure containing 5 input variables along with 3 MFs for each variable and single output neuron

Two-Level Spin System (Quantum Phenomenon). Once the content priority has been defined by FIS module logically, it is now time to physically divide the content to be stored. Setting the priorities for the content was just to help encode the content to classify it into two parts for physically storing it in quantum memories (low priority content is expired so it will not be stored anywhere). For that purpose, data can then be encoded in the form of spin ½ particles (electrons), representing +½ spin (upward spin) and −½ spin (downward spin). Highly prioritized data can be encoded in spin down particles and medium prioritized data can be encoded in spin up particles. An electron has a magnetic field due to its spin. But this magnetic field is cancelled out by an opposite spin type electrons in an atom. There are some paired electrons as well as some unpaired electrons in the atom. So the spin effect is usually determined by the unpaired electrons left in the orbitals. When there are large number of atoms, there is high likelihood of splitting into two distinguished beams while passing through a magnetic field if these particles are accumulated in the form of a beam.

At beginning, all the particles are in mixed state because their state is uncertain yet. These particles have mixed state because they have half-half probability to be in either of the pure sates. A pure state is the quantum state where we have exact information about quantum system. On contrary, mixed state is where we are uncertain about the state of the system. A non-uniform magnetic field is created by placing two magnets in vertical direction (along z-axis) as shown in Fig. 3. Now, as the beam passes through the magnetic field, the particles are deflected along this particular axis by an amount proportional to the z-component of their spin angular momentum. A screen can be used to detect that the incoming beam is split into two distinguished beams along z-axis. These two beams can now be separately stored in two quantum repositories. The $|Z+\rangle$ state shows Repository 1 particles having pure state $|0\rangle$, where medium prioritized content is to be stored, and $|Z-\rangle$ state represents Repository 2 particles having pure state $|1\rangle$, where highly prioritized content is to be stored. Hence these particles having some content information are classified using two-level spin system according to the set priorities. The two above mentioned repositories will help in storing the updated content every single time. The density matrices for both mixed states and pure states are also shown in Fig. 4 below.

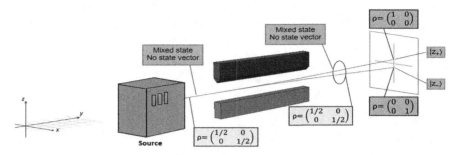

Fig. 4. Electron beam splitting in two while passing through a magnetic field. The matrices for mixed and pure states are also shown.

An ion-trap architecture can be used in this particular scenario, to store quantum data as qubits in the form of atomic ions which are trapped using potential formed by combinations of static and oscillating electric fields. Quantum information can be processed or transferred by collective quantized motion of the ions, known as quantum parallelism. This parallelism leads to increased processing speed in contrast with classical architectures.

5   Results and Discussions

In this section, results for MATLAB simulations for FIS Module have been analysed. The 5 input variables are defined here with 3 triangular membership functions (trimf) each, to determine low, medium or high priority of content as output. Different ranges have been defined for each membership function between 0 and 1 as shown in Fig. 5 below.

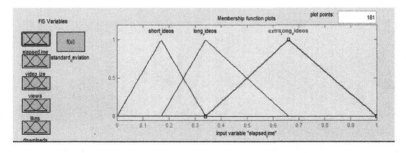

Fig. 5. Illustration of triangular membership functions for each input variable in MATLAB.

After rules development phase in which 243 rules have been made, the system is trained, then tested and validated through data samples for training, testing and checking. The results obtained are given below in Figs. 6(a), 6(b) and 6(c) with respective error rates.

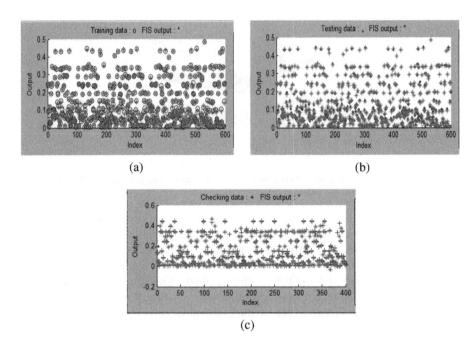

(a)   (b)

(c)

Fig. 6. (a) FIS Output for Training Data with 0.0052016 average error rate. (b) FIS Output for Testing Data with 0.0052016 average error rate. (c) FIS Output for Checking Data with 0.04176 average error rate

Surface graphs are used for 3D analysis of any two input variables and the respective FIS output using the rules developed. We can analyze the effect of any two inputs on the generated output using these graphs. Different surface graphs for random pairs of input variables are generated below in Figs. 7(a) and 7(b).

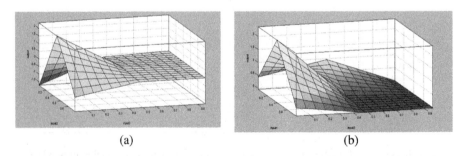

(a)   (b)

Fig. 7. (a) 3D Surface Graph between *video_size* and *views* Input Variables for Checking Data. (b) Surface Graph between *video_elapsed_time* and *views* Input Variables for Checking Data

6 Conclusion

Hence, an edge caching model for overall caching content management in F-APs has been proposed in which caching content is being managed and updated through Adaptive Neuro-Fuzzy Inference System for cache resource management or logical content placement technique and a Quantum Two-Level Spin phenomenon for physically categorizing the content and storing it in two separate quantum repositories. The proposed framework has been proved to be better in dealing with latency related issues in F-RANs as the content is being managed intelligently and efficiently, considering few parameters like content delivery time, content popularity and user preferences, etc. Furthermore, the idea to incorporate quantum memory in F-APs opens new doors for the limited storage constraints in these high power nodes, as storage will no more be an issue in post-quantum era, also providing fast computation in contrast with the classical scenarios currently in consideration.

References

1. Ku, Y.-J., Lin, D.-Y., Lee, C.-F., et al.: 5G radio access network design with the fog paradigm: confluence of communications and computing. IEEE Commun. Mag. **55**, 46–52 (2017). https://doi.org/10.1109/mcom.2017.1600893
2. Peng, M., Wang, C., Lau, V., Poor, H.V.: Fronthaul-constrained cloud radio access networks: insights and challenges. IEEE Wirel. Commun. **22**, 152–160 (2015). https://doi.org/10.1109/mwc.2015.7096298
3. Bonomi, F., Milito, R., Zhu, J.Z.J., Addepalli, S.: Fog computing and its role in the Internet of Things. In: MCC 2012, Helsinki, pp. 13–16. ACM (2012)
4. Mikhail, G., Dmitri, M., Roman, F., et al.: Cooperative radio resource management in heterogeneous cloud radio access networks. IEEE J. Mag. **3**, 397–406 (2015). https://doi.org/10.1109/access.2015.2422266
5. Liu, J., Bai, B., Zhang, J., Letaief, K.B.: Cache placement in Fog-RANs: from centralized to distributed algorithms. IEEE Trans. Wirel. Commun. **16**, 7039–7051 (2017). https://doi.org/10.1109/twc.2017.2737015
6. Arun, G., Mishra, V.: A review on quantum computing and communication. IEEE, Surat, India (2014)
7. Thaker, D., Metodi, T., Cross, A., et al.: Quantum memory hierarchies: efficient designs to match available parallelism in quantum computing. In: 33rd International Symposium on Computer Architecture (ISCA 2006), Boston, USA. IEEE (2006)
8. Sillanpää, M.A., Park, J.I., Simmonds, R.W.: Coherent quantum state storage and transfer between two phase qubits via a resonant cavity. Nature **449**, 438–442 (2007). https://doi.org/10.1038/nature06124
9. Vignesh, R., Poonacha, P.G.: Quantum computer architectures: an idea whose time is not far away. In: International Conference on Computers, Communications and Systems, Kanyakumari, India. IEEE (2015)
10. Almudever, C.G., Lao, L., Fu, X., et al.: The engineering challenges in quantum computing. In: Design, Automation and Test in Europe Conference and Exhibition, Lausanne, Switzerland. IEEE (2017)
11. Peng, M., Yan, S., Zhang, K., Wang, C.: Fog-computing-based radio access networks: issues and challenges. IEEE Netw. **30**, 46–53 (2016). https://doi.org/10.1109/mnet.2016.7513863

12. Liu, D., Chen, B., Yang, C., Molisch, A.F.: Caching at the wireless edge: design aspects, challenges, and future directions. IEEE Commun. Mag. **54**, 22–28 (2016). https://doi.org/10.1109/mcom.2016.7565183
13. Jiang, Y., Ma, M., Bennis, M., et al.: User preference learning-based edge caching for fog radio access network. IEEE Trans. Commun. **67**, 1268–1283 (2019). https://doi.org/10.1109/tcomm.2018.2880482
14. Wang, M., Wu, J., Li, G., et al.: Fog computing based content-aware taxonomy for caching optimization in information-centric networks. In: IEEE Conference on Computer Communications Workshop, Atlanta, USA. IEEE (2017)
15. Wang, X., Leng, S., Yang, K.: Social-aware edge caching in fog radio access networks. IEEE Access **5**, 8492–8501 (2017). https://doi.org/10.1109/access.2017.2693440
16. Tandon, R., Simeone, O.: Cloud-aided wireless networks with edge caching: fundamental latency trade-offs in fog Radio Access Networks. In: International Symposium on Information Theory (ISIT), Barcelona, Spain. IEEE (2016)
17. Vu, T.X., Chatzinotas, S., Ottersten, B.: Edge-caching wireless networks: performance analysis and optimization. IEEE Trans. Wirel. Commun. **17**, 2827–2839 (2018). https://doi.org/10.1109/twc.2018.2803816
18. Wang, S., Huang, X., Liu, Y., Yu, R.: CachinMobile: an energy-efficient users caching scheme for fog computing. In: IEEE/CIC International Conference on Communications in China (ICCC), Chengdu, China. IEEE (2016)
19. Ma, G., Wang, Z., Zhang, M., et al.: Understanding performance of edge content caching for mobile video streaming. IEEE J. Sel. Areas Commun. **35**, 1076–1089 (2017). https://doi.org/10.1109/jsac.2017.2680958
20. Bastug, E., Bennis, M., Debbah, M.: Living on the edge: the role of proactive caching in 5G wireless networks. IEEE Commun. Mag. **52**, 82–89 (2014). https://doi.org/10.1109/mcom.2014.6871674

Challenges and Limitation of Resource Allocation in Cloud Computing

Sadia Ijaz[(⊠)], Tauqeer Safdar, and Amanullah Khan

Department of Computer Science, Air University Multan Campus,
Multan 6000, Pakistan
engrsachaudhry017@gmail.com

Abstract. Cloud computing is internet-based computing era. The resources that are provided by cloud computing is easily accessible by the cloud clients when they are demanding. The infrastructure of cloud computing is dynamic in nature and resources are optimally allocated. These resources shared in cloud computing, like any other paradigm resource management is main issue in cloud computing. It is very challenging to provide all demanding resources, as the number of available shared-resources are increasing. This paper reviews sharing of resources (like servers, applications and data) over cloud and consider techniques to make adaptive algorithms for management of resources in cloud computing.

Keywords: Cloud computing · Resource allocation · Shared resources · Min-Min · Max-Max · Max-Min algorithm

1 Introduction

Cloud computing is new remote computing model where it exposes number of resources. In modern era due to benefits of high availability, less-service cost, more accessibility and scalability of resources the cloud computing is becoming the most suitable platform. It provides internet based computing services by managing and using large amount of resources. Resource management term states the capability of computing environment and focus on the way that how they provide services to other users, applications and entities. These resources are provided on demand [12] over internet [13, 14] and [15] by application programs. Cloud computing is based on distributed and parallel computing [16]. To locate the resources globally and make use of resources economically, it deals with distributed computing. When the demand of users are changes, resources are also changes accordingly. Due to dynamic nature of computing environment, it becomes very complex to deal with vast amount of resources.

Cloud, computing has many problems of the resource-allocation including its infrastructure and corresponding services. According to [1], resource scheduling is the major problem of cloud computing. One of another crucial problem in cloud computing environment is making techniques of resource management, which used to determine the placement of each modules [10] with other devices to increase the throughput and reducing the latency. Data-centers in cloud computing [11] have problems in implementing the methods to migrate and manage the resources. This inappropriate

© Springer Nature Singapore Pte Ltd. 2020
I. S. Bajwa et al. (Eds.): INTAP 2019, CCIS 1198, pp. 723–737, 2020.
https://doi.org/10.1007/978-981-15-5232-8_62

management of resources resulted into wastage of resources and poor transfer of services in datacenters. Resources such as Servers, Hard disk, memory and CPU required to be managing and recognizing. These problems are analyzed by various resource allocation models with the motivations of proper management of resources and accurate transfer of services in datacenters. So this paper provides a complete sequential vision on management of resources in cloud computing. The motivation of this paper is sequential view of resources in cloud computing. In this context resources are classified in cloud computing.

This section covers cloud-computing concept, resource allocation main problems in computing environment. Rest of paper is arranged as follows: Sect. 2 describe framework of resources, Sect. 3 describe major challenges in cloud, Sect. 4 discuss review of literature and compare methods of resource allocation in computing environment, Sect. 5 discuss analysis and comparison of adopted tools\methodologies\algorithms. Taxonomy on Resources Allocation Methods, concluding remarks and future work presented in Sects. 6, 7 respectively.

2   Framework of Resource Allocation

The basic components of Cloud are Users/Bokers, Services, Storage, Application, Platform and infrastructure [19, 20]. The flow of resource allocation in cloud environment starts from identification of requests from users. These requests are treated in such a manner that satisfies distinct goals of cloud provider. The goals in computing environments could be cost optimization [21] or energy optimization [22] etc. Based on information of resources like monitoring of resource, the brokers (cloud provider) requests information and the scheduler identifies solution for allocation of resources (see Fig. 1). Resource allocator could only ensures the static and initial allocation of resources after receiving any request or confirm both dynamic [23] and static allocation [24] of resources to manage resources in sequential manner and readjust previous requests.

Schedulers could just ensure the initial and static resource allocation [25] after request arrival or ensure both static and dynamic resource allocation to manage resources in a continuous way and to further optimize and readjust the old requests. The broader adoption of virtualization and cloud computing technologies has led to cluster sizes extending from increasing number of nodes for small and huge cluster centers respectively [26]. Based on reasons of high electricity consumption [27] and rise of carbon footprints [28], efficiency of energy is becoming highly important for clouds and data centers. Therefore, resolving the issue of resource allocation in computing environment is a big challenge [29]. This issue is also termed as NP-hard [4, 30] that discussed in cloud computing context.

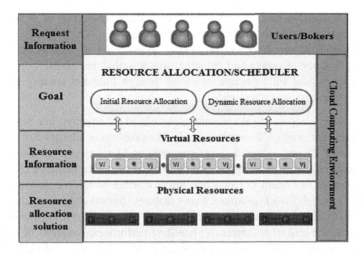

Fig. 1. Resource allocation in cloud computing.

The focus of paper is to discuss the efficient allocation of resources in cloud computing in sequential manner. Various dimensions will be considered in the study, which are cloud service model, scheduling of resources, sequential resource view and static features of solutions.

3 What Is Resource Allocation Challenge?

One of major challenge in cloud computing is allocation of resources because of dynamic nature of resources [31] end-users can access resources ubiquitously (at anytime and anywhere). Meanwhile, Cloud datacenters provides large number of resources, and computing models of clouds capable of supporting on demand adaptable allocation of resources. However, such plenty of resources also causes non-optimal allocation of resources. The objective of allocation of resource for any cloud brokers can either be optimization of applications [32, 33], efficiency of energy or improve utilization of resources irrespective of the sort of ICT resources: elastic IP, blob storage and servers [34] are assigned to end-users. Some of energy efficient challenges with allocation of resources [35, 36] that is find in study includes:

1. From different workloads, select most suitable interference and workload category like consumption of power, performance and usage of resource.
2. Evaluating layout of cloud infrastructure by improving technology and tools, topology and resources of cloud.
3. From different workloads, select most suitable interference and workload category like consumption of power, performance and usage of resource.
4. Facilitate consolidation of resources by evaluating inter dependencies of applications to return on investment and growing performance.

5. Evaluating standardized, federated and centralized resources of datacenters for provisioning and runtime utilization of resources.
6. Recovering from any letdown: improving accessibility of network, utilization of assets, efficiency of power and reducing time to utilize resources.
7. Planning practical Infrastructure of cloud through business security support and elasticity for mission critical bids.

The term resource in cloud computing is defined as anything like storage, CPU, bandwidth and memory (ICT resources) [37]. The problem of allocation of resources is very complex [38] and required some assumptions like: (a) cost of used resources, (b) reduction in wastage of energy (c) set of active servers. Furthermore, cloud brokers assigns resources of system to CPUs and limits whether to receive incoming requests conferring to availability of resources. Many features like: (a) observing accessibility of resource, (b) tracing requirements of services, (c) observing service demands of users, (d) identifying the cost of resources, (e) handling performance requests of service, and (f) tracking actual allocation of resources make it complex and difficult task (see Fig. 2).

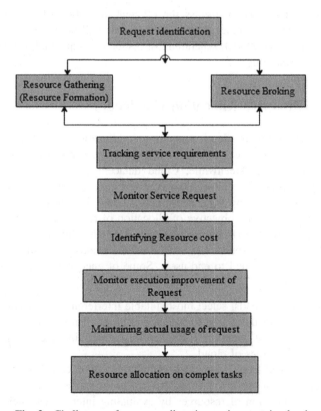

Fig. 2. Challenges of resource allocation assignment in cloud

Furthermore, allocation of resources is challenging because of increasing rate of workloads that causes various demands of resource from brokers for cloud computing model.

4   Literature Review

To achieve more benefits and cloud client-satisfaction, different resource allocation methods are used in cloud computing. Several methods regarding allocation of resources in cloud computing and their related algorithms analyzed under the observed parameters (discussed in next Sect. 6).

In [17], author present efficient-green enhancements as a new frame- work in scalable architecture of cloud computing. In a cloud-based datacenter efficiency of complete system will be improved with overhead of minimal performance by use of minimal VM design, variable management of resources, live-migration and power-aware methodologies. Author present efficient scheduling of energy to describe potential of our framework and propose new methods to save large volume of energy without affecting performance.

In [2], Author presents allocation and migration algorithms in clouds data-centers for management of resources by using CPU management and memory as resource. The author propose DRMA (Dynamic Resource Management algorithm) which make use of best-fit concept for better results and reduce server cost by choosing appropriate algorithm for effective use of resources. Author proposes techniques to reduce under-utilized resources that produce useless relocations due to random loads.

A protocol for resource management and offloading of tasks presented in [3], in which central-controller is used both for mobile cloud and for C-RAN. The author analyzed the performance of vertical scaling of cloud, which indicated that the scaling resources (RAM, CPU, and Storage) in mobile cloud are the major cause to change scaling time-delay trends. Moreover, author concluded that real-time scaling of computation resources could not be appropriate for delay application.

An inclusive framework proposed in [46] containing JCC (joint communication and computation) resource- effective techniques for operators of network and resource effective computation-offloading techniques for users. In order to reduce user's effective-resource offloading problem authors of this paper first focus on defining optimal resource-profile of computation and communication with least utilization of resources and satisfaction of "Quality of service" constraint. After that author, propose techniques to handle admission control problem of users for allocation of JCC resources. To tackle out this problem, author show NP-hard. Therefore, it make low complexity solution by designing ranking criteria of user and provide derivation of guarantee of its performance. A critical value approach was used to make ingenuous system for allocation JCC resource.

In two-tier heterogeneous wireless network author [6] discussed the issues of resource allocation and offloading joint computation. The author proposed a framework for computation offloading of multi cell, multi task and multi user. To verify the possibility of issues in different methods, the multi-tier computation system is used. Author proposed bisection search approaches and less complex algorithms that reduces optimized binary variables and make it scalable in practical heterogeneous wireless network. In this work for heterogeneous wireless network, desired performance of suggested algorithms have conformed through numerical results that may leads to large amount of energy saving.

In [5], author guaranteed to solve the important issue of timestamp and focused on efficient distribution of resources by applying Max-Min scheduling algorithm. The major aim of this work is to increase cloud-scheduling performance and reducing the gap between users of cloud-resource and providers of cloud- services. On faster existing machine, authors propose Max-Min algorithm with selection of Max time execution or Min time execution for resources. Sometimes this algorithm has problem, the Maximum task time of execution causes to increase make-span and Minimum resource execution causes to delay in execution time of tasks. To cope with this drawback, Cloud-Sim algorithm is used with Max-Min algorithm. The results of this paper provide much-improved make-span than Data-Aware and Max-Min algorithm.

In cloud computing infrastructure, the responsibility of resource manager is to give the efficient way of execution of tasks, decreases response-time, improve performance of system and effective utilization of resources. To meet these requirements a standard scheduling algorithm proposed in [7]. Authors present RAMM (Resource Aware Min-Min) algorithm, which follow Min-Min classic algorithm. In RAMM algorithm the task is selected which contains shortest execution time and passes this task to the resource, which contains minimum achievement time and if the selected minimum resource time is not free at that time then RAMM algorithm must looking for next shortest time-resource. The proposed algorithm provides improved results than standard Min-Max, Max-Min and Min-Max algorithm.

In [9] author presented the resource-allocation problem in automotive systems of cloud computing. Authors treated both public and private cloud standard; where public-cloud handle all pledged vehicles and maintaining decentralized binding scheme in which prerequisite is to derive time delays with not any earlier knowledge on the random-bidding from vehicles, while private-cloud serves a particular organization maintaining centralized-binding scheme in which prerequisite is to minimize QoS (Quality of Service) cost. Author showed how the changing of task dead- line and workload effect on policy of optimal bidding. In this work, proposed frame- works demonstrated by numerical examples.

5   Analysis

5.1   Evaluation of Core Resource Allocation Approaches

This section discusses detailed comparison on several resource-allocation methods, algorithms, objectives and main concept of each literature work. The following Table 1 gives a summary of core approaches.

The most common adopted environment is cloud computing [6, 7, 9, 18] whereas green computing [17] and Mobile Cloud Computing (MCC) and Cloud radio access networks (C-RAN) [3] were also discussed. Each paper considered different or common objectives with its limitations such as best performance with saving of energy [6, 17] and less cost [18] and completion of task in specific time [3, 4, 7, 9]. According to each researchers work comparison different resources are considered in each paper with few overlapping resources. The limitations, objectives and major concepts are discussed and compared, which provide better overview of suitable resource in computing environment. The contribution should contain no more than four levels of headings.

Table 1. Comparison between resource allocation approaches.

Researchers	Domain/ Environment	Objectives	Major concepts	Limitations	Future work
Younge et al. [17]	Green Computing	New techniques for saving large volume of energy without effecting performance	Cloud infrastructure for the development of efficiency of system	Cloud infrastructure, both in the commercial and academic sectors not well enhanced	Improve a scheduling system to rise energy saving from physical server and thermal systems
Ngenzi and Nair [2]	Cloud Computing	Maximum allocation of resource with fewer costs, minimum servers used with less transfer of tasks	In cloud data centers for resources management allocation and migration, algorithms implemented	In migration, the cost may exceed the benefit	Efficient resource allocation methods with less migration cost
Magurawalage et al. [3]	Mobile Cloud Computing and (C-RAN)	Effective management decisions for resources on both mobile cloud and C-RAN	C-RAN offered approaches for growth of mobile traffic. While MCC handle compute-intensive tasks to the cloud	In delay sensitive applications, it may not appropriate. Due to major scaling delay	For high auto-scaling it would be made practical in real-time
Chen et al. [4]	Edge Computing	The task will finished in given time. With Minimum usage of the resources	Effective computation offloading and JCC (Joint communication & computation) procedure for net operator resource allocation	On demanding resources, is challenging for brokers to offer all resources	Dynamic case for user departure from mobile edge cloud system. Make effective online algorithms

(continued)

Table 1. (*continued*)

Researchers	Domain/ Environment	Objectives	Major concepts	Limitations	Future work
Nguyen and Bao [5]	Cloud Computing	Multi-tier computation system with allowable latency and practical limitations on bandwidth, optimize the computation offloading, Minimize the maxi- mum weighted energy	In practical wireless HetNets decrease the binary optimization variables and make them able for optimization of scalable computation offloading	Sometimes in terms of consumption of energy, offloading shows the worst performance	Sufficient radio resources would make available; Offload selection to attain first lowest weighted energy with largest weighted energy at end
Nguyen and Long [6]	Cloud Computing	Reduction of performance in cloud resource between users and brokers cloud resource. Cloud scheduling performance is Improved	Max-Min scheduling algorithm used to efficient optimization of resource allocation in the cloud and increase efficiency	Delay in execution of tasks that first enhance makespan time	Extended to phenomenon of simultaneous executing tasks with max-min performance time
Ali and Alam [7]	Cloud Computing	Reduce task's waiting time and better utilization of re- sources. Reduce makespan and resource load balancing	Selects shortest implementation task time and assign it to the resource, which takes shortest completion time.	Resources are pre- sent in a single Cloud environment	Virtual Machines (resources) are expended in multiple Clouds environment
Li et al. [8]	Cloud Computing	On-demand resources are Effectively used; holds an important potential to expand fuel economy, vehicle comfort and safety in future	For automotive sys- tem, problem of re- source allocation un- der both public and private cloud models were treated and managed	Decentralized model developed for public cloud. a centralized (auction based) model is developed for private cloud	More general re- source provisioning models developed for public/private clouds

6 Taxonomy on Resources Allocation Methods

As already mentioned, there are numerous resource allocation techniques in computing environment. A detailed description is discussed on resource allocation method, algorithms/techniques and this analysis section consider various resources in suitable environment. Resources such as energy/power [4, 17], memory/storage capacity [4, 18], CPU [3, 18], bandwidth and latency [6] are considered in different computing environment (Table 2).

Table 2. Comparison between tools/algorithms in cloud.

Researchers	Methods	Resources	Algorithms	Tools
Younge et al. [17]	Power-aware VM scheduling techniques	Energy, power resource	Greedy based algorithm, Cluster scheduling algorithms	Amazon's EC2
Ngenzi and Nair [2]	VMware's Distributed Resource Scheduler (DRS), First Fit and Best Fit method	CPU and memory	DRMA, Bin packing algorithm, Best fit algorithm,	Live migration of VMs
Magurawalage et al. [3]	Methods of task offloading	Scaling computing resource (CPU, RAM, Storage)	Task offloading protocols in C-RAN and mobile cloud for management of resources	USRP N210 and one X300 have been set up as RRHs of LTE & (OAI)
Chen et al. [4]	Cross Entropy method	Joint communication and computation (JCC), Storage and power resource	Power control algorithm, Delay-Aware Task Graph Partition algorithm, Admission Control for JCC Resource Allocation	Numerical evaluation through algorithms
Nguyen and Bao [5]	Bi-section search method	Bandwidth, latency and radio resource	Multi-task and Multi-user Computation Offloading Algorithm, Low-complexity Algorithm with Decoupled MC-SC Optimization	Numerical evaluation through algorithms

(continued)

Table 2. (*continued*)

Researchers	Methods	Resources	Algorithms	Tools
Nguyen and Long [6]	Max-Min method, Binary Integer Programming method	Many Computer resources	Max-Min scheduling algorithm	Cloud-Sim Toolkit
Ali and Alam [7]	Min-Min methods	CPU, (RAM) resources	RAMM (Resource Aware Min-Min) Algorithm, Task Scheduling Algorithm	CloudSim toolkit and for graphics MATLAB Toolbox
Li et al. [8]	Dynamic bin packing method, centralized resource provisioning model, decentralized auction-based model	Bidding based Resource	Deep Deterministic Policy Gradient (DDPG) algorithm, RL algorithms, deterministic actor-critic (DAC) algorithm	Amazon EC2, MATLAB

These techniques have not reviewed with management of energy efficient allocation of resources in sequential manner in cloud datacenter. To do so, make a comparison based on different dimensions: resource adaption policy in sequential view and objective function of why scheduling is needed in allocation of resources [39].

6.1   Adaptation Policy in Resource Allocation

In this dimension, energy aware allocator of resource is able to manage ambiguous or dynamic conditions. These ambiguities come from number of aspects like capacity demand of resources (storage, memory and bandwidth), failures (in hosting application of CPU and network links) and workload patterns of users and locations (see Fig. 3).

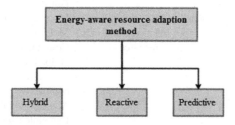

Fig. 3. Adaptation policy of resource allocation assignment in cloud

The main purpose of paper is allocation of resources in sequential manner it considers three categories in adaption policy of resources like: hybrid [40], reactive and predictive (see Fig. 3). This refers to degree to which scheduler or an energy aware allocator capable to adapt uncertain or dynamic condition [41].

6.2 Need of Scheduling in Resource Allocation

The first benefit of scheduling of resources in cloud is to find or select appropriate resources for scheduling suitable workloads and to enhance efficiency of utilization of resources. For better scheduling of resources, it required best mapping of resources. The second goal of scheduling of resources is to find the appropriate workload to support multiple workloads scheduling, to make it able to fulfil various requirements of services like reliability, CPU utilization, availability, and Security etc. for workloads in cloud [42].

In Cloud computing, management of resources includes two steps: resource scheduling and resource provisioning. Resource scheduling is defined as mapping and implementation of cloud user's workload based on nominated resources over resource provisioning. Whereas, resource provisioning is the identification of adequate resources for services, based requirements described by cloud users (see Fig. 4). In start, user's passes request for implementation of workload. On behalf of these user's requirements, resource provisioner identifies appropriate resource(s) for workload. Based on Quality Service requirements, it limits the probability and easiness of provisioning of resources [43]. After effective resource, provisioning service provider of cloud sends resources for scheduling.

Resource provider in cloud has responsibilities like manage performance to insert or delete resources in cloud, from pool of resources releases extra resource and contains

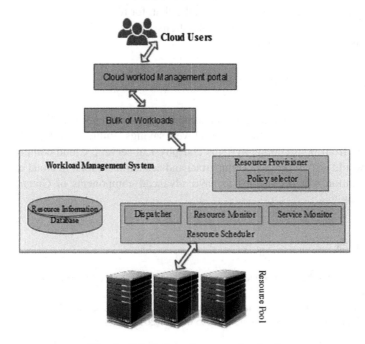

Fig. 4. Scheduling of resource in cloud

all information about resources that are provisioned. In second stage, resource scheduling is completed after provisioning of resources.

The resources that are not provisioned are kept in resource pool. While, others are moved in resource queue [44]. The workloads that are submitted transferred in workload queue where scheduler maps resources to intended workload, then execute and releases it back to the pool after workload is done. The resource scheduling is quite challenging task. To better meet, the scheduling process, there is prior need to consider quality of service requirements [45]. There is dire need to expose the challenges in scheduling of resources to implement workloads without effecting quality of service of other requirements.

7   Conclusion

This paper has offered a precise review of the applications of theories in cloud networking to resource management. As the large number of shared-resources are available in cloud computing, it is very challenging to provide all demanding resources. This paper reviews sharing of resources (like servers, applications and data) over cloud and consider techniques to make adaptive algorithms for management of resources. Different algorithms like Max-Min, Min-Max, and Min-Min scheduling algorithms were considered in which RAMM (Resource Aware Min-Min) algorithm proposed to be best for efficient resource allocation. Virtual Machine (VM) Systems are constructed which provides new ways for preservation of power. DRMA (Dynamic Resource Management Algorithm) make use of bin packing algorithm for CPU and memory resources management. This paper concludes that, for resource allocation, each method has some objectives as well as some limitations. However, the focus is on sequential-efficient allocation of resources.

8   Future Work

To report the remaining challenges in computing environment it continued with some future research. To maximizes the power savings future could explore system scheduling from both cooling-systems and physical-servers. Cloud-computing infrastructure would also improve in commercial and academic sectors. In cloud environment next generation would expected to have advanced components of Green computing technologies.

References

1. Sharma, S., Pariha, D.: A review on resource allocation in cloud computing. Int. J. Adv. Res. Ideas Innov. Technol. 1, 1–7 (2014)
2. Ngenzi, A., Nair, S.R.: Dynamic resource management in Cloud datacenters for Server consolidation. arXiv preprint arXiv:1505.00577 (2015)

3. Magurawalage, C.S., Yang, K., Patrik, R., Georgiades, M., Wang, K.: A resource management protocol for mobile cloud using auto-scaling. arXiv preprint arXiv:1701.00384 (2017)
4. Chen, X., Li, W., Lu, S., Zhou, Z., Fu, X.: Efficient resource allocation for on-demand mobile-edge cloud computing. IEEE Trans. Veh. Technol. 67(9), 8769–8780 (2018)
5. Nguyen, T., Bao, L.L.: Joint computation offloading and resource allocation in cloud based wireless HetNets. In: GLOBECOM 2017 IEEE Global Communications Conference. IEEE (2017)
6. Nguyen, T.T., Long, B.L.: Joint computation offloading and resource allocation in cloud based wireless HetNets. arXiv preprint arXiv:1812.04711 (2018)
7. Ali, S.A., Alam, M.: Resource-Aware Min-Min (RAMM) algorithm for resource allocation in cloud computing environment. arXiv preprint arXiv:1803.00045 (2018)
8. Li, Z., Chu, T., Kolmanovsky, I.V., Yin, X., Yin, X.: Cloud resource allocation for cloud-based automotive applications. Mechatronics 50, 356–365 (2018)
9. Ghobaei-Arani, M., Khorsand, R., Ramezanpour, M.: An autonomous resource provisioning framework for massively multiplayer online games in cloud environment. J. Netw. Comput. Appl. 142, 76–97 (2019)
10. Saraswathi, A.T., Kalaashri, Y.R., Padmavathi, S.: Dynamic resource allocation scheme in cloud computing. Procedia Comput. Sci. 47, 30–36 (2015)
11. Beloglazov, A., Abawajy, J., Buyya, R.: Energy-aware resource allocation heuristics for efficient management of data centers for cloud computing. Fut. Gener. Comput. Syst. 28(5), 755–768 (2012)
12. Buyya, R., Yeo, C.S., Venugopal, S., Broberg, J., Brandic, I.: Cloud computing and emerging IT platforms: vision, hype, and reality for delivering computing as the 5th utility. Fut. Gener. Comput. Syst. 25(6), 599–616 (2009)
13. Wang, L., Kunze, M., Tao, J., von Laszewski, G.: Towards building a cloud for scientific applications. Adv. Eng. Softw. 42(9), 714–722 (2011)
14. Wang, L., et al.: Cloud computing: a perspective study. New Gener. Comput. 28(2), 137–146 (2010)
15. Wang, L., Fu, C.: Research advances in modern cyber infrastructure. New Gener. Comput. 28(2), 111–112 (2010)
16. Voorsluys, W., Broberg, J., Buyya, R.: Introduction to cloud computing. In: Cloud computing, pp. 1–41 (2011)
17. Younge, A.J., Von, L.G., Wang, L., Lopez-Alarcon, S., Carithers, W.: Efficient resource management for cloud computing environments. In: International Conference on Green Computing, pp. 357–364. IEEE (2010)
18. Shyamala, K., Rani, T.S.: An analysis on efficient resource allocation mechanisms in cloud computing. Indian J. Sci. Technol. 8(9), 814 (2015)
19. Liu, N., et al.: A hierarchical framework of cloud resource allocation and power management using deep reinforcement learning. In: 2017 IEEE 37th International Conference on Distributed Computing Systems (ICDCS), pp. 372–382. IEEE (2017)
20. Arfeen, M.A., Pawlikowski, K., Willig, A.: A framework for resource allocation strategies in cloud computing environment. In: 2011 IEEE 35th Annual Computer Software and Applications Conference Workshops, pp. 261–266. IEEE (2011)
21. Singh, P., Talwariya, A., Kolhe, M.: Demand response management in the presence of renewable energy sources using Stackelberg game theory. In: IOP Conference Series: Materials Science and Engineering, vol. 605, 1, no. 1, p. 012004. IOP Publishing (2019)
22. Mohan, N., Kangasharju, J.: Placing it right!: optimizing energy, processing, and transport in Edge-Fog clouds. Ann. Telecommun. 73(7–8), 463–474 (2018)

23. Brady, S.J.: Dynamic resource allocation with forecasting in virtualized environments. U.S. Patent Application No. 10/203,991 (2019)
24. Sun, P., Zhang, H., Ji, H., Li, X.: Task allocation for Multi-APs with mobile edge computing. In: 2018 IEEE/CIC International Conference on Communications in China (ICCC Workshops), pp. 314–318. IEEE (2018)
25. Kesidis, G.: Scheduling distributed resources in heterogeneous private clouds. In: 2018 IEEE 26th International Symposium on Modeling, Analysis, and Simulation of Computer and Telecommunication Systems (MASCOTS). IEEE (2018)
26. Wang, L., Ma, Y., Yan, J., Chang, V., Zomaya, A.Y.: pipsCloud: high performance cloud computing for remote sensing big data management and processing. Fut. Gener. Comput. Syst. **78**, 353–368 (2018)
27. Vafamehr, A., Mohammad, E.K.: Energy-aware cloud computing. Electr. J. **2**(31), 40–49 (2018)
28. Khosravi, A., Rajkumar, B.: Energy and carbon footprint-aware management of geo-distributed cloud data centers: a taxonomy, state of the art, and future directions. In: Sustainable Development: Concepts, Methodologies, Tools, and Applications, pp. 1456–1475. IGI Global (2018)
29. Habibi, M., Mohammad, A., Ali, M.: Efficient distribution of requests in federated cloud computing environments utilizing statistical multiplexing. Fut. Gener. Comput. Syst. **90**, 451–460 (2019)
30. Kumar, D., Deepti, M., Rohit, B.: Metaheuristic policies for discovery task programming matters in cloud computing. In: 2018 4th International Conference on Computing Communication and Automation (ICCCA). IEEE (2018)
31. Nayak, J., Naik, B., Jena, A.K., Barik, R.K., Das, H.: Nature inspired optimizations in cloud computing: applications and challenges. In: Mishra, B.S.P., Das, H., Dehuri, S., Jagadev, A.K. (eds.) Cloud Computing for Optimization: Foundations, Applications, and Challenges. SBD, vol. 39, pp. 1–26. Springer, Cham (2018). https://doi.org/10.1007/978-3-319-73676-1_1
32. Yan, H., Ping, Y., Duo, L.: Study on deep unsupervised learning optimization algorithm based on cloud computing. In: 2019 International Conference on Intelligent Transportation, Big Data & Smart City (ICITBS). IEEE (2019)
33. Megahed, A., et al.: Optimizing cloud solutioning design. Fut. Gener. Comput. Syst. **91**, 86–95 (2019)
34. Mohammed, R.M.: Notavailable. Storage allocation scheme for virtual instances of cloud computing (2019)
35. Wang, J., Pan, J., Esposito, F., Calyam, P., Yang, Z., Mohapatra, P.: Edge cloud offloading algorithms: Issues, methods, and perspectives. ACM Comput. Surv. (CSUR) **52**(1), 2 (2019)
36. Javadi-Moghaddam, S.M., Alipour, S.: Resource allocation in cloud computing using advanced imperialist competitive algorithm. Int. J. Electr. Comput. Eng. **9**, 2088–8708 (2019)
37. Hameed, A., et al.: A survey and taxonomy on energy efficient resource allocation techniques for cloud computing systems. Computing **98**(7), 751–774 (2016)
38. Mann, Z.Á.: Allocation of virtual machines in cloud data centers—a survey of problem models and optimization algorithms. Acm Comput. Surv. (CSUR). **48**(1), 11 (2015)
39. Cheng, D.: Adaptive scheduling parallel jobs with dynamic batching in spark streaming. IEEE Trans. Parallel Distrib. Syst. **29**(12), 2672–2685 (2018)
40. Nguyen, F., Elias, F.: Red Hat Inc. Hybrid security batch processing in a cloud environment. U.S. Patent Appl. **10**(067), 802 (2018)

41. Ilager, S., Kotagiri, R., Rajkumar, B.: ETAS: Energy and thermal-aware dynamic virtual machine consolidation in cloud data center with proactive hotspot mitigation. Concurr. Comput. Pract. Exp. **31**(17), 5221 (2019)
42. Singh, S., Chana, I.: QoS-aware autonomic resource management in cloud computing: a systematic review. ACM Comput. Surv. **48**(3), 39 (2015)
43. Singh, S., Chana, I.: Q-aware: quality of service based cloud resource provisioning. Comput. Electr. Eng. J. Elsevier (2015). https://doi.org/10.1016/j.compeleceng.2015/02/003
44. Singh, S., Chana, I.: QRSF: QoS-aware resource scheduling framework in cloud computing. J. Supercomput. **71**(1), 241–292 (2015)
45. Chana, I., Singh, S.: Quality of service and service level agreements for cloud environments: issues and challenges. In: Mahmood, Z. (ed.) Cloud Computing. CCN, pp. 51–72. Springer, Cham (2014). https://doi.org/10.1007/978-3-319-10530-7_3
46. Yu, R., Yan, Z., Stein, G., Wenlong, X., Kun, Y.: Toward cloud-based vehicular networks with efficient resource management. arXiv:1308.6208. arXiv (2013)

NFC Payment Security with Cloud Based Authentication System

Saira Raqib[✉] and Muhammad Rizwan

Department of Computer Science, Kinnaird College for Women,
Lahore, Pakistan
sairarqb47@gmail.com

Abstract. Near Field Communication is a new medium of wireless communication. NFC technology is now widely introducing in smartphones. NFC technology in smartphone has made them capable of contact-less payment on POS terminals. The security protocol used for contact and contact-less payments is named as EMV (Europay Master Visa). EMV sets the security standards for online transactions in contact and contact-less payments. When deeply analyzed, EMV protocol has security vulnerabilities in (1) Mutual Authentication and (2) Exchange of banking information between payment device and payment terminal. As NFC payment involves exchange of sensitive data in open environment within a range of 10 cm, risks are involved for data being theft. We introduced cloud hosted security protocol to overcome vulnerabilities in EMV standards. The authenticity of this protocol is analyzed using Scyther tool. The protocol uses an authentication server hosted on cloud and asymmetric encryption in mutual authentication and exchange of banking data between payment device and payment terminal.

Keywords: Near Field Communication (NFC) · Europay Master Visa (EMV) · Cloud · Point of Sale (POS) · Security first section

1 Introduction

Near Field Communication (NFC) is a wireless communication technology that is now being widely used for contacting less payments. NFC operates by transmitting radio waves at frequency of 13.56 MHz, It allows two NFC enabled devices to exchange information without contact with in a distance of 10 cm.

NFC payment is simply done by just keeping a smartphone with NFC feature close to NFC POS terminal. NFC payments are micro and macro level payments. Micro payment limits up to Maximum 20 Euros and no PIN or Signature is required for micro transactions where as if transaction is greater than assigned limit, that is called as Macro Transaction and is confirmed by client by entering PIN code or Signature [1]. The standard transactions performed using debit/credit cards and contactless payments uses security protocols defined by EMV (EuroPay Master Visa) [2]. As the NFC payments progressed, some security vulnerabilities are found in EMV standards. NFC payments work on radio waves and hence it involves a big risk of sensitive NFC bank card data being theft by an attacker using a radio antenna near the payment terminal [3, 4].

© Springer Nature Singapore Pte Ltd. 2020
I. S. Bajwa et al. (Eds.): INTAP 2019, CCIS 1198, pp. 738–751, 2020.
https://doi.org/10.1007/978-981-15-5232-8_63

A new security protocol is introduced in this paper to overcome flaws that are found in EMV standard. An authentication server is introduced in proposed solution for security and confidentiality of issuing and acquiring bank. The issuing banks and acquiring banks are connected in live environment with proposed authentication server. This solution is envisioned to secure NFC payment procedures performed through NFC bank cards that lacks the 4G or Wi-Fi capability. In this model we are using asymmetric cryptography, protocol in the proposed model ensures: (1) Mutual authentication (2) Reliability of banking data (3) Bank card validity. A symmetric session key is generated at the event of authentication to make sure the confidentiality of banking data. The justification of our proposed model will be done using scyther tool.

2 Related Literature

As NFC technology is a breakthrough for Contact less payments and it carries a very sensitive monetary data when used as a mean of contact less payment, so there must be a proper safe and encrypted environment for the data exchange between the actors involved. Several attacks are possible like data insertion, eavesdropping, replay attacks etc. when NFC payments are operated in normal open environment. Attackers can change the data transmitted between NFC communication. Attackers can steal the sensitive monetary information between NFC communication in payment environment. Many studies have been conducted to overcome the possible NFC attack and different solutions are proposed to overcome proposed NFC attacks. For possible eavesdropping attack, an attacker can intercept data transmitted using a large antenna between two NFC devices communicating with each other [8]. Elbagoury has defined a solution by introducing a noisy wireless channel [9]. This channel gets a provable key and share it among players to prevent eavesdropping.

Urien and Piramuthu has proposed a solution for authentication of NFC devices using protocols based on Elliptic Curve Cryptography [10]. They have proposed a solution to secure NFC payment system using NFC smartphone in a physical retail store environment. ECC approach offers a low complexity (low storage and less messages) for NFC Smart Phone resources (ram, storage capacity) but the attacks can be attempted easily on bank data because of NFC radio waves carrying sensitive data.

Ceipidor et al. has secured the banking data transfer between NFC payment terminal and NFC POS device by introducing mutual authentication protocol by sharing keys (symmetric) between both devices using authentication server [11]. This ensured mutual authentication between phone and terminal and privacy of sensitive banking data shared between both devices. This system lacks behind transactional data veracity and the legitimacy of the phone (transactional data are not withdrawn).

We anticipated a protocol that overwhelms the EMV weaknesses based on cloud architecture by utilizing asymmetric cryptography. In our protocol, NFC payment terminal is a connected object that is connected in real time with cloud based authentication server with Wifi or 4G and is responsible for communication with cloud over a secure channel. Hence our proposed protocol doesn't require any extra hard wares to be installed but in fact it makes use of the smart phone resources for secure communication and exchange of certificates between actors. The proposed protocol make sure mutual authentication between NFC terminal and NFC smartphone as well as non-repudiation between the proposed actors such NFC smartphone and NFC POS and secrecy of banking data.

3   EMV Risks and Weaknesses

EMV procedures are executed Online Mode or Offline Mode [5, 6]. Online mode works with a connection with internet between payment device, its acquisitioning bank and between acquisitioning bank and issuing bank. The security procedures performed by issuing and acquiring bank are well managed in online mode. Where-as in offline mode security procedures are managed in payment terminal [7].

In this paper we are dealing with two vulnerabilities 1) Lack of authenticity between clients' payment device and payment terminal 2) Transfer of banking data in open format without encryption. EMVco assumptions is NFC transactions are made in open environment with distance ranging of 10 cm, so it's difficult for attackers to steal sensitive banking information [3] but the study in [4] explicitly says that this assumption is very weak. Following are the sensitive information that can be theft 1) PAN (Personal Account Number) 2) Expiration Date, However, card holder name and CVV cannot be retrieved. Some of the ecommerce websites don't get the CVV value when performing online transactions, so the stolen information can be used on ecommerce websites to make fraudulent purchases.

3.1   Principal

In this paper, we have proposed a security protocol that successfully over comes the weaknesses found in EMV. In our proposed model we are using asymmetric cryptography for online communication of AS (authentication server). We are keeping the PAN (personal account number) secret in our model. Instead of PAN our proposed model will be using an identifier Idc to recognize NFC card in AS and issuing bank. Due to unconnected object, card C can transfer data to AS by POS only. Whereas POS is capable of direct communication with AS (Table 1).

Table 1. Abbreviations

nPOS	NFC enabled POS
nBC	NFC enabled BC
AS	Authentication Server
CA	Certificate of Authority
CIB	Cards Issuing bank
TAB	Terminal acquiring bank
H(M)	Hashing Function
BD	Data stored in banking card
TD	Transactional data generated by nPOS
C(X)	Cert. of X
pK(X)	Public key of X
sK(X)	Secret key of X
Key(nBC, nPOS)	Key produced during POS and card communication
Key(nPOS, AS)	Key produced to protect the exchange of information between AS and nPOS

3.2 Actors

In this model, we are overcoming the weaknesses of EMV protocol. Our proposed model includes three actors each have a specific role given below:

1. AS(Authentication Server). AS is used to authenticate NFC bank cards. It is used to increase the security element of issuing and accruing bank. Suppose that this server will be available to us at any time and at every place. It also stores a list of certification authority and for the verification of certificates and signature it has some security application.
2. nPOS(NFC point of sale). nPOS is responsible for all NFC payment operations. It communicates with AS directly through TLS (Transport Layer Security) [11], instead of communicating with issuing and accruing banks. Every time when a connection establishes between nPOS and AS, authentication is performed and new session key K(nPOS, AS) is generated.
3. nBC(NFC bank card). For transactions with a NFC card, the client needs to keep it close to nPOS. Also, nBC stocks the certificate of server to converse for the safety with the AS, it utilizes the public key of server

4 Details of Proposed Protocol

Step1: Authentication Request for nBC (nPOS -> nBC)

- In first step, nPOS sends TD (random values, date, time) in clear format which is one-time TD and exclusive for every transaction. This helps to overcome replay attacks, auth request for nBC, Request-nBC, Certificate (TAB), Certificate (nPOS) and Signature-nPOS. The Signature-nPOS is generated by sK(nPOS) of "nPOS, nBC, TD, Request-nBC" message after performing the hashing operation.

- Certificate (nPOS), Certificate (tAB) and Signature-nPOS collectively perform the authentication of nPOS ensuring the reliability of "nPOS, TD, nBC, Request-nBC" message. This step also makes sure that nPOS can't refuse sending the Signature-nPOS in future.
- nBC has no application installed for verification of nPOS authenticity, but it is able to send the message received (1) to AS by the help of nPOS to execute verification process for nPOS (Fig. 1).

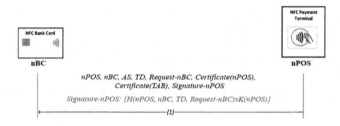

Fig. 1. Authentication request for nBC

Step 2: Authentication and Session Requests for nPOS (nBC -> nPOS)

- In this step, authentication between nBC and nPOS takes place with the help of authentication and sessions requests generated between nBC and nPOS.
- The received message (1) from nPOS requesting authentication of nBC and provides evidence of nPOS authentication by issuing certificates of Certificate (nPOS), Certificate (tAB) and Signature-nPOS.
- To overcome the replay attacks, nBC generate a random number Random-nBC. Random-nBC is generated by hashing the secret identifier Id-nBC and TD: H (IdnBC, TD) which is sent by nBC to AS through nPOS.
- nBC sends the following data to AS through nPOS:

- Identifier Id-nBC in AS.
- Encrypted information with pK(AS) which has the message (1), Random-nBC, authentication request for nPOS (Request-nPOS) and a session request for payment (RequestS). The Request-nPOS communicate with Authentication Server (AS) sends Certificate(nBC), Certificate(CIB) and Signature-nBC encrypted with pK(AS).
- Signature nBC is created by hashing the message of sK(nBC) consisting of "nBC, nPOS, AS, Random-nBC, Request-nPOS, Request-Session" (Fig. 2).

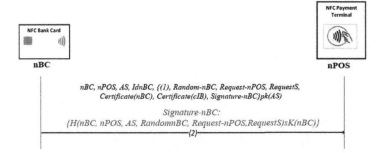

Fig. 2. Authentication and session requests for nPOS

Step 3: Authentication Requests for nPOS and nBC (nPOS -> AS)

- AS decrypt the data sent by session key Key(AS, nPOS) and get the following: TD and Message (2). AS also checks TD validity and in case if fails in validation, It will not send response to nPOS. If the TD comes out to be valid, it decrypts the Message (2) with sK(AS) and get content.
- AS and nPOS are already authenticated through TLS session and securely communicating through session key Key(As, nPOS), so AS will perform nBC authentication to nPOS. It Authentication is successful, another verification is performed other than TLS procedure to authenticate nPOS to nBC. It checks that:

- Certificate(nBC) and Certificate(CIB) are valid.
- The issuing Certification Authority CA3 of Certificate(CIB) is a reliable certification authority.
- pK(CA3) authenticate the signature obtained from Certficate(CIB)
- pK(CIB) validates the signature obtained from Certificate(nBC)
- pK(nBC) authenticates Signature-nBC.

- After successful authentication of nBC, AS performs authentication of nPOS to nBC by the following checks:

- Certificate (nPOS) and Certificate (TAB) are valid and not withdrawn.
- The Certification Authority (CA2) of Certificate (TAB) is a reliable certification authority.
- pK(CA2) performs the validation of signature obtained from Certificate (TAB)
- pK(TAB) performs the validation of signature obtained from Certificate (nPOS)
- pK(nPOS) authenticates Signature-nPOS (Fig. 3).

Fig. 3. Authentication Requests for nPOS and nBC

Step 4: nBC authenticity and session confirmations (AS -> nPOS).

- If nPOS authenticity is positive by AS, a session key is generated Key(nPOS, nBC) to initiate a protected payment transaction between nPOS and nBC.
- AS sends encrypted text to nPOS with Key(AS, nPOS) Conf1 and Conf2 to confirm legitimacy of nBC and nPOS that contains the session key Key(nBC, nPOS).
- nPOS decrypts the message received and check TD and Random-nBC validates the nBC with Auth-nBC message. nPOS also obtain the session key between nPOS and nBC Key(nPOS, nBC), Conf2 and Certificate(CIB). Conf2 cannot decrypt by nPOS because it is encrypted with pK(nBC) and it sent from AS to nBC by means of nPOS. It mainly contains a confirmation message of nPOS validity and Signature-AS.

- Signature-AS is generated by hashing message obtained from session key sK(AS) of "nPOS, nBC, AS, K(nPOS, nBC), TD, Random-nBC, Auth-nPOS" (Fig. 4).

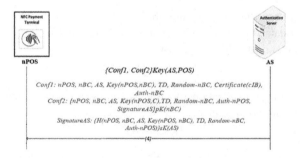

Fig. 4. nBC authenticity and session confirmations

Step 5: nPOS session confirmations and Authenticity (nPOS -> nBC)

- The received (Conf2) message from AS is sent by nPOS to nBC in this step and confirms nBC to initiate transaction session by sending a Random-nPOS value in a cipher text along with session key Key(nPOS, nBC).

- nBC also gets Conf2 with secret key sK(nBC) and checks TD and Random-nBC and obtain Key(nPOS, nBC), Auth-nPOS and Signature-AS.
- nBC trust and stores the authentication server certificate Certificate(AS) which has the pK(AS) and verifies Signature-AS by using pK(AS) to authenticate AS and make sure the authenticity of "nPOS, nBC, AS, Key(nPOS, nBC), TD, Random-nBC, Auth-nPOS". It also makes sure that AS cannot refuse to send Signaturre-ASs in the future.
- nBC also ensures the authenticity of nPOS with Auth-nPOS and decrypts using session key Key(nPOS, nBC) {Random-nBC, TD, RandomnPOS} Key(nPOS, nBC) and gets a Random-nPOS value (Fig. 5).

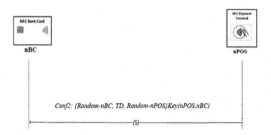

Fig. 5. nPOS session confirmations and authenticity

Step 6: Confirmation back to nPOS and Exchange of Banking Data (nBC -> nPOS).

- nBC starts a secure payment session with nPOS using session key Key(nPOS, nBC) by sending: Random-nPOS-1, the BD and their signatures. The signature of BD is sent by using sK(CIB) to ensure data reliability for nPOS.
- nPOS decrypts and check the Random-nPOS-1 and gets BD and its electronic signatures. It also check signature send using pK(CIB) obtained in step (4) (Fig. 6).

Fig. 6. Confirmation back to POS

Illustration diagram of our propose protocol is shown below in Fig. 7. The diagram describes the steps of messages exchanged at each step in the propose protocol. The fig shows all the 3 actors of our proposed protocol that how they are communicating with each other and the certificates and keys exchanged between each actor. Our proposed actors are Bank Card (nBC) which is not a connected object and can communicate with nPOS. Point of Sale (nPOS) which is a connected object using TLS connection and is responsible for communication with authentication server (AS) and Bank Card (nBC). Last but not the least is authentication server (AS). AS is the main key player responsible for mutual authentication.

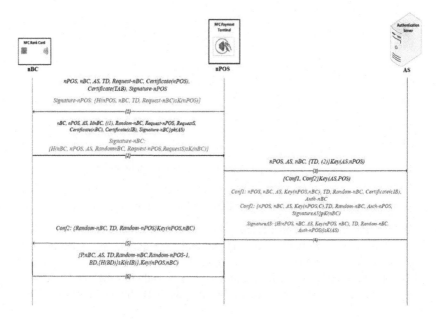

Fig. 7. Diagram of our propose protocol

5   Results

If nBC and nPOS performs all steps that are proposed in protocol, its firmly assured that both nPOS and nBC are authenticated mutually as step no. 4 assures the authenticity of nBC and Authenticity of nPOS is assured in step (5). They can't deny each other's validity because of electronic signatures being sent i.e. Signature nPOS and Signature nBC. The validity of BD that is stored on nBC and its confidentiality is assured in step (6).

6   Scyther Verification

We verify our protocol in the proposed model using scythe tool. Security Protocol Description Language is the language used in scyther tool. Scyther tool can be freely downloaded at [12]. The study also identify numerous breaches and creates a graph for breaches found related to the stated claim [13]. We have written the current system which is working now and our proposed protocol using SPDL language [14].

6.1   Existing System

Following is the SPDL program that we have run on scyther tool for current system. In this system the POS(nP) and bank-card (nB) are communicating with each other without mutual authentication and thus encountered attacks in it (Fig. 8).

```
 role nP
{
fresh tD,RP1:Nonce;
fresh ReqnB:text;
var K(nB,nP):SessionKey;
var id,ReqnP,ReqS:text;
var bD:BankData;

send_1(nP,nB,nP,nB,tD,ReqnB,CertnP,CertAqB,{h(nB,nP,tD,ReqnB)}secK(nP));
recv_2(nB,nP,nB,nP,id,{tD,ReqnB,CertnP,CertAqB,{h(nB,nP,tD,ReqnB)}secK(nP),CertnB,CertIsB,
h(id,tD),ReqnP,ReqS,{h(nB,nP,h(id,tD),ReqnP,ReqS)}secK(nB)});

send_3(nP,nP,nB,{tD,id,{tD,ReqnB,CertnP,CertAqB,{h(nB,nP,tD,ReqnB)}secK(nP),CertnB,CertIsB,
h(id,tD),ReqnP,ReqS,{h(nB,nP,h(id,tD),ReqnP,ReqS)}secK(nB)}}K(,nP));

role nB
{
var tD,RP1:Nonce;
var K(nB,nP):sessionKey;
fresh id,ReqnB,ReqS:text;
fresh bD:BankData;

rev_1(nP,nB,nP,nB,tD,ReqnB,CertnP,CertAqB,{h(nB,nP,tD,ReqnB)}secK(nP));

send_2(nB,nP,nB,nP,id,{tD,ReqnB,CertnP,CertAqB,{h(nB,nP,tD,ReqnB)}secK(nP),CertnB,CertIsB
,h(id,tD),ReqnP,ReqS,{h(nB,nP,h(id,tD),ReqnP,ReqS)}secK(nB)});
```

Fig. 8. SPDL program for existing system

6.2   Scyther Claims for Existing System

We have run the program for existing system using scyther tool. In the program, there is no mutual authentication system existing between nP and nB and thus attacks are found in the scyther results. The Fig. 9 shows the attacks that are found for nP, and nB in current system. Replay, reflection and man in the middle attacks are detected by the authentication claims such as Alive, Weakagree, Niagree and Nisynch. SKR (Session Key Reveal) and Secret in the fig proofs the confidentiality of sensitive data.

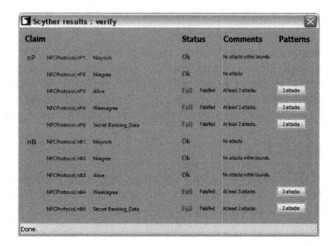

Fig. 9. Scyther verification results for current system

```
role nP
{
fresh tD,RP1:Nonce;
fresh ReqnB:text;
var K(nB,nP):SessionKey;
var id,ReqnP,ReqS:text;
var bD:BankData;

send_1(nP,nB,nP,nB,tD,ReqnB,CertnP,CertAqB,{h(nB,nP,tD,ReqnB)}secK(nP));
recv_2(nB,nP,nB,nP,id,{tD,ReqnB,CertnP,CertAqB,{h(nB,nP,tD,ReqnB)}secK(nP),CertnB,CertIsB,
h(id,tD),ReqnP,ReqS,{h(nB,nP,h(id,tD),ReqnP,ReqS)}secK(nB)});

send_3(nP,nP,nB,{tD,id,{tD,ReqnB,CertnP,CertAqB,{h(nB,nP,tD,ReqnB)}secK(nP),CertnB,CertIsB,
h(id,tD),ReqnP,ReqS,{h(nB,nP,h(id,tD),ReqnP,ReqS)}secK(nB)}}K(,nP));

role nB
{
var tD,RP1:Nonce;
var K(nB,nP):sessionKey;
fresh id,ReqnB,ReqS:text;
fresh bD:BankData;

rev_1(nP,nB,nP,nB,tD,ReqnB,CertnP,CertAqB,{h(nB,nP,tD,ReqnB)}secK(nP));

send_2(nB,nP,nB,nP,id,{tD,ReqnB,CertnP,CertAqB,{h(nB,nP,tD,ReqnB)}secK(nP),CertnB,CertIsB
,h(id,tD),ReqnP,ReqS,{h(nB,nP,h(id,tD),ReqnP,ReqS)}secK(nB)});

role AS
{
var tD:Nonce;
fresh K(nB,nP):sessionKey;
var id,ReqnB,ReqnP, ReqS:text;
rec_3(nP,AS,nP,nB,AS,{tD,id,{tD,ReqnB,CertnP,CertAqB,{H(nB,nP,tD,ReqnB)}secK(nP),CertnB,CertIsB
,h(id,tD),ReqnP,ReqS,{h(nB,nP,AS,h(id,tD),ReqnP,ReqS)}secK(nB)}pubK(AS)K(AS,nP));
```

Fig. 10. SPDL program for proposed system

7 Proposed System

Following is the SPDL program that we have run on scyther tool for proposed security protocol validation. In this we have introduced our new authentication server (AS) that is the key player of mutual authentication between nPOS and nBC. In the proposed system the POS(nP) and bank-card (nB) are communicating with each other through AS (authentication server) and found no attacks in it. Figure 10 shows the program that is run on scyther tool using SPDL with our proposed actors and its clear from the output generated by the program that there are no replay, reflection and man in the middle attacks found in it.

Following code which we have run on SPDL language will generate the following output as shown in Fig. 11. The fig below is the proof for scyther claim that no attacks are found for nP, nB and AS. Replay, reflection and man in t Scyther claims.

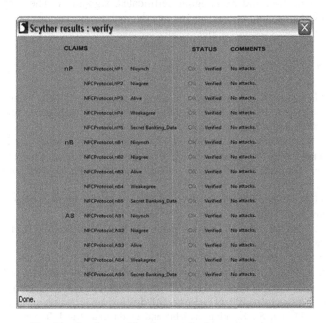

Fig. 11. Scyther verification results for proposed system

7.1 Scyther Claims for Proposed System

The Fig. 11 below is the proof for scyther claim that no attacks are found for nP, nB and AS. Replay, reflection and man in the middle attacks are detected by the authentication claims such as Alive, Weakagree, Niagree and Nisynch. SKR (Session Key Reveal) and Secret in the fig proofs the confidentiality of sensitive data.

8 Conclusion

We introduced a new cloud-based protocol to fill the loopholes in EMV protocol for NFC contactless payments. We have introduced a cloud-based authentication server which is the main representative for security between Banks, NFC Cards and Payment Terminal in our proposed protocol. The proposed protocol performs mutual authentication and non-repudiation between NFC card and NFC point of sale, confidentiality and reliability of private banking information (compared to [15]) Moreover, session keys secrete keys, hashing and cryptography techniques are used to ensure the payments security [16]. Our proposed protocol is accurate and reliable because we are using certificate, signatures and asymmetric cryptography approach for authentication which is different when considered objective and online/offline payment environment. Our approach is practical as well as it doesn't involve any extra hardware infrastructure except the authentication server. We are using the NFC enabled smartphone resources to establish connection and exchanging certificates, signatures. The proposed model can also be used to secure contact payment systems.

References

1. Pasquet, M., Reynaud, J., Rosenberger, C.: Secure payment with NFC mobile phone in the SmartTouch project. In: 2008 International Symposium on Collaborative Technologies and Systems (2008). https://doi.org/10.1109/cts.2008.4543921
2. Madhoun, N.E., Guenane, F., Pujolle, G.: An online security protocol for NFC payment: formally analyzed by the scyther tool. In: 2016 Second International Conference on Mobile and Secure Services (MobiSecServ) (2016). https://doi.org/10.1109/mobisecserv.2016. 7440225
3. Integrated Circuit Specifications for Payment Systems (2019). http://mathdesc.fr/documents/ normes/emv_book4.pdf
4. Lifchitz, R.: Hacking the NFC credit cards for fun and debit. In: Hackito Ergo Sum Conference (2012)
5. Ward, M.: EMV card payments–an update. Inf. Secur. Tech. Rep. **11**, 89–92 (2006)
6. de Ruiter, J., Poll, E.: Formal analysis of the EMV protocol suite. In: Mödersheim, S., Palamidessi, C. (eds.) TOSCA 2011. LNCS, vol. 6993, pp. 113–129. Springer, Heidelberg (2012). https://doi.org/10.1007/978-3-642-27375-9_7
7. Porkess, R., Mason, S.: Looking at debit and credit card fraud. Teach. Stat. **34**, 87–91 (2011). https://doi.org/10.1111/j.1467-9639.2010.00437.x
8. Eun, H., Lee, H., Oh, H.: Conditional privacy preserving security protocol for NFC applications. IEEE Trans. Consum. Electron. **59**, 153–160 (2013). https://doi.org/10.1109/ tce.2013.6490254
9. Elbagoury, A., Mohsen, A., Ramadan, M., Youssef, M.: Practical provably secure key sharing for near field communication devices. In: 2013 International Conference on Computing, Networking and Communications (ICNC) (2013). https://doi.org/10.1109/iccnc. 2013.6504182
10. Urien, P., Piramuthu, S.: Framework and authentication protocols for smartphone, NFC, and RFID in retail transactions. In: IEEE Eighth International Conference on Intelligent Sensors, Sensor Networks and Information Processing (2013). https://doi.org/10.1109/issnip.2013. 6529768

11. Ceipidor, U.B., Medaglia, C.M., Marino, A., et al.: KerNeeS: a protocol for mutual authentication between NFC phones and POS terminals for secure payment transactions. In: 2012 9th International ISC Conference on Information Security and Cryptology (2012). https://doi.org/10.1109/iscisc.2012.6408203
12. Cremers CIn: Cas Cremers (2019). https://people.cispa.io/cas.cremers/publications/index.html
13. 2nd International Workshop on Automated Specification and Verification of Web Systems. In: 2nd International Workshop on Automated Specification and Verification of Web Systems (WWV06) (2006). https://doi.org/10.1109/wwv.2006.2
14. Cremers, C.J.F.: The scyther tool: verification, falsification, and analysis of security protocols. In: Gupta, A., Malik, S. (eds.) CAV 2008. LNCS, vol. 5123, pp. 414–418. Springer, Heidelberg (2008). https://doi.org/10.1007/978-3-540-70545-1_38
15. Cremers, C., Mauw, S.: Operational semantics. In: Cremers, C., Mauw, S. (eds.) Operational Semantics and Verification of Security Protocols Information Security and Cryptography, pp. 13–35. Springer, Heidelberg (2012). https://doi.org/10.1007/978-3-540-78636-8_3
16. Lowe, G.: A hierarchy of authentication specifications. In: Proceedings 10th Computer Security Foundations Workshop. https://doi.org/10.1109/csfw.1997.596782

Resource Utilization in Data Center by Applying ARIMA Approach

Farhan Nisar[1](✉) and Bilal Ahmed[2](✉)

[1] UET Peshawar, Peshawar, Pakistan
farhansnisar@yahoo.com
[2] GC University, Lahore, Pakistan
bilal_ahmdll@yahoo.com

Abstract. Resource administration is basically an important dire function in the data center that may be affect Service level agreement and operation cost provided by the data center known as OPEX and SLA. Efficient resource is the key factor of resource utilization and provided guarantee SLA to each application to maximize the resources in data center. Accurate prediction support each application in data center is the key requirement to provision an efficient resource management. However, Under-estimating and Overestimation in the application workload result shows the resource under provision or overestimating. In this paper, our approach to apply ARIMA model for workload applications in data center, it is forecasting technique and capture autocorrelation in the series by modeling it directly. The key concept of ARIMA model is ordering and differencing only with linear data capturing when data graph in straight line. We applies different operation model to fit applications workload time series. Performance of ARIMA can be tested by MATLAB simulation. We are using the ARIMA model parameters to find out prediction errors during the day and month calculated (i.e. Day = 7.01% and Month = 6.73%) to provide accuracy of ARIMA prediction model.

Keywords: Prediction model · Simulation result · Related work · Comparison survey

1 Introduction

Data centers [1] basically deliver an elastic environment to their users and running applications. The environment has a potential design like Agile Resource Management strategy. For example, Resource provisioned to each application in data center are dynamically allocated with respect to changes of workload accommodate and each users budget is reduced by leasing flexible resources. In contrast on the other hand, Agile resource can also advantage the data center deliver to reduce its operation cost (OPEX) by applying minimum resources to each application in the data center applications. Therefore, Minimum resource is defined as "A minimum resource that are supplied by data center to running a specific application by data center manager, and utilization of resources is maximized and satisfied SLAs". However, the data center cannot provide suitable resources targeted for each application with existing source

I. S. Bajwa et al. (Eds.): INTAP 2019, CCIS 1198, pp. 752–761, 2020.
https://doi.org/10.1007/978-981-15-5232-8_64

strategies for each application. They describe basically the memory utilization, memory utilization and I/O disk running in data centers on main server was calculated 17.76%, 77.93% and 75.28% respectively [2]. For example, the custody are overestimated in the data center specially most of the time the CPU utilized more resources as compare to other applications. It is a great benefit to providing the authentic agile resource management mechanism and other resources to data center and demand of application as well.

The management Architecture consist of two parts i) Global Resource Manager ii) Local Resource Manager. Global Resource Manager is basically to collect the application workload and depend on number of application arrival request. Data can trace from front end server for each time slot. They basically analyzing the data historically, the GRM forecasts module predictor in a period of time for each application (For example forecasting time period). Second it can be estimated application workload in data centers and allocate resource module in GRM essential determine the minimum provisioning resource for each application in next forecasting time period. It should be noted that forecasting time period is different from time slot that GRM collect data workload from each front-end server and based on our configuration setting, each front-end server upload data in each 10 s and application workload predictor would forecast the workload for the next 10 min for each application. The proactive resources for each application's and allocating different resource for predicting the workload for each application is necessary for Global resource management, because implementing Global resource management suffers live relocation and Virtual machines (VMs), which take too much time to complete the process [3]. After words, Global Resource allocator for each application's required to record least source provisioning of application to the servers physically and depend on number of total awaked servers. Computational Complexity of global resource manager are optimized for each forecasting time period in the data center (i.e. 10 min).

The Local Resource Manager is small time scale resource optimization and introduced to provide finer granularity. The figure shows that the Xen-base server and base on real time resource application of each Virtual machines in the server. Recently many database demands for each application have proposed many dissimilar types of reserve allocation strategies. CPU Scheduling Resources [4, 6], Memory Resource Scheduling [4, 6] and Input/Output Scheduling Resource [7, 9] and Memory Resource Scheduling [10, 12] to each Local resource Manager efficiently and impartially share the server-based resources among its presenting VMs. Therefore, designing such optimal Global resource allocation still challenging strategy to determine the poor performance and complexity to estimating the minimum application resource provisioning in the future.

Based on the GRM architecture, application workload prediction prerequisite to manage the data center resources. Poor request capable to estimate the inefficient resource management therefore it provide an application workload model which is precise application and necessary un resource management. Prediction is a prerequisite to manage the resources of a datacenters. Poor enactment of a request capability estimate leads to inefficient resource management. In this paper, we apply ARIMA (Auto Regressive Integrated Moving Average Model) to forecast application workload in data center for the next forecasting time period.

The paper is organized into different Sections. In Sect. 2, we explain our ARIMA model-based application workload Prediction Algorithm. In Sect. 3, we describe the application performance based on application workload on MATLAB simulation with results. In Sect. 4, we describe the related works of the reviewers. The conclusion and future works is presented in Sect. 5.

2   Application Workload Prediction Model

Different Application workload is time series base model application and heterogeneous. Time series model are the collection of well define data through measurement over time. Time series may be cyclical, seasonal and regular event base if the data used ARIMA model then series are stationary and depend on linear relationship and if series doesn't depend on time when it capture then series doesn't stationary. When some revelation sudden huge spikes over time. Apply ARIMA model to guess the workload in data center because ARIMA model automatically each application workload first and after checking the data nonstationary then select different kind of mathematical models. For example, AR (Auto Regressive model), MA (Moving Average model) and ARMA (Auto Regressive Model) forecast application in the data center for next time slot. The method of ARIMA model can be summarized in Fig. 1.

Table 1. ACF/PACF models

Model	AR	MA	ARMA
ACF	Geometric	Significant till p lags	Geometric
PACF	Significant till p lags	Geometric	Geometric

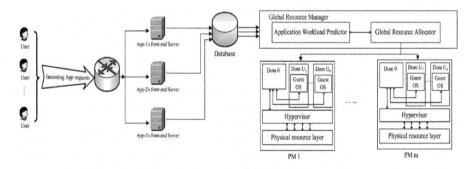

Fig. 1. GRM architecture

2.1   Stationary Testing

Input of ARIMA model can be obtained by application workload time series, and denoted by capital $S = \{s(0), s(1), s(2), s(3)\ldots\ldots\ldots s(n-1)\}$ where n denoted the length of the data and we would predict future applications workload with time slot $s(t)$ $(t = 0, 1, 2, 3\ldots\ldots\ldots n-1)$ (Table 1).

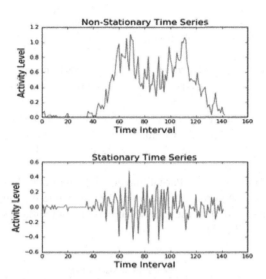

Fig. 2. Stationary and non-stationary graph

In 1st step it checks the historical data is stationary. If the data is stationary it moves to model recognition section as shown in Fig. 2.

In 2nd step if the data is not stationary time series i.e. statistical properties of time series is not in constant with time then model should not be fitted for testing then we take differential of the data by applying different operation.

S' (i.e. S' = {s'(t)s'(t)} = s(t)−s(t−1), 0 < t ≤ n−1)

We Apply the Dickey-Fuller test [13] in the time series.

  i. It checks value of AR (p) series less than 5%.
 ii. If AR (p) value greater than 5% then concept is null hypothesis and time series has unit root.
iii. First take differential and then analysis.
 iv. Current value depend on fraction of previous value of the series.
  v. It built a regression line of previous value.

It is noted that difference operation is applied iteratively until the smooth time series to convert it stationary S'.

2.2 Model Recognition

In model recognition, we apply AR (p), MA (q) and ARMA (p, q) Operations to predict workload based on historical data S'. p and q indicates the order of autoregressive portion and order of moving average portion. ARIMA (p, d, q) shows order, regressive and average of the data center. First apply differencing of order d with lag-1 differencing and seasonal for removing trend.

$$S'(n) = C + \alpha S'(n-1) + \ldots \ldots \alpha PS'(n-p)$$
$$\beta(n) + \beta 1(n-1) + \ldots \ldots \beta q(n-q) \tag{1}$$

Where C is Constant and $(\alpha 1, \alpha 2, \ldots \ldots \alpha p)$ is set of Coefficient at different lag and set of AR. $(\beta 1, \beta 2 \ldots \beta q)$ is the Coefficient at different lag and set of MA. $\alpha PS'(n-p)$ is the set of lag value with mean zero and variance V^2. N−1 up to N−P is the set of lagged value βn.

Autocorrelation function and Partial functional are introduce for smooth time series S'. ACF is basically the correlation between the two value of same variable X1 and X1+K. PACF is association measure between two random variables with the effect set of random variables (Fig. 3).

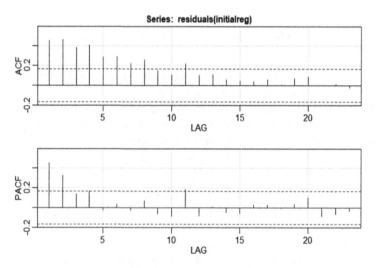

Fig. 3. ACF and PACF

When apply AR, MA and ARMA operation in ACF model, then it shows Tailing off, Truncation and Tailing off. When apply AR, MA and ARMA operation in PACF model, then it show Truncation, Tailing off and Tailing off again. The ACF and PACF decays very slowly and spikes at higher lags.

2.3   Evaluate Model Parameters

In evaluate parameter it predict the value of S' (n) base on Eq. (1) p, q and variance can be calculated by historical data S'

Akaile information Criterion [15] is fitted model provide suitable time series S'.it optimize the value p and q and calculate

AIC base on the equation:

$$AIC\,(p,\,q)\; =\; \ln\,(L) + 2K \tag{2}$$

L is basically likelihood function and depend on modeling data in time series and K is the number of free parameters.

$$K = p + q + K + 1$$

Optimal value of p and q, innovation algorithm [16] and determined the value of $\alpha 1$, $\alpha 2$.....αp and $\beta 1,\beta 2$.....βq and denoted the linear prediction of $S'(n)$.

$$\text{Where } S'(n)\; =\; \sum\,\left(S'\,(n-i) - S'\,(n-i)\,\right) \tag{3}$$

$K(I, J)$ as CF and $S'(i)$ and $S'(J) = E(S'(i)\,S'(j))$ it can be calculated by the following equation:

$$\alpha\; =\; \left(k(n+1,\,J+1) - \sum \alpha - vi\right) \tag{4}$$

$J = 0$, 1,......$n-1$ and $Vn = K(n+1,\,n+1) - \sum n = 0$ and $K(1,1)$. It provide among AR coefficients $J = 1$, $2,,,,,,P+Q$. Substitute $j = q+1$, $q+2$........$q+P$ in Eq. 5

$$B\; =\; \beta n, j - \sum \alpha\beta \tag{5}$$

Once ARIMA model can be fitted to time series and find optimal parameters, it can easily predicted S′ base on the following equation.

$$S'(n)\; =\; \sum \left(S'(n-1) - S'(n-1)\right)\}1 \le n \le m$$
$$\sum S'\,(n-i) + \sum \left(S'(n-i) - S'(n-i)\right),\, n \ge m$$

Where $m = \max\,(p,\,q)$

3   Simulation Results

Assume the application follow to trace the request for accessing the world cup 98 website [18]. For each application 10 s, server send application in term of application request within GRM period. GRM collect application workload data trace and ARIMA prediction model for forecast for every next 10 min. Suppose GRM has already the application workload in data center.

Suppose GRM has obtained the application workload on 51 day of World Cup which shows the workload in the data center. The red line shows predict workload and almost match actual workload line. Prediction error is less than 10% most of the time. Table 2 shows the statistical of workload prediction during the day and month. The 44.5% application workload values are under-estimate and underestimate. To maximize and minimize and average overestimate error are (Max) 73%, (Min) 6.3%, and (Average) 7.17%. On Other hand, prediction value of Minimum, Maximum and Average is 39%, 5.7% and 6.4%. Moreover, the maximum overestimate and underestimate during the day periods noted 19:20–19:30/17:30–17:40 when application workload suffers from sudden huge spikes. The curve automatically increase and decrease which is hard to predict. The average of total predication error during the day is around 7.1% (Figs. 4 and 5).

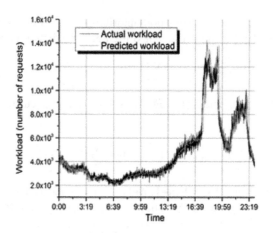

Fig. 4. The distribution of application workload prediction error during the day

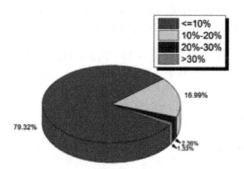

Fig. 5. Predicted workload for one day

Table 2. Prediction results during the day

	Total prediction error	Overestimated prediction error	Underestimated prediction error
Occupation ratio	100%	44.40%	55.60%
Min	5:7 10^5%	6:3 10^4%	5:7 10^5%
Max	73.90%	73.90%	39.60%
Average	7.01%	7.17%	6.42%

Next, predict application workload for each workload for 10 min within one month from 52th day of world cup and the result shown in Table 3. The total average overestimated and underestimated are similar one day prediction result have a little bit improvement. This is because at the beginning of the month, the application workload time series are smoother than the rest of the days in the month.

Table 3. Prediction results during the month

	Total prediction error	Overestimated prediction error	Underestimated prediction error
Occupation ratio	100%	49.20%	50.80%
Min	2:3 10^6%	4:5 10^5%	2:3 10^6%
Max	78.50%	78.50%	42.30%
Average	6.73%	6.89%	6.14%

4 Related Works

Many Algorithms have been recently proposed forecast workload for data center applications, Virtual machine and servers for data center facilitate different proactive resources management. Zhen [17] proposed efficient resource network predict network resources of each virtual machine demand for CPU memory for internet applications. However they proposed First UP and Slow Down Algorithm by predict network resource for smooth quantity weighted moving average (EWMA) model when algorithm is fluctuation i.e. FUSD algorithm always over predicts depend on the source request of the virtual machine for avoid a SLA violation. Experiment results shows that 75% for resource demand forecast are more complex than actual demands resource with mean error of 9.4%. Kashifuddin [19] proposed are using chaotic theory of Virtual machine prediction workload in data center. Virtual machines trace workload can't exhibit by cyclic pattern. For example Similar workload can't appear in virtual machine and fixed period of time can't predicted accurately for long tern scheduling for example prediction error is increasing depend on time in order to improve the workload of VM follows a chaotic time series, they basically calculate MLE (Maximum lyapunoy Exponent value) related to time series from Google cluster Data Trace and NASA [20, 21] and trace data positively and find value of MLE indicated the time series chaotic theory [22]. Choatic theory predict virtual machines and their experiment shows that mean error occur between predicted Virtual machine workload and actual Virtual Machines capability is among 0.005 and 0.015 depend on different data traces running on the virtual machines. Dynamic features of server workload. Nidhi and Rao [23, 24] simulation propose collaborating learning method for forecast each server work correctly. The method is to apply to set different algorithm to forecast server workload and final workload forecast result design for weighted completely result from different prediction algorithm in the set. Weight of each prediction algorithm is directly proportional to accuracy prediction in previous time slots. The experiment results shows it proposed accuracy up to 87.8% Virtual machine and servers in data centers are finished altering energetically due to VM reallocation and VM migration for example VM that is rent base service to running it application and workload may be suffer from huge spikes. When server was running CPU intensive application and I/O application for virtual machine reallocation and migration, Network resource and CPU memory consumption suddenly increase and decrease rapidly, However it is impossible to predict such drops and sudden surges. It is more accuracy workload predicting of the Virtual machines and servers. It is more accuracy to predict workload application. Weiner FIR [25] predicts the workload of the web browser. Workload of VM is resource demand resource utilization and it reallocation in term of different dimensional servers. The idea of filter is mean time error depend on capacity and forecast during intermission to solve Yule Walker equations. Similar to our work we proposed the ARIMA [26]. model predict the data center work applications. Therefore they apply Hyndman-khandakar Algorithm applies to determine the order of differencing the data than Dickey fuller test, which is different from our model

5 Conclusion

In this paper we have to study how to apply ARIMA model predict workload applications in term of arrival request for applications for each time slot during the next 10 min depend on data trace and data rates. By selecting such parameters using the existing methods the average application depend on prediction workload error in data center i.e. day calculation 7.01% and month calculation 6.73% respectively.

Our proposed ARIMA model is better for linear forecasting techniques such as AR, ARMA and MA models. These models are very sensitive and time series base which have an ability seasonal and trends component. If the time series is not stationary, the prediction accuracy of this forecasting model will reduce significantly. The chaotic theory describe application workload if workloads exhibit chaotic features. However, the ensemble learning method can alternative solution for predict application workload if system tolerate longer prediction delay and the complexity of ensemble learning method much better then forecasting models.

In future we design novel management resource for suitable resources depend on different size of virtual machine to application in data center based on prediction results, which are obtained from prediction model propose in this paper, however, maximize the total resource application guarantee SLA of the applications.

References

1. Architecture design, Congestion, TCP in cast and power consumption in data center (2013)
2. A large performance study Report 3820 (2012)
3. Live virtual machine migration with adaptive memory (2012)
4. The design and implementation of an operating system to support distributed multimedia (1996)
5. Borrow virtual time Scheduling supporting latency threads in general purpose (1999)

6. Credit Scheduler-Xen {Online} (2015)
7. Memory resources management in VM ware ESX Server (2002)
8. Memory overbooking and dynamic control of Xen virtual machine (2009)
9. Virtual machine memory Access Tracing with hypervisor Exclusive Cache (2007)
10. Fair Cloud sharing network in Cloud Computing (2012)
11. Improving bandwidth Efficiency and fairness in Cloud Computing (2013)
12. A cooperative game based allocation for sharing data center networks (2013)
13. Testing for unit roots in autoregressive moving average model (1984)
14. Farecasting with univariate Box Jenkins model (2009)
15. Prediction of monthly average solar radiation with TDNN and ARIMA (2012)
16. Time series theory method and methods (2013)
17. Dynamic resource allocation using virtual machines for cloud computing (2013)
18. The 98 world Cup websites [online] (2015)
19. Workload Prediction of virtual machines for harnessing data center (2014)
20. Traces of Google workloads [online]
21. NASA data trace [online]
22. Determine Lyapunov exponents form a time series (1985)
23. Online Ensemble learning Approach for server workload prediction in large data center (2012)
24. Ensemble learning for large scale workload (2014)
25. Lad prediction algorithm for multi tenant virtual machine (2012)
26. Workload prediction using ARIMA model and its impact on cloud application (2014)
27. Automatic time series forecasting packages (2008)
28. Testing the null hypothesis of stationary against the alternative of a unit root (1992)

Detecting Duplicates in Real-Time Data Warehouse Using Bloom Filter-Based Approach

Syed Rizwan, Syed Hasan Adil, and Noman Islam[✉]

Iqra University, Karachi, Pakistan
srizwanraziq@gmail.com, hasan.adil@iqra.edu.pk,
noman.islam@gmail.com

Abstract. Data warehousing has been a topic of intense research for past few years. A data warehouse is primarily as a central repository in which data is coming from disparate sources. Generally, fresh data in these warehouses are loaded to the central repository in disconnected mode through batch processing. Hence, there is always a chance of non-real time data available in the central warehouse. This stale data is not useful for most of the commercial real-time applications such as real-time transport monitoring, smart cities, semantic web, online transaction processing and sensor networks. In order to fully realize these applications, fresh data needs to be readily available for critical decision making purpose. In particular, they demand real time and quick accumulation of data from diverse sources in to main data warehouse. This paper focuses on maintaining consistency and providing real-time data updates in data warehouse. In particular, the paper targets the detection of duplicates in streaming environment with a limited amount of memory. For this purpose, it employs a novel concept called Bloom Filter. The bloom filter sets the bits in the array when the information is added in the data warehouse. This technique gives nearly 100% result without any false positive value. The error rate in worst case scenario is 0.01%. For implementation, a data structure called time frame bloom filter (TBF) is used which is essentially a bit map of information. Using this method, one can insert, update, delete and search the messages data in the data warehouse very quickly. To make the bloom filter scalable, one can also add more than one bloom filter to address the inconsistency issues.

Keywords: Consistency management · Data warehousing · Bloom filter · Real-time analysis · Time frame bloom filter

1 Introduction

Data warehousing has been a topic of intense research for quite a long time. One can define a data warehouse as a central repository where information is accumulated from multiple sources such as office branches, university campuses and multiple units of an organization. The updating of data occurs normally daily or weekly in data warehouses and this data can then be used for analysis and critical decisions making by end users. However, the time taken from online transaction processing (OLTP) to analysis is too

© Springer Nature Singapore Pte Ltd. 2020
I. S. Bajwa et al. (Eds.): INTAP 2019, CCIS 1198, pp. 762–771, 2020.
https://doi.org/10.1007/978-981-15-5232-8_65

much in this classical approach to data warehousing. The end user cannot make critical decisions in real-time due to lack of current data. This delay cannot be tolerated in modern applications as discussed earlier and one needs current or real time data for decision making purpose. This new paradigm where information is updated in real-time is called real time data warehouses. However, in this approach [1, 2], the consumer has to deal with several issues and consistency checks to reduce the time from OLTP to Online Analytical Processing (OLAP) for analysis.

There are many approaches proposed to maintain fresh data in real time data warehouse. Amongst these approaches, RiTE (Right-time ETL) talked about proactively furnishing data for data warehousing [3]. The data can be extracted from multiple sites on demand to enable analysis. In another research, authors introduced main memory concepts for improving loading procedure of data warehouse [4]. In these papers, the authors primarily stressed on quick accumulation of data into data warehouse and suggested an improved Extract, Transform and Load (ETL) strategy where loading of data occurred into data warehouse with OLTP system using trigger approach.

In real time data warehouse, new data should also be inserted. The data mart is linked up with incoming new facts in the system. To get critical decision, data inconsistency should be very low in real time data warehouse. Data should be of high quality with the low latency. The term quality is quite subjective and might imply accuracy, timeliness, completeness, consistency and preciseness of data. To get fresh data from multiple sources, one needs to have proper planning and protocols from management side [5, 6]. In addition, to ensuring that data is consistent, one has to perform consolidation till the very end [7].

Over the past few years, bloom filters are being used for different applications. Among these applications include detecting duplicates in data on cloud platform [8] and database consistency management in cross platform database [9]. Besides, variants of bloom filter have been proposed. This includes counting bloom filter [6, 7], extended counting bloom filter [13] and adjustable size bloom filter [14, 15] that have been used in various researches [10, 11, 16–18]. The major contribution of this paper is to employ bloom filter to identify duplicate records and maintaining consistency of the information stored in data warehouse.

2 Proposed Consistency Management Approach

2.1 Problem Definition

Suppose, N is defined as the number of unbounded data records that are stored in multiple disks represented by $S_N = x_1, ..., x_i, ..., x_N$. Assuming a large volume of data is available. This data is to be stored in a very limited amount of main memory, M to detect duplicates. The problem is to put all records x_i in S_n. Since, M is a small number it can't hold all different records in $x_1 ... x_{i-1}$. To solve this problem, one needs to design a data structure such as a bloom filer. This data structure keeps the record of what data is available in the memory with a very small error rate. When error rate P reaches to threshold or certain values, then bloom will refresh to create common explanation.

2.2   Bloom Filters

Primarily, we define the bloom filter as one that is optimized for efficient storage of data. It is used to perform membership check of an element in a set [7]. The bloom filter is based on a hash function that should be independent and uniformly distributed. A hash function takes an input, performs a mathematical function and returns a fixed bit of information called a message hash. In a bloom structure, false positive can occur however false negative can never occur.

Bloom filter is a well-defined collection of bit array of m-bits i.e. {1, 2, ..., m} with initial values as 0. There are K different hash functions i.e. $H = \{h_1, ..., h_K\}$ each of which mapped to array positions. A hash function takes certain input and output mapped to index m. While inserting the record x on the filters, the x records passes through each hash functions the bit K indexes sets $h_1(x), ..., h_K(x)$ to value *true* or 1 in the memory. If all bits are mapped or indexed in memory m with the hash functions, this infers records are duplicated otherwise records are not duplicated.

In this paper, the application of bloom filter is used to solve data inconsistencies (duplication) problem in real time data warehouse. The paper studies the relationship between accuracy Vs number of records (N), error rate (P), number of hash functions (K) and size of memory (M) for inconsistency detecting using bloom filter. These values can be calculated by the help of following formulae i.e.

$$N = M * (ln(2))^2 / |ln(P)| \tag{1}$$

$$K = M/N * ln(2) \tag{2}$$

$$M = N * |ln(P)| / ln(2)^2 \tag{3}$$

$$m = M/K \tag{4}$$

$$P = p^K \tag{5}$$

We can project the number of records N to insert in the filter or memory with limited memory size M and error rate P using above formulae.

Suppose we have M memory size or filter is 96 bits with maximum error probability P i.e. 1% then we can easily find projected value N i.e. 10 and K number of hash function i.e. 7. This tabulated result given below.

Table 1. Projected error rate P increases with N of records

n	M	m	K	N	P	$P = p^K$	$Diff$
1	96	14	7	10	0.068937	7.3991E−09	0.01
2	96	14	7	10	0.133122	7.4089E−07	0.009999
3	96	14	7	10	0.192882	9.9322E−06	0.00999
4	96	14	7	10	0.248523	5.8555E−06	0.00994
5	96	14	7	10	0.300327	0.00022038	0.00978

(continued)

Table 1. (*continued*)

n	M	m	K	N	P	P = p^K	Diff
6	96	14	7	10	0.348561	0.0006251	0.00938
7	96	14	7	10	0.393469	0.00146008	0.00854
8	96	14	7	10	0.435282	0.0029607	0.00704
9	96	14	7	10	0.474212	0.00539272	0.00461
10	96	14	7	10	0.510458	0.00903072	0.00097
11	96	14	7	10	0.544206	0.01413654	−0.00414

As it is shown in the Table 1, the projected error rate P can change from record to record. The error rate P rises with N and decreases with m and K. There can be chances of false positive. It can happen when we check for the availability of a given x record using the K hash functions i.e. $h_i(x)$. In that scenario, all the K-hash function passes despite there is no record in the data warehouse. In order to reduce the false positive rate further, one can increase the number of hash functions K or size m can also be altered. The chances of false positive rate can be calculated from the given formula:

$$P(x) = p^K \tag{6}$$

where,

$$p = (1 - exp(-N * K/M)) \tag{7}$$

where, the probability of bit 0 for observing n distinct records is denoted by $P(x)$.

The proposed bloom filter approach can be used to tell if a set of records occur or not occur. One can use bloom filter for any volume of data. But, this would require an appropriate amount space to set number of different records using bloom filters. In these days of advanced computing capabilities, capacity is not a very big issue. Additionally, the memory requirement is not very huge as compared to data set. Furthermore, when number of records increases, the chances of number of 0 bits being output decreases and the chances of false positive therefore increases continuously.

2.3 Counting Bloom Filter

It is a variant of Bloom filter where removal of bit is possible when bit is greater than zero. A wide range of applications are possible using the counting bloom filter [11, 12]. As discussed above, a record can be inserted in bloom filter, but records cannot be removed. In counting bloom filter, a counter is used ranging from 1 to b bits. Most of the paper uses 4 bit counter which is fixed. In counting bloom filter, when a record is inserted the counter increases and similarly when record is removed, counter is decreased. However, for decrementing the counter, the value obviously should be greater than zero. When the counter is 0 this means bloom filter has no record.

When counter bit is fixed to 4 then, counter should go from 0 to 15. When the value of counter reaches to 15, an overflow will occur. The chances of over flow are minuscule that is why 4 bit is often used. In counting bloom filter, generally counter 4 of bits are used. Hence, the capacity of counting bloom filter is 4 times compared to the conventional bloom filter. When the value of counter bit is 0, the space is not in used. The memory usage is not useful. To efficiently use memory, some researchers introduced an enhanced version of counting bloom filter. This enhanced version is called variable length Counting bloom filter (VLCBF) [13, 15] and variable length increment counting bloom filter [14]. In VLCBF there is no chance of overflow in memory because bit number is changed dynamically.

2.4   Proposed Approach

Figure 1 demonstrates the proposed approach to move data from Online Transaction Processing System (OLTP) system to Online Analytical Processing System (OLAP) system in real time. As discussed, in the proposed approach, bloom filter has been used. In particular, the paper employs a novel technique called time frame variable length counting bloom filter. This approach is a variation of conventional bloom filter. Figure 2 shows the detail. This is further illustrated in Algorithm 1.

Suppose time is denoted by T and C represents counter. The counter C distributes the bloom into a range of sub-blooms. A *TBF* can be defined as an array of integers i.e. *TBF[1], ..., TBF[m]*. The values are from 0 to *max. b*-bits are required for each hence, max = $2^b - 1$. Here, we use the concept of cell for every element of the TBF. Each bit is represented with the concept of cells with each cell comprising several bits. The cell value is initialized to 0.

Let T indicates time and C is counter. We distributed the available blooms into a set of sub-blooms. A TBF is defined as an array of integers *TBF[1], ..., TBF[m]*. There are number of bloom which can be divided as time or date wise. Every bloom contain

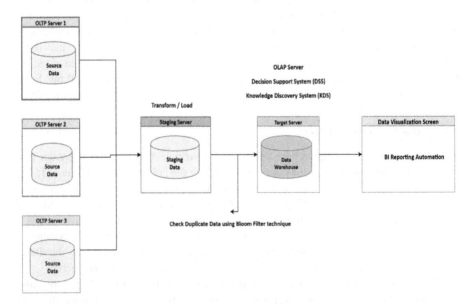

Fig. 1. Proposed approach

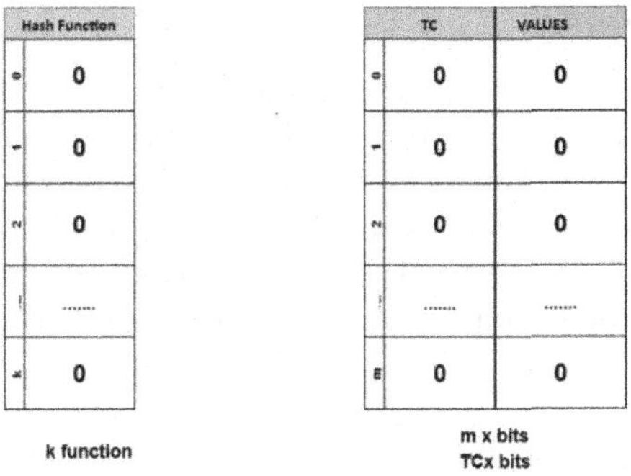

Hash Function			TC	VALUES
∞	0		0	0
$-$	0		0	0
$\sim$	0		0	0
$\vdots$	....		....	....
$\sim$	0		0	0
k function			m x bits	
			TCx bits	

Fig. 2. Illustration of hashing function used

contains m cells. In the initial TBF[1], every bloom contains U different cells i.e. *TBF [j₁], ..., TBF[j_U]* Where $U \in \{1...m\}$ in this array there are "m" cells and every cell contains $1 ... b$ bits. Each b bit can be used as a counter which comprises record with values ranging from $0 ... 2^b - 1$. But in counting bloom filter, counter length is constant. For this reason, that counter size is 0 and the space is naturally unused. In addition, the value of each cell is 0 initially.

Algorithm 1: Pseudo-code for duplicate data detection using Bloom Filter technique.

Data: "N" is number of records $Z = \{x_1,...,x_N\}$
Result: values set in the filter as "1/ 0" or "TRUE/FALSE"

```
Start
Set all of the TBF [1],...,TBF[m] =0
T ∈ TCVL (Time Counter Variable Length)
   For every T ∈ BF:
   For every xᵢ ∈Z:
   scan cells TBF [h₁(xᵢ)],...,TBF[h_K(xiᵢ]
   If every TBF [h₁(xᵢ)],...,TBF[h_K(xiᵢ] are not 0 then
          Duplicate = "TRUE"
      Else
          Duplicate = "FALSE"
Pick a different cells at random        TBF [j₁],..., TBF[jₚ] P
∈ {1....m}
   For every cell TBF[j] ∈ {TBF [j₁],...,TBF[jₚ]}:
      If TBF[j] ≥ 1 then
         TBF[j] =TBF[j]-1
   For every cell∈{TBF[h₁(xᵢ)],...,TBF[h_K(xᵢ)]} :
      TBF [h (xᵢ)] = Max
      Output = Duplicate
Finish
```

In this method, data from raw data table is moved to filter data and log data table. There are total n number of attributes in the Raw data which can be divided into key and date. Each Key have one or more attributes. First of all, the attributes will be concatenated to one column and used as single record x which is then passed through autonomous hash function.

2.5   Insertion of Record

To find a record, we pass it to the hash functions h_i $(i = 1, 2, ..., K)$. User can find the h_i elements in the set of array which then hashes the record x and passes through hash function h_i $(i = 1, 2, ..., K)$. For a hash response of 0, one should not consider the records in the array or data set. In this case instead, the record from raw data is inserted to filter data. In case of hash value as 1, the record is considered to be already present in the array. In this case the record from raw data is we are inserted to log data.

3   Results

Assuming a huge volume of data is coming from transaction servers to a central repository called *RawData*. It is the requirement that that data is accessible, complete and accurate in the given environment. To meet this objective, bloom filter technique is used to remove inconsistent or duplicate data prior to moving the information into the central data warehouse. In *RawData* file, there are two key attributes i.e. date attribute and value attribute that are separated. There are n number of columns or attributes in the table i.e. $\{A_1, ..., A_n\}$. All attributes are linked together and distributed through K number of hash functions.

First, we perform concatenation of these attributes. This concatenated data is then evaluated by hash functions. More blooms in the memory can be considered based on date attribute. Since the memory size is very limited, if memory is found to be short of capacity, one can be release older bloom and new data can be considered.

Let's apply the proposed approach with different number of records to check accuracy (Fig. 3). There are likely 50,000 records on each bloom. We are calculating best error rate P using formula, $1/N$ where N is number of records. When N is 50,000. Now we can find P error rate or threshold value (0.002%). Similarly using Eq. 2 and 3, M no of bits and K number of hash functions can be observed i.e. 11,25,998 and 16 approximately. We can see for the best value case, there is minimal chance to produce error, but we are compromising with memory as shown in Fig. 3a. We can see P error rate changes from record to record. When we reduce or fixed P error rate i.e. 0.01%, one can find M and K which is 9,58,506 and 13 approximately. There is no error and it gives result with excellent accuracy. When we reduce more P error rate i.e. 0.1%, we can find M and K i.e. 7,18,879 and 10 approximately. It gives 2 errors out of 50,000 record, still it shows 99.999% accuracy (Fig. 3b).

If we further reduce the number of records, then error rate might be increased. When we take P error rate i.e. 1% (Fig. 3c). We can find M and K i.e. 4,79,253 and 7 approximately. It gives 75 errors out of 50,000 records, it shows with 99.98% accuracy. When error rate P decreases, then memory consumption can more reduce but we have to balance where we can find result with excellent accuracy. It has been shown in Fig. 3 that when number of records changes, then error rate P also changes. Similarly, when size of memory rises then error rate also decreases.

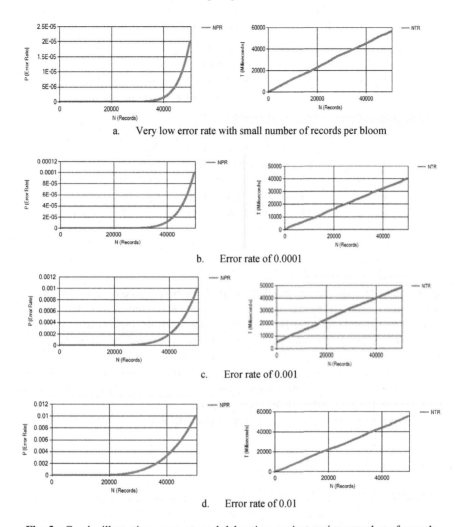

a.   Very low error rate with small number of records per bloom

b.   Error rate of 0.0001

c.   Eror rate of 0.001

d.   Error rate of 0.01

Fig. 3. Graphs illustrating error rate and delay time against various number of records

Let's compare results with multiple values of hash functions (K). One can see the optimal result near optimal value of K. When we increase or decrease the value of K, our false positive rate will be increases which is shown in Table 2.

Table 2. Impact of hash function on Fp (False positive)

n	M	m	K	N	P	Fp	Diff	Fp%
1	95.9	14.4	6.6	10	0.5	0.01	0	1
2	96	14	7	10	0.517689	0.009965	0.000035	0.9965
3	96	19	5	10	0.405975	0.011028	−0.001028	1.1028
4	96	32	3	10	0.268384	0.019332	−0.009332	1.9332
5	96	48	2	10	0.188064	0.035368	−0.025368	3.5368
6	96	96	1	10	0.098925	0.098925	−0.088925	9.8925
7	96	11	9	10	0.608394	0.01142	−0.00142	1.142
8	96	9	11	10	0.682041	0.014856	−0.004856	1.4856
9	96	7	13	10	0.741838	0.020607	−0.010607	2.0607
10	96	6	15	10	0.790389	0.02935	−0.01935	2.935

4   Conclusion

Duplicate data detection is very challenging problem in real time data warehouse. After comprehensive analysis based on star schema of adventure works, the paper has concluded that the bloom filter is very suitable approach for inconsistency (duplicate) detection for real time data warehouse. In order to avoid duplication of data, consistency should be managed in such environments. By means of accurate data, one can take good decisions in future. Bloom filter is very simplistic and efficient approach to detect duplicate problem. In future data updates will be very fast. Therefore, one needs approaches that can handle volatile data in data warehouse. In order to meet this important requirement in real-time data warehouses, Bloom filters have been proposed.

References

1. Zuters, J.: Near real-time data warehousing with multi-stage trickle and flip. In: Grabis, J., Kirikova, M. (eds.) BIR 2011. LNBIP, vol. 90, pp. 73–82. Springer, Heidelberg (2011). https://doi.org/10.1007/978-3-642-24511-4_6
2. Vassiliadis, P., Simitsis, A.: Near real time ETL. In: Kozielski, S., Wrembel, R. (eds.) New Trends in Data Warehousing and Data Analysis. AOIS, vol. 3, pp. 1–31. Springer, Boston (2009). https://doi.org/10.1007/978-0-387-87431-9_2
3. Thomsen, C., Pedersen, T.B., Lehner, W.: RiTE: providing on-demand data for right-time data warehousing. In: Proceedings of the 2008 IEEE 24th International Conference on Data Engineering, ICDE 2008 (2008)
4. Santos, R.J., Bernardino, J.: Optimizing data warehouse loading procedures for enabling useful-time data warehousing. In: Proceedings of the 2009 International Database Engineering & Applications Symposium, IDEAS 2009 (2009)
5. Rudra, A., Yeo, E.: Key issues in achieving data quality and consistency in data warehousing among large organizations in Australia. In: Proceedings of the 32nd Hawaii International Conference on System Science (1999)

6. Prakash, D., Prakash, N.: A Requirements driven approach to data warehouse consolidation. In: 11th IEEE International Conference on Research Challenges in Information Science, RCIS 2017 (2017, to be presented)
7. Bloom, B.H.: Space/time trade-offs in hash coding with allowable errors. Commun. ACM **13**(7), 422–426 (1970)
8. Li, Z., He, K., Lin, F.: Deduplication of files in cloud storage based on differential bloom filter. In: IEEE 7th International Conference on Software Engineering and Service Science (ICSESS) (2016)
9. Goyal, A., Swaminathan, A., Pande, R., Attar, V.: Cross platform (RDBMS to NoSQL) database validation tool using bloom filter. In: 2016 International Conference on Recent Trends in Information Technology (ICRTIT) (2016)
10. Talpur, A., Newe, T., Shaikh, F.K.: Bloom filter based data collection algorithm for wireless sensor networks. In: IEEE International Conference on Information Networking (ICOIN) (2017)
11. Lu, Y., Prabhakar, B., Bonomi, F.: Perfect hashing for network applications. In: Proceedings of ISIT 2006 (2006, to appear)
12. Fan, L., Cao, P., Almeida, J., Broder, A.Z.: Summary cache: a scalable wide-area web cache sharing protocol. IEEE/ACM Trans. Network. **8**(3), 281–293 (2000)
13. Bonomi, F., Mitzenmacher, M., Panigrahy, R., Singh, S., Varghese, G.: An improved construction for counting bloom filters. In: Azar, Y., Erlebach, T. (eds.) ESA 2006. LNCS, vol. 4168, pp. 684–695. Springer, Heidelberg (2006). https://doi.org/10.1007/11841036_61
14. Rottenstreich, O., Kanizo, Y., Keslassy, I.: The variable-increment counting bloom filter. IEEE/ACM Trans. Netw. (2014). https://doi.org/10.1109/TNET.2013.2272604
15. Xuan, S., Man, D., Wang, W., Yang, W.: The improved variable length counting bloom filter based on buffer. In: 2015 Eighth International Conference on Internet Computing for Science and Engineering (ICICSE), pp. 74–78. IEEE Conference Publications (2015)
16. Zengin, S., Schmidt, E.G.: A fast and accurate hardware string matching module with bloom filters. IEEE Trans. Parallel Distrib. Syst. **28**, 305–317 (2016)
17. Mun, J.H., Lim, H.: Cache sharing using bloom filters in named data networking. J. Netw. Comput. Appl. **90**, 74–82 (2017)
18. Xu, Z., Chen, B., Meng, X., Liu, L.: Efficient detection of sybil attacks in location-based social networks. In: College of Information Engineering, Inner Mongolia University of Technology, Hohhot, China Institute of Computing Technology, Chinese Academy of Sciences, Beijing, China Department of Computer Science, Michigan Technological University, Michigan, USA (2017)

Restricted Boltzmann Machines Based Fault Estimation in Multi Terminal HVDC Transmission System

Raheel Muzzammel[(✉)]

Department of Electrical Engineering, University of Lahore, Lahore, Pakistan
raheelmuzzammel@gmail.com

Abstract. The facilitation of bulk power transmission and non-synchronized interconnection of alternating current (AC) grids convince engineers and researchers to explore high voltage direct current (HVDC) transmission system in a comprehensive way. This exploration focuses on control and protection of HVDC transmission system. Fault estimation is a core component of protection of HVDC transmission system. This is because of sudden built up of direct current (DC) fault. In this research, DC fault is estimated in multi terminal HVDC transmission system based on restricted Boltzmann machine. Restricted Boltzmann machine is a generative stochastic artificial neural network in which learning of probability distribution is conducted over the set of inputs. Three terminal HVDC transmission system is simulated under normal and faulty conditions to analyze variations in electrical parameters. These variations serve as learning parameters of restricted Boltzmann machine. Contrastive divergence algorithm is developed to train restricted Boltzmann machine. It is an approximate maximum likelihood learning algorithm in which gradient of difference of divergences is followed. It is found that fault is estimated with the testing of variations in minimum time steps. Simulation environment is built in Matlab/Simulink.

Keywords: Multi terminal high voltage direct current (MT-HVDC) transmission system · Restricted Boltzmann machine (RBM) · Contrastive divergence algorithm (CDA) · Fault estimation (FE) · Direct current (DC) fault

1 Introduction

HVDC transmission system is gathering attention of engineers and investors because of its promising attitude towards bulk power transfer with the aim of improving the standards of living. In addition to this, HVDC transmission system is superior to conventional AC transmission system because of its low losses, ability to interconnect unsynchronized grids, minimum right of way, capability of transferring bulk power, and installation as submarine cables. Therefore, HVDC transmission is basically the renaissance of DC currents in the war of currents [1–24].

Researches have been conducted passionately over the decades for development of methods of fault detection, classification and location in HVDC transmission lines. It is equally important along with the growing concept of smart grids to build an intelligent

© Springer Nature Singapore Pte Ltd. 2020
I. S. Bajwa et al. (Eds.): INTAP 2019, CCIS 1198, pp. 772–790, 2020.
https://doi.org/10.1007/978-981-15-5232-8_66

system of fault monitoring and diagnosis (FMD). Protection system must be capable of detecting, classifying and locating faults in a better way [23–41].

Detection, classification and finding location of faults in HVDC transmission are found to be the most blazing research areas in power system. This is entirely because of the intentions of interconnection of non-synchronized grids and bulk power transfer in a reliable fashion. Developments in digital signal processing techniques, artificial intelligence, global positioning system (GPS), communication and machine learning algorithms have opened doors for the researchers to carry out studies in a way so that the confinement associated with the traditional methods could be dealt and addressed successfully and effectively [24, 26, 28, 30–41].

When a DC fault occurs in HVDC transmission line, it grows rapidly and reaches a very high steady state value. Because of this sudden growth and higher steady state value, converter stations and equipment associated with HVDC transmission undergo severe danger of failures. In addition to this, this sudden growth and higher value of DC fault current are beyond the current interrupting and limiting capacity of conventional circuit breakers. Increase in DC fault current is required to be detected rapidly so that its effects could not be expanded to system. Therefore, in order to overcome this issue of DC fault, extensive studies are carried out over modified forms of relaying mechanisms. In short, there are basically two ways or strategies to counter DC fault current. In selective fault clearing strategy, only circuit breakers associated with the faulted line is used to interrupt fault current but in non-selective fault clearing strategy, fault current is interrupted by combined actions of multiple components such as the converters with the facilities of fault interrupting and limiting capability. Because of too much complexity in non-selective fault clearing strategy and fear of increasing capital expense of converter stations, it is practically not feasible to apply over large power systems [23, 24, 42–59].

DC fault at the terminals is detected by the rate of change of electrical parameters such as voltage and current. Sudden rise in current or sudden drop in voltage is a clear indication of origination of DC faults. Changes in voltage and currents are observed by optical transducers installed to measure these values. These values are converted to lower levels to make them applicable for relay sections. Relay senses them and prepares an action according to the rated capacity of flow of current or of voltage at terminals. This rate of change of voltage or current is compared with the threshold values of voltage or current to prepare a prompt action. When the fault is very closed to the converter stations or magnitude of fault is small, then this rate of change of voltage or current is not sufficient to prepare an interrupting action [42–45, 47, 55]. There must be additional techniques required to extract an in-depth knowledge available in these electrical parameters. This strikes an idea to implement analysis based on time and frequency domain. Fourier transform (FT) technique is applied to analyze the voltage and current signals in frequency domain [60–67]. Because of less information, wavelet transform (WT) technique is developed to observe time and frequency domain of electrical signals simultaneously. Fine analysis requires extensive computation in WT. In addition to this, although discrete WT is computationally efficient yet discretization involves reduction in efficiency of wavelets. Therefore, alternative techniques are taken into consideration or these techniques are supported with further advanced methods [47, 60–74].

Machine learning is an emerging approach for fault diagnosis in HVDC transmission lines. It is a technique in which information is acquired without the need of accurate programming. Hence, this reduces computational burden without questioning the accuracy and efficiency. Features are extracted from the voltage and current signals to prepare a testing and training data. In this way, algorithms are trained for a particular event so that they could respond to testing data accordingly [75–84]. In the literature, there are a vast number of machine learning algorithms. Broadly, they are classified into two techniques. Firstly, is the supervised learning, in which information is evaluated on the basis of available pre-defined tags. Secondly is the unsupervised learning in which unknown data (testing data) is evaluated without the existence of preset tags. Classification and regression are the examples of supervised learning. Clustering and association are the examples of unsupervised learning [85–87].

In this research, HVDC transmission line is simulated under normal and faulty conditions. Moreover, restricted Boltzmann machine learning (RBML) algorithm is developed and implemented. This algorithm is applied and tested for fault estimation in HVDC transmission lines. Matlab/Simulink is used for the simulation.

This research paper consists of following sections: Sect. 1 covers the introduction and literature review regarding fault estimation in HVDC transmission system. Section 2 consists of explanation of HVDC transmission system. Restricted Boltzmann machine is explained in Sect. 3. Contrastive divergence based learning approach of restricted Boltzmann machine is covered in Sect. 4. Steps involved in methodology of fault estimation in three terminal HVDC transmission system is added in Sect. 5. Section 6 contains simulation analysis of test model of three terminal HVDC transmission system. Conclusion is given in Sect. 7.

2 HVDC Transmission System

In high voltage direct current (HVDC) transmission system, direct current (DC) is used for transmission of bulk power. This transmission system possesses significantly low losses in the case of long distanced transmission but has an expensive infrastructure. This system is used as submarine cable transmission without taking into consideration of charging and discharging of capacitance of line in each cycle with heavy currents. In case of short distances, its high cost of deployment is justified because of numerous advantages of HVDC transmission system. Voltage range between 100 kV to 800 kV is usually utilized in HVDC system. In the end of 2019, a new voltage value of 1100 kV will be operational for HVDC system in China [2–6, 8, 9, 15, 18, 20, 23, 24].

Non synchronized alternating current (AC) transmission systems can be interconnected with HVDC transmission link. AC transmission systems working at different frequencies like at 50 Hz and 60 Hz can be integrated with help of HVDC link. Hence, stabilization can also be achieved with HVDC transmission systems in the case of incompatible networks. Control of HVDC link is independent of phase angle between load and source. This concept helps in stabilization of power networks against any disturbances resulted from the change in power [2, 20, 23, 24].

Practically, most of HVDC transmission technology deployed around the globe is the technology developed in 1930s in Sweden and in Germany. In 1951, commercial installation was made between Moscow and Kashira in Russia. In 1954, 100 kV and 20 MW system was installed between Gotland and Mainland Sweden. Rio Madeira link is the longest link established in Brazil consisting of two bipoles of ±600 kV, 3150 MW. Porto Velho in the Rondonia is connected to Sao Paulo Area with long DC link of 2,375 km. ABB group is going to build an ultra-high voltage direct current (UHVDC) land link of 1100 kV and 12 GW for a distance of 3000 km. It is going to be the largest DC link with the highest bulk power capacity [2–6, 18, 20].

The idea of transmission at high voltage is driven because of significant losses and reduction in the lives of equipment deployed in the case of transmission at high currents. High voltages are beneficial for long distance transmission. Because of AC generation systems, three phase AC voltages are converted to high DC voltages. Due to advancement in power electronics in 1970s, it is practically feasible to convert AC to DC and vice versa with the semiconductor components like thyristors, insulated gate bipolar transistors (IGBT), etc. Therefore, based on the semi-conductor technology, HVDC transmission system is broadly classified into two categories: First is Line Commutated Converter in which thyristor technology is deployed for conversion. External AC circuit is provided for turning off and on the thyristor. Second is the voltage source converter (VSC) in which IGBT based converter stations are developed. IGBT technology provides more variants than thyristor based technology. Multiple grid connections, effective controlling, renewable energy integration and self-commutation are the notable features of VSC based HVDC system. Recently, researchers are very much attracted towards development of VSC based HVDC system as an advantageous substitute of thyristor based HVDC system [2–4, 17–22]. Comparison of LCC - HVDC and VSC - HVDC transmission system is presented in Table 1.

Table 1. Comparison of LCC- HVDC and VSC – HVDC transmission system

Function	LCC – HVDC	VSC – HVDC
Converter station	Thyristor based	IGBT based
AC grid connection	Converter transformer	Series reactor and transformer
Filtering and reactive compensation	Filters and shunt capacitors	Only small filter
Smoothing of DC current	Smoothing reactor + DC filter	DC capacitor
Communication link between converter stations	Required	Not required

2.1 VSC Based HVDC Transmission System

Self-commutating switches, e.g. gate turn-off thyristors (GTOs) or insulated gate bipolar transistors (IGBTs) are used in voltage source converters (VSC). These switches can be turned on or off in a controlled manner. High switching frequency based pulse width modulation is utilized in the operation of voltage source converters [23, 25, 27, 28, 31, 40, 47, 56, 58, 62, 64, 69, 78].

Typical configuration of VSC based HVDC system is presented in Fig. 1.

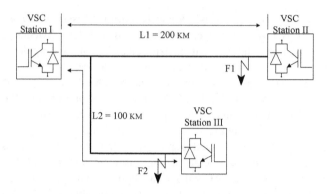

Fig. 1. Typical three terminal VSC – HVDC transmission system

VSC-based HVDC transmission system is composed of two VSCs, transformers, phase reactors, ac filters, dc-link capacitors and dc cables [90–93].

VSCs are connected at the sending and receiving ends of transmission line. Both VSCs have same configuration. One of the VSCs works as a rectifier and the other VSC works as an inverter. Therefore, it can be said that these converters are back to back converters. Normally, transformers are used to connect AC system to converters. In addition to this, transformer also transforms the AC voltage level to DC voltage level. Three winding type transformers are usually deployed and configuration of transformer can be altered with respect to rated power and transformation requirement. Phase reactors act as current regulators for controlling the flow of active and reactive power. These phase reactors also work as AC filters to mitigate the effects of high frequency harmonic contents developed in AC currents because of the switching operation of IGBTs. Two equally sized capacitors are installed at the DC side of converter stations. Sizes of these capacitors are dependent on DC voltage. DC capacitors provide a low inductance path for the turned off current. These capacitors also act as energy storage components in order to control the flow of power. Moreover, these capacitors also decay down the voltage ripples on DC side. Harmonics are blocked by AC filters from entering the AC system. Insulation of DC cable used in VSC based HVDC system is composed of extruded polymer. This material is resistant to DC voltage. Mechanical strength, flexibility and low weight are the notable features of this polymer cable. AC side of VSC station works as a constant current source. Therefore, inductor is used as an energy storage component. Elimination of harmonics is required which is carried out by small AC filters. VSC acts as a constant voltage source on DC side of converter station. Therefore, capacitors are installed which work as energy storage components. In addition to this, these capacitors provide the facility of DC filters. High switching losses are associated with VSC based HVDC system. These losses are reduced by using commutation scheme of soft switching. Controlling of power is done in the same way in VSC based HVDC system as in the case of LCC based HVDC system. Active power is controlled at inverter side and DC voltage is controlled at rectifier station. Fast inner current control loop accompanied by several outer control loops makes the realization of control system of VSC based HVDC system [23, 24, 88, 92–95].

AC currents are controlled by rapid inner current control located at the base level of control system of VSC based HVDC system. Reference AC currents are obtained by outer controllers. These outer controllers are relatively slow and include DC voltage controller, AC voltage controller, Active power controller, reactive power controller and frequency controller. Reference of active current is obtained from DC voltage controller, active power controller or from frequency controller whereas, reference of reactive current can be extracted from reactive power controller or from AC power controller [24, 88–90, 96, 97].

3   Restricted Boltzmann Machine (RBM)

Deep belief networks (DBNs) was introduced by Hinton along with his team at University of Toronto in 2006. It was proposed with a learning algorithm. In DBNs, one layer is trained greedily at a time and unsupervised learning algorithm known as Restricted Boltzmann Machine (RBM) is exploited for each layer. Architectural depth of brain has been working as a source of motivation for neural network researchers to train deep multi-layer networks for decades. Machine learning model is built with multiple hidden layers. Layer feature transformation is applied for training samples layer, for training the samples in the feature space for representation of new features in another space in order to achieve desired results of experiment. Classification, regression, information retrieval, dimensionality reduction, modeling motion, modeling textures, object segmentation, robotics, natural language processing and collaborative filtering are the emerging examples solved by DBNs [98–104].

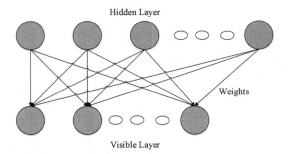

Fig. 2. Graphical representation of Restricted Boltzmann Machine with hidden and visible layers.

Restricted Boltzmann machine (RBM) is composed of two layers of units. One is visible unit represented by $V = (V_1, V_2, \ldots, V_m)$ and other is hidden unit denoted by $H = (H_1, H_2, \ldots, H_m)$. RBM is a probabilistic model in which hidden binary variables are utilized to model the distribution of variables of a visible layer as shown in Fig. 2.

Observed data is represented by visible units. Relation between two observed variables is captured by hidden units. Since all the units are composed of binary variables,

$$(v, h) \in \{0, 1\}^{m+n} \tag{1}$$

Energy function of RBM is defined as:

$$E(v, h|\theta) = \sum_{i=1}^{n} a_i v_i - \sum_{j=1}^{m} b_j h_j - \sum_{i=1}^{n} \sum_{j=1}^{m} v_i w_{ij} h_j \tag{2}$$

Where $\theta = \{w, a, b\}, a = \{a_i, i = i, 2, \ldots, n\}$ and $b = \{b_j, j = 1, 2, \ldots, m\}$ are the biases term associated to visible and hidden units respectively. Conditional probability function is given as:

$$P(v, h|\theta) = \frac{\exp(-E(v, h|\theta))}{Z(\theta)} \tag{3}$$

Where $Z(\theta)$ is a partition function or normalization constant and it ensures the validity of probability distribution given as:

$$Z(\theta) = \sum_{v,k} \exp(-E(v, h|\theta)) \tag{4}$$

Likelihood function provides an information about how well the data summarizes these parameters and given as:

$$P(v|\theta) = \frac{\sum_h \exp(-E(v, h|\theta))}{Z(\theta)} \tag{5}$$

Training of restricted Boltzmann machine is done to evaluate the unknown parameters. The derivatives or gradient of log likelihood function with respect to model parameters θ is calculated to minimize the log likelihood function as:

$$\frac{\partial \log P(v|\theta)}{\partial \theta} = \sum_{t=1}^{T} \{\frac{\partial(-E(v^{(t)}, h|\theta))}{\partial \theta}\}_{P(h|v^{(t)}, \theta)} - \sum_{t=1}^{T} \{\frac{\partial(-E(v, h|\theta))}{\partial \theta}\}_{P(v, h|\theta)} \tag{6}$$

Parameters w, a and b are calculated by finding the gradient of log likelihood function as:

$$\frac{\partial \log P(v|\theta)}{\partial w_{ij}} = \{v_i h_j\}_{data} - \{v_i h_j\}_{model}$$

$$\frac{\partial \log P(v|\theta)}{\partial b_j} = \{h_j\}_{data} - \{h_j\}_{model} \tag{7}$$

$$\frac{\partial \log P(v|\theta)}{\partial a_j} = \{v_i\}_{data} - \{v_i\}_{model}$$

4   Contrastive Divergence (CD) Algorithm

Contrastive divergence (CD) is an approximate maximum likelihood learning algorithm proposed by Geoffery Hinton. This algorithm follows the gradient of the differences of two divergences. This algorithm helps in reducing difficulty of computing log likelihood function.

Training of data is usually conducted by this CD algorithm in RBM [105, 106]. In this algorithm, sample for training, number of hidden layers, learning rate and maximum training cycle are specified and are taken as input. Outputs are usually weight w, bias of hidden layer b, bias of visible layer a. Weights are optimized to train product of expert models. Gibbs sampling is performed in this algorithm and is used inside a gradient descent procedure for the evaluation of weights. Visible layer is usually taken as initialization unit $V_1 = X$ in training. Minimum values of w, a and b are selected randomly.

```
For t = 1, 2, …, T
For j = 1, 2, …, m (for all hidden units)
```

$P(h_{1j} = 1 | v_1)$, $P(h_{1j} = 1 | v_1) = \sigma(b_j + \Sigma_i v_{1i} w_{ij})$ is computed from the

condition of distribution $P(h_{1j} | v_1)$ ∩ $h_{1j} \in \{0,1\}$

```
For j = 1, 2, …, n (for all visible units)
```

$P(v_{2i} = 1 | h_1)$, $P(v_{2i} = 1 | h_1) = \sigma(a_i + \Sigma_j w_{ij} h_{1j})$ is computed from the

condition of distribution $P(v_{2i} | h_1)$ ∩ $v_{2i} \in \{0,1\}$.

```
For j = 1, 2, …, m (for all hidden units)
```

$P(h_{2j} = 1 | v_2)$, $P(h_{2j} = 1 | v_2) = \sigma(b_j + \Sigma_i v_{2i} w_{ij})$ is computed

$-w \leftarrow w + \varepsilon(P(h_1 = 1 | v_1) v_1^T - P(h_2 = 1 | v_2) v_2^T)$

$-a \leftarrow a + \varepsilon(v_1 - v_2)$

$-b \leftarrow b + \varepsilon(P(h_1 = 1 | v_1) - P(h_2 = 1 | v_2))$

In this research, classifier of RBM is constructed. In this classifier model, there are two layers. Lower layer is stacked by a number of layers of RBMs. Upper layer is added containing the desired output variable. This is the classification layer. In the top level units, softmax classifier outputs are used. It is a sample in which probability of different states are added and maximum probability of the state is classified. Proposed flow diagram of CD learning based RBM is shown in Fig. 3.

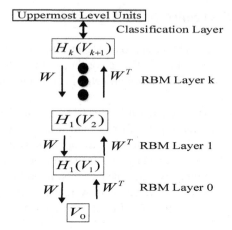

Fig. 3. Contrastive Divergence Learning based Restricted Boltzmann Machine

5   Methodology

Following are the steps involved in the implementation of contrastive divergence learning based restricted Boltzmann machine for fault estimation in MT- HVDC transmission system.

5.1   Data Selection

Voltage and current samples are prepared based on the observations made at converter stations, working as rectifier or inverter, in VSC based HVDC transmission system. Voltage and current values are recorded before and after the occurrence of faults. This data is untagged and it can be employed as pertaining sample. Tuning is done by the application of small amount of tagged samples of current and voltage values recorded at converter stations of VSC based HVDC transmission system.

5.2   Characteristics of Selected Variables

Variables are selected as features of model's input. These variables are basically DC value of the fault, its dominating frequency component and value of total harmonic distortion (THD). These variables depict the normal and faulty state of multi terminal HVDC transmission system. Contrastive divergence (CD) trains the Restricted Boltzmann machine (RBM) on the characteristics of these variables.

5.3   VSC Based HVDC System Status Codes

Fault estimation is basically a multi classification task. This diagnostic technique is divided into following categories based on fault type and fault distance.

1. Pole to Ground Fault
2. Pole to Pole Fault
3. Pole to Pole and Ground Fault

4. AC Fault
5. Fault at Converter Station
6. Fault at 50 km
7. Fault at 100 km
8. Fault at 200 km

In this research, fault distance and measurement points are employed for fault estimation in multi terminal HVDC transmission system.

5.4   Implementation of Fault Estimation Process

Sample and characteristics variables are selected. Classification model is built based on RBM in which training of untagged sample is done through contrastive divergence (CD) algorithm.

Table 2. Parameters of proposed three terminal HVDC transmission test model

Parameters	VSC I	VSC II	VSC III
Configuration	Rectifier	Inverter	Inverter
Power rating (MVA)	2000	2000	2000
Voltage rating (kV)	230	230	230
DC capacitor (microF) (Each Pole)	70	70	70
AC filters (MVARs)	40	40	40
Smoothing reactor (Resistance) (Ohms)	0.0251	0.0251	0.0251
Smoothing reactor (Inductance) (mH)	8	8	8
Three single phase transformers (200 MVA)	200	200	200

6   Simulation Results

Simulation environment is created in Matlab/Simulink. Three terminal VSC – HVDC model is developed as a test specimen. Parameters associated with this test model of VSC HVDC system is given in Table 2.

In this test system, there are basically three converter stations. One is rectifier (VSC – I) and two of them are inverters (VSC – II and VSC – III). The DC transmission cable between VSC – I and VSC – II is 200 km long. The DC transmission cable between VSC – I and VSC – III is 100 km long. This test system is simulated under healthy and faulty conditions to analyze it's working as shown in Fig. 4. Figure 4(a) depicts the current of rectifier station under normal conditions. Values of current are graphically displayed against time. Current is reaching steady state value of 1.463 Amperes in less than 0.2 s. In the similar fashion, current attains a steady state value of 2.48 Amperes and 1.074 Amperes in minimum time at converter station II (inverter) and converter station III (inverter) as shown in Fig. 4 (b) and Fig. 4 (c) respectively. This depicts the achievement of stability of HVDC system in minimum possible time. All the converter stations are working under normal conditions. Figure 4 (d) depicts the variation in DC current measured at converter station I (rectifier) under DC fault on a line of 200 km long. Variations are quite visible under fault condition. DC current increases and is

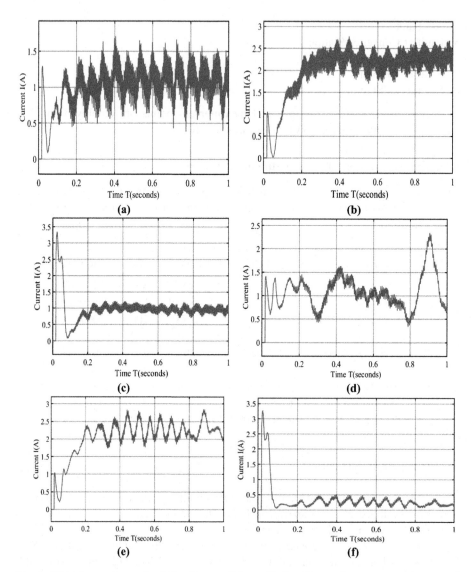

Fig. 4. This figure shows the following conditions. (a) Rectifier station current under normal conditions (b) Inverter station (VSC – I) current under normal conditions (c) Inverter station (VSC – II) current under normal conditions (d) Rectifier station current under DC fault conditions at VSC - II (e) Inverter station (VSC- II) current under DC fault condition at VSC - II (f) Inverter station (VSC – III) current under DC fault condition at VSC - II (g) Rectifier station current under DC fault condition at VSC - III (h) Inverter station (VSC – II) current under DC fault condition at VSC - III (i) Inverter station (VSC – III) current under DC fault condition at VSC – III.

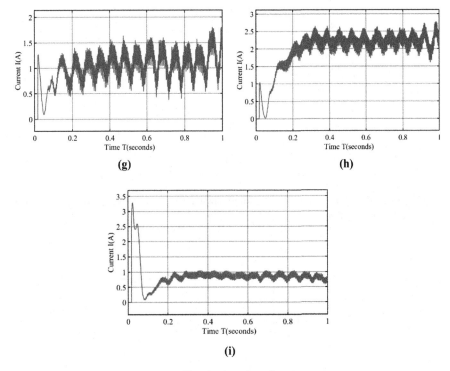

Fig. 4. (*continued*)

found to be of 1.629 Amperes. In the same way, DC current is measured at converter station II and is found to be of 2.334 Amperes as shown in Fig. 4 (e). As the fault occurs at 200 km (very closed to converter station II) from rectifier station, so no significant change in current is observed at converter station II. It is observed that a current decreases to 0.09625 Amperes at VSC – III which is a big variation as shown in Fig. 4 (f). This decrease in DC current is an indication that a neighboring line is under fault condition. When a fault occurs on DC transmission cable connected between VSC – I and VSC – III, increase in DC current is observed at converter station I as shown in Fig. 4 (g). Figure 4 (h) shows that no significant change is observed at converter station III because DC fault is very closed to it. However, decrease in DC current is found at converter station II which is an indication that the neighboring line is under fault as depicted in Fig. 4 (i). Table 3 summarizes the change in value of DC current with respect to different locations of fault and with respect to its measurement points.

Table 3. Nature of DC current under different sates of system

State of test model	DC Current		
	VSC – I	VSC – II	VSC – III
Normal condition	Constant	Constant	Constant
Fault near to converter station (VSC- II)	Increases	Constant	Decreases
Fault near to converter station (VSC – III)	Increases	Decreases	Constant/Little change

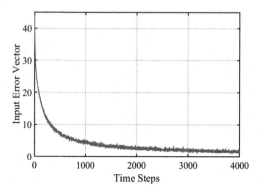

Fig. 5. Error vector with respect to time steps obtained while training RBM with contrastive divergence (CD) algorithm.

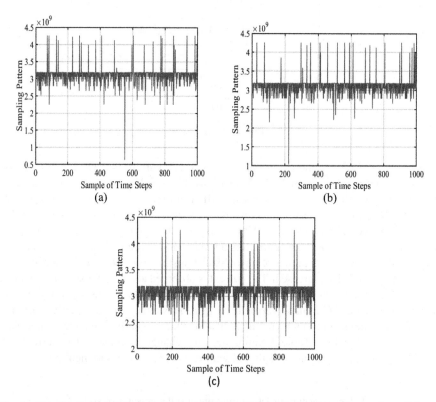

Fig. 6. This figure depicts the following conditions: (a) Sampling pattern of normal condition of test model in 1000 time steps. (b) Sampling pattern of faulty conditions at inverter station (VSC – II) in test model in 1000 time steps. (c) Sampling pattern of faulty conditions at inverter station (VSC – III) in test model in 1000 time steps.

Figure 5 depicts the variations in error vector with respect to change in time steps. It is found that error decreases with the increase in time steps. This error vector is obtained from the contrastive divergence learning of restricted Boltzmann machine (RBM). After training of RBM, this machine is tested under different conditions in a sample of 1000 time steps. Sampling patterns are different under different conditions which help in estimation of fault in MT- HVDC transmission system as shown in Fig. 6. In the normal condition, highest variation in sampling pattern is observed at a time step just before 600 as shown in Fig. 6 (a). In the fault condition of transmission line of 200 km long, highest variation is observed at a time step near to 200 as depicted in Fig. 6 (b). In Fig. 6 (c), highest variation is observed at time step closed to 150. These variations aid in determining the fault in three terminal HVDC test model. These variations are actually the gradient of difference of divergence utilized in restricted Boltzmann machine. These results help in determining the fault conditions established near converter stations.

7 Conclusion

Restricted Boltzmann machine is an emerging technique to estimate fault in VSC – HVDC transmission system. In this research, contrastive divergence based learning is developed for restricted Boltzmann machine. The gradient of the difference of divergence is evaluated under different states of HVDC transmission model. Based on the gradient of difference of divergences, healthy and faulty state of HVDC system are found effectively. Moreover, change in the value of gradient with respect to fault distance helps in determining the fault location in multi terminal HVDC transmission system. In future, this idea can be extended to classification with respect to different type of faults.

References

1. Hingorani, N.G.: High voltage DC transmission: a power electronics workhorse. IEEE Spectr. **33**(4), 63–72 (1996)
2. Ellert, F.J.: HVDC for the long run. Spectrum, 36–42 (1976)
3. Arrillaga, J.J.: High Voltage Direct Current Transmission. Peter Peregrinus Ltd., Stevenage (1983)
4. Padyar, K.R.: HVDC Power Transmission Systems. Wiley Eastern, New Delhi (1990)
5. High Voltage Direct Current Handbook, California Electric Power Research Institute, Palo Alto, California (1994)
6. Starke, M., Tolbert, L.M., Ozpineci, B.: AC vs. DC distribution: a loss comparison. In: IEEE/PES Transmission and Distribution Conference and Exposition, Chicago, IL, pp. 1–7 (2008)
7. Sun, T., Xia, J., Sun, Y., Mao, X.: Research on the applicable range of AC and DC transmission voltage class sequence. In: International Conference on Power System Technology, Chengdu, pp. 374–380 (2014)
8. Meah, K., Ula, S.: Comparative evaluation of HVDC and HVAC transmission systems. In: IEEE Power Engineering Society General Meeting, Tampa, FL, pp. 1–5 (2007)

9. Uhlmann, E.: Power Transmission by Direct Current. Springer, Heidelberg (1975). https://doi.org/10.1007/978-3-642-66072-6

10. Bowles, J.P., et al.: AC-DC economics and alternatives-1987 panel session report. IEEE Trans. Power Delivery **5**(4), 1241–1248 (1990)

11. Bateman, L.A., Haywood, R.W.: Nelson river DC transmission project. IEEE Trans. Power Appar. Syst. PAS **88**(5), 688–693 (1969)

12. Halder, T.: Comparative study of HVDC and HVAC for a bulk power transmission. In: International Conference on Power, Energy and Control (ICPEC), Sri Rangalatchum Dindigul, pp. 139–144 (2013)

13. Ruderval, R., Charpenitier, J.P., Sharma, R.: High voltage direct current transmission systems technology review paper. Energy Week, Washington D.C., USA (2000)

14. Hammad, A.E., Long, W.F.: Performance and economic comparisons between point-to-point HVDC transmission and hybrid back-to-back HVDC/AC transmission. IEEE Trans. Power Delivery **5**(2), 1137–1144 (1990)

15. Chamia, M.: The role of HVDC transmission in the 21st century. In: IEEE WPM - Panel Session (1999)

16. Tenzer, M., Koch, H., Imamovic, D.: Underground transmission lines for high power AC and DC transmission. In: IEEE/PES Transmission and Distribution Conference and Exposition (T&D), Dallas, TX, pp. 1–4 (2016)

17. Long, W.F., Litzenberger, W.: Fundamental concepts in high voltage direct current power transmission PES (T&D), Orlando, FL, pp. 1–2 (2012)

18. Bahrman, M.P.: Overview of HVDC transmission. IEEE PES Power Systems Conference and Exposition, Atlanta, GA, pp. 18–23 (2006)

19. Wang, H., Redfern, M.A.: The advantages and disadvantages of using HVDC to interconnect AC networks. In: 45th International Universities Power Engineering Conference (UPEC), pp. 1–5 (2010)

20. Keim, T., Bindra, A.: Recent advances in HVDC and UHVDC transmission [Happenings]. IEEE Power Electron. Mag. **4**(4), 12–18 (2017)

21. Muzzammel, R., et al.: MT–HVdc systems fault classification and location methods based on traveling and non-traveling waves—a comprehensive review. Appl. Sci. **9**, 4760 (2019)

22. Muzzammel, R.: Traveling waves-based method for fault estimation in HVDC transmission system. Energies **12**, 3614 (2019)

23. Muzzammel, R., Fateh, H.M., Ali, Z.: Analytical behaviour of thyrister based HVDC transmission lines under normal and faulty conditions. In: International Conference on Engineering and Emerging Technologies (ICEET), pp. 1–5, Lahore (2018)

24. Muzzammel, R.: Machine learning based fault diagnosis in HVDC transmission lines. In: Bajwa, I.S., Kamareddine, F., Costa, A. (eds.) INTAP 2018. CCIS, vol. 932, pp. 496–510. Springer, Singapore (2019). https://doi.org/10.1007/978-981-13-6052-7_43

25. Zhang, Y., Tai, N., Xu, B.: Fault analysis and traveling wave protection scheme for bipolar HVDC lines. IEEE Trans. Power Deliv. **27**(3), 1583–1591 (2012)

26. Johnson, J.M., Yadav, A.: Complete protection scheme for fault detection, classification and location estimation in HVDC transmission lines using support vector machines. IET Sci. Meas. Technol. **11**(3), 279–287 (2017)

27. He, Z., Liao, K., Li, X., Lin, S., Yang, J., Mai, R.: Natural frequency based line fault location in HVDC lines. IEEE Trans. Power Deliv. **29**(2), 851–859 (2014)

28. Huai, Q., et al.: Backup protection scheme for multi-terminal HVDC system based on wavelet-packet energy entropy. IEEE Access **7**, 49790–49803 (2019)

29. Leterme, W., Azad, S.P., Van Hertem, D.: HVDC grid protection algorithm design in phase and modal domains. IET Renew. Power Gener. **12**(13), 1538–1546 (2018)

30. Salehi, M., Namdari, F.: Fault classification and faulted phase selection for transmission line using morphological edge detection filter. IET Gener. Transm. Distrib. **12**(7), 1595–1605 (2018)
31. Luo, G., Yao, C., Liu, Y., Tan, Y., He, J., Wang, K.: Stacked auto-encoder based fault location in VSC-HVDC. IEEE Access **6**, 33216–33224 (2018)
32. Hoseinzadeh, B., Amini, M.H., Bak, C.L., Blaabierg, F.: High impedance DC fault detection and localization in HVDC transmission lines using harmonic analysis. In: International Conference on Environment and Electrical Engineering and 2018 IEEE Industrial and Commercial Power Systems Europe, EEEIC/I&CPS Europe, pp. 1–4 (2018)
33. Lan, S., Chen, M.J., Chen, D.Y.: A novel HVDC double terminal nonsynchronous fault location method based on convolutional neural network. IEEE Trans. Power Deliv. **34**(3), 848–857 (2019)
34. Suonan, J., Gao, S., Song, G.: A novel fault location method for HVDC transmission lines. IEEE Trans. Power Deliv. **25**, 1203–1209 (2010)
35. Nanayakkara, O., Rajapakse, A., Wachal, R.: Travelling wave-based line fault location in star-connected multi-terminal HVDC systems. IEEE Trans. Power Deliv. **27**, 2286–2294 (2012)
36. Dewe, M.B., Sankar, S., Arrillaga, J.: The application of satellite time references to HVDC fault location. IEEE Trans. Power Deliv. **8**(3), 1295–1302 (1993)
37. Li, Y., Zhang, S., Li, H.: A fault location method based on genetic algorithm for high-voltage direct current transmission line. Eur. Trans. Electr. Power **22**, 866–878 (2012)
38. Yuangsheng, L., Gang, W., Haifeng, L.: Time domain fault-location method on HVDC transmission lines under unsynchronized two-end measurement and uncertain line parameters. IEEE Trans. Power Deliv. **30**, 1031–1038 (2015)
39. Livani, H., Evrenosoglu, C.Y.: A single-ended fault location method for segmented HVDC transmission line. Electr. Power Syst. Res. **107**, 190–198 (2014)
40. Guoing, S., Xu, C., Xinlei, C.: A fault location method for VSC-HVDC transmission lines based on natural frequency of current. Electr. Power Energy Syst. **63**, 347–352 (2014)
41. Yusuff, A.A., Jimoh, A.A., Munda, J.L.: Fault location in transmission lines based on stationary wavelet transform determinant function feature and support vector regression. Electr. Power Syst. Res. **110**, 73–83 (2014)
42. Azad, S.P., Hertem, D.V.: A fast local bus current-based primary relaying algorithm for HVDC grids. IEEE Trans. Power Deliv. **32**(1), 193–202 (2017)
43. Bucher, M.K., Franck, C.M.: Fault current interruption in multiterminal HVDC networks. IEEE Trans. Power Deliv. **31**(1), 87–95 (2016)
44. Mokhberdoran, A., Silva, N., Leite, H., Carvalho, A.: Unidirectional protection strategy for multi-terminal HVDC grids. Trans. Environ. Electr. Eng. **1**(4), 58–65 (2016)
45. Leterme, W., Azad, S.P., Hertem, D.V.: A local backup protection algorithm for HVDC grids. IEEE Trans. Power Deliv. **31**(4), 1767–1775 (2016)
46. Hertem, D.V., Ghandhari, M.: Multi-terminal VSC HVDC for the European supergrid: obstacles. Renew. Sustain. Energy Rev. **14**(9), 3156–3163 (2010)
47. Kerf, K.D., et al.: Wavelet-based protection strategy for dc faults in multi-terminal VSC HVDC systems. IET Gen. Transm. Distrib. **5**(4), 496–503 (2011)
48. Leterme, W., Beerten, J., Hertem, D.V.: Non-unit protection of HVDC grids with inductive dc cable termination. IEEE Trans. Power Del. **31**(2), 820–828 (2016)
49. Sneath, J., Rajapakse, A.D.: Fault detection and interruption in an earthed HVDC grid using ROCOV and hybrid dc breakers. IEEE Trans. Power Deliv. **31**(3), 973–981 (2016)
50. Elmore, W.A.: Protective Relaying Theory and Applications. Marcel Dekker, New York (2004)

51. Naidoo, D., Ijumba, N.: HVDC line protection for the proposed future HVDC systems. In: Proceedings IEEE PowerCon, vol. 2, pp. 1327–1332 (2004)

52. Sun, J., Saeedifard, M., Meliopoulos, A.P.S.: Backup protection of multi-terminal HVDC grids based on quickest change detection. IEEE Trans. Power Deliv. **34**(1), 177–187 (2019)

53. Farshad, M.: Detection and classification of internal faults in bipolar HVDC transmission lines based on K-means data description method. Int. J. Electr. Power Energy Syst. **104**, 615–625 (2019)

54. Azad, S.P., Leterme, W., Hertem, D.V.: A DC grid primary protection algorithm based on current measurements. In: 17th European Conference on Power Electronics and Applications, EPE 2015 ECCE-Europe, Geneva, pp. 1–10 (2015)

55. Yang, Q., Blond, S.L., Aggarwal, R., Wang, Y., Li, J.: New ANN method for multi-terminal HVDC protection relaying. Electr. Power Syst. Res. **148**, 192–201 (2017)

56. Augustin, T., Jahn, I., Norrga, S., Nee, H.: Transient behaviour of VSC-HVDC links with DC breakers under faults. In: 19th European Conference on Power Electronics and Applications, EPE 2017 ECCE Europe, Warsaw, pp. P.1–P.10 (2017)

57. Li, C., Gole, A.M., Zhao, C.: A fast DC fault detection method using DC reactor voltages in HVDC grids. IEEE Trans. Power Deliv. **33**(5), 2254–2264 (2018)

58. Bertho, R., Lacerda, V.A., Monaro, R.M., Vieira, J.C.M., Coury, D.V.: Selective nonunit protection technique for multiterminal VSC HVDC grids. IEEE Trans. Power Deliv. **33**(5), 2106–2114 (2018)

59. Xie, Z., Zou, G., Gao, L., Zhang, J., Gao, H.: Voltage pole-wave protection scheme for multi-terminal DC grid. J. Eng. **2019**(16), 806–811 (2019)

60. Yeap, Y.M., Ukil, A.: Fault detection in HVDC system using short time fourier transform. In: IEEE Power and Energy Society General Meeting, PESGM, Boston, MA, pp. 1–5 (2016)

61. Brigham, E.O.: The Fast Fourier Transform. Prentice Hall, Englewood Cliffs (1974)

62. Vasanth, S., Yeap, Y.M., Ukil, A.: Fault location estimation for VSC-HVDC system using artificial neural network. In: IEEE Region 10 Conference, TENCON, pp. 501–504 (2016)

63. Elgeziry, M.Z., Elsadd, M.A., Elkalashy, N.I., Kawady, T.A., Taalab, A.M.I.: AC spectrum analysis for detecting DC faults on HVDC systems. In: 19th International Middle East Power Systems Conference, MEPCON, pp. 708–715 (2017)

64. Satpathi, K., Yeap, Y.M., Ukil, A., Geddada, N.: Short-time Fourier Transform based transient analysis of VSC interfaced point-to-point dc system. IEEE Trans. Industr. Electron. **65**(5), 4080–4091 (2018)

65. Ukil, A., Yeap, Y.M., Satpathi, K., Geddada, N.: Fault identification in AC and DC systems using STFT analysis of high frequency components. In: IEEE Conference on Innovative Smart Grid Technologies – Asia, ISGT-Asia, pp. 1–6 (2017)

66. Gaouda, A.M., El-Saadany, E.F., Salama, M.M.A., Sood, V.K., Chikhani, A.Y.: Monitoring HVDC systems using wavelet multi-resolution analysis. IEEE Trans. Power Syst. **16**(4), 662–670 (2001)

67. Murthy, P.K., Amarnath, J., Kamakshiah, S., Singh, B.P.: Wavelet transform approach for detection and location of faults in HVDC system. In: IEEE Region 10 and the Third international Conference on Industrial and Information Systems, Kharagpur, pp. 1–6 (2008)

68. Wang, G., Wu, M., Li, H., Hong, C.: Transient based protection for HVDC lines using wavelet-multiresolution signal decomposition. In: Proceedings IEEE/Power Engineering Society Transmission and Distribution Conference, Asia Pacific, pp. 1–4 (2005)

69. Cai, X., Song, G., Gao, S.: A novel fault-location method for VSC-HVDC transmission lines based on natural frequency of current. Proc. CSEE **28**(31), 112–119 (2011)

70. Liu, X., Osman, A.H., Malik, O.P.: Hybrid traveling wave/boundary protection for monopolar HVDC line. IEEE Trans. Power Deliv. **24**(2), 569–578 (2009)

71. Yang, Y., Tai, N., Fan, C., Yang, L., Chen, S.: Resonance frequency-based protection scheme for ultra-high-voltage direct-current transmission lines. IET Gener. Transm. Distrib. **12**(2), 318–327 (2018)

72. Liu, J., Fan, C., Tai, N.: A novel pilot directional protection scheme for HVDC transmission line based on specific frequency current. In: International conference on Power System Technology, POWERCON, pp. 976–982 (2014)

73. Cheng, J., Guan, M., Tang, L.V., Huang, H.: A fault location criterion for MTDC transmission lines using transient current characteristics. Int. J. Electr. Power Energy Syst. **61**, 647–655 (2014)

74. Wang, D., Gao, H.L., Luo, S.B., Zou, G.B.: Travelling wave pilot protection for LCC-HVDC transmission lines based on electronic transformers differential output characteristic. Int. J. Electr. Power Energy Syst. **93**, 283 (2017)

75. Farshad, M., Sadeh, J.: A novel fault-location method for HVDC transmission lines based on similarity measure of voltage signals. IEEE Trans. Power Deliv. **28**(4), 2483–2490 (2013)

76. Jana, S., De, A.: A novel zone division approach for power system fault detection using ANN-based pattern recognition technique. Can. J. Electr. Comput. Eng. **40**(4), 275–283 (2017)

77. Wang, Y., Hao, Z., Zhang, B., Kong, F.: A pilot protection scheme for transmission lines in VSC-HVDC grid based on similarity measure of traveling waves. IEEE Access **7**, 7147–7158 (2019)

78. Santos, R.C., Blond, S.L., Coury, D.V., Aggarwal, R.K.: A novel and comprehensive single terminal ANN based decision support for relaying of VSC based HVDC links. Electr. Power Syst. Res. **141**, 333 (2016)

79. Tzelepis, D., Dyśko, A., Fusiek, G., Niewczas, P., Mirsaeidi, S., Booth, C., Dong, X.: Advanced fault location in MTDC networks utilizing optically-multiplexed current measurements and machine learning approach. Int. J. Electr. Power Energy Syst. **97**, 319 (2018)

80. Liu, X., Wei, W., Yu, F.: SVM theory and its application in fault diagnosis of HVDC system. In: 3rd International Conference on Natural Computation, ICNC 2007, Haikou, pp. 665–669 (2007)

81. Chang, C.C., Lin, C.J.: LIBSVM: a library for support vector machines. ACM Trans. Intell. Syst. Technol. **2**(3), 1–27 (2011)

82. Breiman, L.: Random forests. Mach. Learn. **45**(1), 5–32 (2001)

83. Tuv, E.: Ensemble learning. In: Guyon, I., Nikravesh, M., Gunn, S., Zadeh, L.A. (eds.) Feature Extraction: Foundations and Applications, pp. 187–204. Springer, Heidelberg (2006). https://doi.org/10.1007/978-3-540-35488-8_8

84. Robnik-Šikonja, M., Kononenko, I.: Theoretical and empirical analysis of ReliefF and RReliefF. Mach. Learn. **53**(1), 23–69 (2003)

85. Abdelgayed, T.S., Morsi, W.G., Sidhu, T.S.: Fault detection and classification based on co-training of semi supervised machine learning. IEEE Trans. Industr. Electron. **65**(2), 1595–1605 (2018)

86. Jarrahi, M.A., Samet, H., Ghanbari, T.: Fast current-only based fault detection method in transmission line. IEEE Syst. J. **13**(2), 1725–1736 (2019)

87. Chen, M., Lan, S., Chen, D.: Machine learning based one-terminal fault areas detection in HVDC transmission system. In: 8th International Conference on Power and Energy Systems, ICPES, Colombo, Sri Lanka, pp. 278–282 (2018)

88. Padiyar, K.R., Prabhu, N.: Modelling, control design and analysis of VSC based HVDC transmission systems. In: International Conference on Power System Technology, PowerCon 2004, vol. 11, pp. 774–779 (2004)

89. Meier, S.: Novel voltage source converter based HVDC transmission system for offshore wind farms. Department of Electrical Engineering Electrical Machines and Power Electronics, Royal Institute of Technology, Stockholm (2005)
90. Undeland, N.M.T., Robbins, W.: Power Electronics: Converters, Applications, and Design (2003)
91. Mohamed, Z.S.A.K., Samir, H., Karim, F.M., Rabie, A.: Performance analysis of a voltage source converter (VSC) based HVDC transmission system under faulted conditions. Leonardo J. Sci., 33–46 (2009)
92. Ana-Irina Stan, D. I. S.: Control of VSC-based HVDC transmission system for offshore wind power plants. Department of Energy Technology, Aalborg University, Denmark (2010)
93. Cuiqing, D., et al.: A new control strategy of a VSC-HVDC system for high quality supply of industrial plants. IEEE Trans. Power Deliv. **22**, 2386–2394 (2007)
94. Bajracharya, C.: Control of VSC-HVDC for wind power. Master of Science in Energy and Environment, Department of Electrical Power Engineering, Norwegian University of Science and Technology, Trondheim (2008)
95. De Oliveira Filho, M.E., et al.: A control method for voltage source inverter without dc link capacitor. In Power Electronics Specialists Conference, pp. 4432–4437 (2008)
96. Machaba, M.B.M.: Explicit damping factor specification in symmetrical optimum tuning of PI controllers. In: 1st African Control Conference, Cape Town, South Africa (2003)
97. Namho, H., et al.: Fast dynamic DC-link power balancing scheme for a PWM converter inverter system. Proc. Ind. Electron. Soc. **2**, 767–772 (1999)
98. Salakhutdinov, R., Mnih, A., Hinton, G.: Restricted Boltzmann machines for collaborative filtering. In: Proceedings of the 24th International Conference on Machine Learning, ACM 2007 (2007)
99. Mobahi, H., Collobert, R. (eds.): Deep learning from temporal coherence in video. In: International Conference on Machine Learning, ACM 09, Canada (2009)
100. Larochelle, H., Bengio, Y. (eds.): Classification using discriminative restricted Boltzmann machines. In: Proceedings of the 25th International Conference on Machine Learning, ACM 2008, Helsinki, Finland (2008)
101. Larochelle, H., Mandel, M.I. (eds.): Learning algorithms for the classification restricted Boltzmann machine. J. Mach. Learn. Res. **13**, 643–669 (2012)
102. Bengio, Y.: Foundations and trends in machine learning **2**, 1–127 (2009)
103. Lei, Y., Jia, F., Lin, J., Xing, S., Ding, S.X.: An intelligent fault diagnosis method using unsupervised feature learning towards mechanical big data. IEEE Trans. Industr. Electron. **63**(5), 3137–3147 (2016)
104. Wong, K.P.: Artificial intelligence and neural network applications in power systems. In: 2nd International Conference on Advances in Power System Control, Operation and Management, APSCOM 1993, vol. 1, Hong Kong, pp. 37–46 (1993)
105. Hinton, G.E.: Training products of experts by minimizing contrastive divergence. J. Neural Comput. **14**(8), 1771–1800 (2002)
106. Fischer, A., Igel, C.: Bounding the bias of contrastive divergence learning. Neural Comput. **23**(3), 664–673 (2011)

Multi-agent Oriented Framework
for University Course Timetable Scheduling

Sehrish Munawar Cheema[(⊠)], Rukhsar Shafiq, Shahid Saleem,
Syed Zeeshan Hussain Shah, and Anees Baqir

Department of Computing and IT, University of Sialkot, Sialkot, Pakistan
sehrishcheema@gmail.com

Abstract. This research proposes a hierarchal, multi-agent based framework that is mapped onto combinatorial real life problems like university course time table scheduling at University of Sialkot that take a lot of hours even days to create or maintain a timetable for different courses. It is a web-based system assisted with an android application. In this paper, we present a multi-agent-based multi-layered hierarchical framework to allocate all events (instructors and courses) to fix predefined resources i.e. timeslots and rooms, where all constraints within the problem must be satisfied. Multiple agents are used for the development of university timetable, course allocation and to manage class held report. The Capturing Agent (CA) takes information from user and saves into database. The Monitoring Agent (MA) searched and justified the user query and pass out data to timetable generator for creation of timetable. The Distributing Agent (DA) publishes the information that becomes available to user's inbox and on university's website. We designed a mechanism for the development of timetable that presents the association and interaction process of different agents of the system. This system is implemented in Java Agent DEvelopment (JADE) framework.

Keywords: Multi agent systems · Course timetable scheduling · JADE · Intelligent agents · Agent based software engineering (ABSE)

1 Introduction

Scheduling is a universal problem for which too many researchers worked to solve it over the years and put solutions using various techniques like operational researches, meta-heuristic methods and intelligent novel methods; also the distributed multi agent systems based approach but with no optimal solution [1, 2]. University course time-table problem is one of the NP-hard problems, with no optimum solution [3]. Most universities schedule it manually that becomes tedious with increasing number of students and courses. It takes a lot of human effort to create and manage timetable. There are a many issues and difficulties at the start of each and every new session to create a time table by a single person or a group involved in task scheduling, which

S.M. Cheema—Both authors contributed equally to this manuscript.

I. S. Bajwa et al. (Eds.): INTAP 2019, CCIS 1198, pp. 791–799, 2020.
https://doi.org/10.1007/978-981-15-5232-8_67

takes parcel of exertion [4, 5]. While scheduling even a smallest constraint can take a great deal of time and the case is even worse when the number of constrains are the amount of data to deal with increases. In manual scheduling there can be a lot of clashes at certain time by default or by preferences that effect on accuracy. We face many difficulties while updating and sharing information to each faculty member. The key problems are to: 1) Keep and manage record of previous data. 2) Meet in person. 3) Manage multiple queries of same subject. 4) Room clashes at the same time. 5) Manage rooms for delivering lectures. 6) Have insufficient information by faculty members during the development of timetable. 7) Notify after every updating of timetable to each faculty member and HOD.

In [6] a framework was proposed for a curriculum based timetable which have different limitations and skins. It deals with the problem in such an environment in which the main agent shares the best portions of the solution with the other agents due to which the universal set of the solutions is improved. In this process, the data of students of two semesters is used for this purpose. And result showed that the sequential search system can be used. This technique shows better results with a greater number of agents.

Other researchers have also worked for the course allocation system [7] where they have used multiple agents. They have used the GAIA methodology for design and analysis. The development framework used for this purpose was Java Agent Development (JADE). In [8] developed a hybrid heuristic algorithm that use different key operator i.e. population, selection, mutation and state replacement for best solution to solve university time table problem. Proposed solution is effective for only small but not for medium and large.

Automation of university course allocation system comes with different kind of problems. One of those problems is the computational social choice and this is the problem which has been least focused. This problem has been suggested a solution based on some protocols and precisions. The researchers have described the problem and its solution using multiple methodologies and tools which are actually unfolding the effectiveness of the approach and the results of the experiment performed for the problem [9].

A system based on hierarchal layered multi-agents oriented was developed that was actually a control system for sake of smart buildings. It was developed to manage electricity load management under real time pricing environment [1]. Therefore, to design, manage and schedule a timetable for education organization is quite difficult and hard job. The general task of solving timetable scheduling problems is reducing human on each semester and reduces time and become more accurate and faster.

Our propose system is a multi-agent based timetable scheduling system (MATSS) for education system as a solution of above mentioned problems which is a web based and android based system it is a time listing detail system for educational institutes of two departments.

Our system consists upon several agents listing the system details for education organization. The information capturing agent (CA) is responsible to catch information by Director, Vice Chancellor, HoD, faculty members and save it into the database. The Monitoring Agent (MA) monitors the environment performs calculations and request DA to publish it on the website and sent it to the user. The Distributing Agent (DA) disseminate on the site, app or sent it to the client as per instruction of EMA. Faculty will mark the attendance of delivered lecture. If any need of makeup EMA checks the free slot of faculty and that section or free room and then notify the faculty with selected slot if (s)he wants makeup lecture. If any clash occurs in any case where system can't handle than system notify the faculty or HOD for arrange meeting for discussion. Also include various component of characterizing and distributing of alarms, warnings, declarations, seeing altering profiles and setting of courses.

The major focus this project is to automate timetable scheduling process for all departments in University of Sialkot, reducing human effort on each semester and reduce time and become more accurate and faster by making it smarter as well as time and cost effective. Our projects objective is to provide the quality of data in a timely fashion. The rest of the paper is organized as follows: Sect. 2 problem definition. Section 2 deals with system design and implementation. Methodology, system components are presented in Sect. 3 followed by conclusion and future work in Sect. 4 respectively.

2 Problem Definition

University course timetabling is a hybrid optimization problem that belongs to one of the class of NP-hard problem [3] that occurs at the start of almost every semester of universities [10]. It includes allocation of different courses, instructors to prefixed resources; timeslots and lecture rooms. This allocation of resources to their events must satisfy some hard and soft constraints to enhance and stimulate the quality of feasible timetable generation [2].

2.1 Basic Definitions of the Problem

- Event: an action that is scheduled for course and instructor.
- Timeslot: a time duration for an event to occur for example daily timeslot form 08:30 am–04:30 pm, Weekly timeslot from Monday to Saturday etc.
- Resource: these are utilized by events like lecture rooms, laboratories, time slots and equipment etc.
- Constraint: during the scheduling of each event constraint is a type of restriction which i.e. hard and soft type. For example, a single course should not be allocated to no more than three instructors, a room capacity, allowed timeslot for a lecture etc.
- People: include HoDs, Directors and lecturers as event's part.
- Conflict: it occurs between two events for example if more than one instructor scheduled for same lecture room in same timeslot.

2.2 Hard Constraints

There are the following few hard constraints of our intended system that MA follows the following rules during the provision of alternatives:

- HOD has the top level priority. So, if HOD selects a course, day, time or room which already has been selected by other faculty member, EMA lets HOD select the course and informs the other faculty member about the situation and asks him/her to offer another course, day, time or room.
- Senior most faculty member has second level priority. This case is also handled like the case 1.
- In case of a subject clash, the subject will be assigned to the teacher who had taught the subject in any previous semester(s).
- In case of a room clash, the priority will be given to the teacher who had been taking classes in this room in the previous semester(s).
- In case of class timing clash, the priority will be given to the teacher who had been taking classes at the same time in the previous semester(s).
- In case of makeup lecture the MA checks the free slot of faculty and respective section and inform the faculty.

2.3   Soft Constraints

- Faculty members choose the offered course. If faculty has highest rank of respective chosen course than course allocate to corresponding faculty. Otherwise system notify for chosen another course.
- Faculty members choose time slots and rooms of corresponding section. If the given pattern exist in timetable generator than assign the slot to faculty. Otherwise view the free slots to adjust the time table.
- Faculty members will mark the attendance of delivered lecture within assign time. If a faculty member forgets to mark attendance system distribute an alarm or notified to mark up the lecture otherwise consider it to absent in that lecture. System checks the free slot of faculty and that section or free room and then notify the faculty with selected slot if (s) he wants makeup lecture.

3   System Design Implementation and Architecture

Figure 1 represents the architectural design to view components of system. The intended system architecture is based on three tiers, which includes presentation tier, logical tier and data tier. Presentation tier includes web portal, android app and Email via which users interact with system. After that logical tier comes it contains logical components that present three agents CA (Capturing Agent), MA (Monitoring Agent), DA (Distributing Agent) and a Timetable Generator in the system. It provides transmission of data between users (faculty members) and agents. It also provides resource handling and high level processing. This tier is based on major features provided by system which are as follow: Capturing agent (CA) capture the time table related information received by HoD and faculty members. And then saves data in database on user's behalf. When data is saved in database the environment got changed. When Monitoring agent (MA) observes these changes in database then it take some pre-decided actions and after that Distributing Agent (DA) then publish this required information on web portal, email and android app for the use system users. At bottom level there is data tier that provides the database and provides collaboration with database to generate some useful results.

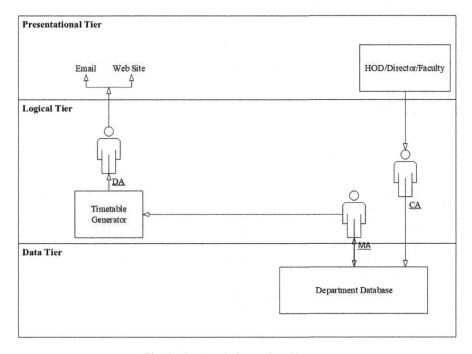

Fig. 1. System design and architecture

4   Methodology and System Components

4.1   System Components

HOD Interactive Module: This component offers courses for current semester. Assign slots of working days minutes of slots and room numbers. It also put the information the program, batch, and section for which some specific course is offered. It also has records of all instructors of current semester.

Faculty Interactive Module: By using web interface of android faculty members choose from offered courses list, choose a room number, slots. If a faculty member wants to conduct a makeup lecture, sends a query to CA via web portal or Android app.

My Lectures: Faculty will mark the attendance of delivered lecture within assigned time duration. If a faculty member forgets to mark attendance, system distributes an alarm or notifies to mark up the lecture otherwise System considers it absent in that lecture. MA checks the free slot of specific faculty member and a specific section and free lecture room then notify the faculty member with selected slot if she/he wants to conduct a makeup lecture.

Meetings: This module of system checks the availability of faculty members in order to conduct department meetings and also inter-departmental meetings to resolve some departmental and interdepartmental issues.

Timetable Generator: After removing all the clashes and issues MA allocate the time slot to faculty member with corresponding course in time able generator and stored in database as timetable generator.

4.2   Timetable Development Process

Timetable generating process starts when following information is feed into system via CA (information capturing agent) by Head of Department and Dean/Director.

- List all the offered courses of current semester.
- Mention the working days where classes can arrange let's take from Monday to Friday and classes on Saturday are arrange for visiting lecturers.
- Mention the Time slots of scheduled lectures. For example lectures can only be conducted from 8:30 am to 3:00 pm each of 1:30 h.
- Information about lectures rooms where classes can be conducted. Director and Head of each department specify the best and comfortable rooms like LR1, LR2.

As MA continuously monitors the environment, MA collects all the information from Director, HoD within specified duration and proper format and request DA to send email to all concerned faculty members requesting them to choose the offered courses from list. The following email has a link where faculty member choose the offer course according to their specialization and expertise. Then these chosen courses are verified from director or HOD. Faculty member choose the day time slot and lecture room.

The faculty member opens the link from email and goes to the web page of link providing the DA. The web page helped to select the courses and preferred day, time slot and lecture room. All the information provides by faculty member are saved in database by CA. In case any clash occur of offering course, day, time slots or room selection MA takes a prompt action and informed the concerned faculty member by DA about the clash and suggest them to resolve or give any alternative solution if not possible then concerned with HOD.

MA follows the following rule or regulation during the provision of alternatives:

- Director or HoD has the highest or top level priority. Director or HoD selects a course, day, time slot, room which if already has been selected by other faculty member, MA Lets Director or HoD select the course and informs the other faculty member about the situation and suggest them to choose another course, day, time slot or lecture room.

- Senior most faculty member has second level priority. Same case is also handled like case of Director or HoD.
- In case of course clash the course will be assigned to that instructor who had high priority and expertise.
- In case of lecture room clash, the priority will be given to that faculty member who had been taking lectures in this room in previous semester.
- In case of lecture time clash, the priority will be given to the teacher who had been taking classes at the same time in the previous semester(s).
- If a clash occurs among faculty members having the same seniority level, then MA asks DA to send an email to all faculty members involved in creating the clash and requests them to have a meeting to resolve the issue.

If a clash still occurs, then MA informs HoD via DA and asks to get resolved the clash. In case of any other clash which is not being resolved by the faculty members themselves, MA informs HoD via DA and asks him to handle the matter and resolve it.

Similarly, if a delay is being faced due to a faculty member in offering the course(s), MA sends them a reminder via DA. If the faculty member does not offer the course even after receiving a reminder, MA prepares a message and asks DA to send it to HoD. Then, HoD may call him/her via mobile number or send him/her notification to select the course(s). When all faculty members have offered the courses and verified by Director or HOD, and there is no clash or delay, MA collects all this information gives it a shape of timetable, forwards it to the HoD for verification from him. If HoD does not verify timetable and makes an objection, MA acts as per instructions of HoD. If HoD verifies the timetable, MA publishes it via DA on the university web page and emails it to all faculty members for their information as well.

During the whole process of developing timetable, no person is involved or participated. The whole process is automatic and intelligent enough to create a consistent and agreed timetable.

4.3   Timetable Development Algorithm

Capturing Agent: The capturing agent (CA) is responsible to catch information from Director, Head of department and Faculty members and save it into the database. Algorithm CA:

1. Gets information relevant to course(s), rooms and timing from HOD.
2. Saves the information in database.
3. Gets data relevant to course(s) offering of a faculty member.

Monitoring Agent: The monitoring agent (MA) monitors the database to take an action if predefined circumstances arise, performs calculations and request DA to publish it on the website and sent it to the user. The logic is performed by this agent.

Algorithm MA:

1. If date=date to offer course(s)
    - i)   Generate a message containing offered courses
    - ii)   Notify/pass message to DA to inform related instructors.
      End if
2. While (offered course(s) == delay || clash!= null) Start
    - a) If (clash == simple)
        - i)   Generate a message for those faculty member caught in clash
        - ii)   Send alert to DA to inform all concerned members
          End if
    - b) If (clash is due to same priority levels of two or more faculty members)
        - i)   "Have a meeting message" is generated
        - ii)   Alert DA to put message on concerned faculty members' screen.
          End if
    - c) If (clash == critical)
        - i)   Generate a message for HoD to resolve the case by his/her input to system
        - ii)   Notification is passed to concerned persons by DA.
          End if
    - d) If (delay in clash resolve process == average)
        - i)   Generate a reminder for concerned faculty member
        - ii)   Notify to members via DA.
          End if
    - e) If (delay in clash resolve process == Critical)
        - i)   Refer the case to HoD.
        - ii)   DA informs to HoD.
          End if
          End While
3. After all clashes resolve, get data from database for timetable.
4. Shape up in a timetable format
5. Verification by dean/director and HoD.
6. If (verification is done)
7. Inform DA for publication timetable on portal and also on android application.
8. Else
    - i)   MA generate a message according to instructions of Dean/HoD via CA.
    - ii)   An alert is given to DA to inform all related members.
    - iii)   Go to step 2
          End if
      End

Distributing Agent: The distributing agent (DA) disseminates on the site or sent it to the client as per instruction of EMA.

Algorithm CA:

a) Get instructions from MA.
b) Publishes data on web site or/and email to the concerned faculty members.

5   Conclusion

A number of efforts have been done to develop and provide intelligent systems for education system. Our proposed framework is a set forward to this. This provides an interface to faculty members, head of department, and dean/directors to manipulate their courses and get a timetable for courses via web and android application. Our developed approach provides scalability in case of distributed environment, independency of scheduling different departments.

As we have provided the initial framework for timetable scheduling problem in educational institutes, it has a room for improvement of unplanned allocation of resources to events by optimizing negotiation and communication among agents for better performance.

References

1. Rasheed, M.B., Javaid, N., Malik, M.S.A., Asif, M., Hanif, M.K., Chaudary, M.H.: Intelligent multi-agent based multilayered control system for opportunistic load scheduling in smart buildings. IEEE Access **7**, 23990–24006 (2019)
2. Babaei, H., Karimpour, J., Hadidi, A.: A survey of approaches for university course timetabling problem. Comput. Ind. Eng. **86**, 43–59 (2015)
3. Marx, D.: Graph colouring problems and their applications in scheduling. Period. Polytech. Electr. Eng. **48**(1–2), 11–16 (2004)
4. Fadiya, S.O., Iruoma, N.E.: University time-table scheduling system: databases design. Int. J. Sci. Res. Inf. Syst. Eng. **1**(1), 45–51 (2015)
5. El-Helly, M., Abdelhamid, Y., Al-Wakeel, M.: A multi-agent pattern based timetabling system. Egypt. Comput. Sci. J. **35**(3) (2011)
6. Abdalla, M.H., Obit, J.H., Alfred, R., Bolongkikit, J.: Agent based integer programming framework for solving real-life curriculum-based university course timetabling. In: Alfred, R., Lim, Y., Ibrahim, A., Anthony, P. (eds.) Computational Science and Technology. LNEE, vol. 481, pp. 67–76. Springer, Singapore (2019). https://doi.org/10.1007/978-981-13-2622-6_7
7. Igulu, K.T., Piah, Z.P.: Multi-agent based course allocator using GAIA methodology and JADE framework. Afr. J. Comput. ICT **8**(2) (2015)
8. Landa-Silva, D., Obit, J.H.: Evolutionary non-linear great deluge for university course timetabling. In: Corchado, E., Wu, X., Oja, E., Herrero, Á., Baruque, B. (eds.) HAIS 2009. LNCS (LNAI), vol. 5572, pp. 269–276. Springer, Heidelberg (2009). https://doi.org/10.1007/978-3-642-02319-4_32
9. Lin, F., Chen, W.: Designing a multiagent system for course-offering determination. In: Boella, G., Elkind, E., Savarimuthu, B.T.R., Dignum, F., Purvis, M.K. (eds.) PRIMA 2013. LNCS (LNAI), vol. 8291, pp. 165–180. Springer, Heidelberg (2013). https://doi.org/10.1007/978-3-642-44927-7_12
10. Chowdhary, A., Kakde, P., Dhoke, S., Ingle, S., Rushiya, R., Gawande, D.: Timetable generation system. Int. J. Comput. Sci. Mob. Comput. **3**(2) (2014)

Author Index

Printed in the United States
By Bookmasters